Exploring Space

Exploring Space:
Spatial Notions in Cultural, Literary and Language Studies; Volume 1: Space in Cultural and Literary Studies

Edited by

Andrzej Ciuk and Katarzyna Molek-Kozakowska

CAMBRIDGE SCHOLARS PUBLISHING

Exploring Space: Spatial Notions in Cultural, Literary and Language Studies;
Volume 1: Space in Cultural and Literary Studies,
Edited by Andrzej Ciuk and Katarzyna Molek-Kozakowska

This book first published 2010

Cambridge Scholars Publishing

12 Back Chapman Street, Newcastle upon Tyne, NE6 2XX, UK

British Library Cataloguing in Publication Data
A catalogue record for this book is available from the British Library

ISBN (10): 1-4438-2143-8, ISBN (13): 978-1-4438-2143-8

CONTENTS

Part III: Metaphoricity of Space in Poetry

PREFACE

The notion of space is as old as the history of human thought. Spatial categories used to predominantly connote immensity, unfathomableness, indeterminateness, or unlimitedness. However, with the passage of time, our perception of space has been substantially modified. Inhabitable space has proved to be insufficient and to have flexible borders, and even outer space, once beyond human reach, has turned out to be conquerable. The space of knowledge has been expanded considerably, although it has also remained impenetrable at points. As is commonly noted, now space seems to be "shrinking" proportionally to the increase in speed and the spread of technology. Consequently, any explorations into the notion of space inevitably reveal oppositions, paradoxes, ambiguities and unresolved questions related to our various perceptions of space.

If we follow the meanders of thought on the nature of space as an ontological-epistemological concept, we will encounter the ancient Greek myth about the creation of the universe. Here, the world emerged out of Chaos. Space was soon betrothed to time, and both generated an insatiable human desire to fathom and order the universe. In Western culture, one of the pioneers of this endeavor was Democritus, "the father of modern science", who formulated an atomic theory for the cosmos, and for whom space was a vacuum. The renowned Greek philosopher Aristotle claimed that space, likewise time, was a "quantity", i.e., it was a whole dividable into parts. Moreover, it was a "multiplicity"—a countable amount of parts in a continuum. To mention other influential conceptions of space, Bernardino Telesio, an Italian philosopher and natural scientist, regarded space as a system of relations between things. Isaac Newton created a theory of absolute space, whereas his contemporary, Gottfried Leibnitz, was the author of a theory of relative space. For Immanuel Kant, the knowledge of space was "synthetic"; by contrast, Ludwig Wittgenstein, in his *Tractatus Logico-Philosophicus*, introduced the notion of logical space and the "ensemble of possible states".

Apart from the philosophy of space (and time), which has greatly influenced modern science, certain spatial categories have penetrated and shaped Western culture and the humanities. The present book demonstrates how the notion of space can be treated as a common axis for research in such diverse disciplines as literary studies, linguistics and cultural studies, and how it has inspired a variety of analyses of textual, linguistic and cultural phenomena from the perspective of English Studies. *Exploring Space: Spatial Notions in Cultural, Literary and Language Studies* falls into two volumes and is the result of the 18th PASE (Polish Association for the Study of English) Conference organized by the Institute of English of Opole University and held at Kamień Śląski in April 2009.

The first volume embraces cultural and literary studies and offers papers on narrative fiction, poetry, theatre and drama, and post-colonial studies. The texts and contexts explored are either British, American or Commonwealth. The second volume refers to English language studies and covers papers on lexicography, general linguistics and rhetoric, discourse studies and translation, second language acquisition/foreign language learning, and the methodology of foreign language teaching. The book aims to offer a comprehensive insight into how the category of space can inform original philological research; thus, it may be of interest to those in search of novel applications of space-related concepts, and to those who wish to acquire an update on current developments in English Studies across Poland.

By exploring various space-related categories, such as distance, proximity, territory, locality and movement, the contributors to both volumes of this book have managed to show that space is a powerful concept capable of conveying human experiences and perceptions across cultural, linguistic and temporal boundaries. It is not to say that space is treated here only in metaphorical terms. In fact some contributions have focused on very physical spaces: from the representations of particular localities (i.e., London or Dublin) in literary texts, to spatial arrangements on stage in theatrical performances; from space-related aspects of dictionary-making and film-subtitling, to classroom spaces that enhance English language learning.

The notion of space has also turned out to be instrumental to insightful analyses of the domain of human psychology. Some contributors have chosen to explore the human psyche with a range of space-related categories: from "neural" and "mental" spaces in our cognitive processing, to spaces that enable emotional "self-discovery", "growth," or, on the contrary, psychological "confinement" or "self-handicapping". This is why some studies in this collection treat space as liberating, blissful and identity-enhancing, whereas others point to its oppressive, sinister or alienating aspects, which only confirms the inherent paradoxes of this concept.

Finally, a large proportion of papers in this collection investigate various social implications and cultural specificities of spatial notions. By applying space-related categories to the analysis of social communication and rhetorical expression, for example, some contributors have demonstrated how the "topos" of space can be used to guide our evaluations of and engagement in social reality. Space has also been shown to inform certain national, religious, moral, aesthetic and epistemological conceptualizations that are still pervasive in the English-speaking world despite its cultural openness and hybridity. Thus, some contributions shed new light on long-standing spatial dichotomies, such as public and domestic spaces, urban and rural landscapes, homeland and diasporic communities, and Western and Eastern geographies.

A conclusion that can be drawn from these studies is that space is by no means a homogeneous category. That is why spatial notions should not be taken for granted, as any attempt at defamiliarizing them makes us discover new meanings in canonical literary texts, linguistic structures and popular cultural phenomena, for example. This is also what this collection hopes to achieve.

—Andrzej Ciuk
Katarzyna Molek-Kozakowska

ACKNOWLEDGEMENTS

The editors wish to thank the PASE Board, particularly its Chair, Aleksandra Kędzierska, for entrusting the Institute of English of Opole University with the task of organizing the 18th PASE Conference, as well as the President of the ESSE Board, Fernando Galván, for his encouragement and support. We owe special thanks to the reviewers of the contributions to this collection: Marek Błaszak, Ilona Dobosiewicz, Jacek Gutorow, and Ryszard Wolny for volume one, and Janusz Malak, Liliana Piasecka, Ewa Piechurska-Kuciel, Tadeusz Piotrowski and Jan Zalewski for volume two. We also wish to express our gratitude to Elżbieta Szymańska-Czaplak, Jarosław Kujath, Tadeusz Lewandowski, Marlena Marciniak, Damian Picz, Tomasz Sutarzewicz and Przemyslaw Wilk for their active support and wholehearted involvement in preparing the conference and the present book.

PART I:

SYNCHRONIC AND DIACHRONIC APPROACHES TO SPACE IN LITERARY STUDIES: DEFAMILIARIZATION OF THE NOTION

Chapter One

Images of Diaspora in Contemporary British Writing: The Island and the Homeland[1]

Fernando Galván

1. Introduction

Travelling, space and settling are notions inherent to the concept of diaspora[2]. Writing recently about the relations between postwar black British writing and space, British critic James Procter has made reference to this by using the image of sowing in association with the term of diaspora, recalling an interesting parallel between *roots* and *routes* initially employed by another Black author, Paul Gilroy, in his 1993 book *The Black Atlantic*. Procter says:

> To sow is not simply to disperse, it is also to deposit, it involves an act of plantation and presumes a ground, land, soil, territory or 'field'. To put it another way, the etymology of diaspora suggests both routes (scattering) and roots (sowing). Diaspora in this sense is inseparable from, and dependant upon, dwelling. A deconstruction of the concept 'diaspora' provides a means of returning to the politics of place, location and territory

[1] This article is part of a larger research project on the metaphors of the postcolonial diaspora in Britain, financed by the Spanish Ministry of Education and Science (code HUM2007-63028/FILO). I am grateful to Dr Jonathan P.A. Sell for comments and suggestions on a first version of this paper, as well as to members of the audience at the 18th PASE Conference (Opole, 19-22 April 2009) who heard and made stimulating suggestions on a shorter version of this text.
[2] I have discussed the meanings of this term in connection with postcolonialism and migration in my recent "Metaphors of Diaspora: English Literature at the Turn of the Century", *ELOPE (English Language Overseas Perspectives and Enquiries)* V (2009) (forthcoming).

within diaspora literature –a politics that too often gets endlessly deferred within its journeying metaphors. (Procter 2003, 14)

This probably explains why Procter's book is entitled *Dwelling Places* (2003), a book which deals with this second aspect of diaspora, that of sowing, or of finding places to settle down. A constant and common topic in the classical Jewish diaspora has been that of space, from the first exile in Babylonia in the year 586 BC to the Sephardic or Ashkenazi diasporas in more recent times. Finding a place to settle and escape from persecutions also means defining and redefining concepts such as the homeland, and that involves a process of imagination and mental construction. Procter explores specifically the places created and recreated by some diasporic writers coming to Britain from the Caribbean or Asia after the Second World War. This is also the aim of this article, although my focus will not be upon the physical locations of those dwellings, but rather on the metaphorical or imaginary spaces inhabited and developed by these writers.

Certainly the physical places are very important, since they constitute a starting point for the process of adaptation to the new environment: how such domestic spaces as bedsits or basements, but also public places like cafés, streets, railway stations, suburbs and the city, London and provincial towns and so on are presented in their writings. Paul Gilroy's book of photographs *Black Britain. A Photographic History* (2007) is an excellent visual record of all these issues. Through these pictures we can contemplate the different phases of adaptation, assimilation, fighting against racism, etc. from the early 20th century—but mainly after the Second World War—until our days.

The immigrants who travelled to Britain after the Second World War, principally to help in the reconstruction of the metropolis, at a time when many of their places of origin were becoming independent from the British Empire, settled in the UK and started a very hard struggle to achieve the status of fully-fledged citizens. From the very beginning this implied asking questions about their own identity, because although many of them believed that they were British citizens and members of a powerful empire—a belief that had been inculcated in them in Asia, or Africa, or the Caribbean—they very soon discovered, upon their arrival at the coasts of Britain, that the "other" British, the white European inhabitants of the island, did not consider them as their equals. This search for identity was closely associated with space and displacements, and involved not only themselves, the exiled people from the former colonies, but also their descendants, their children who came with them, or who were born in Britain after their arrival, and were to be brought up in a place very

different from their places of origin. For many decades their children
would have to answer questions such as "Where do you come from?" or
"Where are you from?", and if the answer was "Bradford", or "East
London", or "Leeds", or any other location in Britain, they would
immediately have to face a second question like "But where do you *really*
come from?", "Where do you *originally* come from?", or "Where are you
really from?", meaning that those British places were not the "real places",
were not the "original places", were not really *their* places. No matter
whether they had been living there for many decades, or even if they had
been born and brought up there, their "real places" were somewhere else.

This concept of "real places" is, then, firmly tied up with the historical
memory of who they are and where they belong. My aim is thus to explore
some of the configurations that this search for an answer takes in writers
of African, Asian and Caribbean origin belonging to these diasporas in
contemporary Britain. In fact, this will enable us to discover that what is
usually referred to as "real places" (the "where are you *really* from"
question) are paradoxically mental reconstructions, configure deterritorialized
locations, and allude more to the imagination than to factual accounts
related to geography. For this purpose I will be using two main aspects of
diaspora, namely the search for emancipation or liberation –sometimes
from the colonial yoke, or from a totalitarian and violent regime, or simply
from a miserable life in a third world country; and the search for identity
and memory, for the consciousness of belonging. Thus I will explore how
some contemporary British writers –migrants themselves or descendants
of migrants—have engaged with and given imaginary/imaginative answers
to those two issues. These answers will take the form of: a) the image of
the island; and b) the image of the homeland.

2. *Diaspora* as an "imaginary":
Avtar Brah and Vijay Mishra

In this connection it is relevant to quote a British sociologist, Avtar
Brah, who in her 1996 book *Cartographies of Diaspora* stressed the
imaginary aspect of the concept of *diaspora*. She said that this concept
"delineates a field of identifications where 'imagined communities' are
forged within and out of a confluence of narratives from annals of
collective memory and re-memory" (Brah 1996, 196); that is to say,
diaspora as a term is not completely synonymous with *immigration* or
migrancy, although they are of course connected. For her, in the concept
of *diaspora* "historical and contemporary elements are understood in their
diachronic relationality" (197) and thus she separates two ideas that may

apparently look the same: that of "home", which is related to the origins, to where one comes from, and that of "feeling at home", which "is not the same as the desire for a 'homeland'" (197). I need to quote further from her to clarify this. Brah writes:

> Contrary to general belief, not all diasporas sustain an ideology of return. Moreover, the multi-placedness of home in the diasporic imaginary does not mean that diasporian subjectivity is 'rootless'. I argue for a distinction between 'feeling at home' and declaring a place as home. Processes of diasporic identity formation are exemplars *par excellence* of the claim that identity is always plural, and in process. The relationship between the two is subject to the politics in play under given sets of circumstances. In other words, the concept of diaspora refers to *multi-locationality* within and across territorial, cultural and psychic boundaries. (Brah 1996, 197)

These ideas, which are at the foundations of the arguments of this article, are basically common to other well-known formulations of diaspora in the last decade. For instance, also in 1996, Vijay Mishra published his essay "The Diasporic Imaginary: Theorizing the Indian Diaspora", where he emphasized the imaginary aspect of diaspora in connection with the way the term "imaginary" has been used by both Lacan and Zizek[3], and which he has further developed in other works to which I will refer later, particularly his more recent version "The Diasporic Imaginary and the Indian Diaspora" (2007). Another critic who has followed this path is Monika Fludernik, who writes in the introductory essay to her book *Diaspora and Multiculturalism: Common Traditions and New Developments* (2003) that "people who identify themselves as part of a diaspora are creating an 'imaginary'–a landscape of dream and fantasy that answers to their desires" (Fludernik 2003, xi). This emphasis on associating *diaspora* with the creation of "imaginary" spaces, because physical spaces are not enough to account for that feeling or need of a place to be identified with, has certainly gone beyond the field of literary

---

[3] This is Mishra's definition of "diasporic imaginary": "The diasporic imaginary is a term I use to refer to any ethnic enclave in a nation-state that defines itself, consciously, unconsciously, or because of the political self-interest of a racialized nation-state, as a group that lives in displacement". He also explains that he uses the word 'imaginary' "in both its original Lacanian sense and in its more flexible current usage, as found in the works of Slavoj Zizek". Thus he quotes from Zizek, remarking that his definition of imaginary is the state of "identification with the image in which we appear likeable to ourselves, with the image representing 'what we should like to be'" (Mishra 1996, 423).

studies and has permeated other areas of the humanities and social sciences.

Naturally a direct consequence of this fact is that metaphorical spaces and metaphorical communities keep springing up in the literature produced by the different contemporary diasporas. Writers belonging to these diasporas and willing to narrate those feelings of belonging, the fight for emancipation and liberation, the search for identity, and so forth, have seen that they cannot simply restrict themselves to the description of their surroundings, their "real" communities, but they need to express the imaginary, the dreams, the fantasies, the allegories, the desires, that usually find expression through metaphors.

3. The image of the island

Ashley Dawson opens his book *Mongrel Nation. Diasporic Culture and the Making of Postcolonial Britain* (2007), with a quotation from Lord Kitchener, a calypso singer who was very popular among the Caribbean immigrants to Britain after the Second World War. The words quoted by Dawson come from a song entitled "London Is the Place for Me":

> London is the place for me
> London, this lovely city
> You can go to France or America
> India, Asia, or Australia
> But you must come back to London City
>
> Well believe me, I am speaking broad-mindedly
> I am glad to know my mother country
> I've been travelling to countries years ago
> But this is the place I wanted to know
> London, that's the place for me
>
> To live in London you're really comfortable
> Because the English people are very much sociable
> They take you here and they take you there
> And they make you feel like a millionaire
> So London, that's the place for me
> (Dawson 2007, 1-2)

The words of this popular song evoke the metaphorical constructions of London and Britain, as well as of its people, developed by the immigrants who came to the country after the Second World War. Books like those by McLeod (2004) or Sandhu (2004) provide countless examples of how London has been imagined and reconstructed by these immigrants. Similarly many other sociologists, political scholars and literary critics have, particularly in the last twelve years, dealt with the constructions of the concepts of Englishness and Britishness (see, for instance, Gikandi 1996, or Mandler 2006). The conception of London as "the place for me" and of Britain as "my mother country" was widespread among the colonized subjects under the British Empire. Within the context of this formulation I wish to tackle the issue of the fight for emancipation and liberation, for becoming independent and more affluent, or in the words of the song, "making you feel like a millionaire". This is linked in the metaphorical constructions of the diaspora to the space of the island. Many diasporic writers make use of this metaphor, but I will concentrate only on two of them, both originally from the Caribbean: one male, Caryl Phillips, and another female, Andrea Levy.

Caryl Phillips, although born on the island of St Kitts, came to Britain with his parents when he was just a few months old. He was brought up near Leeds, and later went to Oxford, where he graduated in English Literature. His first novel, *The Final Passage* (1985), narrates the experience of a young married couple, Leila and Michael, who decide to leave their tiny Caribbean island and change it for the big island of Great Britain.[4] At the bottom of this decision is the utter necessity to escape from a suffocating atmosphere, because Leila feels that her life on the island is, and will always be, a life of humiliation and frustration. Everybody around her knows that her husband does not really love her, and that even after marrying and having their baby Calvin he still likes and goes on visiting Beverly, a former fiancée. Leila is unhappy and senses the commiseration of her fellow countrymen; she is convinced that nothing will really change if she does not leave the island and finds/founds a home elsewhere. Thus this tiny Caribbean island is presented as a sort of prison, whereas Britain, the big island, appears in her imagination as the great hope of liberation, the place that will enable her to start a new life.

This is a story set in the fifties, the period that later came to be identified with the *Windrush Generation* in homage to the ship that transported thousands of Caribbean people to Britain after 1948. The title Phillips chooses for his novel is strongly evocative, since "final passage" recalls of course the "middle passage" of millions of African slaves who were forcefully transported from their countries of origin to the Caribbean colonies of some European nations. Now Leila's decision to come to

---

[4] I have discussed this novel in some more detail, and in relation to other novels by the writer, in my article "Crossing Islands: the Caribbean *vs* Britain in Caryl Phillips's Fiction" (Galván 1997).

Britain is a sort of return, a "final passage", because Britain represents
liberation from a prison, a new land of promise, thus reversing the "middle
passage", which led to slavery. She dreams and fantasises with the idea
that Michael will get a job, will become a different man, will love her
again; she dreams that in Britain, where nobody knows her and their story,
she will get her dignity back. The images that the novelist offers of the
tiny island are gloomy. It is a place where nothing really happens; one day
follows another without any change, seasons and years turn monotonously,
but everything else remains the same:

> Leila woke up alone and feeling sick. Her body had slept but her head had
> not had a moment's peace. Her face felt old and crumpled, like a once-
> read, now-discarded newspaper. Outside a cock began to crow, unsure of
> whether it wanted to go through with another day in this powerful heat.
> The days were lengthening and again the island was preparing itself for a
> small rebirth. It was that time of the year. It had already rained, and the
> mushlike vegetation had rotted and devoured itself, and the winds had
> blown, and the hurricane warnings had been sounded, and the crickets had
> screeched in fear, but there was nothing to fear. (Phillips 1990, 67)

Leila needs to escape from this rotting, self-devouring island, which is
also menacing her with suffocation. However, the story does not have a
happy ending. The big island turns to be a disappointment. All Leila's
expectations are in fact disappointed by a cruel reality: Michael is seduced
by a white woman and abandons her, in another allegory of the white
colonial exploitation of the Black man; her mother, who was already living
in England, dies in hospital; and people around her begin to commiserate
once more, feeling the same sort of pity for her as her fellow countrymen
in the Caribbean. Phillips uses numerous images related to the
idiosyncrasies of both islands to express this. We notice, for instance, that
even as the ship that has taken her from her country to England approaches
the English coast, all Leila perceives around her is gloomy, dominated—
the novelist says—by "a colony of white faces":

> ... she [Leila] watched the drama unfolding around her. The crew in their
> blue woollen hats were preparing to dock. On the decks of the smaller boats
> the owners took a break from their summer repairs. They stood up and
> watched as the emigrant ship slid smoothly past the beacons, the sea wall and
> the lighthouse. Then the ship's engines were cut, almost as a mark of respect,
> and Leila watched as they took their place among the cranes and cargo. A
> colony of white faces stared up at them. The men finished their conversation.
>   'Me, I don't never see so many white people in my life.'
>   'Well, I suppose they don't ever see so many coloured people either.'

'It's true,' said a wise man, 'but we all the same flag, the same empire'
(Phillips 1990, 142)

The echoes of the calypso song are clearly heard here: "the same flag, the same empire" is the usual topical reference to "my mother country". But the description of the new atmosphere is indeed gloomy and "bleak":

> Leila looked at England, but everything seemed bleak. She quickly realized she would have to learn a new word: overcast. There were no green mountains, there were no colourful women with baskets on their heads selling peanuts or bananas or mangoes, there were no trees, no white houses on the hills, no hills, no wooden houses by the shoreline, and the sea was not blue and there was no beach, and there were no clouds, just one big cloud, and they had arrived. (Phillips 1990, 142)

Once she starts walking around she notices that there are announcements hanging everywhere from doors and windows saying "No trespassing", "No blacks", "No coloureds", and "No vacancies for coloureds". Getting a job is an equally grim prospect because racism dominates all social and economic relations. This big island is certainly not what she expected, not the "mother country", but an island of segregation and isolation. The final paragraph of the novel offers a very powerful image of what this island represents, namely old age, decadence, and ultimately death:

> A speckled, burnished light crept in off the street, piercing the awful inadequacy of the curtains. Leila caught sight of herself in a mirror. She looked like a yellowing snapshot of an old relative, fading with the years. She turned suddenly and saw that somebody had pushed a Christmas card through the front door. She stooped, with Calvin, and picked it up and read it, but it was from nobody. (Phillips 1990, 204-5)

The fact that this postcard pushed through the door has nothing written on it, that it comes from nobody, is indicative of the extent to which the imaginary space created by Leila, as by many other diasporians –in their need to construct a home—, is no more than a mirage, like that image of herself in the mirror: "a yellowing snapshot of an old relative, fading with the years".

In her popular novel *Small Island* (2004), Andrea Levy, also from the Caribbean (Jamaica), has similarly addressed this metaphor of the island. The novel starts with the account given by a white woman, called Queenie, of the Empire Exhibition, which took place in London in 1924-1925 and showed an idealized view of the Empire as the domesticated strange places Britain had civilized, all of them contained in a small place, all of them completely under control in a good example of the effectiveness of the exercise of colonial power. The contrast with this idealization comes immediately because Levy presents the encounter of an educated black woman from Jamaica, Hortense, with the "Mother Country".

Hortense had been trained as a teacher in Jamaica and married Gilbert Joseph, formerly a soldier during the Second World War, who had migrated to Britain with the hope of improving their miserable life in the Caribbean. It is an imaginary reconstruction—mentioned explicitly by the narrator (Levy 2004, 99)—of the *Empire Windrush* generation, of those who came to Britain after the War in order to make their contributions to the physical reconstruction of the war-ridden nation. Like Leila in Phillips's novel, Hortense is full of the most optimistic expectations when departing from Jamaica bound for England. We hear her voice as she imagines what will happen to her in the big island:

> I did not dare to dream that it would one day be I who would go to England. It would one day be I who would sail on a ship as big as a world and feel the sun's heat on my face gradually change from roasting to caressing. But there was I! Standing at the door of a house in London and ringing the bell. Pushing my finger to hear the ding-a-ling, ding-a-ling. ... Hortense Roberts married with a gold ring and a wedding dress in a trunk. Mrs Joseph. Mrs Gilbert Joseph. What would you think of that, Celia Langley? There was I in England ringing the doorbell on one of the tallest houses I had ever seen. (Levy 2004, 12)

But those expectations are very soon defeated when she finally arrives in Britain and looks around. She sees that only her fellow countrymen are happy with the arrival of the new ones, whereas the white people seem hostile. When she comes to her husband's dwelling place she also discovers that it is nothing like what she had dreamed on her small island. Gilbert speaks frankly to her, when he shows the ramshackle and dismantled room that constitutes all his lodgings: "This room is where you will sleep, eat, cook, dress and write your mummy to tell how the Mother Country is so fine. And, little Miss High-class, one thing about England you don't know yet because you just come off a boat. You are lucky" (Levy 2004, 32-33). This tiny and dismantled room is thus a metaphor of the big island, of Britain. The experience narrated here is very similar in many other diasporic writers, who have usually written about the shock of arriving and finding their lodgings in London or in other places in Britain[5].

---

[5] Shiva Naipaul does so in his autobiographical record *Beyond the Dragon's Mouth*, as his more famous brother V.S. Naipaul has also done in his autobiographical novel *The Enigma of Arrival,* both in connection with finding

In *Small Island* there is also a revealing example of how this big island of Britain, the Mother Country, turns into another secluded space, a restricted and anti-emancipatory location. It happens when Hortense, very proud of her credentials as a teacher, tries to get a job in an English school. She is of course rejected as her race and colour make her unsuited to perform the job. When after the interview Hortense understands that her studies and training are worth nothing in London, she feels deeply humiliated and makes to leave the room in confusion and anger; by mistake she turns the wrong way and walks into a cupboard, where mops and buckets are stored. That is *her space* in England. The big and promising island has turned into a dark, small, secluded and racist island, like the cupboard which symbolises manual labour, the only place and job for which she is considered adequate, given her race and colour.

Sociologist Avtar Brah has made reference to this racist aspect of the construction of Britishness in contemporary Britain in connection with nativism. She says:

> In the colonies, the Natives were excluded from 'Britishness' by being subjected as natives. But how does this particular nativist discourse reconfigure in present-day Britain? Of course, there is no overt evocation of the term 'native' but it remains an underlying thematic of racialised conceptions of Britishness. According to racialised imagination, the former colonial Natives and their descendants settled in Britain are not British precisely because they are not seen as being native to Britain: they can be 'in' Britain but not 'of' Britain. The term 'native' is now turned on its head. Whereas in the colonies the 'colonial Native' was inferiorised, in Britain the 'metropolitan Native' is constructed as superior. That is, nativist discourse is mobilised in both cases, but with opposite evaluation of the group constructed as the 'native'. (Brah 1996, 191)

4. The image of the homeland

If the island is used to project the most fantastic dreams and imaginary constructions of liberation, of emancipation and progress, only for those expectations to be ultimately defeated, as we have seen in the novels of Phillips and Levy analysed above, what all diasporic subjects also need is, of course, to construct their own image of the homeland. Wherever they live, they constantly feel the need to come to terms with their sense of space, the "real" space they occupy, but also with their history, their memories and traditions, so closely related to the "other space".

accommodation in Earls Court in London. For relevant excerpts from those works cf. Phillips 1997, 152-60 and 186-95.

Salman Rushdie has written in very revealing terms about this concept of the "imaginary homeland" in an essay published in 1982. It is an explanation of how he had come to write *Midnight's Children*. He was living in North London at the time and was struggling very hard to put down on the pages of his manuscript his life in Bombay, the place where he had been born but which had disappeared from his factual reality, particularly since he had left it first for Pakistan and then for Britain. The feeling of distancing from Bombay is similar to that of those migrants who undergo diaspora or dispersion, especially when they have to escape from totalitarianism. Writing in North London about those spaces left behind was very difficult because it was really a search for lost time, and he understood then the utter impossibility of retrieving it as it actually was. What is involved here, as he tells his readers, is mostly memory and the difficulties that memory encounters when attempting to grasp the actual past: "what I was actually doing was a novel of memory and about memory, so that my India was just that: 'my' India, a version and no more than one version of all the hundreds of millions of possible versions" (Rushdie 1991, 10).

Another writer from the subcontinent, who emigrated to the United States and Canada, Bharati Mukherjee, has also discussed this aspect of the diasporic memory, how difficult and, to a certain extent, how artificial and counter-productive it can be to try and capture that reality which is no longer available to the diasporians in their new land. Her words in an interview with Bill Moyers, entitled "Imagining Ourselves", are I think self-explanatory:

> Letting go of the old culture, allowing the roots to wither is natural, change is natural. But the unnatural thing is to hang on, to retain the old world. What is the point of hanging on to a culture that's thousands of miles away, and that probably not you, not your children, not your grandchildren will ever see? Why not adjust and accommodate to the world around you? (quoted from Fludernik 2003, xxviii)

In her comments on these words, Monika Fludernik finds them paradoxical because all diasporic communities try to find their identities through the memories of their origins, but, at the same time, as Mukherjee declares, that seems unnatural. Fludernik wonders, in this respect, if there is a way other than "clinging to what one knows" which might enable one "to face the new and survive the challenge". For her, there's only one way to define one's identity, and that is through narrative, which "needs to start in the past and pace its way to a future that embraces and resolves the discrepancies between past and present". She clearly borrows Rushdie's expression when she tries to explain how that can be achieved: "the memory of the past and its re-invention as an imaginary homeland are of the utmost psychological significance" (Fludernik 2003, xxviii-xxix).

An interesting image Rushdie uses in the above mentioned essay, in order to describe this sort of imaginary homeland, is that of broken mirrors[6]. He sees himself, as I have said, writing from outside India and making an effort to reflect that lost world, but in trying to do that he becomes aware that is dealing with "broken mirrors" (Rushdie 1991, 11), never with the complete and actual reality. The image of mirrors suggests of course substitution (the replacement for the real thing), but as the mirrors are broken, it is also very aptly suggestive of fragmentation. Diasporic migrants are necessarily fragmented, as a consequence of their being dispersed and torn away from their country of origin and their fellow countrymen. Thus, like memory, which is faulty and partial and may lead us into distortions and falsifications of history, the diasporic writer is faced with the challenge of remembering and rewriting the past left behind, which for him are like "broken mirrors". Rushdie then is creating fictions, "not actual cities or villages, but invisible ones, imaginary homelands, Indias of the mind" (Rushdie 1991, 10). In this way fragmentation, which initially might be regarded as a weakness, turns into a strength, allowing the writer to imagine his past, and giving him more freedom to create and to recover lost time and the lost home. Writers like him, who have experienced this sort of diaspora in Britain, feel empowered by precisely the tradition of migration and diasporas of the past. The list of writers he claims as his predecessors in writing in that tradition is revealing of the dimensions of that diasporic condition:

> Let me suggest that Indian writers in England have access to a second tradition, quite apart from their own racial history. It is the culture and political history of the phenomenon of migration, displacement, life in a minority group. We can quite legitimately claim as our ancestors the Huguenots, the Irish, the Jews; the past to which we belong is an English past, the history of immigrant Britain. Swift, Conrad, Marx are as much our literary forebears as Tagore or Ram Mohan Roy. (Rushdie 1991, 20)

The reference to the Jews cannot escape our attention in this context. Rushdie is also alluding to the classical diaspora, and clearly claiming that

---

[6] I have written about this recently in my "Metaphors of Diaspora: English Literature at the Turn of the Century" (forthcoming 2009), from which I adapt a couple of paragraphs.

the Indian, or South Asian, diaspora in Britain bears a strong similarity to that of the Jews.

Other authors, and chief among them Caryl Phillips, have made similar claims about their ancestors. In an anthology which he edited in 1997 (*Extravagant Strangers. A Literature of Belonging*), Phillips collected texts from a wide range of authors and periods. He started with 18th-century writers such as the African Olaudah Equiano but also included contemporary poets and novelists such as Linton Kwesi Johnson, Romesh Gunesekera, Kazuo Ishiguro, David Dabydeen or Ben Okri. He even put in well-known white authors such as William Thackeray, Joseph Conrad, Rudyard Kipling, Wyndham Lewis, or George Orwell, because all of them were born outside Britain and contributed their imagination, their 'imaginary homelands', to English or British literature. Phillips wanted to prove that Britain has always been a country of immigrants, where different diasporas have coalesced in shaping its peculiar identity, an identity that cannot be considered homogeneous at all. The reading of these texts demonstrates the wide diversity implied in the definition of *British*. In Phillips's words,

> readers will come to accept that as soon as one defines oneself as 'British' one is participating in a centuries-old tradition of cultural exchange, of ethnic and linguistic plurality, as one might expect from a proud nation that could once boast she ruled most of the known world. The evidence collected here confirms that one of the fortuitous by-products of this heterogeneous history has been a vigorous and dynamic literature. (Phillips 1997, xii)

In addition to Rushdie and Phillips, many other contemporary British writers could be mentioned, like Romesh Gunesekera, whose novel *Reef* (1994) presents a powerful recreation of an imaginary homeland, corresponding to his native Sri Lanka; or Abdulrazak Gurnah, whose *Admiring Silence* (1996) gathers together the protagonist's memories, but also his lies and fantasies (his mental constructions), about his original Zanzibar. Even writers who are British-born or British-bred have tried to imagine their parents' homelands: Monica Ali, Zadie Smith, Hari Kunzru could be mentioned as examples in the first years of the 21st century.

Let me briefly illustrate these ideas of the imaginary homeland through Monica Ali's successful *Brick Lane* (2003), but not before quoting again from sociologist Avtar Brah, who has tried to define the notion of "home" from a different non-literary perspective. Curiously enough, her conclusions are very much the same as those expounded by writers such as Rushdie or Mukherjee:

Where is home? On the one hand 'home' is a mythic place of desire in the diasporic imagination. In this sense it is a place of no return, even if it is possible to visit the geographical territory that is seen as the place of 'origin'. On the other hand, home is also the lived experience of a locality. Its sounds and smells, its heat and dust, balmy summer evenings, or the excitement of the first snowfall, shivering winter evenings, sombre grey skies in the middle of the day... all this, as mediated by the historically specific everyday of social relations. (Brah 1996, 192)

When reading Ali's *Brick Lane* we notice that for the female protagonist, Nazneen, home is not her everyday reality, that of her pregnancy in her London flat, but another reality, that of the dreams and fantasies of another world:

She looked at her stomach that hid her feet and forced her to lean back to counter its weight. She looked and saw that she was trapped inside this body, inside this room, inside this flat, inside this concrete slab of entombed humanity. They had nothing to do with her. For a couple of beats, she closed her eyes and smelled the jasmine that grew close to the well, heard the chickens scratching in the hot earth, felt the sunlight that warmed her cheeks and made dancing patterns on her eyelids. (Ali 2003, 76)

So space is used here to contrast, to oppose the everyday reality, that of her body, her room, her flat–which paradoxically have nothing to do with her, to what she really feels as home, which curiously enough are aspects linked to the same phenomena mentioned by Brah: smells, sounds of activity (the chickens in this case), and the heat of the sun. The space with which Nazneen identifies is an imaginary place, her imaginary homeland, where she can connect more closely with herself: "You can spread your soul over a paddy field, you can whisper to a mango tree, you can feel that earth beneath your toes and know that this is the place, the place where it begins and ends. But what can you tell to a pile of bricks? The bricks will not be moved" (Ali 2003, 87).

As this female character is initially very dependent, living in London in isolation, locked up in her flat because she cannot speak the language and consequently cannot move freely around, she desperately needs to claim that imaginary homeland as the source of her stability, her identity. That imaginary space gives her a feeling of safety. However, as she progresses and discovers that sewing provides her with money and thus economic independence, she feels more confident, and the appeal of the imaginary places loses ground:

The village was leaving her. Sometimes a picture would come. Vivid; so strong she could smell it. More often, she tried to see and could not. It was as if the village was caught up in a giant fisherman's net and she was pulling at the fine mesh with bleeding fingers, squinting into the sun, vision mottled with netting and eyelashes. As the years passed the layers of netting multiplied and she began to rely on a different kind of memory. The memory of things she knew but no longer saw.

It was only in her sleep that the village came whole again. (Ali 2003, 217)

But this is not always the case. For some diasporians, and particularly for some diasporic writers, the feeling of gaining safety and confidence in their new land does not obliterate the need for an imaginary homeland. On the contrary, as the African writer Abdulrazak Gurnah says, he left his country, Zanzibar, when he was a young man, eighteen years old, and settled in England. Escaping as he was from state terror, the only thing he wanted then was to forget about the hardships and anxiety, and "find safety and fulfilment somewhere else" (Gurnah 2004, 26). It was only after he had achieved that safety in England that he started writing. That act of writing was a way to reconcile himself with the memory of his origins, although that memory did not correspond exactly with the reality left behind:

I realized that I was writing from memory, and how vivid and overwhelming that memory was, how far from the strangely weightless existence of my first years in England. That strangeness intensified the sense of a life left behind, of people casually and thoughtlessly abandoned, a place and a way of being lost to me forever, as it seemed at the time. When I began to write, it was that lost life that I wrote about, the lost place and what I remembered of it. [...] I found myself overcome for the first time by the bitterness and futility of the recent times we had lived through, by all that we had done to bring those times upon ourselves, and by what then seemed a strangely unreal life in England. (Gurnah 2004, 26)

The writer is telling us that his life in England seemed "unreal" (he even refers to "the strangely weightless existence of my first years in England"), and thus the only thing that seemed genuine was the lost life he was recreating from memory. This curiously enough is what gave him the strength to write. Gurnah speculates about the theory that displacement and distance—such as the one he achieved by escaping from his country of origin and settling in Britain—are liberating for the writer, since distance, he says, "intensifies recollections, which is the writer's hinterland" (Gurnah 2004, 27). But at the same time, as he is also aware, distance can be distorting because writing "in isolation among strangers, the writer loses a sense of balance, loses a sense of people and of the relevance and weight of his or her perceptions of them" (Gurnah 2004, 27). This is what can happen with many post-imperial, or postcolonial writers, Gurnah says, because they run the risk of inventing and distorting the realities they talk about. Living far away, without contact with reality, with the real space, may be productive for the imagination, as it might "intensify recollections", but it can also be lethal for good writing and for setting up a fruitful rapport with your potential readers:

> So when I came to write, I could not simply shuffle myself into the crowd and hope that with luck and time my voice would perhaps be heard. I had to write with the knowledge that for some of my potential readers, there was a way of looking at me which I had to take into account. I was aware that I would be representing myself to readers who perhaps saw themselves as the normative, free from culture or ethnicity, free from difference. I wondered how much to tell, how much knowledge to assume, how comprehensible my narrative would be if I did not. I wondered how to do all this and write fiction. (Gurnah 2004, 28)

This is certainly one of the most exciting challenges for these writers of the diasporas: how to tell, how to narrate themselves through their imagination. As Vijay Mishra has said, "diasporas construct homelands very differently from the way in which homeland peoples construct themselves" (Mishra 2007, 9). The history of the Jewish diaspora presents examples of this, which are not only metaphorical constructions such as those I have mentioned from contemporary British writers. Mishra refers particularly to the need diasporic Jews have felt in history to construct their own idea of homeland as a hybrid, which adopts different configurations according to their diverse places of settlement:

> Historically Jewish homelands had been created wherever Jews had settled, in parts of the Middle East, in Poland, and elsewhere. Many Jews looked upon these enclaves as their homeland rather than to the Israel of the Book of Exodus. Their own diasporic episteme was located squarely in the realm of the hybrid, that is, in the domain of cross-cultural and contaminated social and cultural regimes. (Mishra 2007, 17)

So the imaginary homelands of these British diasporic writers are not so strange, if we bear in mind that diasporic homelands have also been

historically deterritorialized spaces, the product of multi-ethnic and hybrid communities in search of their own identity and memories.[7]
In short, and by way of conclusion, I have tried to prove, by showing a few examples of two dominating and powerful metaphors in some writers of the diasporas in contemporary Britain, that the imaginary constructions of space among them respond to a need to come to terms with questions such as the search for emancipation or liberation, for identity and for historical memory, no matter whether their origins are in India or South Asia, in Africa, or in the Caribbean. All these writers, coming from different parts of the world, ultimately resort to common images and metaphors, which, in some cases at least, barely differ from those historically recorded in other diasporas.

References

Ali, Monica. 2003. *Brick Lane*. London: Black Swan.
Brah, Avtar. 1996. *Cartographies of Diaspora. Contesting Identities*. London/New York: Routledge.
Cohen, Robin. 2008. *Global Diasporas. An Introduction*. Second edition London/New York: Routledge.
Dawson, Ashley. 2007. *Mongrel Nation. Diasporic Culture and the Making of Postcolonial Britain*. Ann Arbor: The University of Michigan Press.
Fludernik, Monika (ed.). 2003. *Diaspora and Multiculturalism: Common Traditions and New Developments*. Amsterdam: Rodopi.
Galván, Fernando. 1997. Crossing Islands: the Caribbean *vs.* Britain in Caryl Phillips's Fiction. *Alfinge* (University of Córdoba) 9: 161-69.
—. 2009. Metaphors of Diaspora: English Literature at the Turn of the Century. *ELOPE (English Language Overseas Perspectives and Enquiries)* V (forthcoming).
Gikandi, Simon. 1996. *Maps of Englishness. Writing Identity in the Culture of Colonialism*. New York: Columbia University Press.
Gilroy, Paul. 1993. *The Black Atlantic. Modernity and Double Consciousness*. London: Verso.
—. 2007. *Black Britain. A Photographic History*. London: Saqi in association with Gettyimages.
Gurnah, Abdulrazak. 2004. Writing and Place. *World Literature Today* 78.2: 26-28.

---

[7] Much has been written on the deterritorialized spaces of diaspora. Cf. the second edition of Robin Cohen's book (Cohen 2008, 130-139).

Levy, Andrea. 2004. *Small Island*. London: Headline.

Mandler, Peter. 2006. *The English National Character. The History of an Idea from Edmund Burke to Tony Blair*. New Haven/London: Yale University Press.

McLeod, John. 2004. *Postcolonial London. Rewriting the Metropolis*. London: Routledge.

Mishra, Vijay. 1996. The Diasporic Imaginary: Theorizing the Indian Diaspora. *Textual Practice* 10.3: 421-47.

—. 2007. *The Diasporic Imaginary and the Indian Diaspora*. Wellington, New Zealand: Asian Studies Institute, Victoria University of Wellington. Asian Studies Institute Occasional Lecture 2.

Phillips, Caryl. 1990. *The Final Passage*. Harmondsworth: Penguin Books (first edition 1985).

—. (ed.). 1997. *Extravagant Strangers. A Literature of Belonging*. London: Faber and Faber.

Procter, James. 2003. *Dwelling Places. Postwar Black British Writing*. Manchester/New York: Manchester University Press.

Rushdie, Salman. 1991. *Imaginary Homelands. Essays and Criticism 1981-1991*. London: Granta Books in association with Penguin Books.

Sandhu, Sukhdev. 2004. *London Calling. How Black and Asian Writers Imagined a City*. London: Harper Perennial.

CHAPTER TWO

SACRED SPACES: JOURNEYS OF SELF-DISCOVERY IN MEDIEVAL AND CONTEMPORARY LITERATURE

LILIANA SIKORSKA

Ever Since Aristotle's *Poetics*, philosophers and philologists (in the old sense of the word) strove to make literary analysis scientifically verifiable and objective discipline. Yet, literature has always remained a rather elusive subject with books and their characters living separate lives from their authors. Literary texts continue to occupy the liminal space between the fictional and the real, providing us, the readers, with a glimpse into the author's sacred space but also sometimes leading the critics astray. In what follows, I wish to demonstrate that what we consider "autobiographical" writing can be seen as conscious literary self-creation and what we consider "fiction" can be based on the author's various real-life experiences. Nevertheless, both types of texts confirm that writing has always been a journey of self-discovery in medieval and contemporary times.

1. Introduction

One of the famous early nineteenth century engravings by Charles Mottram presents a scene which for us, the literary scholars, should have the value of a document. Entitled "Breakfast at Samuel Rogers" the picture shows a large room crowded with men, recognizable as the notable men of letters of the early 19th c. The writers were certainly living people, but the scene in the breakfast room never took place. The characters were painted from portraits and the scene created is entirely fictitious. Thus, the picture like many literary texts can be placed in the liminal space between fact and fiction, to which, as will be argued in my presentation, all writing belongs. In what follows, I shall look at two medieval texts, John Capgrave's travelogue *Ye Solace of Pilgrimes* and Margery Kempe's autobiography, *The Book of Margery Kempe*, locating them both in the space of the fictitious, and two contemporary novels, Adam Thorpe's *The Standing Pool* and Andrew Miller's *One Morning like a Bird* placing them in the space of the real.

2. The Space of Literature

I have borrowed the title of this section from Maurice's Blanchot's work *L'Espace Literraire* (1955) translated by Ann Smock into *The Space of Literature* (1982). Blanchot's work is a reflection on the idea of poetry seen through the prism of German philosophy of Hegel and Heidegger. He talks about the "space" of literature as a "void", and of the writer as an exile. Thus, he suggests that the writer always finds himself/herself in the labyrinth of absence, forever corroborating literature's "remove" (used by Blanchot) from the world. The necessary solitude of the endeavour is "concentration" (1989, 21). For Blanchot "To write is to break the bond that unites the word with myself" (1989, 26). Yet, "...from the moment the work becomes the search for art, from the moment it becomes literature, the writer increasingly feels the need to maintain a relation to himself" (1989, 28). Pondering about the process of creation, Blanchot explores the space of autobiographical writing: "The journal-this book which is apparently altogether solitary –is often written out of fear and anguish at the solitude which comes to the writer on account of the work" (1989, 29).

One may not be excited by 1955 views, which in many ways are informed by the post-war existential approach to literature, his book being essentially a long polemic with George Bataille (Smock 1989, 6), but the questions of the space of literature and life remain ever so pertinent in the contemporary world. Blanchot was living in the post war-world without God, a world plagued by moral doubt and artistic inertia, and by the passivity and negativity of existentialism. At the time of historical and social change, philosophers and writers were re-examining the stance of literature and art, asking the question what literature really is.[1] A medieval scholar, John Capgrave (1393-1464)[2], an Augustinian monk, also lived at the time of change. A fervent speaker against John Oldcastle and John Wycliff, Capgrave was a prolific writer of saints lives confident about the

---

[1] See Jean-Paul Sartre. 1998 [1948]. *What is Literature?* London: Routledge

[2] Capgrave entered the convent around 1410 and between 1417 and 1422 he studied theology in London. He was a Prior of Lynn Priory, the largest Augustinian house in England between 1441 and 1453.

validation of his mission. For him, the value of writing was the writing
itself. Capgrave never thought of his works as works of art, rather, he
professed the ultimate aim of creation to be utilitarian. In 1450, Sir
Thomas Tuddenham, lord of the manor of Oxburg (some twenty miles
from Lynn, executed for treason in 1461), sponsored Capgrave's trip to
Rome, probably for the celebration of the Holy Year 1450 (Lucas 1983,
xxii). Following the visit Capgrave wrote *Ye Solace of Pilgrimes*[3], a
description of the city written as he claims: "On to all men of my nacioun
þat schal rede þis present book and namely on to my special maystr sir
Thomas tudenham undyr whos proteccioun my pilgrimage was specialy
sped..." (*SP*, 1)[4]. Capgrave thus acknowledges his patron but unlike in
almost all his other books (save *The Life of St. Katherine*) calls for the
attention of a more general audience, and not only the future pilgrims. He
begins the book listing the famous travelers like Plato, who traveled to
Egypt in order to gain knowledge, and saintly people like St Jerome, who
journeyed as a humble pilgrim. It is perhaps symptomatic that Capgrave
cites secular journeys alongside penitential pilgrimages and seems to be
more interested in the former, describing, for example, a man called
Marcus Paulus who "labored all þe soudanes londe and descryued on to us
þe cuntr þe condiciones of þe men..." (*SP*, 1). He also mentions John
Mandeville, "knight of yngland aftir his labour made a book ful salacious
on to his nacyoun" (*SP*, 1). Having established his intertexts, Capgrave
says: "Aftyr all þese grete cryeris of many wonderfull þingis I wyl follow
with a small pypyying of swetch straunge sitis as I haue seyn and swetch
straunge þingis as I haue herd" (*SP*, 1). He stresses that he uses written
sources, claiming to write solely from "auctores": "...I schal not write but
þat I fynde in auctores & þat is for a principall, or ellis þat I sey with eye
and þat is for a secundari, or ellis þat I suppose is soth lete þat be of best
auctorite" (*SP*, 1). Nevertheless, while discussing other travel narratives
Capgrave does not mention an extremely popular work *Mirabilia Urbis
Romae*, written most probably in the twelve century, which was a much

---

[3] In Furnival's foreword to *The Life of St. Katherine of Alexandria* from 1893,
Furnival lists *Guide to the Antiquities of Rome* of which fragments of this were
found in the fly-leaves of the two MSS of Capgrave's Latin treatise on the creeds"
(2000, xiii) The manuscript was found c. 1907. See C.A. Mills *Introduction*
(1911).
[4] Capgrave, John. 1911. *Ye Solace of Pilgrimes*. Edited by C.A. Mills with an
Introductory note by The Rev. H.M. Bannister. Oxford: Oxford University Press.
Hereafter cited in text.

copied medieval Latin text, and from which he himself borrowed the contents of the first part.[5]

In his life time [6], Capgrave witnessed war, the fall of a dynasty, hunger drought, pestilence, storms and the eclipse of the sun 1461, he was thus no stranger to the marvelous and the supernatural in history. No wonder, he frequently stresses the supernatural/divine intervention in creating Christian Rome. Describing the old temple of Marcellus, he mentions that Marcellus insisted to have "þe grete temple of fals goddis schuld be consecrate to all seyntis" (SP, 140).[7] Capgrave revealed that St. John Lateran "þis church is þe eldest church of þe world" (SP, 146)

> þe first þat euyr was bilid in cristendam and euene ouyr þe auter on þe wal is þe face of our sauiour wheech appered on to all þe puple of rome uisible þe same day þat seynt syluester halowid þe church. And as þe elde stories sey, it was neuyr mad with mannes hand but sodeynly þus it appered. (SP, 73)

Concurrently these are also the churches mentioned by Margery Kempe, who however, concentrates not on the buildings themselves but on her "meeting" with Christ and the Saints in these churches.

Ye Solace of Pilgrimes, written 150 years after the first Jubilee Year 1300, is a curious mixture of the sacred and the profane. Capgrave maps sacred spaces in the city but the city is presented as an amalgam of the real and the historical/tourist places, such as the palaces of Trajan and Hadrian, the coliseum; the mythological such as the tombs of Remus and Remulus and the sacred, including churches and shrines of the Christians. If, indeed the work was dedicated to future pilgrims, there is, however, strikingly little information about hospitals. The tradition of hospitals as shelters for pilgrims went back to the establishing of monastic dormitories for guests (hospes)[8]. Hospes were charitable institutions housing poor not infrequently

---

[5] Capgrave divides the text into: The first part schal declare the disposicious of rome fro his first making. The secunde part schal declar þe holynesse of þe same place from his first crystendom" (SP, 2).

[6] Abbreuiacion of Chronicles continues English history up till the year 1417. It was completed between 1462 and 1463.

[7] S. Marcellus was a Roman by birth, who became Christian. He founded the Catacombs of Priscilla on the Via Salaria, and created twenty five new tituli or Christian parish churches. He was savagely flogged and expelled from the city. This is proved by his epitaph. He appears to have returned shortly afterwards, and to have been condemned to labor in the public stables, where he died (SP, 141).

[8] Hospitals were founded in the late Roman Empire for the treatment of the sick. Later they became houses for ailing Christian soldier-monks such as the Templars.

sick pilgrims. Capgrave, for whom hospitals are of no cultural interest does not write about the hospitals of Rome, and the famous Hospital of St. Thomas is only mentioned once: "In euery sikirnesse I sei a uout mad at rome a ful fayre hous which is a celer at seint thomas hospital euene of þis same maner" (*SP*, 157).

Travel writing has been a much varied genre encompassing works from the Antiquity to modern times. One of the earliest and most interesting motivations of such narratives are discovery and exploration. Although assuring his readers of the religious aim of writing the book, Capgrave does not position himself as a pilgrim, rather, he can be seen as a tourist, admiring the ancient monuments of the eternal city, and providing us with the very first description of tourist attractions. By mentioning Mandeville, he certainly confesses his own "wanderlust", and by balancing secular and Christian elements, he testifies his own proto-humanism, without necessarily compromising the interest in the sacred space of the city.[9] A medieval author would not ask the question Jean-Paul Sartre posed: "why write", rather, a medieval author would write the truth for the glory of God and the benefit of his fellow Christians, and yet somehow always to record somewhat fictional versions of his or her own life.

Likewise, Margery Kempe (c. 1373-1438) did not have a dilemma whether to document her own life or not. On the contrary, she frequently tells the reader about the urge, the need to record her experiences bestowed on her by Christ himself. Concurring with the claim of an eminent medievalist Dee Dyas (a claim delivered during a presentation at Leeds Medieval Congress in 2001) that "we are not medieval Catholics" , we cannot fully comprehend medieval writer's motivation, but we do know literary conventions and many instances of Margery's rather extravagant behavior are downright silly. Throughout the decades scholars have hotly argued about the influence or the lack thereof, of the scribes on her texts, they have also discussed the grounds for her travels. One of the reasons for Margery's travelling was certainly penitence, but her penitence was premeditated as she tried to fashion herself into a mystic and a saint. Accordingly, she always talked about her obligation towards Christ, but rarely declaring that her trips were to be a form of penance prescribed by

---

[9] Capgrave's proto-humanism is best seen in his work on St. Augustine. See Sikorska . "Medieval Confession Manuals and Their Literary (re)Readings. The case of John Capgrave's *Life of St. Augustine* and John Lydgate *The Pilgrimage of the Life of Man*". *in*: Fisiak Jacek –Akio Oizumi—John Scaghill (red). *Text and language in medieval English prose. A Festschrift for Tadao Kubouchi*. Frankfurt,/Main, Nowy Jork: Peter Lang Verlag. 237-254.

her confessors, which suggests that she was also driven by a rather unholy touristic passion.

Arriving at Rome (which was one long stopover on her journey from Jerusalem to England), she is received into the hospital of St. Thomas of Canterbury. Unlike Capgrave, Kempe devotes a substantial portion of her narrative to a description of the hospital, where she undergoes her first trial in Rome. Upon Christ's command she dresses in white, and is afflicted "...with gret wepyng boistows sobbyng, & lowed crying & was hyly belouyd with þe maystyr of þe Hospital & with alle hys brethyr" (*BMK*, 80)[10]. Life would be too good for Margery if she was left in peace so

> ... þer cam a preste þat was holdyn an holy man in þe hospital &also in oþer placys of Rome (...) not-wythstondyng hys holynes he spak so euyl of þis creatur & slawndryd so hir name in þe Hospital þat throw hys euyl language sche was put owte of þe Hospital that sche myth no lenger be schrevyn ne howselyd þer-in. (*BMK*, 80)

Margery welcomes martyrdom by slander. For the glory of God (and undoubtedly her own) she endures difficulties in which she obviously rejoices: the more oppressive people are to her on Earth, the greater the promise of heavenly pleasures. Christ habitually tells her that "...þe more schame, despite & reprefe þat þu sufferyst for my lofe, þe bettyr I lofe þe..." (*BMK*, 81). Later, obeying Christ's order (the fickleness of the Lord?) she changes back into her black pilgrims' clothing, and again she "suffryd sche many scornys of wyfys of Rome" (*BMK*, 85), and did so, as we learn, gladly. Even if we assume Margery's position as a true mystic, the story with her clothes is a bit disturbing, and it is certainly one of the instances of conflation of life and literature.

One of the reasons for travelling to holy places was linked with the strong belief in miracles, primarily the miraculous healing of body and soul. For ordinary pilgrims faith healing entailed the cure of various physical ailments. Contrite and humble pilgrims were better able to obtain divine grace and later be spared the pains of Purgatory. Praying and full participation in mass, however, required confession and Margery did not have a confessor in Rome. Hence, as usual, she turned to Christ for help, praying fervently in the Church of St. John Lateran's. In the church of St. John Laternan a German priest named Wenslawe prayed daily that he

---

[10] Kempe, Margery. 1940. *The Book of Margery Kempe*. Edited by Stanford Meech and Hope Emily Allen. Oxford: Oxford University Press. EEST, o.s. 212. Hereafter cited in text.

might understand her. Although he spoke no English, he was granted the gift of understanding (*BMK,* 82-84).[11] And that aspect, obviously, is a frequent literary element used in a visionary text. Yet another wonderful example of the truly mystical miracle is Margery's ultimate reward from Christ. On November 9th 1414, in the church of "þe Postelys at Rome" (*BMK,* 86), she is married to Christ in the full meaning of the word, as he says "I take þe Margery, for my weddyd wife…" (*BMK,* 87). In this vision (which we might today call daydreaming) she receives a glimpse of heaven, as she sees herself in the center of attention of the Holy Trinity, all the Saints and Archangels.

Suffering misunderstanding, false accusations, hunger and discomfort were part of Margery's thorny path to sainthood. And as a sign of obedience to Christ, she willingly gave away all her means of support. As she now lay prostrate and obviously hungry in "Seynt Marcellys Churche in Rome", she wondered what to do next. Margery is comforted by Christ, who tells her of the friends he has all over the world and that he is not going to let them forsake her. Accordingly, she meets Margarete Florentyn with whom she travelled to Rome, and the lady feeds Margery.[12] For a

---

[11] Notwithstanding the priests good will, to those around her she is a stimulant and hypocrite: "…þe pepil was oftyn-tymes aferd & gretly astoyned, demyng sche had ben vexyd with sum euyl spirit er a sodeyn seknes not leuyng it was þe werk of God but raþar sym euyl spiryt" (*BMK,* 83). And her ill reputation brings about her final trial in Rome, when the company that she met in Jerusalem come to the aforementioned priest and complain that Margery was giving confessions to a Dutch priest who could not understand her. This is the ultimate slander and stain on her holiness, removed through a miracle, when Dutch as the priests' understanding of Margery is proven at a dinner; she tells a story from the Bible in English and the confessor translates her story into Latin. Such a miracle is also granted when Margery visits St. Bridget's chamber and speaks with Bridget's maid, there she is saved by a translator, a nameless man The maiden utters a number of stereotypical expressions about Bridget, which, however, to Margery are not as important as the place itself. She spoke with: "Seynt Brydys mayden in Rome, but sche cowd not vndirstondyn what sche seyd" (*BMK,* 95).

[12] We must assume that Margaret Florentyn was an elderly rich widow, who sought consolation in religion and warded off solitude with good works and alms for people such as Margery. It is most probably, Margaret Florentyn, who earns for Margery the respect of the people, who had previously despised her and had thrown her out of the Hospital. Now, they no longer claim she is possessed of the devil and Margery is invited back to the Hospital of St. Thomas, which in a way is her metaphorical resumption to a safe h(e)aven and out of the Purgatory of Rome. At that point, Margery spared worries of everyday life, Margery becomes a holy tourist who visits places connected with her greatest model and co-luminary (rival), Saint Bridget. Characteristically, Bridget is only a figure to confirm

time, spared from the cares of daily living, Margery visits the church in which the body of "St. Ierom[13] lyth berijd (which was miraculously translatyd from Bedlem in-to þat place…), to þis creaturys gostly sight aperyng, Seynt Ierom seyd to hir sowle, "that she is blessed" and "..drede þe nowt, for it is a synguler & a special 3yft þat God hath 3ouyn þe a welle of teerys þe which xal neuyr man take fro þe' (*BMK*, 99). St. Jerome was a well recognized authority on tears, so Margery's vision is not a accidental one but, one could say, well in line with her personal politics of sainthood. In the fourteenth century anonymous work entitled *Speculum Christiani*, tears are treated as one of the means of cleansing the soul from sin (1999, 214)[14]. The Church in which Margery receives the vision of St. Jerome is that of St. Maria Maggiore. It was a place of the burial of many holy people: "In the "auter of þe church restith þe body of seynt mathie þe apostil. And in a noþir auter by þe body of ierom doctor" (*SP*, 85). The building of the church was connected with the vision of the Virgin, who did not have a church in Rome. In the church there was a portrait of the Virgin executed by St. Luke.[15] Santa Maria Maggiore was famous for a number of other relics, and it is no coincidence that St. Jerome legitimizes Margery's behavior, for such a support corroborates generic requirements of hagiography.

Both Capgrave and Kempe are fascinated with Rome, but while for Capgrave it is a place full of Ancient as well as Christian relics, for Margery, the city remains the sacred space of churches, in which she receives visions of and from Christ. Capgrave reads Latin inscriptions and quotes various texts he has read, Kempe is a Christian tourist visiting places which affirm her own mystical experiences. In both cases, the space of life is invaded by literature.

3. The Space of Life

In 2007 Lindsay Clarke, an eminent British writer, winner of the Whitbread award for fiction, was our guest at the Literature in English

---

Margery's own sainthood, but the place itself has a touristic appeal because of the famous stone. And so: "Sche [Margery] was in þe chawmbre þat Seynt Brigypt deyed in,… & sche knelyd also on þe ston on þe which owr Lord aperyd to Seynt Brigtpte and telde hir what daysche xuld deyn on" (*BMK*, 95).

[13] St. Jerome (b. c. 347, Dalmatia, d. 419/420, Bethlehem, Palestine)

[14] The text mentions St. Christostom, St. Jerome, St. Bernard amongst others, who express the opinion that tears are "modis laxantur peccata" (1999, 214).

[15] The church was also full of relics, such as the arm of St. Thomas of Canterbury and his vestment, and the arm of Luke the Evangelist.

Symposium in Poznań. Having been obsessed with his work in the past, I kept pestering him about stories which provided the inspiration for his novels. It was Lindsay who told me about the transformations of life into literature, transformations which are multifarious and unending. He claimed that he never inhabits the consciousness of one of the characters but is, in a way, in all them. When Adam Thorpe came to Poznań, I was asking him similar questions about the connections between reality and the worlds invented in his novels. He emphasized that all his characters come to him as voices and names. Even a young boy Gilles in *No Telling* (2003), perhaps more akin to Adam's young self than other characters "... is a totally invented character, but probably the one I identify with most" (an e-mail message of November 13, 2008). Having extracted a number of real life stories which inform Adam Thorpe's novels and short stories, I shall cling to that "probably" and "identify" which Adam duly confessed. One may argue, following Michel Riffaterre that truth in fiction is a matter of linguistic perception. In a realistic novel (and both texts selected for further analysis are certainly realistic), fiction can be seen as "true" by means of verisimilitude created in language.[16]

Adam Thorpe's last to date novel *The Standing Pool* (2008) is about (mis)reading and (mis)interpreting reality around us and mistaken notions we have about it. The novel is set in contemporary France, and the two main characters are historians, namely Nick and Sarah Mallisons. Nick has a sabbatical and the family moves to France for a year to work on their respective projects away from their hometown university. At the end of the novel (2008, 412), Sarah looks at the photos, of herself naked and the children, their three girls showing their tummies and is certain that the schizophrenic handyman, Jean-Luc Maille had taken them, while in fact, the pictures of the girls were taken by the girls themselves, as one of them found the abandoned camera in a tool shed. Thus, Sarah's anxiety is the result of yet another misreading. According to Adam Thorpe the novel,

> ...which definitely uses reality and fiction, since it takes place here in France. Also the very climax is very much to do with how we hover between reality and fiction how what we experience is as valid as hallucination or dream and vice-versa, because there's a schizophrenic in the novel and... (....). Basically my point is that, through narrative, we care more about fictional characters than about nameless Iraqi children (...) trouble is, most of the reviewers didn't get this carefully-wrought and thought-out end, berating it as 'tricksy'. I was disappointed. (an e-mail message of November 13, 2008)

---

[16] Riffaterre claims that "fictional truth" refers to linguistic phenomenon but "fictitious truth is an oxymoron" (1990, i).

Thorpe denies any close connection with Nick Mallison, although, like Nick, he dislikes, cell phones: "Nick felt dismayed: he didn't want to admit that, for ideological reasons, they had never had a mobile" (2008, 19)[17], both of them are nevertheless forced to use them.

Briefly, though Nick shares a dislike for mobiles, he's quite separate from his creator in the same way Mrs Dalloway is from Woolf; i.e. he shares certain characteristics but by making him slightly older, of different politics originally (non-green Marxist) and with a very different biography, I never thought of him as being a version of 'me'. He's basically someone who has compromised and now regrets it; a portrait of disappointment. Also, he's an old father and married to a younger woman, with the attendant insecurity that can bring. And very much the academic! Unfulfilled, basically; stuck in Suez. Yet still in there, fighting. I was dismayed readers hated him so much. (an e-mail message of February 25, 2009)

Denying the association with Nick, Adam has Nick flirting with radicalism (*TSP*, 336)[18], which the younger Thorpe also did. Having made a decision to devote his life to writing (he was a pantomime actor and a teacher before), Adam Thorpe escaped Thatcher's conservatism, on what was supposed to be a temporary arrangement, and moved to France. Far from being happy with the development of the political situation in England, either in the light of the Conservative Party or Tony Blair's Labour government, the Thorpes stayed in France. Nick Mallison claims that "Time had surprised him, especially by dissolving his Marxist foundations, he had drifted from Habermas and Jameson to the unlikely port of Gilles Deleuze, a thinker for whom everything is displacement, contingency and indeterminacy, like worrying medical conditions" (*TSP*, 143). Thus, the story of the academic fighting his own weakness and forcing himself to do research is perhaps the story of a writer constantly misread and misunderstood also forcing himself to go on against all odds. In the novel Nick is angry thinking about the pointlessness of scholarship: "To be read by how many people? Why fly to places like Fez or Gdansk, pretending to be doing our academic duty, and read our papers to seven bored colleagues, who read their papers in turn in incomprehensible monotones, and then we all go out and get drunk. It's a farce" (*TSP*, 339).

---

[17] The hospital experience, the story appears in Adam's poem [in a volume *Nine Lessons from the Dark* (2003)] in a poem "After the Fall" (2003: 3-4), (*The Standing Pool* 2008, 124).

[18] Thorpe, Adam. 2008. *The Standing Pool*. London: Jonathan Cape. Hereafter cited in the text.

An even more ironic comment is given during a conversation with the
Sandlers from whom the Mallisons rent the cottage in France. Lucy
Sandler praising her husband's Adam Sandler's learning says: "'He did his
masters in Flann O'Connolly,' said Lucy, flatly, without raising her eyes
from the murk. 'Harvard. And she was a fervent Catholic' (the writer, LS).
'Flannery O'Connor, doll. A genius.' (Alan replies to Lucy) (*TSP*, 350).

Adam Sandler an art dealer, like Adam Thorpe, who has spent his
childhood in Africa and revisions Africa in *Pieces of Light* (1998), has
remembrances of Africa. For Sandler: "Africa! He'd given up on her, on
equatorial Africa. Wars, disease, corruption. It was Conrad's minus the
exciting story" (*TSP*, 43). Nick Mallison is a historian of colonial Africa, it
is no surprise that the themes of politics and history run concurrently with
the story of the Mallisons' stay in France:

> History had somehow escaped them all; had so far let them off. He'd heard
> it all his life, muffled, like a busy street through a closed window. Even in
> the Congo, with its street-mobs whirling chains and brandishing machetes,
> its bloodied faces and casually murdered neighbours, he had not felt the
> window open. He wondered if one day he could hear the high, unexpected
> smash of a stone in its glass. Impossible, of course: history can never be
> present (…) It is all words. It is only words. It has always happened, it is
> always a kind of ghost. (*TSP*, 150)

And in that respect history is open to numerous, sometimes conflicting,
interpretations. Sarah's, Nick's wife, looking at the withered flowers near
the plaque commemorating Second World War local hero thinks: "That
was sad. But that's what happened to history: it dried up to facts and
opinions. Occasionally it withered to a lethal little point, used by
troublemakers long after, stirrers full of hate and prejudice" (*TSP*,128).
Being an academic Nick is meticulously recreating certain periods in
history just like Adam is painstakingly creating the fictional world of the
novel. Interestingly while working on the proofs of the novel, Thorpe has
already begun his work on a medievalist text, entitled *Hodd* to be
published next year. Thus, it is easy to see the "shared characteristics":
Nick "… envied the Anglo-Saxon chronicler in his draughty cell, setting
down the handful of facts picked up from passing monks knocking the
mud from their boots" (*TSP*, 189). Even if for Nick "history is more about
amnesia than memory" (*TSP*, 324), for Adam literature seems to be about
remembering and transforming reality into texts, and the connection
between his own interest in the Second World War, and the life story of
his Polish-Jewish father-in-law seem to have a lot to do with this attitude.

The small town/village in France is a place where people remember the war, know one another and about one another. For Jean –Luc: "The village is all but dead. This annoys Jean-Luc. He blames the foreigners, the second homers. He blames the Parisians. He blames all those who profit at the expense of others. But he keeps this rancor to himself. He has never been to Paris. He doesn't see the point" (*TSP*, 61). The dislike of foreigners in France is quite universal appearing in many texts by English writers about France, more recently in Stepehn Clarke's *A Year in the Merde* (2004)[19]. Obviously, Jean-Luc shares some such sentiments with other small-town French people, while the Mallisons are trying to blend in with the local community. They listen to the French radio and work on their French which results in throwing French phrases into the conversation (*TSP*, 304), which Adam Thorpe was trying very hard not to do. Jean-Luc is one of Adam's greatest creation. Just like the voice of the mad strangler in Robert Browning's poem "Porphyria's Lover" he is a schizophrenic wrapped up in his delusions with a number of actions being real life events of the surroundings of Nimes, which are transformed in Thorpe's novel. For Thorpe, Jean-Luc is like

> Septimus Smith in *Mrs Dalloway* again, particularly the moment when Smith claims to be able to enter everyone's minds – i.e. he's like the author/narrator, a reference to the intrinsic madness of the inventing artist. Jean-Luc has both a symbolic role (war, any kind of sudden eruption— credit crunch, systems collapse?), but is also the lunatic, lover, poet (artist, in his case). He imagines the massacre in his cartoon strip [a kind of primitive art work, LS] just as I have done in my novel… (an e-mail message of February 25, 2009)

Jean-Luc talks to his uncle Fernand, killed by the Germans during the Second World War and creates art forms out of garbage. He is a sick man and a failed artist, while Nick, in a way, is a failed academic. Both of them "make stories (history) out of a chaotic stream of life events" (Adam Thorpe, in a note sent together with the novel, 17 September 2008).

That is also the case of Andrew Miller's protagonist Yuji Takano, a failed poet, in *One Morning like a Bird* (2008). The novel was written some fourteen years following Miller's stay in Tokyo as a teacher of English. Being alone in a strange world induced Miller to transform his experiences and transfer some of them onto his protagonist. Miller like Yuji felt that he was observing rather than participating in the events that

---

[19] The second volume in the series is *Merde Actually* (2005), both published by Black Swan.

were happening around him.[20] Throughout the text, Yuji slowly learns to overcome his detachment from the world as he tries not to be a passive spectator. "He has a great reluctance to take action though in his case it's indolence as much as anything; he wants to go on living his comfortable and slightly deluded former life, a not unusual ambition for a human being" (Miller, an e-mail message of February 18, 2009).

The title of the novel comes from the work of an ancient Japanese poet, Hitomaro: "One morning like a bird she was gone in the white scarves of death. Now when the child whom she lifts in her memory cries and begs for her, all I can do is lift him and embrace him clumsily" (*OMLB*, 110).[21] Similarly to Nick Mallison's disenchantment with his academic career, Yuji is embittered by his lack of success as a city poet. Seeing his only volume of poems untouched at a bookstore, he thinks:

> How many others there out there, untouched, unread, not even a crease or a thumbprint, no tea ring, no ink splash? Is there anything sadder or more useless in the world than a book of poems [*Electric Dragonfly*] nobody wants? (*OMLB,* 45)

The depth of poetic expression of a poet who is not read is contrasted with the shallowness of the bestselling author Karou Ishihara[22] who claims that poetry is no longer needed, "popular classes dominate societies all over the world. Your poetry, Takano, belongs to a more elegant age, the time, perhaps, of our grandfathers or great grandfathers. It is over. It will

---

[20] Miller, Andrew. 2008. *One Morning Like a Bird*. London Sceptre. Hereafter cited in the text. In the novel at a shrine, Yuji scrutinizes the passers-by: "As they come closer, he hears their little yelps of pain and self-encouragement, and as they draw level with him, he sees how their skin glitters with ice like fish scales. Shrine runners. Middle –aged penitents hoping to earn a year of better luck by dousing themselves with buckets of bitter-cold water at every shrine they stagger into" (*OMLB*, 15).

[21] "Hitomaro's (c.660-708) poem comes from Kenneth Rexorth's translations of classic Japaneses poetry. It is quite a long poem, very sad and lovely" (an e-mail message of March 22, 2009).

[22] Karou Ishihara is a contemporary engineer, but Shintaro Ishihara (b. 1932) is a popular writer, who in the past mobilized Self Defense Forces and police officers for an annual earthquake readiness drill. He was elected the governor of Tokyo in 1999. According to Miller "Isihara, is, very loosely, based on Yukio Mishima. Mishima, of course, was little more than a boy during the war" (an e-mail message of March, 22 2009) Yukio Mishima (1925-1970) pseudonym for Hiraoka Kimitake. Other Miller's intertexts are: Yasunari Kawabata (1899-1972), and Junichoro Tanazaki (1886-1965).

not return" (*OMLB*, 141). The readers want easily palatable entertainment and not intellectual puzzles.

It is wartime, and even though twenty-five year old Yuji has an easy life in his father's house, he, like our medieval protagonists, also lives in the time of change in 1940s Japan, and is facing the necessity to work for his living (which he did not have to do before because of his allowance) and the prospect of being drafted, despite his weak lungs. The allowance has become the main source of income to maintain the entire family, as Yuji's father has lost his job and his pension due to a disgrace having written some year previously a political book criticizing the Japanese system of government. In the medieval Japanese *Essays on Idleness* written between 1330-1332, the author, a Buddhist priest Kenko, writes: "It is bitter for a man sunken in grief over misfortunes to shut his gate and live in seclusion, so quietly, awaiting nothing..." (1999, 55). Yuji, a university graduate, hides himself in a mantle or rather the armor of an intellectual: "Is that how you protect yourself? By reading? By listening to music? Or does the world exert an ineluctable force that only the most exceptional can resist? And is he one of them? Is he exceptional?" (*OMLB*, 35). Afflicted with a writer's block, he nevertheless sees himself as a poet:

> A poet, even one who has not written in almost two years (who has abandoned as mysteriously, as abruptly, as it arrived), has a duty to imagine what imagination baulks at, but the best he can achieve before the air in his lungs starts to burn is something indistinct and swirling, a patch of brightness disappearing into the general dark, like a coin sinking to the bottom of a pond, or the moon through blown clouds, or a head, a face as a mask, peering through smoke... (*OMLB*, 9)

In a highly symbolic opening scene, in which Yuji sits with one hand warming at the brazier, and the other holding a book and reading French poetry thinking of the life of a poet always torn between the material demands of existence, life in the outer world and the intangible needs of inner life of an artist, a life in and through books.

> So the young hero (who confesses to knowing nothing of life except through books) must set out again for the chateau of la Quartfouruche while Yuji examines from every futile angle the latest and most pressing of his difficulties, the matter of his allowance, of its days ago, no warning, no warming up, everything delivered in a kind of distracted aside, Yuji by the door, Father at his writing table, smoking and peering at the end of a bookshelf...Apparently, the allowance had become a burden on the

household economy…It was understood, of course, that he understood.
(*OMLB*, 4)

Yuji did understand the economic necessity, but pondering about the past, somehow he could not envision his own future.[23]

Following the economic crisis of the late 120s and early 1930s Japan tried to build its strength based on "the consciousness of the house" (Kotkin 2005, 101). "Asserting the hierarchy of the 'house' had the effect of reinforcing the authority of parents, firm owners, military and political leaders, and ultimately, the emperor" (Kotkin 2005, 101)[24] Such is the hierarchy of Takano's family, with the Grandfather and the Father as its heads. The other side of what one might label as the "the culture of reputation" is the impossibility of communication. Yuji never talks to his mother and hardly ever talks to his father. Following his brother's Ryuichi's death: "It might have freed them once (these two who have taken a certain pride in not speaking), but now, it seems, the time for it has passed. They have changed. They have been changed. Between them, the tilt of circumstance is quite different" (*OMLB*, 254). Hence, the problems of finding oneself in a world caught between the culturally traditional past and westernized uncertain future. For Yuji it is the metaphorical knot of life, of relationships, power relations and dependences, bringing forth the anxieties about which he cannot talk to anyone.

Yuji is a misunderstood and withdrawn artist lost in the labyrinth of life, just like Miller himself was lost in the maze of Tokyo. In a article published on the internet, Miller admits that he had a hard time getting acclimatized in Tokyo. In the hot summer of 1994, he got constantly lost

---

[23] Seidensticker talks about "the double life" which "refers to the Japaneses way of being both foreign and domestic, of wearing shoes and sleeping on the floors. The double life is at best an expense and inconvenience, we are told, and at worst a torment, leading to crises of identity and such things" (Seidensticker 1983, 90).

[24] Miller is very careful in recreating Japanese culture in the behavior of the characters. When Yuji's father's younger brother, Uncle Kensuke calls, "There is a long pause while Uncle speaks. He is the younger brother and not, therefore, not strictly, the one to proofer advice to the head of the family" (*OMLB*: 24). Yuji is also put off by Alissa's too forward behavior: "(And should a nineteen-year-old-girl in the company of men, all of them, with the exception of Oki, at least a *little* older than her, express herself in such a forthright manner? Even for a foreign girl it is surely slightly improper.) (*OMLB*, 61). Being exposed to a different style of life, he observes traditional Japaneses family. For him Mrs Miyazaki is: "One of the old-style wives, content to kneel at the kitchen door waiting to be told when to bring the sake in. A life lived at the edge of the visible" (*OMLB*, 157). patriarchy, the men separate from the women (*OMLB*, 234).

on the way to work, before finally mastering the routes and trains. For Miller learning (and recognizing) the landscapes of the city was a long journey from chaos to order, yet Japan has never lost the aura of mystery. The novel recreates the topography of old Tokyo[25]: The vibrant Low City with Old Ginza: "To find Makiyama he [Yuji] will have to hunt him, bar by bar, along the Ginza" (2008, 52, 70-71), the famous Ginza crossing[26], the supposed center of Tokyo, Ueno Park and Ueno Museum where Taro and Junzo (*OMLB*, 121), Yuji's friends meet[27], the Shinobazu Pond[28], providing an inspiration for Yuji's writing, the middle class Hongo[29], in High City, where Yuji and his family lives, Kanda, where the Feneons have the house[30], and Sentagaya where Yuji's Grandfather lives. This is the Tokyo of the 1940's:

> As you know I lived in Tokyo for just over a year so had indeed visited many of the places—Ueno park for example—visited by Yuji and friends. Obviously Tokyo was extensively damaged in the war and so I had to reconstruct the lost topography as best I could using pre-war fiction and

---

[25] Edo became Tokyo in 1868, it was the seat of power of the shogunate. The Meiji Emperor departed in 1868 and returned to Kyoto in 1869. The same year returned to Tokyo and that is when the permanent residence in Tokyo started. In 1871 the last court offices were moved from Kyoto to Tokyo.

[26] "Though the matter is clouded by the enormous growth of centers to the west, it might be said that the main Ginza crossing is still the center of the city. There was a span of decades, from last Meiji or from Taisho, when almost anyone, asked to identify the very center, would have said Ginza, and more specifically, the main Ginza crossing (Seidensticker 1983, 198).

[27] "Ueno, the place for expositions, is one of five public parks, the first in the city, established in 1873. The public park is another Meiji novelty introduced under the influence of the West" (Seidensticker 1983, 116) "Ueno Park had the first art museum in the land, the first zoo, the first electric trolley, a feature of one of the industrial expositions, and in 1920, the first May Day observances" (Seidensticker 1983, 118).

[28] "A water chute led down to the lower level, on the shores of Shinobazu Pond, where special exhibitions told of foreign lands and a growing empire. There was a Taiwan pavilion and a Ryukyu pavilion, the latter controversial, because ladies from the leasure quarters were present to receive visitors and make them feel at home. They were considered an affront to the dignity of the Ryukus, whose newspapers protested. (Seidensticker 1983, 116).

[29] Hongo is the university district, with may professors living close to the university. "There were some famous boarding houses in Hongo, which, with Kanda, had more of them than any other part of the city. The most famous produced approximately one doctor of philosophy per year during the quarter of a century after its establishment" (Seidensticker 1983, 242).

[30] "Kanda was almost entirely secular" (Seidensticker 1983, 213)

pre-war maps and photographs. The earthquake in which Yuji's brother
died and the Low City was destroyed was the great Kanto earthquake of
1923. (an e-mail message of March 2, 2009)

Trying to preserve the lost world from oblivion, Yuji's grandfather is
constructing the model of the city that no longer exists.

What will happen to the model and what will happen to Grandfather. The
moment cannot be far away now, no more than another winter, two at
most. Will he build an extension onto the house, turn the twelve mats into
twenty, let the model grow north to Asakusa? Or will the end of the table
be the end of his labours, his memorial to the last of Edo, to the spirit of his
eldest grandson, to a thousand streets shaken to firewood then burnt red
ashes? (*OMLB*, 50)

By writing his novel, Miller is also trying to retrieve the old Tokyo
from the past. The earthquake, ever present in the book, furnishes an
atmosphere of unspecified menace, causing anxiety which people live
with, even the tiniest, least felt quakes of the Earth remind them of their
tragedies.[31] The fact that they cannot in any way prevent it, leaves them
prey to natural forces, in a way which resembles the existential passivity
and the impossibility of right choices Miller's characters face in *Oxygen*
(2001) and *The Optimists* (2005).[32]

One Morning Like a Bird is dedicated to Frieda, and as Andrew Miller
himself says, the book is about himself discovering fatherhood. Yuji learns
to love his son Emile, and appreciate the boy's mother, Alissa Feneon.
"The book's interest in children is a straightforward reflection of my own
experience as a new father (I have a four year old girl called Frieda" (an e-
mail message of February 18th 2009). In the end, Yuji abandons his
parents' already empty house, he also leaves behind the last copy of his
volume of poems, *Electric Dragonfly*, feeling that things have changed
irrevocably, that the past is shut in his family's house, and he alone has to
face his future. Like other Miller's characters whose credo comes from
Beckett's *The Unnamable* he is afraid, and frequently thinks cannot go on.
Yet, for the sake of his son, must go on.[33]

---

[31] On the last day of August 1923 Noriko Takano was shopping with Mrs
Hatanaka, she wounded her feet on the broken glass so severely that she is now
practically an invalid spending her life inside the house and never venturing further
than the garden (2008, 49).
[32] "As a character I think Yuji shares traits with some of the characters in *Oxygen*"
(an e-mail message of February, 18th 2009).
[33] The correct quote is „...I can't go on, I'll go on" (Beckett 1958, 414).

The starting point of David Daiches' *A Study of Literature for Readers and Critics* (published originally in 1948) is a question posed to the students of literature: "Why do you spend time reading and discussing books which tell of events which never occurred?" (1964, xi). For Daiches as for contemporary readers and critics that literature might be a trope of reality can be seen as a rather banal regression to a kind of nineteenth century scholarship, which argued that literary works should be perceived as a reflection of historical and social context, through the prism of the author's life. Acknowledging the autonomy of literature one has to admit, however, that in contemporary (rather eclectic) criticism, space is a term used to analyze such diverse phenomena as cultural marginality vs. centrality, closeness vs. distance, private vs. social space, etc. Accordingly, in a travelogue the author's persona recounts his/her experiences, and in autobiography the narrator relates a version of oneself. Journeys of self-discovery, however, do not concern the unveiling of sacred spaces, but rather, as I have demonstrated, they signal the practices of literary discourse which let the novelists "half reveal, half conceal the truth within."[34]

References

Blanchot, Maurice. 1989 [1955]. *The Space of Literature*. Trans. by Ann Smock. Lincoln/London: University of Nebraska Press.

Bannister, H.M. 1911. Introductory Note to Capgrave, John. *Ye Solace of Pilgrims*, ed. by C.A. Mills with an Introductory Note by Rev. H.M. Bannister). London: Oxford University Press.

Beckett, Samuel. 1958. *Three Novels: Molloy, Malone Dies, The Unnamable*. New York: Grove Press.

Capgrave, John. 1911. *Ye Solace of Pilgrimes*, ed. by C.A. Mills with an Introductory note by Rev. H.M. Bannister. Oxford-London New York: Oxford University Press.

—. 1983. Abbreuiacion of Chronicles, ed. by Peter J. Lucas. Oxford: Oxford Univeristy Press. EETS.

—. 2000 [1893]. The Life of St. Katherine of Alexandria, ed. by Carl Horstmann, with a foreword by F.J. Furnivall. Woodbridge, Suffolk: Boydell and Brewer.

"sometimes hold it half a sin
To put in words the grief I feel;
For words, like Nature, half reveal
And half conceal the Soul within" (5). Tennyson *In Memoriam*

Daiches, David. 1964 [1948]. A Study of Literature for *Readers and Critics*. New York: A.W. Norton and Company.

Furnivall, F.J. 2000. Foreword to Capgrave, John. *The Life of St. Katherine of Alexandria,* ed. by Carl Horstmann. Woodbridge, Suffolk: Boydell and Brewer.

Kempe, Margery. 1940 [1993]. *The Book of Margery Kempe,* ed. by Stanford N. Meech and Hope Emily Allen. EETS, o.s.212. Oxford: Oxford University Press

Kenko, Yoshida. 1999. *Essays on Idleness.* Trans. by Donald Keene. Tokyo: Bilingual Books.

Kotkin, Joel. 2005. *The City. A Global History.* London: Wiefeld and Nicholson.

Lucas, Peter J. (ed.). 1983. Introduction to Capgrave, John *Abbreuiacion of Chronicles.* Oxford: Oxford Univeristy Press. EETS.

Miller, Andrew. 2008. *One Morning like a Bird.* London: Sceptre.

Nichols, Francis Morgan. (ed.). 1986. *The Marvels of Rome/Mirabilia Urbis Romae,* ed. and trans. by Francis Morgan Nichols, with a New Introduction, Gazetteer and bibliography by Eileen Gardiner. New York: Italica Press.

Rifaterre, Michel. 1990. *Fictional Truth.* Baltimore/London: The Johns Hopkins University Press.

Sartre, Jean-Paul. 1998 [1948]. *What is Literature?* London: Routledge.

Seidensticker, Edward. 1983. *Low City, High City: Tokyo from Edo to the Earhtquake.* New York: Alfred Knopf.

Thorpe, Adam. 2003. *Nine Lessons from the Dark.* London: Jonathan Cape.

—. 2008. *The Standing Pool.* London: Jonathan Cape.

CHAPTER THREE

URBAN SPACES AND EXPERIENCE OF LITERATURE: IMAGINARIES, PASSAGES, CEMETERIES

TADEUSZ SŁAWEK

> *Death must be only a temporary interruption, the important thing is to get over it and to go on living.*
> —Talcott Parsons

1.

In the first chapter of *The Scarlet Letter* Nathaniel Hawthorne famously claims that the human existential experience is constituted by three kinds of spaces: a social space of "community", a juridical-disciplinary space of "prison", and an administrative-metaphysical space of "cemetery". "The founders of a new colony, whatever Utopia of human virtue or happiness they might originally project, have invariably recognized it among the earliest practical necessities to allot a portion of the virgin soil as a cemetery, and another portion as the site of a prison" (Hawthorne 1959, 55). As we learn from the passage, the community, which must aim at inclusion and participation, regulates its *modus vivendi* through two areas which are territories of exlusion. The prison excludes by a sophisticated machinery of marginalizion, the cemetary by being the plave of those who are absent, who have left the community, the departed ones. Human virtue and happiness, to use Hawthorne's terminology, although certainly communitary in their character of the social exchange of being-with, are anchored in being-without, either temporarily (prison) or permanently (cemetary). What we do with the sense of loss (a loss of virtue or, more radically, with a loss of life) is crucial for the survival of the community.

2.

Greek tragedy makes such a claim: the unburied corpse, a visible manifestation of the loss, marks the most vulnerable point of the community. There seems to be nothing more perilous than the unconfined criminal, one who mocks the law by remaining at large, outside the walls of prison, but even more dangerous and disruptive is an unburied body which, by its manifest visibility, defies the power of the cemetery to hide what should be hidden. To confine and thus to control what corrodes the vital forces of the virtue of surviving (be it criminality or death), is the task of the human society.

3.

Sophocles's *Antigone* opens with the amplification of suffering. To the already long list of harrowing experiences Oedipus's kin have been subjected to a new element is added by the "heavy hand of God". As Antigone says to her sister: "There is no pain, no sorrow, no suffering, no dishonour/ We have not shared together, you and I./ And now there is something more" (Sophocles 1967, 126). This "something more" is particularly difficult to bear because it is aimed at the very heart of the living, constitutes an attack upon the very center of life which is threatened independent of any conscious or unconscious fault, transgression or guilt. It is an assault on the life itself because life is touched to the quick in its very innocence. Creon's order has a very precise addressee: "It is against you and me he has made this order". But if one wants to profoundly assault the living, one needs to take a path which would introduce death into the very substance of life. Death will now rule over a chosen person or group of persons because it will remain a for ever open wound which nothing will be able to seal. Regime marks its perverted power over people by strictly reglamenting the space of burial: some corpses will be buried escorted to a cemetery which is the space of consolation, some however will be denied this privilege. From this perspective the cemetery fulfils the fundamental role of a place where the dead are honoured by being removed from our sight thus allowing for a continuation of life. The human bond is shattered when the "honourable observances due to the dead" are interrupted. Antigone summarizes this in her speech: "Eteocles has been buried, they tell me, in state,/ With all honourable observances due to the dead./ But

Polynices, just as unhappily fallen – the order/ Says he is not to be buried, not to be mourned;/ To be left unburied, unwept, a feast of flesh/ For keen-eyed carrion birds".

4.

The unburied corpse, i.e. also the corpse not mourned, the corpse "unwept", the corpse which was denied its way to the burial space, lies at the center of the political debate and political action. The heart of the problem is the degree to which the dead dictate the course of events in the world of the living. Antigone's claim to the overwhelming supervision of the living by the dead is based on two principles. First, the ultimate priority of the home, family, of *oikos*, over the public sphere, and, second, the reluctance to admit the right of the authority to determine laws which go outside the realm of the living. Even Ismene withdrawing her support from Antigone's unlawful action and recognizing the secular law signals that her attitude is a mark of weakness rather than virtue: "May the dead forgive me, I can do no other/ But as I am commanded; to do more is madness". What Ismene calls "madness", and what Antigone hastens to reiterate with pride ("Leave me alone with my madness"), in the pragmatic language of power means a impudent gesture of the denial of the state. Who raises his or her hand against the state is "mad", but since "madness" lies outside the territory of legal regulations and thus is hardly punishable, it must be translated into the juridical discourse of "crime". Creon maintains that "No other touchstone can test the heart of a man,/ The temper of his mind and spirit, till he be tried/ In the practice of authority and law". The practice of authority and law must include the dead as the aim of practical political and juridical action is to maintain power, and the corpse becomes an important element of this game. Its significance lies in the fact that when it becomes the object of legal decisions, it clearly demonstrates the intimidating might of the ruler: the king is the one whose decisions are not restricted to the living but who also commands the world of the dead. In a concise but accurate formulation the Chorus says to Creon: "Your will is law".

5.

This "will" wants to strengthen the rule over the living by extending its legal jurisdiction over the world of the dead. Antigone and Creon debate the range of democracy over the unburied corpse. L.V.Thomas rightly says that "the dead body is something fundamental. There can be nothing worse

than an absent dead. What is a corpse? It is a presence that marks absence"
(cited in Ph.Ariĉs and G.Duby, 5, 400). What marks the space of a
cemetery which now is seen as central for the *polis* is sovereignty of the
date; there the human time triumphs, paradoxically, by admitting its own
reduction. Tombs are temples of the date, to be more specific, the
cemetery and the whole process of burial is a kind of chronological sieve,
space which filters the abundance of dates constituting human life to the
two most fundamental ones: born in...., and died in.... Nothing else matters
in the funerary poetics of the tombstone. In a sense this filtering of time,
this radical synthesis of volumes of temporal occurrences, calendars filled
with days and hours each with its allotted preoccupation, is an act of
fundamental justice. In a life time one date competes with another, some
of them which seemed epoch making now are hardly remembered – a
profound injustice of existence. Flaubert famously exclaiming on his
deathbed—"I'm dying, while this whore, Madame Bovary, will go on
living!". Antigone constructs her argument along this line: Creon's order,
on the strength of which the body of Polynices is to remain unburied,
belongs to the domain crowded by dates conflicting with one another, thus
to the realm where justice can be only a negotiable truce, whereas the
corpse calls for a burial because it belongs to the realm of peace
supervised by Justice. Commenting upon Creon's decree she says: "That
record did not come from God. Justice,/ That dwells with the gods below,
knows no such law./ I did not think your edicts strong enough/ To overrule
the unwritten unalterable laws/ Of God and heaven, you being only a
man./ They are not of yesterday or to-day, but everlasting,/ Though where
they came from, none of us can tell". On the one hand, there is a
spasmodic nervous spectacle of human dating, on the other – a quiet, even
sedate, realm of the buried marked just by two year references.

6.

Cemetery stands in an awkward relationship with *polis*. It is a
necessary space which conditions the foundations of the laws of the city, it
is there where from buried bodies democracy finds it rejuvenating force.
From this perspective democracy is a political version of resurrection: the
buried rising again to establish the order of the city. But, at the same time,
the cemetery compromises the extensive system of democracy based upon
precise chronological order which organizes human life and its social
aspects within a network of mercilessly accurate time zones. Edgar Lee
Masters, whose name must inevitably come up in the context of funerary
meditations, is acutely aware of this radical power of the tombstone and its

dates, and in his analysis goes one step further. Not only is the tombstone a radical reduction and concentration of the scattered expansiveness of human social time, but it also demonstrates that these two dates always inscribed there, although certainly referring to a specific individual, lose somehow the personal character. The human individual is released from the pressures of social time but also, more radically, he/she is liberated from his personal time – the two most essential dates, that of birth and death, are shown to be aleatoric, somehow incidentally, and therefore loosely, connected with himself/herself. As if birth and death, to which we normally give an ontological orientation (they bring us to and release us from the general pattern and sense of things and events), are now understood psychologically (they are two categories which provide me with a means to perceive and understand reality). In the first reading of the two dates we belong to history, in the other – we belong to stories and occurrences the time and sense of which are uncertain. "Life not repressed", writes Norman O. Brown, "is not in historical time (…) and gathers to itself ageless religious aspirations" (Brown 1959, 93). In the continuation of Masters's famous work on Spoon River we come across the following inscription:

W.O.Morris

In the beginning God created the heavens
And the earth;
And I was born when I was born,
And died when I died -
One statement tells as much as the other! (Masters 1968, 174)

"I was born when I was born" and "died when I died" are phrases which bitterly parody the structure of the social time: the impeccable logic is brought to its ironic denial – tautology, and the dates turn out to be as imprecise as the "beginning" which marks God's creative gesture. The cemetery with its stone engravings constitutes a necessary corrective for the life of *polis*: not in a traditional sense of reminding us of the frailty of our mortal existence but, first of all, because it alerts us to the fact that the human institutions and their timing is founded upon a time which remains totally indifferent to these measures. Democracy, unredeemably locked in time, must however look back towards its timeless sources.

7.

In another epitaph Masters indicates yet another reason for which the cemetery is a lesson for democracy: it helps us to understand the drawbacks of and disillusionment with the system. The cryptic (and we have to hear the necessary funereal tone in this adjective) engravings on tombstones drastically reduce dates of events constituting human life, and in this way demonstrate their vanity but, by eliminating them, purport that history is a series of misunderstandings. The poetics of tombstones evaporates the events of our life and thus make them insignificant; nothing could be learned from the experiences of one's closed existence. If previously it was the time of the society and its preoccupations that was being revised by the tombstone, now this revision addresses a most central conviction of culture – that of a progress resulting from a steady accumulation of facts and knowledge. If this process of gathering data can work with reference to scientific observations, it fails in the domain of being. Progress applies to data; human history as a history of being remains untouched by this belief. Commemorating James Istel Masters writes:

After you have lived and read many books;
And fathomed Patience, Courage, Friendship, Love,
Through suffering and experience.
And seen how much of hate there is in the world, and why;
And how much of robbery there is in the world and why;
And how much of slander there is in the world and why;
And how much of malice, selfishness and cruelty there is in the world and why;
And after so living you have also learned your age,
Then if you cannot make understandable what you know;
And if the new generation is not interested in what you know,
Are you not buried alive and epitaphed with hieroglyphics?
And are you not the voice of wisdom
Which never yet has bequeathed much of its lore
To the next era? (Masters 1968, 234)

One's essential duty is then to make understandable one's life experience which, however, implies the presence of the addressee of such communication, a recipient willing and interested in learning. Death as a sense-making termination of human life is made possible only on the condition of such presence; without it, we are doomed to live a spectral existence of those who are not only "buried alive" but whose lives remain totally sealed in and by incomprehension, "epitaphed with hieroglyphics". Those can truly die who have worked out ways of sharing their contents of their lives and suffering with the "new generation" which, in turn, will be able to die on condition of being willing to participate in the sharing. It is this sharing which makes our burial possible. The corpse of Polynices lying unburied at the walls of Thebes is a testimony of a dramatic failure to share: Creon, sealed off in his sense of lawfulness and false patriotism, refuses to share the experiences with Antigone and, as we have seen, right from the beginning of the tragedy set her off as an incommunicable adversary. The secret of good, human and humane politics therefore would lie in knowing how to combine these two aspects: an indispensible social and ethical technology of efficient being together (such as Patience, Courage, Friendship, Love, all listed by Masters) and the burning pertinence of one's individual existential experience which needs to be shared so that the living could bury their dead.

8.

Traditionally, interpretations of Sophocles's tragedy hinge upon the conflict between divine and human law. But one who wants to meditate upon the significance of the funerary space in *polis*, has to shift his/her attention: the tombstone, with its minimal poetics of just two dates, is a critique of the whirlpool of temporal designations which constitute the rhythms of urban life from the accurate dating of an alarm-clock waking us in the morning, to the intricate, maze-like patterns of international time-tables which allow Phileas Fogg to find in London the best train connection from Rome to Istambul. The chronologically reductionist poetics of the tombstone is a move from what is "of yesterday" and "of to-day" towards the "everlasting", but not in a theologically orthodoxical manner of focusing upon what is to come, the future life, the better world; minimalism of two dates speaks of the "everlasting" which permeates our lives here and now, the non human sense of Justice which Antigone describes as belonging to the "Gods" but which, in fact, in the same speech, she admits comes from nobody knows where. The laws which are older than human jurisdiction are to be respected "Though where they came from, none of us can tell". The realm of the dead and buried is thus a space of unknown laws and regulations, of a specific organization of a post-mortem being. In the work of a Polish poet Bolesław Leśmian we find numerous examples of this situation, to quote but a few: "Pod ziemią wrzał głucho/ Trzepot żagli, pośmiertną gnany zawieruchą" ("Cmentarz"), "Już się gwiezdne poniszczyły zamiecie -/ Cień się chwieje, poróżniony z mogiłą,/ Coś innego stać się pragnie w zaświecie,/ Coś innego, niż to wszystko, co było!..." ("Za grobem"); "I to życie, co po śmierci nie wie, gdzie żyje,/ Jeno szuka siebie po własnym pogrzebie" ("W przeddzień swego zmartwychwstania") (Leśmian 1991, 229, 230, 115). The funerary *locus* does not celebrate the dead; it points at what goes beyond humanity and yet conditions its operations. The cemetery refers to the non-human within the human, all-too-human community.

9.

At this point the minimalist poetics of the tombstone gives way to a political project which aims at searching for the true foundations of the *polis*, the basis which would allow people to connect what is "of yesterday and to-day" with the "everlasting", and hence opens communication between the clearly demarcated and mapped spaces of human democracy and the unchartered areas of the non-human. At the beginning of his harrowing experience Gregor Samsa feels his transformation into a worm is a major watershed in his life, a breakthrough which frees him from the tyranny of "yesterday" and "today": "Oh God, he thought, what an exhausting job I've picked on! Traveling about day in, day out. It's much irritating work than doing the actual business in the office, and on top of that there's a trouble of constant traveling, of worrying about train connections, the bed and irregular means, casual acquaintances that are always new and never become intimate friends" (Kafka 1975, 68). An escape from the world of the clocks takes him to the grave-like space underneath his sofa: "...he scuttled under the sofa, where he felt comfortable at once, although his back was a little cramped and he could not lift his head up, and his only regret was that his body was too broad to get the whole of it under the sofa" (Kafka 1975, 90).

10.

Gregor's complaint of the lack of "intimate friends" bespeaks the difficulty of adjusting the technologies of being together with individual existential experience we have discussed before. On a larger scale, we could claim that the crucial factor in synchronizing the two spheres is the ability, or more likely inability, to find a language which would be able to relate one's existence to other beings. In Gregor's words: language operates successfully on the level securing "casual acquaintances" but not "intimate friends". Alexis de Tocqueville, in the XVI chapter of the first part of the second volume of his great book on America, locates this difficulty as one of the central problems of democracy which favours languages which serve it and maintain its mechanism in movement, i.e.

discourses of law, administration, economics, politics (*ils serviront principalement ŕ exprimer les besoins de l'industrie, les passions des partis ou les détails de l'administration publique*) (de Tocqueville 1961, 2, 96). At the same time, it ignores the language of, de Tocqueville enumerates two disciplines, theology and metaphysics, that is to say, the language which refers to the sphere of hardly nameable existential experience totally outside the calculus of economic, social or political gain. In fine: as democracy develops, it will be marked by a growing chasm between the ever more pragmatic course of its technologies of social and political communication on the one hand, and diminishing level of interhuman communication on the other. Democracy is a paradoxical construction which combines the efficiency of societal mechanisms with the sense of unfulfilment of each busy and active individual. Restlessness of democracy which constantly changes its laws and regulations seem to counter the nervous restlessness of individuals who, as it was described already by Pascal, seek peace of mind. De Tocqueville's version of the same reads: "As the men who inhabit democratic countries have no superiors, no inferiors (…) they readily fall back upon themselves, and consider themselves as beings apart. (…). Hence such men can never (…) tear themselves from private affairs to engage in public business; their natural bias leads them to abandon the latter to the sole visible and permanent representative of the interest of the community, that is to say, to the state" (de Tocqueville 2001, 293). From this perspective, the cemetery and its phenomenology disclose the hidden separateness of human individuals, and the radical reduction of datings of human existence uncannily accentuates the fact that the modern individual lives "buried alive", unable to share his/her existential experience, and even his/her drastically limited epitaph will be an unreadable hieroglyphics. Let us retrieve the penetrating fragment from Edgar Lee Master's poem:

> And after so living you have also learned your age,
> Then if you cannot make understandable what you know;
> And if the new generation is not interested in what you know,
> Are you not buried alive and epitaphed with hieroglyphics?
> (Masters 1968, 234)

Democracy constantly negotiates between the successes of the technologies of being together and the disappointing failure of the existential fulfilment of the very individuals who participate in the various organized ways of being together. Public sphere in this situation becomes more and more an area of the efficient management conducted by specialized force called "politicians" rather than commitment of individuals; simultaneously, the same individuals who dedicate their efforts to achieve individual success feel disconcerted, if not utterly defeated, in their private lives which state Henry David Thoreau succinctly and masterfully puts in his memorable sentence from early pages of *Walden*—"The mass of men lead lives of quiet desperation" (Thoreau 1965, 7).

11.

Nowhere is it more striking than in Herman Melville's *tour de force* "Bartleby, the Scrivener" with its ultimate sentence being a distillate of despair: "Ah, Bartleby! Ah, humanity!". The mysterious copyist is precisely what Masters has called a being "epitaphed with hieroglyphics", his humanity is a humanity reduced to bare essentials and thus, like the mysterious richness of existence totally absent from the tombstone engraving, eventless and dateless. Melville begins by stating the impossibility of writing Bartleby's biography: "While, of other law-copyists, I might wrote the complete life, of Bartleby nothing of that sort can be done. I believe that no materials exist, for a full and satisfactory biography of this man. It is an irreparable loss to literature" (Melville 1986, 3). There are two types of mortal presences in the novella, the depth of which we cannot explore in this brief essay. One is the funerary epiphany of Bartleby who is—Melville's words—"motionless", "pallidly neat", and "incurably forlorn", all features either of cadavers, funeral gear, or irreversible workings of illness. Later we learn that the scrivener had "nothing ordinarily human about him", once his presence is referred to as "apparition", and at least twice cadaver stands for Bartleby's appearance: he behaves with "his cadaverously gentlemanly nonchalance", and his prevailing impact upon his employer prompts the latter to speak of Batleby's "cadaverous triumph". To read about Bartleby is to trace wanderings of a risen cadaver, a resurrected corpse, a message of the cemetery, which tries to speak to the world of what Williams was to call "corrupt cities" using the minimal discourse of the tombstone. The legendary phrase "I would prefer not" is as close as a language of the living can come to the discourse of the dead who are beyond biography (always filled with colourful details and adventurous events) and time (in "The Encantadas" Melville speaks about "dateless, indefinite endurance" which seems to ideally describe the strange existential status of Bartleby).

12.

The other funerary presence is that of Bartleby's employer, a nameless lawyer, a man whose life is based upon "a profound conviction that the easiest way of life is the best". The motionlessness of Bartleby is contrasted with the seemingly vigorous life of the lawyer ("In my haste ... I sat with my head bent over the original on my desk") living under the dictate of obligations and therefore under the constraint of temporal dating ("Once again business hurried me"). But as we read Melville's text we realize that life has already been profoundly stigmatized by death, that, in fact, it has been overwhelmed by death, and that Bartleby, the visiting apparition, the cadaverous specter, the grave-yard messenger, has a mission, like Derrida's specter of Marx, to reveal this truth to modernity. The Wall Street office is completely walled-in, a grave-like structure in which the office's windows "commanded an unobstructed view of a lofty brick wall, black by age and everlasting shade". The "unobstructed view" which, in fact, reveals nothing but obstruction is an ultimate triumph of the realm of death which has extended its influence upon labour now presented as no more than a "lethargic affair". Appropriately, the epitome of justice, a foundation of the human law ("Halls of Justice") is commonly called "the Tombs". New York depicted in the novella resembles a peculiar vision in which Piranesi presented in 1756 a Roman town as an architectural phantasy in which the living neighbour upon the dead, the *polis* and necro-polis are indistinguishable.

13.

What seems to be at stake is a slow discovery of two things which the world of the living learns from the cadaverous lesson of Bartleby. First: if modernity is to be saved it has to be disturbed and profoundly critiqued on behalf of laws and rights which, like in Sophocles's tragedy, are not under a total jurisdiction of either business or politics. Democracy can grow and move on only under this condition of committed criticism. This is a change undergone in Melville's novella by the lawyer who at one point confesses: "...there was something about Bartleby that not only strangely disarmed me, but, in a wonderful manner, touched and disconcerted me". Democracy must be disconcerted or it will be not. Second: a progress on this path of improving the technologies of being together is not a guarantee of understanding an individual existential existence. Friendship (another huge subject which we cannot approach here) budding in the lawyer ("I feel friendly towards you", he says visitng Bartleby at the Tombs) is necessary to make a first step towards a recovery of the human bond ("For the first time in my life a feeling of over-powering stinging melancholy seized me. (…) The bond of a common humanity now drew me irresistibly to gloom. A fraternal melancholy! For both I and Bartleby were sons of Adam"), but the outcome of this bonding brings us dangerously close to Masters's man "epitaphed in hieroglyphics". In a shattering scene of the visit at the Tombs, when the lawyer presents himself as Bartleby's "friend" the latter responds with "I know you (…), and I have nothing to say to you". "I have nothing to say to you", is it not what we say over and over again trying to share with the other what is truly and personally important? This is one of the questions we can ask now. Another one being: if human bonding is such a dramatic and difficult affair, should we not work harder and harder in our critique of democracy attempting to strive towards more adequate forms of being together?

14.

It is the obsequial and sepulchral space that becomes a place from which modern society is being interrogated. Thomas Gray's 1751 "Elegy Written in a Country Church-yard" is in this respect a paradigmatic text. Its famous beginning prepares a *topos* of such an interrogation.

> The curfew tolls the knell of parting day,
> The lowing herd wind slowly o'er the lea,
> The ploughman homeward plods his weary way,
> And leaves the world to darkness and to me.
> (Gray, Collins and Goldsmith 1969, 117).

First of all, we have to note the scene of withdrawal which clearly stands in opposition to the urban multivocal participation. The cemetery is a *locus* marking the interruption in the smoothness of the social exchange, a space which, while carving itself out of the tissue of the *polis* (its location is most frequently peripheral), in fact, cuts right into its most vital processes (although seclusionary, inconvertible, and inhospitable, it tells us something important about what is missing in the hospitality of the everyday). In the pre-Romantic Europe the story of modernity is a double narrative of a tension between regimes of light (city, traffic, language) and shadows (country, twilight, darkness, silence). The world is left "to darkness and to me"; on the one hand, there is, as we learn from the second stanza, a "glimmering landscape", on the other—darkness and me. This phrase combining darkness and independence of the human subject summarizes a radical reduction of all the factors which intervene between man and the world. I meet the "world" in confrontation with "darkness", i.e. the ostentatiousness of multiplicity of well-lit, literally "brilliant", forms which normally constitute my idea of the "world" is now replaced by the dark background, a kind of maternal space, *chora,* which forms barely begin to emerge. Darkness is the acoustic equivalent of silence, and the cemetery presents itself as a place from which the modern vision of the urban society is being meditated upon. In 1720 James Thomson hinges his juvenile poem "Of a Country Life" precisely on the tension between the cacophony of the town and inarticulate, delicate, barely audible ("zephyrs whispering", "gentle murmurs of purling rills") noises of nature:

> I hate the clamours of the smoky towns,
> But much admire the bliss of rural towns;
> Where some remains of innocence appear,
> Where no rude noise insult the listening ear (Thomson 1908, 494)

The corrective which we need to apply to modern life and which the cemetery enables us to learn is double: first—the periphery, the topographical margin of the funerary space as well as death as the radical periphery of life, is the place from which we need to rethink our community and its vital problems, second – politics and its decisions regulating the practice of the everyday life must somehow return to a place where they remain in touch with the least momentary, least urgent, and least summary considerations, the place symbolically qualified as "darkness" and "silence". Jacques Derrida's political philosophy of friendship and of democracy to come (*à venir*) is a contemporary manifestation of the same direction which postulates the necessity of evaluating structures of modern social life from the perspective of what they try to hide rather than show. The summary justice of modern legal system has to rethink itself from the peripheral position of one radically different from our own. Our meditation emboldens us to claim one again that the cemetery is a topographical description of such a perspective marked by "silence" and "darkness", the elements which stimulate our working through so far accepted and habitually evaluated notions.

15.

Max Picard in his classic book on silence touches upon the point in a claim that "Today words no longer rise out of silence, through a creative act of spirit which gives meaning to language and to the silence, but from other words, from the noise of other words. Neither do they return to the silence but into the noise of other words, to become immersed therein"

(Picard 1988, 172). The reductionist poetics of tombstones of which we have already spoken seem to derive from the need to recognize silence as the element from which significance rises, the significance which is not to be understood merely in terms of pragmatic usage and applicability. The tombstone is a carved minimal articulation of meanings and senses which have remained concealed from life and which social life will not be able to accommodate. Gray's poem, in which silence (to be more accurate the poet speaks of "stillness" which term also freezes the hectic impatience of the hasty decisions of the "summary justice" of the democratic world) rules, human words have been supplanted by animal sounds ("where the beetle wheels his droning flight", and where we hear a "complaint of the "moping owl") marks not only the pre-Romantic convention but, first of all, determines the cemetery as a *topos* of radical revaluation of human words necessary for the critical appreciation of the human community and politics. This withdrawal towards stillness establishes a certain counterposition which invites ud towards reflecting upon the everyday conceived of merely as a sequence of practices habituating us to the repetitiveness of the occurrences. Borrowing from Gray's funerary ode we could call this tendency "weariness", and thus the opening stanza in which the ploughman (whose occupation could serve as an epitome of the action repeated on a larger scale of seasons as well as a narrower level of a monotonous shuttling between the two lines marking the end of a field, a movement the Greeks called *boustrophedon*) turn home with a "weary way" locates the speaking subject of the poem in a position (a country church-yard) from which he sees all these actions anew, i.e. as shedding their "weary" character. Paradoxically, the realm of death, the radical margin of the human society, revitalizes and renews its central practices. In this respect it shares the ground with Nietzsche's metaphor of the open ocean from which, if are bold enough to venture a voyage further from the immediate vicinity of the shore, we "command a view, no doubt for the first time, of its total configuration, and when we approach it again we have the advantage of understanding it better as a whole than those who have never left it" (Nietzsche 1986, 1, 616).

16.

The dead cannot be called back to daily chores to which they dedicated their life, but the phenomenology of the cemetery practiced by Gray does not annihilate the value of the everyday. Just the opposite, it wants to bring it back in a revaluated form of a certain community. The churchyard is seen as the internationale of the poor, a lesson where we study "The short and simple annals of the poor". This unusual gathering is not to be defined exclusively in economic terms of property and wealth or their absence. Interestingly enough, the alternative to the "poor" is not the "rich" but the "Proud" whose mark is memory and its "trophies". The Proud want to fend off death by means of memorialization through history ("storied urn"), aesthetics ("animated bust"), flamboyant architecture of burial ("long-drawn isle and fretted vault"), politics ("the applause of listening senates", "the pomp of power"), knowledge ("But Knowledge to their eyes her ample page/ Rich with the spoils of time did never unroll"). The annals of the poor are "short and simple", the poor represent life, *bios,* in its most immediate concerns, life literally and metaphorically close to the very substance of the world. Following Gray's thought we could refer to this existence as life of restricted desire, life in which the non-humanity of being has not been dominated by the liberated human uncontrolled passion which aims at going beyond any limits. Gray comments:

> Let not Ambition mock their useful toil,
> Their homely joys and destiny obscure;
> Nor Grandeur hear, with a disdainful smile,
> The short and simple annals of the poor.

The commitment to the non-human is reflected in the way in which the graves of the poor look: whereas the Proud has ornamental tombs with "storied urns" and "animated busts" which are made to last (with the purpose of memorialization), the poor have only "frail memorial" with "uncouth rhymes and shapeless sculpture", their Muse is "unlettered" , i.e. not only uneducated and simple but also the one that has consciously abandoned letters, un-done them, resigning herself to the regime of silence. The "rustic moralist" of whom Gray speaks in his elegy is one who does not hope to obtain help from philosophy but who "reads" silently texts of nature and society. The idea is not to merely juxtapose "Ambition" and "Grandeur" on the one hand to the "useful toil" of the poor on the other. What is at stake is a certain model of understanding of the latter by the former free of mockery and disdain. Thus, the lesson of the churchyard, defined by Gray as the "neglected spot", is an admonition concerning the "reading" of life and its social forms.

17.

The caveat formulated in Gray's elegy only in part consists in a typical elegiac indication of the democracy of death, the politics of, as the poet refers to it, "the inevitable hour". More importantly, the "neglected spot" provides us with a reminder of withdrawal, of regression, of removing oneself from view, as an indispensable condition of democracy. The reference to the obscurity of destiny bears not only a metaphysical stigma but also a political significance: the way of the poor follows the way of being and "sobriety" ("useful toil") understood as silent persistence in being through withdrawing into one's preoccupations ("Oft did the harvest to their sickle yield,/ Their furrow oft the stubborn glebe has broke"), thus letting other people appear in space. Klaus Held sees in this attitude of withdrawal which the Greeks called *aidos* one of the fundamental conditions of democracy (Held 2003, 57). The famous stanza from Gray's elegy

> Far from the madding crowd's ignoble strife
> Their sober wishes never learned to stray;
> Along the cool sequestered vale of life
> They kept the noiseless tenor of their way.

plainly speaks on behalf of the sobriety of desires imposing necessary limits upon "Ambition" and "Grandeur", and the manner of being which, emerging from this sobriety, permeates in a "noiseless tenor" all our activities. What "Ambition" is guilty of is precisely the ruination of a certain rhythm of being which also is to be found at the basis of the legal system. Excessive desires destroy law and moral rectitude which ought to be its source. Oliver Goldsmith sees it clearly in his 1764 poem "The Traveller, or a Prospect of Society": "Yes, brother, curse with me that baleful hour,/ When first ambition struck at legal power;/ And thus polluting honour in its source,/ Gave wealth to sway the mind with double force" (Gray, Collins and Goldsmith 1969, 654). It is from the funerary, obsequious perspective of these restrictions commanded upon "wishes" that Gray comments critically upon human history and politics as a territory of the "ignoble strife" where truth falls victim to the manoeuvers of power ("The struggling pangs of conscious truth to hide"), and authority results from the ruthless practices of force (wading "through slaughter to a throne"). Thus, the political lesson of the "secluded spot" of the cemetery is a trimming of excess characteristic of human history, a warning of the dangers of unrestricted desires which has so far dominated human society. Already in 1691 Sir Dudley North gravely observed that "the main spur to trade, or rather to industry and ingenuity, is the exorbitant appetites of men, which they will take pains to gratify..." (de Vries 2003, 44).

18.

Gray's "noiseless tenor" brings back the importance of silence which, as we can learn from a careful reading of the elegy, has not been eliminated but devolved into a parasitic form of repression in which it ceases to be a powerful manifestation of sense to become muffled (in)expression of non-sense. Silence has become a mere absence of words, a taciturn acceptance of the social and political status quo. This is a diseased form of silence diagnosed by Max Picard: "Noise has entered now into that good part of life which used to belong to silence, but silence has taken refuge in that evil part of life—the world of sickness and disease, and silence now approaches man on these evil subterranean ways" (Picard 1988, 217). The "secluded spot" of the churchyard is a place from which a critique of such a disfigured and corrupt form of silence becomes possible. Not only does Gray's meditation among the graves occasion his philosophy of proper reading of the ways of living, a reading which has been considerably distorted by the excesses of "Ambition" and "Grandeur" replacing the honest disinterestedness of commitment with practices aiming at "heap[ing] the shrine of Luxury and Pride", but it also allows him to offer yet another vision of modern society in which it emerges as a series of misreadings or, rather, mis-silences. In this perspective modern society dedicates much of its efforts towards constructing and maintaining life at the cost of life itself; the current of social processes runs a strange course energized by all kinds of strategies aimed at suppressing or freezing life. Gray speaks about it in a straightforward manner in lines 51 and 52 of the elegy in which we read that "Chill Penury repressed their [the poor] noble rage,/ And froze the genial current of the soul". One should not let go unnoticed the rhetoric of these verses in which the essentially sociable character of life ("the genial current of the soul", a phrase in which the adjective "genial" seems to stand for the way of sympathetic being-with as a principal manner of human existence) is put within a disfiguring corset of economic and social deprivation ("Penury") and the choice of brumal adjectives ("chill") and verbs ("froze") describing conditions detrimental to life in which modern society has locked itself.

19.

The "Penury" Gray defines as a diabolical mechanism of repression could be further elaborated on with the help of Goldsmith's "The Traveller..." from which we can deduce a set of processes responsible for the disease of silence among the poor, or—rather—for the imposing silence as a disease upon the poor, a malaise that preventing them from speaking out. Combining Gray and Goldsmith we obtain the following triad: (1) an exchange of useful for useless (as indicated by mockery with which the High and Mighty receive the "useful toil" of the poor, (2) dehumanization of the society resulting from the former (Goldsmith: "Have we not seen, round Britain's people shore,/ Her useful sons exchanged for useless ore?"), and, in a manner of the "great luxury debate" characteristic of the eighteenth century, (3) growing waste through the accumulation of capital and luxury (Goldsmith: "Seen opulence, her grandeur to maintain,/ Lead stern depopulation in her train,/ And over fields where scattered hamlets rose,/ In barren solitary pomp repose").

20.

The funerary meditation uses the space of the cemetery for two purposes: (1) to form a critique of the hegemonic philosophy and political economy of capitalism (Ambition-cum-Grandeur) and speak on behalf of the "poor", and, (2) propose the political philosophy which would empower the individual (Goldsmith complains: "Vain, vain, my weary search to find/ That bliss which only centers in the mind:/ Why have I strayed from pleasure and repose,/ To seek a good each government bestows?/ In every government, though terrors reign,/ Though tyrant kings or tyrant laws restrain,/ How small, of all that human hearts endure,/ That part which laws or kings can cause or cure./ Still to ourselves in every place consigned,/ Our own felicity we make or find:/ With secret course, which no loud storms annoy,/ Glides the smooth current of domestic joy".)

The fact that we need the space of the "secluded spot" to achieve this purpose testifies to the degree to which the dominating tendencies imposed their reign upon the society and its life.

References

Aričs Philippe, Duby Georges. 1999. *Histoire de la vie privée*, vol. 1-5. Paris: Editions du Seuil.

Gray Thomas, Collins William, Goldsmith Oliver. 1969. *Poems*, ed. by R. Lonesdale. London/New York: Longman.

Hawthorne, Nathaniel. 1959. *The Scarlet Letter*. New York: Signet Classic.

Held, Klaus, *Fenomenologia świata politycznego*, trans. by A. Gniazdowski. Warszawa: IfiS.

Kafka, Franz. 1975. *The Metamorphosis, The Penal Colony, and Other Stories*, trans. by Willa and Edwin Muir. New York: Schoken Books.
Leśmian, Bolesław. 1991. *Poezje wybrane*, ed. by Jacek Trznadel. Wrocław-Warszawa-Kraków: Zakład Narodowy Imienia Ossolińskich.
Masters, Edgar Lee. 1968. *The New Spoon River*. New York: Collier Books.
Melville, Herman. 1986. *Billy Budd and Other Stories*. New York: Viking Penguin Inc.
Nietzsche, Friedrich. 1986. *Human, All Too Human. A Book for Free Spirits*, vol. 1-2, trans. by R. J. Holingdale. Cambridge: Cambridge University Press.
Picard, Max. 1988. *The World of Silence*. trans. by Stanley Godman. Washington D.C.: A Gateway Edition.
Sophocles. 1967. *The Theban Plays*, trans. by E. F. Watling. Harmondsworth: Penguin Books.
Thomson, James. 1908. *The Complete Poetical Works*, ed. by J. Logie Roberston. London/New York/Toronto/Melbourne: Oxford University Press.
Thoreau, Henry David. 1965. *Walden and Other Writings*, ed. by Brooks Atkinson. New York: Modern Library.
Tocqueville de, Alexis. 1961. *De la démocratie en Amérique*, vol.1-2. Paris: Gallimard.
—. 2001. *Democracy in America*, trans. by Henry Reeve, ed. by Richard Heffner. New York: Signet Classic.
Vries de, Jan. 2003. Luxury in the Dutch Golden Age in Theory and Practice. In *Luxury in the Eighteenth Century. Debates, Desires and Delectable Goods*, ed. by Maxine Berg and Elizabeth Eger. New York: Palgrave Macmillan.

PART II:

DIVERSIFICATION OF SPACE IN NARRATIVE FICTION

CHAPTER FOUR

THE USE AND FUNCTION OF LAND SPACE IN CAPT. MARRYAT'S SELECTED SEA NOVELS

MAREK BŁASZAK

The idea of examining land space in Capt. Marryat's sea novels may appear a tad strange. This is because the author enjoys the reputation of "the most remarkable writer trained to the sea the English ever had until Joseph Conrad" (Warner 1953, 13). Marryat fathered the sea novel as a fully-fledged fictional genre into British literature, and the fundamental constituents of the genre do not comprise land space as such (cf. Błaszak 2006, ch. 1). Past and modern maritime critical authorities pass it over altogether: the Briton John Peck asserts that both sea fiction and nautical fiction "place their emphasis on events at sea" (2001, 4), while the American Thomas Philbrick reserves the terms 'sea novel' and 'sea story' for those "works of fiction in which nautical elements are predominant rather than incidental" (1961, 292). Consequently, by reversing such claims, it would appear that land space in the sea novel is only incidental or marginal. Therefore, it is worthwhile to see how much, or how little, land space there is in some of the classic sea novels of Captain Frederick Marryat, and to find out what role, if any, it plays in them.

To begin, it should be specified that here the term 'land space' encompasses more than the traditionally conceived fictional setting, that is, the physical locale and the time of the action. The 'more' comprises what S. Rimmon-Kenan calls human or social environment (like family or social class, cf. 1983, 66 and 69). Jeremy Hawthorn recently complained that setting is one of those inconvenient terms about which modern critics have felt increasingly uneasy (cf. 1997, 134-5). He claims that this term involves complex relationships between characters and action on the one hand, and the context within which these take place on the other—the context going beyond a novel's geographical setting and extending to some vital social and historical factors. Such an 'extended' concept of fictional setting corresponds to the term 'space' used in the article.

Another preliminary consideration is Capt. Marryat's personal experience in life on land. He was a Londoner by birth, son of a rich and influential merchant. However, he also had an elder male sibling and, in some measure at least, was bound to pursue a career in the army or navy, being too full of vitality for either the cassock or the gown. Impressed by the victory off Cape Trafalgar and by the state funeral of its hero Admiral Lord Nelson, which he saw in London, Marryat joined the Royal Navy at the age of 14 and remained in active service until his retirement 26 years later, at the end of 1830. Back on dry ground, he lived in several prestigious London residences, keeping company with naval officers on the one hand, and with artistic celebrities on the other: Dickens, Ainsworth and Bulwer-Lytton among the *literati*; Sir Edwin Landseer, Clarkson Stanfield and George Cruikshank among the painters and draughtsmen; and William Charles Macready among the leading Victorian actors. The Marryats also had the honour of being introduced to King George IV and then to his successor William IV, and the Captain even became a temporary equerry or gentleman-in-waiting to the Duke of Sussex. However, as Marryat's modern biographer remarks, "he had been dabbling in the life of a courtier, but found this unsatisfying" (Pocock 2000, 107). He travelled a lot on land, sometimes taking his family with him, but most often alone, which was partly connected with his duties as contributor to, editor, and then proprietor of the *Metropolitan Magazine*. He visited the Netherlands and Belgium, France, Germany, Switzerland and Italy, as well as the United States of America and Canada. Having tasted metropolitan life and mingled with the fashionable bohemian society, Marryat exchanged the capital city for a rural manor house in Norfolk, where he spent the last 5 years of his life, from 1843 to his death in 1848 at the age of 56. Pocock asserts that when he settled down in his estate at the village of Langham, the Captain "took to country life with characteristic enthusiasm" (179), among other things arranging house parties and paying return visits to the Norfolk aristocracy and gentry. It remains to add that although he never received any solid formal education, Marryat was always an avid reader of *belles lettres*, demonstrating his familiarity with a host of writers—novelists, poets and dramatists, native and foreign, classic and contemporary—both directly (through references, citations, mottoes) and indirectly (through all kinds of hints and allusions).

The choice of Capt. Marryat's sea novels for this analysis has been inspired by Ernest Hemingway, who in the "Monologue to the Maestro", published in the October 1935 issue of the *Esquire*, enumerated three novels by Marryat among books that make up the world's literary heritage. The titles in question are *The Naval Officer* (Marryat's first novel published anonymously in 1829 while he was still in active service), *Peter Simple* (his fourth publ. in 1834), and *Mr. Midshipman Easy* (his tenth publ. in 1839). It is interesting to note that Hemingway placed the Captain's name in second position after Tolstoy (represented by *War and Peace* and *Anna Karenina*), and before such writers as Flaubert, Thomas Mann, Joyce, Fielding, Stendhal, Dostoyevsky, Mark Twain, Stephen Crane, George Moore, W. B. Yeats, Guy de Maupassant, Rudyard Kipling, Turgenev, W. H. Hudson, and Henry James (Hemingway 1968, 189).

As regards the question of quantity of land space in Capt. Marryat's first novel, *The Naval Officer* (subtitled *Scenes and Adventures in the Life of Frank Mildmay*), the ratio of chapters set at sea to those set on land amounts to 18 to 11 out of the total number 29, or 62% to 38% in favour of the sea. However, if we classify chapters set on board of a ship while it lies at anchor at a port, or chapters in which the hero is delegated by his captain to destroy an enemy target on shore, as belonging to the marine environment, then the proportion is 20 to 9, or 70% to 30% respectively. Proceeding to the consideration of quality of land space used in the novel, the author opens it with a chapter outlining Frank Mildmay's life on *terra firma* prior to his going to sea. Since he becomes a midshipman while still a boy, this first chapter recounts his childhood, providing basic details about his family and social status, as well as his disposition and temperament. It appears that his "father was a gentleman, and a man of considerable property", and that the hero himself was noted for his "liveliness, quickness of repartee, and impudence" (*Frank Mildmay*, hereafter FM, 11). When he goes to boarding school, Frank experiences a good deal of bullying from older boys and adults, receives useless and ineffective instruction, and unjust corporal punishment imposed by teachers. All this is necessary for the author to justify sending his juvenile protagonist to the navy in the second chapter of the novel. Since he "had an elder brother, who was intended to have the family estates, and who was then at Oxford, receiving an education suitable to his rank in life, and also learning how to spend his money like a gentleman" (FM 20), the law of primogeniture very conveniently and plausibly puts Frank out of the way, and his father simply "procures" for him a berth on a fine frigate at Plymouth. The hero himself does not despair over this unfavourable circumstance because, given his disposition and treatment at school, he can only rejoice, as he actually does, at the news that on the king's ship there is no schoolmaster and that the midshipmen are entitled to a daily ration of a pint of wine.

Once a professional sailor, the protagonist's connections with land space become infrequent; they are regulated by short leaves of absence when his ship calls at a port and he is allowed to see his family residing on the outskirts of London. Capt. Marryat emphasizes, on such occasions, the growing alienation of the sailor, belonging to the water world, from his relations on firm ground. As he himself observes, "my sea manners were not congenial to the drawing-room. My mother, aunt, and sister, were very different from the females I had been in the habit of seeing on board the frigate[1]. My oaths and treatment of the servants, male and female, all conspired to reconcile the family to my departure. They therefore heard with pleasure that my leave was expired" (FM 52). It is on the first of such occasions that the novel's land plot, or rather the terrestrial part of the novel's plot, is launched. Frank Mildmay, still on leave and estranged from his family, begins—almost simultaneously—a relationship with two attractive young women, one of whom is a gentleman's daughter and a rich heiress and the other a strolling player or actress. The first is Emily Somerville, an incarnation of angelic delicacy and innocence. The second is Eugenia, who has imbibed "libertine opinions" as a result of being a half orphan brought up in France by "a weak mother" and almost in the spirit of the Revolution (FM 120). The hero falls in love with the former, a love that is idealized, for he finds her "an angel" and is "ready to kneel down and adore her" (FM 112 and 187), while developing an all-consuming sexual passion for the latter, who becomes his mistress.

This love plot located in the land space of the novel is vital to the construction of the whole work, for Frank Mildmay is a two-faced man also as a sailor and a junior naval officer. Thus, the land plot not only runs parallel to the novel's aquatic plot, but also complements and even conditions it: the hero must grow and reject his duplicity in both dimensions or spaces in order to become a real gentleman and full officer (commander), the happy head of a family and man of success, as well as an instructive example to the reader. That the two spaces interpenetrate and give coherence to the plot is evident from the fact that Frank's lust for and debauchery with Eugenia endanger his professional career, whereas his courtship of Emily serves to boost it. In the first instance he prolongs his leave of absence from the frigate almost to the point of desertion and associates with Eugenia's vagrant troupe, bringing disgrace to his naval uniform. In the second instance his official fiancée Emily actually obliges the hero to do his best in the service and strive for promotion: "she did not like the idea of her name appearing in the *Morning Post* as the bride of a

---

[1] Women were allowed on board the contemporary man-of-war only when it was in port, and even then on special occasions like pay-day.

lieutenant. 'What's a lieutenant now-a-days?' said she; 'nobody [...]. No, Frank, I shall not surrender at discretion, with all my charms, to any thing less than a captain, with a pair of gold epaulettes'" (FM 272).

It can be surmised that the romantic-sentimental aspect of the plot set in the novel's land space has been inspired by the author's reading of Richardson's *Pamela*, rather than suggested by real life. Marryat's Eugenia, who lets Frank seduce her, resembles Richardson's Sally Godfrey, whose little respect for herself makes her unfit to marry her seducer Squire B. For his part, the reformed rake Frank—to some extent like the squire—becomes a convert to virtue who can only more fully appreciate the merits of pure wedded love.

It is worth observing that Capt. Marryat's use of coincidence in land space appears to be highly strained, as contrasted with the marine element where chance meetings and separations, or unexpected changes in fortune, are quite plausibly determined by storms and shipwrecks, naval engagements and pirates, and the like. In the land space of *The Naval Officer*, the eponymous protagonist meets and falls in love with Emily Somerville having first knocked down, with a stone, a postillion boy driving a gentlemen's carriage. As a result, the horses break into a mad gallop terminated with the overturning of the vehicle and injuries to its passengers. Among the latter is Emily, skilfully bled by Frank (unrecognized as the perpetrator of the accident due to darkness), who thus wins favour with the young lady and her father. Even more implausible is the removal from the novel of the hero's cast-off and conscience-stricken mistress Eugenia and their illegitimate son Eugenio. The boy simply "had fallen into a trout stream, where he was found drowned some hours after", while his wretched mother "had been seized with a brain fever, and had died at a small town in Norfolk" right after him (FM 337).

One more point of interest as regards the novel's land space is the author's aversion to France and the French. Modern readers should bear in mind that he took part in the Great War against Napoleonic France, in which Britain's territorial integrity had long been at stake. Such is the novel's temporal-historical setting. Accordingly, in its marine space the French are inevitably presented as a threat to the English, which is also specifically reflected in the terrestrial space: for example, when the war with France is eventually over, the hero visits Paris, where he becomes hopelessly addicted to gambling at the rouge-et-noir card game at the casino of the Palais Royal. He loses considerable sums of money night after night, runs into debts, but still "anxiously awaited the return of the hour when the doors would again be opened, and the rooms lighted up for the reception of company" (FM 327). Even though his luck improves at last, Frank is well aware of the danger of the French disease for the plain-dealing Englishmen: "by a miracle only was I saved from utter and irretrievable ruin. How many of my countrymen have fallen victims to the arts practised in that horrible school of vice, I dare not say! Happy should I be to think that the infection had not reached our own shores, and found patrons among the great men of the land" (FM 326-7).

Peter Simple is a much longer novel of 65 chapters, originally published in the standard Victorian three volumes. The ratio of sea to land chapters is not easy to estimate, as some of them are set on ships immobilized in harbour (e.g. court-martial on board the admiral's ship in Portsmouth), or only partially on dry ground (e.g. funeral of a ship's captain on an island during a cruise in the Caribbean). If such chapters are included in the novel's sea space, the advantage of the former over the latter will amount to 42 to 23, or 64% to 36%. These figures are very similar to their equivalents from Capt. Marryat's first novel.

The extended beginning of *Peter Simple* comprises four chapters in which the title hero, a boy aged 14, finds his way to the navy prompted by circumstances familiar to the reader: his father is a well-connected clergyman of the Church of England (himself forced to take the holy orders as the youngest offspring of a noble family), and the hero's prospects of a leisurely gentlemanly existence are thwarted by an elder brother named Tom. Halfway through the book, the 1st-person narrator-hero voices strong criticism of the centuries-old custom of entailing all the property of the aristocracy upon the eldest son, and sending the younger to the army (or navy), while making the youngest enter the church. As a result, both in the army (and navy) and the church, there have been a number of people "who are not only totally unfit for, but who actually disgrace, their calling" (*Peter Simple*, hereafter PS, 294). As a member of the wealthy middle class, Capt. Marryat was not directly affected by the law of primogeniture, and he was also amply provided for by his father, who left him "a handsome share" of a big fortune (Pocock 2000, 97). Consequently, his reason for disparaging this law was that it contributed to the infesting of the naval service with grossly incompetent senior officers whose prototype was one of the author's own commanders, Captain Lord George Stuart of the 'Newcastle' line-of-battle ship. A prominent naval historian writes that he belonged to "a type which had bothered the navy at least since the days of Pepys" (Warner 1953, 47).

Returning to the novel's early land chapters, the youngster Peter Simple has here his first direct encounter with a sailor. It takes place on a coach travelling from London to Portsmouth and the hero is shocked by the noisy and unruly behaviour of the weather-beaten jack tar who drinks ale whenever the vehicle stops at an inn, and always throws the remainder into the face of the waiter, actually hitting one of them on the head with a heavy pewter pot for his trying to cheat him of his money. Hearing that Peter is going to be a sailor himself, and also wishing to comfort him by imparting his intended profession will not be difficult to learn, the honest veteran gives the following harangue, which is totally incomprehensible to the hero:

> 'Larn', [...] 'no; it may be difficult for such chaps as me before the mast [i.e. for ordinary seamen] to larn; but you, I presume, is a reefer [i.e. cadet, midshipman], and they an't got much to larn, 'cause why, they pipe-clays their weekly accounts [i.e. they only fill in records in their log-books], and walks up and down with their hands in their pockets. You must larn to chaw baccy [i.e. chew tobacco], drink grog, and call the cat a beggar [i.e. elude the punishment of being flogged with a boatswain's cat-of-nine-tails], and then you knows all a midshipman's expected to know nowadays'. (PS 9)

The use of sailors' jargon in land space, and particularly the confrontation of landsmen with it, leads not only to misunderstandings but also to many a comic situation, especially when sailors speak of women in terms of sailing craft. Their jargon also highlights the essential difference between the two worlds. Captain Marryat was actually not the first British novelist to cast sailors ashore and show their incompatibility with the terrestrial environment; his predecessor in this respect was a Scotsman Tobias George Smollett, a ship's surgeon's mate for a short time, who presented Lieutenant Tom Bowling (in *Roderick Random* 1748) and Commodore Hawser Trunnion (in *Peregrine Pickle* 1751) as they blunder about and clash with the world of land-dwellers. Captain Marryat naturally surpasses Smollett in variety and depth of nautical experience, which translates into the peculiarities of his salt-water creations and their otherness in the land space.

The major part of the land chapters—eight in number—occur in the middle of *Peter Simple*, and they are initiated by Peter's captivity (he is wounded and taken prisoner by the French, together with his Irish companion Terence O'Brien, following their sally in a frigate's boat to destroy a battery on shore). Their long spell on land serves several purposes: first, in his nurse named Celeste, who "had such pity [for the wounded hero] in her face, which was remarkably handsome, that she appeared to me as an angel" (PS 136), Peter finds a woman worthy to become his wife in the last chapter of the novel. Second, the hero takes advantage of his time in custody to learn French, teaching at the same time his pretty nurse to speak English—a commendable occupation, indeed, for two young people of the opposite sex: "Our chief employment was teaching each other French and English" (PS 141). Third, the two English prisoners of war who eventually effect their escape from the French prison, set out on a long trek of adventures across the country, evidently inspired by Capt. Marryat's reading of picaresque stories and romances and Shakespeare's plays. For example, the runaways take to hiding in the Forest of Ardennes where they are threatened by an enormous wolf (vide *As You Like It*, though woodland scenery and figures of tramps also appear in *Two Gentlemen of Verona* and in *A Midsummer Night's Dream*). The protagonists also dress up—O'Brien as a French gendarme who escorts a would-be-caught English prisoner, and then Peter who dresses up as a girl (putting on petticoats, etc.) and pretends to be O'Brien's modest sister, of whom his companion is apparently very jealous to discourage potential suitors (dressing up is a starting-point for comical situations in *Two Gentlemen of Verona*). The two officer-prisoners on the run, wandering the forest in bad atmospheric conditions, also recall that "in *King Lear* the weather was tremendous" (PS 163). It seems that O'Brien and Peter, the first dragging the other behind his back with a cord, in their roles of the guard and his escort respectively, also bear some resemblance to the blind Earl of Gloucester conducted to Dover by his son Edgar, who is disguised as a mad beggar. Fourthly, travelling the country, Marryat's protagonists observe the French, who appear to be easy to outwit, intimidate and bribe (all three means are successfully tried on them), and who reek of garlic. Thus, the inferiority of the French to the English in the land space complements that on the high seas.

If the hero's adventures on dry ground examined in the preceding paragraph provide a loosely structured variety in the context of the novel's backbone, which is the naval side of the Great War against France and her allies—Spain and Denmark, then one of its central themes developed consistently both in its land and sea spaces is the maturation of Peter Simple, and his gradual transformation from Peter the Simple, that is a passive and dull youth who once thought of binding himself apprentice to a tailor, into a valiant and smart naval officer as well as a true gentleman. In the novel's sea space this transformation is crowned with the hero's promotion to the rank of commander, and in its land space with his assuming the title of Lord Privilege. The latter distinction does not descend to him automatically, for he must confront – following the death of his elder brother – a scheming uncle named William who has no male offspring, but does not scruple to produce to the world a spurious son as his own in order to defraud Peter of his grandfather's aristocratic title. The fake son belongs to a woman servant who has agreed to exchange him for one of the uncle's (her master's) daughters. However, the truth is not revealed without a thorough investigation conducted by the hero and his faithful companion O'Brien, and not without the former's confinement in Bedlam due to his uncle's machinations. In the end Peter wins the woman servant for his cause by saving her husband from drowning in Plymouth harbour. He assumes the said title, while the rascally uncle is paralysed by an apoplectic fit after his adopted heir leans out of the mansion's upper window, loses his balance and falls to his death upon the stone pavement below. The whole story is marked by a series of amazing coincidences and so incredible as to appear to have been inspired by the author's reading of romances on the missing heir theme, rather than by real-life experiences.

The third and last novel to come under examination is *Mr. Midshipman Easy*, which has the lowest ratio of sea to land chapters amounting to 19 to 22 or 46% to 54%. This is because it contains a couple of interpolated stories, set entirely on land, whose only connection with the plot is that they are related by some of the secondary characters appearing at one or another point. Such is the case of Mesty the Negro sailor's story, related by himself, of his royal descent and exciting adventures on the Black Continent prior to his becoming a sailor. Another example is the rather intricate account of the family feuds in Sicily given by a local nobleman called Don Rebiera.

The novel starts with three chapters devoted entirely to the title hero's parents, and particularly to his father, who is clearly modelled on Laurence Sterne's famous eccentric creation Walter Shandy. His counterpart in Marryat's novel is Nicodemus Easy, a gentleman of Forest Hill and an amateur philosopher obsessed with phrenology. He dies in the 37th chapter of the novel, his head crushed by a machine of his own construction for "rectifying the mistakes of nature", that is, mechanically correcting the flaws in the shape of human cranium (*Midshipman Easy*, hereafter ME, 276). Like Walter Shandy, who has his own theory of Christian names, Nicodemus Easy argues with his wife throughout the whole of chapter two about the choice of a proper name for their newly-born son, who is eventually christened Jack in memory of Shakespeare's Falstaff. The boy is raised in the spirit of equality and respect for the rights of man, of which his father is an ardent advocate. Of all of Marryat's young heroes, Jack's reason for going to sea is most ridiculous, as he hopes to find an environment—"a neutral ground" (ME 42)—where natural equality and the rights of man are not abused. This reasoning, evocative of Romantic ideology[2], is absurd because human rights are nowhere abused as completely as in His Majesty's naval service (as of Marryat's time, of course, and the novel's temporal-historical setting).

Thus we come to one of the main themes of *Midshipman Easy* (apart from the successful naval campaign against the French in the Mediterranean), which is to disparage the popular and oversimplified understanding of the ideal of equality as threatening the functioning of the state and its institutions, and inevitably leading to anarchy. Therefore, in the novel's sea space the hero must learn that discipline among different ranks on board is required if duty is to be carried out, and that only one man in the ship – the captain – can be entitled to command. He also finds out that the articles of war, or rules of the naval service, are essential for the good of all who are bound to adhere to them most rigorously. Developments in the novel's land space complement these findings, and Jack discovers that the noble principle of equality upon which his father has founded the management of the family estate, soon becomes corrupted by unscrupulous tenant farmers, lazy labourers and insolent servants. The first are years behind with their rent, and the rest refuse to do any work. The result is that the whole, once flourishing, estate falls into decay. The hero eventually repudiates his father's unreserved support for unrestricted human rights, telling him "by all the laws of society we have a right to expect civility and obedience from those we pay and feed" (ME 278). Accordingly, after the death of his philosophical parent, the newly-retired and now fully converted naval officer takes the household's reins in his own hands and puts things on the estate back in order, much to the satisfaction of neighbouring landed gentlemen. There is little doubt that such a development and conclusion of the plot was determined by Capt. Marryat's privileged status both as a senior naval officer, wealthy gentleman-about-the-town, and proprietor of a 1,000-acre landed estate.

In the middle of *Midshipman Easy* there is an extensive land section set in Sicily. The eponymous hero and his companion Ned Gascoigne are wrecked on the coast in a storm. Marching inland, they come across a country manor house just as two assailants are about to murder its owner, the aforementioned Don Rebiera de Silva. The Englishmen scare away the *banditti*, earning the gratitude of the nobleman, in whose daughter Jack

---

[2] Cf. Byron's invocation to the ocean in the 4th Canto of *Childe Harold's Pilgrimage*, stanza 179:
   Roll on, thou deep and dark blue Ocean – roll!
   Ten thousand fleets sweep over thee in vain;
   Man marks the earth with ruin – his control
   Stops with the shore;

instantly recognizes the pretty girl he had earlier saved at sea. He marries her in the last chapter of the novel after making a fortune (prize-money) at sea, and after finally settling down in Hampshire as a country squire. This is a familiar happy ending in land setting. An interesting supplement to this conventional – from the literary point of view – love story is a speech in defence of marriage of convenience delivered by the hero's prospective father-in-law:

> 'It is true, that when a marriage of convenience is arranged by parents, the dispositions of the parties are made a secondary point; but then, again, it must be remembered, that when a choice is left to the parties themselves, it is at an age at which there is little worldly consideration; and, led away, in the first place, by their passions, they form connections with those inferior in their station which are attended with eventual unhappiness; or, in the other, allowing that they do choose in their own rank of life, they make quite as bad or often a worse choice than if their partners were selected for them'. (ME 159)

It should be noted that Jack's marriage with Agnes goes beyond the formula prescribed by Don Rebiera, in as much as the young people fall in love with each other and make their choice without parental interference. On the other hand, we realize only too well that the parents, or rather fathers, would never consent to their union should their 'stations' be unequal.

One new element in the novel's land space, found in this middle section of the plot, are the machinations of the Catholic clergy, which are exposed and successfully foiled. The first of such villains is Father Ignatio, the confessor of the late Donna Rebiera. He is a disgusting and commanding man, shows no humility or devotion, and turns out to be her lover, disgracing the whole family by getting the donna – a married woman and mother – pregnant. He is also identified as an assassin, the poisoner of the woman's husband. Another malefactor in the cassock is Friar Thomaso, who stands in the way of the hero's union with Agnes Rebiera. He threatens her family with the prospect of excommunication if she marries a heretic. Since the girl persists in her choice, the friar offers a bribe of money to Jack's faithful servant Mesty, who is supposed to put poison into his master's meal. There is also a scene of flagrant extortion that the hero witnesses on the Spanish island of Minorca, a scene in which three Catholic priests force a dying man to revoke his will and bequeath all his property to their holy church, leaving at the same time his own children penniless. Jack thwarts their villainy by jumping into the old man's house through an open window, scaring the priests away, and then burning the extorted new will by the flame of a candle, all while the dying man breathes his last. The scene is evidently overdrawn, as the hero rushes at the priests in the costume of the devil, happening to be on his way to a masquerade party. We finally observe that in the conclusion of the novel, before she becomes the protagonist's happy wife, the Catholic Agnes Rebiera "conformed at once to the religion of her husband" (ME 315). This anti-Catholic feeling crops up in Marryat's other, particularly later, works. This was nothing new to Englishmen, practically ever since the Reformation and the separation of the Church of England from that of Rome, and it was only strengthened in the following centuries by events like the Gunpowder Plot of 1605, the Great Fire of London of 1666 (the first was the work of the Jesuit party and many attributed the second calamity to the Papists, cf. Trevelyan 1975, 280 and 335), and then by the two Jacobite risings in the 18th century. English readers were also well acquainted with the debauchery and monstrous crimes of the Catholic clergy from diverse works such as the picaresque *Unfortunate Traveller* by Thomas Nashe, the tragedies of John Webster, and—more recently—by a host of Gothic romances.

More generally, as far as the genuine religious feeling is concerned, Capt. Marryat compares the profound religiousness of sailors with hollow religiosity of landsmen:

> On shore, where you have nothing but the change of seasons, each in his own peculiar beauty – nothing but the blessings of the earth, its fruits, its flowers – nothing but the bounty, the comforts, the luxuries which have been invented, where you can rise in the morning in peace, and lay down your head at night in security – God may be neglected and forgotten for a long time; but at sea, when each gale is a warning, each disaster acts as a check, each escape as a homily upon the forbearance of providence, that man must be indeed brutalised who does not feel that God is there. On shore we seldom view Him but in all His beauty and kindness; but at sea we are as often reminded how terrible He is in His wrath. (ME 214)

There is no doubt that the author's observations on faith and religion from the perspective of the sea and land, were dictated by his own experience of both. He was a deeply religious man himself and his daughter testifies that his last words on his deathbed were about God and the spirit of Christianity that must be implanted in the breast of youth (cf. Florence Marryat 1872, vol. II, 300).

Concluding the article, there appears to be no fixed proportion of the land to marine space in the three classics of sea fiction subject to analysis—it varies from approximately one third of the novel's volume in *The Naval Officer* and *Peter Simple*, to slightly more than a half in favour

of land in *Midshipman Easy*. More importantly than the question of
quantity, land space in all three works forms an integral part of the total
organisation or complete structure, the notion of structure comprising—
according to Jeremy Hawthorn"plot, thematics, and form", that is, "a
novel's overall organization and patterning, the way in which its
component parts fit together to produce a totality" (1997, 132). In this
sense, all three novels realize the author's aims and intentions in both
spaces, some of his principal objectives being the inculcation of virtue and
patriotism, propagation of the chivalric code of behaviour in the realities
of contemporary life, and encouragement and commendation of individual
exertion, which contributes to the national welfare, pride in Britain and her
institutions. At the same time, the discrimination between the land and sea
spaces serves to emphasize the specificity of the sailor in juxtaposition
with the landsman, and the purity of the salty element and simplicity of
life in its range, as contrasted with the temptations and traps of life on dry
ground. It seems finally plausible to argue that while the rendering of sea
space in his novels was determined by Capt. Marryat's personal
experience and conforms with the convention of realistic style, his
presentation of land space was clearly nourished with his extensive
reading of *belles lettres*, with the result that it is often fiction in the literal
sense of the term.

References

Błaszak, Marek. 2006. *Sailors, Ships and the Sea in the Novels of Captain
    Frederick Marryat*. Opole: Opole University Press.
Hawthorn, Jeremy. 1997. *Studying the Novel. An Introduction*. Third
    Edition. London: Arnold.
Hemingway, Ernest. 1968. "Monologue to the Maestro: A High Seas
    Letter". *By-Line. Selected Articles and Dispatches of Four Decades*,
    ed. by William White. New York: Bantam.
Marryat, Florence. 1872. *Life and Letters of Captain Marryat*. 2 vols.
    London: Richard Bentley and Son.
Marryat, Frederick. 1998. *Frank Mildmay or the Naval Officer*. Ithaca,
    NY: McBooks Press.
—. *Mr. Midshipman Easy*. Without date. London: P. R. Gawthorn Ltd.
—. *Peter Simple*. 1984. With a Biographical Note by Hilary Bacon.
    Gloucester: Alan Sutton.
Peck, John. 2001. *Maritime Fiction: Sailors and the Sea in British and
    American Novels, 1719-1917*. New York: Palgrave.

Philbrick, Thomas. 1961. *James Fenimore Cooper and the Development of American Sea Fiction*. Cambridge, MA: Harvard University Press.

Pocock, Tom. 2000. *Captain Marryat. Seaman, Writer and Adventurer*. London: Chatham.

Rimmon-Kenan, Shlomith. 1983. *Narrative Fiction: Contemporary Poetics*. London/New York: Methuen.

Trevelyan, George Macaulay. 1975. *A Shortened History of England*. Harmondsworth: Penguin.

Warner, Oliver. 1953. *Captain Marryat. A Rediscovery*. London: Constable.

CHAPTER FIVE

VICTORIAN PANOPTICON:
CONFINED SPACES AND IMPRISONMENT
IN CHOSEN NEO-VICTORIAN NOVELS

BARBARA BRAID

The Neo-Victorian novel seems to focus on several potent postmodernist themes, literal and/or metaphorical imprisonment being one of them. This topic as a subject of postmodern theory has been most famously undertaken by Michel Foucault in his 1977 book *Discipline and Punish*. This paper is going to use the main tenets of Foucault's theory of incarceration and its implications for modern societies to present the way the main protagonists of two chosen Neo-Victorian novels, who due to their gender, class, and/or sexuality are the Other, or as Foucault put it, the marginalised, are put in a space of confinement, as well as the extent to which these characters manage to break free from their, not only special, but also social, mental or metaphorical imprisonment. Both novels discussed below, *Mary Reilly* by Valerie Martin and *Affinity* by Sarah Waters, present the domestic space as the space of physical confinement, but also a metaphorical one.

Foucault opens his work with a 1757 case of regicide and describes the punishment of the criminal, Robert Damiens, with gross and graphic details: the prisoner was drawn and quartered, all to the general entertainment of the Parisians (Foucault 1997, 3-5). This description is then contrasted with a dull list of prisoners' duties, in form of a schedule, taken from a detention centre for young offenders in Paris in 1837 (Foucault 1977, 6-7). Barely a century later, the method of retribution changed but the shift from torture to discipline is caused not by the desire "to punish less, but to punish better" (Foucault 1977, 92). The transition from the pre-modern to modern approach to discipline consists of four elements: from public to discreet; from punishing the crime to punishing the criminal; from judges to experts (psychiatrists, parole officers, social workers) and finally, from retribution to rehabilitation. The modern discipline, therefore, is about changing the criminal, control and reform from the inside (Gutting 2005 80-81). In Foucault's words, "the soul is the prison of the body" (Foucault 1977, 30). However, he is not only talking about the modern penitentiary – he is referring to society in general; the discipline is in all of us. A range of institutions, from hospital through school till university, impose a set of rules and disciplinary methods to instil particular behaviour in us: "time-keeping, self-control over one's posture and bodily functions, concentration, sublimation of immediate desires and emotions" (Mills 2003, 43)—the prison is in our minds, not in bodily restrictions.

No one should know it better than a Victorian woman, especially a domestic servant. Not only were there rules one had to obey at all times, like knowing their place, being invisible to the world above the stairs and having a servile attitude to their masters (May 1998, 12), but also it was often unthinkable to go out of the house too often, as it might be dangerous for servants to have too much leisure time; a housemaid would not know how to use it without falling into some mischief (McBride 1976, 24). As a result, they were most of the time limited to the domestic space, and the compact space of attics and basements at that—almost literally imprisoned by their employers, who treated them like children who need instruction and moral example of their betters (McBride 1976, 21).

Similar rules were obeyed by Mary, the main protagonist of Valerie Martin's novel *Mary Reilly* (1990), which is a reworking of a classic *The Strange Case of Dr Jekyll and Mr Hyde*. It shows the story of the monstrous doctor from a point of view of his housemaid, a character only vaguely present in the original novella (Bryk 2004, 204-205). The novel starts with an image of imprisonment: young Mary is locked by her father in a tight space of a closet with a rat. This ordeal leaves deep scars not only on her body, but also, more importantly, on her soul, and taints her relationship with people and herself. Although on the surface she seems quite calmly in acceptance with her past, and she claims she doesn't hate her father, the abusive childhood did shape her—she calls it "darkness and sadness" which comes back to haunt her every now and then (Martin 1990, 31). The way she describes her lapses of depression resembles a dark space of confinement: "I really am in that blackness my father left me, with no way out and nothing to do but wait until somehow there's this merciful release and I come to myself again" (Martin 1990, 31). To some extent her father, a representative of ruthless patriarchal oppression, is still holding the key to her inner prison. Hyde feels it instinctively inside her, and preys on her fear. He is her father's double: when she hears him in the house the first time, she is surprised how his step resembles her father's: "Then I remembered how my father had that halting way about his walk and how I used to hear my own name in it (…)" (Martin 1990, 35-36). In one of the scenes where Hyde abuses Mary (in a sexually tainted way) it resembles the opening scene of the novel—he bites her in the arm until she begs, repeating the same words she said to her father many years before: "Please, sir. Do not do this." (Martin 1990, 220). There also seems to be a deeper link between the two characters at the level of repressed sexuality. It is most clearly visible in the scene in the park, where Mary thinks about her past and her future:

> Like me, *not touched*. (…) I felt such a sadness come over me, for though I understand why I cannot be like others and look forward to the future, making plans and provisions for shared life, still it is hard to bear. (…) All I could see then was blackness and I could feel his hand pressing against my mouth and the sickening weakness that rushed over me. I heard my own heart racing in my ears, his laughter, the sob catching at my throat, and then at my lips I found a taste of blood (Martin 1990, 151-152, emphasis mine).

The fragment above is slightly ambiguous. Although Mary says she knows why she will never marry, she does not explain that to her reader—is that an allusion to a possible sexual abuse from the hands of her Pa in her childhood, a possibility thoroughly examined by the Tristar film interpretation of the book (Foss 2000, 13)? Or does she simply never trust men anymore? Who is "he"—her father or Hyde? Whichever the case, there is a link between her father's and Hyde's abuse. This time, it definitely has a sexual undertone—the scene resembles rape. Therefore, Mary continues to be a victim of sadistic misogyny (Bryk 2004, 213). "Not touched" seems ironic here, as even though she is unmarried and legally speaking "untouched" by a man, she has been definitely more than touched by Hyde.

The chasm between the world of men and women, the oppressors and the oppressed is symbolised by space as well. Houses throughout the book, especially Jekyll's house, in contrast with his laboratory, are the spaces of imprisonment in Martin's novel. It seems that the wardens and masters in this prison are men— Mary's Pa, Master, Hyde, even Mr Poole. Also, the imprisoned victims are mostly women. Both Mary and her co-servant, Anne, sleep in a tiny attic room, and are usually presented in small confined spaces, like the basement kitchen (Bryk 2004, 211). Mary even calls her room "a cage" (Martin 1990, 214). Interestingly, Anne, the scullery maid, behaves like a typical prisoner—"she seems to have no life but working and sleeping" (Martin 1990, 13). On top of that, in an ironic twist of Mary's tale of abuse, her mother's body is consigned to another closet in a staircase by a greedy landlord who did not want to wait to rent her room (Martin 1990, 164). It seems to represent the limitations of the working class women in the patriarchal Victorian society.

The house as a domestic space seems to be also a place of restriction. To some extent, it is a reflection of Stevenson's novella, where the house represents the traditional, moral rules of the society which Jekyll wanted to reject through his experiments in the laboratory, which symbolises his rebellion against moral limitations. In Martin's novel, Jekyll's experimentations seem to be about breaking free from imperatives of morality as well: "a life in which you could act only as *you* please, *when* you please, with no consequences, no regrets" (Martin 1990, 43, emphasis in original). He even uses the language of imprisonment here—he says that alcohol did not bring the beast out in her Pa, but "*let* him out" (Martin 1990, 24, emphasis in original). The spatial relation reflects both the gender and the class of the characters: Jekyll is an educated, middle-class, privileged man who can roam the boundaries of good and evil (the house and the laboratory) as much as he pleases; Mary, however, is house-bound; she is not allowed even near the cabinet (Martin 1990, 31). She is limited by the strict rules a Victorian servant must obey, and Mr Poole is the warden of this prison. Interestingly, the garden in the yard is also a space of a symbolic meaning. It is a middle ground between the two polar opposites, the house (domesticity, female space and its imprisonment) and the laboratory (transgression and male creativity). It is the place of liberation for Mary and Mrs Kent, the only space of female creativity and female freedom. This metaphorical meaning is underlined by one of the final scenes, where Hyde talks to Mary in the yard and steps on her flowers, saying: "This yard is my last prison" (Martin 1990, 218). By vandalising the garden it took Mary so much time to create, he symbolically reclaims his patriarchal power over her.

However, the most important aspect of imprisonment is the fact that Mary internalized her prison, and she is her own warden. The tightest space is, it seems, the soul. From the very first moments of the novel we see how strong Mary's moral convictions are. She often chastises herself. For example, when she for the first time starts thinking about Master in a more amorous way, she lectures herself: "(…) I gave myself a talking to on the subject of a servant's foolishness and how wrong it is ever to have fancies outside one's station as it always leads to misery, as I've observed myself often enough, (…)" (Martin 1990, 12). She is appalled by her "vanity", as she calls it, when Jekyll calls her fair (Martin 1990, 48-49).

This moral confidence is what Jekyll appreciates in Mary, although it can be sometimes a painful reminder that his deeds are not without consequences (Martin 1990, 43). Even if the house and her social station are Mary's prison, it's one she is happy in—she expresses that in an interestingly masochistic language: Jekyll's household and her role in it is like a "harness that fit [her] at last" (Martin 1990, 151). She stresses several times that she is content with her life as it is (Martin 1990, 43). However, it would be a mistake to think that Mary is morally unbending just for the sake of morality itself; she does admit to Jekyll that she does what is good to stay *safe* (Martin 1990, 71-72). In the light of her Pa's abuse, one could venture to say that through this abuse, which was a punishment (Martin 1990, 11)—for being a child, being a girl, the Other— Mary internalised the restrictions put on her; she is a rehabilitated Other, and her soul became the prison of her body. Even though she despises her abusers, she embraces male domination in her love and devotion to Master—the name she never fails to capitalise in her diaries, whereas she always fails to capitalise 'i' (Martin 1990, 243).

According to Foucault, the imprisoning of the body by the soul is done by three means, one of them being hierarchical observation. The ideal form of modern discipline through observation is the design of a panopticon by Jeremy Bentham. Such a prison was actually built in Victorian London in 1812 in Millbank. It is described in Sarah Waters' *Affinity* (1999), the story of two women—Selina Dawes, a spiritual medium incarcerated in Millbank and Margaret Prior, a middle-class lady, intellectual, and a spinster, who visits Millbank as a Lady Visitor in an attempt to distract herself from her recent nervous breakdown.

Described by Henry Mayhew in his *Criminal Prisons of London and Scenes of Prison Life* (1862), Millbank seen through Margaret's eyes becomes something more than just walls and gates. It is a labyrinthine space, deceitfully simple when looked at from above, with its geometrical harmony of a flower, but scary and unpredictable when one is inside. "It is as if the prison had been designed by a man in the grip of a nightmare or a madness—or had been made expressly to *drive* its inmates mad" (Waters 1999, 8, emphasis in original). She compares the complicated corridors of Millbank to drawings by Piranesi (Waters 1999, 9). Millbank itself metaphorically becomes a woman in the description of the Porter (Armitt and Gamble 2006, 146-148) – she is a leaky, flooded, old grim beast (such a liquid creature is in our culture, according to Elizabeth Grosz, associated with female body [203]); he has "heard her *groan*—plain as a lady" (Waters 1999, 312). This metaphor is extended to the convicts inside: they represent a female in Victorian society. The silence they have to suffer is the silence women experience in the public domain (King 2005, 11); the ridicule and rejection of the idea of "pals," that is, lesbian desire, is its ghostly non-existence in Victorian society; the meaningless work and crude education reflect the lack of substantial intellectual occupation characteristic to Victorian women (King 2005, 18-19). Last but not least, the inmates are constantly observed by matrons and visitors, which constitutes a male gaze, the gaze of power, or discipline to use a Foucaultian term.

The idea of looking, observing, gazing at the convicts is recurring in the fragments where Margaret describes Millbank for the first time. She is invited into the central watch tower, and wonders on the panoptical design of the prison. She can see the convicts having their daily walk, ordered as "dolls upon a clock, or beads on trailing threads" (Waters 1999, 13-14). She is shown how to watch the convicts in their cells through a lap, or "eye" (Waters 1999, 23). She observes the women at their daily routines— work, dinner, lessons. However, the gaze of a "vigilant citizen-observer" (Armitt and Gamble 2006, 143) turns into a lesbian gaze of desire once she peeks at Selina for the first time. The matrons seem to be aware of it in time, and invite Margaret even to watch novices bathe, noticing her embarrassment with satisfaction (King 2005, 85). However, in the wider sense, she is not the only observer. Both her journal and Selina's diary have only two voyeurs: the reader on metafictional level, and, on the fictional one, Ruth Vigers, who is the only character who can have access to both texts (Armitt and Gamble 2006, 152).

Selina's literal imprisonment is echoed in Margaret's domestic one. The main reason for Margaret's "punishment" is her suicide attempt after her father's death. Now she is fed chloral and laudanum by her mother, who tries to make sure Margaret is left alone in her room as little as possible and does not write too much (Waters 1999, 70). She often reminds Margaret that her place is at home (Waters 1999, 252). At the end of the novel, when the her mother's patriarchal rules of behaviour become an almost unbearable oppression, in a Freudian slip of the tongue Margaret almost calls one of the matrons in Millbank "Mother"(Waters 1999, 267). At the age of almost 30, after her father's death and her younger sister's marriage, Margaret is now a spinster, a label she has not yet got accustomed to. In the British Library she used to visit with her father things have changed since she last visited: she notices that "the others, who do not know me, call me 'madam' now, I noticed, instead of 'miss'. I have turned, in two years, from a girl into a spinster" (Waters 1999, 58). In a form of normalizing judgment, discussed by Foucault in his theory of prison (Foucault 1997, 177-184), she is now put at the very bottom in the hierarchy of women, or rather, on its margin, as one who rejected marriage and motherhood, the holy duties of a woman (King 2005, 22). As her mother put it, "you are not Mrs Browning, Margaret—as much as you would like to be. You are not, in fact, Mrs Anybody. You are only *Miss Prior*" (Waters 1999, 252-3, emphasis in original). As the Other, she has to be imprisoned in the house as her mother's "consolation" (Waters 1999, 210). She has to remain in the constraint of the domestic space.

Furthermore, the connection between Margaret's life and the life of the convicts in Millbank Prison, especially Selina, is visible in the emotional climax of the novel, when Selina is sent "in the darks," a space of confinement in total darkness, a punishment reserved to the most difficult prisoners. That night, before having guests to dinner, Margaret takes a rather large dose of chloral, which later makes her overtly honest. She openly admits that if it had not been for her social status, she would be in Millbank Prison now: "I took morphia, Mr Dance! (…). Don't you think that queer? That a common coarse-featured woman might drink morphia and be sent to gaol for it, while I am saved and sent to visit her—and all because I am a *lady*!" (Waters 1999, 255-256, emphasis in original). That night, Margaret identifies with Selina bound in the darkness; she becomes Selina—hiding in the closet, with the velvet collar on her neck, restrained by her own clothes (King 2005, 92). This way the affinity between them is shown at its most powerful. Affinity, a word used by Selina to describe her relationship with Margaret, was the term used by Victorian spiritualists for the holy bond between spirits (King 2005, 88), which in the case of Margaret and Selina symbolises the lesbian bond between them.

Nevertheless, even though after her escape Selina is not constrained by material prison nor by the expectations of a middle-class family, is she really free? Her relationship with Ruth Vigers would put it in doubt. By means of Peter Quick she reveals her real face hidden behind a mask of a loyal and servile housemaid. Peter Quick is ruthless, abusive and manipulative. Although it may seem at the first glance that his rough treatment is reserved for the guests of Selina's séances, a close reading will reveal a disturbing power relationship between Ruth/Peter and Selina. When Ruth for the first time appears dressed as Peter Quick, surprised Selina asks what to call him, he "put his mouth very close to my ear, saying 'Say it is your master'" (Waters 1999, 193). Although there are not many clues in the short fragments of Selina's diary, we can still find more of them; after their first séance together Ruth says a shocking: "Good girl" (Waters 1999, 195); and the famous last words of the novel: "Remember, (…), whose girl you are" would show that Selina is "trapped in a seemingly passive/dominant relationship" (Heilmann and Llewellyn 2007,

200). Metaphorically speaking, Selina's relationship with Ruth becomes her space of confinement.

As Gutting rightly noted, Foucault's theories, including that of discipline and punish, are focused on the Other, the marginalised (Gutting 2005, 88). Those at the margin of society are those who have to hide from the gaze, transgress the normalisation and escape examination. The Other shown in the aforementioned novels—the working-class, the woman, the lesbian, the spinster, the monster, the angel—are imprisoned in a space—mostly houses, but also prison cells, rooms, closets, brothels, etc.—which represent a deeper imprisonment than the confinement of walls and ceiling. The female characters of Mary Reilly and Affinity, as the Other, have to be put in a controlled space by the patriarchal system, but they welcome their closets and cells – there is something deeply masochistic in the relationship of Mary and Jekyll/Hyde, as well as Margaret and Selina, and Selina with Ruth. They also attempt a liberation from the space of confinement and the disciplinary gaze of the mainstream society with a varied degree of success. Some, like Mary, do not even want to leave the domestic space and the abusive relationship; some, like Margaret, attempt at an escape, but fail; others, like Selina, think they managed to free themselves from their prison, just to find another one in a lover.

References

Armitt, Lucie and Sarah Gamble. 2006. The Haunted Geometries of Sarah Waters's *Affinity*. *Textual Practice* 20.1: 141-159.

Bryk, Marta. 2004. The Maidservant in the Attic: Rewriting Stevenson's *Strange Case of Dr Jekyll and Mr Hyde* in Valerie Martin's *Mary Reilly*. *Women: A Cultural Review* 15.2: 204-216.

Foss, Chris. 2000. When 'Good' Men Turn Bad: *Mary Reilly* as Allegory of Domestic Abuse. *Literature Film Quarterly* 28.1: 12-15.

Foucault, Michel. 1977. *Discipline and Punish. The Birth of the Prison*. Trans. Alan Sheridan. New York: Vintage Books.

Grosz, Elizabeth A. 1994. *Volatile Bodies: Toward a Corporeal Feminism*. Bloomington: Indiana University Press.

Gutting, Gary. 2005. *Foucault: A Very Short Introduction*. Oxford: Oxford University Press.

Heilmann, Ann and Mark Llewellyn. (eds.). 2007. *Metaphiction and Metahistory in Contemporary Women's Writing*. Basingstoke: Palgrave Macmillan.

King, Jeanette. 2005. *The Victorian Woman Question in Contemporary Feminist Fiction*. Basingstoke: Palgrave Macmillan.

Llewellyn, Mark. 2004. 'Queer? I should say it's criminal!': Sarah Water's *Affinity* (1999). *Journal of Gender Studies* 13.3: 203-214.

Martin, Valerie. 1990. *Mary Reilly*. London: Abacus.

May, Trevor. 1998. *The Victorian Domestic Servant*. London: Osprey Publishing.

Mayhew, Henry. 1862. *Criminal Prisons of London and Scenes of Prison Life*. London: Griffin, Bohn and Company.

McBride, Theresa M. 1976. *The Domestic Revolution: The Modernisation of Household Service in England and France, 1820-1920*. London: Taylor & Francis.

Mills, Sara. 2003. *Michel Foucault*. London/New York: Routledge.

Waters, Sarah. 1999. *Affinity*. London: Virago Press.

CHAPTER SIX

"FROM THE SPACES OF OPPRESSION
THROUGH THE SPACES OF BLISS
TO THE SPACES OF FAILURE":
THE GROWTH OF AN ARTIST'S MIND AGAINST
THE REALITIES OF IRISH LIFE IN JAMES JOYCE'S
A *PORTRAIT OF THEARTIST AS A YOUNG MAN*
AND PATRICK KAVANAGH'S *TARRY FLYNN*

MARCIN CIENIUCH

> I didn't under understand A.E.'s poem ... but for me it had a meaning
> and a message that had come from the hills of the imagination far beyond
> the flat fields of common-sense...
> How long it took us to get home I do not know, for I was wandering
> among the hills of a timeless world. It was an Eden time and Eve not
> violated. Men were not subject to death. I was happy.
> (Kavanagh, 1987, 194)

In 1940 George Orwell published a small book consisting of three
essays. Its title was *Inside the Whale and Other Essays* and if it is still
remembered, it is mainly due to the famous and still influential text which
gave it its title. In "Inside the Whale", primarily the review of Henry
Miller's *Tropic of Cancer*, Orwell drew a distinction between three
different attitudes towards reality that an artist can adopt. In the generation
of writers who dominated the English literary scene in the 1920s, among
others Joyce, Eliot, Pound, Lawrence and Wyndham Lewis, he noted a
prevailing mood of pessimism, a "cosmic despair" (Orwell 1957, 235),
whose effect was a lack of involvement in the surrounding social or
political reality. In the next generation, that of Auden, Spender, MacNeice
and Day Lewis, Orwell observed a converse attitude. Quoting Auden's
"Spain", he criticised their excessive political involvement, bordering in

his opinion on connivance with the organisers of totalitarian terror in the Europe of the 1930s. For the third attitude with which an artist could approach the surrounding world Orwell used a Biblical story and a metaphor of space. He commended Henry Miller—his Jonah hidden inside a transparent whale (Orwell 1957, 249)—for finding a secure vantage point from which to observe and describe reality without turning one's head from its grosser aspects, and without being affected by it to the point of losing objectivity. Moreover, Orwell's artist safely located in the womb-like space was supposed to *accept* the described reality—see it for what it was and give it an accurate expression, face but not challenge it, being thus able to tell some kid of truth about it.

Despite Orwell's classification as a work whose purpose is "very much up in the air" (Orwell 1957, 233), Joyce's *A Portrait of the Artist as a Young Man* (1914-15), his first novel with good many autobiographical elements, can be claimed to address itself directly to the socio-political and cultural issues which conditioned Irish society at the time of the book's conception[1]. Yet, the novel is interesting from the point of view of Orwell's essay for a different reason. It juxtaposes differently understood notions of space to tell the story of an artist trying to deal with the reality of his country. The forces working on an individual in an environment permeated by ideology are represented here through metaphors of confinement, while in the search for liberation, Stephen is showed to build for himself an alternative, visionary space separate from the immediate reality.

A number of these characteristics figure prominently in yet another work by an Irish author. Eight years after Orwell published his essay, poet Patrick Kavanagh presented to the public his first novel. Despite the different setting, time and main protagonist, *Tarry Flynn* (1948) shares with Joyce's *Portrait* a key interest—that of representing the growth of an artist's mind against the realities of Irish socio-political life. Like Joyce's Stephen, in order to elude the pressures of his environment, Kavanagh's Tarry escapes to an imagined domain of freedom. Both youths try to flee from the cliché Irish oppressive forces: the Church, the family, nationalism and tradition. Yet, it is not the influence of these that is to blame for their artistic undoing. Stephen's and Tarry's fates are sealed by their own inability to confront the sources of oppression, to artistically *accept* and

---

[1] Joseph Valentine opens his essay "Joyce's Politics: Race, Nation, and Transnationalism" with a brief account of post-colonialising Joyce: "Joyce the acerbic anti-nationalist cosmopolitan has largely receded before a Joyce whose alleged cultural nationalism better suits his downclassed Irish Catholic status" (Valentine 2004, 73).

refabricate them into a creative account. Hence, instead of facing the reality they turn away from it and flee to imagined spheres of aesthetic bliss—artistic cul-de-sacks, metaphoric dead end spaces to which the real comes only as a distant echo muffled by their own dreams of grandeur.

A good many elements of the background in which Joyce grew up[2] can be traced in *A Portrait*. From the very beginning the Catholic and nationalist Irish milieu is to the fore there: in the famous first scene, playing with his widow aunt Dante, Stephen is inculcated with the unmistakeably Catholic obligation to admit and repent of his guilt:

> He hid under the table. His mother said:
> – O, Stephen will apologize.
> Dante said:
> – O, if not, the eagles will come and pull out his eyes. (*P*, 8)[3]

Not only is the religious strictness signalled already at this stage, but also the spatial arrangement—the urge to hide from oppression in a hard to access space—is also presented as a pattern which will recur throughout the novel. Moreover, as observed by John Paul Riquelme (Riquelme 2008, 39), the need for apology/ confession results from a very specific offence—Dante demands that Stephen atones for harbouring thoughts of marriage to Eileen Vance, a Protestant girl. Such a marriage would be against both religious and political loyalties of the Dedalus family.

The most striking contrast between the imagery of confinement and open space is presented in two scenes: Father Arnell's hell sermon during the retreat in Chapter Three and the seashore epiphany in Chapter Four. Stephen's consciousness vividly records the delight with which the Jesuit priest luxuriates over each and every instrument of torment with which hell is fitted: among hell's physical terrors he enumerates the four-thousand-miles-thick walls, the crowdedness of the place, its stench, darkness, heat and intensity of hell-fire, the company of the fellow-condemned and the company of the devils themselves (*P*, 135-141), adding to that a list of spiritual ones he includes the loss of God, pangs of conscience, extension and intensity and finally the eternity of hell (*P*, 144-152). Thus, he creates a powerful depiction of a monstrous time-space continuum whose sole aim is subjecting his young audience to the

---

[2] This is well documented in a number of biographies and collections of letters, e.g. Richard Ellmann's *James Joyce* (1972, Oxford University Press) or Edna O'Brien's *James Joyce* (1999, Viking Adult Publishers).

[3] All quotes from *A Portrait of the Artist as a Young Man* come from 1996 Penguin Books edition, further referred to as *P*.

teachings of the Church. Such a vision perfectly resonates with the conscience-stricken state of Stephen's mind. The boy is guilt-ridden over his "beastly" (*P*, 126) encounters with prostitutes, which in themselves are a product of his repressed and alienated selfhood[4]. For him, the vivid description results in a complete surrendering to the voice of the punishing Church—the confession he makes after the retreat cleanses him not only of sin but also of his entire individuality—now he takes on the role of an ascetic. Stephen's exaggerated receptiveness to the fragments of the retreat sermons dealing with guilt and sin[5] proves how faulty his budding artistic sensitivity is: his sole focus of attention—in sin and remorse as well as in repentance and sense of unity with God —is himself.

Yet, with the scene of the seaside epiphany following Stephen's rejection of the offer of joining the Jesuit seminar[6] a moment of hope

---

[4] His first visit to a prostitute happens at the end of Chapter Two, in which Stephen is alienated from his family—especially the father with whom he went on the mortifying journey to Cork—from his friends and from the cumulating pressures demanding his subjection to a variety of causes: "… he had heard about him the constant voices of his father and of his masters, urging him to be a gentleman above all things and urging him to be a good catholic [original spelling, MC] above all things. These voices had now come to be hollow-sounding in his ears. When the gymnasium had been opened he had heard another voice urging him to be strong and manly and healthy and when the movement towards national revival had begun to be felt in the college yet another voice had bidden him be true to his country and help to raise up her language and tradition. In the profane world, as he foresaw, a worldly voice would bid him raise up his father's fallen state by his labours and, meanwhile, the voice of his school comrades urged him to be a decent fellow, to shield others from blame or to beg them off and to do his best to get free days for the school. And it was the din of all these hollow-sounding voices that made him halt irresolutely in the pursuit of phantoms. He gave them ear only for a time but he was happy only when he was far from them, beyond their call, alone or in the company of phantasmal comrades" (*P*, 84-5). This is why just before his initiation, his repressed sexuality makes him casts away all dominating structures which tried to foreclose it—the primeval element in him comes to the fore "He was in another world: he had awakened from a slumber of centuries" (*P*, 114).
[5] According to A. Nicholas Fargnoli and Michael Patrick Gillespie (2006, 139), for Joyce's contemporary Irish readers it would be obvious that at such a retreat other topics would also be present and those referring to hell are given undue prominence by Stephen's tormented psyche.
[6] In accordance with Joyce's established aesthetics, this scene also abounds in images of confinement and rejection of life. The Jesuit director of the college greets Stephen "in the embrasure [1. A slanting in the sides of an opening to a wall for a window or door, so that the inside profile of the window is larger than that of the outside. 2. *Mil.* An opening widening from within made in an epaulement or parapet for the purpose of allowing a gun to be fired through it. *OED*] of the

appears for Stephen to successfully steer clear of the oppressive pull of his environment without losing sight of the world around: "His destiny was to be elusive of social or religious orders ... He was destined to learn his own wisdom apart from others or to learn the wisdom of others himself wandering among the snares of the world" (*P*, 184). Such openness to the world is however a state that lasts only for a short time – at the beach, even the spacious, limitless vistas of air, sunlight and water are but a pretext for loftier thoughts—thoughts of himself as an artist. The joyous cries of his bathing friends shouting his Greek-sounding name send him on a visionary encounter with the hawk-like man, for him, clearly a Daedalus figure, while the physical sight of their bodies appals him:

> Their bodies, corpse-white ... gleamed with the wet of the sea. ... It was a pain to see them, and a sword-like pain to see the signs of adolescence that made repellent their pitiable nakedness. ...
> -Stephanos Dedalos! Bous Stephanoumenos! Bous Stephaneforos!
> Now, as never before, his strange name seemed to him a prophecy. ... at the name of the fabulous artificer, he seemed to ... see a winged form flying above the waves and slowly climbing the air. ... Was it a quaint device opening a page of some medieval book of prophecies and symbols, a hawk-like man flying sunward above the sea ... a symbol of the artist forging anew in his workshop out of the sluggish matter of the earth a new soaring impalpable imperishable being?
> His heart trembled; his breath came faster and a wild spirit passed over his limbs as though he was soaring sunward... His soul was soaring in an air beyond the world
> -One! Two! Look out!
> -Oh, Cripes, I'm drowned! (*P*, 191-192)

Unfortunately for Stephen, throughout this enthusiastic outpouring Joyce's merciless irony shoots through—the hawk-like man with whom he instantly identifies flies sunward—Joyce stresses this repeating the word twice—thus more resembling Icarus than Daedalus. The comment of one of the bathers, naturally made unaware of Stephen's flights of fancy, only reinforces the meaning. There is little hope for an artist more preoccupied with himself than with the world. The oppressive environment has driven him into a space of hiding, from which he is incapable of looking to the outside, his sphere of bliss is self-contained, allowing for no true encounter with anything except his own dreams and self-made images.

---

window, his back to the light" (*P*, 175), playing with a loop that can be associated with a noose (see Kenner 1974, 33). Later in his face Stephen sees "a mirthless reflection of the dying day" (*P*, 182).

Chapter Five, the climactic moment in the scheme of Stephen's artistic development only heaps ironies on the precocious youth's grand ambitions. Walking through the streets of Dublin he is blind to the surrounding city life:

> His morning walk across the city had begun, and he foreknew that as he passed the sloblands of Fairview he would think of the cloistral silver-veined prose of Newman; that as he walked along the North Strand Road … he would recall the dark humour of Guido Cavalcanti and smile; that as he went by Baird's stonecutting works in Talbot Place the spirit of Ibsen would blow through him like a keen wind …
>
> His mind … wearied of its search for the essence of beauty amid the spectral words of Aristotle or Aquinas...
>
> His thinking was a dusk of doubt and self-mistrust, lit up at moments by the lightnings of intuition … in those moments the world perished about his feet as if it had been fire-consumed; and thereafter his tongue grew heavy and he met the eyes of others with unanswering eyes … But when this brief pride of silence upheld him no longer he was glad to find himself still in the midst of common lives, passing on his way amid the squalor and noise and sloth of the city fearlessly and with a light heart. (*P*, 199-201)

Stephen walks through the city contemplating his high-minded ideas and failing to see anything of what he generically calls "common lives", amidst whom he saunters light-heartedly on *his* way. Trying to escape oppression, he loses sight of the world around. When he famously tries to fly be the nets of nationality, language and religion (*P*, 231) he does so with his eyes shut. Declaring his intention to leave Ireland, he explains "The shortest way to Tara is *via* Holyhead" (*P*, 285), revealing thus that his destination is not real Ireland, not real Dublin, but the mythical seat of the High Kings. His flight must end in a mythical fall: the last words of the novel "Old father, old artificer, stand me now and ever in good stead" (*P*, 288) could just as well have been uttered by Icarus spreading wings.

The scale of ambition of Kavanagh's eponymous Tarry Flynn is nowhere near Stephen's ecstatic flights. His lowly background of a small farmer makes him an unlikely candidate for an artist with grand aspirations. Yet, Tarry is an artist, a fledgling poet struggling against the suppression of his aesthetic sensitivity by his community. The novel has little plot: due to his mistake, Tarry's mother spends the family savings on useless fields, Tarry ineptly woos two girls at the same time (one desired but unattainable, one unwanted but easy to have), then gets into a fight with a neighbour and is slanderously rumoured to have made the unwanted girl pregnant. All of this happens amidst descriptions of work in the fields which gives Tarry an excuse for solitary stays in the open, away from people, whose company he finds intolerable. In the end, dogged by the conflicts within the family and community, he decides to leave the loved but oppressive spot.

The novel's real theme is the development of an artist in an environment hostile to aesthetic occupations. Like in *A Portrait*, despite a good deal of autobiographic elements[7], the prevailing tone of the book is irony. Another similarity between the two novels is the fact that both authors distance themselves not only from the cramped and stuffy backgrounds of their heroes, but also from protagonists themselves. Kavanagh's chief distancing device is Tarry's doubleness of vision: on the one hand he operates within the rural Ireland of the 1930s, on the other most of his energy goes into creating for himself a space of a non-existent, dreamy world into which he constantly flees from everyday life. Moreover, Tarry's escapism, his lengthy sojourns in the solipsistic domain, reflects directly on his interaction with his "real" environment. Unlike the Orwellian artist who—hidden inside the whale—could observe reality head-on, contained within his visions, Flynn comes to lose touch with the world around. Hence, he ultimately fails not only as the son, brother, lover and even farmer, but first and foremost he fails as an artist.

Tarry's background is the key instrument of his oppression: the rural Ireland of the 1930s as described by Kavanagh, has little to do with the idyll of Eamon de Valera's famous vision from his St Patrick's Day radio address of 1943:

> That Ireland that we dreamed of would be the home of a people who valued material wealth only as a basis for right living, of a people who, satisfied with frugal comfort, devoted their leisure to the things of the spirit – a land whose countryside would be bright with cosy homesteads, whose fields and villages would be joyous with the sounds of industry, with the romping of sturdy children, the contest of athletic youths and the laughter of happy maidens, whose firesides would be forums for the wisdom of serene old age. The home, in short, of a people living the life that God desires that men should live. (Address by Mr de Valera, www.rte.ie)

By contrast, Tarry's native Drumnay is a place ruled by hatred and envy of one's neighbours, by struggle for power and money within the family and by all-pervasive but only declaratively obeyed moral teachings of the Catholic Church. Tarry's mother—domineering and cunning widow—is the perfect product of such an environment and it is the conflict with her that most affects Tarry. Ordering him about their cramped house,

---

[7] See Kavanagh's autobiographic *The Green Fool*.

she imposes on him an enormous amount of pressure. As her only son, he is favoured with affection beyond whatever his three sisters are likely to receive, at the same time he is responsible for fulfilling all of her material aspirations, to which his unprofitable occupations of reading, writing and dreaming stand in the way.

Again, like in Joyce's *A Portrait* space becomes a metaphor for conveying the oppressive mood of the place. The Flynn's house is a confined area in which the mother reigns over the other members of the family. In fact, the entire neighbourhood is presented as a damaging influence:

> Drumnay was a long crooked valley zigzagging West-East between several ranges of hills in Cavan .... the minds of the natives were shaped by and like the environment. In cul-the-sac pocket valleys ... were small farms ... where the owners were inclined to be frustrated and, so, violent. (*TF*, 20)[8]

Moreover, for most of the inhabitants of Tarry's homeland space is one-dimensional: it only matters as the surface of the land, with the commercial value and status it gives to their proprietors. Only Tarry seems to perceive it in different terms. He is endowed with an aesthetic sensitivity which transports him from the surrounding natural world into an almost mystical domain: "And he saw the Holy Spirit on the hills.... The totality of the scene about him was a miracle... In moments like these he was rapt to the silly heavens" (*TF*, 30). Importantly, the quality of Tarry's visionary spaces, or more specifically, the connection between them and the surrounding world changes with the course of the novel. Initially, the seemingly irreconcilable rift between the oppressive real and the imagined space of bliss can be bridged by the beauty of the surrounding nature:

> O the thrilling daisies in the sun-baked hoof-tracks. O the wonder of dry clay. O the mystery of Eternity stretching back is the same as its mystery stretching forward.
>
> That was Tarry: Eternity and Earth side by side....
>
> Why should a man want to climb out of this anonymous happiness in the conscious day? (*TF*, 19-20)

If initially Tarry does not feel the need to escape from "the conscious day" of his real surroundings, as his troubles begin to accumulate, the chasm between his visionary world and Drumnay starts to broaden. The

---

[8] All quotes from *Tarry Flynn* come from 1978 Penguin Books edition, further referred to as *TF*.

clay of whose wonder he previously spoke becomes material out of which an instrument of escape can be fashioned: "Some day he ... might grow wings and be able to fly away from this clay-stricken place. Ah, clay! It was out of clay that wings are made" *(TF,* 44). The separation of the real and the envisioned continues until at some point Tarry starts talking of an alternative space in which his alternative self is present:

> Was there not a second Tarry of whom nobody in Drumnay was aware... who looked on at the mortal Tarry, watching, laughing, criticising and recording? He saw himself sitting there in the corner with his elbows on the table while his mother and sisters talked. Though he was silent his was the only opinion that would matter in the long run.
> Out of this imagination of himself he suddenly emerged to declare:
> 'In a hundred years from now the only thing that will ever be remembered about this savage area is that I lived here awhile among the pigs. *(TF,* 139-140)

The quoted passage epitomises the exact reason of Tarry's ultimate failure. It is not the pressures of the external world that bring about his personal defeat realised on the level of the story by his departure from his equally loved as oppressive Drumnay. Artistically he is defeated due to transporting all his emotional and imaginative powers outside the real space of his and his family's real lives. Like the Orwellian artist he hides inside a secure space of his imagined whale, but contrary to him, he concentrates solely on himself, never actually looking to the outside.

Earlier on in the novel he had already admitted being incapable of taking in and fully engaging with the surrounding world, especially the people:

> In this field Tarry was cut of from the activities of Drumnay. He could daydream here without being disturbed. ... There was a defect in him which these secluded fields developed: he was not in love with his neighbours; their lives meant little to him, and ... this introversion was leading to aridity. *(TF,* 99)

Tarry cannot succeed as an artist—into his secluded world of imagination he only allows nature and himself. People not only threaten his sense of control and disrupt the unreal bliss which he experiences there, they are also simply not interesting enough, as his attitude towards his sisters clearly shows: "Except on rare occasions Tarry realised that he did not care for his sisters, and was not worried how they fared in life. His own problems were too pressing" *(TF,* 64).

The final condemnation comes when Tarry's self-obsessed mind comes up with nearly messianic-sounding statements of one considering himself a great artist beyond the common measure of men:

> ...his egotistical mind could no more entertain [the though of marrying the disgraced girl, MC] seriously than it could anything in the shape of genuine sympathy for anyone but himself.... there were some people who were fit for nothing else than sympathise, but a man like himself had a dispensation from such side-tracking activities.
>
> A man who had seen ecstatic light of Life in stones, on the hills, in leaves of cabbages and weeds was not bound by the pity of Christ.
>
> Or was he?
>
> If he were, how much that was great in literature and art would be lost. He justified himself by the greatest examples he knew of.
>
> Is self-pity not pity for mankind as seen in one man? (*TF*, 174)

Here the young farmer is altogether lost among his self-aggrandising delusions. Utterly incapable of coming to grips with his own life, he comes to despise all who threaten his self-image and unrealistic ambitions. The sole possibility of facing the reality comes to him when he places himself outside life, in a space above it. Only from there, from the position of ultimate, almost god-like control that a puppeteer-artist has over his show, can he try and look at his reality:

> The net of earthly intrigue could not catch him here. He was on a level with the horizon—and it was a level on which there was laughter. Looking down at his own misfortunes he thought them funny now. From this height he could even see himself losing his temper with the Finnegans add the Carlins and hating his neighbours and he moved the figures on the landscape, made them speak and was filled with joy in his own power. ...
>
> He was in his secret room in the heart now. Having entered he could be bold. A man hasn't to be on his best behaviour in Heaven; he can kick furniture around. He can stoop down and pick lumps of mortality without being born again to die. (*TF*, 178)

The "secret room in the heart" from which he looks at his life situated "on a level with the horizon" is the world of his imagination in which *Tarry Flynn* the novel is being written. Only from there can he accept his mother and neighbours, only from there do his struggles seem laughable. Yet, his failure is unquestionable —the escape from mortality and dying is in fact an escape from life. This is not the kind of acceptance of experience that the Orwellian metaphor expressed. Inside the whale, one was supposed to face reality, while Tarry can only either trivialise it as in the above passage, or romanticise it as in the 'Holy Spirit on the hills' quote, or mythologise it as in the final poem of the novel:

> ... I came to the haggard gate,
> And I knew as I entered that I had come
> Through the fields that were part of no earthly estate. (*TF*, 189)

The ending sections of *A Portrait of the Artist as a Young Man* and *Tarry Flynn* strike a similar note: both young characters talk about eluding threatening nets (*P*, 231; *TF*, 179), Stephen's famous "The shortest way to Tara is *via* Holyhead" (*P*, 285) is mirrored by Tarry's uncle's "The best way to love a country like this is from a range of not less than three hundred miles" (*TF*, 184). Most importantly, they are both embarking on a flight, which however for both of them seems to be a word derived from fleeing rather than flying, as their departures are attempts to escape from something (their backgrounds, their past) rather than to something, from the actual spaces of Ireland, into non-existent spaces of delusion and bliss. Both of them are escaping as failed individuals with high hopes of artistic success, which the reader of Joyce's and Kavanagh's novels knows will never materialise. Inside the whale they will remain, failed artists, looking not through its transparent belly, but at mirrors which they fitted there themselves.

References

Brown, Richard. 2008. *A Companion to James Joyce*. Oxford: Blackwell.

Chance, William M (ed.). 1974. *Joyce: A Collection of Critical Essays*. Englewood Cliffs, NJ: Prentice-Hall Inc.

de Valera, Eamon. 1943. Address by Mr de Valera: A Radio Speech Given on 17th March 1943 on the RTÉ, http://www.rte.ie/laweb/ll/ll_t09 b.html (accessed 9 Apr. 2009).

Fargnoli, A. Nicholas and Michael Patrick Gillespie. 2006. *Critical Companion to James Joyce*. New York: Facts On File, Inc.

Joyce, James. 1996. *A Portrait of the Artist as a Young Man*. London: Penguin Books.

Kavanagh, Patrick. 1978. *Tarry Flynn*. London: Penguin Books.

—. 1987. *The Green Fool*. London: Penguin Books.

Kenner, Hugh. 1974. The Portrait in Perspective. In *Joyce: A Collection of Critical Essays*, ed. by William M. Chance, 29-49. Englewood Cliffs, NJ: Prentice-Hall Inc.

Orwell, George. 1957. *Collected Essays*. London: Penguin Books.

Rabaté, Jean-Michel (ed.). 2004. *Palgrave Advances in James Joyce Studies*. New York: Palgrave Macmillan.

Riquelme, John Paul. 2008. Desire, Freedom, and Confessional Culture in *The Portrait of the Artist as a Young Man*. In *A Companion to James Joyce,* ed. by Richard Brown, 34-53. Oxford: Blackwell.

Valentine, Joseph. 2004. Joyce's Politics: Race, Nation, and Transnationalism. In *Palgrave Advances in James Joyce Studies*, ed. by Jean-Michel Rabaté, 73-96. New York: Palgrave Macmillan.

CHAPTER SEVEN

DOMESTIC SPACES AS THE SCENE OF CRIME IN THE SENSATION NOVEL: *LADY AUDLEY'S SECRET* AND THE SUBVERSION OF THE CONCEPTION OF THE HOME

ILONA DOBOSIEWICZ

In 1864, the Archbishop of York delivered a talk to the Huddersfield Church Institute, which echoed throughout the country thanks to a full report published in the November 2, 1864 edition of *The Times*. The talk was devoted to sensation fiction, considered by the Archbishop to be "one of the abominations of the age." He condemned the authors of the sensation novels, claiming that their plots aim at:

> exciting in the mind some deep feeling of overwrought interest by the means of some terrible passion or crime. They want to persuade people that in almost every one of the well ordered houses of their neighbours there [is] a skeleton shut up in some cupboard. (qtd. in Flint 1995, 276)

The sentiment expressed by the Archbishop was shared by numerous contemporary reviewers who complained that the novels, violating the principles of realism as well as of idealism, "represent life neither as it is nor as it ought to be," and were alarmed by the fact that:

> It is on our domestic hearths that we are taught to look for the incredible. A mystery sleeps in our cradles; fearful errors lurk in our nuptial couches; fiends sit down with us at table; our innocent-looking garden walks hold the secret of treacherous murders; and our servants take £20 a year from us for the sake of having us at their mercy. (Anon. 1870, 422)

"What are the Apennines to us, or we to the Apennines?" asked Henry James in his article on Mary Elizabeth Braddon, pointing out that:

> Instead of terrors of 'Udolpho' we were treated to the terrors of the
> cheerful country-house and the busy London lodgings. And there is no
> doubt that they were infinitely the more terrible. (James 1921, 110)

Flourishing in the 1860s, the sensation novel—controversial, provocative,
and rapidly gaining immense popularity—is a genre difficult to define
with any degree of precision. As Lyn Pykett put it, "sensation novels were
something of a generic hybrid, mixing realism and melodrama, the
journalistic with the fantastic, and the domestic with the exotic" (Pykett
1998, 167). The very term sensation is an ambiguous one: taken in a
psychological sense, it may be used to describe the assault on the senses of
the reader which results, according to various reviewers, in such reactions
as creeping flesh, shocked nerves, elevated blood pressure, and teeth on
edge. In the unsigned 1863 article printed in the *Quarterly Review*, the
sensation novel is defined as one which produces "excitement, and
excitement alone" by "preaching to the nerves;" it abounds in "action,
action, action," the effects of which on the reader are physical. Referring
to the work of Sir William Hamilton (1788-1856), a Scottish philosopher,
the author of the article describes sensation novels in the following way:

> A great philosopher has enumerated in a list of sensations "the feelings
> from heat, electricity, galvanism, &c." together with "titillation, sneezing,
> horripilation, shuddering, the feeling of setting the teeth on edge, &c." and
> our novels might be classified in like manner, according to what sensation
> they are calculated to produce. There are novels of the warming pan, and
> others of the galvanic battery type—some which gently stimulate a
> particular feeling, and others which carry the whole nervous system by
> steam. (Anon. 1863, 487)

Or, the term may indicate that sensation fiction refers to some
journalistic sensation such as the forcible commitment of someone
mentally healthy into an insane asylum, bigamy, or some other lurid crime
described in the popular press (the term "the Newspaper novel" is
sometimes used in reference to sensation fiction, for the extensive crime
and courtroom reports published in the popular press in the 1850s and
1860s provided the novelists with material). The staple elements of
sensation fiction were crime, murder, arson, bigamy, blackmail, madness,
desertion, mistaken identity, or the inheritance received under false
pretenses.

Yet, the defining feature of the sensation genre is that, placing the
characters in sensational situations, it tends to use domestic spaces as
scenes of crime, transforming them into morbid, sinful and secret spaces,
the sites of hostility and violence, deception and illicit sexuality. Sensational

characters and shocking plot developments are located within the ordinary middle-class home. As Henry James indicated, the sensation novel became a domesticated version of the eighteenth-century Gothic novel, admitting into fiction "those most mysterious of mysteries, the mysteries that are at our own doors" (James 1921, 110). Criminalizing domestic spaces, the authors brought horror and confusion into the home, thus posing a serious threat to the conception of the Victorian home and hearth, and provoking an outburst of sharp criticism combined with a spirited defense of the ideal of "home, sweet home."

For the Victorians the space of the home was constituted first and foremost by the sense of safety it gave those experiencing the anxieties of rapidly changing modern life. John Ruskin famously described it his 1865 lecture "Of Queen's Gardens" included in the volume *Sesame and Lilies*:

> This is the true nature of home—it is the place of Peace; the shelter, not only from all injury, but from all terror, doubt, and division. In so far as it is not this, it is not home; so far as the anxieties of the outer life penetrate into it, and the inconsistently-minded, unknown, unloved, or hostile society of the outer world is allowed . . . to cross the threshold, it ceases to be home; it is then only a part of that outer world which you have roofed over, and lighted fire in. But so far as it is a sacred place, a vestal temple, a temple of the hearth watched over by Household Gods . . . so far as it is this, and roof and fire are types only of a nobler shade and light,—shade as of the rock in a weary land, and lights as of the Pharos in the stormy sea;— so far it vindicates the name, and fulfills the Praise, of Home. (Ruskin 1907, 122)

Ruskin's use of the images of shade and light conveys the dual nature of the Victorian domestic space, experienced both as a shelter from the challenges of the outside world and pressures of competitive life of business and industry, and a shelter for those spiritual and moral values that were threatened by the commercial and critical spirit of the age.

The home became a place where the individual could remain at peace, and where he could find refuge from, to quote from Carlyle's 1843 work *Past and Present*, "a world alien, not your world . . . not a home at all, of hearts and faces who are yours, whose you are" (Carlyle 2005, 274). Only at home, he could be truly himself. As James Anthony Froude put it in his 1849 novel *The Nemesis of Faith*:

> When we come home, we lay aside our mask and drop our tools, and are no longer lawyers, sailors, soldiers, statesmen, clergymen, but only men. We fall again into our most human relations, which, after all, are the whole of what belongs to us as we are ourselves, and alone have the key-note of

our hearts. There our skill, if skill we have, is exercised with real gladness on home subjects. . . . We cease the struggle in the race of the world, and give our hearts leave and leisure to love. (Froude 1903, 112-13)

Froude was one of the many Victorian writers to sentimentalize and idealize the home which came to be perceived not only as a safe and peaceful, but also a sacred space. The very expression "the temple of the hearth" indicates that for the Victorians the notion of the home was imbued with a considerable degree of moral authority and altruistic emotions.

Not surprisingly, then, the sensation novel, which portrayed the hearth definitely not as any kind of temple but rather as a hotbed of criminal activity, had literary critics and social commentators fulminating against it. The genre posed a challenge to the order of Victorian society, for the readers of such novels could no longer perceive the home, which used to constitute the core of the Victorian value system, as a refuge from the dangers of modern life, because it was exposed as a space which was not safe and familiar anymore, but could harbor a bigamist, a lunatic, or a cold-blooded murderer hidden behind the mask of respectability. The character types made familiar by domestic fiction of the nineteenth century—the angel in the house, the governess, the loyal servant, the country gentleman, the lawyer or banker—were embroiled in sensational situations and were often guilty of perpetrating hideous crimes. Interestingly, the sensation novelists followed the conventions of domestic realism—the dominant mode of representation in fiction since approximately the 1840s—characterized by the minute observation of the surfaces of ordinary life. They described exhaustively interior home spaces and the adjoining grounds which constituted the settings of their novels, paying much attention to furnishings, dress and jewelry, and familiarizing the reader with the most mundane details, such as shipping labels or laundry lists, which in the course of the novel acquired the status of clues or became significant links in the chain of circumstantial evidence. Yet, in contrast to the domestic realism ethos which celebrated the familiar and familial, in the sensation novel, the domestic life of an average Victorian was revealed as unpredictable and extraordinary, full of the secret skeletons in family cupboards.

It is Charles Dickens, with his murders and madness, his family secrets and hidden ancestries, who is often considered to be "the father of sensation fiction" (Sutherland 1999, 563) and Wilkie Collins is today perhaps the best-known of the sensation novelists. Indeed, the pioneering study of the genre by W.C. Phillips was entitled *Dickens, Reade and Collins: Sensation Novelists* (1919). Yet, in the 1860s sensationalism was most closely associated with contributions of such writers as Rhoda Broughton, "Ouida" (Mary Louise de la Ramée), Ellen Wood, and Mary Elizabeth Braddon, known as the Queen of Circulating Libraries. Ellen Wood's *East Lynne* (1861) and Mary E. Braddon's *Lady Audley's Secret* (1862) were the two most successful sensation novels and two of the best-selling novels of the entire nineteenth century. John Sutherland calls *Lady Audley's Secret* "the most sensationally successful of all sensation novels" (Sutherland 1999, 360), and there is no hyperbole involved in this statement. The novel was published on October 1, 1862 and went through eight editions in three months. The pirated text was immediately turned into a drama, which was playing to full houses at the St James's Theatre as early as December of the same year. *Lady Audley's Secret* was so profitable for its publishers, the Tinsley brothers, that Edward Tinsley considered it his obligation to name his new mansion "Audley Lodge" (Uglow 1987, ix).

The novel opens with the rich and elderly owner of the Audley Court, Sir Michael, getting married to the beautiful and poor young governess Lucy Graham, with whom he is clearly besotted. Becoming Lady Audley, Lucy Graham, the girl of humble origins, violates not only the social order, but the moral order as well, for she is an impostor, a bigamist, a mother who deserted her only child, an arsonist who set fire to an inn, where her husband's nephew, who discovered her secrets, was spending the night, and a woman who attempted to commit murder by pushing her first husband down a well. What is more (if anything more is needed), she inherited insanity from her mother, and she will end her life in a lunatic asylum.

The very first pages of the novel provide a detailed description of Audley Court and the surrounding grounds:

> Audley Court lay low down in a hollow, rich with fine old timber and fertile pastures. You came upon it through an avenue of old oaks, bordered on either side by meadows, where the cattle looked inquisitively at you as you passed, wondering, perhaps, what you wanted; . . . .
>
> At the end of the avenue there was an old arch and a clock-tower, with a stupid, bewildering clock, which had only one hand. Through this arch you walked straight into the gardens of Audley Court. . . .
>
> The house faced the arch, and occupied three sides of a quadrangle. It was very old, very irregular and rambling. The hall door was squeezed into a corner of a turret at one angle of the building, as if it was in hiding from dangerous visitors, and wished to keep itself a secret.
> . . .
> A glorious old place . . . a spot in which Peace seemed to have taken up her abode, setting her soothing hand on every tree and flower; on the still

water and quiet alleys; the shady corners of the old fashioned rooms; the deep window-seats behind the painted glass. . . .

A noble place . . . a house that could never have been planned by any mortal architect, but must have been the handiwork of that good old builder—Time. . . .

Of course, in such a house, there was a secret passage. . . .

. . . there was an avenue . . . so shaded from the sun by the thick shelter of over-arching boughs, that it seemed a chosen place for secret meetings; a place in which a conspiracy might have been planned or a lover's vow registered with equal safety. (Braddon 1987, 1-3)

The passage introduces the idea of deceptive facades, which arises out of gradually emerging tension between the traditional idyllic rural setting and the sense of foreboding and unease suggested by the disturbing presence of the "bewildering clock." The pastoral landscape is conventionally associated with peace and stability, yet even the cows there have inquisitive eyes, as if expecting that something will challenge their tranquility; the house obviously harbors some dark secrets, since it does not welcome visitors gladly. The sense of peace is illusory, for it is undermined by such expressions as "the still water," "the shady corners" and "the deep window seats" which convey the sense of mystery, which is confirmed by the existence of a secret passage and a direct reference to a shaded avenue—a perfect place for clandestine assignations.

In *Lady Audley's Secret*, Braddon often links violence and crime with calm, placid spaces and idealized descriptions of pastoral settings. The narrator points out that:

We hear every day of murders committed in the country. Brutal and treacherous murders; slow, protracted agonies from poisons administered by some kindred hand; sudden and violent deaths by cruel blows, inflicted with a stake cut from some spreading oak, whose very shadow promised— peace. In this very county of Essex there is a meadow in which, on a quiet summer Sunday evening, a young farmer murdered the girl who had loved and trusted him; and yet even now, with the stain of that foul deed upon it, the aspect of the spot is—peace. No crime has ever been committed in the worst rookeries about Seven Dials that has not had its parallel amidst that sweet rustic calm which still, in spite of all, we look on with a tender, half-mournful yearning, and associate with—peace. (Braddon 1987, 46)

The passage obliterates the distinction between the tranquil rural landscape and the degenerate urban spaces of crowded and dilapidated tenements of one of the poorest districts of London: both are equally likely to become the sites of most hideous crimes, although the readers, accustomed to the idealized representations of the countryside, are unwilling to recognize this uncomfortable fact. The narrative voice does not allow them to take anything for granted anymore: whatever looks peaceful, familiar and ordinary may be just a façade hiding the ubiquitous evil.

Once-sacred domestic spaces are reduced to becoming such a façade. Robert Audley, Sir Michael's nephew, who ultimately exposes Lady Audley as the villainess, asks:

> What do we know of the mysteries that may hang about the houses we enter? . . . Foul deeds have been done under the most hospitable roofs, terrible crimes have been committed amid the fairest scenes, and have left no trace upon the spot where they were done. I do not believe in mandrake, or in blood stains that no time can efface. I believe rather that we may walk unconsciously in an atmosphere of crime, and breathe none the less freely. I believe that we may look into the smiling face of a murderer, and admire its tranquil beauty. (Braddon 1987, 121-22)

If foul deeds are committed everywhere, and leave no trace, crime is no longer an aberration, but something common even in the most respectable families. "According to Miss Braddon," the article in the *North British Review* pointed out, "crime is not an accident, but it is the business of life" (Anon. 1865, 104). In *Lady Audley's Secret*, the home is no longer a refuge from horror and evil, for it becomes invaded by a dangerous impostor. Lucy Graham, the future Lady Audley, comes to the village of Audley to work as a governess to the local doctor's children, and easily manages to find a place for herself in the domestic setting, which enables her to meet, enchant, and marry Sir Michael. In order to hide the secret of her previous marriage and protect her status as Sir Michael's wife, she does not hesitate to resort to murder and arson, thus shattering the very foundations upon which her home and hearth are built. If revealed, her dark secrets will completely devastate Audley Court, once "a glorious" and "a noble place," and the values it represents.

Braddon conveys the sense of threat to the home through images of disruption and destruction. For example, one night Robert Audley dreams of:

> Audley Court, rooted up from amidst the green pastures and the shady hedgerows of Essex, standing bare and unprotected upon that desolate northern shore, threatened by the rapid rising of a boisterous sea, whose waves seemed gathering upward to descend and crush the house he loved. (Braddon 1987, 210)

He realizes that exposing Lady Audley's criminal activities will result in the complete tearing down of Audley Court, an erstwhile happy and safe domestic space. He warns Lady Audeley: "I . . . shall level that house to the earth, and root up every tree in these gardens, rather than I will fail in finding the grave of my murdered friend" (Braddon 1987, 236). Although the physical destruction of Audley Court does not take place in the novel, the space of the hearth becomes obliterated: the family is destroyed and Sir Michael decides to leave his ancestral home for ever. The novel directly challenges the conception of peaceful, safe and blessed domestic spaces, ending with a vision of the abandoned Audley Court, supervised only by a "grim old housekeeper" (Braddon 1987, 376).

In its treatment of domestic spaces *Lady Audley's Secret* follows the conventions characteristic for the sensation genre. Turning home spaces into the sites of criminal activity and repositories of dark secrets, sensation novels were undermining the cherished ideals of home and family, which constituted the cornerstone of the Victorian moral order. Not surprisingly, they were castigated and considered socially subversive, yet—or perhaps because of that—they were immensely popular.

References

Anonymous review. 1870. Our Novels. The Sensation School. *Temple Bar* 29: 410-24.

Anonymous. 1863. Sensation Novels. *Quarterly Review* 113: 481-515.

Anonymous. 1865. Sensation Novelists: Miss Braddon. *North British Review* 43: 92-105.

Braddon, Mary E. 1987. *Lady Audley's Secret*. Harmondsworth: Penguin Books.

Carlyle, Thomas. 2005. *Past and Present*, ed. by Chris Vanden Bossche. Berkeley: University of California Press.

Flint, Kate. 1995. *The Woman Reader 1837-1914*. Oxford: Clarendon Press.

Froude, James Anthony. 1903. *The Nemesis of Faith*. London: George Routledge & Sons.

James, Henry. 1921. Miss Braddon. In *Notes and Reviews*, 108-16. Cambridge, MA: Dunster House.

Pykett, Lyn. 1998. A Woman's Business: Women and Writing, 1830-1880. In *An Introduction to Women's Writing: From the Middle Ages to the Present Day*, ed. by Marion Shaw, 149-76. London/New York: Prentice Hall.

Ruskin, John. 1907. Of Queen's Gardens. In *Sesame and Lilies, Unto this Last and the Political Economy of Art*, 109-44. London: Cassell.

Sutherland, John. 1999. *The Stanford Companion to Victorian Fiction.* Stanford: Stanford University Press.

Uglow, Jennifer. 1987. Introduction to *Lady Audley's Secret*, by Mary E. Braddon, ix-xix. Harmondsworth: Penguin Books.

CHAPTER EIGHT

THE RIVER AS THE SPACE OF DEATH IN WILLIAM FAULKNER

AGNIESZKA KACZMAREK

From the moment of the publication of his first novel *Soldiers' Pay* (1926), it became evident for the artistic circles of America that death fascinated William Faulkner turning out to be his predominant theme traced clearly throughout his literary output. With Faulkner's belief in mind, that similarly to "our rivers, our land: [is] opaque, slow, violent; shaping and creating the life of man in its implacable and brooding image" (Faulkner 1985, 30), the article is to show that the river as a scene of demise and destruction occupies a significant place in Faulkner's imagery constituting a recurrent motif in his writing. In order to exemplify the above stated thesis, particular passages derived mainly from *The Sound and the Fury* (1929), *As I Lay Dying* (1930), and "Old Man" (1939)[1] will be discussed.

Following the chronological order of the publications, the discussion should be initiated with *The Sound and the Fury*, where the river provides a central setting for the second narrative of the novel. Quentin Compson designates this watery environment to be the place of his suicide, rehearsed in fact a few times, which is detectable through his futile, even ludicrous attempts at sinking his own shadow: "if only I had something to blot it into the water, holding it until it was drown" (SF 111). Further, it becomes apparent that before he actually performs the act of self destruction, he would like the river to turn into his grave while pondering over the process of decomposition of his bones, which after a long time will definitely be inconspicuous in the sand at the bottom (SF 98). Nevertheless, there is another fragment in which Quentin envisages the waterway to be a passage for carrying his "debris half submerged, healing

---

[1] Hereafter, *The Sound and the Fury* as SF, *As I Lay Dying* as AILD, "Old Man" as OM.

out to the sea and the caverns and the grottoes of the sea" (SF 111), which
alludes to "Kubla Kahn" by Samuel Taylor Coleridge (Ross and Polk
1996, 61), where the Alph River flows "to a lifeless ocean" (Coleridge
1973, 256). In Coleridge as well as in Faulkner the river then embodies the
mythological Styx being a channel to the land of the dead.

The branch behind the Compson estate, being a tributary of the
Yoknapatawpha River, also serves as a setting for a potential scene of
destruction, for this is a site where Quentin tries to persuade Caddy to
commit *felo de se* together. By the time his intention of slitting his sister's
throat is revealed though, Faulkner undoubtedly prepares us for what is to
occur by arousing in the reader's mind a number of strong thanatological
connotations. While Quentin is dashing to the branch, the movement of the
surrounding world seems to be suspended, since crickets that stop chirping
are described poetically as creatures creating first "a small traveling island
of silence" and then simply "vacuum" (SF 186).[2] Next, marking the time
of the day with the words "grey darkness" (SF 185), Faulkner clearly
depicts twilight, which in his works is frequently indicative of passing
away. An undeleted name on the first page of the manuscript of *The Sound
and the Fury*, "Twilight" also constitutes a title of a short story (Millgate
1978, 86), which the novel developed from, and which resulted from the
reminiscence about the death of Faulkner's grandmother, Lelia Swift
Butler (Blotner 2005, 210). Furthermore, what is detectable in the air is the
smell of rain (SF 186), associated with mortality from the very beginning
of the Compson saga. In Benjy's section opening the novel, the scent of
rain has already made a bleak prophecy of the finitude of Quentin and Mr
Compson, because before they die, Benjy, recognized to be a seer by the
black servants, senses that both members of his household "smelled like
rain" (SF 79, 81).

The depiction of Caddy lying partly in the branch similarly calls forth
direct allusions to demise. Having passed through the vacuum created by
the crickets, Quentin finds his unmoving sister resembling a castaway in a
recumbent position with the lower part of her body immersed in the water.
Her pale face, pictured as "a white blur" (SF 186), merging with the sand
she is lying on, is visible only because of the hair contouring her head. The
stuffy odour of a honeysuckle, detected on Caddy's face by means of a
synaesthesia is compared to "a thin wash of lilac coloured paint" (SF 183),
i.e. a coating of paint dyed lilac, which is a colour of the flowers Faulkner

---

[2] The motif of the crickets may come from Eliot's *The Waste Land* (Ross and Polk
1996, 129), where we read: "the dead tree gives no shelter, the cricket no relief"
(Eliot 2003, 1431), which in turn constitutes the author's allusion to the passage
from Ecclesiastes telling about old age before dying (ibid.).

indisputably couples with dying. In 1920, trying his hand at poetry, he wrote a verse entitled "The Lilacs," whose lyrical character is a wounded soldier, and whose subject matter touches upon "death in life," to cite Blotner (Blotner 2005, 78). In addition, one should not forget about "The Waste Land" of Eliot, favoured by Faulkner tremendously, where in the part "The Burial of the Dead" we can uncover "Lilacs out of the dead land" (Eliot 2003, 1430), obviously denoting mourning, as in Whitman's elegy on Lincoln "When Lilacs Last in the Dooryard Bloom'd."

In the scene by the branch, permeated simultaneously with sexual overtones, the wish of death ceaselessly surfaces in Quentin's mind. First, he comes up with an idea of killing Caddy's lover Dalton Ames (SF 187), whose murder, in fact, he later attempts to realize in the vicinity of a watery environment too (SF 198). Then, Quentin puts forward that he will cut his sister's throat taking his life in the same way after that. Besides, while caressing Caddy's neck with a knife, he recalls the day of their grandmother's death, whom they nicknamed Damuddy, which in *The Sound and the Fury* constitutes a moment when the Compsons' children were initiated into a world where death exists, a world which their parents intended to hide them from, but which they discovered against their wish thanks to Caddy, who had climbed up a tree to peep through the window at the funeral (SF 54). Moreover, while recollecting Damuddy's death by the branch, Quentin calls to mind the fact that Dilsey scolded Caddy off for her muddy drawers on that day, and if the words "Damuddy" and "muddy" are set side by side, not only is a phonic overlap noticeable here (Bleikasten 1976, 216), but also an overlap between life and death if vigorous and alive Caddy is juxtaposed with deceased Damuddy buried in the muddy ground. It should be stressed here as well that this imagery triggered off the author's work on *The Sound and the Fury*, and as such haunted him for the following fifteen years until he compiled the Appendix, which, as Faulkner admitted, was "the final effort to get the story told and off my mind, so that I myself could have some peace from it" (Faulkner 1968, 245).

The excerpts derived from *As I Lay Dying*, where "death *wells up* from the whole novel" (Bleikasten 1973, 112; emphasis added), additionally provide us with an irrefutable proof that Faulkner regards the river as the space of destruction. One of the most harrowing experiences the Bundren family undergo is the traverse of the Yoknapatawpha River with their mother's coffin swept into the water, which is pictured by Darl, Addie's son, as a scene of an apocalypse, since "the river crossing, like that of the Styx or Acheron, marks the Bundrens' entry into the underground. We are now in Death's other kingdom" (Bleikasten 1973, 110-111). To reinforce the apocalyptic atmosphere, with the current "thick and dark," the water is depicted to be "cold, [...] like slush ice," and above all as "mournful" (ASLD 90 and 93), which shows beyond doubt the author's implication to collate the waterway with departure from life. Above all, the river environment continuously conjures up various images of dying, which is exemplified in the following fragment:

> Above the ceaseless surface they stand—trees, cane, vines—rootless, severed from the earth, spectral above a scene of immense yet circumscribed desolation filled with the voice of the waste and mournful water (ASLD 93).

Here, what rivets the reader's attention is first of all the recurrent, apocalyptic motif of uprooting (Bleikasten 1973, 112), and then the fact that in such a short passage Faulkner employs so vast an array of words which in the context of death may develop plenty of thanatological associations: the phrase "the ceaseless surface" could apparently be read as a link between the river and death taking its toll every single day; the adjectives "rootless" and "severed" relating to vegetation are definitely to create a picture of withering and lifeless plants certainly reinforced by their "spectral" appearance; and finally, the river referred to as "a scene of [...] desolation" can arouse no other connotations than bareness, devastation, wretchedness or loneliness that have always accompanied decease. Additionally, in another passage, where the waterway is described as a site of bleakness too, the river is likened to "the place where the motion of the wasted world accelerates just before the final precipice" projecting in the reader's mind the image of existence ending up in catastrophe (ASLD 96), which *de facto* takes place in the novel with the coffin slipping into the water from the Bundrens' wagon, equated with "Charon's ferry" (Blaikasten 1973, 110).

The river in *As I Lay Dying* essentially remains a site of constant hazard and actual catastrophe. Rising steadily from the first pages of the novel, so high is its level that even the oldest in the Yoknapatawpha County do not recall it as such, to say nothing of the bridge washed away by the current (AILD 71). For this reason, the river is regarded as intransgressible: "it'll take the Lord to get her over that river now, [...]. Anse cant do it [sic]," Peabody claims (AILD 57). Drifting in the water, the logs "scraping and bumping [...] and tilting end-up and shooting clean outen the water [sic]" pose an ever-present mortal danger (AILD 90):

One part of you knowed it was just water […], yet when them logs would
come spewing up outen it, you were not surprised, like they was a part of
water, of the waiting and the threat [sic] (AILD 90).

And that kind of serious menace both people and animals are acutely
aware, because the horse with the eyes dilated with horror neighs fearfully
when spurred into water by force, and Cash with Darl, who are about to
cross the river in the wagon with Addie's body, "crouch flagrant and
unabashed in all the old terror and the old foreboding" (AILD 93). What is
more, the water in the river seems to be a substance with chemical
properties to decompose a human body, for Cash's "face appears sunken a
little, […], as though the wetting had slacked the firmness which had held
the skin full" (AILD 105).

On top of that, applying the joint phenomenological approach of
Gabriel Marcel and Karl Jaspers presented by William J. Sowder in
Existential-Phenomenological Readings on Faulkner, the space of the
river may be recognized to be a place where relationships between the
living sons and the dead mother are possible to be observed. Having been
dragged out of the water after the unsuccessful crossing, Cash is more
interested in the whereabouts of his carpenter's tools that could still be
useful than in the casket with his mother's corpse left only to be buried;
thus after physical expiration Addie for Cash ceases to be a mother turning
into a thing to be dealt with. From Sowder's viewpoint, such conduct
illustrates purely empirical, only sense-based existence of Jaspersian man
as the Encompassing, being far away from other two modes of living, i.e.
"consciousness-as-such," embracing all kinds of reasoning including
seeking answers, classifying, inferring, etc., and "Spirit" (Sowder 1991,
151-152), being a notion defining the highest mode of existence, during
which the Encompassing creates "his own possible reality," to refer to
Jaspers (qtd. in Sowder 1991, 152). In *As I Lay Dying*, the consciousness
mode stands for Darl, because even though there are moments when he
treats his mother dispassionately, at one point, by letting the coffin float
off, he does his best to make Addie "free and moving again," Sowder
states, which is also discerned by the critic as an attempt of
communication between the living and the dead (Sowder 1991, 156). The
protagonist who has managed to go through all three modes of existence is
Vardaman (Sowder 1991, 158), whose attachment to his mother appears to
be so enduring that a breakdown in communication is unthinkable. As the
youngest of all the offspring, he emphatically denies his parent's finitude
initially associating her departure from this world with his hooking a fish
in the river. Later, while rationalizing matters of life and death, he restores
Addie to being by his belief that she is actually a fish, which on the one

hand is perceived as his yearning for the past union of the child with the mother in her womb (Bleikasten 1973, 97). On the other hand, by his belief in Addie's aliveness, Vardaman, with regard to Jaspers, manages to build up his own reality, which admittedly is illusive, but it surely makes his mamma a living memory.

Bearing in mind Vardaman's own built-up reality, in certain of its aspects, the river presents itself as the imprint of animation drawn by Faulkner through the comparison of Addie's corpse to a fish. Apart from the primary Christian symbol of a fish denoting the Eucharist, and as such the living body of Christ, the significance of the juxtaposition is highlighted in another way. After the mental transformation of Addie into a fish, Vardaman believes that the plunging of the coffin into the water opens up an opportunity to see his mother alive again. When Darl, who was to ford the river with the corpse, appears on the shore with nothing in his hands, Vardamar is both startled and disgruntled: "Where is ma, Darl? [...] You never got her. You knew she is a fish but you let her get away" (AILD 101). And although he obtains no scrap of evidence for his parent's transubstantiation, he continues to give credence to it being convinced of Addie's presence in the river:

> Dewey Dell said, She's in the box; how could she have got out? She got out through the holes I bored, into the water I said, and when we come to the water again I am going to see her. My mother is not in the box. My mother does not smell like that. My mother is a fish (AILD 132).

In the novella "Old Man," starting with the first-sentence information about the great flood of 1927, there may be discerned Faulkner's animistic approach to the Mississippi River, which plainly represents something more than a mere setting. By contrast to Mark Twain, who admittedly does mention precarious water rises, but certainly much more appreciates "the majestic, the magnificent Mississippi" to be a source of invaluable experience (Twain 1963, 22 and 55), the waterway is recognized by Faulkner to be a villain-like protagonist (Bleikasten 1973, 101).[3] Nicknamed "the Father of Waters" (OM 602), and the "Old Man" (OM 543), the River, usually capitalized as it was its name (OM 544, 600), does everything in order to annihilate the tall convict, *nota bene* anonymous,

---

[3] Faulkner's imagery of the Mississippi as such is not only disparate from Twain's. In the article "The Mississippi River as site and symbol," Thomas Ruys Smith claims that in the 1920s and 1930s the Mississippi once again took place of a frontier in American consciousness being identified with freedom and civil disobedience (Smith 2009, 73).

"with furious and deadly intent" (OM 603). With "swiftly accumulating ferocity" (OM 606), "inventiveness and innate viciousness" (OM 605), being its personality traits, the element with every wave keeps striking blows against its victim, at first by capsizing the skiff (OM 547), and then by hitting the convict's nose with the stern of the boat (OM 592). Moreover, the outcome of the fight is surely predictable, since after a great deal of tossing and turning in the water, when the inmate finally manages to get back into the skiff, for a short instant he lies in a pool of water tinted with blood breathing heavily (OM 593). And when another billow flings him on the bottom of the skiff, he again finds himself lying flat with his face down losing blood (OM 591-592). Obviously, the convict is cognizant of the river's deadly intentions: after the woman's hint at his bloody appearance, he admits openly: "I feel like I done already been hung [sic]" (OM 596). In addition, his efforts to survive are futile, the more so as he is just a "toy and pawn" for the medium surrounding him (OM 605).

The force with which the river flows does not constitute the only lurking death-dealing danger—whatever the water carries along with itself and wherever it takes the tall convict to are equally perilous. Replete with traps, time and time again the Old Man sets snares for its prey in the form of floating trunks, planks, dead farm animals, and drifting debris from flooded homesteads (OM 609, 614). However, stagnant woods, farms and towns, partly or wholly submerged, turn out to be even more hazardous, therefore this boundless body of water seems to be a never-ending iceberg. As for the threats issued by people, the crew of the shanty boat, from whom the prisoner expected to receive help with the pregnant woman, boot him in the face stepping on his fingers when he holds the edge of their vessel (OM 609). More importantly, what transpires from their faces being "sullen derisive and grim" is scorn for the man in need (OM 609). There is another incident as well, which shows that encounters with those whom the inmate takes as rescuers lead to more violence: when the prisoner attempts to reach the platform, instead of a helping hand he is treated to a salvo of gun fire (OM 612).

In "Old Man," Faulkner highlights the river to be the place of life threatening situations mostly through two types of comparisons, of which the first refers to weapons, and the second to animals. The vivid illustration of the former is the fragment in which the narrator of the story notices that the route they follow disappears in the water "like a flat thin blade slipped obliquely into flesh by a delicate hand" (OM 538). Further, the harrowing experience up the river where the prisoner has just fought for life makes him envisage the concept of upstream exclusively as a straight line, for other images are for him too disturbing to be grasped "like the notion of a rifle bullet [having] the width of a cotton field" (OM 593). The examples explicating the latter type go as follows: having breakfast on the platform to which the inmates were evacuated, it does not escape the tall convict's notice that the barn he saw the previous day was almost totally overflowed through the night and "as a dead fly vanished beneath the moiling industry of a swarm of ants" (OM 544). Likewise, the impetuous currents tossing the prisoner in the fast-flowing water are compared to the movement of an anaconda, whereas the skiff hitting him in his face is juxtaposed with a mule which kicks him without warning with its hoof (OM 593). To add one more imagery, the treacherous wave constantly coming back to pounce on its opponent is similar to "a frenzied stallion in a lane" (OM 603), or its crest is "shredded like fangs" (OM 610).

While scrutinizing the text of "Old Man" it is impossible not to discern a few similarities between the novella and *As I Lay Dying*, which may apparently be claimed to be repetitions. Interestingly enough, most observable in the short story is Faulkner's attachment for the word "desolation," which the author has already employed a few times in the novel of 1930. Here in "Old Man" the reader uncovers "watery desolation" (OM 542), "gray and limitless desolation" (OM 597), "wet and boundless desolation" (OM 602), "boiling desolation" (OM 604), "dreamy desolation" (OM 610), "vast serene desolation" (OM 664), "teeming and myriad desolation" (OM 668).[4] Also, in "Old Man," it is traceable to decipher what Bleikasten has already noticed in *As I Lay Dying* (Bleikasten 1973, 104), namely, Faulkner treats the space of the river as time. In the novel we read: "It is as though the space between us were time" (AILD 96), and in the short story:

> it no longer seemed to him that he was trying to put space and distance behind him [...] but that both he and the wave were now hanging suspended simultaneous and unprogressing in pure time (OM 610).

In *Faulkner's Questioning Narratives*, David Minter, nevertheless, does not see these repetitions as a lack of originality, yet as one of "the characteristic modes of expression of an imagination that could never give

---

[4] Interestingly enough, English Victorian writers who traveled around the New World discerned the Mississippi identically like Faulkner. Frances Trollope depicted the river as "murky stream [...] utterly desolate" (qtd. in Smith 2009, 68). Moreover, William Makepeace Thackeray described it as "dreary & funereal" (ibid.).

up desiring closure of a kind that it saw little and, finally, no hope of achieving" (Minter 2004, 133).

To sum up, the discussion over the river as the space of death appears hard to close, because like the tall convict in "Old Man" we could keep wondering "whether the river had become lost in a drowned world or if the world had become drowned in one limitless river" (OM 606), but the conclusion which may definitely be reached now is the one Eliot formulated making a reference to *The Adventures of Huckleberry Finn*, namely the "River gives the book its form" (Eliot 1977, 332). In Faulkner's case, it is not exclusively one book, or not only a form, since the river in the Yoknapatawpha County is "a treacherous and capricious dictator," to quote Eliot again (ibid.), on whose territory one either dies or is close to the border between life and death.

References

Bleikasten, André. 1973. *Faulkner's As I Lay Dying*. Bloomington: Indiana University Press.

—. 1976. *The Most Splendid Failure. Faulkner's The Sound and the Fury*. Bloomington: Indiana University Press.

Blotner, Joseph. 2005. *Faulkner: A Bibliography*. Jackson: The University Press of Mississippi.

Coleridge, Samuel Taylor. 1973. Kubla Khan. In vol. 2 of *The Oxford Anthology of English Literature*, ed. by John Hollander and Frank Kermode, 254-257. New York: Oxford University Press.

Eliot, T. S. 1977. An Introduction to *Huckleberry Finn*. In *Adventures of Huckleberry Finn*, by Mark Twain, ed. by Sculley Bradley, 328-335. New York: W. W. Norton & Company.

—. 2003. The Waste Land. In vol. D of *The Norton Anthology of American Literature*, ed. by Nina Baym, 1430-1443. New York: W. W. Norton & Company.

Faulkner, William. 1956. *The Sound and the Fury*. New York: The Modern Library.

—. 1968. Interview with Jean Stein vanden Heuvel. In *Lion in the Garden*, ed. by James B. Meriwether and Michael Millgate, 237-256. New York: Random House.

—. 1985. *As I Lay Dying*. In *Novels 1930-35*, ed. by Joseph Blotner and Noel Polk. New York: Literary Classics of the United States.

—. 1990. Old Man. In *Novels 1936-1940*, ed. by Joseph Blotner and Noel Polk. New York: Literary Classics of the United States.

Millgate, Michael. 1978. *The Achievement of William Faulkner*. Lincoln: University of Nebraska Press.

Minter, David. 2004. *Faulkner's Questioning Narratives*. Urbana: University of Illinois Press.

Ross, Stephen M. and Noel Polk. 1996. *Reading Faulkner: The Sound and the Fury*. Jackson: University Press of Mississippi.

Smith, Thomas Ruys. 2009. The Mississippi River as site and symbol. In *The Cambridge Companion to American Travel Writing*, ed. by Alfred Bendixen and Judith Hamera, 62-77. New York: Cambridge University Press.

Sowder, William J. 1991. *Existential-Phenomenological Readings on Faulkner*. Conway: UCA Press.

Twain, Mark. 1963. *Life on the Mississippi*. New York: Bantam Books.

CHAPTER NINE

DISCOURSE SPACE BUILDING IN ELIZABETH BOWEN'S SHORT STORY "OH, MADAM...": A DEICTIC SHIFT THEORY APPROACH

ANNA KĘDRA-KARDELA

1. Introduction

The paper deals with the construction of the discourse space in Elizabeth Bowen's short story "Oh, Madam...". Following Bernard Moulin (Moulin 1995, 89), we understand discourse space as "a pragmatic form of context which is used to structure knowledge contained in a discourse." For, in order to properly understand the message conveyed, both the speaker and the hearer must, to use Moulin's expression, "position" themselves relative to the knowledge used in the message conveyed. The strategy of "positioning oneself" relative to the said knowledge is essential for manipulating the information conveyed in the process of communication. As succinctly put by Moulin,

> When communicating some information, a person usually presupposes that her interlocutor is aware of the context to which that information must be related. If this contextual relationship is not obvious or readily found, the addressee asks the originator agent to indicate explicitly which is the relevant context for that information. (Moulin 1995, 89)

Asking for the relevant context of information, then, is the principal task of the addressee, or, in the case of a literary work, the reader. For, we claim, engaged in the process of reading a text, the reader attempts to extract the information from the text and thus to reach a viable interpretation of it.

In the theory proposed by Moulin, for instance, reading a literary text can be seen to consist in the establishment of the reader's and narrator's perspectives and attitudes (in Moulin's theory: the agent's and narrator's perspective and their attitudes respectively) and confronting them with inference-related discourse spaces, including conditional, alternative, generalized and counterfactual discourse spaces. In Moulin's theory then—and this is worth emphasizing—discourse spaces are not given in advance; rather they are evoked, created or modified by the speaker and the addressee who negotiate the way the discourse is to be understood.

A different solution to the problem of understanding and interpreting a text, a solution adopted in this paper, is to assume that the discourse space of a literary work is created in the process of subjectivizing the text, a cognitive strategy based on the idea of deictic center. In particular, drawing on the insights of *Deictic Shift Theory* as proposed by Stockwell (2002a, 2002b), Tsur (2003), Green (1992) and others, we claim that the reader, when interpreting a text, identifies a deictic centre (or centers)— the text's speaking, writing or thinking voice. Adopting the *cognitive stance* that accounts for the sense of the text's coherence, the reader mentally projects the deictic centre (or centers) and then follows the different voices which locate themselves in relation to this centre. Depending on how the plot evolves, the deictic centre may be projected by the reader and shift between the protagonist, the narrator and the reader, the different participants in narrative communication. The shift is a means of subjectivizing the text, whereby, to use Stockwell's (2002a, 41) phrasing, the reader gets "immersed in the world of the text, relating to characters, scenes and ideas [...]," "as if a threshold is crossed [so that readers] can project their minds into the other world, find their way around there, and fill out the rich detail between the words of the text on the basis of real life experience and knowledge."

The paper undertakes to show how, following the deictic shifts in "Oh, Madam...", the reader constructs the discourse space which will help him/her interpret the story. In this particular case, the main difficulty that challenges the interpreter is that the text is "incomplete" as only the words of one of its interlocutors are recorded for the reader. This imposes an additional interpretive task on the reader because not only he has to "monitor" the appearance of the deictics in the text in order to establish the deictic centre but, additionally, drawing on the inferences from the "silent" part of the narrator's interlocutor, he has to establish the interlocutor's "hypothetical" deictic centre and identify the deictic shifts taking place between the two centers thus established.

2. Deictic Shift Theory

As already noted, when engaged in the reading of a literary work, the readers "put in" their subjectivity in the text, projecting, "their minds into the other world" (Stockwell 2002a, 41). This "subjective immersion" in the world of the text on the part of the reader, his/her empathy with the protagonists, is conducted by means of *deixis*, linguistic means of grounding (or anchoring) meaning to a context. Grounding elements include personal pronouns: *I* (the speaker), *you* (the hearer); demonstrative pronouns: *this, that*; adverbs of time: *now, then*, adverbs of place: *here, there*. These expressions belong to what cognitive theorists call the *deictic center*. Owing to so-called *deictic projection* we can understand the use of words in context such as *come* (in the direction to me) and *go* (away from me); *to your left, in front of you, behind you*, etc.

The following categories of deixis can be distinguished in cognitive poetics (cf. Stockwell 2002a, 45-46):

> *Perceptual deixis*: expressions concerning the perceptive participants in the text, including personal pronouns 'I/me/you/they/it'; demonstratives 'these/those'; definite articles, definite reference 'the man', mental states 'thinking, believing'. ...
>
> *Spatial deixis*: expressions locating the deictic center in a place, including spatial adverbs 'here/there', nearby/far away' and locatives (in London, upstairs), demonstratives 'this/that'; verbs of motion 'come/go', 'bring/take'. ...
>
> *Temporal deixis*: expressions locating the deictic center in time, including temporal adverbs 'today/yesterday/tomorrow/soon/later' and locatives 'in my youth', 'after three weeks'; especially tense and aspect in verb forms that differentiate 'speaker-now', 'story-now' and 'receiver-now'. ...
>
> *Relational deixis*: expressions that encode the social viewpoint and relative situations of authors, narrators, characters and readers, including modality and expressions of point of view and focalisation; naming and address conventions; evaluative word choices. ...
>
> *Textual deixis*: expressions that foreground the textuality of the text, including chapter titles and paragraphing; co-reference to other stretches of text; reference to the text itself or the act of production; evidently poetic features that draw attention to themselves; claims to plausibility, verisimilitude or authenticity. ...

Deictic expressions, representing the above-mentioned types of deictic categories make it possible for the reader to "get inside" the text and thus prompt him to assume the already mentioned *cognitive stance*, a mental capacity owing to which the reader can see things from the point of view of the characters or the narrator and build, from such a point of view, a rich context by relating to deictic expressions. Because the appearance of deictic expressions is context-dependent, reading a literary text, as Stockwell notes,

> involves a process of context creation in order to follow the anchor-points of all these deictic expressions. *Reading is creative in this sense of using the text to construct a cognitively negotiable world, and the process is dynamic and constantly shifting.* (emphasis mine). (Stockwell 2002a, 46)

The *deictic shift*, involved in "seeing things through the eyes of the other," is precisely the subject of study of Deictic Shift Theory.

According to Stockwell (2002a, 47), the main areas of study of Deictic Shift Theory revolve around the following three questions: (i) how the deictic center is created by authors in texts; (ii) how it is identified through a cognitive understanding of textual patterning; (iii) how it is shifted and used dynamically as part of the reading process.

In cognitive poetics theorists' view, the fictional world of literary texts consists of one or more *deictic fields* which are defined by a set of expressions which point to the same deictic center. Deictic fields are often associated with the characters, narrator or narratee, the central "role-players" in the text, but they can also be arranged around other role-holders, such as animals, plants and other objects. (Stockwell, 2002a, 47)

3. Discourse spaces in "Oh, Madam..."

In this section I shall show, using Deictic Shift Theory, how the discourse spaces are created in Elizabeth Bowen's story "Oh Madam...". The story contains an "incomplete" conversation in which we hear only one speaker's part of the exchange, the interlocutor's words can only be guessed from what the speaker says in response to the words of the former. Based on the speaker's utterances, we gradually start realizing that the interlocutors have been living in the house for some time; that the house has been bombed; that there is another person, Johnson, who was around during the raid, but after the "bad night" he left the house and perhaps went back to his wife; that there are other persons, two girls, who have survived the air-raid, and "will be back for their things;" (Bowen 1983, 578) that the dining room has been damaged; that Madam is in a very emotional frame of mind (she is "white", is "upset" and cannot "sit still"(Bowen 1983, 578-9)); that she likes sherry, and so on and so forth.

The "one speaker-oriented" conversation reveals a great deal more about the actual events of the short story's fictional world and provides answers to several questions that can be asked when reading it: What exactly happened, and when? Who are the protagonists: who are the speaker, Johnson, and the girls? In what relations are they to each other? What social classes do they come from? Answers to these questions, which must be laboriously assembled by the reader from the "bits and pieces" of the "incomplete dialogue", are essential in the reconstruction of the short story's fictional world. It is, among others, by identifying deictic expressions that the reader can gradually build the discourse space of the story and reconstruct the story's fictional world. Deictics then are important building blocks of the discourse space which play a crucial role in interpreting the story.

"Oh, Madam…" begins with the following words:

> Oh, madam, Oh *madam*, here you are!
> I don't know what you'll say. Look, sit down just for a minute, madam; I dusted this chair for you. Yes, the hall's right really; you don't see so much at first—only, our beautiful fanlight gone. No, there is nothing in here to hurt: I swept up the glass. Oh, *do* sit a minute, madam; you look quite white… This is a shock for you, isn't it! I was in half a mind to go out and meet you, but I didn't rightly like to leave everything. Not with the windows gone. They can see in. (Bowen 1983, 578)

In this quotation, the deictic centre is established by means of three important elements: the speaking "I" (perceptual deixis), the reference to the place "here" (spatial deixis) and the temporal "now" (temporal deixis). Establishing this *zero point* in the story enables us to understand the context in order to move within the fictional world of the narrative and make sense of it. In the passage the speaker addresses "madam", the character, whose responses and reactions can only be figured out by following closely what the speaker says. Thus the *perceptual deixis* directs the reader's attention to the perceptive participants in the text: the speaker and Madam. One can notice constant shifts between the two interlocutors and thus the two deictic centers: the speaker's centre and Madam's (hypothetical) centre. The narrative is structured by the perceptions of the two protagonists, although in the case of Madam's perception, we are informed about it indirectly. Let us look at the following passage, for example:

> No, I'm all *right* madam, really… Do I? Not more than you do, I'm sure. This *is* a homecoming for you—after that nice visit. I don't *know* what to say to you—your beautiful house! There usen't to be a thing wrong in it, used there, madam? I took too much pride in it, I daresay … I *know* madam, the stairs—all plaster. (Bowen 1983, 578)

The question "Do I?" indicates that this is the speaker's response to Madam's comment about her. There is no doubt that Madam commented on the speaker's gaunt look, a result of the shock she experienced the previous night. Perceptual deixis is limited in the story to the two protagonists, but while in the case of the speaker, we know exactly what the perception is related to, in the case of Madam's perception, the reader may only hypothesize about her feelings and thoughts. The deictics which appear here make it possible to identify this hypothetical deictic centre. When attempting to see things from Madam's perspective, the reader projects his deictic centre as a result of the deictic (perceptual) shift.

Consider now two other "one-person" exchanges:

> Oh, *I'm* quite all right, madam. I made some tea this morning... Do I? Oh well that's natural, I suppose. I'd be quite all right if I wasn't feeling so bad. (Bowen 1983, 578)

and the passage:

> No, I'm all *right* madam, really.... Do I? Not more than you do, I'm sure. (Bowen 1983, 578)

The formal manner of addressing Madam is a clear case of *relational deixis*, which encodes the mutual relationship between the two persons. The interlocutor is no doubt socially inferior to Madam; her role must be that of a housekeeper, who, as we learn in the course of the story, has lived in this house for several years and has taken care of it and now is cleaning the house after the bombardment; she removes the dirt and dust and keeps an eye on the household.

Observe also that Madam clearly treats her interlocutor with kindness and concern, which shows in the latter's reactions, as the following "one-person dialogue" appears to indicate:

> Excuse me, madam—Madam, it's nothing, really. I—I—I—I'm not really taking on. I daresay I—got a bit of dust in my eye ... You're too kind—you make me ashamed, really ... Yes, I daresay it's the lack of sleep ... The sun out there .... If you'll excuse me madam—I'll give my nose a good blow—that clears a thing off... Yes, I'll try, when I've just run up to my sister's. I'll try a good nap. (Bowen 1983, 582)

The spatial dimension of Bowen's story is limited to Madam's house—the "here" of the story. In the first paragraph the protagonists are in the hall of the house. By referring to "this chair", when inviting the lady to sit down, the speaker directs the attention to one of the pieces of furniture in the hall, through which Madam enters the house. The speaker adopts the "from within the house" perspective, which is intended to show to the Madam and to the reader the degree of the destruction. What the reader learns from this opening paragraph is that the house is severely damaged, that the speaker failed to meet Madam, who was absent from the house when the disaster happened, because "the windows [are] gone" and "they can see in". (Bowen 1983, 578)

It is by following the speaker's and Madam's movement inside the house, by identifying all kinds of locatives, verbs of motion such as *come* and *go*, *bring* or *take*, the reader gradually reconstructs the interior of the house as well as the extent of the destruction: "the dining room door won't—I'm *afraid* madam, I'm afraid, it's the ceiling in there gone ..." (Bowen 1983, 578) During the blast of the previous night the housekeeper and other servants sat in their sitting room in the basement. The floor in the telephone room appears to be all right: "It's all right here in the little telephone room." (Bowen 1983, 579) Next the housekeeper, together with Madam, goes upstairs; they pass the broken landing window, and go to the balcony from which one can see the park and the ruined surroundings. Then the second flight is mentioned: "The plaster's worse on the second flight." (Bowen 1983, 582)

That the story is "spatially" limited to just one house is confirmed by the reference to the places where the speaker did not have time to go:

> No, I don't know yet, madam; I haven't heard. I didn't care to go asking out on the street. I expect I'd hear in good time, if—It doesn't do to meet trouble. (Bowen 1983, 580)

The space inside the house—the "here" of the story—is divided into several subspaces, referred to as "here" or "there", where the pronoun "here" is used to refer to different things in different parts of the story. This points to the fact that the interpretation of these adverbs depends on the context. Thus in the "exchange": "Yes, look at the sun out there. Autumn's always the nicest season just around here, I think," (Bowen 1983, 582) the word "here" acquires a different meaning than it had at the beginning of the story, where it was used by the speaker to refer to the house; now the adverb "here" refers to the whole area. Still, the sentence which appears somewhat down below: "The sun out there" (Bowen 1983, 582) reestablishes the distinction between "here"—i.e. inside the house and "out there", i.e. outside the house. This clearly shows that the understanding of such expressions as "here" or "there" depends on the identification of the deictic centre in which these expressions are anchored.

In the absence of the "yet to be established" Madam's deictic centre, the reader has to follow carefully what the housekeeper says in order to complete the gaps and "write the unwritten text". Because the housekeeper's part remains the only source of information, it is only through reading and rereading the parts of the text before and after the gaps (i.e. Madam's presumed part) that one can hope to "reconstruct" the missing parts of the conversation. Dotted gaps in the story indicate the points of Madam's inaudible replies, which are consistently used throughout the story and foreground the story's textuality by acting as its signposts. They are examples of *textual deixis*, marking the shift from the servant's into Madam's deictic centre and indicating that we are dealing with two equivalent deictic centers between which the shift takes place. It is on the basis of the housekeeper's responses, then, that the contents of what Madam says can be guessed. I will call Madam's deictic centre a "hypothetical deictic centre" as it is built only on the basis of the reader's guesses. Still, there is little doubt that the "here" and "now" are two important points of anchorage for both the speaker's and Madam's parts. In Stockwell's view, "a set of expressions which point to the same deictic centre can be said to compose a given deictic field." (Stockwell 200a, 47) What we encounter in "Oh, Madam…" instead are expressions originating from one deictic centre but indicating another one. Although the story appears to lack expressions originating directly from the second deictic centre, it is clear that we are dealing with two distinct deictic centers. It is owing to the establishment by the reader of the discourse space, based on perceptual, spatial, temporal, textual and relational deixis, that the deictic shift can be traced and thus readerly interpretation of the story be provided.

4. Conclusion

In his book *Six Walks in the Fictional Woods* Umberto Eco introduces a wood as a metaphor of a narrative text. If we take a walk in a wood, says Eco, we have to make constant choices as to which way to go: to pursue a beaten track or create our own path, turning, for example, left or right or going straight. Like a stroller in a wood, the reader is thus forced to make constant choices and predict their consequences. Sometimes, Eco notes, we are given a free hand, having to imagine ourselves how the narrative is going to develop. That is, we have to find out to what extent our choices as readers will be sensible. This, in turn, is determined by the so-called model reader i.e. the reader who is extrapolated from the text and is treated as a "partner" in the author-speaker "narrative dialogue." On Eco's analysis, in order to interpret the text, the reader has to choose the right paths in the narrative wood.

The analysis of "Oh, Madam…", presented here, although similar in spirit to Umberto Eco's walking-in-the wood metaphor, is based on a different metaphor: on the metaphor of a destroyed house. The sense of uncertainty and a loss, evident in the story, is enhanced in "Oh, Madam…" by the destruction of the stability which, under normal circumstance, a house can provide. The interlocutor's expressions "Your beautiful house! There usen't to be a thing wrong in it, used there, madam?" (Bowen 1983, 578) or "I know how I'd have felt if I'd thought there ever was dust in here," (Bowen 1983, 580) etc. stand in sharp contrast with the descriptions of "the fallen ceiling," "the windows gone" and of the satin curtains, "torn and torn, like a maniac been at them." (Bowen 1983, 580) Behaving like an architect who examines a ruined house, the reader—on the basis of what has been left of the house—fills the missing elements, thereby restoring the stability. Unlike Umberto Eco's fictional woods, where the reader has unlimited choices as to which path to pursue, in Bowen's story, reading the text and building the deictic-based discourse space is severely restricted by Madam's "inaudible part" in the dialogue.

References

Bowen, Elizabeth. 1983. "Oh Madam…" In *The Collected Stories of Elizabeth Bowen*, 578-582. London: Penguin Books.

Eco, Umberto. 1995. *Six Walks in the Fictional Woods*. Cambridge MA/London: Harvard University Press.

Green, Keith. 1992. Deixis and the poetic persona. *Language and Literature*. 1(2): 121-34.

Moulin, Bernard. 1995. Discourse spaces: A pragmatic interpretation of contexts. In *Conceptual Structures: Applications, Implementation and Theory*, ed. by Gerard Ellis, Robert Levinson, William Rich and John F. Sowa, 89-104. Berlin/Heidelberg: Springer-Verlag.

Stockwell, Peter. 2002a. *Cognitive Poetics. An Introduction*. London/New York: Routledge.

—. 2002b. Miltonic texture and the feeling of reading. In *Cognitive Stylistics. Language and Cognition in Text Analysis*, ed. by Elena Semino and Jonathan Culpeper, 73-94. Amsterdam/Philadelphia: John Benjamins Publishing Company.

Tsur, Reuven. 2003. Deixis and abstractions: Adventures in space and time. In *Cognitive Poetics in Practice*, ed. by Joanna Gavins and Gerard Steen, 41-54. London/New York: Routledge.

CHAPTER TEN

SPACE OF CELEBRATION IN DICKENS'
A CHRISTMAS CAROL

ALEKSANDRA KĘDZIERSKA

Concentrating on the initial and closing staves of *the Carol*, this essay demonstrates how, as a result of Scrooge's conversion, the world of spiritual hollowness, represented by his counting house and his private quarters, eventually gives way to the space of celebration of life.

Externalizing the banker's thwarted heart, the two domains, characterizing his public and his private self respectively, demarcate the territory of his existence dominated by cold, gloom, and seclusion; the world in which a relative scarcity of possessions, suggestive of his meanness towards himself, translates into an even greater meanness towards his fellow men. However, when forced out of his inaction and passivity, and made to explore the vast domain of Christmas, Scrooge learns to appreciate people, and this newly discovered sense of belonging and sharing radically impacts his attitude towards space. The "solitary oyster" no longer wants to remain enclosed in the shell of his prejudices, "barred and self-locked within the invisible chain of his own cash boxes and dusty ledgers" (Buckwald 1990), excluded from general rejoicing. The moment Scrooge accepts Christmas, he no longer needs the borders he has been building all his life. The need to re-create his world pushes him towards establishing new relationships with the territories he would never venture into before. This time, crossing the threshold of his own place he will be ready to embrace the crowded streets of the City, the Church he never seemed to notice or the lodgings of Fred he invariably chose to ignore. And, most importantly, his presence—at home or work, or wherever he goes—will "bless" the space with numerous acts of charity which along with his capacity for rendering other people happy and his own enjoyment, will emerge as the most fundamental attribute of the space of celebration of Life. Like a big child he will play his goodwill tricks, thus testifying to the openness of his heart, which expands with every good thought.

A perfect *homo economicus*, Ebenezer Scrooge hated Christmas. If, as he claims, he could have his will, "every idiot who goes about with 'Merry Christmas' on his lips should be boiled with his own pudding and buried with a stake of holly in his heart" (Dickens 1954, 10). He never merry made at Christmas and could not afford—or so he said—to make idle people merry. To quote his famous definition, Christmas was "humbug",

> a time for paying bills without money, ... for finding yourself a year older but not an hour richer, a time for balancing your books and having every item in them ... presented dead against you (Dickens 1954, 10),

in short, definitely not a time for celebration. Hence, fighting it with all his might, he spent his days in his "money-changing hole", a place whose very name indicated the rather degrading and dehumanizing nature of his business. And indeed Scrooge's counting house best reflected the grotesque triumph of his materialism which, instead of granting the man various creature comforts, transformed his life into a prison and himself into a mean warder terrorizing those who dared disturb his splendid isolation.

Imagining that he can warm himself up by the candle light, Bob Cratchit, Scrooge's only clerk, could hardly work in "the Tank," the dismal little cell allotted to him. The conditions in his principal's cubicle, a "mouldy old office" (Dickens 1954, 53), were hardly any better, the only difference being made by the presence of a box of coal Scrooge did not seem to need (for cold could not affect him anyhow), and the freedom to open or close the door through which, from his high stool, he could watch over his kingdom.

Bullying his clerk, making himself unpleasant to his visitors, and, above all, refusing the donation for the needy seemed to belong to the favourite diversions of Scrooge which allowed him to "resume his labours with an improved opinion of himself" (Dickens 1954, 12). Nevertheless, even in this "facetious temper" (Dickens 1954, 12) he could scare a caroller who, chased away with a ruler, fled in terror not having a chance to go through the first sounds of "God bless you merry gentlemen".

Equally Spartan and as joyless as his workplace were Scrooge's private quarters and it was to this "gloomy suite of rooms" (sitting-, bed-, and lumber-room) that Scrooge would return at the end of the day, when, having taken his melancholy dinner, he read his newspapers and beguiled "the rest of the evening with his banker's book" (Dickens 1954, 14). His house "is a lost, isolated cutoff building" which is a proper residence for a lost isolated and cutoff man (Stone 1979, 121). All alone in this "fortress" he was well protected not only by heavy doors, thick walls and solid locks but also by darkness, fog and frost—the self appointed guardians of his deadness. In these dusted chambers which, not surprisingly, resembled a rather spacious coffin, a reduction of life went on, enhanced by Scrooge's passivity, his scorn for the amenities with which he surrounded himself (the basic few he used included a curtained bed, a washing stand, a sofa, a table, and a closet) as well as the scarcity of decoration. In actual fact, its only instance and, simultaneously, the only vestige of Christian ethos in the whole house, was the fireplace whose tiles, paved all around, were designed to illustrate the Scriptures.

Symbolic of Scrooge's spiritual temperature, the fireplace produced meager warmth, indeed a "very low fire" which meant "nothing... on a bitter night" (Dickens 1954, 16): another reflection of the same miserly soul that jealously "guard[ed] the small fire in his office, the fire as nearly self-contained as fire within flint" (Buckwald 1990), to which Scrooge, a covetous old sinner is compared. The fragility of the creed the stove propagates is most dramatically exposed when, suddenly, the Biblical scenes all disappear, swallowed up and replaced by the ghostly head of Jacob Marley, the previous owner of the flat, who, like Scrooge, always minded only his own business and kept his eyes turned down for fear that he might see, or, worse still, have to follow the star of Bethlehem. Thus, when the booming sound signals the opening of the cellar door—the symbolic border between earth and the nether regions—hell, breaking loose in the person of his ex-partner, elevates and establishes itself in Scrooge's quarters.

Marley's mention of Christ's birthplace opens for Scrooge a path of escape from the realm of doom, suggesting the direction in his life which, no longer leading downward, towards self-destruction, may initiate him into a new order of things: where, for once, the meaning of success will be measured by spiritual gains and by man's capacity to appreciate the fullness of life, best expressed through companionship and celebration.

During his journey with the Ghost of Christmas Past, Scrooge revisits the place where he was apprenticed and where his old principal, Fezziwig, used to work in the same room with his apprentices. The desk behind which he would sit was much higher than that in Scrooge's own office, and yet, quite unlike the banker, Fezziwig was the most fatherly of employers. Most importantly, with a single order, he could make a miracle, transforming a mere warehouse into a ball-room, as snug, warm, and bright as one could only desire. There, like Father Christmas, Fezziwig would cater for those whom life has not spared, inviting them for dances and games and treating them like royals with delicious food and drink.

However, sharing and togetherness are not the only aspects of celebration Scrooge learns about during his expeditions with the Spirits. The Ghost of Christmas Present also drives home the significance of decoration and the joy of rebirth. It seems that Scrooge begins to realize the meaning of this word when he sees his own room transformed by "the jolly Giant," the Ghost of Christmas Present. In place of a cold, semi-dark and melancholy domain, symbolic of deprivation of life, the interior of Scrooge's chambers conveys the triumph of life, the message of rebirth rendered (among others) through the abundance of the "living green" which, hanging from the walls and ceiling makes the room look "a perfect grove". This perfection is further enhanced by the glitter of light and the "mighty blaze" which roaring up the chimney annihilates that "dull petrification of a hearth" (Dickens 1954, 40) that had been emblematic of Scrooge's heart. Equally gratifying for the senses—the unappetizing gruel Scrooge would sup upon long forgotten—is a heap of mouth watering delicacies which form a kind of throne to the Spirit; a holy centre whose establishment erases, or at least neutralizes, whatever remains of hell can still be found in Scrooge's residence. And yet, acknowledging as he does the significance of the private as well as the physical/ sensual character of celebration, the Ghost of Christmas Present teaches Scrooge that far more important is discovering as well as embracing the spiritual delights the world has to offer. Hence,

> holly, mistletoe, red berries, ivy, turkeys, geese, game, poultry, brawn, meat, pigs, sausages, oysters, pies, puddings, fruit and punch, all vanished instantly. So did the room, the fire, the ruddy glow, the hour of the night and they stood in the city streets on Christmas morning. (Dickens 1954, 40)

"Much they saw and far they went", (Dickens 1954, 55), making their appearance "in almshouse, hospital, and jail, in misery's every refuge" (Dickens 1954, 56) so that Scrooge could realize the power of Christmas, the ruler of the vast Kingdom of Goodwill, borderless and reaching the most distant foreign lands. In one of its corners, in some desert moor, as if defying frost and the gloom of the night, the miners assembled round a glowing fire singing a Christmas song. In another, taming the frightful sea were the workers of the solitary lighthouse who also sat at a rough table, keeping warm with their grog and a sturdy song. And even on ships "every man hummed a Christmas tune or had a Christmas thought spoke of bygone Christmases" (Dickens 1954, 50).

Once again, taken beyond the limits of his depressing "hole", the limits of the City, London town itself and even England, wrenched out of his routine, Scrooge finally notices what his eyes were kept shut to: the festive aspect of the City, the glory and the "apoplectic opulence" of Christmas shops, the bustling streets alive with noise and excitement of friendly gatherings. And most importantly, men waiting to become noticed as "his business".

When the magic cycle of Scrooge's journeys finally returns him to his chambers, reborn, he will become capable of expanding his world, giving himself to it in a highly symbolic gesture of opening the window in his room. Miraculously "thawed", "a stony-heart Ebenezer" (Vogel 1977, 71) welcomes the glory of Golden sunlight and exposed to the divine warmth finds himself transformed into an innocent whose childlike exultation best expresses itself in his amazement and capacity to laughter.

Ha ha ha. Really, for a man who had been out of practice for so many years, it was a splendid laugh, a most illustrious laugh. The father of a long, long line of brilliant laughs! (Dickens 1954, 72)

On this perfect day which is itself the triumph of Creation, Scrooge, all by himself, starts transforming his quarters into a space of celebration, for once aware how good it feels "to be child sometimes, especially at Christmas, when its mighty Founder was a child himself" (Dickens 1954, 53). He praises Life with every aspect of his being: running, jumping playfully, laughing out loud, and dancing when he shaves. The silence he used to venerate now explodes with all the noises of happiness, including the meaningless sounds he himself articulates, simply to hear himself exist. He discovers the blessed variety of things "incorrigibly plural," himself being all at once "as light as a feather ... as happy as an angel ..., as merry as a school-boy [and] as giddy as a drunken man" (Dickens 1954, 71). Whereas before he would edge "along the crowded paths of life warning all human sympathy to keep its distance" (Dickens 1954, 8) now, bursting with joy, he wants to share it with others, shouting "A merry Christmas to every-body! A happy New Year to all the world!" (Dickens 1954, 71). The sheer need of using kind words makes him spontaneously compliment his first Christmas interlocutor: "an intelligent boy", "a fine fellow", we hear, "remarkable", "delightful", "it's a pleasure to talk to him" (Dickens 1954, 72). For someone who could only growl or grumble this is indeed an impressive performance and Scrooge by no means wants to stop there.

Recognizing in his heart the divine essence of Tiny Tim, Scrooge's first good deed, done with the boy in mind, is at the same time his homage to Jesus, whom the child impersonates (Vogel 1977, 70). Thus begins the first of a series of Scrooge's Christmas jokes: his anonymously sending a great turkey to the Cratchits. "Rubbing his hands, and splitting with a laugh", he imagines the surprise of the family with the gift which will finally make him, a genuine "Founder of the Feast", the role Bob cast him in proposing a toast to his employer. Encouraged with the ease of doing good and with the pleasure generosity yields to the giver, Scrooge is anxious to have more benevolent interaction with those in whom he recognizes his fellow passengers to the grave and with whom he wishes to exchange season's greetings and share his contented smile. Looking for them makes him venture into the street and go to church and simply walk about a bit. Thus he "watched the people hurrying to and fro, and patted children on the head, and questioned beggars" (Dickens 1954, 74) and quickly discovering the rewards of this commitment, he found that in fact "everything could yield him pleasure" (Dickens 1954, 74).

When, determined to improve his strained relations with Fred, Scrooge had turned his steps to his nephew's house, he scored another point on space expansion, entering the realm in which he would undergo a test of his reconciliation and celebration skills. Here his dream to belong may eventually come true, satisfying his hunger for what he saw others experience: acceptance, friendship, and love. Hence, although he knows that his Christmas dinner at Fred's will indeed be a highlight of the day— after all he has already acquired the taste of it when guided by the Ghost of Christmas Present – at the same time he is anxious to make his 'first night' a success. When he finally summons up the courage to knock at Fred's door and is let in, he is launched in his debut as Family Man and the welcome he receives there brings to mind the story of the prodigal son— the reunion so happy that "nothing could be heartier" (Dickens 1954, 74), the biblical allusion enhancing the anticipation of the feast to follow, the feast in celebration of "the man who was dead, and has come back, was lost and is found" (*The English Bible,* Luke 15:32, 797).

As was typical of many other gatherings Scrooge saw during his journeys with the Spirits, the "young party" at Fred's also occupied a bright, gleaming room which was the centre of their making merry, with family and friends clustered round the fire or close to a table with food and drinks to make everybody feel at home. Nevertheless, the excellent dinner followed by dessert and the bottle passed generously around was by no means the sole attraction of the delightful evening, made even more pleasant by a variety of entertainments prepared for the occasion. After blind man's buff there was time for forfeits and other parlour games ("Yes and No", "How, When, Where") allowing Scrooge to convince the company of his cleverness and wit. Then everybody sang "a Glee or a Catch" or listened to the harp or piano playing. And, as befits the space of celebration, peals of irresistibly contagious laughter were heard, a definite sign of the guests having a good time. For

> when Scrooge's nephew laughed "holding his sides, rolling his head, and twisting his face into the most extravagant contortions, their assembled friends being not a bit behindhand, (Dickens 1954, 51)

laughed as heartily. "It was [simply] impossible to keep the infection off; [and so] his example was unanimously followed." (Dickens 1954, 52). One can be sure that, given the chance of real participation in Fred's Christmas dinner, Scrooge would gladly second the narrator in describing it as "Wonderful party, wonderful games, wonderful unanimity, won-der-ful happiness!" (Dickens 1954, 75). It seems, therefore, that finally at peace with the world and himself, "Uncle Scrooge" (called so even by the narrator himself) has returned to the bosom of the family (also to the extended human family).

On the second day of Christmas, taking to his *homo ludens* self, Scrooge will play yet another joke which, revealing his humane side as an employer, will simultaneously bring the spirit of celebration into the counting house, thus finally chasing away the gloomy ghost of Malthus. Pretending he is about to fire Cratchit, Scrooge starts addressing Bob in his "accustomed growl as near as he could feign it" (Dickens 1954, 75), yet he quickly loses heart to continue in the bad boss impersonation. When he leaps down from his stool to meet Cratchit on equal ground, he accepts his clerk as a human being, his equal in the eyes of God. This immediately translates into the attitude of respect and kindness with which he starts treating Bob and in his person all those needy and less fortunate than himself. Confession, as well as atonement, are those attributes that (more than at Fred's) on the one hand reveal the depth of Scrooge's conversion, and on the other characterize his office space as that of class reconciliation, with the employee and his employer united over a libation of "Smoking Bishop".

Converted into the place of celebration of Christmas, the counting house can no longer be a place of oppression. Instead of the impersonal "you" frequently barked at Bob, Scrooge will now use Cratchit's first name, calling him also "my dear fellow". And when he offers his wishes, he expresses them in the spirit of contrition and with a humbleness of the heart no longer controlled by numbness.

"A Merry Christmas, Bob!" said Scrooge with an earnestness that could not be mistaken, as he clapped him on the back. A merrier Christmas, Bob, my good fellow, than I have given you for many a year! I'll raise your salary, and endeavor to assist your struggling family, and we will discuss your affairs this very afternoon over a bowl of Smoking Bishop, Bob! (Dickens 1954, 75)

As if suddenly affected by cold—a clear indication of his newly acquired delicacy of the spirit, he orders Cratchit to "make up fires", a symbolic invitation for the Holy Ghost to become a new patron of the counting house which may some day lend its space to a ball like Fezziwig's, where, surrounded by workers and friends Scrooge will exercise his power to render people happy.

As has been shown, in Dickens's space of celebration, far more important than the usual paraphernalia of merry making, focused on a company, food and drink, are the acts of goodwill and charity which, can accomplish the most with the help of a benign joke and some role playing (Scrooge as a family man, a philanthropist, a founder of the feast, or a good employer): the performance which not only proves Scrooge is very much alive but almost makes us believe that life and celebration are one.

References

Buckwald, Craig. 1990. Stalking the Figurative Oyster: The Excursive Ideal in *A Christmas Carol*. *Studies in Short Fiction* 27 (1): 1-14.

Dickens, Charles. 1954. *The Christmas Books*. Oxford: Oxford University Press.

The New English Bible. 1976. Oxford: The Bible Societies in association with Oxford University Press and Cambridge University Press.

Stone, Harry. 1979. *Dickens and the Invisible World (Fairy tales, fantasy, novel-making)*. New York: Macmillan Press Ltd.

Vogel, Jane. 1977. *Allegory in Dickens*. Tuscaloosa: University of Alabama Press.

CHAPTER ELEVEN

DANGEROUS BEAUTY:
"GOTHIC" LANDSCAPES IN ALGERNON
BLACKWOOD'S SHORT STORIES

JOANNA KOKOT

Most of the turn-of-the-19th-century horror story writers set their tales in the gloomy interiors of old, lonely houses that once witnessed evil deeds and are now haunted by ghosts either demanding justice or continuing their wicked job and constituting a deadly threat to the reckless intruders. Even apparent departures from this conventional type of haunted space eventually turn out not to be departures at all. True, ghosts may manifest themselves—as they do for example in the stories by M.R. James—in a grove, a garden labyrinth or at the village common, but in every case we have to do with what might be defined as "civilised space", while the supernatural events have their origin in some evil deeds committed in the past, when—as it was in the early Gothic romances—the disturbance of the ethic order resulted in shattering the barrier between the world of the living and that of the dead.

Such a setting can be found also in Algernon Blackwood's short stories. Yet in some of his tales which undoubtedly can be recognised as horror fiction both the setting and the nature of the uncanny events are different. There are no ghosts or emanations resulting from occult practices, but the forces of nature with which man is confronted reveal unusual traits, surpassing whatever is conventionally defined as "natural"[1].

---

[1] The Blackwood scholars often stress the role of such experience as a kind of illumination, even if it arises terror. Cf. eg. Cavallaro 2002, 65, or Olson.

1.

The action of such stories as "The Valley of the Beasts", "The Wendigo", "Running Wolf" or "Skeleton Lake" is set in scenery untypical of the British horror fiction: in the wilderness of the Canadian forests. Already the way it is introduced denies the traditional descriptions, the aim of which is to create the atmosphere of horror and uncertainty. What initially dominates in Blackwood's descriptions is a sense of beauty, a rapture over the primeval nature, untouched by the white man's civilisation.

Here is how the young protagonist of "The Wendigo" perceives the whereabouts of the Fifty Island Water where he spends a lonely day:

> A sky of rose and saffron, more clear than any atmosphere Simpson had ever known, still dropped its pale streaming fires across the waves, where the islands—a hundred, surely, rather than fifty—floated like the fairy barques of some enchanted fleet. Fringed with pines, whose crests fingered most delicately the sky, they almost seemed to move upwards as the light faded—about to weigh anchor and navigate the pathways of the heavens instead of the currents of their native and desolate lake.
>
> And strips of coloured cloud, like flaunting pennons, signalled their departure to the stars...
>
> The beauty of the scene was strangely uplifting. (Blackwood 2001, 112)

A similar experience is the privilege of Grimwood, when he enters the legendary Valley of the Beasts:

> He found the valley, though the actual word did not occur to him, enticing; more and more he noticed the beauty, the desolate grandeur of the mighty spruce and hemlock, the splendour of the granite bluffs which in places rose above the forest and caught the sun. (Blackwood and Wilson 1921, 123-4)

In both stories the protagonist is a hunter coming from more civilised regions, traversing the Canadian forests only in a company of a native guide (and in the situations presented above deprived even of that company)—on the one hand experiencing a kind of unity with nature, on the other fully conscious of the fact that he and his race is no longer its part.

This consciousness manifests itself mainly in the emotional reaction to the splendour of the surrounding wilderness. What is significant in both the fragments quoted above is the word "desolate" which apparently does not fit the charming and enchanting landscape, stressing rather the loneliness of the observer than any of the aspects of the place's beauty. This world of grandeur and splendour is not the place where man can feel "at home". Already Simpson experiences that disquieting aspect of the primeval woods:

> The bleak splendours of these remote and lonely forests overwhelmed him with the sense of his own littleness, That stern quality of the tangled backwoods which can only be described as merciless and terrible, rose out of these far blue woods swimming upon the horizon and revealed itself. He understood the silent warning. He realized his own utter helplessness. (Blackwood 2001, 110)

One might seek analogies between Blackwood's descriptions and the ideas over a century earlier—the divagations of Edmund Burke concerning the beautiful and the sublime, perceiving these features in the ragged mountain landscapes, wild and empty spaces, mysterious, awe-inspiring. However, contrary to Burke's observer, the protagonists of Blackwood's stories do not merely appreciate the splendour of their surroundings. The contact with the primal nature affects their psychical powers, and the influence is hard to be defined as elevating or healing. The beautiful, untouched nature appears to be dangerous to the intruders.

The ambivalent aspect of the nature finds its equivalent in the very descriptions of the forest—on the one hand its beauty is stressed, on the other it provokes an inexplicable fear or at least uneasiness in the observer. Simpson's imagination makes the woods alive and threatening, peopling them with strange creatures and turning them into a place typical of gothic fiction. When the young man stays alone in the camp, the surroundings turn into a "world of wizardy and horror" (Blackwood 2001, 130), it seems to him that "the Wilderness holds him in the hollow of its illimitable hands—and laughs" (129). The camping place chosen by Hyde in *Running Wolf* at first seems to the man a "lonely little paradise" (Blackwood and Wilson 1921, 57), but the narrator soon remarks: "Loneliness in a backwoods camp brings charm, pleasure, and a happy sense of calm until, and unless, it comes too near" (59).

Also the dwellers of the Camp at the Skeleton Lake experience the disquieting aspect of the lonely stay in the wilderness, far from the civilization, long before the tragedy takes place:

> The utter loneliness of our moose-camp on Skeleton Lake had impressed us from the very beginning—in the Quebec backwoods, five days by trail and canoe from civilization—and perhaps the singular name contributed a

little to the sensation of eeriness that made itself felt in the camp circle when once the sun was down and the late October mists began rising from the lake and winding their way in among the trunks. ("Skeleton Lake: An Episode in Camp", Blackwood 1916, 301)

It appears that an accident happened in a neighbouring camp—the guide of Rushton, the hunter, drowns in the lake when the canoe carrying both men is upset, while Rushton himself hardly manages to reach the camp at Skeleton Lake. However, both the words of the first-person narrator (whose report is full of understatements and concealments) as well as the other hunters' reaction clearly suggest that whatever happened was something much worse than a mere accident. And the reaction itself is strange. Rushton's tale is defined as full of contradictions, lacks congruity, is anything but convincing, and yet the other men instead of investigating into the case try to silence the teller, or at least to ignore those fragments of his narrative which are evidently inconsistent—thus betraying a deeper knowledge as to the reasons of whatever happened. Even if the state of the guide's body—found later—proves that his death was not an accident, it was evidently neither a premeditated murder or a manslaughter resulting from some violent quarrel: such cause of the death would not explain the strange reaction of the hunters to Rushton's story, or the state in which the man is. He evidently experienced a severe shock caused by whatever happened—this is confirmed both by his compulsive re-iterating the tale the others would rather not hear and by his physical outlook. As the narrator describes him: "I saw his face, grey under the tan, terror in the eyes, tears too, hair and beard awry" (306).

Rushton falls victim to the wilderness of the forests, to the loneliness and the contact with primeval nature. Such are the suggestions carried by the narrator's vague and evasive tale, whereas the terror experienced by the campers is evidently caused by something more than the mere wickedness of the deed. It conceals something unnamed, just as the eventual version of the events at Skeleton Lake is never revealed[2].

---

[2] A similar suggestion of the dangers carried by the contact with wild and pure nature appears also for example in a story "The Camp of the Dog" of the John Silence cycle, where the place of action is no more the Canadian forest, but seemingly familiar uninhabited islets at the Norwegian coast: "The odours of the wilderness - smells of wind and earth, of trees and water, clean, vigorous, and mighty - were the true odours of a virgin world unspoilt by men, more penetrating and more subtly intoxicating than any other perfume in the whole world. Oh - and dangerously strong, too, no doubt, for some natures!" (Blackwood 1997, 177). Here too yielding to the forces of nature (also of human nature) almost ends in a

2.

However, the strange influence of the Canadian forests is not a mere psychological phenomenon, man's reaction to loneliness and a strange environment. A suggestion appears that something mysterious and dangerous lurks in the woods, some forces unknown to a civilized man. In "The Valley of the Beasts" the existence of such forces is prompted already by the reaction of Tooshali—an Indian guide—to Grimwood's resolution to enter the forbidden valley. A seemingly irrational refusal to go there carries a hint that the place is dominated by different natural laws than those which are commonly known and accepted. Seemingly disquieting is the behaviour of Defago: his young companion is evidently infected by the Canadian's fears and—what is important—immediately renounces any natural explanations of the man's reaction:

> Moreover, to add to the younger man's uneasiness, was the difficulty, nay, the impossibility he felt of asking questions, and also his complete ignorance as to the cause... Indians, wild animals, forest fires—all these, he knew, were wholly out of the question. His imagination searched vigorously, but in vain. (Blackwood 2001, 115)

The woods do not merely hide some mysteries. They seem to be endowed with life themselves, or even with consciousness. The sense of loneliness, of the vastness of the primal nature and the smallness of man is accompanied by a sense that the nature follows the actions of the intruders, ready to absorb or destroy them. Such is the impression that Simpson gets when he is observing the forest:

> The details now beat against his trembling mind with concerted attack. They seemed to gather in those deep spaces of the silent forest about him, where the host of trees stood waiting, listening, watching to see what he wanted to do. The woods were closing round him. (125)

As we can see, the woods seem to watch the solitary wanderer, besetting him as a huntsman would beset his prey ("The woods were closing round him"). The roles are reversed—it is not a coincidence that the protagonists of the "American" stories by Blackwood are hunters. The profession stresses the irony of the situation: the hunter turns into the game when the forest takes over the power. Such a reversal of roles is still enhanced by the narrator's comments, when Defago is called by the Wendigo, a kind of

---

tragedy when the suppressed and hidden love finds its material equivalent as a werewolf, being the alter ego of the enamoured man.

a spirit of the forest. The destructive forces of nature are personified due to the use of the capital letters. They do not function as abstract notions, or purely psychical phenomena, but appear as real as the mythical Wendigo:

> For the Panic of the Wilderness had called to him in that far voice—the power of untamed Distance—the Enticement of the Desolation that destroys. (128)

Almost in each case the dangers which result from the stay in the wilderness are connected with a limited spatial circle—it is the effect of entering a forbidden, sacred ground. The Canadian forests are the places still inhabited by old Indian gods or legendary creatures, places which constitute a taboo.

That sacred dimension of the backwoods is suggested already in "The Wendigo", when the Indian gods come back to life in young Simpson's imagination:

> The dusk rapidly deepened; the glades grew dark; the crackling of the fire and the wash of little waves along the rocky lake shore were the only sounds audible. The wind had dropped with the sun, and in all that vast world of branches nothing stirred. Any moment, it seemed, the woodland gods, who are to be worshipped in silence and loneliness, might sketch their mighty and terrific outlines among the trees. (Blackwood 2001, 111-112)

But—as it appears—the presence of the supernatural in the forest is not a mere figment of imagination.

The camping place of Hyde, an enthusiastic angler from "Running Wolf", is near the site of the Indian cult. The cult may belong to the past now (it is an old burial ground), but it still defines the sacred sphere. Here Hyde will be haunted by an unusual timber wolf, that is in reality a spirit of an Indian, suffering for transgressing the taboo—for killing a totem animal[3].

A similarly special place, where the ancient forces are still at work, are the banks of the Fifty Island Water, where Defago hears the call of the

---

[3] A similar motif can be found in another story by Blackwood "The Wolves of God", where the revenge for killing the leader of the pack of the eponymous wolves reaches the protagonist even on the other side of the ocean. It is worth mentioning that contrary to other stories in "Running Wolf" there occurs a communication between the man and the wolf, representing the ancient beliefs: Hyde fulfills all the necessary conditions necessary to set the desecrator's soul free.

Wendigo. For some reasons Defago fears this spot, it is there too where he is abducted by the mysterious creature. "The Valley of the Beasts" is a tale about an enclave hidden in the Canadian backwoods which constitutes a kind of an animal paradise, where the beasts live in harmony, bloodshed is forbidden and man's presence—banned.

Such *loci* constitute an equivalent of the empty houses in a traditional British ghost story. Both here and there the laws of the mimetic world model are suspended, only that the natural enclaves are not haunted by any ghosts from another world—the supernatural, paradoxically, has its source in nature and in ancient cults perceiving nature as *sacrum*.

3.

And it is invading that *sacrum* which usually appears destructive for man, who breaks the taboo with his mere presence, and exposes himself to danger. Yet the danger does not consist in a simple destruction of the intruder by the conscious forces of nature or by the old deities[4]. Man becomes gradually absorbed by natural forces, experiences a change in personality, sometimes acquiring unity with nature—but it is a unity which deprives him of the very essence of his humanity.

The Wendigo embodies the forces of the primitive nature, free of any human intervention, "the inscrutable forces of the Wild" (Blackwood 2001, 128). It is the same nature which evokes admiration in young Simpson and which has charmed Defago. Here is how the narrator characterizes the latter:

> He was deeply susceptible, moreover, to that singular spell which the wilderness lays on certain lonely natures, and he loved the wild solitudes with a kind of romantic passion that amounted to obsession. (103)

Thus what makes the guide susceptible to the influence of the Wendigo is his love of the backwoods, the "romantic passion", as the narrator puts it. A similar passion is the essence of the experience of the Wendigo's victim—here too it is an unrestrained desire, the love of both the beauty of the wilderness and the unlimited spaces:

---

[4] True, in "The Valley of the Beasts" Grimwood is attacked by the animals which eventually sense a stranger, whereas Ishtot, the Indian god of the Valley, called by the hunter, refuses any help. But the aggression results from breaking the laws governing the valley: Grimwood sheds the blood of an animal that seeks refuge in the vale.

His [the victim's] most vulnerable points, moreover, are said to be the feet
and the eyes; the feet, you see, for the lust of wandering, and the eyes for
the lust of beauty. (136)

Defago yields to the potent call of the wild, embodied by the Wendigo.
But the beauty occurs to be destructive. When the mythical creature has
possessed Defago, it possesses his soul; when the guide eventually returns
to the camp, he is deprived of memory, consciousness, of everything that
defined him as a human being:

On his face was no expression of any kind whatever—fear, welcome,
or recognition, He did not seem to know who it was that embraced him, or
who it was that fed, warmed or spoke to him the words of comfort and
relief. Forlorn and broken beyond all reach of human aid, the little man did
meekly as he was bidden. The "something" that had constituted him
"individual" had vanished forever.
[...] His memory had vanished completely. And before the end of the
winter whose beginning witnessed this strange occurrence, Defago, bereft
of mind, memory and soul, had gone with it. He lingered only a few weeks.
(145)

The influence that the Valley of the Beasts, the animal paradise, exerts
on Grimwood is defined by the narrator as charm or glamour—understood
literally, thus not as a source of enrapture, but as a source of a change, here
taking place within the man. As the narrator states: "the spell of this virgin
forest came upon him like a charm" (Blackwood and Wilson 1921, 127),
whereas the protagonist is described as "spell-bound" and his arrival at the
valley as "some magical home-coming" (131). When he watches the
animals that neither feel nor induce fear, the sight is defined as "a
marvellous, even a magical scene" (131)[5].

His memory of what he is decreases, and he starts to think in a way
similar to the dwellers of the valley, considering it an asylum, a refuge
from the perils of the outer reality. He gradually loses the ability to use
language and to think in abstract terms which differs humans from
animals. He not only does not fear the beasts or discards typically human
accessories as the rifle or the beaker, but he also starts to behave as an
animal. This is how he sits ("He sat on his haunches"—131) or laps up
water—not conscious of this fact, as if such a mode of behaviour were the

---

[5] One might compare the Valley of the Beasts to another place from Blackwood's
stories - the town of cats and dreams, where the protagonist, Vezin, also falls
victim of the spell of the place, the spell understood as something more than a
mere metaphor ("Ancient Sorceries" from the John Silence cycle).

only obvious one. Like forest animals he is scared of fire: "Fire! What *was* fire? The idea was repugnant to him, it was impossible, he was afraid of fire" (129). The memory returns only with the touch of an Indian totem, and when he eventually manages to get out of the valley this is how he comments upon his adventure: "He declares it [the totem] saved his soul, but what he means by the expression he has never quite explained" (138)—thus the earthly paradise where all the creatures live in harmony appears to be treacherous: in the Valley of the Beasts man can live only becoming a beast himself, losing all which makes him a human being.

What is interesting, all this happens independently of the actions of the protagonist, of his character or intentions. There is no ethical dimension present. It is rather a confrontation of the civilized man and the primeval nature that ends (or nearly ends) in a catastrophe—both Grimwood's stay in the Valley of the Beasts and Defago's travel at the side of the Wendigo. *The Call of the Wild* appears to be a destructive factor.

4.

Such an ambivalence of the forces of nature and their relation to man will return in other stories by Blackwood, where the setting is not the Canadian wilderness but homely landscapes (one of Blackwood's collections of stories, *Pan's Garden* is subtitled significantly *A Volume of Nature Stories*). A patch in a garden corner may suck the vital force from a person who is careless enough to come near ("The Transfer"[6]), whereas the spirit of the snow takes the form of a beautiful woman, almost bringing the protagonist to his death ("The Glamour of the Snow"). In the famous story *The Willows* an island overgrown with the eponymous trees appears to be a place where the primal forces of nature work, constituting a deadly danger to the intruders. Sometimes the same place may induce fear in some and for others be an earthly paradise, where one can experience unity with nature ("The Touch of Pan"); sometimes the nature defends itself against the destructive actions of man (as the wood does in "Ancient Lights" which is evidently mocking the inspector). In *The Centaur*—a novel where Blackwood develops the ideas of Gustav Fechner and William James, perceiving the Earth as a living organism—the main character, O'Malley, eventually experiences the earthly paradise, but such a vista is fearful to other characters, too much "soaked" with civilization.

---

[6] Montague Summers quite rightly speaks about analogies between the garden patch and a traditional figure of a vampire - only that in the case of Blackwood's story the victim is deprived of vital energy and not of blood (Summers 2005, 323), the latter often identified (e.g. in the Bible) with the essence of life, too.

Similarly ambiguous is "The Man Whom the Trees Loved", where the tree lover becomes one with them, but "the transcendence of human concerns that this implies is carefully balanced against his wife's powerful sense of loss" (Punter and Byron 2004, 90).

We have to do here with a kind of a reversal of the Gothic conventions. In the traditional horror tales the language of description of the space setting—lonely, haunted houses where once a tragedy occurred—does not leave any doubts as to the terrors lurking in a given place as well as to the ethical dimension of these terrors. The haunted places are presented as spots soaked with evil—no matter whether it is the wickedness of the deeds once committed there or some curse cast in the past. It is different in the stories discussed or mentioned here. Even if the forces of nature may appear destructive, the descriptions are dominated with the sense of beauty and harmony, though the beauty may appear perilous. Man by his very presence makes himself vulnerable to the influence of the forces being part of a world strange to him. *Locus amoenus* turns into a *locus horriblus*, yet without losing any of its glamour.

References

Blackwood, Algernon. 1916 [1906]. *The Empty House and Other Ghost Stories*. London: Eveleigh Nash Company Ltd.
—. 1912. *Pan's Garden. A Volume of Nature Stories*. London: Macmillan.
—. 1963. *Tales of the Uncanny and Supernatural*. London: Spring Books.
—. 1997. *The Complete John Silence Stories*. Mineola: Dover Publications Inc.
—. 2001. The Wendigo. In *Strange Creatures VII. Wildmen and Wendigos*, ed. by Chad Arment, 103-146. Londisville, PA: Arment Biological Press.
Blackwood, Algernon and Wilfred Wilson. 1921. *The Wolves of God and Other Fey Stories*. London/New York/Toronto/Melbourne: Cassell and Co. Ltd.
Cavallaro, Dani. 2002. *The Gothic Vision. Three Centuries of Horror, Terror and Fear*. London/New York: Continuum.
Olson P. V. Algernon Blackwood, http://www.horrornet.com. rootsof.htm. (accessed 3 May 2001).
Punter, David and Glennis Byron. 2004. *The Gothic*. Malden: Blackwell Publishing.
Summers Montague. 2005. *Vampires and Vampirism*. Mineola: Dover Publications.

CHAPTER TWELVE

THE SINISTER SPACE OF VLADIMIR NABOKOV'S FICTIONAL WORLD

IRENA KSIĘŻOPOLSKA

All of Nabokov's heroes experience a special kind of anxiety in relation to space, rooted in their sense of being somehow cheated by it: while their movement and achievements signify that it is possible to create, organize and control the spatial realm, the constantly encountered doubles, mirroring of events and places, and quick matter-of-fact deletions of foreseeable futures suggest that there is a dark and ominous lining of the sparkling, glistening, lovely reality. This suspicion seems akin to madness, like in the passage from Nabokov's novel *The Eye*, where the narrator compares his own sharp metaphysical anxiety to the motion sickness:

> On those terrible, pastel-blue mornings, as my heels tapped across the wilderness of the city, I would imagine somebody who goes mad because he begins to perceive clearly the motion of the terrestrial sphere: there he is, staggering, trying to keep his balance, clutching at the furniture; [...] soon, all the swaying and rocking would make him sick; he would start sucking on a lemon or an ice cube, and lie down flat on the floor, but all in vain. The motion cannot be stopped, the driver is blind, the brakes are nowhere to be found—and his heart would burst when the speed became intolerable. (7-8)

Almost every Nabokov's novel induces a sense that the space is not immobile and thus knowable and controllable—that our progress through it is only a weak version of movement, compared to "the motion of the terrestrial sphere". The dark space of Nabokov's universe, with its gaps and spiral stairways, secret passages and blind windows, is like a gothic castle, imprisoning the characters who forever struggle to find a way out into the sunlight—and the worst of it is that this huge castle is an illusion, its solidity is a pure deception and only our fear of it is real.

Nabokov's *Despair* is a deliberation on the theme of one's murderous progress in a hell of mirrors. The novel is a detective story of the confessional type: the murderer telling the story of his crime. The narrator is "spectacularly unreliable" (Carroll 1982, 83): an ecstatic liar, seriously self-deluded in to the bargain, disastrously unobservant, and singularly slow in interpreting the signs. He keeps having trouble with negotiating space and with remembering the recent past. Worst of all, he manages to plot and carry out a murder with the motive of insurance swindling, mistakenly believing that his victim is his exact double.

Hermann's particular method of associating objects and distributing them in space is highly abnormal. For instance, with the obsessive carefulness he describes several times the location of the murder, and each description creates more problems than it solves—mapping something so ephemeral, that it cannot be seen as topographical, stable space. The first description locates the scene within a three-hour northward drive from Berlin, near a small lake:

> a Y-stemmed couple of inseparable birches grew there (or a couple of couples, if you counted their reflections); also several black-alder bushes; a little further off stood fine pine trees and still further inland one came upon a patch of heather, courtesy of the surrounding wood. (33)

An uneasy reference to the theme of doubles appears in the otherwise quite ordinary inventory of a small parcel of land, property of Ardalion, the cousin of the narrator's wife. The "Y" of the birches marks one axis— the vertical one, usually representing time in space-time diagrams, while Hermann is laboriously drawing the "X" line of the other dimension – mapping the space. It is worthwhile noting that X can be seen as the ideal merging of a double: it is perfectly symmetrical from left to right and from top to bottom. Y, on the other hand, appears as only a wishful half of the ideal double: it is symmetrical, but in one direction only. Hermann's writing aims to turn the "Y" into the "X"—or time into space. To Hermann, the two axes cross at the moment of murder, and try as he may he cannot move beyond that point. His problem is confusing space with time: no matter how far back he tries to go, he cannot separate the site from the murder that will take place there:

> The pines soughed gently, snow lay about, with bald patches of soil showing black. What nonsense! How could there be snow in June? Ought to be crossed out, were it not wicked to erase; for the real author is not I, but my impatient memory. Understand it just as you please; it is none of

my business. And the yellow post had a skullcap of snow too. Thus the future shimmers through the past. (37)

There is something singularly sinister in this foreshadowing, in Hermann's *déjà vu*, on which he insists, repeating three times over that the spot was already familiar to him when he first laid his eyes on it, "familiar [...] as a thing of the future" (35, 36, 37).

After the first description of the spot, Hermann proposes a second, even stranger account, this time referring to the actual map that he got from Ardalion (his wife cousin and lover), yet persisting on referring the reader/viewer outside the imaginary page of the document, connecting the points on the map with his own body parts. Berlin becomes his left elbow, railroad stretches along his sleeve "cuffward from Berlin" (52); the town of Eichenberg becomes the lower button of his waistcoat. It seems as if in attempt to give utmost clarity to the description Hermann is overburdening the reader with directions, references and measurements. As a result, the map "marginalizes the information it is meant to convey" (Villeneuve 2008, 26). To confuse things further, there is a map that Nabokov drew and included in the first English edition of *Despair*, self-translated and published in 1937. Almost the entire stock of this printing was destroyed soon after the publication by a German bomb. The map was never reprinted, thus it exists only in the single surviving copy of the unhappy first edition.

The topographical points on Nabokov's diagram are named after the localities of the novel, which, as Philippe Villeneuve claims, have no existence on the real maps of the area. At the same time, the map is identified as showing Kölberg on the Wolziger See, a very real spot of land that Nabokov purchased in 1929 and where his earlier novel *The Defense* was finished, located not northwest (as in the novel), but southeast of Berlin, as if Hermann's map was held upside-down, or seen in some strange mirror. We may note here that Nabokov did like to invert, or turn upside-down his maps: the one he appended to *Speak, Memory* (showing his Rozhdestveno estate in Russia) strangely reverses the poles: North is at the bottom of the page, while South is at the top (369).

Thus the unreal fictional space is twistingly connected with the autobiographical one, with a still further inversion: in the Russian version of the novel, the "Y" of the crime scene corresponds to the "X" of the town in which Hermann takes refuge after the murder. This is changed in the later, Americanized version of the novel, to Pignan, which Nabokov identifies in the preface as the location where *The Defense* was begun, neatly closing the circle, the earlier novel enveloping the later. The fictional space is made to mirror the autobiographical space in temporal reverse.

The third time Hermann speaks about the small piece of land that seems to haunt him, his depiction of space is "indecently sleepy" (162), entirely dream-saturated. While narrating the preparations for the murder, Hermann takes an inordinate amount of time to travel from Berlin to Waldau. The journey that should have taken him merely three hours swallows up a full day; and the people whom he meets and sometimes talks to on the way have the moody transparency of ghosts, unwilling to pay attention to the still living. Proceeding at this nightmarishly slow speed Hermann sometimes feels that he is driving very fast, his car "lapping up the road, like a conjurer swallowing yards of ribbon" (162). The space seems to have taken control over Hermann, hypnotized him into submission. The murder itself, pre-planned in every detail, seems to be effected by a sleep-walker, who pays attention to insignificant things and ignores the tell-tale objects, leaving the victim's stick with his name on it in the abandoned car which allows the police to identify him and thus spoils Hermann's entire plan. It is as if Hermann was fulfilling the will of the place marked by the yellow post, as voiced by his wife, Lydia, during their first visit there: "What a creepy spot [...] one could get robbed, murdered—anything..." (37).

The ominous lining of the space is clearly connected with the layers of possibilities that it contains—hence Hermann's *déjà vu* and Lydia's forebodings. These futures are brought into the foreground even when Hermann is not talking or thinking about the all-important murder: he notes that the land-selling enterprise from which Ardalion purchased his land is marking the space that does not exist:

> [there are] numerous yellow signposts: one, for instance, points "to the bathing beach," but there is yet no beach to speak of – only a bog on the lip of the Waldau lake; another points "to the casino," but the latter is likewise absent, though represented by something looking like a tabernacle, with an incipient coffee stall; still another sign invites you "to the sports ground," and sure enough you find there, newly erected, a complicated affair for gymnastics, rather like gallows, but there is nobody who might use the thing. (53)

From the list of advertised attractions only one is actually in place, remaining unused, and grimly mimicking gallows. Here is Nabokov's space at its best: routinely breaking promises, boasting of something not really there, hiding traps under the guises of innocent-looking objects. The future, in which casino, cafe, beach, etc. exist, seems singularly unreal in Hermann's narrative: he hints that the whole enterprise is bound to be bankrupt rather sooner than later. Therefore, the village of Waldau with its yellow signposts falls through the surface of space, mapping the region which is unreachable from any point in time—it is a dream space. Hermann's crime scene is similarly unreachable—it is somewhere between "now" and "never". With all the information about distances, time of departure and time of arrival, even the speed of Hermann's movement, his story of the pre-murder journey reads like a twisted mathematical problem about the object that travelled from point X to point Y, but got lost on the way. The locations of space are replaced with the points in time, coldly abstract, making any movement between them impossible.

There is another non-place in the novel: the strange town of Tarnitz, where Hermann goes to meet Felix by appointment. The moment he enters the town he seems to fall into another of his unreal, time-loaded spaces:

> Well do I remember that little town—and feel oddly perplexed: should I go on giving instances of such aspects of it, which in a horribly unpleasant way echoed things I had somewhere seen long ago? It even seems to me now that it was, that town, constructed of certain refuse particles of my past, for I discovered in it things most remarkably and most uncannily familiar to me: a low pale-blue house, the exact counterpart of which I had seen in a St. Petersburg suburb; an old-clothes shop, where suits hung that had belonged to dead acquaintances of mine; a street lamp bearing the same number [...] as one that had stood in front of the Moscow house where I lodged; and nearby the same bare birch tree with the same forked trunk in an iron corset. (70)

The "Y" sign of the birch tree reappears as a double-remembrance: it is a double of the double of doubles near Ardalion's lake, and of another double in Hermann's entirely inaccessible, but silently ominous Russian past. The double becomes a triple, and threatens to outturn the neatness of Hermann's equation (self=double). The narrator's trip to Tarnitz is equivalent to an illicit visit to the past, through the back-door of memory dulled by sleep, producing out-of-context images that torment the dreamer by their irrelevance mimicking importance. In view of this, the name of Tarnitz seems especially apt: as Stephen Saugee surmises, it probably comes from the German *tarnen*, meaning "to veil"—something is hidden there while it is indicated that something is being revealed. Saugee's suggestion that "the town of Tarnitz is a kind of illusion within the book, composed of tantalizing clues and meaningless repetitions" (Saugee 1974, 56, 58) seems very well justified. Philippe Villeneuve also supports this assumption by pointing out that there is no town of Tarnitz in Saxony (where it should be located according to the novel)—it is an invented city.

While the sinister nature of space is clearly apparent, it is more difficult to understand what makes it so terribly dangerous, so unmanageable. It seems that there is more to it than simple incompetence on the part of the hero. And there is: the space of Nabokov's novels is impossible to control because it is irredeemable. His characters try in vain to return to the places they have known, to find the locations they have visited before – the space disintegrates as soon as the present becomes the past – that is, while we read. This is the source of the problem: the weird connection between space and time that exists in Nabokov's universe.

It is often noted that with his employment of memory as a creative method Nabokov rebels against the notion of time's irreversibility, absurd, when contrasted with the reversibility of spatial realm. Paradoxically, in an effort to transcend time's boundaries, he makes the space as incredibly unrepeatable as time, and just as hopelessly irreversible.

A perfect illustration of the phantom space may be found in *Glory*. The hero, Martin Edelweiss, always feels attracted by the distant lights, spread like a handful of diamonds in the velvet folds of the night, as he travels by train. One day he decides to get off the train to chase his dream. He is directed to the village of Molignac: "So this was where they sparkled at night, the lights which had beckoned to him ever since his childhood!" (161). In the village he leads for a while a simple, happy life. When he leaves, he carries with him the satiety of a fulfilled dream, but this feeling is quickly ruffled:

> The night express pounded into the station [...] and Martin experienced a momentary urge to jump out and return to the happy, fairy-tale farm. But the station had already ceased to exist. He stood looking through the window, waiting for the appearance of his beloved lights, to bid them good-bye. Here they came, far away, spilled jewels in the blackness, unbelievably lovely—"Tell me," Martin asked the conductor, "Those lights there – that's Molignac, isn't it?" "What lights?" the man asked glancing at the window, but at this moment everything was shut out by the sudden rise of a dark bank. "In any case, it's not Molignac," said the conductor. "Molignac can't be seen from the railroad." (165-166)

The space of his dream disappears as soon as he leaves its charmed circle, and it is impossible to recover. And this prefigures the end of the novel, when Martin decides to cross the border into the Red Russia—without any particular purpose, it seems, just for the sake of adventure—and disappears there. Martin's plan is not as idle as it seems: though his desire to break through the forbidden boundary has nothing to do with politics, governments, or even with the special kind of angel-winged nostalgia, nursed by many Russian *émigrés*, it is justified as a daring and romantic attempt to overcome the limitations of the three-dimensional reality, finding an entrance to the fourth. Martin's fate is to blend into the texture of his dreams, disappearing from sight in the space which contains the ghastly fourth dimension and, therefore, is invisible to the others, who remain, sadly, in the grey reality of their grieving.

Nabokov's short story "The Visit to the Museum" continues the theme of fantastically folded pattern of space through which the narrator/hero of the story has the misfortune to fall. Asked by a friend (whose "capacity to remain this side of fantasy" (277) the narrator doubts) to check out a certain portrait, the hero of the story walks into a small museum in Montisert, where everything is "as it should be: gray tints, the sleep of substance, matter dematerialized" (278)—and finds the painting. The director of the museum refuses to sell it, claiming that it does not exist, and the hero comes back to prove that it does. Suddenly, the museum's two modest exhibition halls become an endless labyrinth, hosting (to begin with) an entire skeleton of a whale, a locomotive, complete with tracks and signal lights, "an infinitively long passage containing numerous office cabinets and elusive, scurrying people" (283), a greenhouse, a laboratory, a section with fountains and brooks, and so on, until the terrified hero finally finds the exit, only to realize that somehow he has emerged in the Communist Russia.

The story, from the very start skirting the borders of fantasy, with each sentence develops what Ludmila Foster calls "phantasmagoric narrative magnetism" (Foster 1972). What is happening is clearly a dream, yet the hero cannot wake up, and experiences it as definitive and terrifying reality. The dematerialization of the matter, noted at the beginning by the narrator, in fact includes him as well as the absurd collection of dead objects the museum displays. This happens because he is drawn into somebody else's dream, motivated by "the insanity of others" (285) in the space that is at the same time fantastic and inescapably real. As merely a character in someone else's nightmare he exercises no control over its absurd proceedings, and the only thing he can do in the circumstances is to accept it as a kind of reality and try to edge his way back into "this side of fantasy".

The wanderings of the hero through the endless galleries of the museum are strangely akin to time travel—starting from the halls of ancient history and ending up in the hopelessly "factual Russia of today" (285). Even though the hero several times tries to retrace his steps, he never quite manages to do so: there are no returns in the space that is synonymous with time. While there seems to be no method at all in the way he wanders through the rooms of the museum, the historical events abbreviated by these exhibits remain in an unperturbed chronological order, making it seem some phantom-organized tourist tour through history of civilization, from the prehistoric past to the present moment. The space is random, the time is deliberate—and it controls space, which becomes a bleak, imperfect copy of its master.

This is a condensation of the usual fictional space in Nabokov's novels—all the strange and sinister qualities of the phantom territory are magnified, as if providing a case study of the method. The time-permeated dream space is the only space the characters of Nabokov's fiction know before they leave our field of vision. In that realm an illusion of continuity or repetition – of any motion or direction at all—exists only in memory or imagination, with the truth of irreversibility of space sometimes glimpsed by a character in a flash of madness or inspiration. And yet, paradoxically, Nabokov's strange time-space contains an indication that there is something else further beyond, outside the Camera Lucinda of fiction:

> if, in the spiral unwinding of things, space warps into something akin to time, and time, in its turn, warps into something akin to thought, then, surely, another dimension follows—a special Space maybe, not the old one, we trust, unless spirals become vicious circles again. (Nabokov 1996, 620)

References

Carroll, W. C. 1982. The Cartesian Nightmare of *Despair*. In *Nabokov's Fifth Arc: Nabokov and Others on His Life's Work,* ed. by J. E. Rivers and C. Nicol, 82-104. Austin: University of Texas Press.

Foster, Ludmila A. 1972. 'Poseshchenie muzeia' Nabokova v svete traditsii modernizma. *Grani* 85: 176-187

Nabokov, Vladimir. 1971. *Glory*. New York/Toronto: McGraw-Hill.

—. 1989. *Despair*. New York: Vintage.

—. 1990. *The Eye*. New York: Vintage.

—. 1995. *The Stories of Vladimir Nabokov*. New York: Alfred A. Knopf.

—. 1996. *Novels and Memoirs, 1941-1951: The Real Life of Sebastian Knight; Bend Sinister; Speak, Memory*, vol. 1, ed. by B. Boyd. New York: The Library of America.

Saugee, Stephen. 1974. An Artist's Memory Beats All Other Kinds: An Essay on *Despair*. In *A Book of Things about Vladimir Nabokov*, ed. by C. R. Proffer. Ann Arbor: Ardis.

Villeneuve, Philippe. 2008. Topographic Nightmares in *Despair*. *The Nabokovian*, 61: 23-31.

CHAPTER THIRTEEN

UNBEARABLE SPACES:
"THY HEART'S DESIRE" BY NETTA SYRETT
AS A STUDY OF CONFINEMENT

MAŁGORZATA MILCZAREK

"Thy Heart's Desire" is a New Woman short story published in the *Yellow Book* magazine in 1894. Belonging to the *fin de siècle* era, it is one of the texts which mark the transition from the Victorian to modernist modes of literary representation. The space in Syrett's story does not exist only on the physical level as described by the language, but what is physical becomes a metaphor of the psychological construct. In other words, what is focused upon is not how the imagery in the story renders the external, but rather, how the perception of space conveyed through this imagery stems from mental processes. Moreover, the way the story is narrated creates another spatial dimension, namely that between the story and the reader, which becomes most prominent towards the end of the story. The story will be looked at through the lens of Stephen Kern's notion of "positive negative space". As he put it in the context of the beginning of the twentieth century:

> The traditional view that space was an invert void in which objects existed gave way to a new view of it as active and full. A multitude of discoveries and inventions, buildings and urban plans, paintings and sculptures, novels and dramas, philosophical and psychological theories, attested to the constituent function of space. I will refer to this new conception as "positive negative space." Art critics describe the subject of the painting as positive space and the background as negative space. "Positive negative space" implies that the background itself is a positive element, of equal importance with all others. The term is somewhat unwieldy, but it is accurate and suggests the historical sense of the developments in this period, since it implies that what was formerly regarded as negative now has a positive, constituent function. (Kern 2003, 152-153)

The space in "Thy Heart's Desire" is no longer only a passive background. The present discussion aims at a deconstruction of the process in which space confines the female character.

"Thy Heart's Desire" opens as a story of a woman and her husband in a British colony. The accumulating feelings of isolation and madness are revealed to the reader gradually in each of the five parts of the story. It revolves around Victorian binary oppositions of the household, represented by tents as its colonial substitute and the freedom of the space outside the tents, symbolized by the heroine's ability to breathe more easily. Nevertheless, the space created by Syrett becomes a confinement also as a result of the construction opposite to what most of the female writers of the time did, since "Thy Heart's Desire" annuls the natural physical boundaries of confinement as represented by the household, which stands for the Victorian relegation of the woman to the private sphere. The setting of Syrett's story is, paradoxically, the limitless landscape of a plain in the colony. The landscape undergoes the process of defamiliarization in the perception of the reader. Thus, the distance between the reader and the heroine is created at the very beginning. What the reader learns becomes immediately undermined by what the heroine has already discovered for herself. The story begins quite abruptly:

> The tents were pitched in the little plain surrounded by hills. Right and left there were stretches of tender, vivid green where the young corn was springing; farther still, on either hand, the plain was yellow with mustard-flower; but in the immediate foreground it was bare and stony. A few thorny bushes pushed their straggling way through the dry soil, ineffectively as far as the grace of the landscape was concerned, for they merely served to emphasise the barren aridness of the land that stretched before the tents, sloping gradually to the distant hills.
>
> The hills were uninteresting enough in themselves; they had no grandeur of outline, no picturesqueness even, though at morning and evening the sun, like a great magician, clothed them with beauty at a touch.
>
> They had begun to change, to soften, to blush rose red in the evening light, when a woman came to the entrance of the largest of the tents and looked toward them. (Syrett 2001 [1894], 52-53) [1]

What is presented as an attractive potentiality of the space described here becomes negated in the next or even in the same sentence. However, the instability is even intensified by the impressionist quality of the landscape.

---

[1] Syrett, Netta. 2001. "Thy heart's desire". In *A New Woman Reader: Fiction, Articles, and Drama of the 1890s*, ed. by Carolyn Christensen Nelson, 52-69. Ontario/New York: Broadview Press. Hereafter cited in text.

The surroundings are not a typical enclosure imposed by civilization. Rather, strange to its new inhabitants, the landscape eludes the familiar definition of space with angles and horizontal and vertical lines.

The linear aspect of space is abandoned for that of the senses only. With no clear boundaries, that which one may term micro-space and, thus, confinement, are marked only by the human gaze. The word probably most frequently used by Syrett is "eyes": "her eyes wandered over the plain and over the distant hills" (Syrett 2001, 53), "[h]er eyes travelled toward the hills" (Syrett 2001, 58), "[h]er eyes wandered to Broomhurst's hands" (Syrett 2001, 58). Eyes are all the time used by Kathleen Drayton—the main character—and she is constantly followed by the eyes of others. When her husband notices the change in Kathleen caused by her affection to Broomhurst who comes to their isolated place to cooperate with Drayton, he mutely starts to demarcate his space and Kathleen as a part of it through his gaze: "[h]is eyes furtively followed his wife" (Syrett 2001, 61), "[h]is eyes sought her face piteously. She noticed that too, and stood before him torn by conflicting emotions, pity and disgust struggling in a hand-to-hand fight within her" (Syrett 2001, 61) and, as the woman says after her husband's death, "His eyes used to follow me like a dog's, and I was stabbed with remorse, and I tried to be good to him, but I couldn't" (Syrett 2001, 67). It is the gaze, the actual physical act being a manifestation of the mental processes that creates the confinement. What is mediated through other senses is only an extension of the impression of confinement.

Another significant use of sight is through the eyes as the expression of mental processes. The narrator does not give the reader much access to the character's thoughts, and the case of Drayton is the most enigmatic one, as, although an important figure, he exists only as a physical presence. Thus, with no revelation of his thoughts, the knowledge we gain about Drayton is only through the judgements made by the other two characters. A very negative assessment of Katheleen's husband by herself as mediated by the narrator is qualified by "his eyes, even, looked colourless" (Syrett 2001, 54), they are the eyes of a man who lacks the intelligence Kathleen craves for. Only when he realizes what his wife's attitude to Broomhurst is do his eyes become active as an externalization of his concern. A similar externalization can be detected in Kathleen, whose entrapment makes her "large gray eyes, unusually bright and rather startling in effect, for they seemed the only live thing about her. Gleaming from her still, set face, there was something almost alarming in their brilliancy" (Syrett 2001, 53). The contrast between her husband's eyes and hers, and the contrast between her body, which emanates the feeling of confinement, locates the medium for what the heroine struggles to suppress. Her

> eyes, for the moment's space in which they met the startled ones of her husband, had a wild, hunted look, but it was gone almost before his slow brain had time to note that it had been there—and was vaguely disturbing. (Syrett 2001, 55)

As Kathleen and her husband walk Broomhurst to their camp, "she felt his [Broomhurst's] keen eyes upon her" (Syrett 2001, 57). When Broomhurst tells Kathleen he has to leave, he "still kept his eyes on her face" (Syrett 2001, 63), "once more their eyes met in a long, grave gaze" (Syrett 2001, 63). Finally, when some time after Drayton's death and after he has been rejected by Kathleen, Broomhurst finds her after some time and "He came up to her without a word, and seized both her hands, devouring her face with his eyes. Something he saw there repelled him" (Syrett 2001, 65). Eyes are everywhere at every stage of the story. What happens outside as well as inside the characters is expressed and defined through sight. For Kathleen, since throughout almost the whole story she suppresses her emotions, eyes are always the most prominent signifier of her internal split.

The exceptional nature of "Thy Heart's Desire" as a study of confinement rests on the fact that the confinement is constructed with the plain as a background. In most of New Woman fiction, the space in which a woman gains freedom from the oppressive household would be that of a city.[2] In the case of Syrett's story this is reversed from the outside as liberating to the outside as overwhelming.[3] The city implies anonymity and the plain means only isolation. The city functions on the metaphorical level as a living organism, always in the process of becoming. In "Thy Heart's Desire", though the only change is observable with the changing light, the stasis of the place is nevertheless problematized. Paradoxically, the movement does not result from the visual, but rather it is evoked by the auditory. Apart from "eyes", another key word in the story is "silence".

---

[2] The liberating function of the city is emphasized in novels like *The Odd Women* (1893) by George Gissing, *The Daughters of Danaus* (1894) by Mona Caird, *The Heavenly Twins* (1893) by Sarah Grand or even Syrret's later novel *The Day's Journey* (1906). Although in some of these the female *flâneur* was prone to the male gaze of strangers, being lost in the crowd allowed them to penetrate the city freely.

[3] The landscape is also a very significant setting in another New Woman novel, *The Story of an African Farm* (1883) by Olive Schreiner.

Outside there was a deep hush. The silence of the vast empty plain seemed to work its way slowly, steadily in toward the little patch of light set in its midst. The girl felt it in every nerve; it was as though some soft-footed, noiseless, shapeless creature, whose presence she only dimly divined, was approaching nearer—nearer. The heavy outer stillness was in some way made more terrifying by the rustle of the papers her husband was reading, by the creaking of his chair as he moved, and by the little fidgeting grunts and half-exclamations which from time to time broke from him. (Syrett 2001, 54-55)

Space is represented as a living organism.[4] Such a rendering of space represents the shift from the nineteenth- to twentieth-century fiction discussed by Kern:

The beasts of nineteenth-century novels were generally tangible—forces of nature, vices, machines, institutions. ... As terrifying and overwhelming as these things seemed, they could at least be named. But the beasts of the twentieth century would be far less identifiable, living in the mysterious realm of negativity we find in Conrad, James, and Strindberg. For them the void supplies the focus. Their characters seek meaning outside themselves – in a jungle, in a cemetery, behind a door—and find only the horror of nothingness within. (Kern 2003, 169-170)

Kathleen's entrapment is projected onto the space of the plain and its auditory aspect. Broomhurst notices the strangeness of the silence as a newcomer. Kathleen is obsessed with it and as she explains to the man: "'I don't mind the day so much; it's the evenings.' She abruptly checked the swift words, and flushed painfully. ... 'Oh, you have no idea of the awful silence of this place at night ... It is so close, isn't it?'" (Syrett 2001, 60). The noun "silence", like in this passage is qualified throughout the story by adjectives expressing the tactile. The moment of Broomhurst understanding Kathleen's position is marked by his recognition of the entrapment:

He looked up at the star-sown sky, and the heavy silence seemed to press upon him like an actual, physical burden. ... 'Considering that she has been alone with him here for six months, she has herself very well in hand—*very* well in hand'. (Syrett 2001, 61, emphasis original)

---

[4] Such a representation of space stands in opposition to the representation of the outside by other New Woman authors, who usually write about the liberating potential of the city. A *flâneuse* enters the city in order to be immersed in the movement of the whole form of the city.

Another representation of silence that imparts its significance for the construction of confinement is that in which "[t]he whirring of insects, and the creaking of a Persian wheel somewhere in the neighbourhood, filtered through the hot silence" (Syrett 2001, 63).

Kern describes silence in the context of space in the literature of the times contemporary to "Thy Heart's Desire" as "positive negative time", "creative silences" being meaningful in the construction of a literary work (Kern 2003, 170). Silences in Syrett's story have multiple functions which either lead to or express Kathleen's confinement, the hysterical suppressed voice being a powerful expression. What emerges with hysteria is more than just a result of confinement. In fact, hysteria is one of the ways to escape confinement or at least to mark uncontrollable intimate spaces in the space that is defined for the protagonist. The already discussed elements of the story only suggest Kathleen's hysteria and its sources. Silence does not only function as a signifier of endangering madness, but also, like violent weather in gothic stories, it precedes the heroine's recognition and even acknowledgement of madness. Following the passage about silence perceived as an encroaching creature, the woman exclaims to her husband:

> "For heaven's sake—please, John, talk!" ... Her eyes, for the moments space in which they met the startled ones of her husband, had a wild, hunted look, but it was gone almost before his slow brain had time to note that it had been there—and was vaguely disturbing. She laughed a little unsteadily.
> "Did I startle you? I'm sorry. I"—she laughed again—"I believe I'm a little nervous. When one is all day alone—"She paused without finishing the sentence. (Syrett 2001, 55)

Syrett uses all the recognizable symptoms of hysteria. Again, as is the case with the perception of confinement, it is not only what Kathleen receives or perceives but also what she expresses through her body that is represented by the auditory and the tactile. The woman responds to the silence by crying. She suppresses her rage just like the silence represses her. In the scene in which she expresses the attitude to her husband "I am his *wife*—I *belong* to him!" (Syrett 2001, 55, emphases original) we learn that the actual expression cannot be achieved, since the exclamation is followed by another of Syrett's linguistic means of defamiliarization: "she cried, almost aloud" (Syrett 2001, 55). Kathleen's repression is visible in almost unnoticeable distractions like "except for a slight tightening of the muscles about her mouth, her face remained unchanged" (Syrett 2001, 54), "silent momentary clinching of the hands" (Syrett 2001, 60) or "[s]he pressed both her hands tightly against her breast, and set her teeth, fighting to keep down the rising flood that threatened to sweep away her composure" (Syrett 2001, 59). However, she also suffers from more obvious symptoms like *globus histericus*:

> She stood lingering a moment after he had entered the tent, as though unwilling to leave the outer air; and before she turned to follow him she drew a deep breath, and her hand went for one swift second to her throat as though she felt stifled. (Syrett 2001, 54)

Kathleen recognizes and names her state. However, she immediately undermines this form of manifestation by the superimposition of foolishness on hysteria: "Oh, what a fool I am! What an hysterical fool of a woman I am!" (Syrett 2001, 60). She tacitly accepts the silence between her and Drayton on the hysteria:

> "It's all right, John," ... "I'm not mad—yet. You—you must get used to these little outbreaks," ... "and, to do me justice, I don't often trouble you with them, do I? I'm just a little tired, or it's the heat or—something. No—don't touch me!" she cried, shrinking back; for he had risen slowly and was coming toward her.
> She had lost command over her voice, and the shrill note of horror in it was unmistakable. The man heard it, and shrank in his turn ... "I'm so sorry, John," she murmured, raising her great bright eyes to his face. They had not lost their goaded expression, though they were full of tears. "I'm awfully sorry; but I'm just nervous and stupid, and I can't bear any one to touch me when I'm nervous". (Syrett 2001, 57)

What actually stifles Kathleen is even the recognition of the cause of her hysterical fits. The woman is driven by the feeling of guilt, since she had never loved her husband. Hence, it is not only the presence of his male controlling gaze, which, in fact, is not a manifestation of the man's wish for actual power that is so oppressive. Kathleen is not subject to constant examination by the man, but rather, to the examination of herself by herself.

The focus on perception results in the impressionist quality of the narrative. The language is tense and the overall structure of the story is fragmented. Kahane points to the hysteric voice as a predicate of modernist fiction (Kahane 1995, xv).[5] Kathleen finally escapes Broomhurst's

---

[5] Kahane discusses the fragmented narrative of *The Story of an African Farm* by Olive Schreiner as a "hysterical structure of fragmentation" arguing that

expectations of a fulfilled relationship after Drayton's death, since she rejects him with the claim of not loving him anymore. The reader learns about that from the final part of the story that is introduced abruptly as taking place several months later. It turns out that the woman, in spite of Drayton's death, talking to Broomhurst, still "clasped her hands tight, with the old gesture he remembered when she was struggling for self-control" (Syrett 2001, 66). It is not only Broomhurst's expectations, but also the expectations of the reader used to clearer Victorian solutions that are undermined. Towards the very end of the novel, Kathleen says, "It is a mistake to think our prayers are not answered—they are. In due time we get our heart's desire—when we have ceased to care for it" (Syrett 2001, 69). This sentence can be transferred to the structural plane of the text and read as a summary of its idea. The desire of the plot cannot be fulfilled unproblematically if it is to present an elusive female subject. Thus, the proper way to achieve this end is to transcend and open a conventional Victorian ending.

Netta Syrett renders space as a physical as well as psychological construct. In "Thy Heart's Desire", the two dimensions intermingle in the form of hysteria. The hysteric expression blurs the distinction between the two levels to the extent that the unproblematic definition of what is external and what is mental is no longer valid. As a result, the confinement is presented both in terms of the overwhelming space as perceived by senses as well as how mental states affect the protagonist's sensitivity. The protomodernist hysteric voice in "Thy Heart's Desire" disrupts the narrative on several levels. The hysteria of the main character deconstructs the coherence of narration. What is more, it defamiliarizes the perception of various aspects of space by linguistic means. Just like Kathleen remains ungraspable for Drayton as well as for Broomhurst and just like our understanding of the woman turns out to be illusory, the distance between the narrative and the reader reveals itself in the elusive form of the open ending. Although the Victorian realistic modes of fiction are to a large extent preserved by Syrett, "Thy Heart's Desire" marks the transition to the more free impressionist or modernist fictional representations of the external reality as well as internal subjectivity.

Schreiner's "narrative voice is a precursor to present-day representations of a subject-in-process" (Kahane 1995, 84).

References

Kahane, Claire. 1995. *Passions of the Voice: Hysteria, Narrative and the Figure of the Speaking Woman, 1980-1915*. Baltimore/London: The Johns Hopkins University Press.

Kern, Stephen. 2003. *The Culture of Time and Space, 1880-1918: With a new Preface*. Cambridge, MA/London: Harvard University Press.

Syrett, Netta. 2001[1894]. "Thy Heart's Desire". In *A New Woman Reader: Fiction, Articles, and Drama of the 1890s*, ed. by Carolyn Christensen Nelson, 52-69. Ontario/New York: Broadview Press.

CHAPTER FOURTEEN

INNER SEA SPACE IN JOSEPH CONRAD'S
YOUTH AND THE MIRROR OF THE SEA

JOANNA MSTOWSKA

In his book entitled *The Poetics of Space*, Gaston Bachelard distinguishes two major kinds of space, outer one (that is geometrical space visible and perceptible through the senses) and inner one (that is invisible space existing in thoughts, memories, and dreams). As Bachelard perceives space as a spiritual relation between a human being and his or her surrounding, in *The Poetics of Space* he investigates the impact of various spaces upon human inhabitants and vice versa. Bachelard stresses the fact that any outer space, if inhabited and experienced, may become inner one. Once a space becomes intimate, "not open to just anybody" (Bachelard 1994, 78), it is then interiorized and starts to exist in man. Being a phenomenologist of space, Bachelard refutes absolute space. He is convinced that "[i]nhabited space transcends geometrical space" (Bachelard 1994, 47) and, rejecting Aristotelian sense of space, supports that of Heidegger. Aristotle stressed the priority of a place to a thing. According to him, the place is a condition for the thing to exist. The thing depends on the place, however, the place can exist independently of the thing, being empty or filled with the thing. Heidegger, by contrast, strongly rejected Aristotelian sense of space and believed that the place is never empty but exists thanks to its physical or spiritual content.

Being convinced that thanks to human impact on each inhabited space, this space is no longer an object but is elevated to the role of a subject and has a kind of "psyche", in his book Bachelard explores what he calls "topoanalysis", that is "the systematic psychological study of the sites of our intimate lives" (Bachelard 1994, 8). What is more, Bachelard asserts that children perceive and interiorize intimate spaces in a totally different way than adults. As in childhood the boundary between the real and the imagined gets disturbed and blurred, children perceive spaces not only through the senses but also through the prism of their great imagination.

By contrast, adulthood is characterized by "dry" rationalism. In the chapter devoted to nests, Bachelard writes: "But the dreams of today do not go this far, and an abandoned nest no longer contains the herb of invisibility" (Bachelard 1994, 94). Once a child achieves maturity, its great imagination vanishes forever.

Hanna Buczyńska-Garewicz's book entitled *Miejsca, strony, okolice. Przyczynek do fenomenologii przestrzeni* echoes Bachelard's phenomenology of space. Also according to Buczyńska-Garewicz, a place is characterized by its spiritual content, not by its size or by distance from other places. In her book, she goes beyond a physical sense of space and concentrates on its spiritual aspect. Much as Bachelard and phenomenologists, she is convinced that once a space is experienced and interiorized, it exists in human consciousness and psyche. Buczyńska-Garewicz insists that space is by no means empty but full of memories, wishes, dreams and desires. Interpreting space in terms of geometry means for her concentrating only on its physical aspect and reducing space to technological pragmatism and utilitarianism. Geometrical space is finite, limited and measurable, whereas inner one, existing in memories and dreams, is infinite, limitless and immeasurable.

In her book Buczyńska-Garewicz concentrates on the urban spaces of Venice and imagined cities, whereas Bachelard mainly explores significances of the house. Both, however, seem to ignore sea space. This paper thus intends to investigate sea space, which seems to have been left unnoticed by phenomenologists of space but, having its *genius loci* and being filled with spiritual content, it is much more than just a travel channel for ships. In this paper I shall draw on sea space presented in Joseph Conrad's short story, *Youth,* and his collection of reminiscences, *The Mirror of the Sea,* in order to show how sea space exists in sailors and how they give spirituality to the sea. The second point that will be stressed concerns a different way in which young and mature seamen perceive and interiorize the sea, as well as different features of character they ascribe to the salty element.

Young and inexperienced seamen, such as twenty-two-year-old Marlow from *Youth*, regard sea space as the extension of the experienced space of ships. On the ship there is no place for women, therefore personified and feminized ships become the loves of young seamen's lives. In *Youth* the ship called Judea is ancient, outmoded, dilapidated and unseaworthy. Nevertheless, in the men on board she inspires faith, a sense of security, hope, loyalty, and fidelity. Although dirty and rusty, in the eyes of Marlow the ship is beautiful and precious. He loves her unconditionally, and is fully aware that the ship will never be able to requite his feelings. "There was a touch of romance in it, something that made me love the old thing" (Conrad, 1967, 5). He idealizes the ship, speaking about it in a highly elegiac tone and treating the Judea as a beloved old wife. For Marlow the vessel is not only capable of human emotions, but she also, like all human beings, has a soul. Although the Judea is not of breathtaking beauty, Marlow remains blind to her weaknesses and perceives her as precious and unique.

Also for the narrator of *The Mirror of the Sea* ships are not just objects but living creatures who have iron hearts and are able to feel. Here the ships are also feminized figures who are to be admired and adored. The narrator admits that he idealizes ships which fascinate him and in his eyes are attractive mistresses to whose imperfections he remains blind. A ship is a figure that men "shall learn to know with an intimacy surpassing the intimacy of man with man, to love with a love nearly as great as that of man for woman, and often as blind in its infatuated disregard of defects" (Conrad, 1946, 58). In his unreasonable, inexplicable, and overwhelmingly strong love for ships, Conrad regards them as delicate creatures who "do want humouring" (Conrad, 1946, 51). Each of the ships, much as each woman, is not only unique and exceptional, but also mysterious: "You must treat with an understanding consideration the mysteries of her feminine nature" (Conrad, 1946, 56). The above-mentioned examples illustrate Bachelard's statement in which he claims that "[i]f we look at it intimately, the humblest dwelling has beauty" (Bachelard, 1994, 4).

Sailors' relationship with the vessels they adore and admire is beyond any doubt intimate. Apart from perceiving the ships as women, young seamen regard the vessels as their natural homes, as "the non-I that protects the I" (Bachelard, 1994, 5). Gaston Bachelard characterizes the space of the house as *l'espace intime* (intimate space), stressing the fact that in each house there are corners where the inhabitants can hide to find solitude, essential for meditations and reflections upon the world and human condition. Being convinced that houses are to be experienced and interiorized, Bachelard gives primacy to the spiritual aspect of home over the physical one. Bachelard also claims that to inhabit a particular place means to interiorize it and to be in that place not only physically but also spiritually. He goes even a step further claiming that it is possible to inhabit places that do not exist in a physical sense; thus, he stresses the value of oneiric phenomena. Bachelard believes that the houses seen in dreams may never materialize and, as imagined and desired places, remain forever only in the sphere of human psyche. Nevertheless, they always evoke reminiscences and dreams of safety, security, and happiness.

However, as "the space we love is unwilling to remain permanently enclosed" (Bachelard, 1994, 53), in the eyes of young seamen intimate space extends beyond ships and encapsulates also the sea. Young Marlow loves, admires and respects the sea which for him belongs to the sphere of the sacred and is contrasted with the profane of the land. Displaying a kind of naivety, bold and energetic Marlow refuses to believe in his insignificance and regards himself as powerful enough to domesticate the sea. Young Marlow associates sea space with the feelings of safety and security, as the sea, like all "really inhabited space[s], bears the essence of the notion of home" (Bachelard, 1994, 5). The vast majority of young seamen, much as Marlow, are men of extremes; no limitations are placed upon their imagination. They are often subject to flights of imagination, live on the verge of reality and dream, and seem incapable of making a clear-cut distinction between illusion and waking reality. In their perceiving the world through the prism of imagination, they resemble children. Hence, the quality of their experience is phantasmagoric and dreamlike. It is their extreme sensitivity and their susceptibility to daydreaming that enable them to inhabit the sea oneirically. In their eyes, sea space becomes greater than reality, is inscribed in them and "engraved in [their] soul[s]" (Bachelard, 1994, 11). Thanks to the unimaginable depths of their psyche and imagination, they feel enclosed and protected even while seafaring.

In *The Poetics of Space* Gaston Bachelard gives an example of a hermit who feels safe and at home within the intimate space of his hut, despite the fact that the hut is situated in the middle of a wood and it is snowing heavily. The feeling of security given by the intimate space of the hut, makes the hermit able to reduce the outside world to just one word, snow. To quote Bachelard, snow "reduces the exterior world to nothing. [...] It gives a single color to the entire universe which, with the one word, snow, is both expressed and nullified for those who have found shelter" (Bachelard, 1994, 40). Bachelard's statement, which constitutes a very interesting way of perceiving vast spaces, is also applicable to sea space. Young seamen who feel safe on their ships are powerful enough to reduce the immensity of the salty element and to regard sea space as intimate one. Sea space becomes for them what Bachelard calls *l'immensite intime* (intimate immensity). Bachelard believes that there is "correspondence between the immensity of world space and the depth of "inner space"." (Bachelard, 1994, 205) He also states that "the impression of immensity is in us, and not necessarily related to an object" (Bachelard, 1994, XXXIX). If it were not for immature sailors' "inner immensity", they would never be able to domesticate the sea and, in consequence, to become inhabitants of the world.

According to Hanna Buczyńska-Garewicz, only human beings are capable of inhabiting spaces. For her, much as for Gaston Bachelard, inhabiting a place means interiorizing it in one's consciousness and psyche and giving spiritual life to it. A place becomes home when its spiritual content harmonizes with that of the inhabitant's soul. Without that harmony, she regards space as abstract and empty and people as homeless. Buczyńska-Garewicz insists that inhabiting space should be perceived as a spiritual relation, as not only human beings live in space but space also exists in them, in their memories and dreams. She claims further that by inhabiting numerous spaces, man broadens his horizons, as well as realizes his freedom of wandering. According to Buczyńska-Garewicz, a wanderer is open to otherness and it is possible for him to transform strangeness into familiarity, as was the case of young sailors domesticating the sea. A stimulus for every wandering is not emptiness but a kind of fullness characterized by a tendency to exceed. The wanderer's openness to broaden his horizons does not signify that he inhabits empty space but, on the contrary, that he has interiorized numerous spaces. Being a wanderer means extending one's home and becoming an inhabitant of the world, at the same time enlarging the capacity of one's soul. Buczyńska-Garewicz seems to support Bachelard's thesis, also claiming that the ability to domesticate vast spaces in a spiritual way, signifies the immensity of a particular human being's inside (Buczyńska-Garewicz, 2006).

By contrast, sea space interiorized by mature and experienced sailors is by no means intimate but hostile, cruel and malicious. They start to regard the sea as an opponent, fighting with which becomes the essence of their existence. When Marlow's unconscious youth is replaced by disillusioned maturity, he realizes that the sea is not static and approachable but monumental and awe-inspiring. It is indeed its overwhelming vastness and great ferocity that is both frightening and enchanting for mature Marlow. He regards the sea no longer as intimate space but as hostile immensity. Also the mature narrator from *The Mirror of the Sea*, in all likelihood Conrad's *porte parole*, perceives the sea space in a totally different way than young Marlow from *Youth*. Having spent twenty years at sea, having experienced various kinds of enchantments and bitterness associated with the sea life, and having achieved maturity through various ups and downs of life, he has acquired a considerable knowledge concerning the true nature of the sea. Enthusiasm and optimism, which he used to be full of when he was a youthful and inexperienced seaman, vanished forever. Looking from the perspective of twenty-five years, in the Author's Note to

The Mirror of the Sea, Conrad confesses that his feeling towards the sea was neither "the lyric illusion of an old, romantic heart", nor "a foolish infatuation", but "it was great passion for the sea – something too great for words" (Conrad, 1946, VIII). In his youth, his attitude towards the sea used to be like that of a young inexperienced lover towards his mistress: "I surrendered my being to that passion which various and great like life itself had also its periods of wonderful serenity which even a fickle mistress can give sometimes on her soothed breast, full of wiles, full of fury, and yet capable of an enchanting sweetness" (Conrad, 1946, VIII). The great love for the sea quickly became the essence of his existence: "Beyond the line of the sea horizon the world for me did not exist" (Conrad, 1946, VIII). As the young narrator is fascinated and enchanted by his beloved mistress, his attitude towards the sea is similar to that of young Marlow from *Youth*. However, when the narrator achieved maturity, he learned to look beyond the surface, and realized that the ocean "is ready to beguile and betray, to smash and to drown the incorrigible optimism of men" (Conrad, 1946, 137) and that regarding the sea as a tempting mistress giving sweetness and delight was just the vision of his youth.

The older the narrator grows, the more ambiguous becomes the way he perceives the sea. He recollects a moment, and calls it the moment of initiation, when he realized that the essence of a seaman's existence is not showing love and admiration for the sea, but constant fighting with this malevolent force, and loving it at the same time. This is the moment when he adopts a new role, that of a real seaman: "I had looked coolly at the life of my choice. Its illusions were gone, but its fascination remained. I had become a seaman at last" (Conrad, 1946, 142). It was in his maturity that he became fully aware of the inherited cruelty and malevolence of the sea, carefully hidden beyond its tempting and encouraging surface—the only layer visible to the eyes of an enthusiastic and naive youth. While spinning his reminiscences, the narrator once again recollects the moment of initiation and confesses to the reader: "Already I looked with other eyes upon the sea. I knew it is capable of betraying the generous ardour of youth as implacably as, indifferent to evil or good, it would have betrayed the basest greed or the noblest heroism. [...] Open to all and faithful to none, it exercises its fascination for the undoing of the best" (Conrad, 1946, 148).

The mature narrator regards the sea as a testing-ground of his strength and of his character. He also sees the sea as a force that invites him to come out of himself and to extend beyond all limits. The salty element is brutal and hostile, but at the same time encouraging, and affording a chance of success. If it had not been for the sea, the narrator of *The Mirror of the Sea* would have never been tested and he would have never adopted the role of a respected and reasonable commander. As it stimulates the longing for distanced, unknown and limitless spaces, the immensity frees from limitations and opens to new horizons. Experienced sailors become aware of the possible inspiring function of the immense sea space.

In *The Poetics of Space*, Bachelard underlines not only the impact of geometrical space upon human beings but also their influence on space. Young and inexperienced seamen regard sea space as the extension of the intimate space of their ships and love it so blindly and unconditionally as they adore feminized and idealized ships. It is their strong attachment to the sea that elevates sea space to the role of a subject. In their eyes the sea takes on the form of a seductive mistress who is to be admired but who will always remain an impenetrable mystery to a human being. By contrast, mature and experienced seamen do not live in a phantasmagoric world but the way they perceive the sea is deeply rooted in reality. They no longer regard the sea as a mysterious woman but personify sea space as a fierce enemy, fighting with whom becomes the essence of their existence. Having spent years at sea, they are aware of the changeable and the malevolent nature of the sea. However, the sea is still tempting for them, as fighting with this element helps them to go beyond all limits, to test their characters and to rediscover their latent strength. Despite numerous disillusionments, disenchantments, and tussles with the malicious sea, the mature narrator from *The Mirror of the Sea* can neither resist his great passion for the sea, nor is able to hate it. His love towards the impenetrable and heartless salty element turned out to be unimaginably strong and lasting eternally. He confesses in the Author's Note to *The Mirror of the Sea*: "My relation with the sea [...] went on unreasoning and invincible, surviving the test of disillusion, defying the disenchantment that lurks in every day of a strenuous life; went on [...] without bitterness and without repining, from the first hour to the last" (Conrad, 1946, VII-VIII). If it were not for both young and mature seamen's attachment to the sea, the sea space would never gain its spirituality and would exist only in a physical sense. Having interiorized the sea, the seamen gave to its either intimate or immense space a part of themselves.

As has been shown, the transcendental geometry of Gaston Bachelard is applicable also to the interpretation of sea fiction. Beyond any doubt, his concept of interiorized space reshapes the way of perceiving sea space and gives to it enchanting significances. We can observe various ways in which the protagonists of Conrad's fiction approach sea space, as well as different features of character they ascribe to the salty element. On the one hand, young and inexperienced seamen, who live on the verge of dream and waking reality, regard the sea as the extension of the intimate space of the house. Displaying a kind of naivety, they feel powerful enough to domesticate sea space and to reduce its immensity to intimacy. In their youthful dreams sea space exists as a tempting lover who, much like ships, is to be blindly admired and adored. On the other hand, mature sailors are aware of the hostile and ferocious immensity of sea space. Thus, they perceive and interiorize the sea as a malevolent opponent, fighting with whom enables them to rediscover their latent strength and to make sense of their lives. In his book Bachelard concentrates on spirituality of various spaces, stating at one point that "the desert is reflected in the wanderer" (Bachelard, 1994, 204). Conrad's *Youth* and *The Mirror of the Sea* may well exemplify that the sea is not only reflected in sailors' memories and dreams but also, being personified either as a seductive woman or as a malicious opponent, the sea reflects human feelings and emotions.

References

Bachelard, Gaston. 1994. *The Poetics of Space*. Boston: Beacon Press.
Buczyńska-Garewicz, Hanna. 2006. *Miejsca, strony, okolice. Przyczynek do fenomenologii przestrzeni*. Kraków: Universitas.
Conrad, Joseph. 1946. *The Mirror of the Sea*. London: J. M. Dent and Sons Ltd.
—. 1967. *Youth*. London: J. M. Dent and Sons Ltd.

CHAPTER FIFTEEN

ARCHITECTURE OF INSANITY: ALIENATING SPACES IN J.G. BALLARD'S *COCAINE NIGHTS*

STANKOMIR NICIEJA

Undoubtedly, the recently deceased J. G. Ballard was a unique phenomenon of the post-war British literature. Although he was certainly not the most popular among the contemporary English novelists, his writing spawned a remarkably dedicated community of enthusiasts and fans. Only a cursory search of the Internet would reveal many websites and blogs devoted to the author's rich output. Additionally, Ballard's appeal was impressively broad and reached far beyond the narrowly defined confines of the literary world. Numerous musicians, photographers and painters openly conceded Ballard's impact on their art. Notably, his novels provided the base for several interesting films, the most famous of which were Steven Spielberg's *Empire of the Sun* (1987) and David Cronenberg's *Crash* (1996). Another testament to Ballard's wide influence may be the inclusion of the term "Ballardian" into Collins English Dictionary (McKeown 2008; Baxter 2008, 1; Sellars 2009).

One of the most interesting aspects of Ballard's writing was his specific approach to architecture. As a novelist he was evidently fascinated by the way space can be shaped by human activity and the impact architecture might have on common behaviour or values. Later in his life he became particularly attracted to gated communities as both intriguing architectural constructs and also as expressions of specific expectations and beliefs. He not only drew attention to the unsettling significance of such places but used them as broader metaphors for the human condition in post-industrial times. They emerged as powerful symbols of the manner in which capitalism and consumer lifestyle transformed such notions as work and leisure. Architecture and artificially modified space also played a crucial role in Ballard's symbolic re-enactments of the conflicts between the consciously expressed human aspirations and the unconscious irrational drives. He delighted in stark juxtapositions and collisions where dogmatic rationalism crashed with the gritty experience of the every-day and where the conscious urges surrendered to the unconscious desires.

The first striking feature characterising Ballard's fictional explorations of architecture was his peculiar selectivity. He focused almost exclusively on modern structures and usually set his novels well beyond historic centres or heritage sites (Litt 2008, viii). Simultaneously however, his fictions did not usually feature spectacular modern urban projects. With the notable exception of his novel *High-Rise* (1975), Ballard did not write about grand and dazzling architectural designs—the ones occupying the most expensive quarters in the centres of big cities. His novels did not usually evoke bold, ostentatiously futuristic buildings; the kind of "mega-architecture" most often associated with visionaries like Frank Ghery or Norman Foster. Instead, Ballard was interested in much more utilitarian and unspectacular constructions that could be labelled as architectural catastrophes rather than triumphs. He delighted in describing architectural creations responsible for the overwhelming blandness and ugliness of urban areas situated beyond the immediate city centres. As a consequence, the universe that emerged from his novels was conspicuously austere and rough—apparently, more brutal than the infamous British "brutalist architecture" of the 1960s and 1970s (architecture much admired by fellow architects but commonly despised by the general public). Ballard's novels are typically set in a territory featuring tangles of motorways, mazes of car parks and fenced industrial estates. As Toby Litt characterizes it: "His fictional project seems to have been based on a cold assessment of what (apart from woods and fields) takes up most of our country's surface area, what is most obtrusive when viewed from space. [...] No other novelist has paid such close attention to the quiddity of where we now live and work" (Litt 2008, vii).

Most of Ballard's later novels have a very similar, if not identical, structure. They usually take the form of quests or journeys in which a protagonist—typically an outsider – is forced to enter into the alien world that later seduces and overwhelms him. Hence Ballard's output is often compared to that of Joseph Conrad's and particularly his *Heart of Darkness* (1902). Moreover, Ballard's novels portray individuals who manage to throw down the constraints of "culture" and regress to an apparently more comfortable form of social functioning. Remarkably, Ballard's explorations of the meanders of human psychology did not lead him to remote and exotic locations but to run-down tower blocks, motorway exit ramps and pedestrian underpasses. Thus, Ballard is sometimes described not only as a writer but also as a significant chronicler or even sociologist of the modern middle class, their manners and follies. His fictions foreground territories usually ignored in common discourse. Ballard proved that post-industrial cultural as well as environmental wastelands can be very interesting terrains for social observation and analysis. With remarkable artistic success, Ballard negotiated the confusing maze of identical suburban drives, vast and empty supermarket car parks or industrial estates guarded by CCTV cameras and barbed wire fences. The rationale for such a choice of background becomes evident the moment one is drawn into the perversely intriguing universes of Ballard's novels.

Ballardian landscapes may be unsightly but they prove particularly effective in symbolic demonstration of the conflicts and paradoxes of modernity. The tension between the positive and negative symbolic connotations epitomized by modern architecture is probably most dramatically evident in the case of motorways—man-made constructions often associated with Ballard's novels today. His books, with the leading example of *Crash* (1973), invite readers to reconsider the ambiguous symbolism of the motorway. Superficially, motorways are just mere pieces of infrastructure, essential for efficient transfer of goods and people. In the 20th century, however, they gained symbolic significance and have become important cultural symbols strongly connected to the notion of personal freedom. However, as Ballard frequently liked to remind his readers, stripped of these romanticized connotations, motorways prove to be spaces surprisingly hostile and dangerous to humans. For him motorways were spaces of violent death and injury. Moreover, they are a true menace to local ecosystems and landscape and are also rather bizarre places from the viewpoint of social interaction. Large masses of people converge there, yet they stay insulated in the private spaces of their rushing cars. Fellow traffic participants are usually treated as obstacles and possible sources of menace. Moreover, motorways are very restrictive: they exclude non-motorised individuals. Characteristically, it is both illegal to drive too slowly and walk around the motorway.

In the final stage of J. G. Ballard's literary career he often evoked another social product of late modernity, gated communities. For anyone intrigued by contemporary social tendencies, regardless of whether they are sociologists or novelists, gated communities are uniquely attractive terrains for exploration. They also provide numerous purely literary advantages. As, for instance, Sarah Blandy points out: "a number of perennial motifs can be played out against the background they provide: for example, social inclusion and exclusion; order and disorder; nature and human artifice. As well as the rich possibilities of exploring the psychological impact on those living within the walls" (Blandy 2001). Importantly, gated communities may offer effective delineation of the characters in physical space in a similar manner that university campuses, ships, prisons, desert islands or secluded country houses are habitually used in plays and novels. Demarcation within a gated community also opens enormous symbolic and metaphorical potential that Ballard managed to utilize to full extent. Gated communities become symbols of something more than just banal aspirations of modern consumer society. In Ballard's novels they foretell the coming of a new form of social organisation—a form unsettlingly similar to the vision sketched out by Aldous Huxley in *Brave New World* where seemingly benevolent and open society restricts individual choices and constrains unorthodox forms of self-expression.

Gated communities, holiday resorts and marinas, so frequently described in Ballard's novels, serve to illustrate the failure of rationalism and consumerism to address real human desires and aspirations. In theory gated communities are man-made spaces designed to suit the most sophisticated needs and provide ultimate comfort. In the end however, they become—quite literally—sophisticated prisons, alienating and stupefying the dwellers by radically narrowing their horizons and expectations.

Within his considerable literary output, J. G. Ballard created many imaginary gated communities. One of the first visions of the kind appeared already in 1975, in his novel *High Rise*—written well before the term gated community went into wider circulation. The next gated community appeared in 1989 in the novella entitled *Running Wild*. Other significant evocations of the theme can be found in *Millennium People* (2003) and to some extent in Ballard's last novel, *Kingdom Come* (2006). Probably the most memorable and simultaneously most celebrated was Ballard's analysis of life in a gated community sketched out in *Cocaine Nights*, published for the first time in 1996.

From the formal point of view, *Cocaine Nights* has a structure of a classic detective story. The protagonist and at the same time narrator, Charles Prentice arrives in Costa del Sol, a famous tourist destination in southern Spain. However, Charles does not come there for a holiday. He is on a mission to help his younger brother Frank, a former manager at a local Club Nautico. Frank is awaiting a trial in a Spanish jail following his confession to murdering five people in an arson attack. Although almost no one believes in Frank's quilt (not even the police), the narrator's brother faces life imprisonment. But murder is not the only mystery that

needs urgent solution in the novel. On arrival Charles has to face yet
another mystery—namely the phenomenon of Estrella de Mar, a
residential retreat for the rich Northern Europeans where his brother used
to work.

Ostensibly, Estrella de Mar resembles many similar places along Costa
Del Sol; nevertheless, it stands out. While all other communities are
conspicuously lifeless and lethargic, Estrella de Mar teems with cultural
life and social activity. It boasts an extremely busy sports centre and local
residents attend a surprisingly wide array of arts classes and workshops.
Shows of classic films are organised there as well as a retrospective of
Tom Stoppard's plays. In other words, Estrella de Mar thrives in the very
middle of the spiritual and cultural desert.

For anyone familiar with Ballard's output the answer to the mystery of
Estrella de Mar becomes very easy to figure out. What keeps the town's
inhabitants alive is violence, carefully administered to the inhabitants by a
charismatic sports instructor and an informal local leader, Bobby
Crawford. Ostensibly, minor assaults, acts of vandalism or theft,
reintroduce adrenalin into inhabitants' bloodstreams thus making them
more alive and responsive. Hidden beneath the veneer of detective story,
the novel soon reveals another layer and becomes a philosophical quest. In
consequence, Charles Prentice's role as a protagonist becomes soon
redefined. From a clumsy, self-appointed sleuth, he changes into an
anthropologist who infiltrates the community of the residents in an attempt
to understand their strange customs and values (Gąsiorek 2005, 171).

One of the most attractive dimensions of *Cocaine Nights* is the
surrealist manner in which Ballard portrays the architecture of the Spanish
resort and the people who inhabit it. He creates a particularly well-
qualified narrator/protagonist for this task. Charles Prentice is a travel
journalist who lives from writing about the most remote corners of the
globe. Theoretically, Marbella and the surrounding towns, barely two
hours' flight from London, should not impress this jaded and seasoned
globetrotter. "Costa del Sol was off my beat. I prefer the long-haul flights
to Jakarta or Papeete", he notes at the very beginning of the novel
(Ballard, 9). Nevertheless, he quickly becomes seduced by the unsettling
aura of the place. Almost immediately after the arrival he becomes
intrigued by the particularly odd and alienating landscape of the freshly
erected holiday settlements tightly arranged on the hills above the
coastline: the stark whiteness of the innumerable villas alternates with the
radiant greenness of the golf courses. At a first glance, the panorama
resembles some misplaced lunar colony rather than a fashionable holiday
destination. In fact, Prentice sometimes likes to refer to himself in a

fashion similar to an astronaut who returns to earth after a very long absence. This is a classic Ballardian frame. A perceptive and intelligent outsider is plunged in the middle of a seemingly mundane environment which in reality is strange and alienating (Gąsiorek 2005, 171). What is more, the protagonist of *Cocaine Nights* behaves like a modern-day Gulliver who is forced to live among the alien race whose habits and values he is determined to investigate.

One of the first things Prentice notices about Marbella's vicinities is the pastiche nature of the architecture of the holiday villages. Like the doomed French Empress Marie Antoinette who liked to rest from the opulence and conceit of Versailles in a mock-village she ordered to create outside the residence (complete with mock shepherds and milkmaids), the rich Northern Europeans in Costa del Sol chose to settle in pseudo-pueblos. Inside, their houses are fitted with the most expensive furniture and the latest electronic gadgetry, but on the outside they look like old cottages. This is how Ballard describes one of such strange places: "White walled Andalucían pueblos presided over the greens and fairways, fortified villages guarding their pastures, but in fact the miniature townships were purpose-built villa complexes financed by Swiss and German property speculators, the winter homes not of local shepherds but of Düsseldorf ad-men and Zürich television executives" (15). Here we become faced with the perfect example of what Michel Foucault called heterotopias. Places where utopian values and abstract ideas gain physical presence (Foucault 1967). Architecture of Costa del Sol must assist the residents in their desire for maximum relaxation and comfort or more precisely how those ideas should be realised. Ballard seemed visibly intrigued by the values and ideas guiding people who populate such settlements. According to his diagnosis, the atmosphere of leisure and the isolation from the immediate social or political concerns results in a gradual estrangement of the inhabitants. On the hills surrounding Costa del Sol from *Cocaine Nights* everything soon becomes blighted by an almost hypnotic aura of ennui:

> this silent world: the memory-erasing white architecture; the enforced leisure that fossilized the nervous system; the almost Africanized aspect, but North Africa invented by someone who had never visited the Maghreb; the apparent absence of any social structure; the timelessness of a world beyond boredom, with no past, no future and a diminishing present. Perhaps this was what the leisure-dominated future would resemble? Nothing could ever happen in this affectionless realm, where entropic drift calmed the surfaces of a thousand swimming pools. (35)

As we can clearly see from the above quotes these are specific places populated by the new leisure class. The new meritocracy—lawyers, accountants, engineers, middle management and small business owners whose notions of a good life are not shaped by the ideas derived from Greek philosophers but by TV commercials and Hollywood blockbusters. In such mental and physical circumstances the response of the inhabitants is uniform and takes the form of atrophy of any social interaction.

Deprived of strong external stimuli, like anxiety and risk, people quickly turn into automatons, possessing only enough initiative to surf TV channels. One of the most memorable passages of *Cocaine Nights* is the scene when the narrator is taken on a tour of the newly-built complex, neighbouring Estrella de Mar called Residencia Costasol. While Estrella de Mar was built in the 1970s and is one of the oldest places of the kind, Residencia Costasol is described as "pure 1990s" where "security rules [and] [e]verything is designed around an obsession with crime" (212). This is a territory variously referred to as "Zombieland", "the kingdom of vodka and valium" or "brain-death disguised as a hundred miles of white cement" (43).

The gated community, closed to outsiders resembles a "fortified medieval city" forming a "cascade of patios, terraces and swimming pools" (usually not used), where not a single resident is visible and the only moving objects are ubiquitous security cameras. The area is even adorned with and an appropriately Orwellian slogan: "The Residencia Costasol: Investment, Freedom, Security". When Prentice has a chance to peek into one of the lounges, he sees:

> A three-dimensional replica of a painting by Edward Hopper [...] visible below the awning. The residents, two middle-aged men and a woman in her thirties, sat in the silent room, their faces lit by the glow of a television screen. No expression touched their eyes, as if the dim shadows on the hessian walls around them had long become a satisfactory substitute for thought. They are watching TV with the sound turned down. (215)

Ballard's descriptions of gated communities highlight two objects as possessing particularly symbolic significance. These are satellite dishes and empty swimming pools. The omnipresent satellite TV dishes not only underline resident's dependence on this medium of mass communication but also their separation from the Spanish society. The space they inhabit becomes exterritorial (Gąsiorek 2005, 174). The remaining traces of Spanish culture are predominantly artificial, created for foreign residents and tourists. Swimming pools, always described by the narrator as unused, play another function. They emphasize the inertia engulfing the entire area. Pools are more status symbols than practical facilities.

In *Cocaine Nights* Ballard constantly draws attention to the special symbolic status of the settlements like Residencia Costasol that, of course, has nothing to do with the uniqueness of its architecture or atmosphere. Instead, right from the beginning of the novel various characters emphasize the futuristic aspect of the entire Costa del Sol project. They picture it as a harbinger of a new, gradually emerging social order. As Ballard seems to suggest, Western societies inescapably evolve towards communities of incessant leisure. As a result of the increasing life spans and further developments in technology, many Westerners can expect to spend several decades of their lives in comfortable idleness. In such society, as Ballard suggests, all human relations undergo inevitable redefinition. Both religion and politics lose their traditional power to excite imagination or stir one's conscience.

In *Cocaine Nights* Ballard sketched a new paradigm for a fictional dystopian project and an innovative pattern for the development of the genre. A truly dystopian uniformity found in Residencia Costasol is not imposed here from above, as it usually happens in dystopian narratives, but results from a supposedly informed consumer choice. *Cocaine Nights* is a dystopia created and maintained by apathetic customers. Although they live in a world of supposedly limitless choice, people settling around Costa del Sol willingly become a part of a disturbingly uniform, monotonous and deracinated environment.

The value of Ballard's fiction depended largely on his high originality in the approach to his dystopian visions. Instead of speculating about fictitious worlds, he managed to extract dystopian elements from the already existing reality. In consequence, in his representations he did not have to rely on realistic description and could emphasize surrealist qualities of the described landscapes and spaces. This combination of innovation in the approach to the construction of fictional stories and heightened sensitivity to the absurdities of the social order puts Ballard's writing on the par with the most distinguished authors of the speculative and dystopian fiction in the English language like Aldous Huxley, George Orwell, Anthony Burgess or Margaret Atwood and makes him an indispensable reading for anyone interested in understanding the paradoxes of modernity.

References

Ballard, J. G. 1996. *Cocaine Nights*. London: Flamingo.

Baxter, Jeanette. 2008. J. G. Ballard and the contemporary. In *J. G. Ballard*, ed. by J. Baxter. London: Continuum.

Blandy, Sarah. 2009 [2001]. *Enemies Within? Gated Communities Unhinged,* http://www.jgballard.ca/criticism/jgb_gated_communities.html (accessed 10 April 2009).

Foucault, Michel. 2009 [1967]. *Of Other Spaces.* http://foucault.info/documents/heteroTopia/foucault.heteroTopia.en.html (accessed 10 April 2009).

Gąsiorek, Andrzej. 2005. *J. G. Ballard, Contemporary British Novelists.* Manchester: Manchester University Press.

Litt, Toby. 2008. Foreword. In *J. G. Ballard*, ed. by J. Baxter. London: Continuum.

McKeown, Cormac. 2008. *Collins Dictionary*. Seventh edition. Glasgow: HarperCollins.

Sellars, Simon. 2009. *About.* http://www.ballardian.com/about (accessed 10 April 2009).

Chapter Sixteen

The Double Face of London: Crime and Space in *Oliver Twist* by Charles Dickens

Edyta Świerczyńska

In 1841, shortly after the first publication of *Oliver Twist*, the *Punch* magazine contained among its "Literary Recipes" some advice how to cook up "A Startling Romance":

> Take a small boy, charity, factory, carpenter's apprentice, or otherwise, as occasion may serve—stew him well down in vice—garnish largely with oaths and flash song—boil him in a cauldron of crime and improbabilities. Season equally with good and bad qualities—infuse petty larceny, affection, benevolence, and bulglary, honour and housebreaking, amibility and arson—boil all gently. Stew down a mad mother—a gang of robbers— several pistols—a bloody knife. Serve up with a couple of murders—and season with a hanging-match.
>
> N.B. Alter the ingredients to a beadle and a workhouse—the scenes may be the same, but the whole flavour of vice will be lost, and the boy will turn out a perfect pattern. Strongly recommended for weak stomachs. (Collins 1965, 257)

The poignant tone of this critique not only aimed at attacking the notorious Newgate School of Novelists, but also clearly pointed to Dickens's newest work as falling into the category of fiction glorifying the tradition of glamorous thieves and their "ladies", depicting the glitter and romance of the criminal underworld. However unsubstantiated and injurious such accusations seemed to Dickens, he nevertheless found it inevitable to defend himself from being so pigeonholed by providing "a few words of explanation of (his) aim and object" in the preface to the 1841 edition of *Oliver Twist*:

(...) It appeared to me to draw a knot of such associates in crime as really do exist; to paint them in all their deformity, in all their wretchedness, in all their squalid poverty of their lives; to show them as they really are, for ever skulting uneasily through the dirtiest paths of life, with the great, black ghastly gallows closing up their prospect, turn them where they may; it appeared to me that to do this, would be to attempt a something which was greatly needed, and which would be a service to society. (Collins 1965, 259)

Indeed, in defiance of all his critics, Dickens successfully depicted a gloomy and terrifying facet of crime, stripping "the most debased and vicious kind" of all their picturesqueness (Schor 2007, 20), most notably by means of space presentation, investing the criminal domains and territories with the prevailing infernal qualities accompanied by decay, rottenness and dirt. At first glance the poetics of space in *Oliver Twist* does not significantly differ from Dickens's later novels- *The Old Curiosity Shop* with its *leitmotif* of the innocent's wanderings through the metropolis and the country, *Little Dorrit*'s desperate and futile attempt to escape the evils of immersion in physical and imaginary imprisonment, or *Martin Chuzzlewit*'s ubiquitous premonition of danger lurking around the corner. However, the very structural syncretism of spatial imagery renders *Oliver Twist* a paragon of Dickens's strength in orderly arranging idiosyncratic symbols around a polarised pattern characteristic of the novel's urban space. Hence, London's heterogeneity appears in its dualism, with contrastive spatial representations confronted in the course of the narrative; the most prominent symbol of this polarisation is the clear demarcation line between the "respectable" London and "underworld" London – West End and East End respectively, with bridges serving as intransgressible borders separating the two. Such a treatment of urban space allows for arbitrary valuation of distinct city facets and hence facilitates the analysis of intricate relations between the city's topography and the nature of crime. However, this dualism is manifested not only on the obvious horizontal level; more importantly, the boundaries between two cities within a city are also delineated on the vertical level, with the aboveground and underground invested with prominent symbols of this peculiar two-fold binary opposition. Hence, apart from the east-west division, there emerges a picture of the world existing under the level of the metropolitan ground, a dimension the more mysterious as it is hidden from the Londoners' eyes. On the surface, the criminal London does not come into collision with its "respectable" double, guided by the same laws of society and nature: throughout the novel criminal acts are referred to as "trade" or "business", and night seemingly operates as a check to the daily bustle of the entire metropolis:

> Midnight had come upon the crowded city. The palace, the night-cellar, the jail (...) midnight was upon them all. (Dickens 2000, 301)

However, it is under cover of darkness that wickedness is performed; night seems to be the natural element for Fagin and his gang who crawl out from their underground hideouts into the open space of the city only when they cannot be observed and thus personalised. Respectable and criminal "cities" cannot coexist in one space and time, and hence the outcasts are driven to the *under*world, the domain of night[1]:

> Dark and heavy it is, too. A good night for business this. (Dickens 2000, 293)

> The Jew was evidently too familiar with the ground he traversed, however, to be at all bewildered, either by the darkness or by the intricacies of the way. (Dickens 2000, 121)

Interestingly, darkness awakens the labyrinthine quality of the city which in the daylight does not seem hostile or confusing. After dusk the streets, turnings, narrow courts and passages acquire the character of maze, rendering the city a natural ally of criminals who not only seem perfectly acquainted with its topography, but also take advantage of its labyrinthine potential which contributes not only to the city dynamics, but also to its mysterious, gothic qualities. The metropolis shelters outcasts and their proceedings – it is only too telling that every time when Oliver is led to Fagin's or Sikes's "kens" he is escorted under the cover of darkness by the most complicated routes:

> Darkness had set in; it was a low neighbourhood; no help was near; resistance was useless. In another moment he was dragged into a labyrinth of dark narrow courts, and forced along them at a pace which rendered the few cries he dared to give utterance to wholly unintelligible. (Dickens 2000, 96)
> (...) their course indeed being rather to lengthen the distance by various circumlocutions and discursive staggerings like unto those which drunken men (...) are prone to indulge. (...) It was not until the two boys

---

[1] As they are creatures of the underground, it is only natural that the criminals frequently refer to one another as "rats".

hadscoured, with great rapidity, through a most intricate maze of narrow streets and courts, that they ventured to halt. (Dickens 2000, 76)

Oliver is confused and deprived of the sense of directions not only by the horizonless sky characteristic of every city (Bachelard 1994, 27), but mainly by the vastness and intricacy of urban space; having lost his way in Clarkenwell, the boy lost his chance of escaping the gang; as he does not belong to the underworld, the hero is discarded and left unaided by the metropolis. It is also the place of Oliver's losing his identity as a result of his displacement; hence on the very onset of his London adventures the hero has become a nuisance to the metropolis which in this case shows a truly human trait of disinterested malice. For criminals, in contrast, the streets provide a living and replace the walls of a safe home; although they do not dare assume their true form in the broad daylight or transgress the tacit border separating East and West Ends, they still unconsciously perceive London as their safest hideout. As if acting according to Weber's philosophy stadtluft macht frei (Rewers 2005, 5), the thief Noah Claypole seeks refuge within the boundaries of the capital; this is also the case with Sikes who, having murdered Nancy, decides to return to London; after Fagin is arrested Charley Bates, Toby Crackit and Mr. Chitling all remain—quite unreasonably—on Jacob's Island. Interestingly, the criminals always avoid crowds and open spaces, not to mention police or prison neighbourhoods[2]; their "kens" are located either between hills (Field Lane) or surrounded by water (Jacob's Island), representing self-sufficient towns in miniature, "colonies" or "emporiums". They feel safe only in the districts inhabited or frequented by other outcasts, which are referred to as their "element", as if criminals and their allotted space constituted one substance:

> Here he (Fagin) walked even faster than before; nor did he linger until he had again turned into a court, when, as if conscious that he was now in his proper element, he fell into his usual shuffling pace, and seemed to breathe more freely. (Dickens 2000, 161)

Ironically, the belief in the unrelenting protective quality of the city proves illusory as the mere death of one girl shatters to pieces the intricate structure of the underworld, rendering even the most crowded slum area

---

[2] Although the members of Fagin's gang avoid approaching or directly naming the locations of prisons or "traps" stations, they are well aquainted with the proceedings and anatomy of Newgate: Mr. Dawkins (otherwise the Artful Dodger) frequently amuses himself by drawing a ground-plan of the prison on the table with a piece of chalk.

and source of cholera epidemic an unsafe and no longer anonymous hideout. Hence, the dialectics of the city manifest itself in an interplay of contradictory forces, a paradoxical struggle between the false sense of safety on the part of the criminals and parallel rejection of the immaculately innocent protagonist. In this way, the city gains not only the status of a battlefield, but also becomes a reasoning entity itself, controlling the fate of its inhabitants. Such a construct ceases to be a flexible, easily moulded substance in the hands of Fagin and his gang; it eventually manifests its independence and strength by gradually limiting the antagonists' range of movement, allowing them fewer and fewer places of refuge (invariably of the closed character) in the course of the narrative, only to deprive the criminals of their last resort in the climactic scene ending with Sikes's horrifying death. Such a presentation of ever-shrinking urban space, along with the closed and limited dimension of the underworld creates the atmosphere of oppression; even the sole open space familiar and inviting to Fagin's gang, Smithfield, the London's most famous cattle market, is a place where animals are slaughtered and sold on the spot (Lynch 1986, 129). Sikes feels at ease and slackens his pace after reaching the market, what bespeaks not only his dehumanised, animal-like personality, but also the inevitability of fate, "living within the shadow of the gallows itself" (Dickens 2000, 262). Paradoxically, Smithfield is located in the close proximity not only of St Paul's Cathedral, but also of Newgate where public executions took place; the narrative of Oliver Twist abunds in parallels drawn between the situation of the condemned and slaughtered animals, most prominently on the level of discourse; Fagin in his cell asks bitterly:

Strike them all dead! What right have they to butcher me? (Dickens 2000, 354)

Sikes expresses no sympathy with "fine young chaps" who, like cattle in Smithfield, are publicly "butchered":

Well, they're as good as dead, so it don't much matter. (Dickens 2000, 99)

Hence, it is not only space, but also discourse that bespeaks the characters' personality or situation: Fagin is shown as a "butchered" animal, Sikes—as a dehumanised creature. In Nancy's case, it is her place of origin that defines and invests her with identity, rather than discourse which does not reveal her as a streetwalker on the onset of the narrative. Instead of being informed that Nancy is a prostitute, the reader is presented with a passing mention of "remote but genteel suburb of Radcliffe" (Dickens 2000, 81) as her former place of residence. The phrase not only fails to serve its fundamental informative function, but it also misleads the reader by adopting formal vocabulary suggesting Nancy's respectable character; after all, it may be argued that she merely inhabited the district. However, if the same passage was analysed in terms of space symbolism, the reader would notice that Ratcliffe was notorious for its numerous brothels and streetwalkers. Hence it is space that endows Nancy with the character of prostitute, although the text remains neutral.

The figure of Jezebel plays the key function in the analysis of the symbolic dichotomy of city imagery; it is Nancy who brings the "respectable" and criminal Londons into contact by attempting to transgress the border between its West and East Ends. However, she never manages to cross the bridge and thus symbolically rejoin society. London Bridge stands for an extended border (but also, as all bridges, acts as a connection) on which the two worlds can meet but never mix. With her attempts at transgressing and constant occupation of walking, Nancy represents the most active character in Oliver Twist and it seems only natural that it is she who represents the underworld in the clash with the Westenders whose constantly passive attitude prevents the reader from becoming acquainted with the brighter facet of London. On the contrary— instead of representing the counterbalance to the underworld, the respectable characters offer yet another glimpse at Nancy's "home":

> Come. I would not have you go back (...) or take one look at any old haunt, or breathe the very air which is pestilence and death to you. (Dickens 2000, 306-307)

However, the girl is incapable of betraying and leaving her companions; this false sense of loyalty will cost her life:

> (...) never from the first moment I can recollect my eyes and senses opening on London streets have known any better life, or kinder words than they have given me, so help me God!(...) the alley and the gutter (...) will be my death-bed. (Dickens 2000, 263)

Convinced that her fate is sealed, Nancy realizes the myth of Persephone abducted and deceived by Hades—she has already eaten the seeds of Hades's pomegranate by voluntarily taking part in criminal proceedings, and thus has been chained to the underworld, both literally and metaphorically. Indeed, the criminal underworld resembles the inferno (or the world of the dead) in many respects. Constantly referred to as "devil", "the old'un", or "evil spirit", Fagin stands for the prince of darkness (or Hades); his emergency hideout, "the infernal hole" (Dickens

2000, 257) is located in the underground, and his face many a time "wrinkled into an expression of villainly perfectly demonical" (Dickens 2000, 124). Resembling Satan, the Jew is not satisfied with appropriating Nancy; when the girl's mysterious behaviour awakens his suspicions, Fagin wonders:

> How (...) can I increase my influence with her? What new power can I acquire? (Dickens 2000, 296)

Similarily to Persephone who found Hades irresistible, Nancy's attraction towards both Sikes and Fagin bears all the hallmarks of love and devotion, although she is aware of the coming destruction:

> (...) bitter as were her feelings toward the Jew, who had led her, step by step, deeper and deeper down into an abyss of crime and misery whence was no escape... (Dickens 2000, 292)

Hence, the closed space of the criminal world not only represents Oliver's literal imprisonment, but also the girl's metaphorical confinement to the "other" London. The final proof of Nancy's belonging to the *under*ground, both literal and symbolic, is delivered by Sikes who, returning to London after the murder, enquires about the girl's funeral. As his companions inform him that no funeral has yet taken place, Sikes's comment reveals his assurance of the undeworld's appropriating the girl as its natural element:

> Wot do they keep such ugly things above the ground for? (Dickens 2000, 333)

This passage acts as a strong reminder of a two-fold nature; Sikes expresses his belief in Nancy's being an inseparable element not only of the criminal world, but also of the world of the dead, both of which bear the common name of the underground. In this sense, these two domains merge and constitute one dimension, and hence all who belong there appear dead to society as outcasts or renegades. At this point it can be noticed that the ontological status of urban space involves underlying interconnections existing between the spheres of criminals, cemetery and prison on the one hand, and the sphere of the "respectable" society on the other.

Many critics have pointed to the intricate relations between the "parish boy's progress" and "harlot's progress" whose lives are constantly interwoven in the course of the narrative (Schor 2007, 20-27). However, this interrelation acquires even deeper meaning when investigated within the frames of time reference. Nancy represents the extended potential future awaiting the innocent boy and thus solely dominates the second part of the novel; by the same token, Oliver's exposure to the temptations of criminal life can be read as a retrospect of the girl's past, virtually excluded from the earlier portion of the narrative. By sacrificing her life and, in fact, her innocence, Nancy is able to save Oliver's life, but proves helpless in preventing his appropriation by the underworld; as her own story reveals, no effort on the part of a benevolent persona suffices to save another from becoming an outcast. This can only be achieved by the hero's determination in defending himself from Fagin's influence; however, Oliver is not strong or even willing enough to resist the temptation; throughout the narrative he is presented as passive and weak, submissive to others and conveniently fainting in the critical moments of the plot. The hero is spared only by a happy coincidence, so typical of Dickens's love for the sentimental fairy tale convention in which the suffering innocence is rewarded and lives happily ever after. Hence Nancy, by no means an innocent (but still inseparable) part of the underworld, cannot appear in the novel's last chapter devoted to the bliss of living in the world *above* the ground, and this symbolic exclusion seems to be the strongest division line between the "respectable" society and urban criminal underground, more striking and deeper than the delineation of borders symbolised by any other spatial representations discussed above.

References

Bachelard, Gaston. 1994. *The Poetics of Space*. London: Beacon Press.

Collins, Philip. 1965. *Dickens and Crime*. London: Macmillan.

Dickens, Charles. 2000. *Oliver Twist*. Ware: Wordsworth Editions.

Lynch, Tony. 1986. *Dickens's England. A Traveller's Companion*. London: B. T. Batsford Ltd.

Rewers, Ewa. 2005. *Post-polis. Wstęp do filozofii ponowoczesnego miasta*. Kraków: Universitas.

Schor, Hilary M. 2007. *Dickens and the Daughter of the House*. New York: Cambridge University Press.

CHAPTER SEVENTEEN

THE WORLD OF DELIGHTFUL TOPSY-TURVYDOM: LAURENCE STERNE'S SPATIAL EXPERIMENTS IN *THE LIFE AND OPINIONS OF TRISTRAM SHANDY* (1759)

RYSZARD W. WOLNY

For 250 years, Laurence Sterne's renowned novel has been notorious for its multifarious illogicalities and nonsensical humour even though it has also been popularly admitted that its pointlessness is Sterne's point and the denial of fundamental logic it offered was a serious challenge to reason, which came as a particular shocker in the Age of Reason. Sterne's apparent craziness in crossing the boundaries of physicality has been reflected, for instance, in using closing for opening and the peculiar arrangement of words/worlds on the page or leaving empty space for the reader/narratee to fill in. Therefore, the aim of this paper is to disclose the novel's topsy-turvydom in relation to its experiments with space, fundamentally its own space understood as the space of the sheet(s) of paper that collectively come into making of a book.

The Life and Opinions of Tristram Shandy is an unusual novel in very many respects,

> [y]et Sterne's oddity is neither an accident nor mere perversity; it is the strategy of an inventive, thoughtful comic talent. His novel dismantles previous conventions of narrative, substituting baffling changes of perspective and a subjective, fragmentary psychological presence for the clear storyline and the reliable story-teller. It thus points the way to later experiments..., though not all of these would be conducted with that vein of good humour, delicate yet often dark, which runs so riddlingly through Sterne's work. (Ousby, ed. 949)

While speaking of Laurence Sterne's experiments with the formal structure of his book, it is good to bear in mind that the publication of Daniel Defoe's *Robinson Crusoe*—commonly regarded as the first English novel—came just 40 years earlier, thus *Tristram Shandy* should rather be considered as one of the possible solutions or suggestions of how the English novel is to be constructed. Apart from obvious affinities with Cervantes, particularly the second part of his *Don Quixote* (the genre-defying structure and the renowned "Cervantic humour" that his main characters possess: "[g]entle Spirit of sweetest humour, who erst did sit upon the easy pen of my beloved CERVANTES," 1985: 598), Rabelais (the opening sex scene) or Montaigne, the home influence will come from John Locke, the philosopher,

> whose *Essay concerning Human Understanding* seemed to Sterne 'a history-book... of what passes in man's own mind'. Throughout his work he parodies, with a virtuosity that has proved inimitable, the developing conventions of the still-new 'novel', and its problems in presenting reality, space, and time. His sharp wit, often sly and often salacious, is balanced by the affection and tolerance he displays towards the delights and absurdities of life. (Drabble, ed. 947)

Carter and McRae (1998) basically repeat the same, arguing that the novel seems "to parody the developing conventions of the novel as a genre, pointing up the absurdities, contradictions, and impossibilities of relating time, space, reality and relationships in linear form" (186), and add that "it was Sterne who took up Locke's ideas—on the relativity of time, on random association, on the nature of sensation—to break the newly set rules of novel writing, and to escape from the moral and social restrictions of the genre" (187). Laurence Sterne's experiments with the formal structure of the novel, then, led to a complete confusion in the readers who, particularly in the early decades of the shaping of the genre, were used to the classical Aristotelian structure consisting of the beginning, the middle and the end. It was also anticipated—very much as it is nowadays—that the author's preface (if there is one) should pre-face the book, i.e. introduce, foreword it, be a prologue, prelude. But that is not the case in *Tristram Shandy*. The spatial reshuffle is apparently attributed to the narrator/author having some spare time in Vol. III, Ch. 20 for author's preface:

> All my heroes are off my hands: – 'tis the first time I have had a moment to spare, —and I'll make use of it, and write my preface.
> THE
> AUTHOR'S PREFACE

No, I'll not say a word about it.—here it is;—in publishing it,—I have appealed to the world,—and to the world I leave it:—it must speak for itself.

All I know of the matter is,—when I sat down, my intent was to write a good book; and as far as the tenuity of my understanding would hold out,—a wise, aye, and a discreet, taking care only, as I went along, to put into it all the wit and the judgement (be it more or less) which the great author and the bestower of them had thought fit originally to give me, —so that, as your worship see, 'tis just as God pleases. (202)

The spatial shift within the whole composition of the book is attributed to time the author has got now to somehow start it properly and express his purpose. His words also indicate, among other things, that he has given a complete liberty to his characters ("All my heroes are off my hands"), enabling them to speak for themselves, thus contributing to what much later Mikhail Bakhtin called a polyphonic or dialogic novel (see Bakhtin's *The Problems of Dostoevsky's Novels*, 1929). The organization of the book's own space lies in the narrator's consciousness rather than anything else. Throughout the whole text of his novel, he explicitly questions Horace's concept of history as starting from *ab ovo*, saying that he will confine himself neither to his rules nor to any man's rules that ever lived, thus attempting to invent what we may nowadays refer to as Shandean logic, the logic of the unpredictable, the irrational, the nonsensical.

Believing in words' inadequacy or/and their inability of conveying the authorial "truths," Sterne, in Vol. VI, Ch. 38, offers a blank page, which is actually extended to an extra quarter of a page (pages 450-451), to the narratee so that he may fill it out with their mental construct of Widow Wadman:

To conceive this right,—call for pen and ink—here's paper ready to your hand. —Sit down, Sir, paint her to your own mind—as like your mistress as you can—as unlike your wife as your conscience will let you— 'tis all one to me—please but your own fancy in it. (450)

After the blank page, the narrator and the narratee are swapping their opinions in regards to what the latter has written (painted) in the blank page, the result of which is an entire integration of the narratee into the narration:

–   Was ever any thing in Nature so sweet!—so exquisite!
–   Then, dear Sir, how could my uncle Toby resist it?

> Thrice happy book! thou wilt have one page, at least, within thy covers,
> which MALICE will not blacken and which IGNORANCE cannot
> misrepresent. (452)

By this little ploy, which at the same time may seem to be self-defamatory and auto-destructive (malice and ignorance on the side of the author: the author is devoid of his *author*-ity), the narrator again changes the spatial dimensions of the book since he incorporates into his narration the element of the novel that is basically and fundamentally placed outside of it, that is the narratee. It is true, however, that the narration cannot go ahead without the cooperation of the so called narratee whom the narrator has in mind while constructing the narrative line, but, on the other hand, that sort of "cooperation" is essentially mental, not physical. Sterne, therefore, seems to be not only playing with his reader/narratee but also trying to reverse or mingle what we now may call the traditional roles assigned to both of them, thus making the dividing line between them to shift or vanish completely in the above-mentioned pages. Likewise, in Vol. VII, Ch. 37, the narrator leaves some space for the narratee to "swear his oaths" alongside him, but the blanks in Chapters 17, 18 and 19 of Volume IX are of a different character since their spatial function is rather to invite the narratee's (reader's) unspoken imagination than anything else. Ch. 17 finishes with the narrator's request to enter his country house in which lives a solitary life, outdoing Rousseau ("Let us go into the house," 591), and is followed by a blank. Then, Chapters 18 and 19 are blanks, too, and Ch. 20 starts with a series of asterisks separated from the text by two long dashes to indicate an innuendo, a hint or allusion of what might have happened before the narration was resumed:

> —You shall see the very place, Madam; said my uncle Toby.
> Mrs. Wadman blushed—looked towards the door—turned pale—blushed
> slightly again—recovered her natural colour—blushed worse than ever;
> which, for the sake of the unlearned reader, I translate thus—
> > *'L— d! I cannot look at it—*
> > *What would the world say if I looked at it?*
> > *I should drop down, if I looked at it—*
> > *I wish I could look at it—*
> > *There can be no sin in looking at it.*
> > *—I will look at.'*
> While all this was running through Mrs Wadman's imagination, my uncle
> Toby had risen from the sopha, and got to the other side of the parlour
> door, to give Trim an order about it in the passage. (594)

The chapter finishes with the continued play on it, that is to say, on "it," to prove how little communication can be maintained by words, how inefficient they appear to convey the unspeakable and that we need an extra space (a spare room) for imagination to walk in:

> —You shall lay your finger upon the place—said my uncle Toby.—I will not touch it, however, quoth Mrs Wadman to herself.
> This requires a second translation —it shews what little knowledge is got by mere words—we must go up to the first springs.
> Now in order to clear up the mist which hangs upon these three pages, I must endeavour to be as clear as possible myself.
> Rub your hands thrice across your foreheads—blow your noses—cleanse your emunctories—sneeze my good people!
> —God bless you—
> Now give me all the help you can. (594-595)

To counterbalance the blank pages, in Vol. I, Ch.12 the narrator offers the narratee two black pages to commemorate Yorick (61-2), which, in fact, are the two identical sides of the same sheet of paper, the same blackness: an extended, bottomless space of sorrow after the parson's death—technically being of a thickness of a sheet of paper—which may pass for a graphic representation of the sadness that is supposed to pervade the two pages; a slab of sorrow separating the deceased from the outside world—the metaphoric tomb cover (60):

> He lies buried in the corner of his church-yard, in the parish of—, under a plain marble slab, which his friend Eugenius, by leave of his executors, laid upon his grave, with no more than these three words of inscription, serving both for his epitaph and elegy,

> | Alas, poor YORICK! |
> | --- |

This boxed inscription seems to be an obvious sign of the writerly (written) text represented on the sheet of paper with all its evident spatial limits, while the unboxed one—repeated below—is supposed to represent the verbal, readerly text (60):

> Ten times a day has Yorick's ghost the consolation to hear his monumental inscription read over with such a variety of plaintive tones, as denote a general pity and esteem for him;—a foot-way crossing the church-yard close by the side of his grave,—not a passenger goes by without stopping to cast a look upon it,—and sighing as he walks on,

> Alas, poor YORICK!

The pages 233 and 234 are another spatial riddle. Not only do they interrupt the flow of the narration in Vol. III, Ch. 37, but also—because of their representation of the marble – they may serve as the two sides of the same coin, the dialogicity of the novel, the impenetrable character of the word: the signifier and the signified. Introducing the reader to them, the narrator commands:

> Read, read, read, read, my unlearned reader! read,—or by the knowledge of the great saint Paraleipomenon—I tell you beforehand, you had better throw down the book at once; for without *much reading*, by which your reverence knows, I mean *much knowledge*, you will no more be able to penetrate the moral of the next marbled page (motley emblem of my work!) than the world with all its sagacity has been able to unravel the many opinions, transactions, and truths which still lie hid under the dark veil of the black one. (232)

The metaphor of the marbled page (technically paginated as two) seems to be the right one for several reasons. In literal sense, the page breaks down the Latin sentence, starting on page 232 (*"'Nec est cur'"*) and finishing on 235 (*"paeniteat,'"*), into two parts, which – apart from the obvious difficulty caused by foreign words—serves also as an indicator of words' impenetrability, a shield protecting the truths of themselves and of the things they are supposed to convey:

> As the *dialogue* [emphasis added, R.W.] was of Erasmus, my father soon came to himself, and read it over and over again with great application, studying every word and every syllable of it through and through in its most strict and literal interpretation,—he could still make nothing of it, that way. Mayhaps there is more meant, than is said in it, quoth my father.— Learned men, brother Toby, don't write dialogues upon long noses for nothing.—I'll study the mystic and the allegoric sense,—here is some room to turn a man's self in, brother. (235)

The marbled page represents, in the narrator's words, "motley emblem of my work," which may be interpreted as a symbol of the text's diversity, complexity, impenetrability; a kind of a hard stone that separates the signifier from the signified, the reader from the meaning of the text. The marbled page is a mosaic of various, assorted, contrasting and dissimilar texts; at the simplest possible syntactic level—a combination of the blank (white) page and the black one, motley of meaning.

Whereas pointers used quite frequently by the narrator (the famous one illustrating the importance of experience gained in childhood, 131, or the one about Trim's posture, 139) have primarily a didactic role in the text, the line, as a spatial form, plays a significant role in the novel's construction. In, for instance, Vol. VI, Ch. 6, when the narrator feels he cannot narrate the story of the fever in a straightforward manner—that is, in a straight line—he addresses himself and the narratee, "Ask my pen,—it governs me,—I govern it not" (403), thus reducing himself to a mechanical hand or, to use a more contemporary expression, a typewriter if not a word processor. In Vol. III, Ch. 3, we are dealing with zig-zaggery—the diagonal movement of Tristram's father (173), while in Vol. IX, Ch. 4 we are shown the graphic representation of man's freedom exemplified by the movement of corporal's stick (576). In Vol. VI, Ch. 40, the narrator solemnly declares that:

> I am now beginning to get fairly into my work; and by the help of a vegitable [sic!] diet, with a few of the cold seeds, I make no doubt but I shall be able to go on with my uncle Toby's story, and my own, in a tolerable straight line. Now, [what follows is a sequence of four single zig-zagged lines, R.W.] These were the four lines I moved in through my first, second, third, and fourth volumes.—In the fifth volume I have been very good,—the precise line I have described in it being this: [again, a line with various curves marked with letters, R.W.] (453-454)

to finally arrive at a line

> which is drawn as straight as I could draw it, by a writing-master's ruler, (borrowed for that purpose) turning neither to the right hand or to the left. (454)

By mocking the statements by men of "wit and genius," the narrator ridicules straight-line narration in the belief that in nature nothing is straight and simple:

> This *right line*,—the path-way for Christians to walk in! say divines—
> —The emblem of moral rectitude! says Cicero—
> —The *best line!* say cabbage planters—is the shortest line, says Archimedes, which can be drawn from one given point to another.—
> I wish your ladyships would lay this matter to heart, in your nest birth-day suits!
> —What a journey!
> Pray can you tell me,—that is, without anger, before I write my chapter upon straight lines—by what mistake—who told them so—or how it has come to pass, that your men of wit and genius have all along confounded this line, with the line of GRAVITATION ? (454-455)

These and many other examples of various types of extra-textual devices convince us that the stories narrated by different narrators are not pursued in a straight line, but are crosscut with a plephora of non-narrative texts, detours, drawings, etc., and, as Sanders argues, "[e]verything – digressions, hiatuses, absences, lacunae, dashes, asterisks, and the famous black, blank, and marbled pages – is so co-productive of the novel's peculiar energy and essential to its questioning of meaning...*Tristram Shandy* suggests that all information is contingent, all interpretation relative" (318).

This brings us closer to a final statement that *The Life and Opinions of Tristram Shandy* is a constructed work: a "poetic" novel, a real "builder's" novel (from a definition of the poet as the maker, the doer), and the spatial experiments within its body only make it more "literary." Therefore, it may be conclusively stated that the common feature of all nine volumes is that none of them is complete in a conventional sense: they have hardly got a beginning and an end. They indicate the complex character of literary language, which is neither straightforward nor predictable. The many blanks, asterisks, understatements catch the reader's (narratee's) attention and extend an invitation to enter into a dialogue with the text. The spatial experiments Laurence Sterne carried out in his novel are, doubtless, unique. The book operates not only with words, but with graphics as well; therefore, a black page, a blank page, a marbled page, and drawings, like lines, serve to add up to the words and allow for the free game of associations, allusions, imagination. Functioning in the text, these devices *replace*, *misplace*, and *relocate* the words' meaning, leaving an extra space for the readers/narratees to contribute towards the novel's final structure.

References

Carter, Ronald and John McRae. 1998. *The Routledge History of Literature in English*. London: Routledge.

Drabble, Margaret (ed.). 1996. *The Oxford Companion to English Literature*. Oxford: Oxford University Press.

Ousby, Ian (ed.). 1988. *The Cambridge Guide to Literature in English*. Cambridge: Cambridge University Press.

Sanders, Andrew. 2000. *The Short Oxford History of English Literature*. Second edition. London: Oxford University Press.

Sterne, Laurence. 1985. *The Life and Opinions of Tristram Shandy*. London: Penguin Classics.

CHAPTER EIGHTEEN

REPRESENTATIONS OF SPACE IN AMERICAN GOTHIC FICTION: THE EXAMPLE OF CHARLES BROCKDEN BROWN

DAGMARA ZAJĄC

Charles Olson, the founder of the field of American studies, begins his epochal essay on Melville with these words: "I take SPACE to be the central fact to man born in America, from Folsom Cave to now. I spell it large because it comes large here. Large, and without mercy" (Olson 1967, 3). The emphasis represents a profound preoccupation with Space, which has become an integral part of the United States culture. I believe that American Gothic fiction is a genre in which this preoccupation is symbolically realized on multiple levels of representation.

Interestingly enough, while trying to define the Gothic as a literary entity, scholars and critics frequently reach for spatial metaphors that refer to the genre's haunted locales. For instance, in his introduction to *The Gothic*, Fred Botting writes: "The re-evaluation of Gothic productions over the ages manifests a curious dynamic of expulsion and assimilation, denigration and celebration: from being *the dark underside* of suppressed elements and energies, the genre has moved *from the shadows* and into the spotlight" (Botting 2001, 4; my emphasis). Another example may be a statement by David Oakes: "In many ways, the United States proved to be a perfect *spawning ground* for Gothic fiction" (Oakes 200, 6; my emphasis).

What I intend to discuss is the importance of Space in American Gothic and the two levels of its representation. First of all, Space will be considered as landscape and scenery: the central point here is adapting the genre for American setting. Another aspect, which is social Space, is strongly connected to the first one. On both levels mentioned, American

Gothic fiction reveals what we may describe as the forgotten, the repressed, the uncomfortable.

Most definitions of the genre, found in encyclopedias as well as in specialized dictionaries, emphasize the importance of the haunted castle as the most prominent and common element of Gothic literature[1]. In his 1927 study *The Haunted Castle*, Eino Railo argues that the castle serves as "scene of innumerable horrors, capable of touching the imagination each time we see it" (7). Like many other critics, Railo is convinced that the haunted castle plays an immensely important role in Gothic fiction, and without it "the whole fabric of romance would be bereft of its foundation and would lose its predominant atmosphere" (8). The significance of this element comes, in part, from the connection of the term "Gothic" with architecture in the eighteenth century. Most of the earliest works of Gothic literature, including Walpole's *The Castle of Otranto*, are set in the Middle Ages and therefore utilize a castle as the setting for the events of the story.

As David Oakes rightly points out in his *Science and Destabilization in Modern American Gothic*, "The writers of British Gothic fiction could draw on a long history and tradition for their works, enabling them to set their works in the Middle Ages or the Renaissance" (Oakes 2000, 6). The United States does not possess such a long history as a social unit, so writers of American Gothic fiction had to find a way of compensating for that fact when adapting the Gothic form to American setting. The haunted castle had to be replaced with other locations that would evoke the disturbing atmosphere, which is essential to the convention as the genre's constitutive feature.

The author responsible for "Americanizing" the Gothic is Charles Brockden Brown. Oakes argues that the strategy of the author of *Wieland* consisted in "imbuing the ancient forests and natural settings prevalent in nineteenth-century America with the same immense antiquity found in European castles" (2000, 6). In other words, according to Oakes, Brown simply transforms the haunted castle into a wilderness, "a realm of spirits and fantastic events" (2000, 5). Nevertheless, it may be argued that Brown's adapting of the Gothic form was in fact a process much more complex, having to do with the complexities inherent in the "American setting" itself.

What escapes the attention of David Oakes is well described by Ezra Tawil in his essay *"New Forms of Sublimity": Edgar Huntly and the*

---

[1] e.g. Microsoft Corporation. "Gothic Novel." *Microsoft Encarta.*
http://encarta.msn.com/encyclopedia_761553321/Gothic_Novel.html,
Sucur, Slobodan. "Gothic Literature." *The Literary Encyclopedia.*
http://www.litencyc.com/php/stopics.php?rec=true&UID=1216.

European Origins of American Exeptionalism. First of all, Tawil draws our attention to what he describes as "Brown's quest for an indigenous literature" (Tawil 2006, 106). In other words, the author of *Wieland* was consciously seeking to establish a distinctly American literary mode. In a 1978 prospectus for his novel *Sky Walk*, Brown announces the forthcoming publication of "a tale that may rival the performances of this kind which have lately issued from the English press" and one that "will be unexampled in America" (Brown 1859, 3).

Brown keeps referring to those terms throughout the advertisement, as if attempting to claim at once a kinship with English forms—through adapting the Gothic form—and at the same time trying to assert some kind of "native" originality: "To the story-telling moralist, the United States is a new and untrodden field. He who shall examine objects with his own eyes, who shall employ the European models merely for the improvement of his taste, and adapt his fiction to all that is genuine and peculiar in the scenes before him, will be entitled at least to the praise of originality" (Brown 1859, 5).

To achieve this originality, Brown is "using putatively distinctive features of an American landscape to announce the arrival of a distinctively American literature" (Tawil 2006, 111). For example, in *Edgar Huntly* the land provides a natural labyrinth which not only assists, but makes possible the madman Clithero's concealment: "The track into which he now led me was different from the former one. It was a maze, oblique, circuitous, upward and downward, in a degree which only could take place in a region so remarkably irregular in surface, so abounding with hillocks and steeps, and pits and brooks as Solebury" (Brown 1859, 23).

Nevertheless, Brown's use of Gothic locales is not limited to merely substituting one type of setting—the haunted castle—with another location, namely the American wilderness. Tawil argues that we should take a more literal reading of Brown's stated aesthetic goal, "to exhibit a series of adventures, growing out of the condition of our country" (Brown, 1859, 3). Instead of understanding the statement in connection to political and social circumstances, "the condition of the country" might be interpreted as referring quite specifically to certain geographical and topographical features of the New Republic (Tawil 2006, 114). In *Edgar Huntly*, as well as in *Wieland*, which is not discussed by Tawil, the landscape provides the material conditions of possibility of the Gothic plot elements Brown uses to produce readerly pleasure. "In this respect, geography is not merely significant; it is determinative and generative. Thus the preface's peculiar assertion that the book is 'growing out of the conditions of our country' turns out to designate quite perfectly the fantasy of an autochthonous literature in the literal sense of the term: one growing out of the earth itself. The American landscape doesn't only inspire, it effectively authors an American literature" (Tawil 2006, 115).

This "American landscape" obviously differs in many respects from the one depicted by British Gothic. Tawil discusses those differences in detail: Brown frequently employs rural settings—*Wieland, Edgar Huntly,* and the first section of the *Memoirs of Carwin the Biloquist* are all located in the "rude precincts" of Pennsylvania, as the author repeatedly emphasizes the same set of natural features. Rather than cultivated landscapes, these are wilderness settings:

> Brown's America is evidently a place of extremity and verticality, abounding in cliffs and cataracts, which repeatedly subjects inhabitants or visitors to dizzying ascents and precipitous declivities. Just as importantly, it is also a land of negative spaces scooped out of the landscape in a kind of reverse relief: a topography carved with caverns, cavities, recesses, hollows, and chasms, to name just a few of the most frequently repeated ones. These features make up a particularly American type of wilderness supposed to be distinct from typically British uncultivated spaces such as the heath, the moor, or the fen. (Tawil 2006, 116)

Nevertheless, the most important difference is the fact that the British novels were, almost without exception[2], set in foreign locales—that is, in places marked foreign to their authors and intended readership. This predilection of the British authors, such as Walpole and Radcliffe, for mainly European settings, results from the association of "ignorance, violence, and transgressive excess with the residual spaces of semi-feudal, Catholic, and outlying Europe" (Tawil 2006, 117). The important point made by Tawil is that, for nearly all British productions in the genre, "Gothic" events take place, as if by a formal necessity, in foreign settings. The Gothic is by definition supposed to reside *elsewhere*: as a consequence, the readerly pleasure is derived from observing the foreign and exotic—from the vantage point of the domestic and familiar.

The unprecedented situation which results from Brown's setting the Gothic "here and now" is connected with the relation to his implied American reader, who is situated in the same zone as Brown's fictional madmen and antiheroes. For the first time, the Gothic is "brought home." In Tawil's essay, this collapsing of the distance between the reader and the

---

[2] The two most prominent examples of British gothic novels with an English setting, Clara Reeve's *The Old English Baron: A Gothic Story* (1777) and Sophia Lee's *The Recess, or, A Tale of Other Times* (1783) substituted the distance in space with the distance in time in defamiliarizing their fictional worlds.

story-world is analyzed in mainly aesthetical context. Nevertheless, it may be argued that the complex relationship between Gothic narrative space and American Space as such goes beyond the realm of aesthetics.

When the first settlers arrived in the New World, America was still a mysterious, largely unexplored land—a kind of *Neotopia*. The history of Puritan settlement and the subsequent territorial expansion is inevitably connected with what we might call "the national mythology": The United States of America was indeed established on the foundations of optimism and progress. The new country promised the new beginning for a multitude of people, offering an escape from "moribund and oppressive societies in Europe" (Oakes 2000, 6). The New Republic, ideally, offered its citizens an opportunity to pursue their own dreams to the best of their ability—in this way the American *Neotopia* was to be transformed into a universal *Utopia*.

In order for this transformation to take place, the land itself had to be transformed so as to accommodate its new inhabitants. The American settler as well as the American pioneer, whether escaping religious persecution or simply trying to build a home for himself, was invariably seeking to create a "Space of safety." Some of the first settlers imagined themselves to be returning to the bower of paradise. Others saw themselves as bringing Christian redemption to the pagan land. They all shared a belief that they had embarked on what Perry Miller called an "errand into the wilderness," in order to create an improved Christian community.

Nevertheless, The New Land turned out to be a place quite different than the envisaged Paradise on Earth. The settlers had to face multiple dangers, ranging from hardships of climate, through wild animals, to the menacing character of the savage and bloodthirsty Indian. The conquest and rational ordering of this truly "Gothic" Space was the priority: the Nature needed to be subdued. First of all, the land had to be *acquired*—the Native Americans had to be swept aside and the woods had to be cleared. Eventually, the industrial society replaced landscape with technoscape, as the face of the land was entirely transformed.

In *Foundational Space/ Technological Narrative,* David E. Nye refers to the concept of a "fundamental narrative," which every society must construct in order "to make sense of its existence" (2003, 119). Basically, it may be described as a story that explains how a people came to live in a particular place and legitimates their presence there. As far as the United States are considered, the fundamental narrative is revealed through "frontier stories" and early forms of journalism. Nye points out that these stories rarely mention the original inhabitants as they usually present the

New World as an uninhabited region. In such foundation stories, "an unknown and unused abstract space is transformed into a technologically defined place" (120). Nye defines this kind of fundamental story as "the technological foundation narrative" (121). In the American beginning, towards the end of the eighteenth century, the former colonies "re-imagined themselves as self-created community" (120). The author proposes the term "second creation[3]" by means of technology as a phrase to describe the American story of origins[4].

In spite of all the optimism inherent in this fundamental narrative, one is aware that it does not tell the whole story. The transformation of the New Land was not as *constructive* as the technological foundation narrative would have it; as a matter of fact, it was rather *destructive*. In the process of the second creation, the American Space was violated. The accurate description of this abuse and violence is provided, for instance, by Robin Morris Collin and Robert W. Collin:

> The history of environmental injustice in the United States can be traced back to the colonization efforts of Western European Nations. Before their arrival, the North American continent was sparsely populated with other humans, and ecosystems flourished. As the Colonialists and subsequent settlers searched for natural resources, the land, lives, and livelihoods of indigenous peoples were taken and often destroyed. Natural resources were transformed into the commodities of a newly global trade, and the people themselves were converted to labor commodities as colonies began to use slaves to provide labor to grow agricultural commodities such as indigo, rice, cotton and tobacco. This was the beginning of the extract, consume and pollute economies that continue to devastate poor and indigenous peoples and ecologies throughout the world. (2005, 139-140)

In other words, the settlers had left behind the terror of Europe only to experience new and special guilts associated with the rape of nature and the exploitation of the indigenous as well as black people (Fiedler 1966, 31). Although those guilts were absent from the foundation narrative, as well as from dominant ideology as a whole, they could not be made to disappear. They were merely repressed, haunting the generations to come. At the same time, the pervasive optimism did not go unchallenged in literature.

---

[3] As opposed to God's first creation, but in perfect harmony with it at the same time.
[4] Nye analyzes the technological foundation narrative in detail. He argues that the numerous stories contain similar elements that unfold in a specific sequence.

In this particular context, American Gothic fiction acquires a very special function: a function which many critics perceive as fundamental for the entire genre. As Leslie Fiedler points out in his influential study, the Gothic serves as a mirror of "darkness and the grotesque in a land of light and affirmation" (1966, 29). In other words, it destabilizes the reader by problematizing the comfortable, given readings of the world, which usually consists in disputing the cherished national ideologies. It does so by expressing the views of suppressed or marginalized groups, capitalizing on the fear of the outsider, or those who differ from accepted societal norms. Perhaps such an approach to Gothic is best summarized in the statement made by Margaret Anne Doody: she describes the gothic novel as "a momentous invention first wrought by women and homosexuals who could not be happy with the conceptual 'reality' on which domesticated Realism was founded" (1997, 294).

The American Gothic's preoccupation with Space is thus manifested on a deeper, symbolic level: Julia Kristeva has linked the cultural impulse behind the gothic mode to the psychic process of abjection, the "throwing-off" of unacceptable psychic contents or threatening social contradictions onto ghostly or grotesque figures (Kristeva 1982, 17-55). This monstrous Other plays an important role: what the dominant culture cannot incorporate within itself, it must project outward onto this hateful creature[5]. What is worth emphasizing is the fact that the very idea of abjection has to be understood and explained in the context of (metaphorical) Space, since inside and outside are key terms to the concept: the subject emerges as a subject only after the opposition of *I— not I* is realized.

In her study of abjection, *Powers of Horror*, Kristeva associates "dung, guts, and blood", as well as other forms of bodily effluvia, with the kinds of processes that are at work in Gothic fiction. The matter that is detached, produced, and corrupted by the body are all signs of abject identification. "Excrement and its equivalents", she says, "(decay, infection, disease, corpse, etc.), stand for the danger to identity that comes from without: the ego threatened by the non-ego, society threatened by its outside, life by death" (1982, 22). The abject is therefore connected to idea of *removing* something or someone from the personal Space of the subject: it is linked to an act of repression. The abject experience brings out the repressed: in literature, it may be represented as the *return* of the marginalized groups of society.

---

[5] Many critics wrote about the relationship between the Gothic and the abject: see for instance Gross, L. 1989. *Redefining the American Gothic*. Ann Arbor: UMI Research.

The American Gothic, frequently marginalized as a genre itself, continued to reveal "the gaping hole between appearance and reality" (Goddu 1997, 48) also in the nineteenth and twentieth century. The eerie locales of Charles Brockden Brown were gradually replaced by deserted cities, lunatic asylums, and even haunted spaceships in Stephen King's writing. The ambitious project of establishing a "Space of safety" in America fell through, as the city turned out to be a place as dark and dangerous as the wilderness.

Nevertheless, Space still remains the key concept in the contemporary, post-Gothic writing. It can manifest itself as an uncanny metaphor in King's *Trucks*: the area familiar to the reader—a truck shop—is transformed into a haunted castle where a few representatives of a vanished civilization struggle to maintain their fortress against a new order that threatens to crush them. It can be realized as the social space, this disturbing realm in which the "patriarchal scheme of heterosexuality" (Jarraway 2000, 17) becomes the death of a teenager, as it happens in Jim Grimsley's *Dream Boy*. Finally, it may manifest itself at the most intimate level: in American Gothic, "the incomprehensible is first and foremost the deep recesses of the self, the unacknowledged personal motivations that come under the rubric of the conscience" (Wald 1995, 2). The characters populating American Gothic novels represent abjection in Kristeva's sense, as the disturbing continuum established between internal and external spaces threatens the very boundaries of the body.

To sum up: there is much more to American Gothic than a simple shift of scenery. The authors ranging from Charles Brockden Brown to Stephen King make use of Space on multiple levels in order to make possible the return of the repressed, the marginalized, the abjected, the othered.

References

Bachelard, Gaston. 1994. *The Poetics of Space*. Boston: Beacon Press.
Botting, Fred. 2001. *The Gothic*. Cambridge: D. S. Brewer.
Brown, Charles Brockden. 1859. *The Novels of Charles Brockden Brown: Consisting of Wieland; or, The Transformation. Arthur Mervyn; Or, Memoirs of the Year 1793. Edgar Huntly; Or, Memoirs of a Sleepwalker. Jane Talbot. Ormond; Or, The Secret Witness. Clara Howard; Or, The Enthusiasm of Love. With a Memoir of the Author.* Philadelphia: B. Lippincot & Co.
Collin, Robin Morris and Robert W. Collin. 2005. Waste and Race. An Introduction to Sustainability and Equity. In *Space in America:*

Theory, History, Culture, ed. by K. Benesch, 139-152. Rodopi: Kerstin Schmidt.

Doody, Margaret Anne. 1996. *The True Story of the Novel*. New York: Rutgers University Press.

Fiedler, Leslie Aaron. 1966. *Love and Death in the American Novel*. New York: Stein and Day.

Goddu, Theresa A. 1997. *Gothic America: Narrative, History, and Nation*. New York: Columbia University Press.

Jarraway, David R. 2000. Divided Moment 'Yet' One Flesh. *Gothic Studies* 2 (1): 90.

Kristeva, Julia. 1982. *Powers of Horror: An Essay on Abjection*. New York: Columbia University Press.

Miller, Perry. 1978. *Errand into the Wilderness*. Harvard: Harvard University Press.

Nye, David E. 2003. *America as Second Creation: Technology and Narratives of New Beginnings*. Cambridge, MA: MIT Press.

Oakes, David. 2000. *Science and Destabilization in Modern American Gothic: Lovecraft, Matheson and King*. Westport, CT: Greenwood Press.

Olson, Charles. 1967. *Call Me Ishmael*. Boston: City Lights Books.

Railo, Eino. 2003. *The Haunted Castle: A Study of the Elements of English Romanticism*. New York: Kessinger Publishing.

Tawil, Ezra. 2006. "New Forms of Sublimity": *Edgar Huntly* and the European Origins of American Exceptionalism. *Novel: A Forum on Fiction* 40 (1/2): 104-124.

Wald, Priscilla. 1995. *Constituting Americans: Cultural Anxiety and Narrative Form*. Durham: Duke University Press.

PART III:

METAPHORICITY OF SPACE IN POETRY

CHAPTER NINETEEN

"THE BREAKDOWN OF BELFAST": CIARAN CARSON'S URBAN POETICS OF SPACE

GRZEGORZ CZEMIEL

His passion and his profession is to merge with the crowd. For the perfect idler, for the passionate observer it becomes an immense source of enjoyment to establish his dwelling in the throng, in the ebb and flow, the bustle, the fleeting and the infinite. (Baudelaire 1972, 317)

The famous definition of a *flâneur* given by Baudelaire in the *The Painter of Modern Life* has become the ground for the definition of the experience of modernity. It is to this day seen as an accurate diagnosis of the epistemological value of the city both to the ordinary passer-by and to the artist. A sense of immersion in the fabric of the city, its everyday life and its catastrophes is also a recurring motif in the poetry of Ciaran Carson, a Northern Irish poet and writer, born in 1948.

Belfast, the home town of Carson, is omnipresent in his work. It serves him not only as the source material for his poems, but also as a literary vehicle for presenting his ideas about the issues that have been at the heart of post-war Northern Irish poetry during the last decades, i.e. identity, violence and history. Carson's poems are not photography-like snapshots which capture Belfast at a specific moment. His poems freely merge the childhood memories of the 1950s and contemporary times, which results in a certain blurring of time boundaries. Even the riots and outbursts of violence usually bear no marks of time. Belfast is unstable and metamorphic.

For Belfast is changing daily: one day the massive Victorian façade of the Grand Central Hotel [...] is *there*, dominating the whole of Royal Avenue; the next day it is gone. [...] Everything will be revised. (Carson 1989, 57)

Although Carson pays great attention to detail and is an extremely close and careful observer, his Belfast is always on the move and escapes fixity.

Trying to focus on the imagined grey area between Smithfield and North Street [...] I catch glimpses of what might have been, but it already blurs and fades; I wake or fall into another dream. (Carson 1989, 66)

Carson is basically an anti-essentialist thinker and consequently his vision of Belfast is a dispersed one. The city itself always regresses in infinity beyond our scope of investigation.

In terms of space, Carson is acutely aware of the fact that it is impossible to totalize and enclose the city in a birds-eye view. Rather than stepping into the role of a detached observer, Carson follows Baudelaire and adopts an attitude of active participation. His urban poetics is not objective in the traditional sense, but rather purely subjective. He lives the city, always placing himself at the very centre of events, merging elements of autobiography and geography, mixing facts with untrustworthy, second-hand narratives. He allows himself to be guided by the peculiar logic of Belfast rather than by rationality. His experience of the city is continuous—information is not sorted, except for the organization of the poem. In this way, he forms a model of a lyrical I that merges with the crowd and incorporates the city, transgressing the boundary between himself as the subject and the city as an object.

Thus, Carson elevates the city to the level of a subject which speaks to us in its own language through poetry. It has its own personal traumatic history and deserves a psychological treatment rather than a topographical one. This tension is clearly developed in the theme of the map.

Jorge Luis Borges sums this issue aptly in his short prose piece "On Exactitude in Science":

In that Empire, the Art of Cartography attained such Perfection that the map of a single Province occupied the entirety of a City, and the map of the Empire, the entirety of a Province. In time, those Unconscionable Maps no longer satisfied, and the Cartographers Guilds struck a Map of the Empire whose size was that of the Empire, and which coincided point for point with it. The following Generations, who were not so fond of the Study of Cartography as their Forebears had been, saw that that vast Map was Useless [...]. (Borges 1999, 34)

No, don't trust maps, for they avoid the moment: ramps, barricades, diversions, Peace Lines. Though if there is an ideal map, which shows this city as it is, it may exist in the eye of that helicopter ratcheting overhead, its searchlight fingering and scanning [...]. (Carson 1989, 58)

The city is a map of the city. (Carson 1989, 69)

Maps are always a version of a city, an interpretation. The ideal map coincides with reality and is impossible, "[f]or maps cannot describe everything, or they describe states of mind [...]" (Carson 1989, 67). The realistic mode of description is just another "legend"—it reveals that a metaphorical, poetic mechanism lies at the core of "mapping out." Thus, a topographical analysis merges with the linguistic dimension. This comes to Carson as no surprise since he sees the city specifically as a text, in the Latin understanding of the word—*textus*, i.e. woven cloth, or a web. In one of his best-known poems "Belfast Confetti" Carson employs the metaphor of overlaying the city with its purely linguistic map, showing how violence operates in the very gesture of mapping and how the city is always constructed as a textual entity:

> And the explosion
> Itself—an asterisk on the map. This hyphenated line, a burst of rapid fire…
> [...]
> All the alleyways and side-streets were blocked with stops and colons.
> (Carson 1989, 31)

Carson usually interprets the terrible impact of the Troubles on the city of Belfast in terms of maps and weaves that are falling apart, as if the violence was taking place equally on the symbolic and material level. He relates that "[t]he sleeve of Raglan Street has been unravelled" (Carson 1989, 107), "[t]he linen backing is falling apart—the Falls Road hangs by a thread" (Turn Again) and "[m]uch of this is unintelligible, blotted out by stars and asterisks / Just as the street outside is splattered with bits of corrugated iron and confetti" (Carson 1989, 33). Carson's Belfast, although decidedly particular, is to a certain extent an unreal city, much like the ones that are the product of Marco Polo's imagination in Italo Calvino's *Unreal Cities*.

Belfast is always a narration—time seems to be the key element here, but this dimension is left out in the topographical thinking, "[f]or everything is contingent and provisional; and the subjunctive mood of these images is tensed to the ifs and buts, the yeas and nays of Belfast's history" (Carson 1989, 67). The city is often construed as an indecipherable hieroglyph, a "ubiquitous dense graffiti of public houses, churches, urinals, bonding stores, graving docks, monuments, Sunday schools and Orange halls" (Carson 1989, 81).

Ewa Rewers observes that it is only thanks to the historical account of the city that it becomes narratively available to us (Rewers 1998). Still, Carson stresses that the tale of Belfast cannot be reduced to a single map, a single narrative. The city is for Carson the site of a constant linguistic struggle between opposing forces. "At times it seems that every inch of Belfast has been written-on, erased, and written-on again: messages, curses, political imperatives [...]" (Carson 1989, 52). Thus, it can be both read and written-on, its texture can be both torn apart and mended.

Having granted Belfast a linguistic status, Carson lifts it somehow to the level of a subject, not just a mere object. Thus, its changes and internal movements—"intestine war" as as he calls it (Carson 1989, 75)—can be read as symptoms of the processes that are taking place at the "unconscious" level of the society and nation as a whole. By way of metaphors that lead us along such lines of thinking, Carson establishes certain interesting relations between the dynamics of the city and the more general mechanisms of violence, identity and history.

In the essay "Walking the city" John Goodby investigates an interesting connection between walking, thinking and writing, showing how Carson's Belfast is at the same time a narrative and real space. The turns and directions that the *flâneur* of Carson's poems takes, or the obstacles he runs into, are very telling if we treat the Belfast of these poems as a psychic space that can be psychoanalyzed. The urban neurosis of Belfast is particularly striking in this light. This city has undergone a series of traumatic events whose meaning has been on many occasions condensed and displaced. These two terms are not accidental—their Freudian meaning which was originally applied to the analysis of dream-work was linked by Roman Jakobson to metaphor and metonymy—the two basic linguistic and consequently poetic operations.

By looking at the city from this perspective, we can observe that its libidinal economy is seriously disrupted. In "Queen's Gambit" the gun is stashed "somewhere in a mental block of dog-leg turns and cul-de-sacs" (Carson 1989, 36). In "Turn Again" the protagonist relates "I turn into / A side-street trying to throw off my shadow, and history is changed" (Carson 2009). Andrzej Leder who has undertaken a fascinating psychoanalysis of Warsaw writes that "[s]treets are like chains of associations; the flow of thought that is smooth and clear in some areas, in others is stuck in a melancholic, poisonous inertia" (Leder 2008, 63). His diagnosis of an urban neurosis that reveals an underlying trauma can be applied to Carson's Belfast. The Peace Line, the no-go areas and the obsessive tensions are all symptoms of a repression that envelops the traumatic impact of violence. It is not our task to determine how far back in history it goes. The uncovering of difficult events from Ireland's past is not the kind of a preoccupation that Carson would approve of. He seems to be unsettled about such a view of history: "there's any God's amount / Of Nines and Sixes: 1916, 1690, The Nine Hundred Years' War, whatever" (Carson

1989, 35). The usual historicist attitude seems to be trapped in a repetition compulsion that perpetuates violence and sentences the Ulster society to a vicious circle of war and oppression. The litany of Ireland's heroic failures is not only a worn out cliché, but also a mechanism of slowly stiffening the culture: "[w]ith so many foldings and unfoldings, whole segments of the map have fallen off" (Carson 1989, 35). Carson deals with the problem from an altogether different standpoint by projecting the whole situation onto the plane of the city, toying with two ideas that are crucial for the understanding of his urban poetics: psychogeography and panopticon.

In "Intelligence" Carson observes that "[k]eeping people out and keeping people in, we are prisoners or officers in Bentham's *Panopticon*, except sorting out who's who is a problem for the naïve user" (Carson 1989, 79). The panoptic structure of the society is not only a relationship between the army and the local people, but also between the paramilitaries on both sides, which amounts to the creation of "panopticons within panopticons" (Carson 1989, 79). The result of this process is an "ultimate nightmare" in which the city is "made totally transparent and accessible to power" (Goodby 2009, 79), meaning also that it is open to uncontrollable violence. Yet, this power struggle, which bases on fear and feeds on trauma, is what Carson abhors mostly. The panoptic mechanism, which metaphorically recurs in his poems in the form of a circling helicopter, is freezing the city in a stasis of terror.

The surveillance and disciplining of the urban space was acutely felt by psychogeographers—members or supporters of The Situationist International, an avant-garde movement led by Guy Debord. To a large extent they have inherited the tradition of *flânerie* which was transmitted from the thought of Baudelaire by Walter Benjamin onto the surrealists and ultimately to situationists. Anna Zeidler-Janiszewska observes that *flânerie* is not only a "certain practice of reading the streets" but can also be understood today as the experiencing of the city as a labyrinth in order to criticize its architectural and urban functionalism (Zeidler-Janiszewska 1999). Deron Albright in his discussion of situationism quotes the so-called "unitary urbanists" who claimed that what we lack today is a "living critique" that would help us "defend ourselves from the poetry of the bard of conditioning" and "jam their messages, to turn their songs inside out" (Albright 2003, 94). Psychogeographers, whose activity boiled down to "the act of urban wandering" in "the spirit of political radicalism, allied to a playful sense of subversion" (Coverley 2006, 14) were thus challenging the panoptic mechanism and propagating a different experience of the city—one that would work through the oppressive mechanisms and bring up the pleasures that a walk can provide. Ewa Rewers in her analysis of works by Bernard Tchumi notes that there is no architecture without violence, but at the same time there is no architecture without pleasure (Rewers 1998). Indeed, the practice of psychogeography is "an analysis of the space itself—the pleasures it affords, the difficulty it raises, the violence it renders" (Albright 2003, 93). It is the restoration of the fullness of experience and a means of transgressing the guilt- and fear-ridden mechanics of a society that has been paralyzed by an ongoing power struggle.

A similar combination of the subversive and the aesthetic can be found in the work of Walter Benjamin whose quotation from *A Berlin Chronicle* serves as an epigraph to *Belfast Confetti*:

> Not to find one's way in a city may well be uninteresting and banal. It requires ignorance—nothing more. But to lose oneself in a city—as one loses oneself in a forest—that calls for quite a different schooling. Then, signboards and street names, passers-by, roofs, kiosks, or bars must speak to the wanderer like a cracking twig under his feet in the forest, [...] like the sudden stillness of a clearing with a lily standing erect at its center. (Benjamin 1986, 8-9)

Following the usual routes—the kind of automatism that everyone under the all-seeing eye of the panopticon is forced to adopt—was diagnosed by Benjamin as utterly alienating. His criticism of commodification and urban estrangement is taken up by Carson in many ways, especially in the form of free wandering that allows him to detach from symbolic violence. Only through the defamiliarization of the city can one find oneself anew and reinvent both personal identity and the identity of the city. "Fruitless searching is as much a part of this" writes Benjamin and Carson is deeply aware that if he wants to shed and expose the language of violent ideologies that perpetrate hate, he has to "proceed in the manner of a narrative" and "delve to ever-deeper layers" (Benjamin 1986, 26). Yet, there is no fixed and stable omphalos at the bottom similar to the one that Seamus Heaney sought. Benjamin speaks of a negative, quasi-mystical experience of "dark joy" (Benjamin 1986, 26). A counterpart to this kind of epiphany can be found in the poem "Smithfield Market". Carson describes in it an exploded market. After everything got "unstitched, unravelled" and showed its "mouldy fabric" (Carson 1994, 37) he:

> [...] glimpsed a map of Belfast
> In the ruins: obliterated streets, the faint impression of a key.
> Something many-toothed, elaborate, stirred briefly in the labyrinth.
> (Carson 1994, 37)

[…] it was either nonsense, or a formula—for
Perpetual motion, the scaffolding of shopping lists, or the collapsing city.
(Carson 1994, 33)

Thus, the map that he proposes is a fluid and ever-shifting entity that cannot be transmitted otherwise than in a poetic language. The same goes for identity—its map is not a fixed construct. Whoever fashions it in that way is crossing out the possibility of a difference that allows people the space necessary to live a normal life.

In the prose poem "Question Time" Carson describes the experience of roaming freely through the city, which is interrupted by a violent intrusion of paramilitaries who subject him to a questioning so as to establish his identity. They are verifying his map against theirs:

The map is pieced together bit by bit. I am this map which they examine, checking it for error, hesitation, accuracy; a map which no longer refers to the present world, but to a history, these vanished streets; a map which is this moment, this interrogation, my replies. (Carson 1989, 63)

The result of this sectarian, panoptic mania is pure, unjustified violence. Carson's political and ethical struggle is against the deadness of constant surveillance that erases any authentic experience and is based on a violent imposition of maps that are always out of date and miss out on real life.

Zygmunt Bauman speaks a great deal about the political side of map-making (Bauman 1998). He notes that maps are always drawn from a specific point of view that assumes its own privileged status—an assumption that hides behind a seemingly "objective" approach. The negation of all other possible maps, like the ones drafted by psychogeographers which show the emotional impact of certain areas of the city, marks a totalitarian approach that has only one aim: to subject everyone to a single, unitary vision of space and block all sense-making initiatives. Both Carson and Bauman, though employing different discursive modes, point to the same task. They claim that the opening up of urban space to various interpretations does not necessarily lead to chaos. It is rather a different kind of balance, possibly one that might be free from the violence that lies at the heart of the division of Ulster society. This new equilibrium is a dialogic state that allows the flourishing of otherness and thus lets freedom be born, outside the trap of an "in or out" approach.

"He's caught between / Bel*fast* and *Bel*fast" (Carson 1989, 93) notes Carson in an attempt to overthrow this damaging separation which hinders the peace process. He does not want to stand on any side. His task is to link, combine and bridge. In another prose-poem "Farset", he plays with the etymology of the name "Belfast" arriving at surprising conclusions: "let Belfast be the *mouth of the poem*" (Carson 1989, 49). In an atmosphere of inclusiveness, he goes on: "the river Farset, this hidden stream, is all these things: it is the axis of the opposed Catholic Falls Road and the Protestant Shankill [...]" (Carson 1989, 49). Thus, Carson imagines a poetics that would allow the city to overthrow its artificial, ideological burden and speak through verse, coming alive not in the form of an official map, but rather a hybrid labyrinth of narratives.

In this light, the task of the poet is to "try to piece together the exploded fragments" (Carson 1989, 108). However, it is not a matter of shoring fragments against our ruins (to employ T.S.Eliot's phrase), but rather of participating in the reconstruction of new wholes. Joining loose ends is the position that Carson occupies most eagerly: "I am a hyphen, flitting here and there: between" (Carson 1989, 55). Carson knows that "the *flâneur* can no longer stand at the wayside or retreat to his armchair but must face up to the destruction of his city" (Coverley 2006, 77). The role of the poet is not to produce streams of ideology-infested slogans on the basis of a repetition automatism, but rather rest as a voice-box to the constant, unintelligible, but chaotically meaningful text of the city of Belfast.

References

Albright, Deron. 2003. Tales of the City: Applying Situationist Social Practice to the Analysis of the Urban Drama. *Criticism* 45 (1): 89-108.

Baudelaire, Charles. 1972. The Painter of Modern Life. In *Selected Writings on Art and Literature*, trans. by P.E. Charvet, 395-422. New York: Viking Press.

Bauman, Zygmunt. 1998. O ładzie, który niszczy, i chaosie, który tworzy, czyli o polityce przstrzeni miejskiej. In *Formy estetyzacji przestrzeni publicznej*, ed. by J.S. Wojciechowski & A. Zeidler-Janiszewska. Warsaw: Instytut Kultury.

Benjamin, Walter. 1986. *Reflections.* New York: Schocken Books.

Borges, Jorge Luis. 1999. *Collected Fictions*, trans. by Andrew Hurley. Harmondsworth: Penguin.

Carson, Ciaran. 1989. *Belfast Confetti.* Winston-Salem: Wake Forest University Press.

—. 1994. *The Irish for No.* Loughcrew, Oldcastle, County Meath: Gallery Press.

—. 2009. 'Turn Again.' BBC NI—Schools—Poetry—Study Ireland—A Sense Of Place—Page 3. http://www.bbc.co.uk/northernireland/schools/11_16/poetry/ senseofplace3.shtml (accessed April 15, 2009).

Coverley, Merlin. 2006. *Psychogeography*. Harpenden: Pocket Essentials.

Goodby, John. 2009. Walking in the City: Space, Narrative and Surveillance in *The Irish for No* and *Belfast Confetti*. In *Ciaran Carson. Critical Essays*, ed. by Ellmer Kennedy-Andrews, 66-85. Dublin: Four Courts Press.

Leder, Andrzej. 2008. Nerwica miejska. Warszawa. In *Res Publica Nowa* 193 (3): 62-69.

Rewers, Ewa. 1998. Zdarzenie w przestrzeni miejskiej. In *Formy estetyzacji przestrzeni publicznej*, ed. by J. S. Wojciechowski & A. Zeidler-Janiszewska. Warszawa: Instytut Kultury.

Zeidler-Janiszewska, Anna. 1999. Dryfujący flâneur, czyli o sytuacjonistycznym doświadczeniu miejskiej przestrzeni. In *Przestrzeń, filozofia i architektura*, ed. by Ewa Rewers. Poznań: Studia kulturoznawcze.

CHAPTER TWENTY

UNDER A STARRY MANTLE:
A LATE-MEDIEVAL SENSE OF SPACE
IN ENGLISH COUNTER-PESTILENCE POEMS

BARBARA KOWALIK

In many a medieval and renaissance painting the Blessed Virgin Mary is portrayed dressed in a blue cloak, usually ultramarine, as in the Wilton Diptych, but sometimes nocturnal blue sprinkled with gold stars. The blue was taken to symbolise heaven, with reference to the coronation of the Virgin as the Heavenly Queen. Together with the brilliance of gold it was there to remind believers that the Christian religion was one of joy and that their destiny was to share in divine glory. Not only were these the most precious colours spiritually, they were also the most costly to obtain. The deep blue, produced by lapis lazuli, was expensive because the main sources of supply were far distant in Asia. In the late Middle Ages, when Western Europe was ravaged by the Black Death, Mary's mantle became a symbol of protection from the disease: in the works of art associated with the plague she is depicted sheltering the faithful beneath her mantle from the javelins of the plague cast on them by God (Mâle 1949, 200-201).

This paper reconstructs a late-medieval sense of space in several English poems against the plague from the fifteenth century. Many of them were composed in the aureate style, which transposes readers with their problems to splendid and radiant heavenly halls or more literally to the planetary spheres, which were believed to influence human affairs. One of the most artistically accomplished of such poems was Robert Henryson's *Ane Prayer for the Pest*, in which the Middle Scots poet creates a style fitting to address "eterne God of power infinyt":

Superne Lucerne, guberne this pestilens,
Preserve and serve that we not sterve thairin!

Declyne that pyne be Thy devyne prudens!
   Trwth, haif rewth—lat not our slewth us twin!
   Our syt full tyt, wer we contryt, wald blin.
   Dissiver did never quha-evir The besocht.
Send grace with space, and us embrace fra syn!
Latt nocht be tynt that Thow so deir hes bocht! (Elliott 1963, 124)

In the quoted ninth stanza, initiating the poem's triple-strophe coda, the prosodic effects are enhanced and re-orchestrated. The word "pestilens" is shifted from the *C* rhyme in the refrain *CbC* to the initial rhyme of the eight-line stanza, *ababbCbC*, and the pace is quickened by three internal rhymes per line, the first of which echoes the poem's opening word, "eterne". Another Scottish poet William Dunbar employs similar devices in his *Ane Ballat of Our Lady*, as illustrated by the opening stanza:

Hale, sterne superne! Hale, in eterne,
   In Godis sicht to schyne!
Lucerne in derne, for to discerne
   Be glory and grace devyne;
Hodiern, modern, sempitern,
   Angelicall regyne!
Our tern inferne for to dispern,
   Helpe rialest rosyne.
Ave Maria, gratia plena!
   Haile, fresche flour femynyne!
Yerne us guberne, virgin matern,
   Of reuth baith rute and ryne. (Mackenzie 1970, 160-161)

Filling five lines of his twelve-line scheme with triple internal rhymes, Dunbar manages to repeat the same feminine and sonorous rhyme on *eterne* throughout the stanza. The poems illustrate spatial implications of the "natural" music of verse, to use the term introduced by Eustace Deschamps.[1] In this particular case, the rhythm suggests ascending the stairs of a sumptuous celestial palace and throne, imitating and surpassing in splendour the accoutrements of mundane monarchies.

Both poems are often quoted as examples of aureate diction, introduced into English poetry by John Lydgate. This kind of diction was

---

[1] Deschamps was a French court poet contemporary with Chaucer. In his poetic treatise *L'Art de Dictier et de fere chançons, balades, virelais et rondeaux* (*Ouevres* 7, 266-292) he distinguishes between the artificial music produced by the singing voice or musical instruments and the more difficult and sophisticated natural music, consisting in skillful versification in the fixed forms and recited rather than sung.

aptly described by another fifteenth-century poet, John Metham, as "half chongyd Latyne", for it was Latin Englished by means of minimal changes.[2] The polysyllabic Latin words were particularly suitable for religious poetry since they produced a sonorous musical effect appropriate for addressing celestial patrons. Lydgate was the first to pile such words one upon another, particularly in his Marian invocations, such as the *Ballade at the Reverence of Our Lady Quene of Mercy*. Henryson and Dunbar imitated and sometimes outdid Lydgate, adding elaborate rhyme patterns and repeating crucial words. Critics observe that this style places the divine "at a distance from the everyday" (Schirmer 1961: 154), while the "language ... seems to lose touch with referents in reality and to exist solely as a form of hieratic symbolic ritual" (Pearsall 1969: 29). The style changes Jesus from the Man of Sorrows into the mighty and unconquerable Hero King, comparable to Samson and Hercules, as in Lydgate's Passion poems, while Mary becomes the magnificent Queen of Heaven.

Not all counter-pestilence prayers, though, employ aureate diction and are totally removed from everyday reality, witness the short lyric found in the Sarum Hours written in France in the fifteenth century and being a translation of *Stella celi extirpavit*, an anthem to Mary praying for her protection against the plague[3]:

The stern of heven, modre Marye,
    That with hir mylke fed Cryst Jesu,
Of deth that Adam folily
    Had plantid, she the roote up dreu.

That same stern, vochsave she now
    The sterns above to stil and pees,
Whose stryfe and batailles as is to trow
    Arn cause of folks dedely dissees. (Gray 1992, 73)

One observes here a retreat to the intimate space of the maternal body and to the microcosm of wholesome nourishment, even though the

---

[2] Isabel Hyde has proved the accuracy of Metham's description by juxtaposing Lydgate's *Ballade at the Reverence of Our Lady* with a corresponding passage in the *Anticlaudianus* of Alanus de Insulis and showing that Lydgate translates, say, "oliva fructificans" as "fructifying olive" and "cedrus redolans" as "redolent cedyr".

[3] Another two-stanza version of the *Stella celi extirpavit* was written by the Franciscan James Ryman, "a prolific if not very talented writer" (Gray 1992, 136, 140).

macrocosmic image of Mary as the star of heaven, more powerful than other stars, is present as well.

Spiritual space is often underwritten with subtle medical allusions in counter-pestilence poems. More generally in medieval lyrics, Mary and Jesus are called upon as physicians, as in the ejaculatory prayer to "Jesu Crist, my soule leche" (Gray 1992, 54) or in the courtly choice of Mary to "paramour" on the grounds that she is "synguler leche" of the lover's "doloure" and possesses the healing properties of plants and minerals known from herbals and lapidaries (Gray 1992, 59). In particular, Mary is likened to a "pentafiloun" planted in the "herbere" (garden) of the speaker's heart. The *Grete Herball* (1529) describes this five-leaf herb and specifies its numerous healing properties, including remedy "agaynst bytyng of serpents" (Gray 1992, 133-34). In the poem the plant is introduced as a visual pattern underlying the acrostic on the name Maria and as such a cure for lovesickness, a real physical malady in medieval understanding. In the final envoy the poet sends his "lytil balett" (song) to Mary, implying that poetic composition combined with piety, contemplation of nature, and intellectual games are healthy pastimes therapeutic for the pangs of love. This "hygienic justification" of literary activities (Olson 1982, 39), encouraged by medieval physicians as beneficial for the emotions, underlies medieval literature.

A similar nexus of spiritual and scientific lore and constant shifting between macrocosm and microcosm dimensions occurs in Lydgate's writing occasioned by coming of the Black Death to England first in 1348-49 and persisting with varying intensity throughout the later Middle Ages.[4] Apart from composing prayers against the plague—two versions of *Stella celi extirpavit* and *De Sancta Maria contra pestilenciam*, Lydgate wrote a miracle legend in verse about St. Sebastian, *How the Plague was Sesyd in Rome*, adapting an old story to the plague in London. He also wrote a legend about St. Petronilla, another saint believed to give protection against the plague, whose skull was a relic preserved in his home monastery of Bury St. Edmund's as a cure for feverish illness, where a leper hospital bearing her name was also maintained. Furthermore, Lydgate is the author of *A Doctrine for the Pestilence*, instruction on how to cure the disease forming the initial part of his

---

[4] The Black Death ravaged the country in 1362 and 1369, and the renewed outbreaks continued until 1450. The plague raged particularly fiercely in 1433-34, causing the Parliament to be adjourned and King Henry VI to spend several months in Lydgate's home monastery of Bury St. Edmund's.

Dietary, a book about rules of health.[5] More generally, the plague underlies Lydgate's rendering of the *Dance Macabre*, imbuing its depiction of death with a sense of tangible reality, while a general concern with issues of health and hygiene runs through his entire work. Thus, the theme of health underlies his *Nine Properties of Wine*, which states that wine "clears the eyes, delights the heart, warms the stomach, heals wounds, and cleanses the gums" (Schirmer 1961, 111), and is touched upon in the introductory section of *Resoun and Sensuallyte*, giving advice upon the art of living, and in the moralistic reflection upon the inconstancy of health in *God is myn Helpere*. Lydgate's preoccupation with cleanness is in turn visible in his *Treatise for Lavenders* (laundresses), instructing a servant on how to take care of her lady's attire. The poet's last though unfinished work was a translation of the *Secreta Secretorum*, a book very popular in medieval times, including an exhaustive doctrine on hygiene and physiognomy.

In particular, the argument of Lydgate's longest prayer lyric against the plague, *De Sancta Maria contra pestilenciam*, composed in eleven rhyme royal stanzas with the final word *serpent* repeated as refrain (*ababbcC*), to a considerable extent relies on medical and astronomical science, associating physiological processes with cosmic phenomena, in accordance with the medieval holistic worldview whereby "the macrocosm-microcosm relationships provide explanations for everything" (Taavitsainen 2002, 383). In the first stanza the discourse of medieval astronomy, whereby the planets are considered the most important forces affecting the body and human lives, is discernible in the stellar invocation of the Virgin Mary:

> O Hevenly sterre, most Comfortable of lyght,
> Which, with thy goostely gracious Influence,
> Haste Claryfyed and put vnto flyght
> Alle mysty wedrys parlyous for pestilence,
> Preseruyd thy peple from olde violence,
> Plantyd be Adam whan he first gaff asse[nt]
> To evys Councell, take of the serpent. (Brown 1939, 206)

In medieval cosmology the influence of the stars was part of God's working and thus fully consistent with the teachings of theology. Lydgate does his utmost to underline this connection in the first six stanzas of his

---

[5] Another such didactic work of a medical or pseudo-medical nature occasioned by the Black Death is the Middle English mnemonic plague tract described by R. H. Bowers.

poem, each of which addresses Mary as a star, including the lode star and the pole star.

While the first stanza evokes cosmic space, in the second the astronomical metaphor quite abruptly gives way to an erotic image of Mary's breasts, Mary being visualised as a breastfeeding woman:

> Thow art the sterre, with brestis softe as sy[lke],
> That gave owre lorde at his Natyvyte
> Ffull offte sowke of thy Celestyall Mylke,
> Whos gracious Condyte had Angelyke plente,
> Tryacle, & Bawme Ageyne all Mortalyte,
> Plantyd be Adam when he first gaffe Assent
> To evys Councell, take of the serpent. (Brown 1939, 206)

Drawing upon the popular belief in milk as excellent nourishment, Lydgate builds an image more ethereal and intellectual. He extends a link between the maternal milk and the milky white starlight and clear air, purified from misty weathers believed to be the cause of the plague. This pure air is contrasted throughout the poem with "vnholsome Eyres Cawsyng greete syknesse", "pestilence eyre", "Infeccyon", the mists "of Infecte Eyres", and "wedris of Corrupte Pestilence" (Brown 1939, 206-210). Milk enters thereby the medical discourse informing this stanza and the whole poem. It is compared to a balm for healing wounds and soothing pain, and to an antidote against all mortality. In a later line Lydgate implores Mary: "Off thy Chaste mylke make owre preseruatyffe" (Brown 1939, 207).

Although the milk as nourishment for Christians is to be interpreted spiritually, this does not exclude dietary implications. Medieval regimens of health included advice on food and drink. One is reminded of the poor widow in the Nun's Priest's Tale, whose "bord was served moost with whit and blak—milk and broun breed" and whom Chaucer presents as "a model ... of the healthy body consequent upon a healthy lifestyle" (Voigts 2002, 49-50). Let us recall Lydgate's own *Doctryne for Pestilence* in the *Dietary*, his "most popular work, to judge by the number of extant manuscripts!" (Pearsall 1969, 25). In this guide to good health Lydgate interweaves recommendations on moderate eating and drinking with moral advice, prescribing for example piety. It is recommended that for "pestilence", which here means feverish illness, one should be cheerful, avoid bad air, drink good wine, and take walks in the garden. Mary's milk is a metaphor of such a healthy lifestyle in Lydgate's prayer against the pestilence. The poem calls the plague the new poison parallel to the old one of the small apple eaten by Adam and takes the vinegar and gall drunk by Christ on the cross to be an antidote against both maladies. The focus on Christ's blood in the second part of the poem, activating Eucharistic symbolism and particularly the idea of the Eucharist as a feast, completes this chain of imagery of proper and improper refreshment.

After the focus on the microcosm of the female body in the second stanza, astronomical discourse at the macrocosmic level prevails in the third:

> O glorious Sterre, do not now disdeyne
> Contraryous planetis to Appeeese & Represse,
> Whos dredefull werrys do men full Mortall peyne,
> Be vnholsome Eyres Cawsyng greete syknesse,
> Roote & Begynnyng of eche ffeverus Accesse,
> Toke his Orygynall when Adam gaff assen[t]
> To evys Councell, take of the serpent. (Brown 1939: 206)

The war of the planets as the plague's chief cause continues to be associated with medical discourse through such words as "pain", "unwholesome", "sickness", and "feverous". The presentation of the original sin as "root", implying a venomous herb causing successive fits of illness, likewise triggers medical connotations.

The ruling spatial image of the fourth stanza is the sea, with Mary being invoked as a star by which a ship can be steered amidst stormy waves:

> O loode sterre of this [tempestuous] se,
> In which we be fordryve with many a [wawe]
> And forpossed by Many aduersyte,
> Be owre freele flesh to froward lustis drawe,
> Ageyne all such pereyles lette □i lyght a-dawe
> On all thy peple that serue the of Intent
> And children of Adam, disseyved be a serpent. (Brown 1939, 206)

Again, the apparently macrocosmic image of navigation (Lydgate was familiar with navigation by the stars for he digresses about it in his *Troy Book*, I, l. 670) is imbued with medical significance since the tempestuous sea is an allegory of emotions, or "passions of the mind" as they were called by medieval physicians (Voigt 2002, 48), which are here associated with frail flesh and presented as a source of perverse desires. Emotions were part of the so-called "non-natural" component of health and disease in the pre-modern medical science. These non-naturals (*res nonnaturales*) were facets of one's physical, social, and psychological environment and included, apart from emotions: "air and environment; food and drink;

sleep and waking; motion and rest; repletion and evacuation" (Voigt 2002, 48). Lydgate's poem alludes to most of these factors.

The fifth stanza connects the image of the macrocosm illumined and governed by the pole star with the depiction of Mary as a royal figure receiving homage, endowing her with power and authority over the entire physical cosmos, including the plague:

> Sterre of the poole, bryghtest of sterrys alle,
> Whos bryght beames all derkenesse doth enchase,
> Be thow owre socowre when we to the Calle,
> Crying for helpe, knelyng Afore thy face.
> Helpe, noble Pryncesse of pyte & of grace,
> Be pestylece eyre that we be not shent –
> We chyldren of Adam, deceyued be a serpent. (Brown 1939, 207)

Lydgate's picture of Mary as the empress of the universe, radiant with mercy, elevates her above the stance of a breastfeeding mother or even that of a courtly lady, but still the image apes mundane political and social hierarchies. The speaker kneels in prayer, which is the posture of humility and subjection, a lowering of the self before something or someone better and desired. In a later stanza he asks Mary to hold up the "Banner" of her Son's cross, a visual symbol functioning not unlike the badges and arms of medieval nobility.

In the sixth stanza a number of thematic threads are gathered together: the metaphor of the beneficial star, with several kinds of stars being mentioned; the healing properties of starlight; the feudal hierarchies; and the image of the sea knocking about the vessel of the human body. The evening star, presiding over people's nightly rest, is mentioned along with the morning star, guiding humans in their daytime activities and journeys. Thus, two more pairs of non-natural factors of health are introduced into to the underlying medical-astronomical discourse of the poem: sleep and waking and rest and motion. The importance of well-governed emotions for health is reinforced first by the reiterated image of the tempestuous sea and then by the emphasis on the destructive impact of false sorrows, "Treynys", prompted by the devil.

> Sterre of Jacob, owre myschevis to Releve,
> Caste down thy streemys, thi seruauntis to socowre
> Ageyn blake nyghtis, owre Esperus at Eve,
> Day sterre A-morowe, for folkys ☐at labowre
> Helpe that karybdis owre vessell not devowre
> With froward Rokkys, ☐at it be not to-Rent
> Be noo false Treynys of the olde serpent. (Brown 1939, 207)

The allusions to ancient mythology betray Lydgate's interest in the new humanist learning, looking back to Greek and Roman antiquity, which enriches his medieval Christian view of the influence of the celestial spheres as part of God's working with pagan mythological motifs. The two attitudes need not be perceived as clashing and yet in a devotional Marian poem they come somewhat as a surprise because, although pagan deities often appear for example in Chaucer's works, Chaucer does not insert them into, say, his *ABC*. Lydgate contrasts the Virgin Mary with the dangerous sea monsters, Scylla and Charybdis, but his invocation of Mary as Hesperus, the evening star, and his addressing her as the morning star are daring for they bring Mary close to Venus, a widespread allegory of sensuality.

In sum, as illustrated by Lydgate's *De Sancta Maria contra pestilenciam*, writing about the Black Death was an occasion for interweaving in the narrative space[6] diverse discourses, mixing theology, medicine, astronomy, hygiene, and mythology. Thus, Lydgate, a master of this kind of interdisciplinary discourse, has managed to make even a short poem an encyclopaedic "pageant of knowledge", as his contemporary John Shirley put it (Lindenbaum 1999, 297). At the same time, the Blessed Virgin Mary remains in sharp focus throughout "thys dyrge" (dirge), as Lydgate calls his song in the final stanza, dedicating it to the Heavenly Queen to be received at her grace. Thus, in counter-pestilence verse, cosmic space has the body contours of the feminine and maternal figure of the Virgin Mary, with the starlit sky as her sheltering mantle and Mary becoming something like a benevolent planetary goddess and empress, shielding her worshippers even from the righteous wrath of God Himself. This kind of space is much more personalised, humanised, and consequently more cosy and homely than our modern sense of limitless galaxies. On the other hand, the late-medieval space is also invested with scientific significance, in accordance with the pre-modern intellectual construct. Mary provides remedies against the Black Death that reflect the current state of knowledge. Lydgate thus strikes a balance between a mythical and a scientific sense of space. The narrative self of his poem proves to be strikingly plural and fluid: both immersed in medieval spirituality and embracing a rational and pragmatic stance as well. Soon

---

[6] Narrative is here understood very broadly in accordance with recent developments in narratology whereby narrative is no longer taken to be the narration of a succession of fictional events, as defined by Shlomith Rimmon-Kenan (1983), but "a manner of perceiving, organizing, construing meaning, and a mode of cognition different from logical or discursive thinking" (Rimmon-Kenan 2006, 195).

after Lydgate, though, medieval representations of the Virgin Mary in her blue starry cloak will cease to be comprehensible as a symbol of wholesome environment and will be discarded as mere icons of idolatry.

References

Bowers, R. H. 1956. A Middle English Mnemonic Plague Tract. *Southern Folklore Quarterly* XX: 118-25.

Brown, Carleton (ed.). 1939. *Religious Lyrics of the XVth Century.* Oxford: Clarendon Press.

Brown, Peter (ed.). 2002. *A Companion to Chaucer.* Oxford: Blackwell.

Elliott, Charles (ed.). 1963. *Robert Henryson. Poems.* Oxford: Clarendon Press.

Fyler, John M. 2002. Pagan Survivals. In *A Companion to Chaucer*, ed. by Peter Brown, 349-59. Oxford: Blackwell.

Hyde, Isabel. 1955. Lydgate's 'Halff chongyd Latyne': An illustration. *Modern Language Notes*, LXX: 252-254.

Grabes, Herbert and Wolfgang Viereck (eds.). 2006. *The Wider Scope of English.* Frankfurt am Main: Lang.

Gray, Douglas (ed.). 1992. *English Medieval Religious Lyrics.* Exeter: University of Exeter Press.

Lindenbaum, Sheila. 1999. London Texts and Literate Practice. In: *Medieval English Literature,* ed. by David Wallace, 284-309. Cambridge: Cambridge University Press.

Mackenzie, W. Mackay (ed.). 1970. *The Poems of William Dunbar.* London: Faber & Faber.

Mâle, Emile. 1949. *L'art religieux de la fin du Moyen Âge en France.* Paris.

Olson, Glending. 1982. *Literature as Recreation in the Later Middle Ages.* Ithaca, NY: Cornell University Press.

Pearsall, Derek. 1969. *Gower and Lydgate.* London: Longman.

Rimmon-Kenan, Shlomith. 1983. *Narrative Fiction: Contemporary Poetics.* London: Methuen.

—. 2006. Narrative as Paradigm in the Interface between Literature and Psychoanalysis. In *The Wider Scope of English*, ed. by Herbert Grabes and Wolfgang Viereck, 195-204. Frankfurt am Main: Lang.

Schirmer, Walter F. 1961. *John Lydgate. A Study in the Culture of the XVth Century.* London: Methuen.

Taavitsainen, Irma. 2002. Science. In *A Companion to Chaucer,* ed. by Peter Brown, 378-96. Oxford: Blackwell.

Voigts, Linda E. 2002. Bodies. In *A Companion to Chaucer,* ed. by Peter Brown, 40-57. Oxford: Blackwell.

Wallace, David (ed.). 1999. *Medieval English Literature.* Cambridge: Cambridge University Press.

CHAPTER TWENTY-ONE

THE NOTION OF SPACE IN JOHN ASHBERY'S POETRY

PAWEŁ MARCINKIEWICZ

The notion of space in poetry used in this paper is based on a few assumptions. First, space is understood as an imaginary landscape evoked by a literary work, where word/image connection is taken for granted, with little consideration for poststructural doubts about the nature of meaning. Secondly, the notion of space developed here neglects the spatial organization of the text, including physical shape on the page, which was the main interest of early Modernist visual poetry (the most influential visual poet was Christian Mogernstern).[1] Later, visual poetry evolved into concrete poetry, which often employed collages, used by legion of artists, from Modernists, like Kurt Schwitters, to postmodern tycoons of pop art, like Richard Hamilton.

In twentieth-century American poetry, space had various representations in verse, as many poets were trying their hands at pinning down the plainest level of human existence, which is our physical presence in the world. Most obviously, space-rendering strategies could be divided on the basis of mimetic verisimilitude. On the one hand, there are poets linguistically faithful to perceptual clichés, like Robert Frost or Robinson Jeffers; on the other, there are those ontologically dubious, and who mock our common spatial sensations, like Wallace Stevens or Marianne Moore. A more rhetorically focused division would take into consideration particular poets' uses of metaphor, according to which the non-metaphorical William Carlos Williams stands in contrast to the highly metaphorical Hart Crane. Or, the criterion for the division could be determined on the basis of philosophical tradition represented by diverse and antagonistic poetic schools: Wittgensteinian "city impressionists," like

---

[1] This problem is elucidated by Witold Sadowski (2004) in his comprehensive history of visual forms in European poetry.

Frank O'Hara or James Schuyler, could be seen as competing with Kantian "objectivists," like Louis Zukofsky or Charles Reznikoff.[2] Whatever the critical benchmark applied, one predicament is certain: the further into the twentieth century, the more problematic the issue of spatial representation becomes. As John Koethe wittily observes,

> the exemplary poem of thirty years ago (...) rarely acknowledged its status as writing, and its attitude toward the impulses of romanticism was one of irony and condescension. The generic poem of today seems quite different. (1995, 85)

A typical poem of the present historical moment—the moment par excellence of John Ashbery—boldly withdraws from representational claims, forcing the reader to accept its arbitrary panoply of recycled meanings.

This quality is poignantly expressed by Jonathan Morse: "All that is real in [contemporary poetry] exists in the language itself (1995, 24)." For Ashbery, language is, first of all, a means to express his primary bond with the "community of language users—of human beings who share one world," which is the main argument of Kacper Bartczak's enlightening study of the New York poet's rhetoric, *In search of communication and community* (2006, 205). This attitude distinguishes Ashbery from Language poets, who explore the very conditions for linguistic meaning, rejecting the model of the voice poem and demolishing the conventional relationship between the (active) poet and the (passive) reader. Ashbery distances himself from experimenters, such as Charles Bernstein, claiming that "language finally depends on references to meanings generated outside language."[3] A typical Ashbery poem is profoundly a voice poem: it keeps the reader in mind by putting to test all possible applications of the pronoun "you," which makes the poem's scope available, and serves as the gateway to its imagery.[4] Needless to say, entering Ashbery's poetry has always been difficult due to the poet's adherence to fixed forms, his excessive use of clichés and puns, his self-referentiality, his unapologetically mixed diction, and his esoteric allusiveness. What makes his mature works even more problematic is the fact that their disjunctive language, in which

---

[2] For a thorough study of Wittgenstein's influence on American poetry see Marjorie Perloff (1996).

[3] For more detail see Linda Reinfeld (1992, 24).

[4] The poet's increasingly keen and affectionate attention to his readers has recently been examined by John Emil Vincent (2007).

words are unhinged from their traditional meanings, occasionally evolves into crystal clear splinters of realistic representation.

The linguistic complication of the poets belonging to the "tribe of John" does not mean that it is easier for us to understand the nature of spatial representation in the more traditional poetry written today. From the Renaissance until Modernism, our perception of space in arts and literature had been governed by two principles—first, centralization and, second, unification of vision, whose aim was mimetic representation. According to Tadeusz Sławek, the early twentieth-century avant-guard movements distorted the impersonal fixity of post-Renaissance perspective, which was no longer a crucial part of artistic vision, and lost its power to organize space (1984, 166). Cubism and Surrealism exemplify two contrasting attitudes towards the treatment of space in Modernist art. Cubism uses reason to perpetuate the object, which exists in a real space, while Surrealism abandons reason and places the object in an imaginary space. The first emphasizes the existence of the object, reconstructing its form; the second destroys the object, highlighting its inherent formlessness and lack of structure. Therefore, in Cubist vision, thought dominates over image; in Surrealist vision, thought and image are unified and cannot be separated. It seems that the two strategies for rendering space in visual arts have their analogues in literature, and they are common for most twentieth-century poets. In verse, however, reason-based or/and irrational presentations of space are not necessarily mutually exclusive, which is proved by John Ashbery's prolific oeuvre.

Ashbery uses a variety of strict procedural forms, such as sestina, canzone, and pantoum. Additionally, he relies on the seriality of verse patterns, borrowed from numerous sources, for example paraphrastic hemistitches taken from the *Kalevala*, a collection of Finnish oral epic poems, which he employed in his "Finnish rhapsody"; or haiku, which he brought back to its original shape as a long-line poem in his "37 haiku." According to John Emil Vincent, Ashbery often invents his own formal restrictions, like a double-sestina, which is *Flow chart*'s climax (2007, 66). Another type of restriction typical of Ashbery is writing for a given time and for a given number of pages, both of which were used in *Flow Chart*, whose one-hundred-page manuscript was written in a predetermined time, with the poem's finale composed on Ashbery's sixtieth birthday (Vincent 2007, 47-48). Actually, Ashbery finished the poem some time earlier, which is also quite significant because he never treats formal restrictions rigorously, and breaking them is also a part of his game. Ashbery inherited much of his formal inclination from Modernists, especially Auden and Bishop. However, for Auden, any formal pattern is a means to create a fairly conventional lyrical picture, while for Ashbery it is a method of withdrawal from traditional lyricism. According to Joseph M. Conte, for postmodern poets, "procedural form presents itself as an alternative to the well-made metaphorical lyric" (1991, 5). Both procedural forms and seriality help to respond to the cognitive challenges of contemporaneity: discontinuity of experience, skepticism of imposed hierarchical orders, and confrontation with chaos. A good example of Ashberian non-lyrical space generated by a procedural pattern is a sestina called "The Painter," originally published in the poet's debut book, *Some trees*.

The sestina's sense develops along the six end words permutated in identical form in all seven stanzas: "buildings," "portrait," "prayer," "subject," "brush," and "canvas," whose unpoetical bluntness mocks the idea of the Audenesque lyric poem. According to Bartczak, *Some trees* presents poems that are "programmatically noncomplex" as if they were designed to resemble exercises in formal closure and regularity (2006, 18). This is definitely true about "The painter," which, quite typically for the early Ashbery, describes the conflict between the artist and the world confining him or her. On a metaphorical level, the poem focuses on the relation of the work of art to its models in nature, expressing distrust towards representational realism (which the poem itself pretends to employ!). Initially, the artist in the poem sanctifies transcendental nature and strives to iconize its essence. However, he tries to avoid the taint of creative artifice, and, as a result, is defeated by his own grandiose ambition, unable to recognize that the fate of his artistic endeavor is, from the start, determined by the strictly artificial character of his enterprise. Finally, mocked by the public, the painter is crushed by what he wished to represent unfailingly—the sheer chaos of the raging natural element.

The limitations of the sestina—the permutated order of seemingly accidental end words—create a box-like space of an artificial environment in which nothing is "natural." However, the mind bouncing in such an environment often explores the unknown senses which, paradoxically, lurk within the known angles. Such new senses are revealed by the different collocations of the end words, for example "buildings." In the course of the poem they undergo a sequence of transformations, from dwellings inhabited by the people into ruins, the conflagrations sites, some other artists' homes and, finally, into the site of the protagonists' death, which blurs the obviousness of their meaning. The "portrait" is first the portrait of the sea, then the artists' self-portrait, and eventually, the artist himself. Although the set of angles is strictly limited, the final effect is that of a new territory or a newly charted landscape, where reality loses its shapes and evolves into the ever-new dimensions of strangeness. The physical objects appearing in the box-like space of the poem—the brush, the canvas, the sand—are rather generic, with almost no adjectives endowing them with individual character. The poem's space is permeated with the speaker's ironic undertone, which gives the reader interpretational directions.

It would be tempting to find an analogue of Ashbery's meticulously structured spaces from *Some trees* in visual arts, in the paintings of Edward Hopper from the same period. Many of the Hopper's late oils, programmatically incomplex, such as "Rooms by the sea" or "Sun in an empty room," focus on the contrast between the natural and the artificial, following a predetermined tripartite scheme. According to Ivo Krasnzfelder, the illumination in the first painting disregards the actual, physical configuration of the room, with perspective gone askew, which leads to a sense of insecurity, negating—quite similarly to Ashbery's poems—naive representational realism (2006, 188).

The box-like contrived space of Ashbery's early pattern-poem reveals a proximity to another visual artist—the American surrealist Joseph Cornell, whose assemblages (framed wooden boxes with dime-store trinkets, like metal rings, pipes, glass balls, but also photographs, etc.) create inscrutably meditative landscapes, where "the thing is in its thingness" (Ashbery 1989, 16). In his *Central park carrousel, in memoriam* (1950), we can see a broken net wiring covering a moon-like bluish shape, with a black-and-white lithograph of a lady or an angel, soaring in the air.[5] On the very bottom of the box, behind the moon, and on the left vertical part of its frame, there are two stripes of a mirror. The title of the assemblage created in 1950 ironically refers to the fire, in which the famous Central Park carousel had been destroyed in the same year. *Central park carrousel* produces meanings by a complex juxtaposition of images and concrete objects: the moon (dreams, wishes, aspirations), the angelic lady in the air (love, passion), and net wiring (power, control) enable the reader to construe a number of interpretations. The space generated by such imagery seems to be based on everyday experience, yet it is astonishing, and indicates unforeseen connections. In an interview with Peter Stitt, Ashbery admits that he found inspiration in Cornell's art, and he thought of his own poems as assemblages—autonomous sets of objects woven of the familiar scraps of reality (1983, 45).

Quite a different space emerges in Ashbery's free verse poems from the same period, which avoid artificial principles of reason. According to

---

[5] *Central park carrousel, in memoriam*, together with 22 other works by Cornell, is a part of MoMA's collection, *The Museum of Modern Art*, http://www.moma.org./collection/object. php?object_ id=80771.

Bartczak, Ashbery uses the less formalized texts in his collections to shed more light on the workings of his stricter formal procedures (2006, 21). In the course of his career, the poet developed his own specific and novel concept of a free verse poem. He started with a highly disjunctive language, rejecting any notions of regularity whatsoever. Semantic indeterminacy, which takes the shape of colliding chunked phrases, no longer forming sentences, constitutes the bulk of his second collection, *The tennis court oath* (1962). The volume presents Ashbery's vision of the atomized self, and it engages with the tiniest bits of visual and auditory experience. However, these disjunctive techniques were still a coherent method of representation of experience for the poet. In an interview with Alfred Poulin Jr., commenting on one of the most notorious pieces in the collection, "Leaving the Atocha Station," Ashbery expressed his conviction that the poem furthers the cause of the close mimesis, representing the very physical actualities of the given moment:

> [T]he dislocated, incoherent fragments of images which make up the movement of the poem are probably like the experience you get from a train pulling out of a station. The dirt, the noises, the sliding away seem to be a movement in the poem. (1981, 245)

The poem's space is that of a collage or assemblage, with clippings of linguistic ready-mades and found objects, like fragments of dialogues or vague citations, in the spirit of Gertrude Stein's linguistic experimentation, distrusting lucid narration.

If the reader feels disoriented in this space, it is primarily because of the poem's veered deictics: "we," "he," "you," and "I" give the poem a conversational character; however, it is impossible to recognize the speakers involved in it. As John Emil Vincent claims, "Often, as many poets do with image, Ashbery seeks to create density with pronouns... in order to provide an effect of richness or innovative polyvalence" (2007, 52). Obscure personae, metamorphosing from line to line, and their stylistically wide vocal range force sudden changes on the level of the poem's interiority: the here and now of writing borders on a terrain of meditation ("the menace of your prayer folds"), quotidian close-ups ("Leaving the Atocha Station/steel/ infected bumps the screws"), or semi-confessional riffs ("for that we turn around/experiencing it is not to go into/the epileptic prank"). Characters change, as well as narrative modes and verb tense; however, the poem's shifts are not random swervings: the seemingly stable locale—a train car, which offers a view of a station, with realistic details ("Other people ... flash," "blazing pigeons from the roof," or "Air pollution terminal"), help the reader to get oriented in the text, and they do provide connectives between the opening gesture, which is the beginning of the journey ("pulling us out of there experiencing it"), and the closing gesture, which is leaving the Atocha station behind ("next time around"). There is no epiphanic overtone in the poem to reduce the impurity of images or sounds entering its space. Hence the reader may finish the poem with no purchase on meanings or patterns. There is no allegorization and, therefore, no cumulative message for the reader to be construed. Yet, because of the poem's autonomous character, the reader builds a feeling of attachment to it.

In visual arts, we could find an analogue to Ashbery's disjunctive free verse poems in dislocated spaces of abstract expressionists, like Arshile Gorky, Jackson Pollock or Willem de Kooning.[6] According to Barbara Rose, a common feature of the above painters was automatism of artistic creation achieved with such techniques as "drip" and "all-over," or by usage of unconventional tools, such as rollers (1980, 87). Abstract expressionists generated semi-figurative forms, and they developed surrealistic poetic spaces, Whitmanesque in their essence—exalting pristine energies of nature—dominated by "hybrid biomorfism" (in André Breton's parlance), which used graphic allusions to human or animal anatomical details, vegetative ornaments or landscapes (Rose 1980, 72). A good example is de Kooning's oil *Excavation* (1950), which shows a tangle of intriguing flat shapes—parts of human body, like teeth, an arm or an eye—cut in quick black lines.[7] The picture's colors are smudged shades of gray and brown, resembling flesh, illuminated by red, yellow and blue spots and splashes. The shapes' contours overlap, giving a feeling of chaotic movement in diverging perspectives. The title of the picture evokes an image of destruction: the viewer examines a site of a natural disaster or a landscape after a war. The shapes clash, generating a discontinuous unstable space, lacking any specific ambiance or a center, yet recognizable and homogeneous. This resembles very much the multi-vocal space of "Leaving the Atocha station."

Interestingly, Ashbery did not reprint the poem, or in fact any of his linguistic collages, in his 1985 *Selected poems*. His search for poetic space ran in the direction of the free flux of thoughts introduced by his next

---

[6] In her *American painting. The twentieth century*, Barbara Rose explains that "abstract expressionism" – the term coined by the art critic Robert Coates – is not a very fortunate designation for the New York school of painting, which gained recognition in 1950s. The artist themselves preferred such names as "abstract impressionism" or "inter-subjectivism" (1980, 72).

[7] The Painting is exhibited in The Art Institute of Chicago and also available on-line at http://www.artic.edu/aic/collections/artwork/76244.

collection, *Rivers and mountains* (1966). Two poems from this collection are particularly important for understanding of the notion of space in mature Ashbery's poesies—"Clepsydra" and the "Skaters." Both narratives are meditations, with a number of hardly discernible speakers, whose voices explore the free rhythms of thought. Their sheer extensiveness puts to test our reading habits: they are not so much traditional poems as linguistic games, played until a certain size or heft is achieved. This strategy is even clearer in Ashbery's next collections, *The double dream of spring* (1970), with its virtuoso "Fragment" made of fifty dizains, and *Three poems* (1972), with its vast prose poem "The system." Ashbery's lyrical space is inclusive and contains multitudes of tropes, objectifying the speakers' consciousness. According to James McCorkle, the poet's porous narratives are "fluid mnemonic structures that move from the personal to include the polyphonic social" (1995, 103). Their constant inner oscillations between the singular and plural, the surface and depth of images, representation and voice—cause a deferral or dispersal of meaning. Instead, the poem's shifting tonalities suggest a transmission, flux or exchange of meanings. Therefore, the Ashberian space is truly "indeterminate," as Marjorie Perloff puts it, which means that it lacks any "content" (1981, 54). According to McCorkle, this feature of Ashbery's space resembles Derrida's anagrammatic and polyphonic poetics from *Signesponge/Signsponge*: For Derrida and Ashbery, poetic language inscribes "excess or the possibility of overflowing and invokes a libidinal energy no longer centered upon the self" (1995, 106). "Clepsydra" is probably one of the most accessible of Ashbery's indeterminate landscapes. In the opening fragment of the poem, like in its full 253-line text, a dense array of autobiographical elements lurks beneath the opaque images. Perhaps the greatest riddle in the poem is the very opening sentence, "Hasn't the sky?", whose rift cannot be sealed without a recourse to some extratextual interpretative structure, and, therefore, proves that Ashbery's poetry, in its decentering drive, is not a passive register of the world, but it also recognizes the role of the reader in the act of interpretation, which is always social. According to Bartczak, the opening movements of the poem are those of consciousness waking up from the incomprehensible tongue-twisters of dream-talk (2006, 27). The lines that follow organize the dream-like vision into a landscape, which combines the speaker's farsightedness with his myopia: steamy "clouds" and "hills" suddenly dissolve to show "the half-meant, half-perceived/Motions of fronds" or "nets drying in the sun." The poem develops temporally like a movie played frame by frame, each line being a mini-clip, made of an image, a metaphor, and an introspection purged of personal details, with some general emotional traits left. Interestingly, glimpses of the apparently real world enter the poem with metaphors or similes as their tenors (or vehicles): "The reply wakens easily, darting from/Untruth to willed moment, scarcely called into being/Before it swells, the way a waterfall/Drums at different levels." Thus, the "waterfall" is a part of the landscape, but only as a fragment of a trope—a reference to the ambiguous "reply," belonging to the main course of the poem's narration. The further into the poem, the more profound the disparity between the landscape of the self and the physical world becomes. The only way for the self to ascertain its surroundings is the mnemonic movement of language, in which reality is not represented by language, but simply becomes this language. Our experience lacks centers, and memory's debris, linguistic in form, is constantly redistributed, enabling us to adapt to the selves' new moments. This is where the speaker arrives in the poem's finale:

> What is meant is that this distant
> Image of you, the way you really are, is the test
> Of how you see yourself, and regardless of whether or not
> You hesitate, it may be assumed that you have won, that this
> Wooden and external representation
> Returns the full echo of what you meant
> With nothing left over, from the circumference now alight
> With ex-possibilities become present fact, and you
> Must wear them like clothing, moving in the shadow of
> Your single and twin existence, waking in intact
> Appreciation of it, while morning is still and before the body
> Is changed by the faces of evening. (2008, 146)

Technically speaking, this single sentence is a multi-leveled series of metaphors, with clauses dispersing in all possible directions. The first level, introduced by "What is meant", implies an authority beyond the narrative level of the poem—an omniscient voice, which produces the poem's inert protagonist, referred to as "you", in a gesture of artistic creation. The second level is the "you" level, where most of the poem's descriptive elements are contained, such as its story and, possibly, its message. The new day, which wakes the addressee, with its splendid "circumference now alight" seals cracks and rifts between fragmented chunks of his existence. Although the addressee's linguistic representations are "wooden" and "external," they still enable him to regain his present "I" through a meticulous survey of bits and pieces of himself shaped previously (although it is not really sure: "it may be assumed that you have won"). Therefore his existence is always "single" (lived at the present moment) and "twin" (made of present and past selves). The message of the poem is only seemingly clear and straightforward: this is all only "meant", and it "may be assumed" with hesitation. This is a very important feature of Ashberian space from his mature middle period: the space created by the poem is only hypothetical since it exists in an unreal present, as a supposition made in the moment of writing/reading, which gets erased by the conditional mood.

In his subsequent volumes (excluding, perhaps, the illustrated *The Vermont notebook* from 1975), *Self-portrait in a convex mirror* (1975), *Houseboat days* (1977), and *As we know* (1979), Ashbery perfected his polyphonic and decentered mode of writing, combining it with tropes, which enabled immediacy of experience, whose concoction became his trademark. The Ashberian poem swings between the existence of an autotelic vision, in which dream logic replaces knowledge, and the existence of a referential pastiche, romantic in spirit, engaged in intertextual and tropical play.[8] The space revealed by the poem is multidimensional, disrupted and uncanny: the speaker's fragmentary observations, from trivial declarations to philosophical statements, border with realistic descriptions, creating a specific Ashberian *Dasein*. Each poem offers a nebulous continuum, which is haphazardly relocated and extended, with use of various associative techniques, like formal patterns (stanzaic division, meter) or sound structures (alliterations, homophones, puns). "A Tone Poem" from *As we know*, as convincingly as any of Ashbery's later poems, gives a feeling of shifty, solipsistic topography:

> It is no longer night. But there is a sameness
> Of intention, all the same, in the ways
> We address it, rude
> Color of what an amazing world (…).
>
> But this is the same thing we are all seeing,
> Our world. Go after it,
> Go get it boy, says the man holding the stick.
> Eat, says the hunger, and we plunge blindly in again,
> Into the chamber behind the thought.
> We can hear it, even think it, but can't get disentangled from our brains.
> Here, I am holding the winning ticket. Over here.
> But it is all the same color again, as though the climate
> Dyed everything the same color. It is more practical,

---

[8] The problem of dream logic in Ashbery's poetry is the main topic of Marjorie Perloff's essay "'Fragments of a buried life': John Ashbery's dream songs." (1980, 66-86).

Yet the landscape, those billboards, age as rapidly as before. (2008, 689-690)

In the poem, the speaker occupies an indeterminate position between the real world and an illusionary verbal continuum, where the "sameness" of intention is "all the same," and everything is "the same color again." In the realistic perspective, the poem offers a description of a breaking dawn: the speaker (and some people he associates himself with, or human beings in general, hence the pronoun "we") marvels at the color of the city, with landscape spotted with disheveled billboards, his conclusion being that the view seems to be artificial, yet recognizable since the billboards age as rapidly as *before*. The second perspective involves motives, actions and personae, which cannot be combined in a comprehensive picture of a situation. "The man holding the stick" and the personified "hunger" have some allegorical potential, while the "chamber behind the thought" or the "winning ticket" are simply puzzling or even comical. Interestingly, the realistic perspective contributes to the poem's atmosphere, but it does not contain the poem's logical argument, which is conveyed in disjunctive and highly metaphorical discourse.

The reader may only hypothesize that the poem deals with the problem of aesthetic representation in literature: the Emersonian trope of nature, according to which "the poet, the painter, the sculptor, the musician, the architect, seek to concentrate (…) radiance of the world on one point," is mockingly inverted and presented as a means of producing artistic banalities (Emerson 1969, 12).[9] Tradition is perceived to be an oppressive school, where students/poets are told what to write about and how: "go get it [beauty of the universe] boy, says the man holding the stick." The tropes used subsequently blur the Emersonian reference, which finally gets erased in the glimpse of suburban neighborhood provided by the poem's closing gesture. Therefore, the poem eludes an Aristotelian plot or *praxis*, with strong sequential causality, and resists heuristic interpretation. This quality was perspicaciously grasped by Kacper Bartczak:

> Ashbery (…) builds a habitat for thought, a field of connections can can be entered, lived in or observed from the outside. Especially Ashbery's shorter poems are best approached as habitats, seemingly independent from our daily sanity. (2006, 46)

---

[9] On the other hand, Ashbery shares Emerson's most primal view that "a work of art is an abstract or epitome of the world. It is a result or expression of nature, in miniature" (Emerson 1969, 12).

Being a habitat, the Ashberian poem annuls the distinction between fictions of fact and fact itself, and it shares the same quality, the same violation, the same coexistence in our lives as have real events.

An interesting gloss on space in Ashbery's mature poems is Angus Fletcher's theory of the environment-poem (which is not a poem *about* environment, but a poem intended to surround us in the way an actual environment surrounds us).[10] According to Fletcher, in the most general sense, the function of space in literature is to provide a limited cosmology: the literary and artistic cosmos is a constellation of images and actions we usually call "allegory" (2004, 237). However, allegory is an ideological fiction, which derives poetic elements from fundamental axioms according to the law of logical derivation. In the Coleridgean vision of poetry, ideas correspond to images on a one for one basis, like "a simple lever in a machine matching a simple rotor in the same machine" (2004, 226). Post-romantic poetry dealt with various aspects of art, which negotiated between the real and the fictive, seeking causal consequence. The environment-poem does not recognize the above dialectics, trying to reconstruct the world as an immense informational network.

Furthermore, the environment-poem is the opposite of allegory: it discovers a manifold in nature that has no isolating wall around it. It also lacks any superimposed hierarchic system of images and is always self-organizing and non-linear. The environment-poem seeks symbolic control over the drifting experience of being environed, and it introduces an experience of an outside that is developed for the reader inside the experience of the work:

> While this outside/inside game closely resembles a stream of consciousness technique intended to reveal elusive states of mind, the environment-poem converts natural surroundings and their common surrogates, like the furnishing of a house, for example, into a surrounding that actually has more presence than any state of mind. It is as if the dream had become real. (Fletcher 2004, 227)

Thus, the environment-poem is a double of nature herself, which questions all unexamined versions of causal dramatic structure. It expresses a complete order, as that of an ecosystem, with no wish to achieve a cohesiveness of poetic action.

It seems that in the 1970s, Ashbery's poetry discovered a new way of presenting space, beyond the modernist reason-based or/and irrational dialectic of Cubist or/and Surrealist vistas. The New York poet developed

---

[10] For more detailed description see Angus Fletcher (2004, 227).

various precursor traditions, from the romantic directness of Beddoes and Clare, to the modernist synchronous unity of Mallarmé. Due to Ashbery's influence, poems written at the end of the twentieth century were more and more often environment-poems, resembling chaotic habitats rather then allegorical visions. Their frenetic speed and condensation of their images helped them to reveal their order over minimal time, as if duration was compressed into an epiphany of complex emergent properties. Their coherence as a source of unity was obviously much looser than any neoclassical or Aristotelian norm. Among the environment-poets, we should mention such different artists as James Tate, particularly in his early period, from *The lost pilot* (1967) to *Distance from loved ones* (1990); Glyn Maxwell, especially in his early books of poems, like *Tale of the mayor's son* (1990); or those poets who have made their debut quite recently, like Mary Jo Bang, the author of *The eye like a strange balloon* (2004). The ubiquity of the environment-like spatial presentation is also reflected by the annual cross-sectional anthology of American poetry, *The best American poetry*, edited by David Lehman.[11]

A visual analogue of the last type of space discussed here would be a space of a multi-channel installation, using a variety of media, like painting, film, text and sound. Among many contemporary artists, who have won international acclaim, there is a Belgian, David Claerbout, who operates on the borders of photography and video. In his 2005 *Shadow piece*, which has been recently exhibited in the Pompidou Center in Paris, in MUMOK in Vienna, or in the Hamburger Banhof in Berlin, the artist presents a black-and-white projection, with studio sound, of a spacious staircase in an entrance hall of an office building from 1950s.[12] The viewer can see people approaching the entrance door to the building and can hear their footsteps, together with the buzz of the nearby street. It is an evening of a sunny day when the setting sun casts long shadows of the people, far onto the office floor. The visitors come to the door, try to open it, check time, sometimes peep into the hall, and, as the door is closed, they walk off. The projected image fills the entire wall, and the viewer has a feeling of being inside the building, standing on a landing overlooking the entrance. Moreover, all the viewers entering the semi-dark room cast shadows on the floor of the imaginary landing. The dramatic tension of the installation comes from the play of the two sets of shadows: the fixed

---

[11] The latest volume of the series was published in September 2008, with a guest-editor, Richard Wright.

[12] This and many other installations by Clarebout are available on-line at a number of Websites, among others at http://www.hauserwirth.com/artists/4/david-claerb out/images-clips/26/.

shadow pattern played in the movie by its characters, and the unpredictable pattern created by the viewers, who are an integral part of the work. Among other artists, whose work is based on a similar rationale, we should mention Carole Benzaken, Shinji Ogawa, or Doris Salcedo. *Shadow piece* discovers a random environment, which does not simply reveal art/nature equivalence, but also works like a natural order, surrounding the viewer in such a way that the world "within" and the world "out there" become one. The same principle propels John Ashbery's poetic spaces. In the poet's latest volume, *A worldly country* (2007, 26), we find a brief quote that grasps its most conspicuous quality: "It's been real. I mean really real/like you can't imagine it."

References

Ashbery, John. 1989. *Reported Sightseeings: Art Chronicles, 1957-1987*, ed. by David Bergman. New York: Knopf.
—. 2007. *A Worldly Country*. New York: Ecco Press.
—. 2008. *Collected Poems 1956-1987*, ed. by Mark Ford. New York: The Library of America.
Bartczak, Kacper. 2006. *In Search of Communication and Community. The Poetry of John Ashbery*. Frankfurt am Main: Peter Lang.
Claerbout, David. 2005. *Shadow Piece*. Houser & Wirth: Artists. http://www.hauserwirth.com/artists/4/david-claerbout/images-clips/26/ (accessed on 24 July 2009).
Conte, Joseph, M. 1991. *Unending Design: The Forms of Postmodern Poetry*. Ithaca/London: Cornell Unniversity Press.
Cornell, Joseph. 1950. *Central Park Carrousel, In Memoriam*. MoMA: The Collection. http://www.moma.org/collection/browse_results.php?object_id=80771 (accessed on 24 July 2009).
Emerson, Ralph Waldo. 1969. Nature. In: *Selected Prose and Poetry,* ed. by Reginald L. Cook, 3-38. New York: Holt, Rinehart and Wilson.
Fletcher, Angus. 2004. *A New Theory for American Poetry. Democracy, the Environment, and the Future of Imagination*. Cambridge, MA/London: Harvard University Press.
Koethe, John. 1995. The absence of the noble presence. In *The Tribe of John. Ashbery and Contemporary Poetry*, ed. by Susan M. Schultz, 83-90. Tuscaloosa/London: The University of Alabama Press.
Kooning, Willem de. 1950. *Excavations*. The Art Institute of Chicago. http://www.artic.edu/aic/collections/artwork/76244 (accessed on 24 July 2009).
Kranzfelder, Ivo. 2006. *Edward Hopper. Vision of Reality*. Köln: Taschen.

McCorkle, James. 1995. Eros and reverie in the poetry of John Ashbery. In *The Tribe of John. Ashbery and Contemporary Poetry,* ed by Susan M. Schultz, 101-125. Tuscaloosa/London: The University of Alabama Press.

Morse, Jonathan. 1995. Typical Ashbery. In *The Tribe of John. Ashbery and Contemporary Poetry,* ed. by Susan M. Schultz, 15-25. Tuscaloosa/London: The University of Alabama Press.

Perloff, Marjorie. 1980. 'Fragments of a buried life': John Ashbery's dream songs. In *Beyond Amazement: New Essays on John Ashbery,* ed. by David Lehman, 66-86. Ithaca: Cornell University Press.

—. 1981. *The Poetics of Indeterminacy: Rimbaud to Cage.* Princeton, NJ: Princeton University Press.

—. 1996. *Wittgenstein's Ladder: Poetic Language and the Strangeness of the Ordinary.* Chicago: The University of Chicago Press.

Poulin, Alfred Jr. 1981. The experience of experience: A conversation with John Ashbery. *Michigan Quarterly Review* 20 (3). 242-255.

Reinfeld, Linda. 1992. *Language Poetry: Writing as Rescue.* Baton Rouge: Louisiana University Press.

Rose, Barbara. 1980. *American Painting. The Twentieth Century.* Rizzoli Editore: New York.

Sadowski, Witold. 2004. *Wiersz wolny jako tekst graficzny* [*Free verse as graphic text*] Kraków: Universitas.

Sławek, Tadeusz. 1984. *Wnętrze. Z problemów doświadczenia przestrzeni w poezji* [*The interior. The problems of spatial experience in poetry*]. Katowice: Uniwersytet Śląski.

Stitt, Peter. 1983. 'The art of poetry XXXIII.' Interview with John Ashbery. *Paris Review* 90, 31-59.

Vincent, John, Emil. 2007. *John Ashbery and You.* Athens GE/London: The University of Georgia Press.

CHAPTER TWENTY-TWO

"A PLACE YOU'VE NEVER BEEN": A NOTE ON THE CONCEPT OF SPACE IN MARK STRAND'S POETRY

MACIEJ MASŁOWSKI

1. The invisibility of space and the "spatiality of one's own body"

In one of his most frequently quoted poems "Keeping Things Whole" from the 1964 debut collection *Sleeping with One Eye Open* Mark Strand writes:

In a field
I am the absence
of field.
This is
always the case.
Wherever I am
I am what is missing.

When I walk
I part the air
and always
the air moves in
to fill the spaces
where my body's been.

We all have reasons
for moving.
I move

to keep things whole. (1981, 10)[1]

Leaving aside the metaphoric uses of the term space which reduce its function to that of a relative modifier, denominating always the space of something (the space of politics, the space of the city etc), Strand focuses upon the irremovable presence of space itself as central to human experience and yet mysteriously invisible; in the text under discussion this invisibility finds its expression in the text's failure to name space, which is allowed to exist only between the lines. In an attempt at explaining the invisibility of space (which shall be discussed in greater detail further in this paper), the philosopher Maurice Merleau-Ponty notices that "space represent[s] . . . a communication with the world more ancient than thought," and, as such,

> it can neither be observed, since it is presupposed in every observation, nor seen to emerge from a constituting operation, since it is of its essence that it be already constituted, for thus it can, by its magic, confer its own spatial particularizations upon the landscape without ever appearing itself. (2002, 296)

In other words, as a necessary condition of all perceptions space remains forever beyond the eye's scope.

A question that arises at this point is what enables the I-speaker of Strand's poem to recognize this perfectly transparent presence. Arguably, at the beginning of Strand's exploration of the concept of space lies the discovery of what Merleau-Ponty labels the "spatiality of one's own body," which differs radically from the spatial existence of an object. The philosopher writes: "The outline of my body is a frontier which ordinary spatial relations do not cross" (2002, 112). The edge of one's own body (*le corpse propre*) demarcates within the world a special kind of locus that is impenetrable to the spatial structure of external reality; as Kant notices (1996, 77), space can be conceptualized only as existing outside the limits of the subject's body. The initial observation that the I-speaker of "Keeping Things Whole" makes is therefore that he exists spatially and that, consequently, his being constitutes a rift within the world, that "in a field" he is literally the "absence of field."

Thus in Strand's poem space is linked with identity. The fact of the spatiality of one's own body noted in the opening lines of the text makes it possible for the subject to exist among things, which is to say to inhabit

---

[1] For the sake of the reader's convenience, the parenthetical references to Strand's texts shall be, wherever possible, limited to the 1981 edition of his selected poems.

the world of objects and yet remain different from them. Spatiality enables the emergence of singularity by means of which fragments of the world seal themselves off from one another with their impermeable surfaces. As a special kind of object, one's own body, Merleau-Ponty asserts (2002, 105), is "divorced from [other] objects, and reserves among them a quasi-space to which they have no access." When Strand writes, "Wherever I am / I am what is missing," it is therefore precisely the presence of space that allows the I-speaker to say the "I am" necessary for a subject to become. In this way, as Merleau-Ponty concludes, space announces, "at the very core of the subject, the fact of his birth" (296). Yet for Strand self-identification is a negative process: what the I-speaker is is always that which "is missing," that which is not the world, a gap in its otherwise homogenous structure. At the core of his being the I-speaker identifies a radical absence around which presence crystallizes in the midst of space, irreversibly disrupting its unity. Quite significantly, another name given by Merleau-Ponty to the "quasi-space" delineated within the world by the body is "void" (2002, 105). To quote the philosopher,

> Bodily space can be distinguished from external space . . . because it is the darkness needed in the theatre to show up the performance, . . . the zone of *not being* in front of which precise beings, figures and points can come to light. (115, emphasis added)

2. "I am what is missing": The hospitality and the hostility of empty space

Being that-which-is-missing is linked also with the notion of hospitality. As was demonstrated above, for Strand the emergence of being is possible only against the backdrop of space which is always and already there, embracing, with infinite patience, all phenomena. This unlimited capacity of space to take in being, to host things, marks what Klaus Held refers to as the world's "openness." According to Held, "the world happens as . . . a giving-place." Proposing as if a secular version of the Jewish concept of *tzimtzum*, that is, God's withdrawal from the universe that creates space for being to come into existence, Held contends that "the being of the world" is the "granting of open space for events to emerge. In this sense, the world is the all-embracing dimension of openness" (1997, 157). Significantly, Held links this openness with the Greek *uranos*, meaning sky—but also the world in its infinite totality (157)—and with the Platonic *chora*, place, and the derivative verb *choreo*, which Held proposes to translate as "to give place by withdrawing and becoming an

embracing space" (158). In order for being to be-come, the world has to
retreat, inviting the thing to inhabit it as its lack and to become, in the
world, the absence of world. Thus defined hospitality of the open space
forms the central intuition around which Strand's text is structured.

For Strand, then, space is that which makes being possible, that which
lets itself be parted on the arrival of the thing. Yet although in the poem
under discussion presence seems to be privileged, it is always
simultaneously called into question. "When I walk," Strand notes, "I part
the air / and always / the air moves in / to fill the spaces / where my body's
been." In Strand's poem, space becomes the otherness whose presence
enables the becoming of the subject while simultaneously threatening his
being; it is, to quote Merleau-Ponty (2002, 336), "the absolute 'outside',
correlative to, but also the negation of, subjectivity." Just like in Edward
Hopper's paintings (which became the subject of Strand's 2001
monograph[2]), in "Keeping Things Whole" space constitutes at once the
condition for subject's existence and the agent of its annihilation that dogs
the I-speaker's footsteps, erasing all traces of his presence. It is a void that
absorbs the subject's being, as in a poem "A Piece of the Storm":

> From the shadow of domes in the city of domes,
> A snowflake, a blizzard of one, weightless, entered your room
> And made its way to the arm of the chair where you, looking up
> From your book, saw it the moment it landed. That's all
> There was to it. No more than a solemn waking
> To brevity, to the lifting and falling away of attention, swiftly,
> A time between times, a flowerless funeral.
> No more than that
> Except for the feeling that this piece of the storm,
> Which turned into nothing before your eyes, would come back,
> That someone years hence, sitting as you are now, might say:
> "It's time. The air is ready. The sky has an opening." (1998, 20)

Empty space, the opening in the material structure of the world which
makes being possible, now turns out to be the vacuum that sucks in all
existence. And since, as Strand repeatedly insists in his oeuvre, the world
was not "planned / With us in mind" (1981, 9), the pact on whose strength
space offers us its hospitality is most fragile. This intuition is further
developed in the poem "Taking a Walk with You":

> We live unsettled lives
> And stay in a place

---

[2] *Hopper.* New York: Alfred A. Knopf.

Only long enough to find
We don't belong.
Even the clouds, forming
Noiselessly overhead,
Are cloudy without
Resembling us and, storming
The vacant air,
Don't take into account
Our present loneliness.
And yet, why should we care?
Already we are walking off
As if to say,
We are not here,
We've always been away. (9)

As in "Keeping Things Whole," space—conceptualized here as *uranos*, the sky—is characterized by its absolute otherness from the human form. Yet whereas in the former text space remained perfectly homogenous, in "Taking a Walk with You" it reveals its inner-structure marked by the presence of the clouds it secretes and rearranges according to the unfathomable rules of the sky. In the poem under discussion, space is a silent machinery, constantly operating at the heart of "vacant air" and sustaining—but also destabilizing—all being. By thus thinking space, Strand places himself in the American tradition that, from James Fenimore Cooper's *The Last of the Mohicans* (1826) to Cormac McCarthy's *The Road* (2006), has seen it as at the same time the welcoming openness of nature and the threatening vastness of the American landscape; as Charles Olson declares (1947, 11), "I take SPACE to be the central fact to man born in America, from Folsom cave to now. I spell it large because it comes large here. Large, and without mercy."

3. "Becoming a horizon": The dynamics of empty space

Significantly, both "Keeping Things Whole" and "Taking a Walk with You" represent being as movement: their I-speaker(s) "walk," "are walking off," "move," "part the air," and these itineraries are always reflected in complex reconfigurations of empty space. In the analyzed texts, being is therefore presented as transition, or rather transience, the process of passing itself materialized in the bodily form. In *Phenomenology of Perception* Merleau-Ponty insists on seeing "the human body as the outward manifestation of a certain manner of being-in-the-world" (2002, 64); to this formulation Strand adds: this manner of bodily being is not so much being as becoming, that is, an impossible synthesis of presence—

which is always necessarily pinned to some specific "here"—and an ongoing movement towards an infinitely distant destination. The "I"—this observation constitutes the central discovery in "Keeping Things Whole"— cannot exit space; it is inherently somewhere, able neither to disappear from the world nor to transcend the spatiality of its own body that can be only where it already is, since the slightest movement inevitably throws it beyond its current location into a new "here," while space fills in its tracks. In this sense, in Strand's poetry the subject is always simultaneously in and out of place, a "prey," to use Merleau-Ponty's phrase, "to an active nothingness" (191). This dislocation is encapsulated in the poem "Breath," where Strand writes (1981, 67): "by being both here and beyond / I am becoming a horizon." Leaving is therefore the only available way of existing within a world where, on the one hand, one always is and, on the other, one has "never been" (61). At this point, in Strand's oeuvre empty space becomes a correlate of nothingness, which, as Merleau-Ponty insists (1996, 64, trans. mine), cannot be thought otherwise than as "the edge of being," "perceivable only out of the corner of one's eye." If being is movement (as was suggested above), it is therefore a passage through nothingness, with no point of departure and no destination, and thus marked by the ultimate impossibility of arrival, as announced in Strand's poem "Black Maps":

Not the attendance of stones,
nor the applauding wind,
shall let you know
you have arrived,

nor the sea that celebrates
only departures,
nor the mountains,
nor the dying cities.

Nothing will tell you
where you are. (61)

Paradoxically, however, this hardly visible nothingness of empty space manifests itself by precisely withdrawing, and here lies another reason for its invisibility: its unfathomable nature is realized precisely in its disappearance. As Held observes in the already quoted text, space, taken up/occupied by the thing, withdraws, enabling being to exist in a specific "here," and this granting of co-present potentialities consists precisely in the escaping from our attention of the withholding. Thus, its total inconspicuousness belongs to this happening; the space-giving of the original emptiness completely disappears in favor of that for which it leaves place. (1997, 157-158)

By rediscovering this invisible existence, Strand defamiliarizes space, revealing its presence. Thus his poetic discourse necessitates a radical restructuring of the Western ontology, which, since Plato, as Held points out (161), has seen the thing as the privileged mode of being. In this tradition, whatever is real is ultimately that which exists object-ively. Accordingly, space is conceptualized as a container where the thing is to be found. For Strand, however, space cannot be viewed in negative terms as a lack of something. Rather, in his works empty space functions as pure potentiality. This dynamic character of space is repeatedly suggested by the poet in the recurring images of the wind, storm, gale, or blizzard; all these phenomena are manifestations of empty space in motion—in the random patterns outlined by the whirling snowflakes or leaves the untraceable architecture of emptiness is momentarily exposed, which is why the storm, the blizzard, or the gale are in this poetry moments of sudden realization of the instability of all seemingly fixed forms. In "Violent Storm" Strand writes:

Deeper and darker than ever, the night unveils
Its dubious plans, and the rain
Beats down in gales
Against the roof. We sit behind
Closed windows, bolted doors,
Unsure and ill at ease
While the loose, untidy wind,
Making an almost human sound, pours
Through the open chambers of the trees.
We cannot take ourselves or what belongs
To us for granted. (1981, 6)

Situated in this perspective, the thing ceases to be the primary mode of existence, which is instead conceptualized in Strand's poetry as a process, or, as Held points out, referring to the phenomenological tradition, appearance. In Strand's oeuvre, being is what Held labels "e-vent" or "e-mergence" "that come[s] forth out of the world due to its space-giving character" (157). Being in these poems happens, appearing at the heart of emptiness; it takes place, constantly emerging from and simultaneously disappearing in space. It is, to quote Strand (1998, 20), a "piece of the storm," a seemingly solid entity exuded and at once absorbed by the void.

4. "To keep things whole": Ethics of empty space

However, although empty space in its incomprehensible vastness incites anxiety, Strand proposes a way of thinking about this emptiness which goes beyond the traditional alternative of resignation in the face of nothingness on the one hand and the naïve belief in the primacy of being over inexistence on the other.

In the final section of "Keeping Things Whole," Strand states (1981, 10): "We all have reasons / for moving. / I move / to keep things whole." The openness of space in which the hospitality of the world manifests itself inspires gratitude and imposes upon the subject an ethical imperative which seems to organize Strand's oeuvre. In this sense, Strand's poetry constitutes what Dick Kirby refers to as a "program of self-effacement" (1990, 7), an attempt at the restoration of the original emptiness and at savoring, to quote Strand, "the honey of absence" (1981, 91). From book to book, Strand's I-speaker(s) consistently submit(s) themselves (himself?) to the hard, monkish practice of "giving oneself up," initiating, as Richard Howard notes (1974, 104), a "celebration of the empty place." As Strand himself admits in an interview with Michael O'Keefe, "self is a kind of sickness" and "forgetting of the self is a kind of antidote." In a poem entitled "The Remains" Strand therefore writes:

> I empty myself of the names of others. I empty my pockets.
> I empty my shoes and leave them beside the road.
> At night I turn back the clocks;
> I open the family album and look at myself as a boy.
>
> What good does it do? The hours have done their job.
> I say my own name. I say goodbye.
> . . . .
> Time tells me what I am. I change and I am the same.
> I empty myself of my life and my life remains. (1981, 51)

Here, the self itself is conceptualized in spatial terms as a container which can be emptied of or filled up with numberless artifacts that, however, eventually prove perfectly disposable. What is more, in Strand's poetry even the body seems sometimes to be merely an addition to the underlying emptiness, as in the poem "Giving Myself Up," which constitutes a record of the physical self-decomposition of the subject:

> I give up my eyes which are glass eggs.
> I give up my tongue.
> I give up my mouth which is the constant dream of my tongue.

. . . .
I give up my clothes which are walls that blow in the wind
and I give up my spirit that lives in them.
I give up. I give up.
And you will have none of it because already I am beginning
again without anything. (1981, 52)

For Strand, these repeatedly undertaken efforts at baring oneself of
everything that on the surface appears to be essential to one's being are
thus not an extravagant intellectual exercise but a program of returning to
the source of existence and the original freshness of being. In this sense,
his meditation on the nature of empty space and the resultant resolution "to
keep things whole" is a radical gesture that runs counter to the traditional
politics that, as Jacques Derrida notices, relies upon the practice of
assigning fixed positions and thus creating a structured, governable space
(1999, 43).

Interestingly, writing constitutes a vital part of this practice. In the
quoted interview with O'Keefe, Strand remarks: "you have to forget self
when you write," which finds its conceptualization in "A Poem," where a
personified text visits the I-speaker:

He leans over my bed and he says he has come
to kill me. The job
will be done in stages.

First, my toenails
will be clipped, then my toes
and so on until
nothing is left of me.
He takes a small instrument
from his keychain and begins.
. . . .

How much time passes,
I cannot tell. But when I come to
I hear him say he has reached my neck
and will not be able to continue
because he is tired. I tell him
that he has done enough,
that he should go home and rest.
He thanks me and leaves. (1981, 15).

In a sense, the I-speaker's attempts "to keep things whole" prove futile: in
the end something inescapably remains and forms a centre around which

presence crystallizes anew in emptiness. Yet in the process the underlying distinction between being and nothingness is suspended and what is left for the I-speaker to do is to consciously participate in the mysterious mechanics of appearance. In the poem "The Guardian" from the 1970 collection *Darker*, Strand notes:

> The sun setting. The lawns on fire.
> The lost day, the lost light.
> Why do I love what fades?
>
> You who left, who were leaving,
> what dark rooms do you inhabit?
> Guardian of my death,
> preserve my absence.
>
> I am alive. (1981, 58)

Arguably, the effort at the preservation of absence and the continuous meditation on empty space form, at least to date, the central imperatives of Strand's poetic project.

References

Derrida, Jacques. 1999. Χώρα / *Chora*, trans. by Maria Gołębiewska. Warszawa: Wydawnictwo KR.

Held, Klaus. 1997. World, emptiness, nothingness: A phenomenological approach to the religious tradition of Japan. *Human Studies* 20 (2): 153-167.

Howard, Richard. 1974. Review of *The Story of our Lives*, by Mark Strand. *Ohio Review* 15 (3): 104-107.

Kant, Immanuel. 1996. *Critique of Pure Reason*, trans. by Werner S. Pluhar. Indianapolis: Hackett.

Kirby, David. 1990. *Mark Strand and the Poet's Place in Contemporary culture*. Columbia: University of Missouri Press.

Merleau-Ponty, Maurice. 2002. *Phenomenology of Perception*, trans. by Colin Smith. London: Routledge.

—. 1996. *Widzialne i niewidzialne*, trans. by Małgorzata Kowalska et al. Warszawa: Fundacja Aletheia.

Olson, Charles. 1947. *Call me Ishmael*. San Francisco: City Lights.

Strand, Mark. 1981. *Selected Poems*. New York: Atheneum.

—. 1998. *Blizzard of One*. New York: Alfred A. Knopf.

—. 2003. Interview by Michael O'Keefe. *Post Road Magazine* 13.
    http://www.postroadmag.com/13/etcetera/Okeefe.phtml
—. 2006. *Man and Camel*. New York: Alfred A. Knopf.

CHAPTER TWENTY-THREE

VARIOUS DEPICTIONS OF CEMETERIES IN GRAVEYARD POETRY

JAROSŁAW MIHUŁKA

John Young, in *A Criticism on the Elegy written in a Country Church Yard. Being a continuation of Dr. Johnson's Criticism On the Poems Of Gray* (1783, 20), wonders "What is the most proper Church-yard?" and "Whether there be a Taste in Church-yards." Graveyard poets, the loose group of poets who flourished in the mid-eighteenth century, tried to answer these questions. The graveyard poets included mainly Thomas Gray, Thomas Parnell, Robert Blair and Edward Young, although we can find more poets who discussed similar topics in their poems. They all wrote their works in the age called Pre-Romanticism, also known as Post-Augustanism. Although Augustan and Romantic are theoretically opposites, in practice "post-Augustan" and "pre-Romantic" are often used interchangeably. The use of these terms suggests certain ambiguity which can be also noticed in the case of the various presentations of cemeteries by the graveyard poets.

Thomas Gray calls graves "The mansions of the dead" ("Elegy" l. 39) but the presentation of the surroundings of the churchyard is neither violent nor terrifying. On the contrary, the environs are calm and quiet—a village, herds and laborers returning home, a brook running over pebbles, a wood (in Young 1783, 21)—a normal, everyday life of people and nature. Among all these usual things and situations there is "the surface swelling here and there with common graves" (21), which seems to be perfectly blended with the presented scenery. Gray does not give a description of a churchyard which is overwhelming and abounding with scary visions; it is just one of the components of an everyday life. Thomas Parnell's description of a churchyard in "Night-piece on Death" (1722) is more accurate and detailed than that of Gray. The surroundings are also regarded as very essential:

In distant prospect, a lake: resting on its bosom, the Moon, surrounded by Stars, having for ground a sky deep azure: on the right, rising grounds, "*retiring from dimness from the sight*:" on the left, the Church-yard; or (as he, in imitation of Hebrew simplicity, calls it) the *Place of Graves*, surrounded by a wall, which is laved by a silent stream: a steeple belonging no doubt to the Church: a charnel-house, over-canopied with yew: graves, with their turf osier-bound: other graves, with smooth flat stones inscribed: and others still, splendidly done out with marble. (in Young 1783, 20-1)

The general impression is similar to Gray's "Elegy" due to the fact that both in Gray's and in Parnell's poems calmness of the scenery and the obvious, natural place of a graveyard appear in the foreground. There are differences as to the images but they convey the same meaning: in Gray there is a village with its residents coming back from work, which symbolises an idle atmosphere and so is the impression when Parnell mentions "lake: resting on its bosom". In Gray's "Elegy" there is a brook running over pebbles and Parnell presents a silent stream which washes a wall that surrounds the graveyard. Brook or stream may symbolise a boundary of two worlds which in those two poems is blurred and hence the brook runs over the pebbles close to the graveyard and the stream washes the graveyard's wall.

1. Trees and other plants in graveyard poetry

One of the common images present in the graveyard poetry of the eighteenth century is the picture of the dead buried by a tree. Young points to the fact that "A human body buried at the foot of a large tree, with strong spreading roots, is more consonant to the poetry, than to practice" (1783, 22). Here, the first traces of Romanticism are exposed— the poetry goes beyond the real life and it is the same with the poetry of tombs and graveyards. In the poems discussed, it is easy, as Sutherland in his *Preface to the Eighteenth Century Poetry* (1966, 22) asserts, "to meet with entirely fresh and original observation, a seizing upon the thing seen however unusual or infrequent it may be." The origins of focusing on trees as often indispensable components of burial place can be traced back to the ages of high antiquity (Young 1783, 86). There is no certainty as to the reason why the trees appear by the graves. One explanation is presented by Wright in *The Grave, by Robert Blair; to which is added Gray's Elegy*. According to Wright, those trees (for example, yews, beeches, cypresses, elm trees or oaks), being evergreens, may be treated as emblems of the immortality of the soul due to the fact that they never shed leaves. The pictures of trees by the grave appear in almost every single poem of the era in which the graveyard poetry flourished. Many churchyards presented in that poetry are planted or hedged around with yew trees, as they add a gloomy and somber air to English churchyards. Yew, or "you," trees invoke in the minds of the poets a representation of the ultimate end of us all. They appear, for instance, in Robert Blair's "The Grave" (1743) where they are called a (ll. 22-23) "Cheerless, unsocial plant! that loves to dwell / Midst sculls and coffins, epitaphs and worms." The tree is displayed as having a lack of desire for the company of others, not only plants but also living creatures (besides worms). The yew needs no company but the dead buried by it.

In the above cited extract from *A Criticism on the Elegy...*, Young elevates the role of the yew tree by the fact that he compares it to a canopy which hangs over the charnel-house resembling the baldachin hanging over the altar as a symbol of authority (ll. 53-54): "Now from yon black and fun'ral yew, / That bathes the charnel-house with dew." The primary function of a canopy is to provide shade or other shelter and the yew tree bestows such a protection upon the dead so that they can rest in peace. In his "Elegy," Gray also mentions the yew tree when he writes that (l. 13): "Beneath those rugged elms, that yew-tree's shade."

Another plant that often appears in the graveyard poetry is an elm tree. The origin of this word has some religious and funeral connotations: the word "orme" (French word for "elm") is derived from such ancient languages as Sumerian and Babylonian, and means "serpent" or "worm." Both these words have some associations with eternity and death—a serpent shown swallowing its own tale represents eternity and the worms midst which the graveyard tree (a yew) dwells ("The Grave") refer to death. Similarly to Thomas Parnell in "The Night Piece on Death," Blair also elevates and shows a great respect to the graveyard tree—in his case it is an elm tree—by calling it "reverend" (ll. 45-49):

> Quite round the pile, a row of reverend elms,
> (Coeval near with that) all ragged show,
> Long lash'd by the rude winds. Some rift half down
> Their branchless trunks; others so thin at top,
> That scarce two crows can lodge in the same tree.

Cypress tree, which designates hope, was an indispensable element of any Roman funeral and its branches adorned the vestibule while the body lay in the state. Among the graveyard poets it was Edward Young who made use of the cypress tree in his presentation of a cemetery in "The Complaint, or Nine Thoughts on Life Death and Immortality: in Nine Nights" (1742-45). As in the case of the yew in Gray's "Elegy," Young mentions the shading function of the cypress but it is not presented in a positive way; on the contrary, Young writes (Night I 4): "The vale funeral, the sad cypress gloom; / The land of apparitions, empty shades!" or (Night V 61): "Beneath Death's gloomy, silent cypress shades." The cypress tree presented by Young brings beyond any doubt some negative connotations: the tree is gloomy, sad, silent and its shades are of death. The tone is completely different than that in Gray's work in which the yew and its role is praised.

Thomas Gray seems to be the most concerned of all graveyard poets of the 18th century with presenting symbols in the forms of plants. Besides the above mentioned yew and elm trees, he touches upon the presence of an ivy and a thorn in a cemetery. The ivy is a symbol of immortality, friendship and faithfulness and due to the fact that it is an evergreen that climbs over a tomb it signifies the need for protection. One of the elements of the graveyard surroundings presented in Gray's "Elegy" is a tower which is covered with an ivy (l. 9): "Save that from yonder ivy-mantled tower." A thorn is treated by Gray in the same way as the yew or other cemetery trees. It is associated with Christ's crown of thorn and represents earthly sorrows. In "Elegy," Gray presents a thorn as a plant under which the dead is buried (l. 116): "Graved on the stone beneath yon aged thorn."

Trees and other plants one can find in the graveyard have a symbolic significance and, as it has been already suggested, it is more typical of poetry than of real life. The role of yews, cypresses, elm trees, beeches or oaks is clearly explained: they represent immortality and, as the yews in Gray's "Elegy," provide shelter (shade) upon the buried. The graveyard trees are either praised (the yews in Gray's work), highly respected (a "reverend" elm tree in Blair's "The Grave") or there appear negative associations with them (as the cypress in Edward Young's "Nine Thoughts on Life Death and Immortality: in Nine Nights.") Regardless of its various connotations, the tree by which the deceased is lying is clearly marked and its role in the poetry of the graveyard poets is highly symbolic.

2. The grave as an element of nature in graveyard poetry: The overground and underground perspective

James Sutherland (1966, 112) argues that "The normal eighteenth-century preference was for the natural scene that showed welcome signs of Man's occupation, for the cultivated landscape with smoke rising from cottage chimneys, and the spire of the decent church topping the neighbouring hill." In the footnotes (112) we can find the explanation of the word "decent" used in this context: "The decent church: decent because appropriate to its surroundings, customary, unostentatious, assuming its due and proper place in the landscape and in the life of the community."

For the graveyard poets not only churches but also churchyards were among those "decent" places in the country scenery. The poets differ as regards the perspective they take while "looking at" the graves and their surroundings. One group of graveyard poets focuses their attention on what is on the ground and the other is interested in the underground.

The key representative of "the overground" fraction is Thomas Gray's "Elegy Written in a Country Churchyard" (1751). Gray wrote this poem in the time when burying in open-air cemeteries was becoming more and more popular among all social classes. Even those who belonged to the upper classes, which in the 16th and 17th centuries preferred to be buried in churches, in the 18th century wanted to have their graves outside. According to Joshua Scodel (1991, 360), "Gray's contrast between church and churchyard in terms of social class and the distinction between art and nature both exemplifies and influences the new eighteenth-century sense of distinction between indoor and outdoor commemoration."

In *L'Homme devant la mort* (1977, 345) Philippe Aries argues that choosing churchyard as a place of burial instead of church was a general tendency which indicated the return to nature. Scodel seems to agree with this saying that the choice was motivated by a desire to assert in death their links to "simple" nature and to the socially humble, who were regarded as the closest to nature. Both the private gardens of the upper classes and the public churchyards present this new cult of natural simplicity. The public churchyard (Aries 332) at the end of the 17th c. and in the 18th c. was often a kind of a pasture where the parson's cattle and sheep were grazed. The graves of the rural cemetery were as if blended with that scenery constituting a component of everyday life. Consequently, grave (the image of death) approached nature (life). Gray's "Elegy" is an exemplification of such presentation of cemetery which plays here the role of a metaphor of death.

From the 18th century onwards, the rural churchyard with its lying or standing gravestones united with nature seemed to be a calm and quiet picture where the fear of death weakened. The manner in which death was perceived changed and it appeared that certain balance of melancholic simplicity, represented by English cemeteries, would be reached. However, as Aries (335) notices, the recurring thoughts of a minute character of all things eventually led to the thoughts of nothingness. It is a kind of a dramatic return of a melancholic life to its empty centre. The moment of this return was the time of the retreat from life, of the solitude. The eighteenth century required plunging into the thoughts of death, which might have led to the increased popularity of the 17th-century concept of nothingness which preceded Chaos which came before Creation. This way of perceiving things might have resulted in the emergence of the fraction of graveyard poets that focused on the dark and the underground.

Grażyna Bystydzieńska, in her work devoted to the life and output of Edward Young (1982, 131), claims that "The Romantics were more fascinated with the images coming from the kingdom of vaults (minerals, jewels, etc.) than with what is on the ground and in the sky. Life was hidden deep in the ground and the mystery of creation can be found there." [trans. mine] The fascination with the underground can be already observed in the 17th century when John Donne, in his "Meditation 2" (1624), argues that (in Wolny 1999, 6) "*Earth* is the *center* of my *Bodie*, *Heaven* is the *center* of my *Soule*; these two are naturall places of those two." Ryszard Wolny, in his book entitled *The Ruinous Anatomy. The philosophy of death in John Donne and the earlier seventeenth-century English poetry and prose* (1999, 168), says: "What is of particular importance for us, [...] is that the concentric scheme of nature leading inevitably to decay [...] is a vertical movement downward." This idea of "downwardness" may have some connections with an ancient image of death which depicted Thanatos in the guise of the youth or genius turning his torch downward. As Karl S. Guthke, in *The Gender of Death: A Cultural History in Art and Literature* (1999, 134-5), asserts, this personification of death is also most appropriate for the eighteenth century. The attention is directed downwards, to the underground which resulted in the growing tendency towards the fascination with the "treasures" of the underground. Consequently, in pre-Romanticism, it is not an open-air graveyard any more that arouses interest, but the grave itself with its darkness and gloom.

3. Robert Blair as a representative of the "underground" fraction of Graveyard Poets

The idea of the concentration upon the underground features of grave is clearly depicted in "The Grave" (1743) by Robert Blair. The poem was influential in giving rise to the graveyard school of poetry and Blair himself is sometimes regarded as the "founding father" of the whole movement, although Thomas Parnell's "Night Piece on Death" (1726) was in fact written much earlier.

From the very beginning of the poem, there is no doubt that Blair focuses upon the underground, on the grave which resembles dark and deep cellar (ll. 13-16):

> Where naught but silence reigns, and night, dark night,
> Dark as was chaos, ere the infant Sun
> Was roll'd together, or had tried his beams
> Athwart the gloom profound.

Here, one can see a reference to the previously mentioned concept of nothingness. In this short excerpt the emphasis is put on the dominating role of dark over light. It is the Night which is the mother to the Sun ("infant Sun"), it is superior to the Sun due to the fact that the dark (of Chaos) came before the light and despite the power of the Sun's beams the gloom pervades. Darkness is one of the characteristic features of the grave which Blair calls a (l. 9) "dread thing." The grave evokes bad associations and its name arouses fear (l. 10 "men shiver, when thou'rt named.") The grave with all its attributes has also a great impact upon nature which is disturbed (ll. 10-11): "Nature appall'd shakes off her wonted firmness." This image can be understood in at least two ways: on one hand the grave and its powerful companion (darkness) have a potent influence upon everything, even upon the nature which is the symbol of balance. On the other hand, however, it might be the ground as the representative of nature whose "firmness" has been violated by the grave. This understanding is close to Rousseau's "Everything is good as it comes from the hands of the author of nature, but everything degenerates in the hands of man." Blair also depicts nature from another, more holistic point of view: nature which is understood as the representative of everything that lives is afraid of the grave symbolising death, that is the parting of body and soul (ll. 374-376): "Nature runs back and shudders at the sight, / And every life-string bleeds at thoughts of parting; / For part they must." First, nature in the form of the ground is "senseless" due to the fact that it is disturbed and violated by the burial practices (which symbolise Death) and then, nature, perceived as everything that lives, loses its firmness and fears Death to such an extent that it quivers at its sight.

In "The Grave" Blair, like Gray, also uses the metaphor of turf in order to emphasise the recurring character of nature (ll. 487-90):

> The very turf on which we tread once lived;
> And we that live must lend our carcases
> To cover our own offspring: in their turns
> They too must cover theirs.

Here, the dead human body is compared to a carcass which plays the role of a fertiliser that enriches the ground and, eventually, serves as a burial ground upon which the living ones tread. Then the living ones die and "lend" their bodies to be used as a ground covering for the bodies of the next generation. This is an example of depicting death in its very physical sense. Blair uses the word "carcass" in the poem two more times (ll. 341-6, 169-74):

> To his own carcase, now lies cheaply lodged.
> By clamorous appetites no longer teased,
> Nor tedious bills of charges and repairs.
> (…)
> Why this ado in earthing up a carcase
> That's fallen into disgrace, and in the nostril
> Smells horrible?

Cemeteries and graveyards changed its appearance throughout the centuries. At first they were mass graves outside the city, later they were situated by the church; cemeteries reflected people's status but also became the main places where the new attitudes towards death could be observed. The dual nature of pre-Romanticism—on one hand going back to Neoclassicism, and, on the other, preceding Romanticism—is clearly visible in the various perceptions of cemetery. Gray and Parnell, being called in this article the representatives of the "overground" fraction of graveyard poets, showed cemetery as an element of an everyday scenery; in their poems they often refer to the co-existence of cemetery and nature. Although one can also notice the links between graves and nature in the poems by Blair or Young, the peaceful co-existence of these two can be seen only in "Elegy" and "The Night Piece on Death." In Young's "Night Thoughts," cemetery plants bring negative connotations whilst in Blair's poem the grave makes the nature disturbed, it arouses fear and is called a "dread thing." In contrast to the poems by Gray and Parnell, in "The Grave" we can clearly observe the Romantic fascination with the underground.

References

Aries, Phillipe. 1977. *L'Homme devant la mort*. Paris: Le Seuil.

Bystydzieńska, Grażyna. 1982. *Między oświeceniem a romantyzmem. Studium o twórczości Edwarda Younga*. Lublin: Maria Curie-Skłodowska University Press.

Guthke, Karl S. 1999. *The Gender of Death: A Cultural History in Art and Literature*. Cambridge: Cambridge University Press.

Scodel, Joshua. 1991. *The English Poetic Epitaph: Commemoration and Conflict from Jonson to Wordsworth*. Ithaca/London: Cornell University Press.

Sutherland, James. 1966. *Preface to Eighteenth Century Poetry*. Oxford: Oxford University Press.

Wolny, Ryszard. 1999. *The Ruinous Anatomy. The Philosophy of Death in John Donne and the Earlier Seventeenth-century English Poetry and Prose*. Perth: Polish-Australian Cultural Society Press.

Wright, George (ed.). 1787. *The Grave, by Robert Blair; to which is added Gray's Elegy*. London: Scatcherd & Whitaker.

Young, Edward. 1854. The Complaint, or Night Thoughts on Life, Death and Immortality. In *The Poetical Works of Edward Young*, ed. by Milner and Sowerby. Halifax: Milner and Sowerby Press.

Young, John. 1783. *A Criticism on the Elegy Written in a Country Church Yard. Being a Continuation of Dr. Johnson's Criticism on the Poems of Gray*. London: G. Wilkie Press.

Chapter Twenty-Four

Camelot—
A Vision or an Absolute Reality
an Alfred Tennyson's *Idylls of the King*

Ewa Młynarczyk

Since it was first mentioned in the late 12th century by Chrétien de Troyes in his *Lancelot*, Camelot has come to be inextricably linked with the Arthurian legend. As Jenkins points out, "the idea of the [Arthurian] capital only comes into the story after the general Arthur has been mythologized into a king" (Jenkins 1990, 34). In the sixteenth century, John Leland attempted to identify the place with Cadbury Castle in Somerset. But even though his assumption was partly corroborated by the excavations carried out at the site in 1966-70, which revealed the existence of a large hill fort refortified in the Arthurian times (Lupack 2007, 438), Camelot still belongs to the realm of the legendary rather than to that of the historical. Yet, in Tennyson's long poem, *Idylls of the King*, it seems that the city is not merely a legendary place associated with King Arthur, as its significance as the centre and symbol of the Arthurian reign has been further expanded. Tennyson's Camelot may be perceived as reflecting the Victorian need for an idealized space beyond time, a refuge from the ugliness of the industrial revolution, the hectic pace of the scientific discoveries, and the overwhelming religious doubt. Still, what differentiates Tennyson's depiction of Camelot from its other representations in his predecessors in Arthurian literature is the uncertainty concerning the ontological status of the city, as the Camelot of the *Idylls* seems to be suspended between vision and reality. Apparently, the true significance of the city can be better understood when analysed in the light of Eliade's notions of sacred space and time.

This most important dilemma concerning Camelot is introduced in *Gareth and Lynette*. Gareth, the King's nephew and a would-be Knight of the Round Table, approaches the walls of the city together with his companions, and is subjected to an apparent fallacy of perception:

> At times the summit of the high city flash'd;
> At times the spires and turrets half-way down
> Prick'd thro' the mist; at times the great gate shone
> Only, that open'd on the field below:
> Anon, the whole fair city had disappear'd. (*Gareth and Lynette*, 189-193)

To the newcomers, the city presents itself as changing and unstable, hidden in the mists and illusory. Gareth's companions are afraid that "(...) there is no such city anywhere, / But all a vision" (*Gareth and Lynette*, 203-204). As they draw closer, they are further amazed to see the carvings on the gate to the city move before their eyes:

> Then those with Gareth for so long a space
> Stared at the figures, that at last it seem'd
> The dragon-boughts and elvish emblemings
> Began to move, seethe, twine and curl: they call'd
> To Gareth, 'Lord, the gateway is alive.' (*Gareth and Lynette*, 227-231)

While they try to explain the phenomenon by resorting to folk tales about the King as a fairy changeling, supported by the magic of the great Merlin, the wizard himself undermines this interpretation with his references to optical tricks, which were so popular in the Victorian age. Yet, at the same time, he warns the newcomers that at Camelot "(...) there is nothing in it as it seems / Saving the King" (260-261). Gareth, on the other hand, remains sceptical yet unconvinced by either solution. Even though Tennyson claimed to describe all seemingly supernatural phenomena in such a way as to leave a rational explanation possible, he still insisted on not giving any final answers to the symbolism in his work: "Poetry is like shot-silk with many glancing colours. Every reader must find his own interpretation according to his ability, and according to his sympathy with the poet" (Tennyson 1897, 127).

It seems that this enigmatic state of the city can be explained when projected against the background of Eliade's ideas on sacred space and time. In *The Sacred and the Profane*, he discusses the way in which the religious man (*homo religiosus*) introduces order into amorphous, profane space. He craves to remain in constant contact with the only real, the absolute, the presence of which is revealed to him through *hierophany*, or the manifestation of the sacred into the profane world. As Eliade observes, this break in the homogeneity of space "reveals an absolute fixed point, a center" (Eliade 1987, 21), and thus provides the religious man with the most important point from which to turn the surrounding chaos into a new world, his own cosmos.

While this juxtaposition of an anthropological theory concerning the archaic societies with a 19th century English poem set in legendary medieval times may seem to be somewhat far-fetched, on closer inspection it turns out that the two works display a number of important similarities. All the afore-mentioned key notions, such as chaos and cosmos, the center of the world, and especially the dichotomy between the real and unreal, find their place in Tennyson's version of the Arthurian narrative.

In the pre-Arthurian epoch the land is plunged in confusion and overwhelming chaos:

> For many a petty king ere Arthur came
> Ruled in this isle, and ever waging war
> Each upon other, wasted all the land;
> And still from time to time the heathen host
> Swarmed overseas, and harried what was left.
> And so there grew great tracts of wilderness,
> Wherein the beast was ever more and more,
> But man was less and less, till Arthur came. (*The Coming of Arthur*, 5-12)

Men are degraded to the level of wild beasts and the two merge into one in what Tennyson describes as "wolf-like men" (32), which are "Worse than the wolves" (33), children stolen and raised by their surrogate wolf mothers in the wilderness. Yet, it is not only the heathen hordes and wild animals that are called "wild beasts"; the term is consistently applied to denote the petty kings fighting among themselves to gain temporary and unstable supremacy over one another. In the realm devoid of moral values brother turns against brother as King Leodegran is assailed by King Urien.

The coming of Arthur can be seen as the introduction of Eliade's *homo religiosus*. The passage that is the most important for such identification is his speech to the Knights after they have returned from the quest for the Holy Grail. The quest, which apparently reflects the Knights' need for a spiritual rebirth in the laziness and stagnation of the Arthurian realm, does not appeal to the King, who is too much concerned about his duties in the realm to "(…) follow wandering fires, / Lost in the quagmire" (*The Holy Grail*, 888-889). Instead, when the work of the day is completed, he experiences his personal glimpses into the absolute reality:

> In moments when he feels he cannot die,
> And knows himself no vision to himself,

Nor the high God a vision, nor that One
Who rose again. (*The Holy Grail*, 913-916)

Apparently, in the above-quoted passage, the word "vision" takes on a
pejorative meaning, and instead of being a manifestation of the sacred into
reality it is used here as a synonym of "illusion", "appearance", which
conceals the world of *sacrum* from the eyes of common men. Hence, to
most of the Knights except Galahad the quest does not result in true
spiritual experience, but, on the contrary, turns into a chase of projections
of a feverish mind.

Thus endowed with exceptional insight, the King is the only character
who is able to see through the appearances of transitory life, the only one,
who, as Merlin observes, is not trying to hide his real self at Camelot. His
mysterious speech has its counterpart in Tennyson's conviction that the
two notions of space and time should be annihilated as "matter is merely
the shadow of something greater than itself, which we poor short-sighted
creatures cannot see" (Tennyson 1908, 498).

It seems that Arthur becomes the instrument of Godly intervention on
earth, as he endeavours to create his own realm. His actions in this world
of wasteland and chaos are metaphorically depicted as the introduction of
light:

(...) Then he drave
The heathen; after, slew the beast, and felled
The forest, *letting in the sun*, and made
Broad pathways for the hunter and the knight. (*The Coming of Arthur*, 58-61,
emphasis mine)

These images very much agree with the way in which Eliade describes the
founding of the world through the repetition of the original cosmogony.
He observes that

[w]hether it is a case of clearing uncultivated ground or of conquering and
occupying a territory already inhabited by 'other' human beings, ritual
taking possession must always repeat the cosmogony. For in the view of
archaic societies everything that is not 'our world' is not yet a world. A
territory can be made ours only by creating it anew, that is, by consecrating
it. (Eliade 1987, 31-32)

Thus Arthur creates his own sacred space, and the purity of these "fair
beginnings of a nobler time" (*The Coming of Arthur*, 456) is emphasized
by the "stainless white" (455) of Arthur's attire and the freshness of the

spring in May. At the centre of this sacred universe of Arthurian realm lies the city of Camelot.

One of the images of the Centre of the World according to Eliade is "the cosmic mountain", which, as he comments, expresses "the connection between heaven and earth", thus "it is believed to be at the center of the world" (Eliade 1987, 38). This idea is also present in the *Idylls*, as the location of Camelot is "the Royal mount" (*Gareth and Lynette*, 187), also called "the sacred mount of Camelot" (*The Holy Grail*, 227). Tennyson's intention to depict Camelot as a holy place situated at the top of a mountain can be still better deduced from his sketch in prose written about 1833, where he describes "the sacred Mount of Camelot", rising from "the land of Lyonnesse". The Mount is "the most beautiful in the world, sometimes green and fresh in the beam of morning, sometimes all one splendour, folded in the golden mists of the West", it is surrounded by "gardens and bowers and palaces", and at its top there are "King Arthur's hall, and the holy Minster with the Cross of gold" (Tennyson 1897, 122). Eliade further observes that the sacred mount represents "an *axis mundi* connecting earth with heaven" and thus "it in a sense touches heaven and hence marks the highest point in the world" (Eliade 1987, 38). Again, such imagery can be found in the depiction of Camelot with its spires reaching out to heaven:

Camelot, a city of shadowy palaces
And stately, rich in emblem and the work
Of ancient kings who did their days in stone;
Which Merlin's hand, the Mage at Arthur's court,
Knowing all arts, had touch'd, and everywhere
At Arthur's ordinance, tipt with lessening peak
And pinnacle, and had made it spire to heaven. (*Gareth and Lynette*, 296-302)

Apparently, such a way of crafting the turrets is no mere coincidence; it is clearly stated that the high pinnacles were created "At Arthur's ordinance" (301), which again reveals his need to remain in contact with the absolute by means of the vertical opening upwards.

Thus, the Center proper, defined by Eliade as "precisely the place where a break in plane occurs, where space becomes sacred, hence pre-eminently *real*" (Eliade 1987, 45), in the case of the Arthurian realm appears to be the city itself, and, on a smaller scale, Arthur's hall. It seems that already the gate to Camelot, "the weird white gate" (*Gareth and Lynette*, 648), the like of which has never been seen under heaven (209), is crucial for the significance of the city. With the central image of the Lady of the Lake, her arms stretched in the shape of the cross and a sacred fish floating over her breast, and "Arthur's wars in weird devices done, / New things and old co-twisted, as if Time / Were nothing" (221-223) carved to both her sides, the whole topped with the representation of the mysterious three Queens, the gate both displays the spiritual guardians of the city and introduces the important concept of the suspension of time. It seems that the images on the gate commemorate the coronation scene and place it on the same temporal level with Arthur's victorious battles, thus annihilating the passing of time.

This idea of the sacred time, which is not progressive but cyclical, will be also important in the portrayal of the hall of King Arthur, which can be interpreted as an equivalent of Eliade's temple. It seems to be the centre within the centre, a replica of the cosmic mountain, and hence to "constitute the pre-eminent 'link' between earth and heaven" (Eliade 1987, 39). According to Eliade, the temple is both an *imago mundi*, in which the four parts of the interior represent the four cardinal directions (62), as well as "the earthly reproduction of a transcendent model" (58), which thus participates in the sacred space and time.

While in Tennyson's sketch from 1833, upon the mountain there were situated both King Arthur's hall and the minster, it seems that in the *Idylls* the role of the latter has been taken over by the former. This can be especially visible in the coronation scene, in which the hall is transformed into a sanctuary. The Lady of the Lake, who is also present at the coronation "[c]lothed in white samite, mystic, wonderful" (*The Coming of Arthur*, 284), may represent the living Church, as she appears in "a mist of incense" curling about her (286-287), with her face "hidden in the minster gloom" (288), accompanied by the holy hymns, or even stand for the Lord Himself, since she "Hath power to walk the waters like our Lord" (*The Coming of Arthur*, 293). She bestows upon the King the renowned Excalibur, which becomes the central object in this ritual. It is also the space in which takes place the central hierophany of the whole *Idylls*:

> From eye to eye thro' all their Order flash
> A momentary likeness of the King:
> And ere it left their faces, thro' the cross
> And those around it and the Crucified,
> Down from the casement over Arthur, smote
> Flame-colour, vert and azure, in three rays,
> One falling upon each of three fair queens,
> Who stood in silence near his throne, the friends
> Of Arthur, gazing on him, tall, with bright
> Sweet faces, who will help him at his need. (*The Coming of Arthur*, 269-278)

The colourful light, "flame colour, vert, and azure" (274), which descends from the cross upon Arthur and the three Queens as he binds his Knights with the vows, may be indicative of the stained glass in the windows.

A fuller description of the hall can be found in *The Holy Grail*, in which Percivale, the narrator, portrays it as "the mighty hall that Merlin built" (231). He begins with the exterior and the "four great zones of sculpture" (232), a symbolic representation of the hierarchy in the universe consisting of beasts, men, warriors, and angels, topped with the crowned and winged statue of Arthur facing the east, "whence have sprung all the great religions of the world" (Tennyson 1908, 509). The importance of the directions is also visible in the description of the interior of the hall:

'And, brother, had you known our hall within,
Broader and higher than any in all the lands!
Where twelve great windows blazon Arthur's wars,
And all the light that falls upon the board
Streams thro' the twelve great battles of our King.
Nay, one there is, and at the eastern end,
Wealthy with wandering lines of mount and mere,
Where Arthur finds the brand Excalibur.
And also one to the west, and counter to it,
And blank: and who shall blazon it? when and how?—
O there, perchance, when all our wars are done,
The brand Excalibur will be cast away. (*The Holy Grail*, 246-257)

The eastern and the western end mark the dawn and the decline of the Arthurian reign, the latter foreshadowing the "last, dim, weird, battle of the west" (94) of *The Passing of Arthur*. This may be reminiscent of the significance of the directions in the Christian cathedral, where, as Eliade points out, the East symbolizes paradise, thus marking the beginnings of humanity, while the West stands for the realm of darkness, and is associated with grief, death and the Last Judgement. (Eliade 1987, 61-62). Moreover, such a depiction of all the great battles seems to repeat the motif of the annihilation of time, already present in the images on the gate. Apparently, the hall constitutes an *imago mundi* of the Arthurian world, the centre, from which the main directions of the world can be assigned through the most significant events in the Arthurian legend.

It may be posited that the space of Camelot in Tennyson's *Idylls of the King* can be read as Eliade's irruption of the absolute into the transitory world. To the knights, to whom the world of appearances is the only real one, as they are limited in their perception by their senses, Camelot seems unreal, flickering, unstable, illusory, a shadow. To Arthur, on the other hand, who has managed to transcend the boundaries of human perception in his glimpses into the absolute, Camelot represents the only sacred reality, the centre of his realm, surrounded by constantly threatening literal and metaphoric chaos. This epistemological uncertainty concerning the real state of Camelot is apparently inscribed in "the unending war of humanity in all ages—the worldwide war of Sense and Soul" (Tennyson 1897, 130), which becomes one of the most important themes of the whole *Idylls*. Moreover, such a presentation of Camelot as the manifestation of the absolute reflects the Victorian longing for spirituality, for the safety in unwavering faith in the modern world dominated by rationalism and science.

References

Eliade, Mircea. 1987. *The Sacred and the Profane: The Nature of Religion,* trans. by Willard R. Trask. New York: Harcourt Brace & Company.

Jenkins, Elizabeth. 1990. *The Mystery of King Artur.* London: Michael O'Mara Books.

Lupack, Alan. 2007. *The Oxford Guide to Arthurian Literature and Legend.* New York: Oxford University Press.

Tennyson, Alfred. 1908. *The Works of Tennyson, Annotated. The Eversley Edition*, Vol. 5, *Idylls of the King*, ed. by Hallam Tennyson. London: Macmillan & Co., Ltd.

Tennyson, Hallam. 1897. *Alfred Lord Tennyson. A Memoir.* Vol. 2. London: Macmillan & Co., Ltd.

Chapter Twenty-Five

Dislocated Subject and the Invading Space of the Unknowable in Samuel Beckett's *Ping*[1]

Maciej Piątek

All known, all white, all bare. Light, heat, traces, blurs. All silence, but the wind. Planes shining, infinite. The landscape is a desert, a waste land, a nowhere. Here and there a few repetitive cacti are scattered over the monotonous space. They are no landmarks, they mark nothing, they lead nowhere, traces, blurs, signs, but no meaning. Like a handful of words cast and recast, again and again, upon the white space of paper, almost like dice, searching for the right formula, for the solution to the riddle, and arriving nowhere. And there, in the midst of the desert, as if one of the cacti, a solitary... figure. One is reluctant to say "person," feeling it would perhaps be saying too much. The figure is almost faceless—only the eyes only just—with mouth invisible like sewn, legs joined like sewn, toes joined like sewn, featureless, sexless. A strange, humanoid desert plant, moving in jerks, emitting murmurs with the sewn lips, barely audible, barely comprehensible. The figure is only a trace, a distant echo, a blur of humanity, only just. It is not a person, not a "persona," since the mask has been removed. For what is humanity but the actor's mask which, once dislocated, leaves a blank bare face. There remains only one meaningful detail—"long lashes imploring"—as if glued to the otherwise expressionless countenance. But imploring whom? Imploring what? The silent scream reverberates without answer. The figure escapes definition just as it escapes something more formidable than Aristotelian logic by moving in nervous jolts across the blank space of the desert. For this space—the

---

[1] All quotations, allusions and cryptic allusions to Samuel Beckett's *Ping* refer to the edition of the text in: Beckett, S. 1995. *The Complete Short Prose, 1929–1989*. New York: Grove Press.

space in which the dislocated figure moves and the space in which the
maimed discourse limps—is under invasion by that which resists
comprehension and therefore language, and which becomes enacted (not
symbolized since that would be already saying too much) by this strange,
nonsensical word "ping." It acts as a spoke in the wheel of an attempt at
enclosing the desert in language, an obstacle over which both the subject
and the discourse stumble continuously. The figure falls short of any
definition since it is the figure of mutilated humanity, reduced to jerks and
murmurs. If the capacities for free action and for language be the
distinctively human features, as two modern definitions of humankind
have it (Arendt 1958, Heidegger 1971), then the Beckettian cripple has
only dregs of those. Lips are invisible like sewn, legs joined together like
sewn. The little speech there is—only incomprehensible murmurs, the
little action there is—but movements of a helpless puppet. This fearful
"kenōsis" remains a hopeless void, leading to no exaltation, no
resurrection, no "parousia," be it in the Christian or Hegelian spirit. The
human potential for transcending the determinism of nature manifested in
the elevating faculties of linguistic expression and free action becomes
thus not only degraded into aphasia and paralysis, but also questioned
with regard to its rational basis. The text describes the movement of the
figure always in the same manner: "bare white body fixed ping fixed
elsewhere." What actually happens between one position and another, that
is the action, is enacted—I guess I will stick to that word as "express"
would definitely be too much in this place—by the word "ping." The basis
of action, its motivation, its springs are thus enveloped in the impenetrable
mist raised by that little word deprived of meaning. The ultimate rhyme or
reason, if there is one at all, remains hidden, unknowable. These words,
"hidden" and "unknowable," are, of course, wrong, since they presuppose
the existence of the thing about which one can never be sure if it actually
is. What does then constitute the principle of human action? Is it free will?
Is it nature understood in deterministic terms? Both? Neither? The answer
is "ping," which is, obviously, no answer. The solitary figure escaping
across the wilderness from its fate, or call it what you will, no matter,
becomes gradually invaded by the desert which creeps into its own
"nature", however dwarfed it may be, and takes possession of it. When the
figure produces sounds which come close enough to human speech, this
event is always preceded by the stubborn "ping." And so is silence. What
is the source of language? Why do we speak? What do we speak? Is it we
that speak words? Or perhaps on the contrary: words speak us? Do we
know what we say? Can we? There is only one answer to all these
questions, and you already know it. The invasion proceeds. The subject

becomes dislocated by the unknowable which infects its being to the very core, however rotten it may already be. The sand seeps into the veins making a Gobi of the heart and transforming the figure into a huge dying hourglass that is out of joint. The murmurs that escape it are "always the same all known: perhaps a nature, perhaps a meaning, that much memory." Nature, referring to the figure's movements which have become incomprehensible to itself. Perhaps, then, a nature as a way of accounting for them? Meaning, referring to the bits of language that crop up. Perhaps, then, a meaning as a way of accounting for them? But what is the *meaning* of *nature*? "Ping" silence. Those leftovers of apparently sensible speech are only traces, blurs, sings, but no meaning. They are just "that much memory." They stick to the tongue like the "long lashes imploring" stick to the face, out of habit, having perhaps accidentally resisted the invasion and dislocation. The humanities it had, scraps of memories from a barely remembered past, hold to it still. The crown of all creation in the dust: a deposed king of shreds and patches.

The dislocating experience of the desert, both without and within, makes the subject a blind spot cut adrift in the all-encompassing void. In a way it is directly opposite to the Heideggerian "Geworfenheit," the sense of being thrown into the world, the incessant flux, "samsāra," sequences of phenomena, call it by whatever name you will, it does not matter, since they are all hollow, groundless signifiers referring only to the void they are supposed to cover. The experience of the Beckettian figure, much like the experience of what Buddhism calls "śūnyatā"—the voidness constituting the ultimate reality—is governed by the violent movement of dislodgement. The invading space of the unknowable reveals the emptiness that forms the lining of reality in all its dimensions. In this paradoxical and Socratic sense "all is known," that is all is known to be unknown, unknowable, devoid of meaning and significance. The truth is that there is no truth. This vehemently defamiliarizing experience dislodges the subject out of its safe grounding in the world, transforming that world into a desert which infects the truly human activities with the virus of absolute incomprehensibility. These activities are, as pointed out above, free action and language. Action, as defined by Hannah Arendt, pertains here to ethical, social and political spheres (Arendt 1958), while language, following the later writings of Martin Heidegger, can be termed as humans' actual dwelling place (Heidegger 1971). However, these neatly organized and comforting systems of human thought cannot withstand the overwhelming force of the actual and individual experience which knocks the subject out of its long-standing, traditional illusions, its humanities. The desert has taken hold of the heart, even though the mind may still perform its old tedious acrobatics to the contrary, always the same, all known, that much memory. But the heart, as Pascal aphoristically put it, is subject to a different law than that of the mind. Nevertheless reason may occasionally succeed in throwing a veil over the eyes of the heart. The following sentence appears twice in the Beckett's text: "Ping elsewhere always there but that not known." Changing the location, moving elsewhere, gives rise to a reasonable hope that it is indeed somewhere else, "perhaps way out there," out of the desert. Yet in fact it is always there, "but that known not." Thus Beckett reformulates one of his peculiar paradoxes: reason is not the source of knowledge, but on the contrary, of ignorance. The less I think about it, the more certain I am, to quote *Molloy* (Beckett 1958, 11). "Logos" fools the subject with wily arguments to save it from vertigo and it seems to have been its long-established function. Yet, deep down, the heart knows.

When attempting to describe this Beckettian experience of invasion and dislocation, it is tempting to apply a religious or quasi-religious discourse, which I have already done by referring to the Buddhist category of "śūnyatā" and to Pascal. The reason for this peculiar affinity is the fact the experience of dislocated subject is the antipode, the negative of what one can describe as religious, or even mystical experience. In early medieval Christianity the desert is both a physical and a metaphorical space where the ardent believer transcends the borders of this world and steps into the unknown of divine reality. The aspiring temperament of Desert Fathers took the shape of "contemptus mundi" and "fuga mundi," contempt of the world and disengagement from it. It was an escape ("fuga") from the earthly but at the same time an escape towards embracing the all-transcending Godhead that resisted human powers of comprehension. "Mundi," therefore, stood not only for the basic ties with the world, but also for the worldly, that is human, ways of thinking. A Desert Father was the father of the desert in the literal sense of the phrase. He escaped into a physical desert and *conceived* a mental desert within himself, thus opening the mind and the soul onto the experience of God. The dynamics of this double movement is also invasion, but directed otherwise. For the mystics, the space to conquer is the sky, and their weapon, suffering, to paraphrase a passage from Emile Cioran's *Tears and Saints* (1995). It is the mystic who is the willful invader, aspiring to the unknowable by following the "via negativa" of renunciation and "askēsis." It is the desert that is invaded by the holy fools with an inextinguishable passion for the absolute. The fire of the heart burns in the middle of the void. The Beckettian cripple, on the other hand, is not the father but the son of his desert, born into it in the agony of invasion and dislocation. He strives to escape, but the desert is boundless and it has already wreaked havoc in his heart, leaving but cinders and "scattered ruins same grey as the sand" (Beckett 1995, 197). Invaded by the unknowable in the deepest recesses of his being, the dislodged subject becomes a will-less mystic and therefore a failed or "dud mystic." The enforced disengagement and severance of all ties wrought by the all-permeating "śūnyatā" seem to create conditions for mystical experience, but its failure is inevitable. The fire of the heart is dead in the middle of the void. "Kenōsis" then, but no exaltation, no resurrection, no "parousia."

As the text draws to its end, "pings" proliferate: "Ping fixed last elsewhere." Death, the final and the ultimate unknowable, the negative and the lining of life, is approaching. "Head haught eyes white fixed front old ping last murmur one second perhaps not alone eye unlustrous black and white half closed long lashes imploring ping silence ping over."

References

Arendt, Hannah. 1958. *The Human Condition*. Chicago: University of Chicago Press.

Beckett, Samuel. 1958. *Three Novels: Molloy, Malone Dies, The Unnamable*, New York: Grove Press.

—. 1995. *The Complete Short Prose, 1929–1989*. New York: Grove Press.

Cioran, Emil M. 1995. *Tears and Saint*, trans. by Ilinca Zarifopol-Johnston. Chicago/London: University of Chicago Press.

Heidegger, Martin. 1971. *On the Way to Language*. New York: Harper and Row.

Chapter Twenty-Six

The Theatrical Lesson of the Pearl-Poet's *Patience*

Piotr Spyra

The Middle English *Patience*, found in the *Pearl* manuscript, is usually seen as a negative exemplum that foregrounds the follies of impatience through presenting the figure of the fallen prophet Jonah in his self-righteous refusal to subordinate himself to the will of God. What structures this tale of irony is Jonah's escapism and reluctance to acknowledge his own role as part of God's masterplan. God, in turn, proves patient enough to withstand the peevish moods of his prophet and persists in showing him the right path not only by divine interventions but also by exposing Jonah to interactions with the rest of the Creation, which functions as an impeccable model of obedience. In this, the entire world becomes something of a theatrical stage where Jonah is made to participate in the unveiling of divine Providence. The prophet, however, vehemently refuses to become involved in this ongoing process, and instead he engages God in what effectively becomes a game of hide and seek, time and again seeking refuge from the eyes and demands of the Lord with the "petulance of a spoiled child" (Benson 1991, 148) and shunning any interactions whatsoever. The three places where he finds himself set apart from the rest of the Creation—the ship, the whale and the woodbine bower—are key to the didacticism of *Patience* and to the understanding of the uneasy relation between God and man.

The story of Jonah lends itself most easily to an exploration of the nature of this relation. While Job may seem to be a more obvious exemplar of the virtue of patience (Anderson 2005, 127), his story significantly involves an intermediary—the Devil. Making his only real appearance in the Old Testament, the fiend in the Book of Job is far from what later representations would have him be. Rather than a direct adversary and arch-enemy of God, he emerges as an evil yet God-fearing spirit that cooperates with the Lord in testing the fortitude of Job. By allowing Satan to take away the man's earthly possessions and to plague his body with pox, God indeed establishes a sort of communication with Job, but it is the Devil that actually effects the interactions between the two through his actions. By drawing from the Book of Jonah instead and thus adopting a less obvious example of patience, the text of the poem foregrounds the directness of the relationship between God and man.

God is the one who demands. As soon as the narrator moves to the tale of Jonah, even before the readers have a chance to visualise the scene as such, he immediately outlines God's command:

> Hit bitydde sumtyme in the termes of Judé
> Jonas joyned was therinne jentyle prophete.
> Goddes glam to hym glod that hym unglad made,
> With a roghlych rurd rowned in his ere:
> 'Rys radly,' he says, 'and rayke forth even;
> Nym the way to Nynyve withouten other speche,
> And in that ceté my sawes soghe ale aboute
> That in that place, at the poynt, I put in thi hert. ['] (61-68)[1]

God is just as straightforward as the narrator, and he makes it clear that this ought to be done "withouten other speche"—without any delay. Jonah's adversity to these words is also established instantly, and the prophet, fearing that the wicked Ninevites, whom he is to chastise for their sins, might channel their anger onto the herald of woe, decides to shrug off the dangerous call and remove himself to a place where God would not find him.

He embarks on a ship bound for Tarsus, and as he boards the vessel, the text presents a curiously detailed image of the sailors and their actions as they set sail:

> Then he tron on the tres and thay her tramme ruchen,
> Cachen up the crossayl, cables thay fasten,
> Wight at the wyndas weyen her ankres,
> Spynde spak to the sprete the spare bawelyne,
> Gederen to the gyde-ropes—the grete cloth falles.
> Thay layden in on laddeborde and the lofe wynnes;
> The blythe brethe at her bak the bosum he fyndes,
> He swenges me thys swete schip swefte fro the haven. (101-108)

This picture of a "faultless sequence of action and response" (Stanbury 1991, 78) has an almost mechanical quality to it. The sailors work in unison,

---

[1] Quotations from *Patience* are identified by line numbers.

and the alliterative verse coupled with the mention of one or two specific activities in each line intensifies the overall impression of a gradated mechanised procedure with the men acting as cogs in the wheel, undifferentiated by the text. The ship has neither a captain nor a clear command structure; when the storm comes, the "spakest" (wisest) of the sailors offers his counsel, but even he is "dispayred wel nere" (169), and in this respect merges with the rest of the crew, who are all equally bewildered and confused in the chaos of the tempest.

A passage similar to the one above shows the sailors in the attempt to save their ship and lives (153-160), but it is not the only instance of the text presenting the world acting like a well-formed mechanism. C. David Benson observes that there is something inhuman about the repentance of the Ninevites, noticing the overdrawn and almost comical quality of their "much too perfect" reaction to Jonah's words:

> The alliterative verse emphasises their maniacal [...] response, as they all instantly strap on hair-shirts ("Heter hayres thay hent that asperly bited"), which are luckily at hand, and cover themselves with dust [373-76]. Not to be outdone, the king races from his throne, tears off his "ryche robe," and dives precisely into a pile of ashes: "And of a hep of askes he hitte in the myddes" [377-380]. (Benson 1991, 155)

What is more, the king has even children and animals participate in this communal penitence, "bothe burnes and bestes, burdes and childer" (388). He decrees that all shall willingly fast, which is a curious turn of phrase, for why should a decree be needed if they did indeed act "frely":

> Thenne sayde he to his serjauntes: 'Samnes yow bilyve;
> Do dryve out a **decré**, demed by myselven
> That [...]
> [...]
> Alle faste **frely** for her falce werkes.
> Seses childer of her sok, soghe hem so never,
> Ne best bite on no brom, ne no bent nauther,
> Passe to no pasture, ne pike non erbes,
> No non oxe to hay, ne no horse to water. (385-387, 390-394, emphasis mine)

This phrasing puts into question the very notion of free will with regard to the Ninevites, whose sudden repentance proves as energetic as their commitment to sin at the beginning of the tale, when God raged against their wickedness, so odious to him that he could no longer tolerate it, saying "her malys is so much, I may not abyde, / Bot venge me on her vilanye and venym bilyve" (70-71).

Men and beasts in Nineveh act alike, as the whole city begs God for mercy. Benson argues that the Ninevites actually "act more like brute nature [...] than like real human beings" (Benson 1991, 155). Indeed, the storm scene provides a parallel to the uniform actions of the residents of the city and the sailors on Jonah's ship in its depiction of the elemental forces that obey God's commands. The very moment the Lord calls upon two easterly winds, "Ewrus and Aquiloun" (133), "out of the north-est the noys bigynes" (137) and both the winds and the waves work in concord to waken the whale which instantly rises to the surface of the ocean just in time to swallow Jonah. "Thenne was no tom ther bytwene his tale and her dede" (135)—God's commands are followed by an immediate, well-timed and mechanically obedient response of nature.

Consequently, rather than a study of the sin and repentance of the Ninevites under the influence of Jonah's teachings, *Patience* is a story of Jonah and his interactions with the whole of God's Creation. The people of Nineveh are presented not so much as actual flesh and blood characters whose tale of salvation the story purports to tell, but as signs and portents from God, who communicates thus with his prophet.[2] Only Jonah is presented with any psychological depth; where the Bible merely states that Jonah did not wish to preach in Nineveh without specifying the reason[3], *Patience* provides a clear psychological motivation, underlining the prophet's fear of death and bodily mutilation at the hands of the wicked Ninevites.[4] By contrast, it is impossible to fathom the psychological motivations of men other than Jonah, and rather than following their own individual human inclinations, all they seem to do is conform blindly, alongside animals, the weather and all the elements, to a pre-ordained script imposed on them by God himself.

While it would be difficult to argue that the world around Jonah functions as a proper allegory, it does create the impression of being there exclusively for the purpose of instructing the prophet and to function solely within the exigencies of this purpose. Sarah Stanbury describes this world as a kind of "zoned theater" (Stanbury 1991, 74), with Jonah

---

[2] Alongside providing Jonah with signs, God remains directly in touch with him at all times, unlike with Job.

[3] "But Jonah rose up to flee unto Tarsus from the presence of the Lord, and went down to Joppa" (Jonah 1.3).

[4] "'Oure Syre syttes,' he says, 'on sege so hyghe, / In his glowande glorye, and gloumbes ful lyttel / Thagh I be nummen in Nunnive and naked dispoyled, / On rode rwly torent with rybaudes mony'" (93-96).

moving, or prompted to move, from one zone, or stage, to another. J. J. Anderson concurs that Jonah appears to be "set apart from the rest of the Creation" (Anderson 2005, 151), and the juxtaposition finds its fullest realisation in a number of enclosed spaces in which the prophet finds himself literally at a remove from the surrounding reality. The use of those spaces and the way the text endows them with meaning is critical for the didactic force of the exemplum.

The first of these is the hold of the ship, where Jonah sleeps through most of the tempest, unaware of the frantic activities of the sailors in the raging storm. The narrator informs the readers that there the prophet "slypped upon a sloumbe-slepe, and sloberande he routes" (186). The onomatopoeic alliteration underscores the physical torpor that characterises Jonah's body, but it also reflects on the depth of his spiritual lethargy as he lies huddled in a murky corner at the very bottom of the boat. The text compares the kick he receives from the sailor who hurries him on board to being woken up suddenly by the devil—"Ther Ragnel in his rakentes hym rere of his dremes" (188)—and this sort of imagery contextualises Jonah's withdrawal from the world and escape from the eyes of God as embarking on a path of sin.

"[P]hysically sluggish as Jonah is, he is made to seem even more inactive by contrast with the veritable frenzy of activity by which the poet characterises the other human and divine characters in the poem" (Stock 1991, 167). While God is busy orchestrating the events around his prophet and controlling the elements, acting as a true Aquinian first cause and prompting an endless chain of actions and reactions, Jonah retreats to what might be termed *cavities of torpor*—enclosed spaces where he wishes to attain a condition of total isolation from the surrounding reality. Stock observes that "it is difficult to imagine a more inert character than the Jonah in *Patience*" (Stock 1991, 167). He also notices how the texts plays with the notion of prophetic voice, ironically underscoring Jonah's shortcomings by contrasting his predominant silence with the noises that surround him, whether the "clere strenthe" of the "crye" of the Ninevites (395), the "noys" of the storm (137) or the sailors' "loude" (195) questions (Stock 1991, 169-170). The scene of the tempest provides the best example of such contrast when Jonah has to explain to the crew who he really is and what brought him to the ship; only with the help of signs and gestures, "unnynges that thay undernomen" (213), does he eventually manage to explain "That he was flawen fro the face of frelych Dryghtyn" (214).

The belly of the whale seems similar to the hold of the ship in the sense that there too Jonah finds himself alone in an enclosed space. Sandra

Pierson Prior points to the passage which openly identifies the parallelism: "As in the bulk of the bote ther he byfore sleped. / So in a bouel of that best he bidez on lyve" (292-293).[5] She rightly observes that despite this, however, the similarities are only superficial:

> [...] this is a hiding place of a very different kind: it is not *away from* God, but *with* God, and it is not of *Jonah's* making but of *God's* making, and in it Jonah does not sleep [...] much less snore. [...] [He is] rather turning toward both God and his mission. (Prior 1994, 88)

What is more, in the description of the whale, the imagery of hell mingles with that of heaven. The place "stank as the devel" (274) and "savoured as helle," but at the point of entry into the creature's mouth, the text compares Jonah to a "mote [...] at a munster dor" (268), which communicates both the sacred character of the space he is about to enter and the inevitability of the process of submission which he will have to undergo.[6] The contrast appears particularly striking if one considers the tradition of presenting the jaws of Jonah's whale as the Hell-mouth, "the standard iconographic representation of the infernal realm [...] by the fourteenth century" (Schmidt 1991, 183). In terms of imagery, Patience connects the entry to Hell with the door of a cathedral, the house of the Lord.

Such a juxtaposition of imagery has puzzled critics, and a number of interpretations have been offered. Schmidt supports S. L. Clark's and J. N. Wasserman's claim that the reference to the cathedral is one that merely communicates proportions and Jonah's helplessness in the encounter with the monstrous whale (Schmidt 1991, 184-185). Still, one could also read this apparently paradoxical juxtaposition in a different way. The moment Jonah recognises his faults, he finds a comfortable nook where he can escape the stench of the creature's guts; as the narrator expounds, "bot ever is God swete," and the sweetness of the reunion with God clearly contrasts here with the hideous smells Jonah initially had to endure. Since it is Jonah's escapism and unwillingness to accept his role as part of God's creation that the poem admonishes against, the imagery of hell functions here just as in the storm scene, where the space of withdrawal figures as a

---

[5] Anderson's edition, which breaks the text into quatrains, suggests the two lines quoted here are not linked together in a comparison, with the second line starting a new line of thought. Nevertheless, the parallelism is also identified in the lines that immediately precede this passage: "Ther he sete [...] / As in the bulk of the bote [...]" (291-292).
[6] For an exposition of the indebtedness of *Patience* to traditional representations of Jonah's whale as Hell, cf. Schmidt 1991.

place of sin. The cathedral-like architectonics that the text imposes onto the skeletal structure of the whale's ribs and the olfactory transformation the readers witness point, on the other hand, to the fact that, as Prior puts it, it is all "of God's making" (Prior 1994, 88) and leads to a change of heart in the prophet himself. God proves wise and gracious enough to encourage Jonah to participate in the unveiling of divine Providence by teaching him a lesson on his own terms—within an enclosed space of the sort that Jonah sought, but one which Jonah cannot help but dismiss as odious and loathsome.

With the prophet finally willing to carry out God's plan, the whale spits him out onto the very land that he had earlier wanted to avoid venturing into—by the city of Nineveh. Here, for a brief moment he merges with the rest of Creation in mechanically following God's instructions, his voice for once sounding "cler" and sonorous in delivering the message to the wicked city and eliciting an equally sonorous penitential response. When God takes pity on the Ninevites, however, Jonah loses his patience and returns to his old ways, "al joyles and jangland" (433) removing himself to a provisional bower he constructs in the open space of the plain. He sees God's mercy as undermining his reputation, for his words of doom now seem to have amounted to nothing more than empty threats.

It is then that God decides to provide yet another lesson for his erring prophet. It is a lesson of mercy, and the poet faithfully follows the biblical Book of Jonah in presenting God's motivations behind it. When the prophet wakes from his uneasy sleep, he finds himself sheltered from the heat of the sun by the leaves of a lovely woodbine[7], more pleasant to the eye than anything man could imagine—"Such a lefsel of lof never lede hade" (448). Jonah is overjoyed with his discovery and remains in the bower throughout the day. The next morning, however, he finds the woodbine withered completely and himself exposed to the elements once again. This pushes the prophet into a fit of anger:

> With hatel anger and hot heterly he calles:
> 'A, thou maker of man, what maystery the thinkes
> Thus thy freke to forfare forbi alle other?
> With alle meschef that thou may, never thou me spares.
> I kevered me a cumfort that now is caght fro me,
> My wodbynde so wlonk that wered my heved.
> Bot now I se thou art sette my solace to reve;

---

[7] *Wodbynde* is the Pearl-Poet's name for the plant which features as *gourd* in the King James Bible.

Why ne dyghtes thou me to diye? I dure to longe.' (480-488)

Jonah feels cheated by the Lord and he sees himself as a victim of a cat and mouse game, tempted with solace and then returned to the pit of his own misery. God's motivations were, however, far from this, for all he wanted to do was to help Jonah understand divine compassion. If the destruction of a mere bower inspires such powerful emotions and an overwhelming sense of loss in the prophet, should he not approve of sparing a city that dons penitential robes and houses "lytel barnes [...] that never bale wroght" (510)?

Jonah is not impressed with the woodbine exemplum, though, and his reaction to the situation makes it clear the ordeal of the whale had only a short-term effect. His sinful refusal to participate in God's masterplan finds its reflection in yet another curious reference to the devil, similar to the previous two, the narrator this time mentioning the devil in an interjection—"the devel haf!" (460). Jonah returns to his old ways, and having done his duty with regard to the Ninevites, he believes he can simply leave and avoid any further burdensome quests God might want to trouble him with. His withdrawal reaches ludicrous proportions when at one point (457-464) he declares that he would actually like to take the bower home (sic!), the passage reinforcing the image of one who "enacts the drama of the small man, the individual who believes first in what he sees close at hand" (Stanbury 1991, 90) and who does not wish to get involved with what lies beyond his own comfortable niche of existence and take on greater responsibilities. Presented with another space of refuge, he succumbs to passivity instead of recognising the didactic aspect of the sign.

This connects with the way the text of the poem posits patience, the virtue Jonah fails to exhibit. It is not so much a quality one may or may not possess as something that needs to be tirelessly exercised on a daily basis. The message is that "everyone's role, like Jonah's, is to participate patiently in God's plan" (Prior 1994, 89) and that "human beings in general are deluded if they think they are in control of their lives," (Anderson 2005, 139) or ever can be. Patience is an action, as the opening line of the poem asserts, stating clearly that "Pacience is a poynt, thagh it displese ofte" (1). As the poem itself makes abundantly clear, patience only makes one's life easier by eliminating the anxiety that comes with opposing the decrees of divine providence, and yet it is often displeasing. This is precisely because it is an action which requires constant effort, difficult to be consistent in and displeasing in the demands it puts on those who faithfully follow its course. The "seemingly anticlimactic episode of the woodbine" reinforces this understanding of patience, for it is God who is the true exemplar of the virtue here (Prior 1994, 89), and the open ending of the story, providing no clear conclusions, leaves the readers with the Maker persisting in waiting for Jonah to reform, just as he did for the Ninevites.

The lesson of what patience really is, which Jonah repeatedly fails to understand, comes in clearly theatrical terms. God, "that Syre that syttes so hyghe" (261), "guides the entire drama" (Stanbury 1991, 84), orchestrating the events around his prophet so as to prompt him to acknowledge the need to become actively involved with the rest of the Creation and to help him comprehend the futility of his attempts to withdraw to his own secluded world. Through presenting the three spaces of refuge and creating an interplay between inner and outer space, the Pearl-Poet manages to convey the image of a struggle in man's soul, the drama of one always steered astray by his own fallible nature from the understanding of the divine and its demands. Significantly, unlike the other three works of the manuscript, the poem does not end with a prayer. Instead of engaging the reader in appealing to the divine for succour, it ends on a more affirmative note—that God indeed has the patience we need to be saved.

References

Anderson, J. J. 2005. *Language and Imagination in the Gawain-poems*. Manchester: Manchester University Press.

Benson, David C. 1991. The Impatient Reader of *Patience*. In *Text and Matter: New Critical Perspectives of the Pearl-Poet*, ed. by Robert J. Blanch, Miriam Youngerman Miller and Julian N. Wasserman, 147-161. Troy, NY: Whitston.

Cawley, A. C. and J. J. Anderson (eds.). 1976. *Pearl, Cleanness, Patience, Sir Gawain and the Green Knight*. London: Dent.

Gardner, John, trans. 1975. *The Complete Works of the Gawain-Poet*. Chicago: University of Chicago Press.

Prior, Sandra Pierson. 1994. *The Pearl-Poet Revisited*. New York: Twayne.

Schmidt, Gary D. 1991. 'This Wrech Man in Warlowes Guttez': Imagery and Unity of Frame and Tale in *Patience*. In *Text and Matter: New Critical Perspectives of the Pearl-Poet*, ed. by Robert J. Blanch, Miriam Youngerman Miller and Julian N. Wasserman, 177-193. Troy, NY: Whitston.

Stanbury, Sarah. 1991. *Seeing the Gawain-Poet: Description and the Art of Perception*. Philadelphia: University of Pennsylvania Press.

Stock, Lorraine Kochanske. 1991. The 'Poynt' of *Patience*. In *Text and Matter: New Critical Perspectives of the Pearl-Poet*, ed. by Robert J. Blanch, Miriam Youngerman Miller and Julian N. Wasserman, 163-175. Troy, NY: Whitston.

CHAPTER TWENTY-SEVEN

SPATIAL METAPHORS ON MAN-GOD RELATIONSHIP IN THE CHOSEN POEMS OF GERARD MANLEY HOPKINS

KATARZYNA WINIARSKA

Whenever the arts are concerned with the question of God, the paradox appears: how is it possible to articulate the realm of religious experience, one that escapes categorization and balances on the brink of language? It seems that in order to penetrate to the heart of the mystery, it is necessary to turn to the world of metaphors which "incarnate" what appears inexpressible. The sacred texts themselves often present man-God relationships in terms of spatial metaphors. The spiritual situation of after the fall is depicted in terms of the growing separation. The very etymology of the word "devil" is rooted in the spatial relationship since gr. *diaballein* literally means "to throw across, to tear apart". On the contrary, the Incarnation of Christ diminishes the distance as His Cross unites heaven and earth.

The aim of the paper is to analyse the use of spatial metaphors in the depiction of man-God relationship in the chosen poems of Gerard Manley Hopkins. The work is going to be divided into two major parts. The first will deal with the poems expressing the separation of man from God. The literary means used by Hopkins range from the description of physical distance and God's concealment to the disintegration on the level of the poems' language, the words and verses, just as the poet (man) in the real world, undergo actual and visible disintegration. Paradoxically, experience of desolation is often a catalyst to a more profound intimacy with God, hence the second part will discuss the poems undertaking the subject of transgressing the dividing chasms.

1. Separation of man from God

1.1. Vertical trajectory

Inscribing man-God relationship into vertical trajectory is the most prevalent representation of the chasm that exists between Creator and His creation. While God is usually depicted as dwelling in the highest, human beings are associated with what is "down", either to show their insignificance and **sub**-mission or humbleness and meekness. Often the very movement of men, as bowing or kneeling, additionally underlines their lowliness and humility in relation to God.

Hopkins often refers to such traditional depictions, especially in his early (pre-conversion) poems of desolation. Interestingly, the more the speaker feels his unworthiness to receive God's love, the more the vertical distance seems to be exposed. In one of Hopkins's early poems, "My prayers must meet a brazen heaven", not only is God's dwelling up above in the unreachable height but also heaven is described as "brazen" and "brass", as if additionally iterating its inaccessibility. What is interesting is that the chasm between the Deity and man is so great, that God himself is absent from the poem and speaker's lamentation. God's presence is evoked only through negative references to the hopelessly remote heaven. The division appears to be even more profound because of the description of the lowliness of a man. Hopkins turns to typical Biblical image of man as clay: "Like clay in the hand of the potter, so are you in my hand, O house of Israel" (Jer 18, 6). "Clay" is associated with what is down and, axiologically, it introduces the idea of weakness and unworthiness. The sins of a man who is likened to "this clay uncouth", prevent him from reaching heaven with his prayer: "I cannot buoy my heart above;/ Above it cannot entrance win" (Hopkins 1970, 27). "Hopkins is—as Delli-Carpini notices—gravity-bound, unable to transcend worldly allurements" (1998, 40). Yet this human clay is mingled with iron. This striking image seems to refer to the Book of Daniel, and particularly to the description of an enormous statue whose feet were made of iron and clay. Such statue appeared in king's vision and Daniel interpreted it as the revelation of future: "so this will be a divided kingdom; yet it will have some of the strength of iron in it (…) And just as you saw the iron mixed with baked clay, so the people will be a mixture and will not remain united, any more than iron mixes with clay" (Daniel 2, 41-43). In that respect the division between the realm of "brazen heaven" and the realm of "clay uncouth" is mirrored by the division within the very nature of man.

A parallel image of dividing chasm inscribed into vertical trajectory appears in the "The Half-way House". The very title points to the category of space by introducing the idea of a way and hence pilgrimage and spiritual journey. God, even though He is prayed to and addresses directly as Love, is still remote as He dwells in an inaccessible realm of the above: "Thou on wings dost ride (...) Love it grows darker here and Thou art above" (Hopkins 1970, 28). Unlike in the previously discussed poem, man is not described in terms of unworthiness of clay, but of a worm. The speaker says: "See, Love, I creep", as if clearly indicating his "identity". Worms traditionally relate to what is down and, axiologically, they bear associations with what is lowly and ignoble. Yet again, such image has its source in the Bible: "How then can a man be righteous before God? If even the moon is not bright and the stars are not pure in his eyes, how much less man, who is but a maggot—a son of man, who is only a worm!" (Job 26:4-6). Out of his miserable position of a mere maggot, unable to reach the heaven with his prayers, the speaking persona asks God: "Love, come down to me if Thy name be Love" (Hopkins 1970, 28). And here he reaches the verge of blasphemy since he denies that silent and distant God may be called Love. Hence, an interesting paradox is evoked, while the speaker bemoans the unbridgeable chasm separating him from God, he keeps on calling his Creator "Love". The very name "Love" introduces, after all, the idea of closeness and amity. Even though the speaker calls God Love, he does not experience him as such, and, therefore, doubt arises. Christ warns against such attitude: "Not every one that saith unto me, Lord, Lord, shall enter into the kingdom of heaven" (Mt 7:21). The speaker seems to face the very core of faith—it is not the knowledge of God as Love that grants closeness but the actual experience of love. The speaker points finally to the silent presence of God in the Eucharist: "He is with you in the breaking of the bread" (Hopkins 1970. 29). It appears that yet again the very condition of a man (division between his actual state of faith and the way he addresses God, between knowing and being) mirrors the perceptible chasm between the height of God and the lowliness of a man.

1.2. Horizontal trajectory

When it comes to horizontal metaphors expressing the unspeakable drama of faith, Hopkins often refers in his poems to the dichotomy of East and West. In Christian tradition the east-west axis carries a great importance in terms of its ritualistic function, e.g. the churches were oriented along it. In Hopkins poetry, East is associated with light, whiteness, sunrise and pattern, and West—with darkness, night, chaos and matter. In such case the visual and spatial metaphors and images are inseparably connected. Two poems that best exemplify such use of metaphors are "God's Grandeur" and "Spelt from Sibyl's Leaves". The first of the two poems introduces the demarcation line between West associated with the worldliness and darkness devoid of God's presence and East that brings new hope of life. The blackness of the West may be also associated with the character of the Western civilization, particularly—industrialism: "all is seared with trade; bleared, smeared with toil" (Hopkins 1970, 66). The world of technical progress is a place where man, "being shod", finds it difficult to discover that "the world is charged with the grandeur of God". The blackness of West is contrasted with the brightness of East and the rising sun that is equated with the Holy Ghost. Interestingly, despite the overwhelming power of God's grandeur, men remain passive, disengaged from the Love that seeks them, just as West is disengaged from East.

In "Spelt from Sibyl's Leaves" West is even more strongly associated with the overwhelming and all-permeating night that annexes the world and deprives it of the blessed daylight. The last rays of the sun fade in the west: "Her fond yellow hornlight wound to the west" (Hopkins 1970, 97). To paraphrase poem's words: the light is "waste" in "the west". The darkness that approaches from the west seems to be the beginning and end to all, since it is "womb-of-all, home-of-all". The earth becomes strange and disorganised as if returning to primal chaos and matter is bereft of form; in the darkness all things lose their selfhood and distinctiveness. The world is "diremembring, dismembring". The absence of God seems to be so overwhelming that it allows even for the occurrence of the pagan elements in the form of the oracle and the reference to Sybil.

1.3. Disintegration on the level of language

Apart from employing traditional spatial metaphors and imageries, Hopkins, most of all, worked on the very tissue of language in order to express man-God relationship. In some of the poems it is the very language used that implies the distance between man and God. In the sonnet "Let me be to Thee as the circling bird", the speaker points that God as Love is the source and ultimate goal of all being: "Love, O my God, to call Thee Love, and Love" (Hopkins 1970, 28). Interestingly, the thrice repeated word "love", though similar, is not the same. Hopkins, cleverly, uses it as: (1) an apostrophe to God, (2) a name he wants to attribute to God and (3) a verb that is a call to particular action. Heidegger pointed that "the depth of the divine God is such that it continually withdraws behind every name which is addressed to it" (Caputo 1982, 275). It seems therefore that God sustains the distance and remains unreachable even though the speaker addresses Him with the most intimate name. At the same time the speaking persona makes an attempt to break through the appearances created by the seeming sameness of the word and to experience the true revelation of the Divine Word, instead of just calling God Love.

A similar, if not greater distance is sustained in the poem "Thou art indeed just, Lord". Calling just God "sir" ("Sir, life upon thy cause", Hopkins 1970, 106) implies not only unexpected distraction and additional tension, but, first and foremost, builds a further reservation between man and God. However, apart from a distance, calling someone "sir" reveals also a great deal of respect. Hence the distance does not tend to break the relationship but, paradoxically strengthens it.

In yet another poem of desolation, "My own heart", just as the speaker undergoes impenetrable spiritual darkness, the words of the poem undergo displacement:

> At God knows when to God knows what; whose smile
> 's not wrung, see you; unforeseen times rather—as skies
> betweenpie mountains-lights a lovely mile. (Hopkins 1970, 103)

The space is not only metaphorically evoked but it is visible on the very surface of the text. The word "smile/'s" is not only divided by the apostrophe, but is also broken into enjambment. It seems to dissolve itself, as if to make the clearing for the appearance of the mystery it represents. The tangible breaking of the text strengthens the evoked image of the mountains, into which the world of difficulties is translated, and the sudden appearance of the sky between two mountains, that is God's smile. Yet again a paradox is introduced here—the promise of the closeness of God's consolation is available within gaps, distance. In other words, the distance may bring proximity.

2. Transgressing the chasm

As it was already pointed, the distance between man and God may often, paradoxically, become a catalyst to a more profound intimacy. Hopkins often underlines in his poems that in order to transgress the dividing chasm, the double movement has to take place—the movement of God's grace and the movement of man's sincere and humble faith. The direction of the movement is of great axiological importance. The movement of grace is directed "down" and the true believer has his eyes always fixed "up".

2.1 God

To express the downward movement of grace, Hopkins often invokes the images of "rope", "rod" or "lightening". "Rod" and "lightening" are traditionally understood as a directing line of God and symbol of His authority. They are often associated with tools of punishment and discipline. In the Second Book of Samuel we read: "I will be his father, and he will be my son. When he does wrong, I will punish him with the rod of men" (7:14). Even though God describes Himself as just and ready to punish for the wrongdoings, He also invites man to the most intimate relationship of father and son. Hence even though rod and lightening may arouse horror and anxiety, they may, by the very fact of transgressing the space between God and man, become the tools of salvation.

The imagery of "rod" is introduced, among others, in the already discussed poem "God's Grandeur". The speaker asks: "Why do men then now not reck his rod?". He is grieved to see people rejecting the law of God and not caring either for God's love or wrath. The rod is designed to "crash human self-will under religious discipline" (McChesney 1968, 54) and in that sense it is a parallel image to the "the ooze of oil/ crushed". God hence manifests himself to men either in the beauty of creation or by imposing stress until the spiritual significance is discharged.

When it comes to the imagery of "lightening", Hopkins referred to it in his poems of spiritual wrecking: "The Wreck of Deutschland" and "The Loss of Eurydice" as well as in the sonnet "The shepherd's brow fronting forked lightning". In the "Loss of Eurydice" the speaker cries: "But to Christ lord of thunder/ Crouch; lay knee by earth low under" (Hopkins 1970, 76). In "The Wreck", the speaker, similarly, recognizes "glow, glory in thunder" and in the sonnet the speaker points to "the horror and the havoc and the glory" of the lightening. In the three poems the play of lightning's light and thunder's darkness reveal both the horror and majesty of God. The lightning tears the sky apart, but at the same time it connects the heaven and the earth; the suddenness of the lightning makes Deity "un-conceal". The encounter with God is possible only when one accepts the ways of God: "I did say yes/ O at lightning and lashed rod" (Hopkins 1970, 52). What is needed is just one word: *fiat*.

Finally, the rope imagery recurs in "The Wreck of Deutschland" and it introduces a striking clash of two possible ways of conduct in the face of extremity. In Part the second devoted to the drama of the ship, Hopkins recalls that when "hope was twelve hour gone", a brave man decided to save a woman on the decks below: "One stirred from the rigging to save/ The wild woman-kind below/ With a rope's end round the man, handy and brave" (Hopkins 1970, 56). Unfortunately, there was nothing he could do on his own since "He was pitched to his death at a blow". The exceptional courage of the sailor proved only to be his sin of pride. He was so very much confident in his own strength that he seemed to have forgotten that only God is the "giver of breath and bread" (Hopkins 1970, 51). Mariani points out that "he was brave but against the terrifying perspective of the storm he made but a poor *dues ex machine* transformed suddenly into a headless manikin swinging from a string, a grotesque pendulum for the others to 'tell' the terrible 'hours'" (1970, 60). Quite the reverse image appears in Part the first of the poem—here it is God who fastens his people with the rope of his love and grace:

> I am soft sift
> In an hourglass (…)
> But roped with, always, all the way down from the tall
> Fells or flanks of the voel, a vein
> Of the gospel proffer, a pressure, principle, Christ's gift. (Hopkins 1970, 52)

Man is, Hopkins claims, sustained by God at every moment. "Christ's gift", his blood shed on the Calvary for our sins has become the stream of grace and the best proof of God's love. Through Christ and in Christ man is "roped" to God, his Creator.

2.2 Man

The movement of a man of faith is always directed "up". Apart from common metaphors implying reaching up (e.g. tower), Hopkins uses striking reversal of perspective. Spatial and visual categories are here inseparably interwoven. An example of such reversed perspective is to be detected in "Hurrahing in Harvest":

> I walk, I lift up, I lift up heart, eyes,
> Down all that glory in the heavens to glean our Saviour;
> And, eyes, heart, what looks, what lips yet gave you a
> Rapturous love's greeting of realer, of rounder replies. (Hopkins 1970, 70)

In this fragment, the sense of direction becomes hazy: the speaker lifts up his eyes to look down at "all that glory". The speaker is granted a vision as if from God's site. He becomes what he sees. The caring gaze and uncovering of the veil of nature allow the speaker to experience the holiness of nature, since "all that glory in the heaven" is right here, on earth, in the harvesting field. In the intractable logic of God up becomes down, covered is uncovered, everything, literally, stands on its head. According to Heidegger, a true gaze abolishes the distance and it may bring the onlooker to the place where the thing he is looking at is situated. Hopkins literary put such theory into practice, since the speaker of the poem is granted the vision as if from the place he was looking at. Interestingly, the speaker not only lifts up his eyes, but also heart, as if to underline that physical perception may be one with religious investigation. The image of hearts lifted up is an echo of the Eucharist since identical phrase occurs in the Eucharistic prayer: "Lift up your hearts. We lift them up to the Lord". The prayer develops into the praise: "Holy, holy, holy Lord, God of power and might, heaven and earth are full of your glory". It seems that the poem develops along the lines of the Eucharistic prayer and points that mystical vision is inseparable from mystical union.

The aim of this paper was to analyse the occurrence of spatial metaphors illustrating God-man relationship in the chosen poems of Gerard Manley Hopkins. The poet appears to be very much indebted to the traditional depiction of man-God relationship, especially when one thinks of his metaphors and imageries drawing on horizontal and vertical trajectories, as well as on Biblical figures of "rod" or "lightening". The novelty of Hopkins's treatment of the spatial metaphors reveals itself in his extraordinary approach towards language and the interweaving of the visual and the spatial. The literary means used by Hopkins serve to present the fundamental paradox of faith: distance between God and man often grants intimacy. Due to the limited space of the paper some of the problems and interpretations oh Hopkins's poems are merely hinted at and require some further research.

References

Caputo, John D. 1982. *Heidegger and Aquinas. An Essay Overcoming Metaphysics*. New York: Fordham University Press.
Delli-Carpini, John. 1998. *Prayer and Piety in the Poems of Gerard Manley Hopkins*. Lewiston: The Edwin Mellen Press.
Holy Bible. King James Version. http://www.biblegateway.com
Hopkins, Gerard Manley. 1970. *The Poems of Gerard Manley Hopkins*, ed. by W.H. Gardner and N.H. MacKenzie. Oxford: Oxford University Press.

Mariani, Paul L. 1970. *A Commentary on the Complete Poems of Gerard Manley Hopkins.* Ithaca and London: Cornell University Press.
McChesney Donald. 1968. *A Hopkins Commentary.* London: University of London Press.

PART IV:

DIMENSIONS OF SPACE IN DRAMA AND THEATRE

CHAPTER TWENTY-EIGHT

THE EXHIBITED IN THE ORDER
OF EXHIBITION:
ADAPTATIONS FOR THE STAGE

EWA KĘBŁOWSKA-ŁAWNICZAK

In *Colonising Egypt*, Timothy Mitchell expounds on the experience of
the Middle Eastern visitors who were taken to the theatre, "a place where
Europeans portrayed to themselves their history," to the public and
zoological gardens as well as to the museums where they "saw the cultures
of the world portrayed in objects arranged under glass" (Mitchell 1991, 6-
7). The conviction that the space of exhibitions and collections, through its
choice and method of displaying artefacts, offers more tangible insights
into a nation's/society's or culture's identity than myths has become
commonly quoted knowledge (Lunnon 2009, 54). The visitors in
Mitchell's report were, as it seems, curiously exposed to renderings of the
Heideggerian world picture, a Vor-stellung (a setting in place) where truth
"has been transformed into the certainty of representation" (Heidegger
1977, 127). The world picture, according to Heidegger, means "the world
[what is] conceived and grasped as picture"—not meaning an "imitation,"
but a setting of whatever is "fixedly before oneself" (Heidegger 1977,
129). As opposed to the earlier concept of man as *Vernehmer* who
apprehends, the modern man brings before oneself (represents) as the
normative realm what is at hand (*das Vorhandene*). Thus constituted by
himself, man as *subiectum* "gets into the picture" in precedence over
whatever is (Heidegger 1977, 131-132). Hence, "whatever is, is considered
to be in being only to the degree and to the extent that it is taken into and
referred back to this life [...] and [thus] becomes life-experience"
(Heidegger 1977, 134). In this way man becomes the central relationship
that gives measure and draws guidelines employing his "unlimited power
for moulding" and for research discipline. Among consequences
experienced by the modern man Heidegger enumerates, there is the *Vor-*

stellung of remote realities in their "everydayness" and a mania for "excelling" (134). This leads to the effect of spectacle where objects on display, imported from spatially and temporally distant realities, are to be investigated and experienced by an observer whom Mitchell reduces metonymically to the dominant European gaze.

Apparently, not only traditional nineteenth-century public museums, but a considerable number of modern plays makes use of these concepts and the ensuing strategies of representation. Apart from a spate of playwrights focusing on science and research plays, a specific sub-genre, numerous mainstream authors seem to have employed the patterns and methods of the spatial rhetoric of exhibition as a way of implementing and, sometimes, foregrounding the very *Vor-stellung*. Among others, there are such diverse figures as Tom Stoppard, Howard Barker, Joe Penhall, David Mamet, Harold Pinter, and David Storey. The present discussion will focus on one playwright, Caryl Churchill, and her classic, *Top Girls*.

The play had its first production, an all-female stage picture, in 1982 and was received, according to Elaine Aston, as "a socialist-feminist critique of bourgeois feminism" (2003, 23). The 1991 revival, with its original director, Max Stafford-Clark, and several members of the 1982 cast, was called "a state-of-the-nation debate about the Thatcher legacy" (Aston 2003, 23), which shift indicates an ongoing process of re-evaluation Churchill's open and provocative theatre invites. Commenting on *Top Girls*, Janelle Reinelt and Amelia Howe Kritzer[1] argue interestingly and perhaps on a more abstract level emphasizing Churchill's attack on a glorification of bourgeois individualism and personal achievement (Reinelt 2000, 180). According to the feminist critics, it seems, individualism and feminist pursuit of success are staged in *Top Girls* as an American-style infusion into the British welfare state epitomized by Marlene's, the main character in Churchill's play, memories of and her fascination with the American adventure as well as her faith in the "stupendous eighties" (*Top Girls,* 137). Contradicting the second wave feminist beliefs, the play can be approached as a dramatisation of the price paid for adherence to traditional male images of competitiveness and success. By 1991, with the Thatcher era behind, Aston comments interestingly on the play's revival stating that the "images of glamorous, shoulder-padded executive businesswomen felt like a museum or media [...] pieces" adding that "[t]hese had been replaced [currently] by glamorous images of professional working mothers"(Aston 2003, 25). Further on, Aston defines her own subject/observer position in

---

[1] The above refers to A.H. Kritzer, *The Plays of Caryl Churchill: Theatre of Empowerment.* New York: St Martin's Press, 1991.

relation to a thus defined exhibitionary order of the play's spectacle by stating that her gaze is that of a professional working mother.

The conviction that our present reception of *Top Girls* involves the mechanisms of *vor-stellen*, in introducing an exhibitionary regime just in order to ironically subvert it, is also traceable in the context of the first production. Interestingly, juxtaposing *Top Girls* with Benjamin's "Theses on the philosophy of history" (also translated "On the concept of history"), Peter Buse suggests that what remains from the staged past is the "overall picture" we produce concealing a more complex pattern (Buse 2001, 114). Following Benjamin, Buse doubts in the presence of the exhibitionary order of progress in Churchill's play (2001, 120). Whatever the answer is, the playwright does seem to implement some exhibitionary order. Implementing the order, she seems to look back to the feminist artist, Judy Chicago, and her 1979 installation entitled *The Dinner Party*.[2] The idea of staging an all-female party in the form of a restaurant or dinner celebration, found in Chicago's work, is very rare in an all-female context and therefore Winsome Pinnock's analogous but considerably later scene in *Mules* (1996) invites comparisons with the 1982 *Top Girls* only.

The purpose of Chicago's work was defined by the artist as an attempt to terminate the ongoing cycle of omission in which women were absent from historical records. Therefore the artist endeavoured to give prominence to compensation for the vision of women history as "achievement obscured" (Synder 1981, 31). The installation was supposed to restore their names to public memory. Caryl Churchill's Marlene, in a surrealist manner, also rescues a selection of women from obscurity and isolation in diverse historical periods, but essentially the idea is to celebrate her own promotion to a managerial post in a traditionally masculine setting of restaurant scenery. *The Dinner Party* installation has a vast banquet table resting on a triangular Heritage Floor whose opalescent porcelain tiles bear the names of 999 women inscribed in gold. The three-winged table is laid for 39 women, recognized but not sufficiently honoured in historical accounts. They are seated in temporal order. The first wing is given to women from Prehistory to Roman Empire; the second from the beginning of Christianity to Reformation while the third from the American to Women's Revolution. The triangular shape of the table as well as the remaining visual symbolism on plates and

---

[2] *The Dinner Party* was conceived by Judy Chicago and realized by a collaboration of many individual women and men in the years 1974-1979. The first exhibition was launched in June 1979 at the San Francisco Museum of Modern Art. Since 2002 it has been permanently housed at the Brooklyn Museum within the Elizabeth A. Sackler Center for Feminist Art.

the accompanying inscriptions on mats promote feminine symbolism and iconography in an exhibitionary order which supposedly inverts "Leonardo's male world" (Synder 1981, 32). Churchill's table can be either round or rectangular but she provides no definite instructions (absence of stage directions) concerning its shape. Perhaps despite the artist's intensions, the installation which precedes Churchill's premiere and whose message seems to be straightforwardly feminist—the triangle being part of the staple feminine symbolism—turns out to produce uncontrollable ironies/ambiguities and tensions whose analogues are to some extent traceable in *Top Girls*.

Irony may arise from an interplay between the exhibitionary order created by the artist/curator/collector, on the one hand, and the order of the exhibits, here the individual women, as well as the position of the imagined observer on the other. In *The Dinner Table*, the visitor/observer is likely to be involved or interested in some feminist activity while Churchill's play has been exposed to a mixed theatrical audience. The exhibitionary order in Chicago's composition generates a strong contrast between the glowing table and the engulfing darkness. The guests we never meet but only imagine as seated at the impressive table are, according to the artist, "contained within a domesticity," "served and ready to be consumed" (Chicago 1979, 22). Synder reminds us of the fact that one of Chicago's early slogans for the introduce tory stage of the project was "Twenty-Five Women Who Were Eaten Alive" (1980/81, 31). Indeed, the observer may be in dilemma, whether the female guests come to eat or to be eaten. The answer is essential. Pervasive hesitation traceable in the history of Chicago's installation is indicative of difficulties in establishing "a transcendental entity called culture, a [...] cognitive map by whose mysterious existence," according to Mitchell, "'the world' is lent its 'significance'"(Mitchell 1991, 62). The exhibitionary order of *The Dinner Table*, as stated above, marks a strong contrast between the outside and the inside but the supposedly new picture encourages a fragmented, truncated and citational vision of women history/achievement whose conciseness recalls the annals. Somewhat ironically, though in an attempt to give artistic status to feminine crafts and despite a heavily feminine symbolism, Chicago inscribes her project in the pre-existent symbolic system depriving, paradoxically, her exhibits of a chance to reshape their identity in a new language: they remain silent, focused on their symbolically defined bodies and named by the attached labels. Indeed, it seems that the effect of domesticity objectifies and contains the exhibits within the well-known, traditional world picture. Further, careful inspection of Judy Chicago's composition reveals the oversize chalices/goblets matching the almost ecclesiastical splendour of the spectacle transubstantiating the profane concept into the disembodying sacred frames, which contradicts the earlier announced attempt to subvert *The Last Supper*.

Both in the installation and in the play, the collectors' gender is foregrounded: Judy Chicago and Marlene. If care, creativity, nurturance and preservation are feminine collector traits (Ekström 2007, 3; Belk and Wallendorf 1994, 242),[3] the exhibits invited to dine onstage might be addressing consuming practices as a kind of feminist performance suggesting, as stated by Marcy J. Epstein, "that eating [...] comments on and *allows* both physical embodiment and the embodiment of women's material conditions, including gender" (1996, 21). In *Top Girls* Churchill's characters give surprisingly precise and individual orders concerning food. Joan, the *papessa*, who orders cannelloni and a salad (*Top Girls* 1996, 59), speaks explicitly on the importance of "matter" admitting that "[b]ecause angels are without matter they are not individuals. Every angel is a species" (58). Hence the scene of ingestion can provide individualising and liberating space. Even though Marlene's guests refuse to put food before sexuality as a mark of gender, which the ongoing dialogue proves, food does generate their actual bodies and distinct identities. As Epstain states, generalizing, to use food is "to incorporate cultural signs into bodies whose material performances provide the gesture of selves" (1996, 23), which is paraphrased in the dietary slogan of you are what you eat. Churchill's female exhibits seem to enter the order of progress and success, another adventure, or step that "makes for a party" (1996, 55). The order of the table does not promise to subvert Leonardo's *The Last Supper*, but paraphrases a stock masculine scene.[4] The attitudes to cuisine and ingesting are atemporal and contemporary at the same time though the individuality of each figure is carefully preserved. The opening lines feature a bottle of Frascati (55) followed by further bottles of wine, whiskey and cups of coffee (59, 61, 73, 78). Joan's order encourages and justifies the following list of food-signs: Isabella is paired with nourishing soup and chicken; Nijo orders Waldorf salad—the 1983 invention of the luxurious Waldorf Hotel finding its way into Cole Porter's "You are the Top": "you are the Waldorf salad." The simple Dull Gret has soup, bread and potatoes while the masculine Marlene orders "Avocado vinaigrette,"

---

[3] Stereotypical masculine *collector traits* include aggressiveness, competitiveness, mastery and seriousness. Hence *maintaining* has been considered feminine while acquisition masculine (Belk and Wallendorf 1994, 242, 250)

[4] In theatrical tradition, there are numerous masculine scenes in pubs. An often-quoted masculine restaurant scene appears in David Mamet's *Glengarry Glen Ross* (first produced in 1983).

two rare stakes and "a lot of potatoes"(58-59). Marlene's masculine load of food emphasizes her recent empowerment but it matches both her collector traits and a drive towards embodiment. Thus she is also having pudding and "getting nice and fat" (74). She worries about the most spiritually-minded and supposedly anorectic (74) exhibit, the patient Griselda who does not care for food and never eats pudding (73-74). The binge ends with zabaglione, apple pie with cream, cake, cheese and biscuits (75). In the background, evoked by Dull Gret, there appears the image of the gaping mouth of Hell conflated with that of a street in a besieged city—this time an image of destructive ingestion and devouring energy (82). An analogy, hardly intended, emerges from the vaginal references on Chicago's round plates, which turn body parts into food and, potentially, into waste. This constricting and self-destructive cannibalistic concept is left unexplained. In Churchill's play, the wasted bodies of children and babies enter from Breughel's painting, the visual source of Dull Gret.[5] Within the exhibitionary order of success promoted by Marlene, the wasted lives and bodies emerge from the darkness engulfing the restaurant scene to become more real in the ugly domesticity of act 2 and act 3, when Angie, Joyce and Marlene's mother come to fore and so does the question of waste and cannibalism.

In *Top Girls*, Caryl Churchill, a socialist feminist, produced an exhibitionary spectacle the effect of which was to set the capitalist Thatcher era as a picture. The *objectness* of the exhibits was supposed to evoke, by its method of organisation, some larger meaning Mitchell defines in his study as Empire, History or Progress (1999, 297). All three seem to be present in Churchill's drama which reveals the means of producing both the certainty of a thus grasped world (including the dangers it poses) and its loss—the latter especially in the revival production. On the level of particular exhibits, Churchill preserved the quasi-realistic, historically credible, convention. Each of the figures is traceable to its sources and therefore a typical figure on loan. Isabella Bird, the Victorian travelling woman who visited America, Scotland, Australia, Canada and Hawaii is known from her own writing openly used by Churchill in constructing dialogues. Lady Nijo's *Confessions* are often referred to as an autobiographical novel from the 14th century. Pope Joan, more often considered a historical fake, is supposed to have succeeded Pope Leo IV in the middle of the 9th century. Dull Gret derives from Flemish folklore and, more tangibly, from Peter Breughel's painting.

---

[5] Pieter Brueghel the Elder painted *Mad Meg* in 1562.

Patient Griselda's Christ-like figure[6] derives from literary sources including *Decameron* and Geoffrey Chaucer's adaptation of Boccaccio's tale in his *Canterbury Tales*. Marlene is a pure construct: the curator and the staged observer of the exhibition. Hence she can be excluded from the exhibitionary order. Staging a model of success, the exhibition preserves a sense of distance from the represented reality by foregrounding the precedence of the model and by introducing it on a surreal level. In spite of this distanciating technique, the revival production Aston finds so different from the first, indicates the model's extension in the shift from emphasis on act 1, the restaurant scene, to focus on acts 2 and 3 which reveal Marlene's "family life" and professional environment.

Though the present thesis assumes that Caryl Churchill's *Top Girls* was inspired by Judy Chicago's famous project, it argues that, even if the audience remains unaware of this source, the effect of a peculiar collection or exhibition is inherent in the construction of act 1. Easily noticeable, it pervades the comments of several critics. The concept of exhibitionary order can obviously be referred to Heidegger's world picture but, on the level of praxis, its presence implies also involvement in definite practices of collecting, which might be traceable in Churchill's theatrical project. Indeed in the sixteenth century ideal collections were referred to as *theatrum* or *universo theatro* and were defined either as places or as texts (Schultz, 176).[7] Hence an exhibitionary model located on stage follows tradition. The play's collecting and curating activity includes miscellaneous objects from Europe and outside the west. However, the pressing question of *alterity* is referred to gender rather than cultural identity. Excluding the nineteenth-century guardian/keeper model of a public museum, with its national identity concepts based on ownership, and excluding also the international modernist concepts of art institutions on the other hand, our discussion indicates the prevalence, in *Top Girls*, of a trans-national model characteristic for global exhibitions. This model, conveniently for Churchill's critique of the Thatcher era policy, asserts its neo-imperial reach concurrently advocating emphasis of trans-national and diasporic networks. Accordingly, the collector's role shifts from that of a keeper to one of active engagement (Deborah Cherry, ES), clearly discernible in Marlene's role. The global model brings together restitution and hospitality.

---

[6] According to some interpretations Griselda stands for *pharmakos*, a *figura Christi* whose spirituality stands in opposition to the model of *vita activa* promoted by the Thatcherite woman of success, Marlene. See Marga Cottino-Jones, 1973, 41-44.

[7] Encyclopaedias, for example.

Restitution as repayment of debts appears as part of Marlene's promotion and Howard's, her opponent's, demise. Her managerial position is, according to Isabella, "just the beginning of something extraordinary" (*Top Girls,* 67) as it locates her "[o]ver all the women [...] And the men" (67). It means liberation from Chicago's cycle of omission. The characters/exhibits are not negatively dislocated and therefore no restitution to their original location is required. On the contrary, the arrival of Marlene's guests can be compared to an invitation extended to diasporic communities which are encouraged to comment and thus bring about a restitution of interpretation. While Chicago's display of silent ghosts follows what Clifford defines as the "ethnographic" manner, Churchill's collection consists of "moving performances" (Cliffird 1999, 188). The life-stories told by the exhibits are interrelated in the course of broken and overlapping dialogue, which reveals their relevance for the current political or social situation. One of the painful subjects raised by the celebrating community is child-birth and child abuse. Both find extensions in the contemporary, untold family life story of Marlene, Joyce and Angie. A thus constructed collection becomes a *contact zone* (Clifford 1999, 192) signalling co-presence and hospitality. Hospitality assumes, as a rule, that host (exhibitionary order, curator) and guest (exhibit) are charged and changed. The question whether the high-flying lady is affected by the encounters is left unanswered. Certain remains Angie's indescribable fear (141), which makes us wonder whether, as opposed to the outspoken visitors, she does not remain a fully tamed, objectified exhibit ready for consumption within the order of *studium.*

Churchill's project departs in many ways from the fixation of the world picture underpinning traditional European public collections in particular. Apart from the series of interactive, overlapping narratives, the characters resist a *Vor-stellung* by cultivating mobility. Marlene herself is a high-flyer and adventurer who "can't bear sitting still" (55). Isabella Bird spends her life on therapeutic travelling. Lady Nijo becomes a vagrant nun (57); Pope Joan is a high-flyer in pursuit of truth and Dull Gret leads an army of women to pillage hell (57) but also enjoys walking (66). Patient Griselda's life is the least active and the most contemplative. By their mobility, the exhibits resist incorporation into the picture and into a *studium* display. Resisting subjection and showing, in this way, preference for a *punctum* representation, they fail to either learn or edify remaining in the sphere of the Heideggerian *Erlebnis*, that is, *mere* experience and not *Erfahrung* (experience as gaining knowledge). In a thus constructed *heterotopic*[8] collection, various and often contradictory forms of spatial organisation can coexist and the exhibits tend to oscillate between *punctum* and *studium*. There is space for the aesthetically minded collector of roses (*Top Girls*, 99) as well as for the microcosmic collection, a summary of the universe,[9] emerging from Pope Joan's *De Rerum Natura* by Titus Lucretius Carus, quoted in Latin. By referring to the world picture concept, which guarantees stability to the observer/subiectum, Churchill provides a basis for a eulogy of extreme individualism only to destabilise the model and launch its thorough critique. Its echoes ring in Pinnock's story of women-mules where Bridie, Marlene's counterpart, comments on her inability to cease travelling as it would require her to "establish some sort of relationship"(50) with herself. Resisting subjection, Bridie, like Marlene and unlike Griselda, reminds us of the dangerously liberating lack of self-possession.

References

Aston, Elaine. 2003. *Feminist Views on the English Stage: Women Playwrights, 1990-2000.* Cambridge: Cambridge University Press.

Belk, Russell W. and Melanie Wallendorf. 1994. Of Mice and Men: Gender Identity in Collecting. In *Interpreting Objects and Collections*, ed. by Susan M. Pearce, 240-253. London/New York: Routledge.

Buse, Peter. 2001. *Drama+Theory. Critical Approaches to Modern British Drama.* Manchester and New York: Manchester University Press.

Cherry, Deborah. 2007. Transnational Practices in Collecting. Seminar: *Collecting and Identity.* Van Abbe Museum. www.becomingdutch. com/docs/Transnationalcollecting%20Deborah%20Cherry.pdf (accessed 14 March 2009).

Chicago, Judy. 1979. *The Dinner Party: A Symbol of Our Heritage.* New York: Anchor.

Churchill, Caryl. 1996. *Top Girls.* In *Plays: 2*, 51-142. London: Methuen.

---

[8] Michele Foucault defines the place as outside times and epochs, capable of enclosing "all forms, all tastes," "an immobile place." Among the examples the author refers to is both the library and the museum (1986:26). Further on, Foucault distinguishes several types of heterotopias of which the heterotopias of illusion and compensation (27) are relevant to Churchill's play.

[9] Schulz considers Pliny's *Historia Naturalis* a collection (1994:175) text stating further that the task of the text was to collect the constituents that were to be examined as well as to instruct scholars on what was to be collected. In the 16th century works of art and artistically arranged naturalia were often displayed in the same collection (176).

Clifford, James. 1998. On Collecting Art and Culture. In *Visual Culture Reader*, ed. by Nicholas Mirzoeff, 94-107. London: Routledge.
—. 1999. Museums as Contact Zones. In *Routes, Travel and Translation in the Late Twentieth Century*, 188-219. Cambridge MA/London: Harvard University Press,
Cottino-Jones, Marga. 1973. Fabula vs Figura: Another interpretation of the Griselda story. *Italica* 50: 38-52.
Ekström, Karin M. 2007. Zooming in the Collector's Identity. In *Proceedings of the Nordic Consumer Policy Research Conference*. 1-3. Göteborg; Göteborg University. www.consumer2007.info/wp-content/uploads/Proceedings0Cover.pdf (accessed 27 March 2009).
Epstein, Marcy J. 1996. Eating Acts and Feminist Embodiment. *The Drama Review* 40, 4, T 152: 20-36. New York: New York University and the Massachusetts Institute of Technology.
Foucault, Michel and Jay Miskowiec. 1986. Of Other Spaces. *Diacritics* 16: 22-27. Published by the Johns Hopkins University Press. http://www.jstor.org/stable/ 464648 (accessed 29 March 2009).
Heidegger, Martin. 1977. The Age of the World Picture. In *The Question Concerning Technology and Other Essay*, trans. by William Lovitt, 115-154. New York, London, Toronto: Harper Perennial.
Kahn, Miriam. 1995. Heterotopic Dissonance in the Museum Representation of Pacific Island Cultures. *American Anthropologist*, New Series 97, 2: 324-338.
Kritzer, Amelia Howe. 1991. *The Plays of Caryl Churchill: Theatre of Empowerment*. New York: St Martin's Press.
Mitchell, Timothy. 1991. *Colonising Egypt*. Berkeley, Los Angeles, London: University of California Press.
—. 1999. Orientalism and the Exhibitionary Order. In *Visual Culture Reader*, ed. by Nicholas Mirzoeff, 293-303. London: Routledge.
Pinnock, Winsome. 1996. *Mules*. London: Faber and Faber.
Reinelt, Janelle. 2000. Caryl Churchill and the Politics of Style. In *The Cambridge Companion to Modern British Women Playwrights*, ed. by Elaine Aston and Janelle Reinelt, 174-193. Cambridge: Cambridge University Press.
Schulz, Eva. 1994. Notes on the History of Collecting and of Museums. In: *Interpreting Objects and Collections*, ed. by Susan M. Pearce, 175-188. London/New York: Routledge.
Snyder, Carol. 1980-1981. Reading the Language of *The Dinner Party*. *Woman's Art Journal* 1: 30-34. Woman's Art, Inc. http://www.jstor.org /stable/1358081 (accessed 7 April 2009)

CHAPTER TWENTY-NINE

IN BALLYBEG AND BEYOND: PRIVATE AND PUBLIC SPACE IN BRIAN FRIEL'S *DANCING AT LUGHNASA*

KATARZYNA OJRZYŃSKA

In *Dancing at Lughnasa*, a play written in 1990 and considered by most critics one of Brian Friel's "high point[s] of critical and commercial success" (Coult 2003, 103), the Irish dramatist focuses on the presentation of a poor female-dominated household situated on the outskirts of the mythical village of Ballybeg in County Donegal. The retrospective nostalgic story depicts the last joyful moments of a family facing threats posed by the "encroaching materialism and industrialization" (Cave 2006, 189) which eventually lead to its disintegration. On the visual level, the play presents the audience with a typical Irish domestic space, comprising a house and its surroundings. At the same time, it explores the complexities of the geographic location of the Ballybeg community and the diversity of mental spaces of the characters which find a concrete expression in *Dancing at Lughnasa,* providing valuable hints for possible interpretations.

The paper examines the use of both physical and psychological spaces in the play. Beginning with the macrotopographic level of Friel's masterpiece, it gives attention to the location of the house of the Mundy family with reference to the distinction between the public and non-public spheres. The further analysis adverts to the issue of methods in which the mental spaces of the female characters are realized on the visual level, with particular attention devoted to the use of movement as a means of characterization in the focal dance scene of the play.

In terms of space, the central opposition established in *Dancing at Lughnasa* is the one between the village and the back hills. Governed by the stringent rules of Catholic propriety, the former area belongs to the public sphere, whereas the hills are where the hidden, subconscious tendencies and desires of the Ballybeg society are realized in the form of pagan ritual and celebration. Replete with allusions to Bacchic rituals, the space is presented in the official discourse as subversive and dangerous. The unsanctioned celebrations of Celtic origins are thus endowed with clear satanic references and shrouded in a certain mystery. Kate learns from the local gossips that "They were doing some devilish thing with a goat—some sort of sacrifice for the Lughnasa Festival; the Sweeney was so drunk he toppled over into the middle of the bonfire" (Friel 1990, 35). The story of the unfortunate boy grows into truly monstrous proportions, as we discover that "He was anointed last night [. . . .] Not an inch of his body that isn't burned [. . .] He knows he's dying [. . .] Just lies there moaning" (Friel 1990, 16). The rumour, however, seems more than exaggerated, for, towards the end of the play, the audience is informed that the injuries were altogether not that severe.

The vilification of the Celtic rituals by the Ballybeg gossips reflects the antagonism between the official and the unofficial, the village and the back hills. Consequently, the story of the Sweeney boy can be interpreted as both a projection of the social fears of wild instincts inherent in the ancestral rituals and as an element of the tactics of the Catholic Church aimed at deterring potential participants from joining the pagan celebrations. As Kiberd puts it, "These people's access to the traditional interior of the ancestral culture—the fire-festival of Lughnasa celebrated in the back hills of Donegal—has been blocked by the codes of a prim Catholicism, epitomized by the censorious but not bad-hearted Kate" (2007, 154).

In terms of geographic location, what remains striking about the setting of the play is the intermediary position of the house of the Mundy family, situated half way between the village and the back hills, occupying certain undefined space and thus reflecting the social position of the sisters as outsiders who belong to neither area. They are social outcasts whose presence cannot be fully accepted in the official sphere, with Christina's illegitimate child or Father Jack who indulges into, as Kate euphemistically puts it, "his own distinctive spiritual search" (Friel 1990, 60). Nor do the sisters belong to the world of back hills—the unofficial space which serves the function of Jungian collective unconscious of the Ballybeg community, symbolizing both the ancient religion suppressed first by the invaders, then by the Church, and all the desires of the local people that cannot be realized in the public sphere.

Considering the location of the play in the wider topological context, Cleary indicates that "The Ireland or Ballybeg of *Dancing at Lughnasa* is essentially conceived as a transient and ephemeral limbo suspended somewhere between the worlds of Ryanga and London and destined to move only in the direction of the latter, since the hour of its industrial revolution is at hand" (2007, 228). One of the elements which supports this view is the interest of the Mundys in foreign, rather than local issues. The foreignness invades the household by the agency of Marconi—a wireless which, in historical terms, "brought outside voices and ideas into previously isolated rural areas" (Lojek 2006, 82). Kiberd argues, "Apart from a passing line urging people to vote for de Valera, there is no reference to the politics of the new Ireland. In fact, there is more interest in the wars in Abyssinia and Spain" (2007, 153). This may suggest a form of escapism, realized both on the physical and psychological level. As regards the latter, it is, among others, the presence of the foreign music, such as popular American tunes, that releases the desires and emotions of the sisters, which otherwise remain suppressed by the strict Catholic morality, in this way opening the female characters to wider mental horizons and spaces.

Surprising as this may seem, what provides a stimulus for the eruption of the untamed dance in the famous kitchen scene is a reel tune—"The Mason's Apron," played by a *céilí* band. The unusual character of this accompaniment consists in the fact that, on a number of other occasions, the author chooses to introduce popular foreign songs such as Cole Porter's "Anything Goes." In terms of psychological space, the non-Irish music sets the sisters free from the narrow mental confines of the village community and its despotic morality. As Friel himself stated in 1991, "I think what's interesting is that it's music from a different culture that liberates them. They haven't absorbed it into their life and into their culture and tamed it. It's still slightly exotic" (in Lahr 2003, 215).

Yet, there exists a well-grounded justification for selecting a piece of traditional Irish music for the pivotal scene of *Dancing at Lughnasa* and thus endowing it with a truly subversive flavour. The unbridled dance of the sisters takes place in the domestic space—a location associated with familistic, patriarchal order and a particular model of femininity. "Recogniz[ing] the Family as the natural primary and fundamental unit group of Society, and as a moral institution possessing inalienable and imprescriptible rights," the Article 41 of the 1937 Constitution ascribes a very specific role to the Irishwoman. It states:

> In particular, the State recognises that by her life within the home, woman gives to the State a support without which the common good cannot be achieved. (*Bunreacht Na hÉireann* 1937)

As Lojek puts it:

> In the independent state that emerged in the 1920s the image of suffering Mother Ireland joined the ideal of the 'sainted' Irish mother to become a hall mark of national patriarchal assumptions. The Republic's 1937 Constitution famously incorporated not only the tenets of conservative Catholicism, but also a romantic vision of Irish woman, a term that clearly meant 'wife and mother.' (2006, 78)

Consequently, it seems that the house is supposed to serve as space within which de Valera's idea of womanhood was to be fulfilled. With their wild behaviour in the central dance scene of *Dancing at Lughnasa*, the Mundy sisters contradict or even subvert this model, which is accurately described by Michael for whom the music and dance "derange those kind, sensible women and transform them into shrieking strangers" (Friel 1990, 2).

Another crucial historical fact which contributes to this interpretation is the introduction of the Dance Hall Act in 1935, a year before the time when the play is set. The regulation was aimed against the phenomenon of *céilithe* held in private houses, and it approved of organizing dances in special halls licensed for such a purpose. In other words, the private space was considered improper for this form of entertainment as, contrary to the public space, it lacked formal supervision which could lead to certain "baleful affects [. . .] upon rural morels" (qtd in Brennan 2001, 125), especially with reference to drinking and sexual activities. One's household was no longer a proper place, also in legal terms, to organize dancing parties or other forms of social gatherings.

Although the dance of the sisters cannot be considered a social occasion or a communal event, as it is a unique experience reserved exclusively for the female characters of the play, the Mundys seem to be conscious of violating this rule. It is particularly conspicuous in the case of the oldest of the sisters, Kate, who "identifies most with repressive religious authority" (McMullan 1999, 97), but simultaneously "fights against her moments of 'otherness', because her return to her mundane self is the harsher for the contrast" (Cave 2006, 194). At one point she performs

> a weave of complex steps that takes her quickly round the kitchen, past her sisters, out to the garden, round the summer seat, back to the kitchen; a pattern of action that is out of character and at the same time ominous of some deep and true emotion. (Friel 1990, 22)

However liberating and rebellious this idea of abandoning the domestic space may seem, in truth it is nothing more than a gesture of submission and obedience. As Terry John Bates, the choreographer of *Dancing at Lughnasa* under Patric Mason's direction, suggests, in this scene,

> You have to have that feeling of claustrophobia. If they all start to prance around the stage, you've lost that claustrophobia in the kitchen. I think you've got to keep the frustration of these women. There's only Kate who goes out to the garden and dances because she doesn't want to be seen to be dancing inside houses (in Coult 2003, 193)

and in this way tarnish the domestic space. Furthermore, it is possible to argue that the oldest sister escapes to the garden because she is unable to withstand the pressure and the intensity of emotions within the house which "bubbles with desire and repression" (Praga-Terente 2006, 84); thus Bates puts forward another suggestion: "They [the sisters] are doing extreme things. I mean Kate would never dance in that kitchen, but maybe she's been driven to do it. She has to get out of the house, and this is a very awful moment, really. They're all letting off steam" (in Coult 2003, 196).

The other four sisters remain within the spatial confines of the house throughout their dance. As regards stage directions, Friel's instructions concerning their initial movements do not stress the idea of reunion and togetherness of the women, but rather their individuality and separateness, which also serves as a form of characterization. Each sister interprets the music in her own distinctive way. Their individual mental spaces gain visual dance representations, giving the reader[1] an impression as if they were occupying, or perhaps creating, separate physical spaces which may or may not overlap. This depends on the way the choreographer or the director decides to interpret Friel's stage directions and to what extent they wish to highlight the bonds among the sisters, for it is only after the initial phase of individual performance when they all, except for Kate who joins in later to present her lonely private dance, "*meet* [and] *retreat* [. . .] *form a circle and wheel round and round* [. . .] [with] *their arms tightly around one's another's neck, one another's waist*" (Friel 1990, 21-22). Yet before this collective performance, each of them dances on her own as if enclosed in her private mental space which gains a specific visual on-stage equivalent.

---

[1] The choice of the word "reader" is purposeful in this context, for Friel leaves the choreographer some freedom of interpretation, which may be exercised to minimize the effect of separateness of the sisters and which, in turn, may lead to a different reception of the dance scene by the theatre audience.

The one who initiates the dance is Maggie. Both her *"look of defiance, of aggression* [and] *crude mask of happiness"* and wild exclamations *"Come and join me! Come on! Come on!"* (Friel 1990, 21) serve as a perfect reflection of her mental space that is, in McMullan's words, being "the most subversive, with her wicked, provocative sense of fun, her parodic dances, and her 'Wild Woodbines'" (1999, 97). Maggie's dance provides also a potent allusion to the African motif in the play—a grotesque mockery of a primitive ritual, presenting her as belonging more to the world of back hills or distant Ryanga than to the ordered and repressive village. Yet the symbolism of the mask may also allude to her desire to hide disappointment and disillusionment or a reference to the Bakhtinian idea of the carnivalesque.[2]

Compared with the dancing styles of other sisters, Rose's movements seem to be most authentic and deprived of any deliberate theatricality. Her disability makes the woman respond to her instincts eagerly and in an uninhibited way. With her *"wellingtons pounding out their own erratic rhythm"* (Friel 1990, 21), Rose's dance visually expresses her unrefined, simple-minded nature.

Agnes is the one who *"moves most gracefully, most sensuously"* (Friel 1990, 21). As Mason recalls, "He [Friel] was very specific about Agnes— she was a very nice dancer. She was the *best* dancer. I think he had a soft spot for Agnes" (in Coult 2003, 193). Consequently, her dance may be read as reflecting Agnes's being "highly intelligent and sensitive but harbouring deeply repressed desires" (McMullan 1999, 97), which becomes even more evident in the scene of her dance with Gerry imbued with erotic tension and ambiguity.

Finally, Christina tosses in her dance Father Jack's surplice over her head. Apart from being an allusion to the carnivalesque idea of a masquerade, the gesture serves as a fierce mockery targeted at the religious and secular patriarchy, "hint[ing] at priestly femininity" (Lojek 2006, 87) and posing Michael's mother in opposition to the Catholic rules of propriety.

On the physical level, the individual spaces created by the sisters through the diversity of their dancing styles serve as a reflection of their personalities and tempers. Yet, more importantly, they function as private microspaces in which the female characters can give voice to the repressed

---

[2] Discussing the idea of the carnivalesque in his work *Rabelais and His World*, Bakhtin writes: "Even more important is the theme of mask, the most complex theme of folk culture. The mask is connected with the joy of change and reincarnation, with gay relativity and with merry negation of uniformity and similarity; it rejects conformity to oneself" (1984, 39-40).

feelings and anxieties, thus creating a temporary opportunity for a certain degree of self-realization. The differences among the sisters in terms of movement further suggest the fragmentation of the appropriated communal space and the promotion of individuality rather than conformity to the uniform rules governing the society also visible in reference to the strict canon Irish dancing introduced at the beginning of the 20th century.[3]

Analyzing social space as a social product and "a means of control and hence of domination" (2000, 26), Lefebvre argues that "The violence of power is answered by the violence of subversion [. . .] State-imposed normality makes permanent transgression inevitable. As for time and negativity, when even they reemerge, as they must, they do so explosively" (2000, 23). In *Dancing at Lughnasa*, such an uncontrolled and violent outburst of repressed emotions is not, however, endowed with this revolutionary potential. Although violating the domestic sphere, it takes place outside the sanctioned area of the village—in the private and not the public space, and, therefore, it does not pose any threat to the existing order. Being just a momentary release of tensions and anxieties, the dance finishes as soon as the music ceases, leaving the sisters "*slightly ashamed* [though] *slightly defiant*" (Friel 1990, 22). Consequently, the scene appears very close to the Bakhtinian idea of the carnivalesque. Like the medieval *festa stultorum*, the pivotal dance in the play implies a temporary rather than permanent transgression of the social decorum, performing the role of a safety valve and providing the sisters with an opportunity to release all the negative feelings which otherwise might lead to either rebellion or severe despair and depression. Conforming to Bakhtin's idea of the carnivalesque, the untamed emotional outburst of the sisters "sanction[s] the existing pattern of things and reinforce[s] it" (Bakhtin 1984, 9). The anarchic, revolutionary potential of the dance remains unfulfilled; despite giving the impression of "*a sense of order being consciously subverted*" (Friel 1990, 22), the activity aims at sustaining rather than abolishing the existing social rules.

A moment after the sisters finish their dance, Kate immediately restores order within the domestic space, suppressing the last signs of rebellious defiance and scolding all the participants of the physical outburst of emotions. She criticises Chris's "corner-boy language" (Friel 1990, 22), Rose's wellingtons, Maggie's smoking and untied laces as well as Agnes' low income. Kate also insists on Christina's instantly taking off the surplice, thus depriving her of this carnivalesque attribute, which could

---

[3] For further information, please consult Brennan's chapter entitled "The Fleshpots of Egypt and Gaelic Mayo: Dance and the Gaelic League" (2001, 29-43).

be interpreted as a gesture corresponding to the medieval uncrowning of the king of the feast of fools and an act of reinstating the rules of propriety. All in all, the topographic analysis of physical and mental landscapes in *Dancing at Lughnasa* reveals a number of interrelations and nuances incorporated in the play. Although the space presented visually on the stage is limited to one household and its surroundings, Friel provides us with sufficient information concerning its location within a wider context, revealing tensions between the public and the non-public spheres of the local community. Yet, more importantly, both on the individual and collective levels, the space in *Dancing at Lughnasa* is used as a representation of the mental landscape either of the given character or the whole community, revealing their nature, fears and anxieties, and thus greatly contributing to the psychological dimension of the play.

References

Bakhtin, Mikhail. 1984. *Rabelais and His World*, trans. by Helene Iswolsky. Bloomington: Indiana University Press.

Brennan, Helen. 2001. *The Story of Irish Dance*. Lanham: Roberts Rinehart Publishers.

Bunreacht Na hÉireann. Constitution of Ireland. 1937. www. taoiseach.gov.ie/upload/static/256.htm (accessed 14 March 2009).

Cave, Richard Allen. 2006. Questing for Ritual and Ceremony in a Godforsaken World: *Dancing at Lughnasa* and *Wonderful Tennessee*. In *Brian Friel's Dramatic Artistry: 'The Work Has Value'*, ed. by Donald E. Morse, Csilla Bertha and Mária Kurdi, 181-204. Dublin: Carysfort Press.

Cleary, Joe. 2007. *Outrageous Fortune Capital and Culture in Modern Ireland*. Dublin: Field Day Publications.

Coult, Tony. 2003. *About Friel: the Playwright and the Work*. London: Faber and Faber.

Friel, Brian. 1990. *Dancing at Lughnasa*. London: Faber and Faber.

Kiberd, Declan. 2007. *Dancing at Lughnasa*: Between First and Third World. In *Ireland on Stage: Beckett and After*, ed. by Hiroko Mikami, Minako Okamuro and Naoko Yagi, 153-176. Dublin: Carysfort Press.

Lahr, John. 2003. In *Dancing at Lughnasa*, Due on Broadway this Month, Brian Friel Celebrates Life's Pagan Joys. In *Brian Friel in Conversation*, ed. by Paul Delaney, 213-217. Michigan: University of Michigan Press.

Lefebvre, Henri. 2000. *The Production of Space*, trans. by Donald Nicholson-Smith. Oxford: Blackwell Publishers.

Lojek, Helen. 2006. *Dancing at Lughnasa* and the Unfinished Revolution. In *The Cambridge Companion to Brian Friel*, ed. by Anthony Roche, 78-90. Cambridge: Cambridge University Press.

McMullan, Anna. 1999. 'In touch with some otherness': Gender, Authority and the Body in *Dancing at Lughnasa*. *Irish University Review* 29: 90-100.

Praga-Terente, Inés. 2006. 'Those five Glenties women': Echoes of Lorca in *Dancing at Lughnasa*. *Estudios Irlandeses* 1: 81-89.

CHAPTER THIRTY

A SENSE OF EPISTEMOLOGICAL VERTIGO IN TOM STOPPARD'S SPATIAL CONSTRUCTIONS

ANNA SUWALSKA-KOŁECKA

We live in an Age of scepticism, claims Stuart Sim, and explains that postmodernism, with its disdain for authority and received wisdom, challenges any theory "claiming to be in possession of ultimate truth, or of criteria for determining what counts as ultimate truth" (Sim 2001, 3). Epistemologically postmodernism states its opposition against the enlightenment quest for certain knowledge through rationality and logic. Reason can no longer assume the position of the great clarifying force for it is impossible to know anything with absolute certainty. In essence, the crisis of epistemology, sparked off by the distrust of totalising mechanisms, leads to the increased emphasis on the importance of competing explanations and a plurality of voices, none of which can claim authority. Erosion of authority and dismantling of boundaries provoked a shift towards the acceptance of fragmentation, discontinuity, and indeterminacy.

In the light of above observations, Tom Stoppard seems to respond to the problem of epistemological doubt for the playwright produces plays in which "meanings are stated, countered, and cross-countered in a dizzying display of linguistic and philosophical paradox" (Heuvel 2001, 217). The main aim of this paper is the analysis of the techniques employed by Stoppard to problematise the epistemological uncertainty through the space the playwright produces in his plays. The plays chosen for examination are his early pieces: *Rosencrantz and Guildenstern are Dead*, *After Magritte*, *The Real Inspector Hound*, and *Jumpers*. The plays display diverse spatial constructions, from space anchored in the already existing text to dystopian England under a ruthless political regime, but they all have salient characteristics in common.

The predominant feature of space created by Stoppard is its ambiguity. It can be therefore stated that the atmosphere of the epistemological uncertainty pervades most of his plays. The stories he creates have epistemological emphasis for they remind the recipient repeatedly that it is impossible for man to know anything. Inscrutability of the surrounding reality permeates the plays with an interrogative mood and all the plays show man's efforts to encompass the world through reason. In fact, all the plays under discussion contain an enigma of a criminal type and a detective story is an epistemological genre *par excellence*. Stoppard, however, plays parodistically with specific texts or with stock elements of the convention and these intertextual practices give rise to the creation of his dramatic space. In this way the playwright rethinks cognitive frames used to embrace human individual experience. Ros and Guil want to understand Hamlet's behaviour and consequently their own place in an alien surrounding and a host of searching questions are asked in the course of the crime investigations in the three other plays. Puzzled by what is around them and intrigued by what happened in the past, the dramatic figures pursue to impose upon the world an element of logic and cohesion. Ros and Guil play their question-answer games, Inspector Foot tries to match a witness report with his casual observation into a full-scaled reconstruction of the crime, and George suffers tortures to close his ramifications in the frame of the lecture. In the same way, Moon and Birdboot lay bare the conventions underlying the performance they are watching to assimilate its meaning. No surprise then that Stoppard frequently uses detectives and scholars in his plays for their very profession entails the interrogation of the reality.

The very interrogation, even if it concerns trivial problems like a family disagreement over the identity of a passer-by glimpsed casually from the street, serves a limited purpose. Space, as it is constructed by Stoppard, resists man's efforts to enclose it in a rational system of thought. Many a time the epistemological uncertainty is fuelled by the playwright's intertextual practices which provide scaffolding for the construction of the play's space. For example, it seems that the heart of the originality of his *Rosencrantz and Guildenstern are Dead* lies in the clash of two kinds of time and space continuum and in the discrepancy between the level of awareness of the major figures and the recipient. The play opens with two, well-dressed Elizabethans in "a place without any visible character" (9). They pass their time tossing coins and announce loudly the result: eighty-five heads in a row. The result arouses mixed feelings: Ros shows no sign of surprise, Guil, on the other hand, is gravely worried about the implications. What upsets him is not the fact that he has been losing (his moneybag is nearly empty!), but the violation of the law of probability. Once lost equanimity will never be restored, because all the attempts lead to a disturbing question about the beginning of the game, but that neither of the courtiers remembers. What they do remember is that they have been summoned to the court by a messenger and his arrival initiated the disturbance in the expected course of events.

The construction of the very first scene conveys directly a message that from the point of view of the courtiers the surrounding reality is empirical. Thus they take for granted it is subjected to physical laws, one of them being probability. This belief in the probability rule gives them a kind of harmony and confidence, both of which are seriously undermined once the coins keep falling down on heads. Meanwhile they make another attempt to stifle the feeling of uneasiness and disbelief and decide to go. They are, however, unable to carry out the command "Forwards!" until they locate where "Backwards" is and that is beyond their capacity for they do not remember the direction they have arrived from. Thus the moment the messenger banged on their shutters, they are "within un-, sub- or supernatural forces" (13), which belie the rule of probability, memory and a sense of direction. It is worth stressing that being dramatic figures, Ros and Guil are not capable of discerning that this space has a direction imposed on it, direction connected with the time and course of ensuing events[1]. The recipient, however, due to their prior knowledge of Shakespeare's text, knows that the road goes to Elsinore and that the courtiers are supposed to come across the tragedians on the way. And it is exactly what happens: for an appropriate payment, travelling actors promise Ros and Guil to transfer them to a world of intrigue and illusion, suggesting it will cost more to get caught in the action.

Their offer acquires additional importance in the light of the ongoing scenes. Once the coin finally lands on tails, the light changes from exterior to interior, and the courtiers are drawn into *Hamlet*'s action. When the royal procession leaves the first words uttered by Ros are indicative of what they feel after this confrontation: "I want to go home"—says Ros and adds quickly "I am out of my depth here" (29). The pair will try to fight ferociously the feelings of loss and exasperation, but they will hang on to the attendant lords till the end of the play. It seems the price for "getting caught up in the action" is very high. This time and space jump seems yet again to be indicative of some unnatural forces being set in motion in their

---

[1] Jerzy Limon in his *Między niebem a sceną* discusses the differences between the physical space and the fictional space conjured in the course of a theatrical performance. This juxtaposition proved immensely helpful in the analysis of the dualism of space in *Rosencrantz and Guildenstern are Dead*. (2002 28-53).

world. From a country road they have been somehow transferred to a place which is, due to the recipient's knowledge of *Hamlet*, immediately recognised as the court of Elsinore.

Aesthetisation of the language is a theatrical convention and the inhabitants of the court speak blank verse. Even Ros and Guil switch from modern English to archaic Elizabethan one, but the change escapes their attention. Elizabethan blank verse is a strong authorial signal of the theatre convention, which, however, passes unnoticed by Ros and Guil. It is the language that differentiates these two realities and two time and space continuums, and the language makes the juxtaposition between them ostensibly visible. These authorial signals are identified by the recipient who consequently discerns the dichotomy between the world of the theatre and the persistence of Ros and Guil to treat it as the empirical reality, governed by natural forces. The recipient, from the position of the superior level of awareness, is able to reconstruct the theatre world as subjected to completely different rules. Intertextuality will be instrumental in this respect: on the more abstract level it is the familiarity with theatrical conventions connected with the construction of the dramatic world. On the more particular level, the familiarity with Shakespeare's text proves helpful because every intertextual remark conveys a set of relations from *Hamlet* to Stoppard's play.

Since the world of *Hamlet* is instrumental in building the space of Stoppard's play, it is essential to consider its so-called geography. McElroy observes that it consists of three parts and the court of Elsinore occupies the most prominent position of all three of them because it is where the action is set (1973, 29). We are presented with a mere fragment of the fictional world but it is implied metonymically and can be reconstructed on the basis of the figures' words and movements. The castle comprises numerous chambers and halls: soldiers guard its walls, Gertrude retreats to her bedroom where Polonius hides himself behind a curtain, Hamlet drags his dead body to the castle's chapel and so on and so forth. All in all, the figures move from one place to another with ease and confidence. We are also invariably informed about the world outside the castle from which numerous people arrive and where many depart. It has its stream where Ophelia drowned and its graves dug by gravediggers. It has universities where Hamlet, Rosencrantz and Guildenstern used to study and where Leartes returns. It has its cities from which the players bring news about bad times. We are aware it is surrounded by a kingdom when Claudius welcomes ambassadors from Norway and sends Hamlet to England, when Fortinbras threatens its sovereignty by his invasion and when pirates attack Hamlet's ship. The third realm of *Hamlet's* world is the metaphysical sphere, which makes its disquieting presence with the appearance of the Ghost and which "is never far from the mind of the hero" (McElroy 1973, 29).

As a rule, it is the author of a play who decides which segment of the fictitious world to display for the recipient. Space spreads in different directions in accordance with the author's will and it is closely connected with time. In other words, time and the course of the plot equip space with direction. Due to Stoppard's intertextual operations the shape and direction of *Hamlet*'s space is transferred to the modern play.

It is this "modelled" and "directed" space that Ros and Guil enter, apparently against their will. As it has already been mentioned, the very first encounter with the play-world provokes a nagging anxiety that will not be relieved till the end of the play. They make an attempt to foster a sense of harmony by harking back to past days when they used to remember their names and were able to introduce themselves when asked. In contrast, today, not only does the queen mistake them, but they themselves have problems with asserting their own identity. Guil begins to question the validity of everything they can remember and ponders that the man who banged on their shutters might have been just a mere coat and hat on the stick. The only thing that is certain is that they came and that the beginning of their journey is marked by birth and the end by death. Ros insists on coming back home, but to be able to do so he would have to succeed in locating his position. His attempts end in failure because he applies to the space the direction dependant on his point of view, unaware that the play-space has already been given direction by somebody else. As early as the first encounter with the play-world, Guil tries to define the nature of the situation they found themselves in:

> GUIL: We've been caught up. Your smallest action sets off another somewhere else, and is set off by it. Keep an eye open, an ear cocked. Tread wearily, follow instructions. We'll be all right.
> ROS: For how long?
> GUIL: Till events have played themselves out. There's a logic at work— it's all done for you, don't worry. Enjoy it. Relax. To be taken by hand and led, like being a child again, even without the innocence, a child—It's like being given a prize, an extra slice of childhood when you least expect it, as a prize for being good, or compensation for never having had one ... Do I contradict myself? (30)

"We are impressed not by the absurdity of the situation, but by its terrible sense, one senses the chilling presence of *Hamlet* waiting menacingly in the wings"—says Gruber and the very presence casts a sinister shadow on Guil's words (1981-1982, 302). The superior level of awareness enables the recipient to note that at times Guil approaches the answer they seek. They did not have childhood because they are literary figures that exist within the frame of the script which in their situation does not provide them with one. Guil feels also that some mechanism has been set in motion and they have to submit to it, but the true extent and nature of the problem apparently goes beyond his comprehension. The discrepancy between their expectations and the course of events known in advance by the recipient, endows Guil's words with a poignant character. Even the title, *Rosencrantz and Guildenstern are Dead,* hangs over their heads like ominous *memento mori* and sneers at their arrogance and naivety.

Therefore in the external communication system this prior knowledge makes it possible to somehow recreate the space and time of the play nearly out of nothing, relying on a few signals which activate the recipient's intertextual competence. Neither stage directions nor elaborate word-scenery is needed to set up the walls and chambers of Elsinore castle. In this respect the recipient has basic familiarity with the world of Stoppard's play. This familiarity generates new meanings because it creates a considerable tension between similar and dissimilar. On the one hand, the recipient recognizes the setting, on the other; however, they must change the angle of vision and apply it to the figural perspective. It is from Ros and Guil's perspective that the world discloses its inscrutability. Whenever the pair wants to impose cohesion upon their world they fail and their condition is marked with a prevailing sense of insecurity and fundamental perplexity. A firm grasp on reality is impossible because, unlike the recipient, they lack the key to unlock the secrets of the world surrounding them. Though the Player instructed them that „uncertainty is the normal state" and that one acts „on assumptions" (48-49), their uncertainty is the outcome of the fact that they made an erroneous assumption. Insisting on finding their bearings in the spatio-temporal continuum, they are unable to transcend the limitations of a dramatic figure. There is yet another reason for the inscrutability of Stoppard's play-world.

Intertextuality weaves a web of correlation between Shakespeare's and Stoppard's plays and draws a parallel between the qualities of the presented worlds. Maynard Mack in his article "The World of *Hamlet*" draws our attention to the fact that it is prevailingly in the interrogative mood and that it resounds with questions, expressing anxiety, fear and contemplation (1952, 502-23). These questions are provoked by mysteriousness and inscrutability of Hamlet's world, established as early as the first line of the play with its question "Who's there?" shouted into the darkness of the night. The world is a riddle and the obscure language of the main figure, overflowing with puns, and his strange behaviour constitute a riddle for many a resident of the court, including Rosencrantz and Guildenstern. "This is the problematic nature of reality and the relation of reality to appearance"—writes Mack—that is another chief attribute of Hamlet's world (1952, 247). To resolve a conflict between appearances and reality, to see what is beyond the masks put on by people to hide their true intentions—is the central problem of the play. The problem is written deep into the language of the play which has in abundance a few central expressions like: seems, put on shape and act. Is Ophelia, kneeling with her prayer book, what she seems: an embodiment of purity and innocence? Has the devil assumed the shape of the ghost? What is beneath the mask of an antic disposition Hamlet acts in front of all? The play parries all the probing questions, partly due to the fact that things are not what they seem because almost everybody is a player.

Familiar as the world of *Rosencrantz and Guildenstern are Dead* might seem to the recipient due to their textual background, its salient features become transferred from the pre-text by the same means. Therefore here appearances and reality also clutch tightly with each other. Moreover, the world of *Hamlet* is the world where mistakes can be fatal, where poison is poured into the ears of the sleeping ones, glasses of wine, or applied to the blades of swords, where you can be stabbed while praying or even hiding behind a curtain. In this world young innocent women lose their mind and drown and the bodies of the dead are dragged along the floor. Therefore when Ros and Guil look around full of anxiety, the recipient knows their fear is justified.

The effect exerted on Ros and Guil by the space they were thrown into resembles the situation of Birdboot and Moon—two theatre critics from *The Real Inspector Hound*. As the courtiers, they are drawn into space that has already been modeled by another text of art. And again once the wheels are set in motion they move around the space towards a direction common to them all: violent death. From the outset of the play two distinct planes are established. It is the audience, occupied by among others Birdboot and Moon, and the acting area, which is constructed upon the parodied forms of the whodunit best represented by Agatha Christie's *The Mousetrap*. The inner play is in itself a travesty of many devices utilized by detective stories and by Christie's play in particular. The division between the two continuums is underlined repeatedly by boundary markers of different kinds. The result of these diversification practices is the creation of the opposition between the fictionality of the inner play and the "reality" of the outer plane. In the course of the play, however, there emerge striking parallels between the conversations of the critics and the action of the whodunit by means of which both planes get closely interwoven. On top of that, the figures of both levels of theatricality begin to intermingle, the inner play absorbs the figures of the outer plane whereas the figures of the whodunit are thrown out of the margin separating so far the two levels and replace the positions occupied by the two critics. The process of the fusion is further reinforced by cyclicity which duplicates roughly everything that took place earlier. The action of the inner play is repeated with two figures of the outer plane being new members of the cast and it is commented on, this time, by two figures of the inner play. By means of the circularity of design both planes blend together and form a new construct in which the conflict between what is signalled to be real and fictional becomes hardly soluble.

Birdboot and Moon make desperate efforts to escape the inscrutable and unlimited power of the script. Their situation seems to be easier in comparison with the predicament of Ros and Guil because the courtiers had just a premonition of the existence of the mechanism they are thrust against, but Birdboot and Moon know perfectly well the way it works. Not only do they, as theatre critics, know the rules that operate in the world of crime stories, but what is more, they have seen the development of action with their own eyes, sitting in the auditorium. Although they are granted with this knowledge they cannot resist the influence of the script. Moreover, the continuum which imprisoned them inside is that of a crime story, with enveloping fog, marshes, and a stalking madman, therefore the outcome of this bizarre situation cannot be optimistic.

Due to the construction of space the perceptual equanimity of the recipient is shaken, which in turn induces a frantic search for meaning. To heighten the effect in many of his plays Stoppard recalls a genre whose nucleus is an enigma—a detective story. Since the genre is highly conventionalised and widely popular, its stock elements such as a dead body, a detective, or deadly marshes function similarly to the snippets from *Hamlet*. They transfer a world model inherent in detective fiction or in a representative work, like for example Agatha Christie's *The Mousetrap* to Stoppard's plays. It is a world model where both time and space reveal all their secrets under a scrutinizing eye of a detective. In this world a splinter of wood or a chip of chine found on the scene of murder fit perfectly all other elements and make a coherent and integrated whole, which, in turn, gives access to the past.

As in *Rosencrantz and Guildenstern are Dead*, however, a change in the angle of vision is needed. Here the world of detective fiction, imbued with rationalism and empiricism, is recalled by a number of devices only to be shattered by means of, for example, a distorting mirror of parody. As a result of Stoppard's stripping away the convention, confusion is in the eye of the beholder and many a time the beholder is a detective. Instead of restoring balance and equanimity lost with the act of murder, which he/she does in the conventional detective story, the detective shrouds both the recipient and the dramatic figures in an even thicker aura of uncertainty. The mainstay of reason and logical order turns into an instigator of chaos and confusion.

The height of Stoppard's parody is achieved in the construction of the time and space continuum of the inner play from *The Real Inspector Hound*. As already mentioned, the inner play derides Agatha Christie's canonical whodunit at almost all its central points. Stoppard imitates humorously, with a hefty dose of exaggeration, Monkswell Manor—a country house, whose tranquillity is disturbed by a howling blizzard and arrival of sergeant Trotter. The policeman comes on skis, alarmed by the appearance of a lunatic in the neighbourhood. Muldoon Manor, where the action of the inner play is set, is cut off from the outside world by swamps, high cliffs and dense fog. A dead body on the floor of the living room and a radio announcement about a madman hiding in the deadly marshes charge the atmosphere with menace and oppression. The host and her guests are as eccentric as the house itself and it quickly transpires that everybody could be the killer. The target of the parody aims also at the detective: Inspector Hound. When the detective arrives at Muldoon Manor on inflated pontoon, each half a meter across, with a foghorn in hand, he does not bring the comfort of a quick solution to the enigma. His arrival aggravates mounting anxiety comparable to the nocturnal visits of the dog from *The Hound of Baskervilles* by Conan Doyle. The allusion to "the other" unquestionable master of the genre is reinforced by the detective's name and by the sound he produces from hooting the foghorn, which resembles "the cry of a gigantic hound" (30). As in the mocked original, the noise frightens the life out of the residents in the house. Therefore owing to the parodic practices, when the treacherous fog rolling off the sea veils this "strangely inaccessible house", nothing is going to disperse it because the world of rationality is replaced by the world of ambiguity.

Another example of the world of reason and logic with its simultaneous juxtaposition with a contrastive model appears in *Jumpers*. The choice to set the action of the play in the dystopian, non-defined future seems to be the author's deliberate strategy. It aims at constructing a purely hypothetical situation illustrating the potential consequences of implementing the principles underlying the detective fiction world model into the political life. Logical positivists, as their factual predecessors, are the admirers of logic, science and empirical verification and they set the tone for the changes taking place in England under their reign. England has become a grim place of utility and rational calculation where all efforts are being made to eradicate the affairs of the heart and soul completely. The Moors' flat is like dystopian England in miniature with all the implications of a new political and ethical order visualised all together in one place.

Yet, simultaneously, throughout the play there appear elements which consistently build a field of associations connected with a diametrically different world model—a world model drifting towards "the irrational, the emotional, the whimsical" (31). In the clearest way this world model is delineated through the discussions of the dramatic figures, in other words, through being a voice in an unresolved debate. On the deeper level, however, the belief in the faculties of the mind which are capable of penetrating the surface reality of sense impressions and gaining the truth beyond the power of reason is conveyed by a set of elements conventionally associated with the *Zeitgeist* of the late eighteenth and early nineteenth century. These are intertextual allusions to Romantic poetry through the names of Keats and Shelley, a stock motif of the silver face of the moon as well as the tunes of highly conventionalised "moon" love songs. These elements evoke a world model which places emphasis on man's emotional capacities and imaginative powers, only to be finally arranged in a set of contrastive pairs with their counterparts from the other model. Therefore the love songs of the past get interwoven in the course of the play when Dotty sings the words of one song to the tune of another. The silver disc of the moon, conventionally associated with a couple of lovers kissing beneath it, is replaced with a satellite picture magnifying its surface and revealing instead deep and ugly pores. Exactly the same transformation occurs to Dotty's body when her silky and translucent skin is examined by a dermatograph and enlarged on the screen.

It needs stressing that many a time it is the arrangement of space with a big television screen as well as props and light that help to emphasize the fundamental principles of the dystopian country, the principles which stand in stark contrast to those of the past. In the here and now of the play, the spiritual crisis is believed to be cured by skin examination and the ideas of fortitude, courage and self-sacrifice negated as non-practical. In the world of *Jumpers*, conditioned by pragmatism and the belief in empirical verification, two bodies enclosed within the walls of one room, appear to be most poignant manifestation of the deficiency of such an attitude. It is the dead body of MacFee, hanging on the door, and the nude body of Dotty, sprawled on her bed and weeping,

The construction of space in the discussed plays questions the postures of rationalism by yet other means. Space does not submit easily to a rational analysis for it resembles an ambiguous combination of erratic parts, a jarring juxtaposition of common objects in an incongruous setting. The opening and closing tableau of *After Magritte* as well the description of a mysterious figure from Ponsoby Place is a representative example of the technique in question. The unusual appearance of the room that is inhabited by figures looking and acting in an odd way creates a need for a rational explanation that would dull a disquieting sense of confusion. As well as that, in the course of *Jumpers* Dotty walks in the gait of a moonwalker with a fishbowl over her head. George opens the door holding a bow and an arrow in one hand and a tortoise in the other, with shaving foam covering his face. The police inspector sits in the bedroom of a suspect wearing a frock, a headdress, and black-face, and beating a waste bin as a bongo drum.

The mysteries lurking in the unexpected juxtaposition of everyday objects resemble the works of Rene Magritte conceived of as visual riddles. In *After Magritte* the arrangement of the dramatic figures, the layout of the stage and typical Magrittean props like a tuba and a bowler hat, are reminiscent of specific paintings as well as the point of view of the artist preserved in the memory of the recipient. Owing to the limitations of the figures' perspective, the effect is achieved solely in the external communication system. Therefore the intertextual modelling of space heightens the sense of incongruity of the presented reality because the name Magritte brings into the play his epistemological convictions. The painter rejected the hegemony of reason and received opinions for he believed man is responsible for the conceptualisation of their world. Keir Elam notices that Magritte brings also to the play his semiotic interest in the arbitrary nature of signs. The conflicting interpretations of the mysterious figure from Ponsoby Place trigger off an interpretational chain which resembles interaction between objects, images and linguistic signs depicted by Magritte in his paintings (Elam 1984, 473-475).

Another technique by means of which Stoppard challenges a world model of detective fiction is the denial of its communally authorized version of truth by the inclusion of a complex network embracing a multiplicity of points of view and contradictory relations. The structure of space dismisses the claim of objectivity that the surrounding world is totally transparent to a perceiving eye; it rather bewilders the figures and reveals the differences in their perceptual worlds. A strong strain of subjectivity, elements of chance or coincidence, as well as patterns employed to perceive the world bring the figures into conflicts which, in turn, emphasise the uncertain state of things around them. Consequently, the eyewitness testimony decreases in value for the police investigation.

The bizarre appearance of the stage appears to be a stimulus that sets in motion the figures' "fervid and treacherous imagination", which conjures up the whole robbery story at the sight of a few coins lying on the pavement or turns a woman in a black bathing cap into a Pakistani with an amputated leg.

The differences in interpretation arise also from the fact that the arrangement of space and the configuration of dramatic figures are open to multiple, often plausible, but still conflicting, interpretations. Space may create the setting both for the love scene and medical examination (*Jumpers*), for dance-competition preparation or surgical operation (*After Magritte*). The visual and aural riddles the figures get caught in constantly prove how difficult it is to account for what we have seen or heard. Many times it is just through the language, through verbal misunderstandings the figures get entangled in, through copious puns and verbal games that Stoppard displays a possibility of competing interpretations and conflicting opinions. Therefore the language of his plays, the language dense with puns, verbal trickery and veiled allusions, sparkling with wit and adding touches of humour to the most serious dilemmas under discussion, has become the hallmark of Stoppard's dramatic accomplishments. In a truly Derridean spirit, Stoppard's predilection for puns and word play demonstrates the instability of language and its creative potential. Verbal riddles inscribed in the tissue of his plays give rise to considerable misunderstandings which, in turn, emphasise emphatically the postmodern notion of "difference" that intrudes into communication and prevents the completeness of meaning.

On the thematic level, the shift towards indeterminacy occurs when Stoppard imbues his plays with a polyphonic quality by sparking off heated debates be it on the problem of the existence of God or the status of art. The proverbial grain of truth which can be found in any opinion or interpretation, the open perspective structure and the open ending device precludes repeatedly the possibility of hierarchical sequence. This technique is masterly used in *Jumpers* where the search for the murderer and the search for the absolute truth run on interconnected levels and share one major point of convergence: lack of solution. The recipient witnesses a parade of suspects and a parade of different points of view but no ultimate resolution is endorsed and conflicting opinions are allowed to coexist freely in the play. The sense of an ongoing philosophical debate is enriched by the shape of the on-stage area for it is divided into three parts: George's studio, Dotty's bedroom—occupied by Archie, and the hall separating the two—along which Inspector Bones enters and leaves the flat. Jim Hunter argues every participant of the debate is predominant over his own territory where they gain most applause and attention. Whenever, however, they change the area they occupy, their power of articulation grows weaker. For example, when in the hall George tries to explain to Bones some of the assumptions of contemporary philosophy Bones takes him for a magician not a logician. On the other hand, Bones bosses around in the hall and it is there that Archie fails to corrupt him. But it is in Dotty's bedroom, the realm of Archie, where he is caught and eliminated out of the play (Hunter 1982, 48-49). And again the layout of the stage area sharpens the sense of an unresolved debate for there are three distinct voices and three areas, but there is no strong voice dominating the whole stage.

To sum up, in many cases it is a strong strain of subjectivity and high valorisation of individuality that is a contributory factor to the creation of space in Stoppard's selected plays. The idea that the reality appears to be the function of human perception, which in turn is determined by a range of relevant factors as for example our assumptions, fertile imagination or faulty memory, is incessantly stressed in the plays under discussion. Therefore, by means of numerous devices, the efforts of the old Newtonian paradigm to enclose the world in an all-inclusive system of thought are toppled and the air of ambiguity and confusion becomes the conspicuous feature of Stoppard's constructions. Instead of achieving one, authorially accepted version, the recipient of Stoppard's plays observes frequently a process of diffraction of meaning, stimulated by the dramatic figures who venture their subjective opinions. As a result, we can see the familiar castle of Elsinore from a completely new angle, an alligator handbag acquires a chameleonic quality, changing from a football to a tortoise, and instead of a voice of a detective declaring at the end of the play the truth, we are confronted with a plurality of voices, each insisting on their subjective interpretation. In the never ending process of semiotization, Stoppard's dramatic figures are always presented as co-producers of meaning. This function is not only limited to the assessment of what they see and hear. It also concerns their actual creation of their personal memories, of the historical past, of the content of the translated texts as it is most neatly illustrated through the structures of space of his later plays like *Arcadia* and *The Invention of Love*. Hardly ever is it possible to trace down elements whose objective, absolute value is indisputable. Instead, the categories of time and space are shown as filtered through subjective, distorting minds of Stoppard's dramatic figures.

In the plays parodying detective fiction, the fruitlessness of man's efforts to reconstruct the past is conveyed by the construction of the dramatic space. It is connected with the fact that contrary to the time of a detective story, time in the plays under discussion does not drive its figures towards progress and solution of an enigma. It makes a circle trapping its figures in the impossibility to tell the truth and appearances, the truth and fiction, apart. The opening and final tableaux of the plays bear striking similarities: it may as well be a pyramid of gymnasts or a family assembly engaged in most bizarre activities. In *After* Magritte, for example an old woman is lying on the ironing board in a black bathing cap with a bowler hat on her stomach and when the play finishes the very same woman is playing on the tuba standing on a chair which is on the table, with her one hand in a woollen sock. The circularity of design emphasises man's predicament which is the difficulty in interpreting the surrounding reality. Therefore the positivist claim of the possibility of moving backwards in time and reconstruct the past with the help of the powers of reason and observation is also dismissed.

To sum up, the stories told by Stoppard have repeatedly epistemological emphasis. His dramatic figures are constantly confronted with questions concerning their capabilities of comprehending the world as well as the possibility of objective knowledge of the past. Stoppard has great dexterity for constructing space which continues to baffle these who attempt to interpret it. The examples cited above prove that many of the techniques Stoppard uses in the construction of his dramatic space stems from his scepticism of the explanations which claim to be valid for everybody. Instead, the foundation for his constructs is the fallible and relative experience of an individual rather than the optimism of objective verification. In the ongoing process of semiotization even the known and familiar acquire a new individual stamp. Elsinore is a place where Hamlet, a lunatic, talks nonsense in the distance and preparations for a dance competition seen by Constable Holmes in *After Magritte* look as an illegal amputation of the Pakistani. Therefore when Stuart Sim claims that "the emphasis on difference (…) is very much characteristic of the postmodern philosophical ethos" (2001, 5), it is possible to discern this paradigm in Stoppard's works. In his plays space is intertextually modelled, divided into distinct ontological realms which are finally fused to capture the shifting and transformational nature of reality and to stress the differences in our conceptual schemes. Spatial parameters of the plays reject the pursuit of objective and authoritarian perspective of detective fiction in favour of an individual, subjective one.

Soon the realisation of the difficulties arising from the attempts to interpret correctly the meaning of events engulfs every figure in the play. Epistemological uncertainty of the dramatic figures constantly reminds the recipient of the impossibility of knowing anything with absolute certainty. It is therefore legitimate to say that the space the dramatic figures move around in is as puzzling and ambiguous to them as it is to the recipient. In other words, a sense of epistemological vertigo is transferred to the external communication system.

References

Elam, Keir. 1984. After Magritte, After Carroll, After Wittgenstein: What Tom Stoppard's Tortoise Taught Us. *Modern Drama* 27: 469-485.

Gruber, William. 1981. 'Wheels within Wheels, etcetera': Artistic Design in *Rosencrantz and Guildenstern are Dead*. *Comparative Drama* 15: 291-310.

Heuvel, Michael Vanden. 2001. Is postmodernism?: Stoppard among/against the postmodern. In *The Cambridge Companion to Tom Stoppard*, ed. by Katherine E. Kelly, 213-229. Cambridge: Cambridge University Press.

Hunter, Jim. 1982. *Tom Stoppard's Plays*. London: Faber and Faber.

Limon, Jerzy. 2002. *Między niebem a sceną*. Gdańsk: Słowo/Obraz terytoria.

Mack, Maynard. 1952. The World of *Hamlet. The Yale Review* 41: 502-23.

McElroy, Bernard. 1973. *Shakespeare's Mature Tragedies*. Princeton: Princeton University Press.

Sim, Stuart. 2001. Postmodernism and Philosophy. In *The Routlege Companion to Postmodernism*, ed. by Sim Stuart, 3-11. London/New York: Routlege.

Stoppard, Tom. 1967. *Rosencrantz and Guildenstern are Dead*. London: Faber and Faber.

—. 1968. *The Real Inspector Hound*. London: Faber and Faber.

—. 1979. *After Magritte*. London: Faber and Faber.

—. 1986. *Jumpers*. London: Faber and Faber.

CHAPTER THIRTY-ONE

GEOMETRY, QUANTUM MECHANICS AND UNCERTAINTY PRINCIPLE: DRAMATIC AND STAGE SPACE IN TOM STOPPARD'S *HAPGOOD*

JADWIGA UCHMAN

Tom Stoppard's dramatic output is characterized by a number of traits one of which is his intensive use of intertextuality, the idea of which was introduced by Julia Kristeva who, while discussing the passage from one sign system to another, argued:

> To be sure this process comes about through a combination of displacement and condensation, but this does not account for its total operation. It also involves an altering of the thetic *position* and the formation of a new one. The signifying system may be produced with the same signifying material; in language, for example, the passage may be from narrative to text. Or it may be borrowed from different signifying materials: the transposition from a carnival scene to the written text, for instance. . . . The term *intertextuality* denotes this transposition of one (or several) sign-system(s) into another but since this term has often been understood in the banal sense of "study of sources," we prefer the term *transposition* because it specifies that the passage from one signifying system to another demands a new articulation of the thetic—of enunciative and denotative positionality (111).

Intertextuality, then, as the term was understood by Kristeva, is not a simple borrowing but involves taking elements from one sign system and incorporating them, in an altered position, into another. What is worth stressing here is that intertextuality may refer either to two works of the same sign system or to works belonging to different sign systems.

Tom Stoppard employs both kinds of intertextuality, his drama containing references to literature is, most obviously, his theatrical debut—

Rosencrantz and Guildenstern are Dead (William Shakespeare, Samuel Beckett and, possibly, Luigi Pirandello). Most of his plays contain, at least, a phrase taken from Shakespeare's masterpieces and there are also two other pieces owing much to the bard: *The (15 Minute) Dogg's Troupe Hamlet* and *Dogg's Hamlet, Cahoot's Macbeth*. *Travesties* employs Oscar Wilde's *The Importance of Being Earnest* as its frame, *The Real Thing* refers to Henry James' short story under the same title and also includes fragments of August Strindberg's *Miss Julie*, John Ford's *'Tis Pity She's a Whore* while *Invention of Love* is connected with both A. E. Houseman's output and Jerome K. Jerome's *Three Men in a Boat (not to Mention the Dog)*. Literature is by no means the only intertextual reference to be noticed in Stoppard's output. The other signifying systems he uses are: philosophy—*Jumpers* (the Viennese Logical Positivists Circle), *Professional Foul* (the already mentioned Vienna Circle and Ludwig Wittgenstein), the latter being also the basis of *Dogg's Our Pet, The (15 Minute) Dogg's Troupe Hamlet* and *Dogg's Hamlet, Cahoot's Macbeth*); art—*After Magritte* being a reference to the great Belgian's output and beliefs and *Artist Descending a Staircase* making a direct reference to Marcel Duchamp's famous picture as well as history—*Travesties* (in which Joyce, Lenin and Tzara appear), *Squaring the Circle* (presenting Polish history between the summer of 1980 and that of 1982), *Arcadia* introducing the off-stage figure of Byron and finally the trilogy *The Coast of Utopia* presenting a group of Russian revolutionaries and romantics.

Stoppard's intertextual references are not limited to the area of humanities only because he also makes use of scientific achievements and discoveries. Such is the case with *Hapgood*, a spy drama which not only parodies "the double agent plot of Le Carré" (Rusinko 1986, 110) but, also, according to Demastes, "is a spy thriller that operates at several science-informed levels" (1998, 42). The plot of the play concerns discovering which of the members of the British Secret Service is a double agent acting simultaneously for the British and the Russians.

In *Hapgood* Stoppard turns to mathematics and physics in order to provide an explanation for the events presented, the numerous references to physics in the play stressing the importance of relativity. It was Clive James who first noticed the parallels between Stoppardian theatrics and Einstein's physics. He argued that Stoppard's plays reflect the new, post-Newtonian outlook based on the proposition voiced by Einstein who "found himself obliged to rule out the possibility of a viewpoint at rest" (1975, 71). In an interview Stoppard said that he considered James' article to be brilliant and added:

What he said was that you get into trouble if you think that there's a static viewpoint on the events. There is no observer. There is no safe point around which everything takes its proper place, so that you see things flat and see how they relate to each other. Although the Einsteinian versus Copernican image sounds pretentious, I can't think of a better one to explain what he meant—that there is no point of rest. (Hayman 1979, 144)

Making numerous references to the discoveries of modern physics, *Hapgood* demonstrates the changes that have occurred in our conception of reality as a result of the shift from Newtonian mechanics to the formulation of relativity and quantum theory. Classical Newtonian physics postulated a permanent external world, fixed, objective and describable. Scientific laws were always based on strict cause and effect principle and were independent of the perceiver. Modern physics has shown that once it is discovered that a law does not hold in conditions in which it has so far been considered to hold, it is necessary to search for new explanations. This notion was expressed by Richard Feynman in his *Lectures on Physics* from which Stoppard takes the motto for his play and to which he often refers in the course of the drama.

In the lecture "Probability and Uncertainty—the Quantum Mechanical View of Nature," Feynman discusses the experiments concerning the nature of light. He describes an experiment during which electrons are supposed to get through two holes. The observation of their movement is to bring the answer whether they are particles or waves. In order to be able to observe, the behaviour of the electrons the experimenter has to use light which "affects the result. If the light is on you get a different result than when the light is off. You can say that the light affects the behaviour of electrons" (1965, 140). The situation provides no solution—it is impossible to state exactly what is happening: either you turn off the light and are unable to watch the electrons because you do not see what is happening, or you turn it on and thus affect their behaviour. Feynman has written:

A philosopher once said "It is necessary for the very existence of the science that the same conditions always produce the same result." Well, they do not. You set up the circumstances, with the same conditions every time, and you cannot predict behind which hole you will see the electron. Yet science goes on in spite of this—although the same conditions do not always produce the same results. That makes us unhappy, that we cannot predict exactly what will happen. (1965, 144)

Feynman's experiment is referred to by Kerner who calls it "a trick of light" (10). In discussing it he does not pay much attention, though, to the changed circumstances (the light being turned on or off) but he concentrates on the perceiver: "Every time we don't look we get wave pattern. Every time we look to see how we get wave pattern, we get particle pattern. The act of observing determines the reality." Furthermore, as Kerner continues, "nobody knows" how this is possible. "Einstein didn't know. I don't know. There is no explanation in classical physics. Somehow light is particle and wave. The experimenter makes the choice" (12). At another point in the play, Kerner makes a reference to Heisenberg's uncertainty principle and compares the particle world to "the dream world of intelligence officer":

> An electron can be here and there at the same moment. You can choose; it can go from here to there without going in between, it can pass through two doors at the same time, or from one door to another by a path which is there for all to see until someone looks, and then the act of looking has made it take a different path. Its movements cannot be anticipated because it has no reasons. It defeats surveillance because when you look what it's doing you can't be certain where it is, and when you know where it is you can't be certain what it's doing; Heisenberg's uncertainty principle; and this is not because you're not looking carefully enough, it's because there is *no such thing* as an electron with a definite position and a definite momentum; you fix one, you lose the other, and it's all done without tricks, it's the real world, it is awake. (48)

In this passage Kerner concentrates not on the perceiver but on the very nature of electrons which seems to escape a clear definition. Werner Karl Heisenberg mentioned by Kerner, an atomic physicist, a specialist in quantum mechanics, has formulated the uncertainty principle which "concerns attempts to measure the position and motion of a quantum object simultaneously. . . . The very act of trying to pin down an electron to a specific place introduces an uncontrollable and indeterminate disturbance to its motion and vice versa" (Jenkins 1990, 174). Feynman paraphrases this uncertainty principle in order to be able to use it while describing his own experiment; "It is impossible to design any apparatus whatsoever to determine through which hole the electron passes that will not at the same time disturb the electron enough to destroy the interference pattern" (143).

The specific behaviour of electrons described by quantum mechanics scientists becomes for Stoppard a skilfully used metaphor to describe what is happening in the world of espionage. The dual nature of the agents, further underlined by the fact that quite often they are literally doubled, appearing in couples as twins, is evocative of the structure of light as both a wave and a particle. This metaphor of the world of the spies being reminiscent of the world of quantum mechanics is enriched by the introduction of the "quantum jump." The probability function, introduced into physics by Feynman, among others, indicates a tendency of the possible course of events as well as our limited ability to know it. The so-called "quantum jump" is an expression of the transition between the "possible" and the "actual." According to atomic physicists the probability function is a mid-stage between the idea of an event (our perception and interpretation) and the actual event. This point is again expressed by Kerner:

> I cannot stand the pictures of atoms they put in the schoolbooks, like little solar system: Bohr's atom. Forget it. You can't make a picture of what Bohr proposed, an electron does not go round like a planet, it is like a moth which was there a moment ago, it gains or loses energy and it jumps, and at the moment of the quantum jump it is like two moths, one to be here and one to stop being there; an electron is like twins, each one unique, a unique twin. (49)

Stoppard uses the notion of the "quantum jump" three times in the course of the play to make it work in visual terms. On the first occasion, it functions as a visual bridge between the first two scenes. Scene One ends with Blair making arrangements to meet Kerner and Ridley at twelve in the zoo. As it ends, "*he puts the radio away and looks at his wrist-watch. The next time he moves, it is twelve o'clock and he is at the zoo*" (9). Later on, a similar "quantum jump" of Blair provides a link between scene 3 and 4 (24). On still another occasion, in the inter-scene, as Stoppard calls it, it is Ridley who makes something like "*a quantum jump.*" The stage directions indicate that the Ridley we see in the inter-scene is "*somebody else*" than the Ridley presented in the preceding one (69). What the audience are watching is Ridley's literal twin materializing out of nowhere. The use of the "quantum jump" in reference to Blair and Ridley is different. In the case of Ridley, it is meant to bring out in visual terms the notion that Ridley is something other than he claims to be, that there are, in fact, two Ridleys, twins taking part in espionage. He is (they are) a double agent in both senses of the word—he is spying both for the British and the Russians and there are two of them. In the case of Blair, the "quantum jump" has another meaning. When the audience see Blair as he appears in the consecutive scenes, they may realize that he has varied faces to show in different situations. In Scene One, appearing at the bath, coming out of the darkness, he does not react to Wates' drawn revolver, remains professional, cool and in control. At several moments in the play, however, especially in some scenes with Hapgood, he appears to care for his people, to be a loving, tender father figure to them. Yet Kerner comments on the other Blair when he says that what counts for him is the "technical" aspect of espionage, not the "personal" one, the espionage at large and not the individual people involved. Kerner clarifies this point when he tells Blair that he would betray Hapgood if he thought it necessary (73). The above discussion of "quantum jumps" concerned the change of the stage space, that is the concrete space where the actual action of drama takes place, the theatre stage (Pavis 1998, 402)—the audience actually witness a change of the place in which the action of the consecutive scenes takes place. The "quantum jumps" are also referred to only in verbal (and not in visual) terms and thus another kind of space is involved—dramatic space which is mentioned in the playtext only and cannot be perceived visually by the audience (Pavis 1998, 400).

At one point in the play, while talking to Ridley, Hapgood argues: "You can't be in two places at once" (61). At the beginning of the drama, while commenting on the scene in the changing room, speaking about the two Russians taking part in the switch, Hapgood said: "The meet this morning went exactly as the Russians planned it, including the arrests. The twins weren't necessary, there must be another reason for them. They were meant to be seen, they were a success—'Now he's here, now he's there, oh my God there's two of them'—Wates nearly cut himself shaving he was so fascinated. He's done a diagram, on pink paper, showing who was where when, all the coming and going" (17). The attempts to solve the mystery of what was happening in front of their (and the audience's) eyes, so within the stage space, did not bring any result. It was provided by Wates' diagram and by Kerner arguing that an electron "is like a moth which was there a moment ago, it gains and loses quantum of energy and it jumps, and at the moment of quantum jump it is like two moths, one to be here and one to stop being there; an electron is like twins, each one unique, a unique twin" (49). Thus the dual nature of electrons as propagated by quantum mechanics becomes an apt metaphor for describing the world of espionage and the people working in the secret service who are not only double agents but also, being twins, sometimes appear in pairs.

The notion of duality or doubling, of such a great importance for the play, is also brought about by means of stage space as most of the scenes are doubled: there are two pool scenes, two zoo scenes, two rugby scenes, two "group meeting" scenes in the office, two "personal" scenes showing Ridley and Hapgood. John Fleming who has noticed this structural characteristics of the drama as far as the use of the stage space is concerned, concludes: "Overall, this doubling structure helps reinforce Stoppard's thematic concern" (181).

Hapgood starts with a bizarre stage image, so that what Stoppard once said about *Jumpers* and *Travesties*, "You start with a prologue which is slightly strange" (Hayman 1979, 12), is also relevant to this play. The opening of the drama takes place in two different kinds of space—the dramatic and the stage space. In the stage space we see a *"part of the men's changing room of an old fashioned municipal swimming baths"* (1). The only person visible on the stage is Wates, a CIA officer who has come from Washington to help the British detect the traitor within their ranks. What happens next is an entrance of a number of men, dressed more or less fully, all of them carrying one thing or another, who go into one of the cubicles and then leave it. When Hapgood, who runs the action, enters the stage, it is discovered that despite all their efforts, the traitor has not been specified as the switch of the suitcases has not been noticed by Wates. It is the first time we actually see Hapgood but earlier, when she was off-stage, her existence was discernible to us thanks to a specific treatment of the dramatic space. While successive men enter and leave the cubicles, the fictitious, dramatic space is evoked by means of a shortwave radio conversation conducted by Hapgood and one of her men:

> RADIO: OK, we have a blue Peugeot. . . stopping.
> Single male.
> It's not Georgi.
> Anybody know him? Carrying a towel, no briefcase, repeat negative on briefcase.
> Are you getting this, Mother?—we have the Peugeot but it's not Georgi.
> He's crossing the road. Fancy tracksuit, running shoes. No sign of the follower.
> Are you getting this?—target is approaching, negative on follower . . .(1)

What we get in the playtext is a way of prompting the reader to imagine the extended space—apart from the actual, visible stage space (the changing room), the off-stage, evoked by the sound of the radio transmission is also imaginatively created in the minds of the audience and thus dramatic space becomes nearly equal in importance to the stage space.

In the original London production the play opened with a red dot moving about the map of London projected onto panels which filled the stage (Billington 1988). The winking red light moving along the streets thus represented a car under surveillance. Hapgood, talking to someone on a short-wave radio provided a verbal commentary to this visual image. By the time the first person comes through the doors of the changing room of the swimming baths which form the set of this scene, the audience know that agents have been following someone all over London. Thus, then, the stage space presents simultaneously two different areas—the changing room (the actual theatre stage) and the streets of London (the panels).

In his stage directions Stoppard writes: "*In the first production, all the foregoing action was done to music and lightly choreographed*" (4). The audience watching this "ballet" become aware that it is impossible to make sense of what is actually happening. Hersh Zeifman has written: "The confusion of this opening scene is deliberate; there is no way an audience can possibly follow all those comings and goings, and Stoppard knows that. We are thus immediately made to experience, structurally, what the play's characters are suffering from thematically: an inability to figure out what's going on, to determine precisely who is the traitor in their midst" (1990, 182). The opening stage image, just as the whole play, brings about confusion and the impossibility of distinguishing what is real and what is a mere illusion. Stoppard has commented on this aspect of the drama:

> The play has been written about as though it were incomprehensibly baffling. It does not seem to me to be borne out by experience. After all these years one thing you learn is what's going on in an audience and by God you know when you're losing them. It's like getting a temperature, you can't miss it. My impression is that an ordinary punter has less trouble with it than some critics. (Billington 1988, 28)

It is undoubtedly true that, while finding it difficult to understand what is actually happening, "the ordinary punter" will find this spy thriller thrilling. On the other hand, the fact that some uncertainty concerning the question of what is taking place remains, adds to the overall impact of the play which is about uncertainty as such, about the difficulty of defining reality and about the prevailing relativity.

The scene at the pool opening the play foreshadows the main thematic and structural interests of the play. Christopher Innes argues that "the whole play is structured on game-playing, using the Kiplingesque image of spying as 'the Great Game,' but taking the metaphor literally" (1996, 316). In his article he discusses the numerous game strategies employed in the drama and argues that the very initial stage picture in the original production was evocative of "a recently issued cops-and-robbers board game called *Scotland Yard*." It may be said that one of the games introduced in the course of the play is the game of interpretation played both by the characters and the audience. One can wonder whether the theatre audience watching the production are aware of the fact that the very first scene presents two pairs of twins—there are two Russians and two Ridleys taking part in it. Even if the theatre audience do not immediately realise that a special doubling effect is employed, they discover it as the play progresses. If the audience are temporarily misled, however, it means that Stoppard, while employing one of the ambushes and withholding information, has made them interpret the situation differently from what it actually is.

The printed text, however, does not permit any misinterpration, as the stage directions are explicit and quite telling:

> The essence of the situation is that RIDLEY moves around and through, in and out of view, demonstrating that the place as a whole is variously circumnavigable in a way which will later recall, if not replicate, the problem of the bridges in Königsberg. . . . As a matter of interest, the RIDLEY who posts the briefcase is not the same as RIDLEY who entered with it. (2-3)

The case of the bridges of Königsberg is explained verbatim by Kerner, the atomic physicist, who provides numerous scientific explanations of what the characters and audience alike are witnessing. In the Prussian city of Königsberg there were seven bridges and "an ancient amusement of the people of Königsberg was to try to cross all the seven bridges without crossing any of them twice." It was the Swiss mathematician, Leonhard Euler (1707-1783) who "took up the problem of the seven bridges and . . . presented his solution to the St Petersburg Academy of Science in the form of a general principle based on vertices." The conclusion the mathematician came to was that it cannot be done, two walkers are needed (45-46). The knowledge of mathematics and Euler's solution enables Kerner to solve the mystery of the dressing room case. In opposition to quantum mechanics which stresses the relative quality of reality and promotes the uncertainty principle, Euler's explanation supplies a scientific explanation which sheds light on reality and explains it. Looking at the situational diagram of the scene at the swimming pool, which Wates has drawn, Kerner comes to the conclusion there must be two Ridleys and thus scientifically supports the earlier suspicions of both Wates and Hapgood.

The situation in which two different areas are evoked is not to be noticed in the opening stage image only. There are several instances in the drama when an onstage character is talking on the radio to an off-stage one and thus from the ensuing conversation we learn what is happening there and are able to visualise the dramatic space which is described in a verbal way. In the first case, it is a continuation of the dialogue between Hapgood and the person who is following the Peugeot (6-7). The next radio conversation is conducted by Blair and indicates that Hapgood (being at that time suspected of treason) is followed by secret agents (31). The participants of the next two dialogues are Ridley and Hapgood and they occur while Hapgood in the double role of herself and her pot-smoking, disorderly, absent minded, bohemian sister—Celia. In both scenes, Ridley and Celia are in a photographer's studio which is supposed to be the living space of Celia. On the first occasion, noticing that Ridley is reaching out to take his radio in order to, most probably, get in touch with Hapgood, Celia quickly leaves the room to talk to him from the kitchen as Hapgood. In this scene, the stage space (the room) is strictly connected with the role of Celia played by Hapgood. While off-stage, in the kitchen, or to put it differently, in the invisible dramatic space, she can again become her real self—the leader of the secret service agents (66). On the second occasion, the stage space presents Hapgood in her role of Celia, sleeping, while Ridley is in vain trying to get in touch with Hapgood. In all the previous scenes which introduced the radio conversations, we had to do with the professional activities of the agents communicating by means of it while carrying out their tasks. In this case, however, the situation is altered, as the sleeping Hapgood/Celia is no longer the professional Hapgood or, in other words, we get a glimpse of her "personal," private self. As can easily be noticed, the specific treatment of space is another way of Stoppard's presenting the duality inherent in quantum mechanics whose premises constitute the metaphoric backbone of *Hapgood*.

It seems noteworthy to mention that space has also an important, even though different, function in Stoppard's *Arcadia*, another drama of his which is characterised by strong intertextual scientific links, the theory employed in this case being that of chaos. In this play, the playwright skilfully presents the off-stage events and reality (especially the garden and the changes it undergoes) by means of incorporating their descriptions into the dramatic text (that is by means of evoking dramatic space). At the same time the stage space is treated by him in a really astonishing way. The drama takes place in a house in Derbyshire and presents two distant in time moments of lives of its inhabitants—the times of Lord Byron (who remains an off-stage yet important character) and the present. At the beginning, the successive scenes are set either in the past or in the present, gradually the two different phases of time start merging. The end of the play, presenting characters belonging to the two periods participating in the same dance, uses stage space as an apt metaphor indicating that even though some things change in the course of time, others remain forever the same.

References

Billington, Michael. 1988. Stoppard's Secret Agent. *Guardian* (18 March): 28.

Demastes, William W. 1998. *Theatre of Chaos. Beyond Absurdism, into Orderly Disorder.* Cambridge: Cambridge University Press.

Innes, Christopher. 1996. *Modern British Drama: 1890-1990.* Cambridge: Cambridge University Press.

James, Clive. 1975. Count Zero Splits the Infinite. *Encounter* 45.5: 68-76.

Feynman, Richard. 1965. *The Character of Physical Law.* London: Cox & Wyman Ltd.

Fleming, John. 2001. *Stoppard's Theatre. Finding Order amid Chaos.* Austin: University of Texas Press.

Hayman, Ronald. 1979. *Tom Stoppard.* London: Heinemann.

Jenkins, Anthony. 1990. Moles and Molecules: Tom Stoppard's *Hapgood.* In *Critical Essays on Tom Stoppard*, ed. by Anthony Jenkins, 164-174. Boston: G. K. Hall & Co.

Kristeva, Julia. 1980. *Desire in Language. A Semiotic Approach to Literature,* ed. by Leon S. Roudiez, trans. by Thomas Gora, Allice Jardine and Leon S. Roudiez. Oxford: Basil Blackwell.

Pavis, Patrice. 1998. *Słownik terminów literackich*, trans. Sławomir Świontek. Wrocław/Warszawa/Kraków: Zakład Narodowy Imienia Ossolińskich.

Rusinko, Susan. 1986. *Tom Stoppard.* Boston: Twayne Publishers.

Stoppard, Tom. 1988. *Hapgood.* London: Faber and Faber.

Zeifman, Hersh. 1990. A Trick of the Light: Tom Stoppard's *Hapgood* and Postabsurdist Theater. In *Around the Absurd. Essays on Modern and Postmodern Drama*, ed. by Enoch Brater and Ruby Cohn, 175-201. Ann Arbor: The University of Michigan Press.

PART V:

POST-COLONIAL AND CULTURAL APPROACHES TO SPACE

CHAPTER THIRTY-TWO

PROPERTY, PLACE AND MOOD IN THREE CLASSIC BRITISH CRIME FILMS

ANTHONY BARKER

When the dramatist David Hare wished to expose white-collar profiteering in early 70s Britain, he used the form of a Chandleresque detective enquiry. The protagonist of his play *Knuckle* (1974) is therefore a hardboiled arms-trader returning home to investigate the mysterious disappearance of his sister. At the heart of the story is a property speculation fraud in Guildford perpetrated by their merchant banker father. Informed by the notion that it is worse to own a bank than to rob a bank, Hare's play offers an attack on the quiet corruption of the City of London. This is Curly the gun-runner on his return home:

> I was ready for England. I was attracted by news of the property racket. Slapping people on top of people like layers of lasagne... When I got back I found this country was a jampot for swindlers and cons and racketeers. Not just property. Boarding houses and bordellos and nightclubs and crooked charter flights, private clinics, horsehair wigs and tin-can motor cars, venereal cafes with ice-cream made from whale blubber and sausages full of sawdust... Money can be harvested like rotten fruit. People are aching to be fleeced. But those of us that do it must learn the quality of self-control. (Hare 1974, 27)

Whereupon his companion shouts to the audience in distinctive anglo-Brecht: "Return John Bloom to your kingdom. Jack Cotton, arise from your grave. Harry Hyams, claim your children" (Hare 1974, 27). This invocation of specific speculators and fraudsters reminds us that Britain awoke at the end of the 1960s to the fact of endemic corruption in public life. A particular conjunction of events raised the volume on a topic which had traditionally been hushed up, that is, the presence of crime and corruption in public places. The Profumo affair of 1963 was a chaser for a series of scandals which broke at the end of the decade. Architect John

Poulson's bankruptcy in 1971 released into the public domain the extent of his building and property operations based upon bribing public officials. In particular, his association with Conservative Home Secretary Reginald Maudling, Labour's Leader of Newcastle City Council T. Dan Smith (aka Mr Newcastle) and Andrew Cunningham, leader of the General and Municipal Workers Union, resulted in a wave of resignations, prosecutions and prison sentences. Scandal touched comedy in 1974 when former Postmaster-General and Labour Cabinet Minister John Stonehouse, having cooked the books of his business enterprises, faked his own suicide by drowning at sea (just as the sister does in *Knuckle*) to evade detection. In *Knuckle*, Curly forces one of the minor perpetrators of the property fraud to consume a bottle of whiskey at gunpoint. Cognoscenti will recognise this as the homage of high-status drama to the low-status British crime film *Get Carter* (1971), where Michael Caine as Carter forces his enemy to do the same before killing him.

As Chibnall and Murphy argue (1999, introduction), crime cinema has possessed very little cachet in Britain. Britons have never learned to look upon gangsters as emblematic immigrant entrepreneur figures as the 1930s American cycle of gangster films did, and have never been able to glamorise either criminals or violence as Coppola so engagingly does in the *Godfather* films. If there is any native British crime tradition, it is either the Dickensian one of Bill Sikes or that of gentlemanly cracksters like Hornung's Raffles or Leslie Charteris's The Saint. British cinema favoured the comedy heist film because at least until the sixties there was social and industry pressure to position films always on the side of the police. When criminals were the protagonists, they were dubiously competent, as in Michael Caine's earlier film *The Italian Job* (1968). *Get Carter* provided a paradigm shift for the British crime film. Maybe for this reason we see Carter reading Chandler's *Farewell My Lovely* in the film's opening sequence. That he is on the train up to Newcastle, site of Britain biggest urban slum clearance programme and soon to be revealed as the centre of one of Britain's most notorious instances of municipal graft, is also no accident.

We also see at the beginning of the film Carter socialising with his gangland bosses, Sid and Gerald Fletcher, disguised versions of the Kray twins. In 1969, the Kray brothers were sent to prison for 30 years each for assorted crimes, including murder. The press coverage of the Krays' trial established some sort of foundation for belief in organised crime in Britain. Although gangs certainly operated in London, the unsubtle and dozy nature of these groups might just as well have suggested disorganised crime. In any event, high-profile prosecutions of senior Flying Squad officers and subsequent purge of the Metropolitan Police and Special Branch in the early 70s made it clear that the relations between racketeering and law had become too cosy. That there were gangsters, bent coppers and crooked public servants in England was evident from the newspapers. Film culture tracked this perception by shifting from the heist or caper film to the gangland film. (most robberies are 'project' crimes (as explained by Gottfredson and Hirschi 1990, 203-204)—criminals come together for these enterprises and then disperse, rather than holding together in semi-permanent groupings). A trio of excellent British films were released within a year, *Performance, Get Carter* and *Villain*, all attesting to a general awareness of a new type of criminal corruption prevalent in English society.

There are other, less parochial ways, to read this phenomenon. The 60s had led to the relaxation of many of the social and legal norms which had held sway since the 19th century. The exercising of these newly-won freedoms and rights were read by many on the right and by uneasy liberals as a form of social breakdown, with urban race and campus riots in America, political protest over Vietnam in the west, strife in labour relations everywhere and radical revolutionary movements on the rise in various countries. The hard-hitting crime film was often a film about **the ungovernability** of western nations. Works such as *Dirty Harry, The French Connection, Klute, The Conversation* and *Chinatown* posit compromised heroes and heroines because they cannot imagine upstanding ones making any impact. In these films, the criminals are likely to get away, be let loose by the courts or be protected by big business or political interests. In films about criminals, like *Point Blank* (1968) or *The Godfather* films, criminals are as likely as not to be 'normalised' within a society that is unsure of the difference between right and wrong. Seen in this light, the sordid 70s were the return of the repressed of the hedonistic/idealistic 60s's. In any event, 70s villainy saw the emergence of an aesthetic of dirty realism and an exploration of degradation. *Performance* is part art-film[1] which merges swinging London with the underworld and *Villain*, closest to the dangerous incompetence of English gangland in the figure of Richard Burton's Vic Dakin, is a study in disorderly, psychotic criminal behaviour. The crime TV series which dominated the 70s, *The Sweeney*, and which generated

---

[1] Two of the best recent crime films have also been complex art films: Neil Jordan's *Mona Lisa* and Peter Greenaway' *The Cook, The Thief, His Wife and her Lover* use performers like Michael Caine, Bob Hoskins and Helen Mirren, who import their personas from the crime films under review here.

two spin-off theatrical releases, centred on two hard-boiled Flying Squad detectives called Jack Regan and George Carter, who took their names and amoral colouring from the protagonist of *Get Carter*.

The British crime film tries to keep some distance from its American counterpart. Although Hodges's conception of Carter is influenced by Lee Marvin's implacable Walker in *Point Blank*, there still remains something ineluctably English about the context in which he operates. His remains a world where guns look strange, shoot-outs don't seem plausible, killing is personal (with a knife or by drowning or a fall), where criminals are strangely maladroit at violence, unfit or uncharismatic. The assassin at the end of *Get Carter* is an anonymous figure with a high-velocity rifle; other gangsters fail to intimidate him. When one looks at the violence in post-70s British crime films, it seems increasingly influenced by the violence which had indeed taken root to those islands, the violence of the Northern Ireland Troubles, that of snipers and car-bombers and punishment beatings. Indeed, *The Long Good Friday* at the end of the decade makes the contrast between two different styles of violence, one outmoded and the other aggressively contemporaneous, its very subject

In this paper, the focus will be on one feature of the British crime film—its sense of place. I want to argue that British crime films articulate an interesting relationship between the provinces and the metropolis, indeed that their crime plots after the early 1970 are often bound up with visions of painful social transformations. Provincial centres are major sites of interest and value in British cinema. One can regard the British New Wave of 1959-63 as the filmic discovery of the industrial north and the Swinging London movement as the centripetal movement of power and influence back to the capital after 3-4 years of literally slumming it in the midlands and the north. Julie Christie's departure for London at the end of *Billy Liar* (1963) to reappear in Schlesinger's next cosmopolitan film *Darling* (1965) or the Beatles deserting authentic Liverpool for Dick Lester's London are emblematic of this. In *Get Carter*, we see the archetypal Londoner, Michael Caine, on a train going back up north to sort out Newcastle. The novel on which the film is based stopped well short of that, in Mrs Thatcher's North Lincolnshire: Mike Hodge's takes the story all the way up to his own native Tyneside (Davies 2002, 47). For this reason, the unreconstructed back-to-back housing, pubs and betting-shops of Newcastle constitute a return to the New Wave north just at a time when it was being swept away. This is a recurrent theme of the three films under review; they capture major urban renovation sites just before the bulldozers arrive and they factor in social demise into their storylines. But because *Get Carter* was made in 1970 before the T. Dan Smith affair became public knowledge, crime had not yet come to assume its full top-down significance. The two shady Newcastle businessmen whose feud is the occasion of Carter's brother's death are Cyril Kinnear, a gambling and pornography operator who has connections to the metropolitan Fletchers, and Cliff Brumby, a slot-machine and bar and restaurant entrepreneur. The omnipresence of gambling, from the race track to the bingo hall, keeps crime local and small-scale here but we see these men and their minions wining and dining their clients and consorting with architects and local politicians, suggesting their movement into more lucrative and ostensibly more reputable activities. In this respect Carter's arrival on the scene brings noise and visibility to what is supposed to go on unseen. Violence as undesirable publicity getting in the way of making semi-legitimate deals becomes a plot motif as the British gangland drama progresses.

John McKenzie's *The Long Good Friday* (1980) started as a made-for-television movie produced by a midlands company ATV/ITC. Its producers lost faith in the project[2], alarmed by the authentic accents of its actors, its complicated opening sequence and its willingness to represent the IRA, contrary to the British government's position, as a force which it would be difficult to defeat militarily. Two things are significant here from my perspective. The first is the fact that it took barely a decade to go from acknowledging the existence of a British gang culture to finding its days numbered. Films about real British criminals—*McVicar, Buster* and *The Krays*[3]—only began to emerge around this time. The second is the merging of that culture with reputable business practice, especially that of property developing. London's docklands is the *topos* of the film only a matter of weeks before the heavy equipment moved in to create Canary Wharf and the dockland developments so recently foregrounded during the London G20 summit.. Because the film was shelved for over two years nearly all its significant locations had gone, and many of their replacements had already been completed, before the film was seen. It is precisely the redevelopment of the docks using American mafia investment that the protagonist Harold Shand (Bob Hoskins) proposes—and we see the crucial days during which the deal goes sour as a result of some petty criminal dealings on the part of his own gang. Shand is a

---

[2] The film was rescued by a high-profile campaign to salvage Bob Hoskins's performance when it was re-dubbed for American audiences inexplicably in an impenetrable Wolverhampton accent.

[3] There is a tradition in Britain of using pop stars to play gangsters –these leading roles were played by Roger Daltry, Phil Collins and Spandau Ballet's Kemp twins.

character who hovers between tragedy and parody, tragic because his delusions of proud regeneration were shared by many, parodic because he is unaware of his own redundancy in the process. The film has many fine and metaphorically suggestive scenes but perhaps the best is Shand's patriotic speech/sales pitch to his investors as his boat glides under Tower Bridge. The film represents his desperate need to preserve his legitimacy in the face of the mayhem that bursts all around him. But under pressure, he reverts to the thuggery which has been the foundation of his empire. His internationalist rhetoric fits ill with the parochial behaviour of his associates, and quickly degenerates into nationalist abuse. Having formerly praised American entrepreneurial spirit, he turns upon his guests when they decline to become his partners. The "Special Relationship" now dead, Harold then proposed to go in with "the Krauts", who've "still got their bottle". Shand going into Europe is a serio-comic view of the Conservative position throughout the 1980s, wanting in but only if we can lead, wanting a rebate because of unfavourable entry conditions, wanting benefits but no pooling of sovereignty and inclining to blame others for our own limitations.

Few films relate a crime story so closely to a cityscape, indeed to the very bricks and mortar of a city. As well as the pubs, clubs, restaurants, hotels and casinos of London, we also have scenes set in public swimming baths, a local church and an abattoir. Shand's ability to function is abetted by two associates: Chief Inspector Smith who tips him off when the heat is on and City Councillor Harris, who is also a major London builder and who slips him planning information. Operating just on the margins of the law, we see Shand lose his bearings. Thomas Leitch has written that

> Although it could be argued that every crime film is a critique of the society crime disrupts, the gangster film is especially concerned with the social order its gang mimics or parodies. This concern begins with the gangster film's obsession with rules. Some rules are so fundamental that they are virtually universal in gangster films. (Leitch 2002, 103)

Leitch's examples include Vincent and Jules's reflections on the erotic limits of foot massage from *Pulp Fiction* or Vincent's injunction that "you do not fuck with a man's automobile." Here, gang boss Shand, in his moment of triumph, finds himself in a situation where the rules are comprehensively not being followed by all around him. The American Mafia seems unwilling to countenance violence because they are courting legitimacy (to Shand, this looks unforgivably like weakness) and the IRA don't behave like any rival gang he has known. Their refusal to be rounded up and intimidated or bought off causes him perplexity, and ultimately costs him his life. The unity of purpose of these two organisations is contrasted with the fragmentation and venality of his own associates. Shand is both patriotic and entrepreneurial but he is unable to match the political focus of the Irish nationalists or the corporate hard-headedness of the Mafia "suits." In the end, he is driven off to his execution a tragically anachronistic figure. If *Get Carter* can be read as an updated Revenger's Tragedy (Carter is 'got' because he operates outside the rules in the pursuit of personal vengeance), *The Long Good Friday* is more like *Othello*, where an old warrior is practised upon by enemies within and without his own camp.

Aware that both films had already become cult classics, Mike Figgis's *Stormy Monday* (1987) reprises the Newcastle locations of *Get Carter* with the mob-financing of a redevelopment plot elements of *The Long Good Friday*. One *Stormy Monday* scene goes to the exact Tyneside location where Carter had met with his brother's elusive mistress Margaret—there, the contending gang figures arrange a meet. But instead of a partnership that fails to happen, British jazz club-owner Finney is the only hold-out preventing the lucrative redevelopment of Newcastle's quayside wanted by local councillors and American investors. *Stormy Monday* pits local Geordies against American interlopers in an unequal struggle in which improbably the locals prevail. But there are intimations that although the skirmish is won, the war is already lost. Many stylistic features of the film represent Britain as a shabby outpost of the American Empire. For example, Newcastle is in the middle of a themed "American Week", where American razzmatazz takes over the street. On another level altogether, the film casts major US stars Tommy Lee Jones and Melanie Griffith in glamorous roles that throw the British protagonists played by Sting and Sean Bean into relief. Sting's Finney, in particular, seems a provincial figure who resents American strong-arm tactics but who is, as a jazz club owner, frankly in thrall to American culture. In one scene, he is seen in moody retreat from the conflict, improvising jazz bass chord sequences alone in his club. As in *The Long Good Friday*, partnership with Europe might be a viable alternative to US imperialism, and here it is represented by the Krakow Jazz Ensemble which comes to play Finney's club and ends up disrespectfully sabotaging Tommy Lee Jones's deal-clinching ceremonials with an *avant-garde* rendering of "The Star-Spangled Banner". But the car bomb which is meant for Finney's associates carries off the Krakow Jazz Ensemble's 9nnocent leader and the strangely enervated crime plot is allowed to dissipate in moody American-style interiors and jazz atmospherics. Revenge is aborted, the Mob leave town and fictional Newcastle's quayside apparently goes undeveloped. But, as Figgis tells us in his directorial commentary to the DVD, the film's urban landscape was in fact swept away within months of the film's completion, presumably without the proceeds of drug money-laundering. The films therefore have the feel of elegies for lost cityscapes, and in their elegiac form also plead for the passing of ways of life out of which the doomed crime gangs come. In a way, the tawdry American marching band sequences from *Get Carter* and *Stormy Monday* stand for the easy implantation of a brasher alien culture. An American presence in a British film is often token of the film's desire to obtain American finance or distribution, and therefore its hope to do well in America. None of the films mentioned here achieved that aim, although *Get Carter* has the dubious privilege of having been remade in an American version in 1999 with Sylvester Stallone

Two things unite these three films, apart from their crime genre identity. Each is virtually the first film of their directors (a curiosity for films which have become classics) and each makes telling use of jazz themes by British composers. Roy Budd's melancholy refrain from *Carter* and Francis Monkman´s driving theme from *Good Friday* contribute significantly to the films' successes (both were classically trained musicians). Figgis himself wrote the score for his film, having converted from professional musician to film director. His voice-over for the DVD tells us that the highlight of making the film was recording the title song in New York with B.B. King—who had never previously recorded the blues classic "Stormy Monday". So geared to jazz was the film that its original title had been "Around Midnight", another jazz classic, which had to be dropped when another film of the same name[4] was released. Musical atmospherics account for the languorous pace of *Stormy Monday*, but they are no less important in establishing the mood of the two other films here featured. When the British gangster film underwent a renaissance at the end of the 1990s, with the release of Guy Ritchie's *Lock Stock and Two Smoking Barrels* (1998), the dominant musical influences had become those of Britpop. Together with the film's fast and tricksy editing, an MTV aesthetic had clearly taken root in the British gangster film. Violence became comedic, carnavalesque even. Of the recent clutch of British gangster films, only Jonathan Glazer's *Sexy Beast* (2000) and Hodge's *I'll Sleep when I Die* (2003) have avoid the pull towards anglo-Tarantino. The transatlantic connection so desired by

---

[4] Bertrand Tavernier's *'Round Midnight* starring jazzman Dexter Gordon was released in October 1986, Figgis's film in late 1987.

British crime figures has dwindled by *Snatch* (2000) to playing weaker supporting roles to glitzy cameos by American stars like Dennis Farina, Benicio del Toro or Brad Pitt. The britgangster film found its niche in small-time jokey violence. Its sense of place has likewise been confined to an indeterminate, media-familiar London setting and there seems little unease about social change. Shand's observations about the decline of Brixton, for example, have given way to the racially relaxed attitudes of the Ritchie films.

References

Chibnall, Steve and Robert Murphy (eds.). 1999. *British Crime Cinema.* London: Routledge.

Davies, Steven Paul. 2002. *Get Carter and Beyond: The Cinema of Mike Hodges.* London: Batsford.

Figgis, Michael (dir.). 1987. *Stormy Monday.* UK: Majestic Films/British Screen.

Gottfredson, Michael R. and Travis Hirschi. 1990. *A General Theory of Crime.* Stanford: Stanford University Press.

Hare, David. 1974. *Knuckle.* London: Samuel French.

Hodges, Mike (dir.). 1970. *Get Carter.* UK: Metro-Goldwyn-Mayer.

Leitch, Thomas. 2002. *Crime Films.* Cambridge: Cambridge University Press.

Mackenzie, John (dir.). 1980. *The Long Good Friday.* UK: British Lion/Handmade Films.

Chapter Thirty-Three

Spaces of Multiplicity in Kathy Acker's Novel *Pussy, King of the Pirates*

Emilia Borowska

Pussy, King of the Pirates begins with the female character named O planning an escape from her familial house and dreaming of a city that "was always decaying" (3). From O's confining familial room Acker takes this tale into new territories, and within these new territories comes not just another map but another type of cartography. Suddenly, from the stable, rigid oppressive pillars of the Oedipal architecture housing a stable identity in a metric, orderly space, O sets off on a symbolical journey into the irrational, multiple and rhizomatic territories somewhere in China, where all the slums in the unknown cities "looked exactly like each other: each one a labyrinth, a dream, in which streets wound into streets which disappeared in more streets and every street went nowhere. For every sign has disappeared" (7). With no more stability of points and signs but within a web of trajectories, flows and thresholds, Acker unfolds turbulent space of multiplicities and schizos.

1. The cartography of turbulence

This article seeks to map Kathy Acker's quest for multiplicity and chaos in examining her new conceptions of space as multiple, chaotic and fluid in her practice of writing against the conception of normative, orderly and solid Euclidean spatiality in her novel *Pussy, King of the Pirates*. Acker's feminine alignments of order and chaos will be read through the lenses of the poetics of turbulence theorized by Gilles Deleuze and Felix Guattari, Michel Serres and other spatial theorists of poststructuralism. The common objective of this collective of theorists is transcending the traditional boundaries between science and humanities and building the bridge that privileges chaos over order, multiplicity over dualisms, fluid over solid, movement and metamorphosis to stasis and death. In their overall polemics, turbulence, one of the forms taken by chaos in non-linear dynamics, disturbs the binary oppositions running across order/chaos, law/violence, war/peace and life/death. Turbulence, as a conceptual tool, cuts through the dominating static order introducing positive chaos and difference that replaces identity equalled with death and dualism. Serres claims that ultimately "identity is death. ... Turbulence disturbs the chain. It troubles the flow of the identical, just as Venus disturbs Mars" (2000, 109-10). Similarly, Acker's project acts as an intermission of turbulent noise in the familial order, stable forms and unchanging institutions. *Pussy, King of the Pirates* is a loose variation on Stephenson's *Treasure Island*. O and Ange, the novel's main characters, decide to escape their static existence in family homes, brothels, prisons, schools and join the girl pirates on a symbolical journey in search of buried treasure, guided by the map that "had come out of Ange's dead mother's box. Just as Ange come out" (265). Reworking the classic text that is so deeply integrated with the conventional notions of Euclidean space, Acker employs tactics of insurgency and turbulence in order to disturb the laminar flow of Stephenson's linear narrative by bringing about the collapse of rigid boundaries of the masculine, solid text and translating it into "the territory named women's bodies" (9).

2. Euclid's prison-house

The building, the house and the body are the recurring tropes that Acker consistently employs as an index to different spatial models, embracing them by the term of turbulent space. Fluctuating between orderly and chaotic territories, Ackerian architecture operates as a device of deformation, a perpetual movement between the states of solidity and malleability, from laminar masculine flow to feminine turbulence and vortex. Here, the architectural design operates as a filter of chaos which renders the buildings constant and shifting, solid and fluid and as both closed and open systems. When the building/home is rendered closed, solid and homeostatic, it is necessarily associated with the patriarchal order—the father. In a brothel, O recalls St. Barbara's theory of religion, according to which "Every revolution starts in a church or in the place of the church because churches and brothels do not have windows that lead to what lies outside" (31). This suggests that the enclosed, hermetic environment such as a brothel or a church can give rise to the emergence of the new, out of the embedded potential for change and revolution—the clinamen. Serres, drawing on Lucretius, speaks of the clinamen as a deviation or the scandal of declination that "opens the closed system" (2000, 77). In Acker's text there is an ongoing opening of the doors and windows of the closed systems and confronting them with forces from the repressed outside. Acker lets in the taboos of incest and sado-masochism which leaves readers confused by O's simultaneous attraction and hatred towards her father. Through deviation, change, the scandal and the taboo, O sets off on her departure from the orderly familial structure, disrupting the Oedipal chain.

Acker uses the house and the body interchangeably to actualize systems far-from equilibrium and she treats their boundaries as mediators between the static and dynamic, solid and fluid, orderly and turbulent as they become thresholds between the states. Prior to transformations, women's bodily space is represented as a container or a house that can be entered, penetrated or be broken into. According to this model, like Euclid, the man in Acker's text is that who appropriates, measures, immobilizes the boundaries, erects the walls, constructs a grid, organizes and coordinates thereby taming chaotic and deregulated flows. Irigaray insists, as if talking to Euclid: "Everywhere you shut me in. Always you assign a place to me. Even outside the frame that I form with you. ... You mark out boundaries, draw lines, surround, enclose. What is your fear? (Irigaray 1992, 24-25). Serres (1995, 108) specifies the main object of this fear as a fear of multiplicity. Multiplicity is the term which represents what Western metaphysics of Mars has feared: liquid, disorder, nonlinearity, the unpredictable, the turbulent–that which shakes the foundations.

3. Inside the labyrinth

The experience of reading *Pussy, King of the Pirates* corresponds to the feeling of entering a maze, a new ontology. Acker lures her readers into the labyrinth, giving them no choice but to move and become lost with the characters. O, disillusioned after Pussycat abandons her, fails to contact her two last remaining friends by phone because no one is any longer traceable:

> Each time I dialled a number on the black phone, that number led to another number ... all these numbers formed a labyrinth around me, a labyrinth inside the phone receiver, a labyrinth from which O was never going to be able to escape. Truly, I was doomed. (161)

Whether represented as a labyrinth, a fold or a fractal, Acker dooms her readers to become lost in her complex text that defies a summary/solution or a straightforward exit point, with its multi-dimensional and poly-episodic structure, shifts of viewpoint, character's multiple personalities, temporal jumps, non-linear narrative, the usage of various fonts, assemblages of disparate genres, fusion of text and images, puzzle maps and maze-like drawings of dreams.

Being an index to Ackerian's models of space, her vulnerable architecture loses its measure, fixity and structure; it becomes connected as a part of a multiplicity, a rhizome. In the pirate world, the buildings are connected to each other by winding, unpaved paths that are emerging and dynamic, housing unexpected encounters. They are like Möbius strips articulating the incompossibilities: stabilization and destabilization, inside and outside, solid and fluid. In the pirate world, it is possible to "trash the house of childhood," to reverse interior and exterior, to go into a building "whose insides were larger than outsides" or "whose walls were coming down." The architectural object loses its symmetry and stability, pierced through with multiple horizontal and vertical openings and cracks, curves and arches, and is now more about movement than rest, where the orientation shifts from the floor towards the staircase and elevator. The staircase becomes both a time and space machine and "a threshold of the unknown." The novel is abundant with passages portraying laminar space becoming turbulent by means of chance encounters, endless rooms, knotted corridors, twisted paths, houses within houses as if they were Russian dolls, hiding various people in them. The space disappears and mutates as quickly as it emerges. In her maze-like travelling, Antigone accidentally meets Andromeda who breaks into her father's house inside which "[a] room beyond this room, though attached, was in another house," then "she began to see more and more houses. They stood closer together. She could no longer distinguish between dirt and concrete. Between what belonged to the country and what to the city" (183). Throughout their quest for the buried treasure, O and Ange experience randomness, be it the accidental encounters with the punk boys, repulsive pirate girls, poets, criminals, whores or be it the surprise of chaotic space itself, an encounter with the unexpected and unplanned.

4. Pointless cartography

Deleuze and Guattari propose a new way of thinking about mapping as "way finding." Against the traditionally conceived map as a representation, self-closure and a-temporality, they propose a map that "is open and connectable in all of its dimensions" that "is itself a part of a rhizome" (1987, 12). Acker's narrative displays a corresponding configuration of mapping, unsettling the classic Western map in a number of ways. Superficially framing the novel within the departure-arrival binary, Acker lures the reader into the linear structure of Stephenson's *Treasure Island* travel narrative, where the plot is concentrated on the protagonists' move from point A to B with an interlude of adventures and obstacles before they reach the target. The arrival at the destination, finding the treasure and completing the quest seem to be an inevitable situation or a steady-state attractor of fiction, and within travel fiction in particular. Accordingly, the act of reading is a process of way finding, revealing the hidden meaning of the text, arriving at the satisfying interpretation–closure. Meanwhile, Acker's turbulent tactics combat the linear order of such schemata via a cartography of becoming which includes locating her text in non-Euclidean spaces, refusing to give maps representational authority, resisting closure and developing "pointless" cartography of variable boundaries and of "monstrous middles."

In the text Acker shifts the focus from the departure-arrival binary to the multidirectional voyages in-between, protecting the narrative from an entropic death. In this way, the text resists closure and final rest, ending with the chapter that is also a beginning of "Days That Are to Come." Maps in the novel are unreliable, signifying multiple orientations, with the buried treasure being a movable target-attractor. Consequently, the roaming of O and Ange is initially directionless, chaotic and essentially intensive rather than extensive. Their actual, physical movement from one place to another is put into question, as rather than move forwards (horizontally, extensively), they move down the vortex (vertically, intensively):

'We're traveling now.' [...]
'Tell me what you're seeing, O.'
'I don't know. I've got to come out of hiding, Ange. It's very scared down here.' (58)

It is the discovery of new zones of intensity, the relationship between speed and slowness as opposed to totality achieved though physical movement from point A to point B that characterizes their becoming-pirate. In Deleuze and Guattari's words: "Voyage in place [...] Voyage smoothly or in striation, and think the same way" (1987, 482).

Maps in Acker's subversive narrative no longer attempt to picture the universe or represent and provide the right instructions. On the contrary, this cartography seeks to disorientate, distort and confuse by merging several orders of representation. The map Bad Dog uses when trying to find her mother who was shopping, resembles the map of the situationists. Situationist cartographers disrupt the map's sense of coherence and totality and open up its rigid order to the surrounding multiplicity: the surprise of the unexpected and unplanned. Following such an unconventional map, Bad Dog "[c]rossed a street which she hadn't seen on the map, then entered a store which hadn't yet been visible."(192) The main map of the book, that had come out of the female body, is another of Acker's situationist/surrealist remakings of a classic map. As Caren Irr has observed by analysing its geographic silhouette, Acker's Pirate Island "might recall Ireland or Cuba as much as North America. In so far as it is a 'place,' it may be one of those 'PLACES OF TRANSFORMATIONS' indicated on the map, where the mathematical logic of latitude and longitude is transformed by dreaming" (2004, 228). The map contrasts the fractal-like nature of the coastline with the rigid architecture of urban housing; the traditional point and nodes are replaced with arrows, lines and girly handwriting takes over the neat text of the conventional map. Finally, the authority of the map is almost completely lost when O and Ange forget about it and choose to follow the rhizomatic trajectories of the pirate girls. The map as an authority becomes significant by the end of the novel when the two girls want to separate themselves from the pirate band and the masculine order is being restored for the two travellers. It is then that the sole purpose of their voyage becomes a commodity.

5. "Safe on a ship which an ocean surrounded"

For Acker everything is in the state of a dream resembling a Deleuzian virtuality awaiting actualization. Whether it is in a dream, imagination, fiction or reality, architecture remains the filter of chaos. Prior to the move onto the ocean, novel's hydraulics are concentrated around the bathroom and the toilet, which Acker frequently makes accessible only from the outside (129). These sanitary spaces she employs as thresholds and mediators between the closure and control of the pipework (the striated space) and what Deleuze and Guattari would call the smooth space of the sea or the ocean. They claim that the logic of the State aims at constraining movement and suppressing the turbulent flow: "the State needs to subordinate hydraulic force to conduits, embankments, which prevent turbulence, [and] constrain space itself to be striated and measured, which makes the fluid depend on the solid, and flows proceed by parallel, laminar layers." The logic of the nomad science and the war machine, on the other hand, "consists in being distributed by turbulence across a smooth space, in producing a movement that holds space and simultaneously affects all of its points" (Deleuze and Guattari 1987, 363). Against the logics of the State, the flows of liquids in the pirate world defy control, allowing for the interruption of the smooth space especially "[f]rom the toilet," where O can "glimpse the ocean. The ocean's freedom." (123).

Acker would call the fluid an ideal state that brings chaos to the surface, being aware, however, that this primordial multiplicity has now been suppressed and solidified into binary, unitary systems of the State. The pirate assemblage's move onto the ocean is a sign of protest against the control and dominance of the apparatus of capture. Acker practices the turbulent tactics of disruption and subversion by deterritorializing the striated space, reintroducing heterogeneity and movement. The pirate-girls are depicted as paradoxical, simultaneously attractive and repulsive, abject figures: "They wore their insides on their outsides, blood smeared all over the surfaces" (265). This idyllic sisterhood, however, is not as anarchic as it seems, revealing a deep structure of order that emerges out of this chaotic assemblage. They have the king Pussy as their leader, who essentially tames the chaotic nature of the group into an organized hierarchical structure, oscillating between monarchy and anarchy.

As it becomes clear by the end of the novel, the turbulence that follows in the wake of these female pirates is both productive and destructive. The shock of turbulence disturbs the temporary order of "conceptual peace" among the girls making their assemblage more complex, forcing it to bifurcate and unwind. While previously their roaming was directionless and aimless, O and Ange, more separate from the girl-pirates than ever, now see "the pirate girls in their true colours" (265) and find the map to steer their journey away from a rhizomatic plane into a linear route with a specified, commodified aim. The turbulent flow is crystallized into a less chaotic system. Again, order emerges out of chaos. Ironically, O and Ange do not metamorphose into the girl-pirates when given an opportunity. They choose to remain within the order of a masculine, unnatural society of death, symbolized by the skeleton's phallus that pointed at the hidden treasure on the Pirate Island. Order is built on fluid foundations of chaotic multiplicities via violence, death and rivalry. As Acker herself admits, neither demonization of the whorehouse or creation of the girl-pirate world is the perfect response to the phallocratic order. Female piracy is, however, "as utopian as I can get at the moment"—she concludes (Garrett 1983, 17-18). There is a feeling of dissatisfaction when the Serresian "third term" is excluded as the process of organization and stabilization steps in. Serres (1982a, 1982b) uses the figure of Hermes or the parasite as the Third Man that negotiates the space between order and disorder, the outside and inside, between pure and ordered multiplicity. Acker's *Pussy,* and her creation piRATes, who in the course of the tale mutate into rats, play the parasites that introduce noise to the finely tuned music of masculine culture. As Maria Assade asserts, "Hermes and the parasite have become paradigms for the intimate relation between order and disorder" and their exclusion "draws a neat line, definitive line between stability and instability and turbulence." (1991, 278). Accordingly, O and Ange exclude the figure of the rat, Ratski, from their voyage. The pirate banner Ratski demonstrates an essence of the rhizomatic and fluid character of their journey. The flag renders Ratski's cartography intensive (rather than extensive) and impossible as it belongs to the realm of multiplicity:

> No one ever finds Ratski: she lives inside the interstices of the world.
> Located between red flowers. The name of each interstice is 'intellect.'
> Ratski's always on the rag.
>
> **...and so the reign of girl piracy began...** (208)

Rather than follow the multiple trajectories and explore the potentiality of Ratski, O and Ange choose to rest at the point designated by a skeleton's phallus. The two girls lose the possibilities ascribed to the pirate world due to their ignorance. Unchanged by the pirate underworld, O and Ange re-enact the myth of Orpheus and Eurydice. For the two characters the masculine order is re-established, while the pirates disappear into the imaginary third/pirate space so that their reign can continue.

Pussy, King of the Pirates is first and foremost a tale of creation. The Ackerian notion of the female pirates and her consistent technique of literary piracy is a repetition with a difference, an emergence of the new within the old regime. Acker provides a new cartography where space, instead of being fitted into a rigorously striated and grid-like coordinate system, is mapped as multiple, turbulent and creative. She maps space on a Möbius strip that rotates around both the outside and the inside, the smooth and the striated, order and chaos—as both are a part of the emerging existence—a life. One of the final chapters Acker entitled: "playing house," where O and Ange dream of having their own house, their private space. O narrates: "we looked for a house in which we could play house 'cause we knew that it wasn't going to be our real home." O, Ange and more than a few readers realize that one needs "islands of stability amidst chaos," however, as Acker's turbulent writing has demonstrated, it is necessary to rebuild the existing systems of oppression and dominance. The pirates as vehicles of multiplicity reintroduce change and transformation, opening doors to positive chaos, calling for inclusion. *Pussy the King of Pirates* is a distinctive example of literature's search for the third term, negotiating between the ordered and the multiple and generating an emergence of the new.

References

Acker, Kathy. 1996. *Pussy, King of the Pirates*. New York: Grove Press.

Assad, Maria L. 1991. Michel Serres: In Search of a Tropography. In *Chaos and Order: Complex Dynamics in Literature and Science*, ed. by N. Katherine Hayles, 278-298. Chicago/London: University of Chicago Press.

Deleuze, Gilles and Felix Guattari. 1987. *A Thousand Plateaus: Capitalism and Schizophrenia*, trans. by Brian Massumi. Minneapolis: University of Minnesota Press.

Garrett, Shawn-Marie. 1983. Interview. Treasure out of Treasure. *Theater* 26.1-2:170-173.

Irigaray, Luce. 1992. *Elemental Passions*, trans. by J. Collie and J. Still. New York: Routledge.

Irr, Caren. 2004. Beyond Appropriation: *Pussy, King of the Pirates* and a Feminist Critique of Intellectual Property. In *Devouring Institutions: The Life Work of Kathy Acker*, ed. by Michael Hardin, 211-233. San Diego: San Diego State University Press.

Serres, Michel. 1982a. *Hermes: Literature, Science, Philosophy*, ed. by Harari, J.V. and Bell, D.F. Baltimore: The Johns Hopkins University Press.

—. 1982b. *The Parasite*, trans. by Lawrence R. Schehr. Baltimore: The John Hopkins University. Press.

—. 1995. *Genesis*, trans. by G. James and J. Nielson. Ann Arbor: The University of Michigan Press.

—. 2000. *The Birth of Physics*, ed. by David Webb, trans. by Jack Hawkes. Manchester: Clinamen Press.

CHAPTER THIRTY-FOUR

THE MEDIEVAL MIDDLE EAST AS A SPACE OF CULTURAL HYBRIDITY IN AMITAV GHOSH'S *IN AN ANTIQUE LAND*

RADEK GLABAZŇA

One of the most lasting obsessions of European modernity, demonstrated by the socio-political reality of the last few centuries—a reality we still inhabit—is the pleasure taken in drawing maps and fashioning clear-cut identities and boundaries between cultures and communities. The resulting products of this map drawing and self-fashioning are then called nations or nation-states. That is, in the hegemonic epistemology of European Enlightenment there is no space left for disruptive in-betweens and subversive hybridity.

However, this "epistemic violence" has recently been challenged by a great variety of theorists, anthropologists, historians, or novelists. Benedict Anderson's intriguing claim that "imagined communities [...] are to be distinguished, not by their falsity/genuineness, but by the style in which they are imagined" (1991, 6) can be seen as a point where all such counter-hegemonic approaches collude, though going in various directions themselves. The Indian novelist and ethnographer Amitav Ghosh has taken upon himself a task running roughly along the lines of Anderson's statement, yet his novel *In an Antique Land* strives to prove a slightly different point.

Rather than tracing a history of enlightened map-drawing and fashioning of exclusive identities, a history with a capital "H", as Ghosh calls it on many occasions in the text, the writer is interested in the recreation of a flexible, pre-modern world, a world of cross-cultural exchange and delicious hybridity, a world of "indistinguishable, intertwined histories, Indian and Egyptian, Muslim and Jewish, Hindu and Muslim" (Ghosh 1998, 339), that is the world that preceded the arrival of aggressive European colonialists. Ghosh situates this world in the area stretching from the North Africa, across the Persian Gulf and Arabian Peninsula, all the way across the Arabian Sea and Indian Ocean, up to the Malabar Coast in India. In doing so, he cunningly blows up the commonly held binary opposition between the supposedly positive term "modern" and its negative counterpart "medieval", and also situates the category of space right in the centre of his narrative. Under the gaze of the Western colonial scholarship the space now known as the Middle East has been epistemologically transformed, to borrow the words of Edward Said, into "a setting that is deeply inscribed with the politics […] and the strategies of power" (1997, 129). The narrator of *In an Antique Land* is also well aware of "the intercourse between power and the writing of history" (82) and writes in such a way as to undo this intercourse. Thus the term "modern" comes to denote Europe as a space of violence, greed and warfare, whereas the "medieval" in *In an Antique Land* refers to the pre-colonial Middle East as a space of "the rich confusions that accompany a culture of accommodation and compromise" (288).

In an Antique Land can certainly be variously interpreted by historians, ethnologists, anthropologists or literary critics, who could all read the text in ways fitting their respective disciplines. However, the variety of readings Ghosh's text can produce should not be used as evidence against its seeming lack of cohesion or meaning. On the contrary, it validates the view expressed by Claire Chambers that *In an Antique Land* is a "[…] multi-faceted, imaginative and open-ended text" (2006, 17). It operates on many levels and mingles together several overlapping narrative lines. Chambers appreciates how "in place of the epistemically coercive discourses of history and anthropology, Ghosh offers a deliberately partial and dialogic narrative" (17).

The two main narrative lines of *In an Antique Land* are divided by at least seven hundred years. The first tracks the story of a 12th-century merchant Ben Yiju, a Jew of Egyptian origin, but of Indian residence, and his venerated Indian slave Bomma. The narrator of *In an Antique Land*, who is Amitav Ghosh's younger self, pieces this story together from fragments of letters originally stored in the Ben Ezra synagogue in Cairo, now possessed by Cambridge University as part of the Taylor-Schechter collection.

The second narrative line is centred around the narrator himself, namely his experiences as a young ethnographer carrying out field work in the Egyptian villages of Lataifa and Nashawy during the 1980s. Apart from these two main narratives, there are many secondary and partial narratives, most prominently of young men from the Egyptian villages heading for Iraq to take jobs vacated by Iraqis engaged in the war against

Iran, and then heading back to Egypt in panic after the eruption of the Gulf War in the early 1990s. The category of space plays a central role in all of these narratives and the strategic function of space in Ghosh's subversive re-mapping and re-imagining of the pre-colonial Middle East will be the subject of the following paraphraphs.

In his rigorous and elaborate study of Ghosh's novel, Javed Majeed claims that "in *In an Antique Land*, the category of the 'medieval' appears as a space into which the artist tries to escape from the consequences of modernity, but the very creation of that space is itself testimony to the inescapability of those consequences" (1995, 48). But what are these consequences of modernity? For the narrator of *In an Antique Land* the answer is clear enough. An ethnographer doing fieldwork in far-off villages of Egypt, young Amitav finds himself in a very precarious situation. Were he an Englishman or Frenchman, he could perform his scholarly duties in keeping with the established code of Orientalism—he would simply observe his indigenous subjects from an utterly disinterested vantage point of a Western scholar and his writing would then take shape of an authoritative scientific treatise. He would be the Centre gazing upon the Periphery, or the Self gazing upon the Other. But he cannot do this. Firstly, though very intelligent, he is NOT of the colonial mindset, and secondly, he is an Indian and as such born of a very troubled history of conquest, territorial and cultural usurpation, and partition. The modern epistemology of exclusive identities cannot possibly appeal to young Amitav, who has seen the rise of aggressive communalism in his homeland. To escape this epistemology, he begins to recreate a medieval story of entirely different qualities—a story of cross-cultural exchange, fluidity, hybridity and flexibility. Amitav's presence in the Egyptian villages of Lataifa and Nashawy is a very disruptive event both for the villagers and Amitav himself. On numerous occasions, the roles of him as an ethnographer and the villagers as objects of his scrutiny are completely reversed. For the villagers, India is a member of the Third World family, a country worthy of sympathy, perhaps, because of a shared history and similar political goals of Nasser and Nehru, but hardly a place worthy of respect or following. Majority of the villagers are in fact ignorant of anything the two countries may have in common, which is why Amitav seldom saves his grace when the villagers start asking questions about India:

> "Tell me, is it true what they say, that in your country you burn your dead?" […]
> My heart sank: this was a question I encountered almost daily, and since I had not succeeded in finding a word such as "cremate" in Arabic, I knew I

would have to give my assent to the term that Khamees had used: the verb "to burn", which was the word for what happened to firewood and straw and the eternally damned. [...] "Yes," I said, regretfully. "Yes, we do—we burn everyone." (168-169)

The critic Shirley Chew points out that though innocent in themselves, such questions "return Ghosh to memories of unspeakable violence, and the trauma of a homeland partitioned and lost" (2001, 207). It is against these memories, against the awareness of such unfortunate consequences of modernity and European colonialism that Amitav attempts to recreate the undercurrent hybrid history of the medieval Middle East. This point is foregrounded in a scene that could well be considered the crucial moment of the whole narrative—the ferocious quarrel between Amitav and Imam Ibrahim in front of a crowd about the meaning of progress and development:

The Imam turned away and laughed scornfully. "He's lying," he said to the crowd. "They don't burn their dead in the West. They're not an ignorant people. They're advanced, they're educated, they have science, they have guns and tanks and bombs." Suddenly something seemed to boil over in my head, dilemmas and arguments I could no longer contain within myself. "We have them too!" I shouted back at him. "In my country we have all those things too; we have guns and tanks and bombs. And they're better than anything you've got in Egypt—we're a long way ahead of you." "I tell you he's lying," cried the Imam, his voice rising in fury. "Our guns and bombs are much better than theirs. Ours are second only to the West's." (236)

And a little later on:

The Imam and I: delegates from two superseded civilizations, vying with each other to establish a prior claim to the technology of modern violence. [...] In the end, for millions and millions of people on the landmasses around us, the West meant only this—science and tanks and guns and bombs. I was crushed as I walked away; it seemed to me that the Imam and I had participated in our final defeat, in the dissolution of the centuries of dialogue that had linked us: we had demonstrated the irreversible triumph of the language that has usurped all the others in which people once discussed their differences. We had acknowledged that it was no longer possible to speak, as Ben Yiju or his Slave, or any one of the thousands of travellers who had crossed the Indian Ocean in the Middle Ages might have done. [...] I felt myself a conspirator in the betrayal of the history that had led me to Nashawy; a witness to the extermination of a world of accommodations that I had believed to be still alive, and in some tiny measure, still retrievable. (236-237)

Reflexive and insightful as the quoted passages are, they need little comment apart from a reminder of what the famous anti-colonial theorist Franz Fanon famously said about the desire of the colonized subject: "The colonised man is an envious man. [...] There is no native who does not dream at least once a day of setting himself up in the settler's place." (1965, 32) Fanon made this statement with reference to the colonial situation, but it is clear from the quotes above that it has currency with regards to the postcolonial situation, too.

Amitav's bitter disappointment with his own reaction to Imam's claims to Egypt's military superiority over India could as well have meant a complete surrender of hope on the narrator's side. But instead, refusing to become engaged in a similar debate again, he embarks on his project of reconstruction of the flexible medieval world with yet more determination and vigour. Chew points out that this determination also manifests itself in the formal layout of the novel, where the episode of quarrel between Amitav and the Imam is immediately followed by a particularly vivid image of the twelfth-century port of Mangalore, the temporary place of residence of Ben Yiju on the Indian Malabar Coast, thriving with bustling life and fertile cross-cultural dialogue. Here is what *In an Antique Land* has to say about Mangalore:

> There were thirteen Chinese vessels in the harbour when Ibn Battuta's ship docked there, and he reports that the city regularly had visitors from China, Sumatra, Ceylon, the Maldives, Yemen, and Fars... A Portuguese sailor, Duarte Barbosa, who visited the city early in the sixteenth century, noted that the city's merchants included Arabs, Persians, Guzarates, Khorasanys, and Decanys, who were known collectively as pardesis, or foreigners. (242-243)

Chew reads such organization of the book as "Ghosh's attempt at expiating what he understands to be his betrayal of 'histories' he quested after" (205). For the critic Majeed, it punctuates the contrast between "the cultures and style of medieval accommodations" and "the 'rigid ladder of Development' on which nations are ranked" (51). In other words, to quote Majeed again, "the medieval world which the author evokes becomes the basis of a critical perspective on modernity and in the polemic of the text the term "medieval" is shorn of its pejorative connotations" (45).

What exactly then does Amitav Ghosh evoke from this unlimited space of cross-cultural fertilization that was the medieval Middle East? As it has been noted above, the whole space of North Africa, the Persian Gulf, the Arabian Sea and the Indian Ocean, and the Malabar Coast of India, is recreated by the narrator as a space lacking any territorial or cultural boundaries. Exactly how much of this space is recovered and recreated depends on the quality of the 12th-century letters from which Amitav pieces together this lost, but up to a certain degree retrievable world. Some of the letters are mere discontinuous fragments with a great deal left to the narrator's, and in turn the reader's, creative imagination. As Majeed notes, "this imaginative historical recovery [...] is presented as the reconstruction of the 'choice of Histories', now supposedly no longer available in the modern world. It is also seen as the creation of a space for those 'intertwined histories' which characterized the pre-modern world" (48). Majeed's stress on words such as "imaginative" and "creation" should remind the perceptive reader that Amitav Ghosh's *In an Antique Land* is a fictional narrative, or rather a "construction of a coherent narrative from fragments which quite literary exist in an archive" (54). The fact that there is not a single hint at the possible distortions and manipulations necessarily occurring in such a process is also very productive, because this apparent lack of questioning of the validity of such a narrative undermines the construction of grand narratives, or Histories, characterized by the same absence of a doubtful voice. It is against such discursive practices that *In an Antique Land* authoritatively asserts itself, using the discursive strategies of modernity and exclusive identity-formation against themselves—that is to re-create a pre-modern space of hybridity and all kinds of border-crossing, be it geographical, cultural, social, linguistic or religious. Such is the space occupied by the 12th-century Jewish merchant Ben Yiju, his many Muslim and Hindu friends, and his slave Bomma, who, after all, does not comply with the contemporary understanding of the word "slave" at all. It is the personal stories and histories (with a small "h") of these people that Amitav Ghosh is primarily interested in and which he recreates with real warmth, because he looks upon them as "tiny threads, woven into the borders of a gigantic tapestry"(Ghosh 1998, 95).

Ultimately, it is this human warmth and intimate personality of Ghosh's presentation of the medieval Middle East that sharply contrasts with the shockingly anonymous coldness of the modern world, punctuated by the spread of TV sets broadcasting atrocities of the 1990s Gulf War. In the final scene of the novel, which describes a televised footage of the exodus of Egyptian migrant workers from Iraq after the break-up of the Gulf War, even the category of space is transformed into a sinister and unsurpassable obstacle. There is no more medieval crossing and melting of boundaries, only "thousands and thousands of men, some in trousers, some in jallabeyyas, some carrying their TV sets on their backs, some crying out for a drink of water, stretching all the way from the horizon to the Red Sea, standing on the beach as though waiting for the water to part" (353).

This is where the novel—to pass the final verdict—really succeeds: through its spatial representation of hybridity and cross-cultural exchange in the medieval Middle East, as opposed to the linguistic, social, political, religious or territorial boundaries drawn by European colonialism, it shakes the reader anywhere on the planet into awareness of the limitations of the "modern" conceptions of identity or nationhood.

References

Anderson, Benedict. 1991. *Imagined Communities: Reflections on the Origin and Spread of Nationalism.* Revised ed. London and New York: Verso.

Chambers, Claire. 2006. Anthropology as Cultural Translation. *Postcolonial Text* 2 (3): 1-19.

Chew, Shirley. 2001. Texts and Worlds in Amitav Ghosh's *In an Antique Land*. In *Re-constructing the Book: Literary Texts in Transmissions*, ed. by M. Bell, S. Chew, S. Eliot, L. Hunter, J. L. W. West III, 197-209. Aldershot: Ashgate.

Fanon, Franz. 1965. *The Wretched of the Earth.* London: MacGibbon & Kee.

Ghosh, Amitav. 1998. *In an Antique Land.* 2nd ed. London: Granta Books.

Majeed, Javed. 1995. Amitav Ghosh's *In an Antique Land*: The Ethnographer-historian and the Limits of Irony. *The Journal of Commonwealth Literature* 30 (2): 45-55.

Said, Edward W. 1997. Orientalism Reconsidered. In *Postcolonial Criticism*, ed. by B. Moore-Gilbert, G. Stanton and W. Maley. London: Longman.

CHAPTER THIRTY-FIVE

FRANK CAPRA'S BEDFORD FALLS
AS AXIS MUNDI

MAGDALENA GRABIAS-ŻUREK

Frank Capra undoubtedly belongs to the pantheon of the great masters of American cinema and his masterpieces like *It Happened One Night* (1934), *Mr. Smith Goes to Washington* (1939), or the audience's beloved *It's a Wonderful Life* (1946) are considered the icons of American culture.[1] Capra is remembered for pioneering and developing the genre of screwball comedy and a slightly more serious populist comedy, within which, as he himself claimed, apart from entertaining he was also able to "say something" (Capra 1971, 185) to his audience. Although the motif of a hero struggling for his ideals on unfamiliar and unfriendly territory can be traced back to Capra's 1920s silent features, it is in his populist movies of the next decade that the Caprasque hero gained his most recognizable traits. Capra's heroes are usually small town dwellers and apparently plain common men who in the course of an action turn out to be uncommon and prove to be "the hope of the world" (Capra 1975, 19). They are romantic idealists willing to stand up and fight for what they believe in and defend their values against the cynical corrupt environment.

The above description largely fits the hero of *It's a Wonderful Life*—Capra's first post-war production, which will be the main concern of this article. The film is based on an idea drawn from a short story *The Greatest Gift* initially distributed as a Christmas card by its author Philip Van Doren Stern. The plot of the film revolves around the small town hero, George Bailey (James Stewart), who spends his life dreaming about big deeds, big travels and adventures, but his sense of duty towards his family, friends and community makes him give up his dreams and remain in a "crummy little town" he hates. As the plot unfolds, on the brink of suicide,

---

[1] All three have been selected for the Library of Congress's National Registry.

George is given a chance to see what the world would be like, had he never been born.

In spite of the subject's gravity, and the fact that for more than half of the film Capra pictures George Bailey's life and his struggles within a small town of Bedford Falls in a gloomy and *noir* like fashion, the film's ultimate message is optimistic and hopeful, indicating that "each man's life touches so many other lives and that if he isn't around it leaves an awful hole."

The world presented in *It's a Wonderful Life* is multi-dimensional. As I shall argue, its spatial pattern consists of three horizontal levels joined together by a vertical pillar. My aim, therefore, is to present the complexity of the organization of Capra's filmic reality and to prove that George Bailey's home town, Bedford Falls, constitutes an *axis mundi*.

According to Mircea Eliade, "an *axis mundi* is a holy place at the world's center, where heaven and earth meet. It is [...] sometimes expressed through the image of a universal pillar, axis mundi, simultaneously connecting and supporting heaven and earth [...]. Such a cosmic pillar can be only at the very center of the universe, for the whole of the habitable world revolves around it" (Eliade in Tuerk 2007, 183). *Axis mundi* may acquire the form of natural objects like a mountain or tree, products of human hands and toil like a spire, a pillar, a church or a skyscraper; it may also be a human body. Nevertheless, *axis mundi* usually expresses a point of connection between heaven and earth. It is "the immovable Spot [...] around which the world may be said to revolve" (Campbell in Tuerk 2007, 183).

The pre-Christian idea of *axis mundi* corresponds with the vision of the universe as to be found, among others, in Slavic culture. The Slavs used to imagine the universe as a giant oak, the three parts of which, would represent the three cosmological levels: the tree-top would be the house of Gods, the trunk—the earthly level of humans, and the roots—the realm of the dead (Gieysztor 1982, 168-172). Such conception similarly seems to recall Dante's vision of the world division presented in his *Divine Comedy* (Dante 1992). Dante enumerates three components the universe consists of, i.e. paradise, purgatory, and inferno. These, in turn, as I am going to prove, constitute the equivalents of the three levels of Frank Capra's filmic space,[2] namely: heaven, the earthly level of Bedford Falls, and Pottersville—the underworld.

---

[2] The parallelism between the universe division of Dante's *Divine Comedy* and Capra's *It's A Wonderful Life* has been discussed by Barbara Bowman (Bowman 1992, 20-29). In my article I shall argue that the spatial division of *It's A*

The multi-level reality of *It's a Wonderful Life* universe is indicated already in the first reel of the movie. The film opens with a picture of Bedford Falls, but soon the camera moves upward and the viewer is offered the vision of the starry firmament. We hear heavenly voices talking and as each voice is heard, one of the stars sparkles brighter than others. The discussion concerns George, and as the celestial intercourse follows, we learn that a divine intervention is going to be provided for the benefit of Bailey. The resolution is reached to send Clarence Odbody (Henry Travers), an angel second class, who has not earned his wings yet, down to earth to rescue George from committing a suicide. However, before Clarence's mission begins, the angel and the viewers are offered a long retrospective sequence presenting all the significant occurrences of George Bailey's life. Thus, the paradisal opening is continued by a detailed insight into the earthly level.

Bedford Falls is a quintessentially American town, where every feature of a typical small town is to be found and which, at a first glance, can hardly be named unusual. With its tree-lined, lively main street, a drugstore, a cinema, its banks, offices, and bars, it constitutes a faithful picture of its times and, in fact, America in miniature. Everything seems to happen here. The joys of the Roaring Twenties, despair of the Great Depression, political, economic and social issues of the 1930s and 1940s, and war dilemmas are all a part of Bedford Falls. The town commemorates traditional small town values and morality and, as in many other Capra's films, celebrates an idea of a friendly neighborhood and small town communities. It is an attractive, quiet, and generally nice place to live, yet it becomes George Bailey's earthly purgatory and the background for cosmological struggle for his soul.

It has been stated by critics on several occasions that, contradictory to the film's title, in some ways George Bailey's life is not wonderful at all. To the contrary: it seems to be a never-ending chain of unfulfilled dreams and lost opportunities. He does not go to college, as he has to protect the Bailey Building and Loan, the financial organization providing the poor with the chance to own a house, against a local robber baron, Mr. Potter (Lionel Barrymore), who urges the dissolution of it as unprofitable. George stays in his home town, marries a local girl, Mary (Donna Reed) and his life revolves around the Building and Loan and struggling against Potter's ambitions to take control over the whole town. The hero's frustrations accumulate over the years and they finally burst out the day his business associate, uncle Billy (Thomas Mitchell), loses eight thousand

---

Wonderful Life is even more complex, as it consists of Dante related horizontal levels and the vertical axis.

dollars—the property of the Building and Loan. The money falls into the hands of Potter, who quickly grabs the chance of destroying George. When in despair George turns for help to Potter, the wealthy mogul accuses him of being a fraud and states that with his five hundred dollars life insurance, George is worth more dead than alive.

Clarence, the angel, intervenes the moment George considers taking his own life. A while later, George pronounces the wish to have never been born, which is granted by the angel, and the hero gets the chance to see the world without him in it. What follows is a bleak infernal sequence in which George experiences the horrifying results of his nonexistence. His hometown, now Pottersville, family and friends are all much altered and the frightening experience makes him beg for his life again. His wish is granted again and, back in Bedford Falls, he can finally appreciate how wonderful his life really is. Thanks to the successful result of the mission, Clarence is entitled to get his wings, and George joyfully rushes back home to learn that his fiscal troubles were miraculously solved by collective endeavours of his Bedford Falls' friends.

The earthly level of George Bailey's reality appears a hopelessly bleak space. Throughout his entire life George Bailey has to face moral alternatives and he usually makes choices for the benefit of the community he lives in, and to his own material disadvantage. "As a moral man, a decent man, he is obliged over and over again to act for others, putting aside his own dreams," Lorraine Mortimer notices (Mortimer 1995/96, 3). Sam Girgus defines this rare altruistic propensity of George as perennial moral masochism (Girgus 1998, 97), while Robert Ray anxiously points out that *It's a Wonderful Life* is a film about possessing all that American Dream promises (a wife, children, a job, friends, a house) and still being unhappy (Ray 1985, 192). Nevertheless, despite the strong evidence for the above views, the audacity of the story lies in the conviction that notwithstanding the everyday and apparently unsuccessful toil of a man, life and the mere fact of being alive is still wonderful. Capra makes his message explicit, as it is expressed within the film: "No one is a failure who has friends." However, George's life is marked with much too many relinquishments and sacrifices to acknowledge this truth with ease, and before it can happen, he has to touch the infernal experience of the underworld. Until then, he is trapped within a claustrophobic axiological purgatory filled with constant doubts about his morality and the rightness of his choices, fear of meaningless life, and the mistaken assumption that he is an utter failure.

Capra shows George Bailey as an exceptional heroic man, who "without quite realizing it, becomes the town's leading citizen, admired and loved for his quiet championship of decent living" (Griffith 1975, 161). He is the only one who dares to oppose Potter and his plans to change Bedford Falls into a place built on inhuman economic rules and human misery. George's biggest drama, then, is suffering within his inner purgatory brought about by the restricted perception of space in which he exists. He needs Clarence to show him the cosmological perspective of Bedford Falls and his life within its reality.

The provincial town of Bedford Falls is, Stephen Handzo suggests, "the archetypal American microcosm" (Handzo 1975, 173). Yet, as I have already stated, its typicality is illusive. In fact, in Capra's filmic vision it becomes the center of the Earth, the *axis mundi*, as the eyes of the powers of good and evil are turned upon it. Moreover, the emissaries of the two competing powers are no longer abstract ideas in Bedford Falls, but are incarnate in human forms of Clarence, the angel, and Mr. Potter, the resident envoy of evil. According to Ray Carney, there is no need for a villain in *It's a Wonderful Life* at all, as the real hell is within George's mind (Carney 1986, 381). Nevertheless, even though Potter does not appear in Pottresville sequence in person, his presence in Bedford Falls and its effect upon the town's inhabitants and George's life in particular is obvious. Even if we assume that George's purgatory is mostly of axiological nature, it is still unquestionable that Potter and the need to resist his inhuman policy was always the reason for George's dramatic choices.

Apparently, Potter remains beyond the laws of biology and passing time. He does not age or change throughout the story. The most striking and suggestive thing, however, is the fact that even though Potter eventually looses in the cosmic battle for George's soul, he neither gets punished nor ever stops spinning his webs of evil.

Another startling fact of the story is that it is not the emissary of evil, but the angel who takes George to the underworld. Clarence saves George not by promises of divine awards in heaven, but by providing him with the abysmal vision of the world without him. Such stratagem enables the angel to gain advantage over the evil power by means of clearing George's perception out of Potter's venomous poison and helping him see and appreciate his life from the perspective unblurred by the purgatorial conviction of being a failure.

The nightmarish Pottersville sequence depicts the underworld level of the film's spatial reality. The vision of the town without George from the start strikes the viewer with unfamiliarity. The town is transformed beyond recognition and as George in panic traverses the streets, Pottersville "exposes the iconography of the 1940s *noir* city: a riot of neon and jazz, the main street is crammed with burlesque halls, dance joints, pawnbroker's stores, and bars" (Krutnik 1997, 85) full of unsmiling hostile people. The druggist that George saved from prison in childhood, is a drunkard and an ex-con, as George was not there to prevent the tragedy. George's mother (Beulah Bondi) is a solitary old woman, and everyone George meets denies ever knowing him. "Bailey Park," the residential quarter built thanks to Building and Loan, is replaced by "Potter's Field," the cemetery, where George finds the grave of his younger brother, who was drowned as a child, as George was not there to save him. His house is in utter ruins, and his wife is an old maid. George's hysterical attempts to convince Mary that he is her husband and the father of her children ends up in a *noir* gangster-like fashion street shooting from which he manages to escape, and having realized what a wonderful gift his life was, he prays to God to let him live again.

The Pottersville sequence presents the reality within which the cosmic balance has been severely disturbed. It is the realm of evil where Potter's rapacious ambitions and cold-hearted philosophy are reflected in every stone, building and institution. The idyllic Bedford Falls is changed into the modern *noir* city where, as Raymond Chandler points out, "the streets [are] dark with something more than night" (Chandler in Krutnik 1997, 83).

The horror of dislocation, homelessness and the inferno of George's nonexistence makes him fully acknowledge the value of his life sacrifices. Clarence's lesson helps the hero regain a clear perspective of his home town reality and to regain his inner balance. Moreover, by George's final choice to get back to life, no matter what it brings, he manages to rescue Bedford Falls from Potter's infernal threat, and thus restore the cosmic balance within the town.

The nightmare vision proved unequivocally that it is solely the person of George Bailey that stops Potter from transforming Bedford Falls into a corrupt urban wasteland and life of its dwellers into hell. However, one can claim even more than that. As Ray notices, the Pottersville sequence showed that George "was not merely a hero; he was the center of the world on whom everything depended" (Ray 1985, 200).

Bedford Falls and George Bailey have frequently been incorrectly defined as common. However, there is surprisingly a lot going on in Bedford Falls for a mundane provincial town. As for George, the film indicates explicitly that he is *spiritus movens* of his home town. The moment he ceases to exist, the reality of Bedford Falls transforms into the infernal Pottersville. Furthermore, if George is an ordinary common man, why is so much fuss made about him both in paradise and in the inferno?

Clearly the battle for George's soul is fierce: Potter exposes George to a perilous trial of inner struggle against the temptation of an easy life in material luxury and moral oblivion, and when the time comes, George's guardian angel comes down for his rescue in person.

As I have indicated, the filmic world of *It's a Wonderful life* consists of three horizontal levels: the paradisal, manifested in a celestial opening, but also in George's choices of good over evil, and impersonated in Clarence; purgatorial—the level of Bedford Falls and the place of George's earthly struggle with his doubts and uncertainties; and the infernal underworld— the nightmarish dream sequence of Pottersville. The film proves that without George Bailey, however, the level of Bedford Falls disappears reducing the spatial pattern to two impermeable levels of paradise and inferno. The above evidence allows for a conclusion that not only is George Bailey not an ordinary man but, in fact, he *is* Bedford Falls and within the entire cosmological spectrum of the presented world he constitutes an *axis mundi* around which everything revolves. The thesis can be supported by numerous facts. George is undeniably the one who makes it possible for heaven and hell to meet on the earthly level. Thus he can be perceived as a physical and axiological vertical axis, a cosmic pillar, and "the point of entry" (Campbell in Tuerk 2007, 183) providing the connection between the three horizontal levels and opening an inter-spatial tunnel between them.

The hole created by the vertical axis allows Clarence to come to earth, and later on further down to the underworld in company of George. However, George's axiological battle is fought on multiple levels of his consciousness which happen to be parallel to the division of the world within which he lives. The paradisal level is expressed in George's innocence, his innate goodness and honesty, his dreams and high hopes for the future. On the level of purgatory he despises his town and his life, he fails to appreciate what he has and does not realize the importance of his achievements. On this level he is also seduced by Potter and almost gives in to the temptation. Finally, in the infernal level George ceases to exist and he crosses the physical boundaries of the earthly level and enters the underworld.

It is through the experience of inferno that George can gain clear sight and a full perspective. Thus, the experience enables the hero to return physically to the earthly level of Bedford Falls, which from this moment acquires the status of George's axiological paradise. Hence, Clarence's lesson and the Bedford Falls community's disinterested initiative to help their lifelong benefactor in his financial troubles makes George fully acknowledge that his life is truly unique and wonderful and recognize the angel's simple moral that no one is a failure who has friends and family. As I have indicated, the spectrum of Capra's narrative space in *It's a Wonderful Life* consists of the combined horizontal and vertical division, where the mediating vertical axis holds the three horizontal levels in place and propels them to a constant revolution around it. The ending of the movie, picturing George Bailey, his wife and children around him, surrounded by a vast group of friends, confirms the fact that the hero's multilevel struggle has been completed successfully and the cosmological balance of the entire filmic world has been restored both axiologically and territorially and the middle level of Bedford Falls once more regained its status of the *axis mundi*.

References

Bowman, Barbara. 1992. *Master Space: Film Images of Capra, Lubitsch, Sternberg, and Wyler*. New York: Greenwood Press.

Capra, Frank. 1971. *The Name above the Title*. New York: The Macmillan Company.

—. 1975. "Frank Capra: One Man-One Film," The American Film Institute Discussion no. 3. In *Frank Capra: The Man and his Films*, ed. by Richard Glatzer and John Raeburn, 16-23. Ann Arbor: The University of Michigan Press.

Carney, Ray. 1986. *American Vision: The Films of Frank Capra*. Hanover: University Press of New England.

Dante, Alighieri. 1992. *Boska komedia*. Warszawa: Ludowa Spółdzielnia Wydawnicza.

Gieysztor, Aleksander. 1982. *Mitologia Słowian*. Warszawa: Wydawnictwo Artystyczne i Filmowe.

Girgus, Sam B. 1998. *Hollywood Renaissance: The Cinema of Democracy in the Era of Ford, Capra, and Kazan*. Cambridge: Cambridge University Press.

Griffith, Richard. 1975. It's a Wonderful Life and Post-war Realism. In *Frank Capra: The Man and His Films*, ed. by Richard Glatzer and John Raeburn, 160-163. Ann Arbor: The University of Michigan Press.

Handzo, Stephen. 1975. Under Capracorn. In *Frank Capra: The Man and his Films*, ed. by Richard Glatzer and John Raeburn, 164-176. Ann Arbor: The University of Michigan Press.

Krutnik, Frank. 1997. Something More than Night: Tales of the Noir City. In *The Cinematic City*, ed. by David B. Clarke, 83-99. London: Routledge.

Mortimer, Lorraine. Winter 1995/96. The Grim Enchantment of *It's a Wonderful Life*. *The Massachusetts Review*, Vol. 36, No 4.

Ray, Robert B. 1985. *A Certain Tendency of the Hollywood Cinema, 1930-1980*. Princeton: Princeton University Press.

Tuerk, Richard. 2007. *Oz in Perspective. Magic and Myth in the L. Frank Baum Books*. Jefferson, NC: McFarland.

CHAPTER THIRTY-SIX

SPATIAL TRANSFORMATION
AND THE SUBVERSIVE DIALOGUE
WITH CONVENTION IN J.M. COETZEE'S
DISGRACE

KATARZYNA KARWOWSKA

Disgrace is Coetzee's first novel published after the collapse of apartheid. It marks the passage of five years from the first democratic elections in the Republic of South Africa, which was the crowning achievement of the process initiated in 1990 with the release of Nelson Mandela after a long-term imprisonment and the lifting restrictions on opposition groups. Logically, the novel might be understood as the author's response to this historical moment of passing away of the old regime. The voice of the white author who despite being born in Cape Town feels alienated from Afrikaners' culture, history, and language (Coetzee 1992, 341-2) is worth listening to especially for his ability to "imagine the subjectivity of that which one is not" (Wright 2006, 119). This paper aims to elucidate how the textual representations of changing strategies of inhabitation and transformations in the field of identity correspond and contribute to the spatial transformations as imagined and experienced by people. This discussion is narrowed down to the analysis of *Disgrace* which is read against the Afrikaner genre of *plaasroman* which had its great share in shaping the symbolic landscape of South Africa and can be recognized as a systematizing strategy for ordering of space.

In order to pursue this subject without confusing the material or the actually existing landscape with its representations or imaginings, one needs to draw clear distinctions and acknowledge certain theoretical conjectures pertaining to the relation between these two concepts. Some of the critics who take as their subject the notions of space, place or landscape in literary texts tend to freely incorporate into the field of literary studies the vast scope of theories which originate within the sphere of such disciplines as anthropology, sociology and cultural geography. Though the inspirational role of such interdisciplinary ventures cannot be undermined, it might prove problematical if those analyses come without the awareness of the huge ontological gap between the physical landscape and the represented spaces. An acclaimed and well recognized theorist of space, Henri Lefebvre, propounds a triadic conceptual classification distinguishing between perceived, conceived, and lived space. Perceived space refers to the social spatial practices, conceived space is linked to the planned activities of scientists, urban planners, engineers and architects, while the lived space is expressed "through its associated images and symbols... space which the imagination seeks to change and appropriate" (Lefebvre 1991, 39). Thus the latter might be considered to be that aspect of the spatial triad which is the effect of the act of representation. Symbolic renderings of space are quite often caught up in the discussions on the concept of landscape. For Cosgrove and Daniels for example landscape is an ideologically infused mode of representation, "a cultural image, and a pictorial way of representing, structuring or symbolizing surroundings" (Keith 2004, 86). Said, inspired by Bachelard's *Poetics of Space*, similarly coins the notion of "imaginative geography" to speak of the invented and arbitrarily imagined visions of physical terrain which participate in its creation (Said 1978, 54-57). Having mentioned this creative potential, it is well justified to inquire into the specific properties of images constitutive of landscape. Even before an image is artistically rendered it is preceded by the activity of perception which is the first stage of the construction of a represented landscape (here I omit the fact that material landscape is already a construct, shaped by the various activities of a society). For seeing involves complex processes in which the observer's prior knowledge, his/her historical and cultural background and ideological beliefs work together (quite unconsciously) upon the object of perception. Added to this first-stage composition is the extrapolation of the image into the realm of textual, narrative reality. Assuming that this effort is to a degree performed consciously and for a certain purpose "textual and discursive practices can have profound material consequences, allowing as they do appropriation of space by rendering it meaningful to those capable of exerting control" (Warf 2004, 146). The construction of the newly colonized exotic spaces as *terra nullis* and the oblivion to the presence of indigenous peoples in travel narratives procured by white western colonizers (Birch 1996, 178) might serve as an example of controlling and taking possession of the land through representation.

Thus South African landscape, as any other landscape, resembles a palimpsest on which one can trace the signs of successive inscriptions (Ashcroft et al. 2007, 158). It has been subjected to various imaginative renderings for centuries since the first white settlements were established by the Dutch East India Company in what today is known as the Cape. The general trend was to describe the newly discovered territories as a "no man's land" and hence the proliferation of travel narratives which participated in the process of colonization as they "implied that the natural resources were only waiting to be used by the European settlers and often disparaged the society and character of the current inhabitants" (Gallagher 1991, 55). As time passed by, new settler societies were founded in the context of struggles and wars over territories between the British, the Boer and the indigenous peoples. The presence on and appropriation of the land were justified and enforced by a discursive process which involved making links between national identity and environment (Darian-Smith et al. 1996, 8-9). The dominant genre in this species of writing is the explicitly Afrikaner type of farm novel, i.e. *plaasroman*, traditionally interpreted as participating in the pastoral convention.

J.M. Coetzee in *Disgrace* continues his discursive dialogue with this genre, which was initiated in his earlier novel *In the Heart of the Country* and exposed the utterly oppressive and disastrous effects of this patriarchal discourse upon the female psyche. Magda, the protagonist, unsuccessfully fights to shake off the strong and enslaving grip of the textually and traditionally enhanced archetypal Afrikaner identity of a white farmer's daughter. So powerful and so long-lasting are the genre's imprints left on the land and the identity of South African people that the writer decided to draw the image of the post-apartheid, transformed landscape by the means of intertextual subversion of this convention. Coetzee in his work on the literary tradition in South Africa entitled *White Writing* writes widely about this particular genre. He explains that this mode of pastoral writing, the program of which "is one of a renewal of peasant order based on the myth of the return to the earth," is a response to the difficult economic situation in South Africa in 1920-1940's and the "emergence of a class of landless farmers" (Coetzee 1988, 79, 82). The main themes and features of the *plaasroman* comprise: concern to preserve traditional rural values of patriarchal society, mystical bond with the owned land which is the seat of lineal heritage, farmer figure who being the good steward of his land owes it the duty of labor and should be able to understand the lessons provided by nature and live in accordance with its rights and cycles, and the preference for the life on the farm as opposed to the corrupting forces present in the capitalistic and material ways of the city (Coetzee 1988, 82-114).

Disgrace thus participates in what Hein Viljoen describes as "the ironic revision [of the plaasroman]" which "culminated in the 1990s in a number of novels in which the subgenre is used in a parodist way as a vehicle of criticism of the ideological order of apartheid" (Viljoen 2004, 109). Central to those rewritings is their preoccupation with the idea of farm "as the essential South African form of habitation" (Viljoen et al. 2004, 10). Coetzee, through questioning of the old and the depiction of the new, alternative ways of inhabiting South African land contributes to the creation of a transformed vision of the country's spatial relations. *Disgrace* tells the story of an aging professor of humanities, David Lurie, who having ventured a romantic liaison with one of his students, is ostracized by the academic society and forced to give up his teaching position. He decides to leave Cape Town and stay for a while at his daughter's farm near Grahamstown in the Eastern Cape. What was intended to be an idyllic repose in the countryside turns into a nightmare when David and Lucy fall prey to violent and savage attack: Lucy is gang-raped and David suffers severe head burns. Furthermore, the method of rendering the picture of the farm itself reinforces the impression that this place cannot correspond with the conventional notion of the Afrikaner rural Arcadia.

The family structure on Lucy's farm does not suit the traditional patriarchal model promoted by the *plaasroman*. Instead of a multigeneric family with an aloof patriarch, morally chaste, strong and subordinate wife and numerous children, Lucy's household comprises only herself (Gallagher 1991, 93). Although she bears some considerable resemblance to a picture of a traditional *Boervru*, at the same time she constitutes its negation at the most essential level, i.e. the young woman is a homosexual and thus she brings no promise of bearing children and prolonging the family line. If Lucy gets pregnant it is only as a consequence of rape. The reversal of power relations is also made apparent by the breaking of the "silence about the place of the black man in the pastoral idyll" (Coetzee 1988, 81) of the traditional *plaasroman*. In *Disgrace* black people, just as the white men, are part of the African rural landscape. Coetzee, however, goes even further and reverses the old master and slave roles by making David, a white scholar, a helping-hand to Petrus, a black landowner to be.

Furthermore, in the genre model of *plaasroman* the white farmers justified their proprietorship of the land through the myth of natural right in which "The farms they [ancestors] carved out of the wilds, out of primal, inchoate matter, become the seats to which their lineages are mystically bound" (Coetzee 1988, 83). Lucy, on the other hand, is not united with the farm land by any rights of heritage; she simply bought the farm. By the standards of the genre the woman's occupation of the land is not legitimate. However, Coetzee leaves the reader with ambiguous feelings: Lucy's stubbornness, her unshakeable will to stay on the farm and finally her decision to give birth to the child put her on a par with the legendary Afrikaner "founding fathers who paid for the farm in blood, sweat, and tears" (Coetzee 1988, 85). Lucy is prepared to offer her suffering and to humble herself in order to live where she has chosen. The conditions that she is forced to accept are indeed severe for they first entail becoming a tenant to Petrus, the black co-proprietor who seems to have his share in the tragic attack, and second participating in an alliance which Lucy describes in the following way: "I contribute the land, in return for which I am allowed to creep in under his [Petrus'] wing" (Coetzee 2000, 203). David cannot comprehend his daughter's refusal to report the crime and her meek acceptance of fate. Lucy in return dismisses her father's accusations that she acts unreasonably and that she "hopes to expiate the crimes of the past by suffering in the present" (112). The young woman however, does not perceive her life as participating in the history of oppression; she approaches the matter from a realistic point of view, caring solely for her own safety and peace. She treats her life as a private matter and does not seem to be interested in the past. Her philosophy is as simple as moderate her expectations are, which she admits by saying "Yes, I agree, it is humiliating. But perhaps that is what I must learn to accept. To start at ground level. With nothing. Not with nothing but. With nothing. No cards, no weapons, no property, no rights, no dignity" (Coetzee 205).

The ending of the novel suggests that Lucy's attitude might help in expiating the overly anti-pastoral vision of the South African country. For as a "forward-looking lady," as Petrus calls her, she tries to build future at all costs, ignoring the wrongs of the past (136). The vision of the white and black people coexisting together, irrespective of the sacrifices it calls for, allows hoping for improvement. One of the final scenes displays a picture of Lucy, visibly pregnant, busy with garden work. The season is that of summer, the garden is full of bright blooming flowers. David is a silent witness to this scene and sees it in the following way:

> The wind drops. There is a moment of utter stillness which he would wish prolonged for ever: the gentle sun, the stillness of mid-afternoon, bees busy in a field of flowers; and at the centre of the picture a young woman, *das ewig Weibliche*, lightly pregnant, in a straw sunhat. (218)

This atmosphere of peacefulness throws David into a pensive mood. However, instead of ruminating on the tragic and painful past, he finally thinks positively about the future: the future of Lucy, of her child and the next generations, "a line of existences with his share" (217), and finally his own future as a grandfather. This optimistic strain allows to believe in the possibility of a "new start" (218) and peaceful coexistence of people of various races in spite of the suffering and pain of the past. The child that Lucy is pregnant with might be perceived as the epitome of this new world, new order to come.

Clearly, *Disgrace* is a narrative which represents a specific way of living in a particular socio-geographical location. Through reversal of the conventions of *plaasroman* it reveals a new strategy for the white and black South African population to dwell in a country which strives to overcome the damaging aftermaths of a system based on racial segregation. This imagined 'habitation', which Ashcroft defines as "a way of being in a place which itself defines and transforms a place" (Ashcroft 2002, 157) involves expiatory actions and supreme personal sacrifice on the part of those whose ancestors belonged to the broad category of the privileged. The readiness to accept even the heaviest blows delivered in the name of reclamation seems indispensible and, as in Lucy's case, marks the turning point in the history of mutual hostility. However, it should not be forgotten that such acts in order to be genuine must be the result of a deep personal acceptance of the new order. The presence of the black people on the map of South African land does not suffice. The power relations, which traditionally found their most vivid epitome in the spatial relations and were ultimately certified by the acts of land ownership, require radical transformation. As becomes clear, one needs to pay (not always in the literal way) for the right to live on the South African land, which is no longer the unknown territory at the disposal of the people whose only justification for its appropriation was a false premise that it belonged to no one.

J.M. Coetzee in his 1987 Jerusalem Prize Acceptance Speech dwells upon the subject of "unfreedom of the hereditary masters of South Africa" whose source lies in the fact that their "love [for] South Africa has consistently been directed toward the land, that is toward what is least likely to respond to love: mountains, deserts, birds and animals and flowers" (Coetzee 1992, 97). The failure to extend this sentiment over the peoples of other races, especially those who were the inherent part of and belonged to this landscape has rendered fraternity and coexistence on equal basis impossible. One solution, which breaks this continuing impasse is that exemplified by Lucy, who resolves to surrender all her claims and legal rights to the farm and to the land. However, she does not simply "start a new chapter elsewhere" (Coetzee 2000, 155), but consciously ties her future with the future of the black people. The baby to come allows hoping that both the ex-slaves and ex-masters will be united by the affinity with and love for the child. David, finally reconciled, admits that "It will be, after all, a child of this earth" (216). Obviously, there is no guarantee that it will be an easy process but as Lucy states "Love will grow" (216).

The transformation depicted in *Disgrace* concerns primarily the issue of land, the ways it is inhabited and consequently the relationships between those who populate it. The vision of the South African countryside which used to be imagined and represented in terms of "a network of boundaries crisscrossing the surface of the land, marking off thousands of farms, each a separate kingdom ruled over by a benign patriarch, beneath him a pyramid of ... children, grandchildren, and serfs" (Coetzee 1988, 6) propagated by the *plaasroman* genre is disappearing. The very phenomenon of 'farm' loses its traditional sense and validity in the new post-apartheid African reality, which becomes obvious when Lucy urges her father: "Stop calling it the farm, David. This is not a farm, it is just a piece of land where I grow things" (Coetzee 2000, 200). Assuming, after Hillis Miler, the possibility that "the text and its reading... are performative speech acts bringing the terrain into existence" (Miller 1995, 5) novels are granted a very powerful (but still ambiguous) capacity to mould reality. Positively interpreted and employed, this potential of literary texts might contribute to the deconstruction of old imperial landscapes and to the creation of the new ones, transformed in such a way as to become the home of emerging communities and national identities. *Disgrace* seems to be just this kind of a text.

References

Ashcroft, Bill. 2001. *Post-Colonial Transformation*. London/New York: Routledge.

Ashcroft, Bill, Gareth Griffiths and Helen Tiffin. 2007. *Post-Colonial Studies: They Key Concepts*. London/New York: Routledge.

Birch, Tony. 1996. 'A land so inviting and still without inhabitants': erasing Koori culture from (post-) colonial landscapes. In *Text, Theory, Space: Land, Literature and History in South Africa and Australia*, ed. by Kate Darian-Smith, Liz Gunner and Sarah Nutall, 173-88. London/New York: Routledge.

Coetzee, J. M. 1988. *White Writing: On the Culture of Letters in South Africa*. Wynberg, Sandton: Radix.
—. 1992. *Doubling the Point: Essays and Interviews*, ed. by David Attwell. Cambridge MA/London: Harvard University Press.
—. 2000. *Disgrace*. London: Vintage.
Darian-Smith, Kate, Liz Gunner and Sarah Nutall. 1996. Introduction to *Text, Theory, Space: Land, literature and history in South Africa and Australia*, ed. by Kate Darian Smith, Liz Gunner and Sarah Nutall, 1-20. London/New York: Routledge.
Gallagher, Susan VanZanten. 1991. *A Story of South Africa: J. M. Coetzee's Fiction in Context*. Cambridge, MA/London: Harvard University Press.
Keith, Lilley. 2004. Denis Cosgrove. In *Key Thinkers on Space and Place*, ed. by Phil Hubbard, Rob Kitchin and Gill Valentine, 84-89. Los Angeles, London, New Delhi, Singapore: Sage Publications.
Lefebvre, Henri. 1991. *The Production of Space*, trans. by Donald Nicholson-Smith. Malden, MA/Oxford: Blackwell Publishing.
Miller, J. Hillis. 1995. *Topographies*. Stanford, CA: Stanford University Press
Said, Edward W. 1978. *Orientalism*. London: Penguin.
Viljoen, Hein. 2004. Land, Space, Identity: The Literary Construction of Space in Three Afrikaans Farm Novels. In *Storyscapes: South African Perspectives on Literature, Space and Identity*, ed. by Hein Viljoen and Chris N. van der Merwe, 107-123. New York: Peter Young Publishing.
Viljoen, Hein, Minnie Lewis and Chris N. van der Merwe. 2004. Introduction to *Storyscapes: South African Perspectives on Literature, Space and Identity*, ed. by Hein Viljoen and Chris N. van der Merwe, 1-22. New York: Peter Young Publishing.
Warf, Barney. 2004. Derek Gregory. In *Key Thinkers on Space and Place*, ed. by Phil Hubbard, Rob Kitchin and Gill Valentine, 141-148. Los Angeles, London, New Delhi, Singapore: Sage Publications.
Wright, Laura. 2006. *Writing 'Out of All the Camps': J. M. Coetzee's Narratives of Displacement*. New York/London: Routledge.

CHAPTER THIRTY-SEVEN

FROM THE OUTSIDE TO THE INSIDE AND THE OTHER WAY ROUND: THE SPACE OF CONTEMPORARY GOTHIC CITIES

AGNIESZKA KLIŚ

The story of Lestat de Lioncourt, told in Anne Rice's *The Vampire Lestat* (1985), starts in Auvergne, France, just before the Revolution. Among the places recalled by the vampire there are those which bring to the readers' minds the typical scenery of early gothic novels: a winter forest, a crumbling castle of the Lioncourts, a monastery in which young Lestat seeks refuge from his aristocratic legacy, all of which might together constitute the centre of a traditional gothic universe. Yet, significantly, the novel as such does not begin by introducing the reader to a typical gothic landscape. Before the reader enters the distant past, s/he first meets Lestat in the Downtown of New Orleans in 1984. It is a contemporary city that proves to be the lair of the vampire, its hunting ground and venture point, and thus, the centre of the presented world.

The space of a contemporary gothic city—or a city that is the major setting in a contemporary gothic text, such as Rice's *The Vampire Lestat*, or Tim Burton's film *Batman* (1989), or a plethora of other films produced in the late twentieth and early twenty-first century, cinema representing the favoured locus of the contemporary gothic—is the main focus of this article, in which the issue of space arrangement is viewed from the perspective of a split in the main character's self. If the gothic is to be considered, as Robert Miles claims (1993, 4), "a mode for representations of the fragmented subject," then the contemporary gothic city may be viewed as a space which perfectly reflects liminal characters, functioning both in the gothic and in the familiar dimension of that space. Defining the urban gothic of the nineteenth century, represented by Bram Stoker's

Dracula, Kathleen L. Spencer characterizes it as manifesting "a concern for purity, for the reduction of ambiguity and the preservation of boundaries," which stems from a deeper concern for the "ultimate distinction between self and other" (2004, 310). Contrary to its Victorian forefather, and somewhat in the manner of E. A. Poe's proto-urban tale "The Man of the Crowd," contemporary urban gothic tends to erase this distinction by introducing the main character who represents a "liminal" figure, and by introducing the city as a space in which the gothic and the familiar dimension remain in the state of fusion, one merging into the other, and secrets/evils/supernatural elements circulate in and out freely, permeating the surrounding of the unaware masses.

The gothic setting has undergone numerous transformations since the rise of the gothic novel, allowing for space arrangements to change in accordance with the demands of particular times. According to Manuel Aguirre, the typical eighteenth-century gothic universe encompassed two spheres: the familiar and the unfamiliar/gothic, joined, but at the same time clearly separated by a threshold (2002). Entering the gothic sphere enabled "renewing and heightening a sense of self and social value... [reconstituting] identity against the otherness and loss" (Botting 1996, 9). Victorian gothic, which included the early urban gothic, by insisting on the "modernity of the setting" and its "*identity*" with the world of the reader (Spencer 2004, 307), allowed for the familiar space, such as the city, to be invaded by evil. Thus, as Agnieszka Izdebska points out, the eighteenth-century clear-cut boundary between the familiar and the Other was blurred, and the familiar site changed into a labyrinthine trap, infected with evil which knew no boundaries (2002, 3). The transformation of the setting mirrored a shift in the way of thinking of bourgeoisie and their questioning of Cartesian distinctions (Aguirre 1998, 206). The uncertainty of the stability of recognized norms resulted in the self dissolving, and "the bestial within the human" emerging into sight (Botting 1996, 12). Still, just as Dracula was finally expelled and order/boundaries restored so the split in the self tended to be overcome, and subjectivity—reconstituted.

The city as a gothic scene emerges in a number of the nineteenth-century gothic writings, which focus on the issues of society, order, natural distinctions, purity and reality. Botting proposes G. W. Reynold's *Mysteries of London* (1945-8) as the representative of the urban gothic, and points to the presence of gothic traits in numerous novels set in the city by Charles Dickens. In both cases, the authors elaborate on the issue of social order, threatened by horrors and tyranny in "the city's labyrinth of immorality" (1996, 125-126). As Botting writes, the "material horrors of social depravity and criminal corruption displayed in Gothic representations of the city, indicate a certain dissatisfaction with the present" (127). Spencer, as she considers Stoker's *Dracula*, states that it repeats the nineteenth-century "drive to purify the inside and expel the foreign pollution," thus reflecting "the cultural crisis Britain experienced between 1880 and 1914" (2004, 314). The struggle to preserve the boundaries between self and other may also be observed in Stevenson's *The Strange Case of Dr Jekyll and Mr. Hide*, which Allan Lloyd-Smith perceives as one of the novels which develop the possibilities of urban setting most fully. For him, these possibilities are, nevertheless, sensed much earlier, in a short story by Edgar Alan Poe, "The Man of the Crowd," which he views as a "foretaste of urban Gothic" (2008, 115).

Contemporary urban gothic—or the gothic utilizing urban setting— owns much to its predecessors. Still, it eradicates the boundary between the familiar and the unfamiliar, the inside and the outside, self and other, portraying the city as a space in which immorality of elites (or criminals, or supernatural invaders) does not "enmesh" the behaviour of the masses (Botting 1996, 125), but is generated by the masses themselves, and, as such, has the power to penetrate the surrounding in an unconstrained manner. It is in this sense that the space arrangement of a contemporary gothic city resembles that of Poe's London in the afore-mentioned short story.

While the space of the Victorian gothic city remains a space arranged according to boundaries—even if blurred—Poe's proto-urban gothic story is set in a space in which boundaries seem to be none, and which is permeated by evil accumulating in the person of one old man, who becomes the city's circulating centre. Initially, the plot of "The Man of the Crowd" concentrates on the narrator—an American convalescent—and the "decrepit old man" (Poe, par. 13), who suddenly attracts the narrator's attention. As the plot develops and the narrator follows the man, two other significant characters emerge in the background: the crowd and the city, closely connected with each other and the character of the old man. As the narrator travels around London, he reports how the city changes in each of the districts, and how the crowd changes accordingly. Yet, what is interesting is the fact that there are no descriptions of physical boundaries between the districts—each turn, each lane, each deserted by-street leads to another place where people gather. The city is one, and so is the crowd, even if the masses may be easily classified into different social groups. Only the old man escapes classification, his garments combining signs of wealth and comfort with those of a beggar's misery. Unclassified, he remains outside the society but, at the same time, represents all of its classes. His aura manifests "[a]ll the qualities of the promiscuous urban throng," which Lloyd-Smith interprets as "suggestive of the dangers of democracy" (2008, 115). Vast mental power, caution, penuriousness, avarice, coolness, malice, etc. (Poe, par. 13), designate the darker face of the crowd, and support the narrator's assumption that the man is "the type and the genius of deep crime" (Poe, par. 20). Thus, the man becomes the abject as described by Julia Kristeva. "[R]adically excluded" (Kristeva 1982, 2), like refuse and corpse, he represents—accumulates, in a sense— what the crowd "thrusts aside" (3) in the space of the city. On the one hand, he is noticed only by the narrator—a liminal figure as well, an outsider capable of distinguishing the man from the crowd and defining the sort of crimes the man has committed. At the same time, he proves a circulating city centre, "[t]he worst heart of the world" (Poe, par. 20), which is only seemingly excluded as it needs the masses to sustain itself as much as the masses need it to survive.

As in "The Man of the Crowd," in contemporary gothic fiction the urban space proves a space which encompasses both spheres of Aguirre's traditional gothic universe, but allows them to merge one into the other up to a point at which they become inseparable from each other. The contemporary gothic city is a familiar site, a common dwelling of masses; still, it is penetrated by evils/criminals/supernatural beings—all possible incarnation of the other—that represent external projections of the sins of the inhabitants of the city. In such a city, otherness originates inside.

Anne Rice's *The Vampire Lestat* is a conspicuous example of a novel which introduces urban space as a space where the boundary between the familiar and the gothic is absent. The city—a powerful symbol of the shift from Cartesian distinctions to postmodern denial of distinctions as such— is juxtaposed with the typical gothic scenery, such as the one described in the beginning of the article. Traditional gothic settings, separated from the world of the mortals by clear-cut boundaries, represent imposed rules and divisions between men and women, aristocracy and peasantry, the living and the dead. By contrast, the city is a site where an aristocrat becomes an actor, and a vampire runs a theatre—distinctions cultivated in the past are suspended. The city becomes the vampire's favourite hunting ground, a place where bloodsuckers mix with the crowd unrecognized, lure their victims in disguise of most compelling humans. The lair of the vampire community, e.g. the Parisian theatre or New Orlean's pub, is not a remote gothic spot, but an inseparable part of the familiar, which remains undiscovered by and large due to the unawareness, ignorance or disbelief of the living (Rice 2002).

The ignorance of the masses, or their inability to distinguish between the other and themselves, is a recurring phenomenon in the contemporary urban gothic. In *The Crow* (1994), Sergeant Albrecht makes friends with the daughter of a waitress who is the lover of a member of the T-Bird's gang. The same waitress serves the gang in the very same club in which Erick Draven, murdered by the gang, used to perform. Detroit—gloomy, rainy and full of Gothic decorations—is home both the police and anarchists but they never happen to meet eye to eye despite the fact that they walk in the same streets. In Ridley Scott's *Blade Runner* (1982), Replicants can be distinguished from humans only with the help of sophisticated equipment. If not recognized, they mix with the crowd which is itself a mixture of different social and ethnic groups with ease. In *Sin City* (2005), a film which presents the world in which overt sin is the norm, individuals who are not thoroughly black-and-white—who hide something, like the policeman who betrays his partner or the prostitute who lies to her mother—are indistinguishable from the masses in the eyes of black-and-white characters. In Norrington's *Blade* (1998), secret vampire communities maintain active cooperation with human individuals (represented by Faithfulls, whose desire is to become vampires) and institutions (the police, scientific circles, governmental organizations). The vampire and the human sphere are congenial, yet not many humans are aware of this fact—those who are have become outcasts. To unmask the conspiracy is to find oneself in the liminal position and discover that the familiar sphere is much more than it seems on the surface. That is why, in each of the afore-mentioned films, those who acknowledge the existence of the gothic sphere condemn themselves to the liminal existence.

In a way, the inability to distinguish oneself from the other—or the inability to notice the other—confirms the statement that the gothic city embraces both the other (the unfamiliar) and the self (the familiar) since otherness originates inside. The gothic city absorbs what is abjected, expelled from the consciousness of those who live in it. In such a city, secrets, crimes, malevolence, etc—in other words, all the vices inherent in "the bestial within the human," which is necessarily eradicated in order to preserve the boundary between the self and other and save the self from splitting in the earlier gothic fiction—originate from the masses of inhabitants. Once expelled, they are projected on the outside, giving birth to the figures of villains, who remain unnoticed until they take action to be seen. Burton's *Batman* leaves little doubt about the "promiscuity" of the people of Gotham. Their "ultimate sin" is greed, manifested through the crowd's readiness to support criminals for money. Primitive instincts of the crowd emerge into sight once triggered, confirm its dubious nature, and explain why Gotham is so fertile a ground to the seed of corruption and crime.

Once evil is projected onto the outside, it invariably returns into the inside. That is why Joker torments the people of Gotham with his range of deadly cosmetics that can kill anybody, anywhere, at any time, and representing evil which knows no boundaries since it originates from the familiar. Thus, the permanent relationship between self and other is established. The other originates inside (human self) and is discarded and projected onto the outside (the criminal/monster/psychopath). Then, it returns from the outside to incite revulsion and terror among the masses. As a result, it will penetrate into the insides of individuals, who will acquire the status of the liminal figures—those, who consciously function in both dimensions of the city space, and are inside and outside at the same time, their subjectivity reflected by the space of city.

The liminal figures are typically represented by the main characters. Erick Draven, the main character of *The Crow*, returns from his grave as a dark avenger as a result of the gang's prior killing him and raping his fiancée, Shelley. With the help of the crow, he is the only person able to detect the gang. Hence, he proves to function in the gothic dimension. At the same time, he cooperates with Albrech and his friend in the familiar. Burton's character of Bruce Wayne functions in the same way—he is Batman because, as a child, he witnessed his parents being shot by the young Jocker. Deckard, the main character of *Blade Runner*, is most successful as a Blade Runner, but, at the same time, he may be a Replicant himself.

By embracing both the familiar and the gothic/secret, the city proves the reflection of liminal characters. Though its space encompasses two dimensions which used to be clearly separated in the urban gothic of the Victorians, it is not fragmented but constitutes a whole. The same refers to the main characters. As the liminal figures, they comprise both the human and the beast; their selves split, but at the same time they represent a new concept of completeness. Initially struggling to define themselves as belonging to one of the dimensions, the characters most often finally accept their liminal status. Such is the case of e.g. Rice's Lestat. Dead, yet still in love with life, craving attention, yet forced to remain unnoticed, he does not reject any of his contradictory natures. He relishes vampiric undeath, at the same time striving to live the human life that that he was deprived of against his will.

As the liminal figure, the protagonist follows, traces and chases the gothic elements in the space of the city. S/he moves from the familiar to the gothic—from the inside to the outside—and the other way round, thus repeating the motion of the other. However, neither entering the dimension of the unfamiliar, nor returning into the familiar sphere allow for regaining the previous status or eradicating the split. On the contrary, the split can be overcome only by being accepted. Being both good and evil, part of the society and an outsider, one can only choose to become "the guardian of knowledge," alienated even if physically present in both spheres. Thus, eventually, Deckard will be chased by Blade Runners like the Replicants who used to be chased by him. Wayne will never cease to be Batman. In *The Dark Knight* (2008), it is he who will finally become the ultimate criminal—the bearer of the secret of Two Faces. Thus, he will save the people of Gotham not from the criminal underworld, but from themselves. Aware that human nature has two faces, one just, the other—monstrous, Wayne will accept the status of the monster to save the faith in ultimate justice, and crystal-clean individuals. Disclosing the true identity of Batman will never become possible, since it would equal disclosing that every individual comprises both self and other, good and evil, and thus may change from a police officer into a criminal any minute. Similarly, Blade will continue his fight with the vampires, feared and rejected by the society which he strives to protect. What will happen to him after he eventually succeeds in *Blade Trinity* (....) is not known—but the fact he will remain the only carrier of the vampire virus is telling.

While in earlier gothic texts the split of the self is feared and rejected, and double identity emerges as a matter to be concealed and necessarily eradicated before one re-enters the respectable society, the discussed contemporary gothic texts introduce a subject who is not meant to eradicate the split, or reject one of the two identities, even if it leads to his or her alienation, or condemns him or her to a double-life. Just as the city proves to be a whole in spite of, or perhaps on the grounds of being inhabited by both the ordinary citizens who function in the familiar space, and the outcasts who function in the gothic dimension, the described characters represent traumatized individuals who are nevertheless most complete, comprising the qualities of both groups of inhabitants, and lacking no type of experience. Analyzing the intricacies of contemporary popular culture, often described as gothic, Alexandra Warwick argues that "[i]n the contemporary experience the anxiety is not of fragmentation, but of wholeness, the sense that subjectivity is in fact not complete *unless* it has been in some way damaged" (2007, 12). Since, as has been mentioned in the beginning of this article, the change of gothic setting—its space and arrangement—usually mirrors the changes taking place on the cultural and social level, perhaps it is this demand for a new completeness that the discussed texts are all symptomatic of, and that is reflected by the arrangement of the space of contemporary gothic cities.

References

Aguirre, Manuel. 1998. On Victorian Horror. In *Gothic Horror: A Reader's Guide from Poe to King and Beyond*, ed. by Clive Bloom, 199–232. London, New York: St. Martin's Press. Originally published in *The Closed Space: Horror Fiction and Western Symbolism* (Manchester: Manchester University Press, 1990).

—. 2002. Geometria strachu: Wykorzystanie przestrzeni w literaturze gotyckiej, trans. by Agnieszka Izdebska. In *Wokół gotycyzmów: wyobraźnia, groza, okrucieństwo*, ed. by Grzegorz Gazda, Agnieszka Izdebska and Jarosław Płuciennik, 15-32. Kraków: Universitas.

Botting, Fred. 1996. *Gothic.* London/New York: Routledge.

Izdebska, Agnieszka. 2002. Gotyckie labirynty. In *Wokół gotycyzmów: wyobraźnia, groza, okrucieństwo*, ed. by Grzegorz Gazda, Agnieszka Izdebska and Jarosław Płuciennik, 33-42. Kraków: Universitas.

Kristeva, Julia. 1982. *Powers of Horror: An Essay on Abjection,* trans. by Leon S. Roudiez. New York: Columbia University Press.

Lloyd-Smith, Allan. 2008. Nighteenth-Century American Gothic. In *A Companion to the Gothic*, ed. by David Punter, 109-121. Malden, Oxford: Blackwell.

Miles, Robert. 1993. *Gothic Writing 1750-1820: A Genealogy.* Manchester: Manchester University Press.

Poe, Edgar Allan. 2008. The Man of the Crowd. In *The Works of Edgar Allan Poe.* Vol. 5 of the Raven Edition, http://www.gutenberg.org/files/2151/2151-h/2151-h.htm#2H_4_0005.

Rice, Anne. 2002. The Vampire Lestat. In *The Vampire Chronicles Collection.* Vol. 1, 1-481. New York: Ballantine Books.

Spencer, Kathleen L. 2004. Purity and Danger: *Dracula*, the Urban Gothic, and the late Victorian degeneracy crisis. In *Nineteenth-Century Gothic: At Home with the Vampire.* Vol. 3 of *Gothic: Critical Concepts in Literary and Cultural Studies*, ed. by Fred Botting and Dale Townshend, 304-330. London/ New York: Routledge. Originally published in *English Literary History* 59 (1992): 197-225.

Warwick, Alexandra. 2007. Feeling Gothicky? *Gothic Studies* 9/I: 5-15.

Films

Burton, Tim (dir.). 1998. *Batman.* DVD. Burbank: Warner Home Video.

Goyer, David S. (dir.). 2005. *Blade: Trinity.* Burbank: Warner Home Video.

Nolan, Christopher (dir.). 2008. *The Dark Knight*. Burbank: Warner Home Video.

Norrington, Stephen (dir.). 2009. DVD. *Blade—Wieczny Łowca*. Warszawa: Monolith Video.

Proyas, Alex (dir.). 2003. *Kruk [The Crow]*. DVD. Warszawa: Imperial.

Rodriguez, Robert and Frank Miller (dirs.). 2005. *Sin City*. DVD. New York: Dimension Films.

Scott, Ridley (dir.). 2007. *Blade Runner: The Final Cut Special Edition*. Burbank: Warner Home Video.

CHAPTER THIRTY-EIGHT

NOTTING HILL'S CALYPSO TENT: HOW SPACE AFFECTS PERFORMANCE

MAGDA KONOPKA

1. Introduction

This paper is concerned with demonstrating how space in both its geographic and physical dimensions may influence cultural practices. As observed by Mike Crang, an attempt to turn "space" into "place" is a common strategy of identity-making processes as "people do not simply locate themselves, they define themselves through a sense of place" (2005, 102). The practices described in the paper are those associated with calypso singing in the United Kingdom, which is used as a case study to raise more general questions concerning the significance of space(s) emergent in the wake of transnational migration and globalisation processes for people's identification as well the conceptualisation of their cultural heritage. To this end, the paper draws on the analysis of ethnographic interviews with major British calypsonians conducted by the author in 2008 in order to outline a brief history of calypso's presence in Britain and discuss the issues surrounding the activity of the London Calypso Tent as well as its significance for local community.

Firstly, an attempt at defining the musical genre of calypso deriving from the Caribbean island of Trinidad and Tobago is made. Secondly, the paper proceeds to discuss the status of calypso in London and describes the main institutions responsible for the popularisation and safeguarding of this genre in Britain. Furthermore, it demonstrates how the change of venue of the annual calypso performances which took place in 2008 may be discussed in the context of "heritage gentrification." Finally, it puts these observations in perspective by demonstrating how global rules of market economy result in culture commodification.

2. Calypso's subversive potential

Calypso, which is regarded as "national treasure" in Trinidad, may be approached from a variety of perspectives. At the beginning of her chapter on British calypso, Tina K. Ramnarine provocatively plays on this proliferation by offering a few simple statements: "Calypso is a prominent Caribbean song genre associated with Trinidad and Tobago. Calypso is a British folk music. Calypso is a commercially recorded, globally marketed genre" (2007, 42). Indeed, all of the above are true of today's calypso, which is poised between its indigenous roots and the forces of global music market. The matter of calypso's origin is also a complex one, since, as pointed out by carnival specialist Peter Mason, it has its roots in a mixture of traditions including African, Hispanic, British and Irish (1998, 20-21.)

Its beginning dates back to the days when slaves used songs as a means of communication. For this reason, even nowadays it remains strongly political. To demonstrate calypso's subversive potential, Dick Hebdige quotes a passage from Alex Haley's novel *Roots* featuring the book's young protagonist Kunta Kinte, an African boy kidnapped by white slavers. In the episode the white crew of the slave ship, who decide to put on an impromptu performance using concertinas and African drums, force the stunned enslaved Africans to dance. On seeing them petrified and confused, the slavers, called by the enslaved "toubob," reach for their whips. However, an old African woman manages to mobilise her compatriots:

> "Jump!" shouted the oldest woman suddenly in Mandinka. She began jumping herself. "Jump!" she cried shrilly again, glaring at the girls and children, and they jumped as she did. "Jump to kill the toubob!" she shrieked, her quick eyes flashing at the naked men, her arms and hands darting in the movements of the warrior's dance. (...) Then the singing of the woman was joined by the girls. It was a happy sound, but the words they sang told how these terrible toubob had taken every woman into the dark corners of the canoe each night and used them like dogs. "Toubob fa!" (kill toubob) they shrieked with smiles and laughter. The naked, jumping men joined in: "Toubob fa!" Even the toubob were grinning now, some of them clapping their hands with pleasure. (quoted in: Hebdige 1994, 28)

In the opinion of Hebdige, this account, although an imaginary one, is helpful in conceptualising both the present and the past meaning of Caribbean music. According to the scholar, it demonstrates that Caribbean music "was the result of two different traditions—the African and the

European—the meeting here of drums and concertinas. Most modern pop and rock, jazz, blues, soul and even reggae can be traced back to that blending of black and white forms" (Hebdige 1994, 28). He goes on to state that the episode skilfully demonstrates another feature of Caribbean music i.e. its ostensive lightness and cheerfulness. However, as Hebdige observes, "underneath the harmonies and the bright, happy rhythms you can often hear those other voices—the angry threatening voices of the slaves and their descendants—the 'rebel sound' of people seeking freedom or revenge" (1994, 28).

The remembrance of the difficult period from which calypso emerged seems to prove of relevance to contemporary performers. Brown Sugar, one of the leading female calypsonians originally from Trinidad, commented on calypso's origins set in the dark days of slavery in the following way:

> When you look back at the history of calypso, it started off when slaves weren't allowed to speak to each other. And they started singing in order to relate how they feel or what they were about to do, or what they were doing. So it's a form of social commentary, a form of informing somebody regarding political situation. (...) And you see it as a vehicle to express your emotions and your take on certain subjects. So yes, it's something very deep to me. (I 5) [1]

As can be seen, Brown Sugar uses the words "social commentary" to describe the role of calypso and the calypsonian who may be viewed as a modern day trickster-like critic of the world's madness, mercilessly exposing nonsense of his or her immediate social context. British calypsonian Alexander D Great identified with this social role and explained it in a following way:

> In the old days, a guy would sit in a rum shop and whatever was going on in the world, he would sing about it. People didn't read and write so you went to the rum shop to find out what was going on in the world. It's usually the calypsonian who, like the Fool in Shakespeare plays, is the most intelligent person. He plays the part of coming from the gutter. The people from the ruling classes look down on him. Especially if he's a true calypsonian, he's gonna be subversive. He's gonna be like Bob Dylan and John Lennon. And Bob Marley. (I 3)

In fulfilment of his role, in the calypso season of 2008, Alexander D Great performed a calypso entitled "Sweet Dominica," in which he

---

[1] The list of interviews quoted in the text is available at the end of the article.

criticised the project proposing the construction of an oil refinery in Dominica. Alexander sang in the chorus:

> Sweet Dominica, you beautiful island
> Shining like a diamond in the Caribbean sea.
> The vultures are gathering to destroy your beauty
> Please do your duty and set yourself free.
> Please do your duty and set yourself free (© Alexander Loewenthal)

This example of political commentary was elaborated upon by the author in the following way:

> This year I'm all fired up about Dominica talked into an oil refinery they don't need. And that's my song. Win, lose, tie, I don't care, I don't give monkeys if I come last. That's not the point. I want the people here to hear about Dominica. I want them to go on Google and say: "What's happening in Dominica? Hey, I never knew that!" I want Dominicans who live here to think about it. (I 3)

As can be seen, ever since its very birth, calypso has had a significant social role to play. It is for this reason that performers are strongly committed to what they consider their vocation. However, this is not to say that calypsonians see themselves as puritanical guardians of the audience's morale, as it needs to be remembered that no matter how serious message they convey, calypsos are never devoid of humour or double entendre. As observed by Dick Hebdige quoted above, the duality marked by cheerfulness and seriousness seems to be a characteristic feature of all Caribbean music.

3. Calypso and London's Notting Hill Carnival

This typically Trinidadian sound arrived in Britain together with the first wave of Caribbean immigrants. Its popularity is said to have spread with the arrival of two masters of this song genre, Lord Kitchener and Lord Beginner on board HM Windrush in 1948, who played in clubs and bars of London with much commercial success (Hall 2002). During the 1960s and the 1970s the genre in Britain was practised by the first generation of immigrants from the Caribbean, mainly from Trinidad. Lord Cloak, one of the most experienced calypsonians of the London Calypso Tent, who came to Britain in 1964, thus described his story:

> Well, I started composing my own songs back in Trinidad but back in those days a little boy could not go into a calypso tent as well as we could

not go into a steelband yard, the pan. So we used to make up songs but our mother didn't know. And I remember I made up a song on my mother. And I went in a tent and I sang this song. And I get a big reception, very, very good. But then the woman came to me around. I ran away. (laughing) Well, I wouldn't run now. (I 4)

In this statement, which yet again emphasises calypso's subversiveness, Lord Cloak remarks that performances in the so-called calypso tents were not considered respectable and therefore were not regarded as something appropriate for a young person. However, calypso tents enjoy considerable popularity in Trinidad, especially in the period leading to the all-encompassing Trinidadian Carnival, the national fete of the Trinis.

In London, calypso has been associated with the Notting Hill Carnival taking place every year on the last weekend of August in one of the most interesting spaces of London: the northern part of the Royal Borough of Kensington and Chelsea. The Carnival, which started as a local initiative in mid-1960s in what was then known as a run-down and impoverished area, has flourished into what we may observe now: a multicultural festival, in which the Caribbean flavour is still predominant, yet transformed by the requirements of market economy (Cohen 1993). The most popular Carnival disciplines are mas (costume section), stationary and moving sound systems, which play a variety of music genres from soca to reggae, dub and house as well as steelbands, i.e. orchestras made up of musicians playing steel pans.. All these disciplines are visible and audible on the Carnival route and the orchestras have an additional opportunity to display their musical talents during the event now taking place in Hyde Park on a Saturday before Carnival, which is known as PANorama.

However, calypso, the fifth traditional discipline of Carnival, remains relatively unknown to the general public. Moreover, without the considerable support from sponsors received e.g. by certain mas bands or steel orchestras, calypso is the least commercialised Carnival discipline. Calypso artists are represented by the Association of British Calypsonians (ABC), which proclaims itself to be "Europe's only representative body for British-based calypso singers and composers" (Yaa Annual Report 2008, 25). The ABC, headed by calypsonian the Mighty Tiger, and the London Calypso Tent were established in 1991. However, even before this date calypso contests were held in London but the capital lacked a formalised organisation. Yaa Asantewaa Arts and Community Centre, an important centre for Caribbean arts established in 1978, provided the ABC with a performance space, where it remained for 17 consecutive years. The Calypso Tent at Yaa was much loved by the audience although it provided only basic amenities. Uncomfortable plastic chairs, stage not big enough to fit all the musicians and backing singers or the lack of air conditioning noticeable already at the beginning of a five-hour show, were some of the inconveniences which the audience learnt to come to terms with over the years. The relative shabbiness of the venue was compensated for by unforgettable, almost homely atmosphere. Yaa was and has remained a place where all those interested in the art of carnival may be certain to receive a warm welcome from volunteers and organisers working there.

4. Performance rules and migration of the Tent

The atmosphere during calypso concerts is characterised by relaxed and unconstrained camaraderie. However, despite the laid-back feeling, the performance is far from being a spontaneous gathering of calypso enthusiasts as it follows a carefully designed scenario repeated every year. The calypso season preceding the Notting Hill Carnival is made up of 6 performances taking place on Fridays and, in the case of the Calypso Monarch competition, on a Thursday just before the Carnival weekend. However, the calypso season of 2008 saw a major change in the organisation of the ABC, associated with the set-up of a new capital partnership known as Carnival Village. In the words of its CEO, Shabaka Thompson:

> Carnival Village will be a flagship cultural venue for the delivery of high quality black arts. It will encourage, train and nurture artists, and also support the development of carnival-related creative industries. Aiming to stimulate and foster the economic and cultural well-being of the communities it serves, its goal will, in essence, be to develop the arts and business of carnival (2007, 59)

The new project managed by four organisations: the ABC, Yaa Asantewaa as well as Mangrove and Ebony steelbands and located at the Tabernacle, a former church and community centre, was not officially open during the 2008 carnival season. However, it was decided that the Calypso Tent will be the first cycle of events to take place under the auspices of the Carnival Village. As a result, the performance venue was moved from the Yaa Asantewaa Community Centre situated off Harrow Road to the new home of Carnival Village in Powis Square at the very centre of Notting Hill.

The new venue appeared much more elegant and "respectable" than its less impressive predecessor. It was to be expected that the change would have an impact on both the performers and the audience. Calypsonians tended to observe that they needed more time to become accustomed to the new venue, as it was bigger and had different acoustics. To most of them the space also seemed unwelcoming:

> It doesn't feel like a tent. The old place felt like a tent. In Trinidad the tents are buildings like the Yaa Asantewaa. They're old, they tumble down, they're usually converted or they're something left over from another building that no one's using. And that creates the feeling of reclamation of recycling for the people. This smacks of a high class theatre and the price has gone up 33% as a consequence and I think that's why people aren't coming as many as we should have. Plus the atmosphere is not there (I 3)

Calypsonian Helena B. supports this view by saying:

> Because we stayed a lot of time in the Yaa, we're not used to here yet. Maybe by next year or so we'll start to get used to here…This year is like "ooooohh" [shuddering a little] we're getting the feel out, you know. We preferred the Yaa. Because we were used to the Yaa, we knew everything in the Yaa, but here is like strange. Maybe next year things will be better. (I 2)

Carnival Village's CEO Shabaka Thompson was aware of the change brought about by the decision to perform at the Tabernacle. As he explained to me:

> In my community, no matter what you do, you can't please everybody. (…) I have heard comments "Nicer venue, higher price". Because the price increases, this place costs a lot, you know. It's a bigger space than Yaa. These are the comments people feed back to me indirectly and directly. And people are still getting used to this Calypso Tent. You know, Yaa that vibe, that over 17 years developed a kind of rhythm known to Yaa, at Yaa everyone was close to one another, all in one place. Here is order, you come in, you pay, you're downstairs, you're told to come upstairs, then you come back down, you have to come back to have a drink and you go back. But, you know, it's a theatre. (I1)

This statement definitely demonstrates that the Association considers itself prepared to begin a new phase in its development. One calypsonian suggested that it would be advisable if calypso nights could have a similar status as e.g. a West End show, for which "people will queue up and pay 35-75 pounds" (I 5). The symbolic move from a venue in the vicinity of the impoverished Harrow Road to the gentrified area of Notting Hill means that there has occurred a break-through in the approach to the marketing of this kind of music. It is not my intention to exaggerate the importance of the change but it is interesting to consider its implications for the future of calypso in Britain. It seems that this "upgrading" movement resulting from the Tent's migration to the heart of Notting Hill may be viewed as a manifestation of what may be called "heritage gentrification." Of course the term "gentrification" is usually employed while referring to processes characteristic of urban spaces, in which neighbourhoods undergo alterations caused by the change of social structure of its inhabitants. As Graham Martin points out, "gentrification is seen as a concurrent symbolic and material recasting of a neighbourhood in accordance with the dominant tastes of the incoming groups. (…) The local incumbent population is disenfranchised from this recasting, and so the re-imaging of such areas represents a violent imposition of a dominant perspective of place" (2005, 67). Drawing on these observations, it seems justified to use the term "gentrification" to symbolically refer to the changes that heritage may undergo as a result of commercialisation. It is not clear which direction the heritage of calypso in Britain will head to. However, with the help of the ABC members' flexible attitude, calypso will neither be stifled by commercialism nor forgotten by the unappreciative audience.

5. Conclusion

As the paper attempted to demonstrate, the change of performance venue may affect the future of British calypso in London. It may be observed that official documents produced by the Association of British Calypsonians, in which the organisation explains the motives behind the creation of the new partnership reflect the newspeak characteristic of the discourse of multiculturalism. This could suggest that this sudden rise in ambition experienced by the ABC, may have been caused by the discourse dominant in the British culture sector, which tends to promote entrepreneurship and capital gains. However, it needs to be observed that this process is not unique to Britain as it has been witnessed for many years in Trinidad, where calypso has become a prominent sector of economy. As stated by calypso specialist Gordon Rohlehr, "market forces have steadily pushed calypso toward commodification, teaching singers to do for profit what their ancestors did for fun, entertainment, relaxation, edification, or self-knowledge. Synchronized now to the heavy life-pulse of a so-called 'world music,' calypso has emerged beyond the confines of its original small communities" (1998, 82).

However, there are reasons to believe that the future looks bright. Shabaka Thompson, who agrees that the new venue is much more "respectable" than the previous "Tent," stated: "Yes, it's more regulated like any mainstream venue. I think people like that. People appreciate this kind of etiquette in terms of a space. But we like the hooligan thing too. (laughing)" And it is this final remark which seems to ensure that the heritage of calypso will not be fossilised or taken over by the mainstream culture.

References

Cohen, Abner. 1993. *Masquerade Politics: Explorations in the Structure of Urban Cultural Movements*. Oxford/Providence: Berg.

Crang, Mike. 2005. Place or Space? *Cultural Geography*. London: Routledge.

Haley, Alex. 1992. *Roots: The Saga of an American Family*. Doubleday Books.

Hall, Stuart. 2002. Calypso Kings, *The Guardian*, www.guardian.co.uk/culture/2002/jun/28/nottinghillcarnival2002.nottinghillcarnival, (accessed 10 September 2008).

Hebdige, Dick. 1994. *Cut'n'Mix: Culture, Identity and Caribbean Music*. London/New York: Routledge.

Martin, Graham P. 2005. Narratives Great and Small: Neighbourhood Change, Place and Identity in Notting Hill, *International Journal of Urban and Regional Research*, vol. 29.1, 67-88.

Mason, Peter. 1998. *Bacchanal! The Carnival Culture of Trinidad*. London: Latin America Bureau.

Ramnarine, Tina K. 2007. *Beautiful Cosmos: Performance and Belonging in the Caribbean Diaspora*. London/Ann Arbor, MI: Pluto Press.

Rohlehr, Gordon. 1998 "We Getting the Kaiso That We Deserve": Calypso and the World Music Market, *The Drama Review* 42 (3): 82-95.

Thompson, Shabaka. 2007. Carnival Village, *Notting Hill Carnival Grooves*, August, 58-59.

Yaa Asantewaa Arts and Community Centre (2008). *Annual Report 2007-2008*.

Interviews

I 1.Interview with Shabaka Thompson, CEO of Carnival Village, (August 14, 2008);

I 2. Interview with calypsonian Helena B, (August 15, 2008);

I 3. Interview with calypsonian Alexander D Great, (August 21, 2008);

I 4. Interview with calypsonian Lord Cloak, (August 21, 2008);
I 5. Interview with calypsonian Brown Sugar, (August 22, 2008).

CHAPTER THIRTY-NINE

SPATIAL METAPHORS IN THE QUEST FOR IDENTITY: DAVID DABYDEEN'S *DISAPPEARANCE*

BOŻENA KUCAŁA

In *The Location of Culture* the leading postcolonial critic Homi Bhabha claimed: "[...] we find ourselves in the moment of transit where space and time cross to produce complex figures of difference and identity, past and present, inside and outside, inclusion and exclusion" (1998, 1). According to Bhabha, the archetypal modern figure is the migrant living in a transitional space where cultural differences permanently clash. In order to describe the interaction between cultures in the era of mass migration, Homi Bhabha has proposed the concept of cultures (in the plural) in relational terms—rather than being self-contained entities separated and differentiated from one another by clear-cut boundaries, cultures are perceived as inevitably interconnected and intercontaminated, alike and different simultaneously:

> It is in the emergence of the interstices—the overlap and displacement of domains of difference—that the intersubjective and collective experiences of *nationness*, community interest, or cultural value are negotiated. How are subjects formed "in-between," or in excess of, the sum of the "parts" of difference (usually intoned as race/class/gender, etc.)? How do strategies of representation or empowerment come to be formulated in the competing claims of communities where, despite shared histories of deprivation and discrimination, the exchange of values, meanings and priorities may not always be collaborative and dialogical, but may be profoundly antagonistic, conflictual and even incommensurable? (1998, 2)

Bhabha posits the existence of an "in-between" space, signifying the site of conflict and interaction, a fluid, contested territory which he terms "the third space" so as to emphasise its evasion of binary divisions.

I want to argue that the unnamed protagonist of David Dabydeen's *Disappearance*, whose identity exemplarily fluctuates between not just two but at least three cultures—involving different geographical locations, notions of race, nations and colour—inhabits a space in-between fixed designations of identity.

The fiction of David Dabydeen has invariably been constructed around his own experience of migration. His characters travel between England, India, Africa and the Caribbean. Dabydeen was born and brought up in Guyana, and perceives himself as a member of the large group of Caribbean writers who arrived in England after the Second World War. Not only his fiction and poetry, but also his academic career centre on his West Indian background.

Even though he was only fourteen on arrival, Dabydeen admits that his self-image continues to be shaped by the experience of moving between the two countries rather than full identification with either. In an interview, he explained:

> I have no problem in calling myself an immigrant. Even though I'm settled here, I was once an immigrant [...] The non-writing part of me, the restrained part of me is Britain. The imaginative part of me is Guyana. But then one can't have these easy dichotomies either; but you know what I mean, there are grey areas as well. (in Nasta 2004, 232-233)

Disappearance draws on autobiographical material, portraying a young Guyanese engineer arriving in England and forming his identity in relation to both places. But apart from the double pull of opposing lands there are, as Dabydeen said about himself, "grey areas" in his experience as well.

The novel is the protagonist's first-person account. He comes to England to assist in a project to shore up a cliff in the Kent village of Dunsmere which is being eroded by the sea. The engineering work done, he goes back to his home country. The boundary between the land and the sea, apart from the obviously literal meaning in the context of the action, generates metaphors in terms of which the protagonist tries to delineate his own position. Predictably, the land connotes fixity and solidity while the sea stands for wildness, uncontrollability, constant change, although on closer inspection this straightforward binarism becomes more complex. In the novel, stress is put on the dividing line and hence on the (fluid) opposition of the two spheres. As in "Dover Beach," the sea in *Disappearance* disturbs the narrator, confusing and frightening him. In frequent interchanges of literal and metaphorical meanings, the sea constitutes a permanent threat to the land, which has to be laboriously protected by a conscious human effort. The narrator's arrival in Kent forces him to confront the significance of the constant clash of stability and fluidity; he is physically and figuratively on (the) edge. Or, to explore another dimension of the metaphor, he is compelled to abandon the surface and acknowledge the unfathomable depth whose existence he has studiously denied.

The beginning of the narration finds him in England, already engaged in his task, and conversing with his landlady, Mrs Rutherford, after work. This opening *in medias res* corresponds to the narrator's tendency to insist on realising his identity in the here and now, in the process of performing his job, which is accompanied by deliberate renunciation of the past and of the places that have previously influenced him. Adhering to what is visible, calculable, knowable was his intuitive reason for making engineering his profession. It is only now, while looking back on his youth, that he begins to understand the psychological mechanism that determined his decisions. His chief dilemma is verbalised in a conversation with Mrs Rutherford: "'It's the future that matters,' I continued, struggling to evolve a cogent answer, 'I'm *me*, not a mask or a movement in history. I'm not black, I'm an engineer'" (Dabydeen 1993, 102).

Engineering offers a professional identity, detached from colour, race, country, history; it nullifies time and place. It is the seemingly innocent and conventional question, posed by Mrs Rutherford as to the protagonist's motives in choosing engineering, that sets off a series of reflections. The very first sentence of the book reads: "Why, Mrs Rutherford wanted to know, did I become an engineer?" The intermingling of current episodes with reminiscences about the past is in fact the narrator's indirect, convoluted and evasive response to that spuriously simple enquiry. A more or less complete answer, although expressed only as an internal monologue, comes at the end of the narrative:

> When Mrs Rutherford asked me why I became an engineer I couldn't answer, but deep down I knew a dam was my identity, an obstacle I sought to put between shore and sea to assert my substantialness, my indissoluble presence, without reference to colour, culture or age (132-133).

The spatial metaphor implies that, like in Matthew Arnold's "Dover Beach," it is not only the sea that connotes danger—the narrator tries to turn his back on the land as well, finding temporary refuge in the narrow volatile space in between.

The narrator's identity is not attached to any existing land. In Guyana he was constantly reminded of his blackness and regarded as inferior by members of the Indian-Caribbean population. An especially unsettling experience was overseeing an engineering project in Guyana, prior to the project in England, where the protagonist was simultaneously socially superior to his workers as their manager but racially inferior as a black man. His hopes that his profession would liberate him from racial affiliation proved futile.

But his escape into professionalism had never been racially neutral. Engineering is a foreign science, taught in Guyana by English instructors. The English Professor Fenwick had a formative influence on the engineer-to-be. Self-possessed, always correct in speech and manners, in the narrator's eyes Fenwick becomes an epitome of the true Englishman and simultaneously an attractive role model, radically different from the typical Guyanese whose nature the protagonist portrays as

> by contrast boastful and boisterous: politicians promising more than they could deliver; professionals displaying their status by driving extravagant cars and honking at every cycle or donkey-cart that got in their way; the common traders bawling their wares from street stalls and open markets or haggling for an advantageous sale. (81)

Accordingly, in the narrator's eyes engineering as personified by Professor Fenwick becomes associated with his idea of English life as more civilised, orderly, neat and rational. Therefore in trying to shed his own cultural background, the protagonist does not become culturally neutral—he becomes English-like. The Indian labourers he supervises rightly sense that this is only an assumed pose, quite fragile due to his lack of confidence, which they exploit by constantly provoking him. On the occasion when he reproaches the most unruly worker he is mocked for playing a white man:

> "You better mind your words and not go spreading discontent among my workers, otherwise you will be in trouble," I said, assuming an ominous tone.
> "'My workers,'" he said, "eh-eh, like you act white man, or what? 'My workers' indeed!" (28-29)

In consequence, the protagonist experiences alienation, avoids human company and feels secure only in the abstract world of numbers. His coming of age coincided with Guyanese independence, hence the prospect of his own future naturally blended with imaginings about the future of his country. The protagonist resolutely renounces the country's history, thereby refusing to accept that his own identity has been shaped by a collective past, and instead decides to look ahead and make his contribution by imposing on Guyana the admirable English-style order.

This attempt on his part materialises in a transformation of the physical space. The protagonist's ideal is to bring the wild landscape under control: build roads and houses, cultivate the land, fend off the continuous onslaught of the sea. He shows an ostentatious lack of interest in the colonial history of Guyana; even less is he interested in his African ancestry. However, aspects of contemporary Guyana preclude his full commitment to his native country. While working on his first project on the Guyanese coast, the young engineer again and again comes up against his fellow countrymen's incompetence, laziness, superstition, racial prejudice—manifestations of attitudes that both disgust and discourage him.

Yet the protagonist's yearning for order is also personally motivated. The metaphors used in the description of Professor Fenwick, "half framed behind an oak desk," "anchored steadfastly in the knowledge of his craft," indicate the narrator's own state of flux and the resultant need to find something stable and reliable to hold on to. A number of conflicting forces affect him: he is devoted to his mother yet feels oppressed by her possessive love, he is shy with women yet surprises himself by his sexual violence, he is black and yet resents black people, he wants to improve Guyana but secretly wishes he were English. The job in England, recommended by Professor Fenwick, seems to give him both a chance to escape from his personal turmoil and an opportunity to reach a rock solid point in the land of his dreams.

England's failure to play this role is metaphorically foreshadowed by the contradictory qualities of the English landscape. Superficially, it gives the appearance of perfect human control exercised over the forces of nature. At first sight, the village encapsulates the protagonist's idea of England:

[Generations] settled down, multiplied and prospered within the boundaries they had marked in the land, marks enshrined in law, protecting neighbour from neighbour. Fields of barley and wheat, hedges that defined territory, a stabilised woodland, secluded cottages and a sense of the Law of the Land—this was Dunsmere. (92-93)

However, the village is precariously perched on top of a cliff which will soon collapse, causing this epitome of pastoral England, an officially recognised national heritage site, to disappear. It is his English landlady that makes the protagonist aware of the land's underlying past and unwittingly deprives him of the illusion of its stability: the land is underpinned by its history of violence, territorial wars and the Norman invasion in nearby Hastings that ultimately made England what it is now.

When she once taught children in an African school, she emphasised the bloodshed and barbaric rituals in English history in order to make the children get "a proper sense of our country as being every bit as dark and diseased as we told them theirs was," echoing Marlow in *Heart of Darkness*, to whom London "also has been one of the dark places of the earth" (Conrad 1994, 7). Mrs Rutherford, full of contempt for English complacency and the game of appearances, insists on a hidden layer of turbulence beneath the quiet surface; according to her, as across the whole nation, the respectable villagers have quite ignoble or irregular life stories. Under her influence the protagonist also begins to see that the settled affluent gentility of the Kent coast "follows inevitably from centuries of plunder." Paradoxically, it is the English woman that alerts him to the possible connection between his colonial background and the spurious attractiveness of the English countryside by insisting that English prosperity stems from centuries of colonial exploitation. Mrs. Rutherford takes for granted her lodger's colonial awareness: "But then you would know that first-hand, coming from the colonies."

Ironically, it was evading his colonial affiliation that the protagonist expected on arrival in England. Yet, like in his native Guyana, he is perceived above all as a black man—a role he resists, irrespective of the intentions of those who label him black. The same situation is enacted—his English workers mistrust his authority as an engineer on account of his blackness:

> I was stared at as soon as I approached the camp. Even the bulldozers seemed to cease their whining. It was to be expected. A black man in a striped suit and shiny briefcase walking an English beach at the crack of dawn was bound to be as barbarous a sight as the Normans and Danes who appeared bearing axes in previous centuries. Professor Fenwick in his naïve goodness had obviously not alerted them to my nature. (108)

The only worker who establishes any personal contact with the Guyanese engineer is an Irishman, Christie. Christie treats the black man like a fellow outsider in a foreign land, at the same time, however, displaying unconscious prejudice. For the sake of the Guyanese, he plays the part of an eccentric Irishman, mistakenly assuming that he and the protagonist share a background of folk tales, superstitions and hatred of the English. Mrs Rutherford, although well-intentioned, also casts her lodger in the role of a black man and appeals to his African ancestry. Instead of introducing him to English culture, as he hoped she would, she tries to turn him into an African.

The chief irony is that it is in England that he confronts Africa. Mrs. Rutherford shares with him stories of her stay in Africa, discusses the meaning of rituals and religious artifacts, taking for granted his familiarity with or at least interest in them. While she is fond of the objects, he is repelled by their strangeness, the terror and brutality they seem to embody. He observes the incongruity of the African masks in a building that typically connotes the peaceful English countryside: "Their ugliness was increased considerably by their prominence on the whitewashed walls of this English cottage. As soon as you caught sight of it you thought you were in the presence of a venerable England" (8). Although the narrator claims that as a West Indian he "cultivate[s] no sense of the past," he finds himself responding to the traces of his very distant ancestors. What enables him to resist the appeal of the masks, however, is Mrs. Rutherford's—"so solid in her presence, so seemingly rational, well-mannered—and English"—mediation. Standing on the cliff, he experiences a strong urge to yield to the brutal spirit of the sea and throw himself down. Yet he manages to find a space between the savagery of the sea and the rational solidity of the land:

> I was seduced by the prospect of falling, the exhilaration of wanting to know what it was to die. What was enthralling was the space between wanting to know and the experience itself, which would instantly annihilate all knowledge. It was the space I had put between myself and the African masks... (14)

During the protagonist's stay in England, he gradually loses confidence in the validity of the distinctions he made between England and his own country. In both places he is treated as a black African, much as he would like to deny his African ancestry and ignore the colour of his skin. On a personal level, a parallel is forged between his mother and Mrs. Rutherford. His mother, after being abandoned by her husband, invested all her expectations in him. In a gesture which the narrator regards as symbolic she sold her wedding ring in order to pay for his education, as a result of which he became, in his own words, "wedded to her ambitions." Many aspects of his filial subjection are reenacted in his relationship with Mrs. Rutherford, who, also abandoned by her husband, is both motherly and seductive towards her lodger. Like his mother before, she sends him out among the English like her "black white knight." Her open criticism of her own nation makes her treat the protagonist as an instrument of her private revenge on her fellow Englishmen whose complacency he is supposed to shatter, whereas his own initial intention was exactly opposed to hers—to integrate with the English.

But the English workers turn out to be as work-shy as the Guyanese workers, and progress is disappointingly slow. The accusations of fraud and corruption among the authorities responsible for the project, including Professor Fenwick, further undermine England's supposed superiority, from the protagonist's point of view dissolving the superficial distinctions between the two countries. He realizes quite soon that England could never be his home:

> I felt that I could still not inhabit the place. It was simply not mine. The hills, the fatted sheep, the cottages, the pub, the church, the language preserved and spoken, the manner of dressing body or meat, the gestures made, the looks exchanged, none of these were intrinsic to me [...] It would take centuries for me to grow into the English landscape... (131)

The inevitable collapse of the cliff becomes a metaphor for the decay of England's imperial glory. Yet as the protagonist admits his foreignness, he does not become any more attached to Guyana although he eventually returns there; instead, he becomes disillusioned with England as the paragon of civilised life and grudgingly acknowledges his both obscure and involuntary bond with Africa.

In a survey of West Indian literature Dabydeen and Wilson-Tagoe claim that confrontation with Africa, a major theme of this literature, functions "in a sense as a confrontation with self, a coming to terms with origin and a purging of fear and shame" (1997, 32). Mrs. Rutherford, "the unlikely catalyst of his enlightenment" (Jaggi 1993, 20), has after all succeeded in making the protagonist develop a postcolonial consciousness; however, he concludes that her rebellion against England is misguided—England is hollow, merely a shadow of its former self, so there is nothing to fight against. The reason why he eventually chooses to go to Guyana is not that Guyana has any more substance, but that its empty space holds the promise of something new: "The land was vast and empty enough to encourage new beginnings in obscure corners," tentatively offering the protagonist the possibility of self-invention.

The ultimate failure of his quest for a stable personal space metaphorically corresponds to the protagonist's realisation that the dam he constructs to stabilise and protect the land will only be a temporary accomplishment. The character's search for solidity ends in a failure: as an engineer, he has to acknowledge the power of the sea. But then presumably, on returning to his native country, he will continue to construct provisional dams in the fluid in-between zone, a project which metaphorically represents his ongoing quest for a tenuous sense of selfhood.

References

Arnold, Matthew. 1901. *Poetical Works of Matthew Arnold*. London: Macmillan.

Bhabha, Homi K. 1998. *The Location of Culture*. London/New York: Routledge.

Conrad, Joseph. 1994. *Heart of Darkness*. London: Penguin Books.

Dabydeen, David. 1993. *Disappearance*. London: Secker and Warburg.

Dabydeen, David and Nana Wilson-Tagoe. 1997. *A Reader's Guide to Westindian and Black British Literature*. Revised edition. London: Hansib.

Jaggi, Maya. 1993. David Dabydeen: *Disappearance*: Review. Times Literary Supplement 12 March.

Nasta, Susheila (ed.). 2004. David Dabydeen with Mark Stein: An interview. In *Writing across Worlds: Contemporary Writers Talk*. London: Routledge.

CHAPTER FORTY

HARNESSING URBAN CHAOS

BARBARA LEFTIH

In 1889 Jane Addams founded, in a poor, immigrant district of Chicago, one of the first American settlement houses—Hull House. Settlement houses, manifestations of the Progressive reforms, were institutions which became sites of contact between the "other half", to use Jacob Riis's designation of the destitute, mainly immigrant, population, and the socially and educationally privileged native-born Americans, who volunteered to live in slum areas to act as facilitators of the immigrants' accommodation to the municipal and national structure. Settlement houses, which mushroomed in other American urban centres at the turn of the twentieth century, proved to be valuable incubators of social reforms desperately needed by the country undergoing turbulent social and industrial transformation. Moreover, as many historians point out, the settlement house movement enabled many middle-class educated women, who resided in the institutions, to appropriate part of the cityscape, create new public roles and gain independence.

Addams and other prominent female settlement house reformers, such as Lillian D. Wald, explained their presence in the city by the principles of "civic housekeeping" (Addams 1960, 114). As Daphne Spain states in *How Women Saved the City*, "[a]dvocates of municipal housekeeping promoted similarities between the home and the city, particularly the need for cleanliness and order, as a way to establish their credentials for civic involvement" (Spain 2001, 9). Thus, female reformers of the era, among them settlement house workers, frequently contrasted male and female visions of the city and abilities to manage it. The space settlement house workers, who were mainly female, appropriated in the cities was "'parochial'—the world of the neighborhood as opposed to the totally private world of the household and the completely public realm of strangers" (Spain 2001, 6). Daphne Spain defines various social amelioration centers established by the turn-of-the-century female reformers, among them settlement houses, as "redemptive places", which, as she explains, were "sites of assimilation, both socially and politically, and of moral influence. ... temporary institutions for a society in flux" (Spain 2001, 14). Therefore, the settlement house, whose status was "liminal" as it situated itself between the private and public spheres, had assimilative and regulatory functions. It served as a buffer zone between the city and the deluge of newly arrived immigrants unfamiliar with American customs, laws, and city life (Spain 2001, 24-25). Most importantly, the settlement house movement facilitated the transition of American cities from the period of unregulated capitalism to the period in which it was controlled by appropriate legislation (26-27). Moreover, for a number of female reformers it created a springboard to political functions (70).

This article discusses the settlement house as an urban space created by female reformers for the purposes of social amelioration as presented in Jane Addams's autobiography *Twenty Years at Hull House* (1910) and Lillian D. Wald's *The House on Henry Street* (1915) and *Windows on Henry Street* (1934). In this article I would like to analyse how Addams and Wald, two prominent female settlement house leaders, depicted immigrant districts in large cities, defined the role of settlement houses in the immigrant quarters, presented and negotiated spatial relations between the settlement residents and the changing neighbourhood as well as the settlement house and the city environment, and finally what change, according to the above mentioned reformers, was instigated in the neighborhoods and cities by the institutions they created.

The first pages and chapters of Addams's and Wald's accounts of their lives in the immigrant districts of Chicago and New York respectively seem to be dominated by the excitement of conquering and transforming a new frontier the city slums constituted. In *The House on Henry Street* Wald portrays her nursing mission in the slums as a "crusade against disease" which necessitates "pioneering zeal" (Wald 1915, 60-63). To explain to the readers why she became involved in the settlement house movement, Wald opens her book with a dramatic story which she characterizes as her "baptism of fire" (7). She is shown, on a rainy day, hastening after a young girl to the rescue of her mother in confinement. Like an intrepid explorer, Wald goes alone through filthy, foul-smelling, and crowded streets to a claustrophobic flat in a dilapidated building where she is treated like a long-awaited savior. Moreover, photographs in the book, present her alone in cluttered and ill-lit staircases or on tenement roofs taking a shortcut to help another needy person. In her social writings Jane Addams frequently pictures herself as venturing into morally-suspect places, such as dance halls, and does not shy away from stating that she lives in a neighborhood in which saloons or "vice" establishments are situated. It seems that both Wald and Addams rely to some extent on a new frontier imagery to conquer a completely new urban space for middle-class women.

However, in their accounts of life in the immigrant districts aspects other than excitement come to the fore. As they are "civic housekeepers" and settlement house workers, they focus on the critique of a contemporary industrial city created by men, which is portrayed as an unregulated structure crushing people's lives and on the portrayal of the immigrant who is perceived as bewildered by the modern city life and alienated from the life of the nation, but capable of becoming a contributing member of American society. Importantly, both Addams and Wald eye the neighborhoods in which they live and the entire cities with a transforming look. They enter the places they describe in order to alter them. This objective turns their books into recitals of investigations and instigated reforms, stories of rescued lives, records of democratic cooperation with the neighborhoods and social initiatives taken by their neighbors.

Both Addams and Wald picture immigrants as people isolated in their ethnic enclaves and extreme poverty from the larger life of the city or nation, neglected and abandoned by the municipal government. Wald describes the East Side in New York as "a vast crowded area, a foreign city within our own, for whose conditions we had no concern. ... The lower East Side then reflected the popular indifference—it almost seemed contempt—for the living conditions of a huge population" (Wald 1915, 2). An immigrant district appears to be a national and municipal limbo. Importantly, however, the immigrant population in many cases emerges from Addams's and Wald's accounts as morally undeformed by their conditions and willing to ameliorate them in cooperation with settlement house residents. Although Addams does not refrain from commenting on bad experiences with the neighbors, such as abandoned, illegitimate babies, battered wives, unscrupulous landlords, women who, in the language of the era, went astray, immigrants who opposed enforcement of the law, she also emphasizes the neighborhood residents' honesty, kindness, tolerance, and an ability to make disinterested sacrifices.

Addams's and Wald's criticism centers on the surroundings in which the immigrant population lives and lack of municipal control. Addams states, "The policy of the public authorities of never taking an initiative ... is obviously fatal in a neighborhood where there is little initiative among the citizens. The idea underlying our self-government breaks down in such a ward" (Addams 1910, 98). Immigrants are not prepared for the life in a city or new country and the municipal government evades taking responsibility for immigrant neighborhoods. Both authors point out sordid living conditions in the immigrant districts—lack of the plumbing system, unpaved streets, omnipresent dirt and foul smells, inefficient garbage collection, overpopulation and congestion which breeds diseases and immorality, ill-lit streets, inadequate education and healthcare systems, sweatshops in tenements, inappropriate housing conditions that guarantee no privacy or proper ventilation, so people are forced to seek respite at summer nights on the streets, fire escapes or in parks, and finally a failure to enforce the existing safety, housing or sanitary laws. All these conditions are generated and exacerbated by an exploitative economic system as well as lack of appropriate municipal control and legislation harmonized with changing industrial conditions.

Thus, one of the objectives of the settlement house was to regenerate space, understood as a neighborhood and municipal structure that surrounded it. In their books both Wald and Addams offer various definitions of the settlement house which became a new field of social activity for upper- and middle-class women. In *Windows on Henry Street*, written long after the heyday of the settlement house movement, Wald asserts that the New Oxford Dictionary formulated one of the best definitions of the settlement house as "an establishment in the poorer quarter of a large city, where educated men and women live in daily contact with the working class for cooperation in social reform" (Wald 1934, 5). In *Twenty Years at Hull House* Addams characterizes the settlement as "an experimental effort to aid in the solution of the social and industrial problems which are engendered by the modern conditions of life in a great city" (Addams 1910, 125) and compares it to "the big brother whose mere presence on the playground protects the little ones from bullies" (ibid., 167). These definitions highlight the aspects of the settlement house that both Addams and Wald as "civic housekeepers" always foregrounded—flexibility, adjustability, cooperation with and service to the neighborhood, social amelioration, protection and guidance offered to the immigrant.

The social centers they established began to provide the neighborhood with the most basic services, such as kindergartens or nursing care, only to branch out into other fields. Activities offered by the settlement houses run by Addams and Wald ranged from social, cultural, vocational to civic activities. Moreover, Addams and Wald portrayed their settlement houses as "interpreters" in an extremely ample sense of this word. Their primary function was to acquaint the new arrivals with municipal institutions and citizenship duties, in other words to teach the immigrant take advantage of the urban environment and simultaneously assume responsibility for this environment, and thus facilitate assimilation and assist in the immigrant's transition from an old reality to the new one. As Addams avers, the settlement "constantly acts between the various institutions of the city and the people for whose benefit these institutions were created" (Addams 1910, 167). One of the gauges of the settlement's success in this educational mission was definitely the immigrant's involvement in local politics—one such initiative was the 19th Ward Improvement Association that Hull House provided with a meeting place (321).

Furthermore, in the eyes of Addams and Wald, the settlement house attempted to promote understanding between various social groups—old country parents and their Americanized children, different nationalities and races. Settlement houses, managed by Addams and Wald, saw themselves as places committed to religious and cultural tolerance and freedom of outlook. Significantly, on some occasions the settlement house performed the role of an arbitrator in industrial disputes by for example providing "the neutral ground where both sides might meet" or by acting as "the 'impartial third party'" (Wald 1915, 282). Finally, one of the objectives of the settlement house was to interpret the immigrant population to Americans by "creating and informing public opinion" (ibid., 310). The settlement house, as a site of direct, unmediated contact between the immigrant population and the representatives of the middle-class, offered insight and knowledge unavailable to American society at large. At the time of antagonism towards the immigrant, the settlement house stood out as a place championing tolerance: "Only through knowledge is one fortified to resist the onslaught of arguments of the superficial observer who dismayed by the sight, is conscious only of 'hordes' and 'danger' to America in these little children" (ibid., 66). Settlement workers, residing in the immigrant districts and interacting with immigrants on a daily basis, deemed themselves more qualified to evaluate the character of the immigrant population and objected to immigration restrictions.

Residing in the immigrant districts gave settlement workers a unique possibility to familiarize themselves with the neighborhood and acquire knowledge of its conditions, which turned settlement houses into investigation and research stations. Settlement house residents carried out a plethora of investigations concerning various aspects of urban life, such as sanitary and housing conditions or employment practices. In Jane Addams's words, settlement house residents "are bound to see the needs of their neighborhood as a whole, to furnish data for legislation" (Addams

1910, 126). Accumulated data was used to lobby for and instigate appropriate legislation that alleviated and regulated living conditions in urban centres. Settlement residents, working with their informants and researching the neighborhood, appear to be field workers who cooperated closely with legislators (Wald 1915, 261).

Jane Addams, however, warned against treating settlement houses as "sociological observatories" designed to conduct investigations, observe and discipline the neighborhood population (Addams 1910, 308). Nevertheless, external observation, which involved visits at home, medical examinations of school children, questioning, was not always welcome by working-class families who frequently interpreted institutional interest as curtailing their privacy and interference, as historians such as Sarah Deutsch or Mary E. Odem point out. In *Salome of the Tenements*, Anzia Yezierska pointedly shows that spatial relations between settlement residents or benefactors and their charges were not equal. The settlement house was an institutional space open to everybody not a private home to which the "other half" was invited as a guest.

Interestingly, neither Addams nor Wald present their settlement houses as institutional spaces. Addams describes Hull House as "a house, easily accessible, ample in space, hospitable and tolerant in spirit, situated in the midst of the large colonies which so easily isolate themselves in American cities" (1910, 91). The settlement is pictured as a site of hospitality and tolerance. Moreover, both Addams and Wald give details of the middle-class way their settlement houses were furnished (the bath was an indispensable fixture in the house), which even further suppresses the settlement's institutionality. Nevertheless, the settlement house was construed as a middle-class space situated in the chaotic, working-class district. Both Addams and Wald perceived their settlements as a "refuge" from the unfavorable economic and industrial system, moral depravity plaguing the city, and paradoxically the working-class home (101).

As soon as they move in, the women set out to tame, transform, regulate and organize the "industrial neighborhood situated in an unorganized city", which surrounds them (148) For example, after Wald moved into Henry Street, she immediately converted the backyard into a playground where a kindergarten for the neighborhood children was organized. As Daphne Spain states, "Male professionals built grand and civic monuments in search of the City Beautiful. Female volunteers built the places of everyday life, the neighborhood institutions without which a city is not a city—hallmarks of the City Social Movement" (Spain 2001, 13). Thus, the neighborhood environment was to serve its inhabitants and facilitate their participation in the industrial system. Hence, the settlement house offered an impressive number of services to the neighborhood, provided a venue for strike organizers and functioned as a cultural and social center for the neighborhood's inhabitants.

Both Addams and Wald construed the urban environment as replete with moral perils and traps for the unwary youth of both sexes. Gin-palaces, vaudeville shows, dance-halls, five-cent theatres, which Addams called "magic places ... responsible for an entire crop of petty crimes", featured prominently on the reformers' maps of moral jeopardy (Addams 1910, 386). In contrast, the settlement house was portrayed as a safe environment which offered moral immunity to the dangers posed by the city by inculcating urban youth with appropriate, namely middle-class, standards of behavior. Supervised entertainment was provided and a variety of social clubs offered an alternative to gangs and constituted "a means of guidance and instruction for the young" (Wald 1915, 179). The settlement house seems to have enjoyed the trust of the neighborhood inhabitants as it was approached by parents unable to cope with their unruly children or girls asking for help (Wald 1915, 179; Addams 1910, 145-146). Furthermore, the settlement was to provide a place where children could study away from overcrowded conditions of the working-class home; in other words, it was to offer the neighborhood children "a quiet corner" (Wald 1915, 102). Study rooms established in settlement houses alleviated unfavorable living conditions in the poor city quarters, but they also were a clear sign that working-class houses were deemed inadequate.

With the passage of time the reformers extended their influence over the entire neighborhood and city. For instance, they cooperated with neighborhood schools so that the children could use school facilities during the summer for recreation (Wald 1915, 87) and with the police that agreed to redirect traffic from certain streets to enable children to play safely in these areas (95). "Civic housekeepers" became involved in the struggle to change the appearance of the city—they contributed to the instigation of the playground movement, the public bath movement and reforms in the housing system (Spain 2001, 14). Interestingly, Wald also gives examples of the appropriation of the city's space by its residents and their impact on the urban environment. During the Fourth of July celebration, the Henry Street Settlement organized a dance on the streets in which all neighborhood inhabitants could participate (Wald 1915, 214-215). The working-class people of New York petitioned for the change of admission days of the Metropolitan Museum of Art so that it could be open on Sundays to all strata of society (80-81).

Importantly, towards the end of their accounts both Addams and Wald enumerate changes that occurred in the neighborhoods and their cities to demonstrate the results of their city housekeeping effort and success in educating people. After twenty years of "civic housekeeping" and lobbying for reforms, the appearance of the city was transformed and regulated. The city was turned into a "livable" space, to use Daphne Spain's term, into whose organic structure settlement houses were embedded (Spain 2001, 13). According to Jane Addams, the objective of Hull House was "to be swallowed and digested, to disappear into the bulk of the people" (Addams 1910, 309). Addams perceived the settlement house as an element of the organic tissue of the neighborhood in which it functioned and an indispensable part of the city organism.

However, it seems that the city organism was not attuned to the needs of its entire population. Residential patterns in the city changed when the African American migration from the agrarian South to the industrial centres of the North began. However, as historians point out, settlement houses, to a great extent, failed to adjust their activities to the needs of black population, as white leaders tended either to establish separate branches of their settlement houses for blacks, support black organizations which paralleled their effort, but in a segregated environment, or engage in work that was directed at the black community, but was not strictly settlement work (Lasch-Quinn 1993, 1-29).

Addams's and Wald's books give tribute to their co-workers and constitute powerful accounts of instigated reforms. Residence in the poor quarters gave settlement house workers unique understanding of the living conditions in the city and maladjustments of the economic and social system. Addams and Wald enumerate investigations that were carried out by Hull House's and Henry Street Settlement's female residents, which resulted in the instigation of Progressive reforms that stressed professionalization, efficiency, regulation of industry and industrial relations. Interestingly, taming the urban space and regulating industrial conditions encountered opposition from the local authorities and businessmen. Addams remarks that the efforts of her female colleagues and her own to prohibit child labor were challenged by male businessmen—"this first modification of the undisturbed control of the aggressive captains of industry, could not be enforced without resistance marked by dramatic episodes and revolts" (Addams 1910, 207). Although Addams and Wald do not overemphasize the element of gender struggle, it is evident in their books and other writings that acquiring control over the urban space required wresting it first from male hands.

The aim of this article was to examine how two female settlement house leaders, Jane Addams and Lillian D. Wald, presented in their books the following spaces—the settlement house, immigrant districts and urban environment. From their descriptions the settlement house emerges as a multilayered institution. On one level it is portrayed as a site of social investigation conducive to valuable social reforms that harness the chaos of an unregulated city. On another level it is an all-female community whose objective is civic housekeeping and saving the city from "predatory", to use Jane Addams's words, male influence. On still another level, it is a middle-class haven in the working-class district, whose mission is to facilitate the transition of the immigrant population into the new, Americanized world. Finally, an important facet of the settlement house is its commitment to social justice, with socialist undercurrents, and promotion of tolerance and understanding.

References

Addams, Jane. 1910. *Twenty Years at Hull House: With Autobiographical Notes.* New York: The Macmillan Company.
—. 1960. Utilization of Women in City Government. In *A Centennial Reader*, 156-159. New York: The Macmillian Company.
Lasch-Quinn, Elisabeth. 1993. *Black Neighbors: Race and the Limits of Reform in the American Settlement House Movement, 1890-1945.* Chapel Hill, NC: University of North Carolina Press.
Spain, Daphne. 2001. *How Women Saved the City.* Minneapolis: University of Minnesota Press.
Wald, Lillian D. 1915. *The House on Henry Street.* New York: Henry Holt and Company.
—. 1934. *Windows on Henry Street.* Boston: Little, Brown and Company.

CHAPTER FORTY-ONE

THE OPEN TRAP:
BETTY FRIEDAN'S CRITIQUE OF SUBURBAN
SPACE IN *THE FEMININE MYSTIQUE*

TADEUSZ LEWANDOWSKI

The America of the 1950s witnessed explosive suburban growth and a widespread commitment among women to housewifery and childrearing, both of which were made possible by the postwar economic boom. As real incomes rose, men achieved sole breadwinner status, and those disenchanted with grimy, cramped city tenements left for the family-friendly suburbs, which promised privacy, larger living spaces, and greater comfort. Central to this new lifestyle was a domestic ideology defined by accomplished female homemakers and strong male providers. This model of the nuclear family was touted as the bedrock of the nation, holding the United States in good stead through the Cold War, and protecting society from the potentially chaotic individualism of the new affluence. Americans responded enthusiastically, beginning a baby boom that brought a new infant into the world every seven seconds by mid-decade. The "new domesticity" featured a clearly delineated ideal for these babies' new mothers, who were expected to find ultimate satisfaction through dedication to homebound pursuits, such as cooking, cleaning, raising children, and catering to the proverbial man of the house (May 1988, 88-91). The idyllic setting of suburbia acted in mutual dependence with this emergent domestic vision. Here was a place where normalcy could return after the wrenching dislocations of the war years, when men fought in the European and East-Asian theaters, and women worked in heavy industry to assist in the war effort. And within this family-oriented arena a new generation of healthy, well-adjusted children could be reared. This suburban lifestyle, however—and the physical space of suburbia itself—soon attracted critics. But while numerous male observers decried the suburbs' conformity and blandness, only Betty

Friedan (1921–2006) offered an assessment that specifically concerned these new domestic spaces' ostensible effect on women. This paper examines the planning and architecture of suburban communities and homes in 1950s America, and the critique of suburban space found in Friedan's groundbreaking social analysis of postwar domesticity, *The Feminine Mystique* (1963).

The Feminine Mystique was written in response to what Friedan saw as the confining and unfulfilling nature of the mid-century feminine ideal for those women who adhered to it. This dim view was directly anchored in Friedan's personal experience. Born in 1921, she grew up watching her mother suffer over the fact that she had given up her job at a newspaper after marriage. As a result, mother constantly urged daughter to pursue a career in journalism, of which she herself had dreamed. Freidan graduated from Smith College in 1942 with highest honors and went on to graduate studies in Psychology at the University of California at Berkeley. In 1947 she gave up her Ph.D. studies, married, moved to the suburbs and gave birth to three children in rapid succession. Although she pursued a journalistic career by writing articles for women's magazines in her spare time, she felt discontented in the role as housewife and mother. In 1957 Friedan sent a detailed questionnaire to her Smith College classmates, inquiring as to the course their lives had taken. She received answers from two hundred female alumni, many expressing profound disappointment with the postwar gender role they had been assigned. When Friedan composed an article on this research, the editors of the women's magazines she had written for refused to publish it. She henceforth resolved to investigate the problem more deeply and turn her findings into a book. *The Feminine Mystique* appeared six years later in 1963, instantly becoming a runaway success, and selling over three million copies (Notable Biographies 2007, online). Friedan was subsequently inundated with letters from women who had struggled to conform to the outlines of postwar domesticity. The missives evidenced prevalent disgruntlement among the housewives of America, and convinced Friedan that she needed to address women's issues on a wider, more active scale. She moved to Manhattan with her family, and in 1966 helped found the National Organization for Women (a divorce followed). Friedan acted as its president until 1970, and continued to agitate for women's rights until her death in 2006. *The Feminine Mystique* is today regarded as *the* book that ignited the modern feminist movement in America (Fox 2006, online).

At the crux of Friedan's monograph was an attack on the postwar feminine ideal and the middle-class lifestyle of suburbia, which she argued were as confining in nature for women as the separate-spheres ideology of the Victorian era. She took direct aim at 1950s "gender experts" and their influence in the media, which had helped reanimate outdated beliefs from the 1800s regarding the "true woman's" inborn passivity, nurturing instincts, and proclivity for the domestic arts—as well the imperative of male dominance (Friedan 2001, 108-10, 130-1). This "biology is destiny" model had given rise to "the problem that had no name", a phrase that Friedan used to convey the quandary that:

> lay buried, unspoken, for many years in the minds of American women. It was a strange stirring, a sense of dissatisfaction, a yearning that women suffered in the middle of the 20th century in the United States. Each suburban wife struggled with it alone. As she made the beds, shopped for groceries—she was afraid to ask even of herself the silent question—"Is this all?" (15)

As such, Friedan denounced "the feminine mystique", which, as she explained, ascribed "the highest value and the only commitment for women...[as]...the fulfillment of their own femininity", meanwhile making "the housewife-mothers...the model for all women" (43). Since this role of "professional housewife", had failed to provide the fulfillment guaranteed by gender experts, Friedan urged women to break away from the mire of the suburban domicile, go back to school, and pursue careers. These were radical sentiments in a culture that branded working wives both a "menace" and a "disease" (Coontz 1992, online). But included in Friedan's analysis was not only this negative appraisal of present-day suburban housewifery, but a critique the very space in which it was meant thrive. Friedan cast modern suburbia as an open trap whose very material structure inherently condemned its female inhabitants to the role of homemaker. Contemporary planning and architecture were thus implicated in the feminine mystique's promotion.

The suburban dream began in the New York World's Fair of 1939 and '40 with an exhibition called "Highways and Horizons", also dubbed "Futurama." It featured a gigantic scale model over 100 yards long and 50 yards wide, which depicted how Americans would live in the year 1960. Urban tenement houses were replaced by free-standing homes surrounded by spacious yards, connected to the city by wide motorways. The absolute wonder felt by the populace who viewed the display was reordered by E. B. White: "A Ride on the Futurama...induces approximately the same emotional response as a trip through the Cathedral of St. John the Divine...I didn't want to wake up" (qtd. in Leinberger 2008, online). This sublime reverie became reality a short decade later, when the US

government constructed a massive highway system that connected the
metropolises with the hinterlands. Eighty-five percent of the 13 million
homes built in America during the 1950s were located along these new
arteries, and life in suburbia soon became inevitable for weary city
dwellers looking to raise children. The suburbs offered a cleaner, crime-
free environment of greater comfort—both spatially and privacy-wise—as
well as key benefits for families; a fact promoted by the building company
Levitt and Sons, which in the '50s created communities across the North
East (called Levittowns) that today stand as the archetype of suburban
development (Boyer, et al. 2000, 827-8).

Levittowns offered a radically new model of spatial engineering and
manufacturing efficiency. Their creators boasted that each was the "most
perfectly planned community in America" (State Museum of Pennsylvania
2003, online). Centering around one master block surrounded by
neighborhoods dubbed "sections", planners created the feeling of a small
town within the seemingly infinite suburban sprawl. The master plan
included numerous family-oriented features, such as public swimming
pools, baseball fields, parks, shopping malls, community centers,
churches, and schools. Emphasizing the child-friendly nature of the
design, promoters insisted that "no child will have to walk more than one
half mile to school or cross any major road" (2003, online). Utilizing
prefabricated housing patterns from the armed services; these suburban
homes were built with rapid construction techniques using standardized
parts and a workforce with specialized skills that constituted a moving
assembly line. The result was a wholly uniform product, from the number
of square feet in the floor plans to the exact number of shingles on each
roof (Hales 2008, online). Architectural critics decried the identical
dwellings on their 60-by-100 foot "cookie-cutter" lots, and similarly
denigrated the taste of the moderate-income groups that purchased them.
Such communities were referred to as "degraded in conception and
impoverished in form" (Binder and Reimer 2000, 220), and as a "uniform
environment from which escape is impossible" (Ruff 2007, online).

Social critics as well deplored such pre-fabricated conformity, where
televisions were built directly into living rooms, the blinds on the
windows were a constant, the streets all curved at the same angles, and
trees were planted at precise distances from one another (Boyer, et al.
2000, 827-30). Particular concern was devoted to contrasting the
cosmopolitan nature of the city with the bludgeoning sameness of the
suburbs. In *The Lonely Crowd: A Study of the Changing American
Character* (1950), David Riesman (1909–2002) lamented the rise of the
"other directed type" who inhabited suburban space. This brand of

individual wanted nothing more than to be a "member of a team", and avoid "offending anyone" with the appearance of "knobby or idiosyncratic vices" (Riesman 1961, 8, 71-82). With respect to urbanity, Riesman later ruefully noted in "The Suburban Dislocation" (1957) that in the suburbs there existed "a tendency…to lose the human differentiations which have made great cities in the past the centers of rapid intellectual and cultural advance" (Riesman 1957, 241-2). William Whyte's (1918–1999) extremely influential book on postwar corporate values, *The Organization Man* (1956), meanwhile argued that, "suburbanization robbed people of the older, tight-knit experience of community" that they had once enjoyed in the city (qtd. in Kaiser 2004, 860). But perhaps the most acidic characterization of suburbia was found in Lewis Mumford's (1895–1990) *The City in History* (1961), described as:

> a multitude of uniform, unidentifiable houses, lined up inflexibly, at uniform distances, on uniform roads, in a treeless communal waste, inhabited by people of the same class, the same income, the same age group, witnessing the same television performances, eating the same tasteless prefabricated foods, from the same freezers, conforming in every outward and inward respect to the common mold, manufactured in the central metropolis. (qtd. in Archer 2004)

Together, such criticisms identified a postwar "problem of conformity" among the nation's suburban citizenry, which provoked much consternation and commentary in intellectual circles. Betty Friedan, however, had a different perspective than her male counterparts. Firstly, she felt that the removal of family life from the city to the suburbs denied women professional opportunity, due the distance from centers of higher education and employment. But perhaps more terrible, in her estimation the very layout of the mid-century ranch or spit-level house held ineluctable dangers for the average housewife.

The irony of Friedan's displeasure with the suburbs was that their organization was largely intended with women and mothers in mind, reflecting the concept of "togetherness" that *McCall's* magazine famously coined to glorify the ideal of the American nuclear family focused almost exclusively on itself when removed from the urban public sphere of work (Spigel 1992, 37). A key element of the new suburban homes she so detested was that the floor plan centered around an open, ultra-modern kitchen. Previously, prewar kitchens had been enclosed in four walls, and stand-alone cabinets and appliances were the norm. But in postwar kitchens, all major appliances, refrigerator, oven, automatic washer and dryer, along with food processors with interchangeable attachments, were compactly built into the surrounding cupboards. Among these luxuries was often a push-button "food center", which did everything from sharpening knives to housing blenders and their attachments. This followed the industry dictum that, "Today, the American housewife demands a coordinated, well-planned kitchen" (State Museum of Pennsylvania 2003, online). Boasted one Levittown architect: "Thanks to the number of appliances in our house, the girls will have three hours to kill every afternoon" (2003, online). Also significant was how the kitchen lost its walls. City tenements constructed at the turn of the century had clearly defined, cordoned off spaces. Forward-looking 1950s architects, however, opened up suburban floor plans to create fully-integrated living spaces, transforming the kitchen from the prewar "fox hole" into the "command center" of the home, thus allowing housewives to carry out their duties while still interacting with family members in adjacent areas. In Levittowns, for example, the kitchen cupboards and domestic devices were positioned on only two walls open to the living and dining areas. Within this exposed spatial arrangement, the kitchen cabinets for the first time were regarded as furniture, and the housewife's domain was symbolically enlarged. Such suburban ranch homes also featured large picture windows in the rear, which allowed mothers to supervise their children from this unified kitchen, living and dinning room complex. The front of the house, however, was usually closed off from the street, focusing attention to the private sphere of the back yard (Hales 2008, online). Hence in this new suburban fastness the family was well sequestered from the public sphere, and always subject to a maternal presence.

Friedan saw little value in the cutting-edge architectural innovations of what she deemed "those ugly and endless sprawls" of suburbia (Friedan 2001, 243). In "the open plan of the contemporary 'ranch' or split-level house…, which has been built in the millions", she found nothing to celebrate and much to bewail (245-6). Rather than being a domestic paradise, she declared that they:

> give the illusion of space for less money. But the women to whom they are sold almost *have* to live the feminine mystique [emphasis in original]. There are no true walls or doors; the woman in the beautiful electronic kitchen is never separated from her children. She need never feel alone for a minute, need never be by herself. She can forget her identity in those noisy open-plan houses. (246)

In conjunction with this loss of privacy and, as Friedan gloomily viewed it, potential loss of identity, came more practical considerations. The plan of the standard suburban home simply demanded more work from its female inhabitants, filling their days with menial cleaning. She writes: "The open plan also helps to expand the housework to fill the time available. In what is basically one free-flowing room, instead of many rooms separated by walls and stairs, continual messes continually need picking up" (246). Adding: "A man, of course, leaves the house for most of the day. But the feminine mystique forbids a woman this" (246). This ideological and physical confinement had dire consequences.

For Friedan, the eventual result was an insidious self-alienation brought on by a simultaneous lack of solitude and real purpose. This was somewhat ironic given supposedly private nature of suburban space. She comments: "It's strange how few places there are in those spacious houses and those sprawling suburbs where you can go to be alone" (246). Friedan's own research purported to show that when women came to realize that they wanted to do something for themselves, they often added "a room with a door to their open-plan house…'so I can have someplace to myself, just a door to shut between me and the children when I want to think'—or work, or study, be alone" (246-7). But this was hardly a cure-all. Friedan states: "Most American housewives, however, do not shut that door. Perhaps they are afraid, finally, to be alone in that room", suggesting that, "even if she had more time and space to herself, she would not know what to do with it" (247). The only option, therefore, is to make "a career of marriage and motherhood, as the mystique tells her", becoming the burdened "executive of the house" (247). Friedan took care to point out that even when the suburban housewife left her orderly abode and entered her immediate environment, she found only a wasteland painfully devoid of real opportunity and stimulation. This was indicative of residential areas designed for children to grow up and men to relax on weekends. What connected such women to the outside world was merely "shopping and gardening and chauffeuring and do-it-yourself routines" (243). Unfortunately, this was little to offer for those with greater ambition, and thus followed a profound malaise.

The Feminine Mystique climaxes with Friedan's controversial and rather hyperbolic depiction of the suburban home as "a comfortable concentration camp" (307). She argues that those females who inhabit it "are in as much danger as the millions who walked to their own death" during the Holocaust (305). The specific threat was the loss of sense of self observed in prisoners so dehumanized that they went indifferently to their destruction, deprived of all frame of reference and individual identity. Like them, the "women who live the image of the feminine mystique [have] trapped themselves within the narrow walls of their homes" (307). So what, then, was Betty Friedan's final solution with respect to the suburban nightmare? Ultimately, she seems to suggest that one of the best options is a return to the city. According to her, urban areas held greater promise for fulfillment for women and mothers. There one could find more jobs for educated women, more universities with evening courses for young mothers who want to pursue graduate degrees, and better access to house-cleaning services, daycare centers, and after-school play programs. As well, unlike in the suburbs there was "less room [in city apartments] for housewifery to expand to fill time available" (244). She cites a sociological study of upper-income suburban housewives who rejected homemaking after years of living the much-vaunted domestic dream. The sociologist found that those who decided to take other paths in their lives overwhelmingly moved back to metropolitan areas. Friedan herself took this advice after *The Feminine Mystique's* publication, moving to New York City to found the National Organization of Women and enlarge the reach of her work. Physical escape, therefore, was the obvious way out of the open trap laid by postwar America's sinister suburban spaces.

References

Archer, John. 2004. Making Difference in the Suburbs.
http://www.designcenter.umn.edu/reference_ctr/publications/pdfs/db10.pdf
Binder, Frederick F. and David M. Reimers. 2000. *The Way We Lived: Essays and Documents in American Social History, 1865-Present*. Vol. 2. Fourth edition. Boston: Houghton Mifflin Company.
Boyer, Paul et al. 2000. *The Enduring Vision: A History of the American People, from 1865*. Fourth edition. Boston: Houghton Mifflin Company.
Coontz, Stephanie. 1992.'Leave it to Beaver' and 'Ozzie and Harriet': American Families in the 1950s.
http://us.history.wisc.edu/hist102/readings/Coontz_Beaver.pdf.
Friedan, Betty. 2001. *The Feminine Mystique*. New York: W. W. Norton & Company.
Hales, Peter. 2008. Building Levittown: A Rudimentary Primer.
http://www.tigger.uic.edu~pbhales/Levittown/building.html.
Kaiser, David. 2004. The Postwar Suburbanization of American Physics. *American Quarterly* 56 (4): 851-888.
Leinberger, Christopher. 2008. The Next Slum? *The Atlantic Online*.
http://the atlanticonline.com/doc/print/200803/subprime?x=41&y=3
May, Elaine Tyler. 1988. *Homeward Bound: American Families in the Cold War Era*. New York: Basic Books.
Notable Biographies. 2007. Betty Friedan.

http://www.notablebiographies.com/Fi-Gi/Friedan-Betty.html

Ruff, Joshua. 2007. Levittown: The Archetype of Suburban Development. http://www.historynet.com/levittown-the-archetype-for-suburban-development.html

Riesman, David. 1961. *The Lonely Crowd.* Third edition. New Haven: Yale University Press.

—. 1957. The Suburban Dislocation. *Annals of the American Academy of Political and Social Science* 314: 226-257.

Spigel, Lynn. 1992. *Make Room for TV: Television and the Family Ideal in Postwar America.* Chicago: University of Chicago Press.

The State Museum of Pennsylvania. 2003. Levittown, PA: Building the Suburban Dream Exhibit. http://server1.fandm.edu/levittown/default.html

CHAPTER FORTY-TWO

THE SARTORIAL REFLECTION OF THE SPATIAL
RELATIONS IN KENNY GLENAAN'S *YASMIN*

HANNA SZEWCZYK

The issue of racial segregation between the white majority and certain minority groups of South Asian origin has been a cause for concern in contemporary Britain, especially after the riots of 2001 and the July bombings of 2005. The authorities have been voicing their anxiety concerning community cohesion, which they have seen as seriously imperilled by the presence of residential segregation in British towns and cities (see Robinson 2005). Addressing the issue of British Asian engagement with the host society, Ceri Peach writes:

> The picture that emerges is one of economic integration but social segregation. In other words, BrAsians are part of the political economy of Britain, but they seem to constitute distinct civil societies within that political-economic frame. This is most acute in the case of the Bangladeshis and Pakistanis, where social encapsulation is manifested within high levels of residential segregation. (2006, 181)

Elsewhere, he gives the following numbers regarding the degree of segregation:

> Within the urban areas in which they have settled, Pakistanis and (particularly) Bangladeshis have shown high rates of segregation. On a scale from 0 (no segregation) to 100 (complete segregation), Pakistanis segregated from whites averaged 54 while Bangladeshis averaged 65. (2005, 28)

Another author, in a study concerning the residential segregation in Oldham (one of the cities where the 2001 riots erupted), notes that the inhabitants' lives "were lived in separate parallel universes" (Sardar 2008, 273), the statement closely mirroring the post-2001 concerns of the British authorities regarding what has been termed as *parallel lives* of white and British Asian (esp. Pakistani and Bangladeshi) populations. There are, however, also more optimistic visions concerning the issue of segregation, with authors such as Phillips et al (2007) claiming that, although admittedly British Asians do tend to cluster residentially, there has nevertheless been a growing trend (evident especially among younger people) to greater mixing and a willingness to integrate, giving the lie to the prevailing notions of a worrying degree of British Asian propensity for self-segregation and self-seclusion.

The reasons for segregation are manifold, not least of them being the presence of racism and, in the case of Muslims (predominantly citizens of Bangladeshi and Pakistani origin), the phenomenon of Islamophobia, a tendency to vilify Muslims, especially evident since the inception of the so-called "War on terror" post 9/11 New York attacks. The director of *Yasmin* (2004), Kenny Glenaan, describes the predicament of Muslims in contemporary Britain as "an invisible war happening in Britain..., he Muslims of our country, it's similar to being Irish in the 70's and 80's..., guilty until proven innocent," (*Yasmin*: the movie). Tariq Modood, in turn, mentions a much vaster "sense of 'siege' and 'threat' that some Muslim peoples have historically felt in the context of western colonialism and cultural domination" (2001, 74), a response to which has been what he calls *defensive traditionalism* (1992 and 2001), i.e. a return to certain traditional cultural practices, frequently evident in the diasporic context. Since in conservative societies it is women who are traditionally perceived as depositaries of family and community honour and vessels of tradition, the demand on many South Asian women in diasporic environment to perpetuate traditional practices is particularly strong. Among those practices, clothing occupies a prominent position as, according to Bakirathi Mani, "in the diasporic context [it] is recognized as one way in which cohesive cultural and religious histories are reproduced" (2004, 125).

These elements are clearly visible in the film, which addresses a whole range of issues generated in the bubbling cauldron of the multicultural society of Britain. From among the wealth of material, the present article focuses on the fascinating interplay between the spatial and the sartorial in the picture, analysing the semiotics of dress and its role in the protagonist's negotiation of identity in the context of contemporary multicultural Britain.

The film tells the story of a young British woman of Pakistani Muslim origin, Yasmin Hussain (played by Archie Panjabi), who lives in a north English town in an area populated chiefly by people of Pakistani origin,

and works in a white-dominated environment. She commutes daily by car
between the two spaces along a rather empty country road. By watching
her repeatedly covering the spatial/physical distance between the two parts
of her world, the viewer appreciates their acute separateness. The
transitional sense of the road to work is further intensified by Yasmin's
twice-daily change of attire, taking place somewhere along the way and
symbolically marking the boundary between the two worlds Yasmin
inhabits and has to reconcile on a daily basis. By adjusting her appearance
in accordance with the expectations of the respective environments
Yasmin thus becomes a physical embodiment of difference and segregation.
In fact, this is precisely the situation when Yasmin first appears on the
screen: she is getting changed from traditional[1] Pakistani Muslim
garments—salwaar kameez (a long tunic with matching baggy trousers), a
black overcoat and a black headscarf, into blue denim jeans (the epitome
of Western fashion) and a low-cut top. The opposition is thus set very
clearly from the outset through the sartorial markers signifying her
membership in the two worlds respectively. When within the confines of
her minority community, she is always seen wearing salwaar kameez
when at home and a black overcoat and headscarf when outside. This
traditional dress, connotative of female modesty, humility and obedience,
is in perfect accordance with the roles she is supposed to play in the home
environment: that of a dutiful daughter and wife. It is worth mentioning at
this point that she has been coerced into an arranged marriage with a
cousin from Pakistan. However, it is evident from the very first moment
that she is too independent to fulfil these roles without demur; thus, she
may cook for her family, and succumb to the arranged marriage but she
refuses her husband sex and keeps reminding him that she will be married
to him only as long as it is necessary for him to obtain leave to remain in
the UK. Any vestiges of this traditional role are cast off together with the
traditional clothing as soon as she reaches the point on her way to work
where she can safely change into her jeans and top. She goes out with her
white friends, visits pubs, pretends to drink beer (she is not so liberated as
to trespass on the Koranic injunction against drinking alcohol), and even
refers to the members of her community as "Pakis". The rather flashy red
car she buys for commuting to work is the perfect accessory to complete

---

[1] The concept of "traditional clothing" is in itself far from unequivocal, as it is a
mistake to perceive ethnic dress styles as fixed and immutable (see Tarlo 1996,
Bahl 2005). For the purpose of this article, however, I will use the term
"traditional" to refer to clothing perceived as non-Western and accepted as
appropriate by conservative members of ethnic minority groups, in this case British
Pakistani.

the image she is keen to present to the world outside her community—that of a modern, independent, thoroughly "westernised" woman. The expensive convertible itself is a statement of defiance against the cultural expectations on both sides of the divide; at her friend John's surprise at her buying such an extravagant "black hole" of a car Yasmin retorts that she was not going to go for "a TP car—Typical Paki".

The September 11 events provide a dramatic turning point for Yasmin and other people from her community. After the New York towers have fallen and a War on Terror has been proclaimed by the US, tensions in society visibly mount, further deepening the gulf between the two communities. Yasmin's aunt, when out shopping in her Islamic outfit, is abused by young white boys. The protagonist herself becomes a target for primitive and childish jokes at work (she finds a note on her locker door saying "Yas loves Osama"; later on, her photograph on the "employee of the month" board is embellished with a burgeoning beard in resemblance to the infamous Al-Qaeda leader and the words "Taliban van" appear on the window of her work van). These experiences of racism and hostility coupled with a major row with her father concerning her inadequate fulfilment of "family obligations" cause her to rebel openly against her Pakistani Muslim identity. She puts on tight jeans and a revealing, flimsy top, accessorised with a profusion of jewellery, her appearance finished off with exaggerated make-up; she makes no effort to cover this shockingly unorthodox attire with the overcoat and hijab when leaving the house. A heightened, desperate need for acceptance outside her ethnic community pushes her towards a desperate attempt to sartorially disassociate herself from her "Asianness". When out with her friends, she even takes the drastic step of actually drinking vodka. It soon becomes evident, however, that in the white majority space she is viewed with suspicion as one of "them"—the threatening "Other". Desperately trying to deny her Muslimness ("I haven't been to a mosque in five years!", she shouts), she demands to know what actually she is being blamed for—and in response she hears from her friend (and romantic interest) John what has been repeated all over the Western world, but especially in the countries with significant Muslim minorities: that no Muslims have "actually come out and said 'sorry'". Later on, when the racist taunts at work continue and she decides to complain, her boss advises her to take some time off and thus remove herself physically from the white-dominated work space. It thus becomes glaringly and painfully obvious that, despite her personal efforts, she has effectively been banished to the other side of the divide, the gulf suddenly expanding to alarming proportions. Even before this final act of banishment, and after her house is brutally raided by the police in search of her husband suspected of terrorist associations, when preparing to leave for work Yasmin is actually hesitant to step out of the house. The two spaces seem to have sprang apart as far as possible and no efforts of hers seem capable of drawing them back together in her life, least of all sartorial ones. In this context, her provocative sartorial attempt from the "night out on the town" takes on a touchingly pathetic quality in its utter futility.

After her husband is detained under the Anti-Terrorism, Crime and Security Act, Yasmin finally receives her divorce papers. When she decides to visit Faysal in custody so that he may sign the documents, she conspicuously takes her Muslim identity with her to the world outside her community: she is wearing her salwaar kameez, black overcoat and headscarf. Since that moment, the viewer never again sees her in her top and jeans combo. One can view her decision as a political gesture, perhaps a sign of solidarity with her oppressed family and community. This would not have been an isolated gesture. In the aftermath of 9/11, in defiance of the worldwide trend to regard people of "Islamic" appearance as potential terrorists (especially the headscarf seems to have been stirring negative emotions), a visible increase has been noted in the number of people, especially young women, adopting traditional sartorial markers of Islam (see Aziz 2003; La Ferla 2007; Roy 2005). Thus, Yasmin's decision can be read either as an act of solidarity and defiance, or perhaps as an outward manifestation of the need to create this physical sartorial boundary between herself and the suddenly very hostile white majority space. In this manner, she physically separates herself from the majority culture and symbolically withdraws into the realm of the culture of her ancestors which she has heretofore only had a superficial affinity with. Analysing the impact the 9/11 events have had on the lives of young British Pakistanis, Bagguley and Hussain notice poignantly: "Although they feel themselves to be British, Islamophobia has excluded them from the 'British nation'" (2005, 219). Indeed, Yasmin has every reason to feel excluded, especially after, instead of being granted access to her husband, she is herself detained for "withholding information" she does not possess. There is an emblematic shot of Yasmin in the cell, only partly visible through the peephole, the door constituting a very real physical boundary between her and the white-dominated space outside. Locked up in the cell, with a supplied copy of the Koran, she actually starts reading the book which has so far been of little interest and relevance to her. The Yasmin who leaves the cell after this humiliating ordeal is a changed woman: she throws out the divorce papers and, conspicuous in her Islamic attire, waits all night outside the police station for her husband, reading fragments of the Koran she has taken from the cell. In this context, the scene immediately following that in the bar, of Yasmin retching into a toilet bowl, takes on a symbolic quality with hindsight: it seems it is not just the inordinate quantity of vodka that she was then expelling from her body; she may have been ejecting her former schizophrenic identity along with it.

The decision to dispose of the divorce documents does not mean, however, that her change is so complete she is going to perform the role of a dutiful wife in a marriage imposed on her. Admittedly, the hapless couple come back home together and there is even a touching scene when their preparations for a prayer end with a distraught Faysal crying on his wife's shoulder; however, Yasmin is as determined as ever to separate from him. Yet the act of divorce itself is truly emblematic of the new Yasmin: after throwing out the documents she asks her husband to divorce her in the traditional Islamic way, by repeating "I divorce you" three times. Thus, she perseveres in her "Western" independence, while at the same time symbolically choosing her allegiance to the Islamic culture rather than to the majority culture which seems to have rejected her. She retains her indomitable free spirit—but it seems as though from now on she will be asserting her identity mainly from within the Islamic context.

There is, however, another highly significant scene connected with yet another change of attire towards the end of the film. It features Yasmin outside her community—in the white majority space—but she is no longer dressed head to toe in "traditional" dress. Although she is wearing a kameez top teamed with a matching dupatta scarf, she has dispensed with the baggy salwaar trousers, opting for a pair of blue jeans instead. She bumps into John, who initially does not recognise her in her "get-up". We learn that she is on her way to a mosque and he is going for a drink. They both decline the other's invitation to come along; it seems that their paths have diverged irrevocably. However, there is a barely perceptible note of optimism concerning Yasmin's membership of multicultural British society, subtly signalled through sartorial signifiers. The "fusion" clothing she is wearing seems to be an expression of a new "hybrid" identity and as such represents a challenge to simplistic dichotomous divisions. The phenomenon of such sartorial "fusion" has been analysed by Claire Dwyer (1999) in an article exploring "the ways in which dress is actively used by young Muslim women in the construction of their identities both through the challenging of meanings attached to different dress styles and in the reworking of meanings to produce alternative identities" (5). In the case of Yasmin, it seems to suggest that she is adamant at carving out her own niche at the intersection of various cultural influences. It seems that her reactive pride, heightened by the post 9/11 climate and manifested through the adoption of certain Islamic practices, seems to have actually deepened into an authentic appreciation of the culture of her ancestors. At the same time, however, she is by no means severing her ties with the host culture, signified in this outfit by the pair of blue jeans. It is also significant that she no longer covers her kameez with the extremely modest black coat and that the austere black hijab has been replaced by the much more chic dupatta. Thus Yasmin seems to have symbolically rid her wardrobe of both the more revealing (and, by Islamic standards, immodest) items of Western clothing, as well as those Islamic garments that seem unnecessarily austere. By carving out this niche for herself she seems to have symbolically erased the stifling boundaries of racial segregation, even though the film's ending (her younger brother departing to fight for his Muslim "brothers" and "sisters" in the East) is far from optimistic. It does not mean that the film's catchphrase— "One woman, two lives"— has abruptly ceased to be relevant to the protagonist's life; it might mean, however, that a new journey has begun, one which may eventually lead her to achieving a more complete sense of belonging in the multicultural space of contemporary Britain.

References

Primary sources

Yasmin. DVD. Directed by Kenny Glenaan. 2004. inD DVD, 2005.

Secondary sources

Aziz, Shaista. 2003. Viewpoint: Why I Decided to Wear the Veil. *BBC. co.uk,* Sep 12. http://news.bbc.co.uk/1/hi/talking_point/ 3093688.stm
Bagguley, Paul and Yasmin Hussain. 2005. Flying the Flag for England? Citizenship, Religion and Cultural Identity among British Pakistani Muslims. In *Muslim Britain: Communities under Pressure*, ed. by Tahir Abbas, 208-221. London and New York: Zed Books.
Bahl, Vinay. 2005. Shifting Boundaries of "Nativity" and "Modernity" in South Asian Women's Clothes. *Dialectical Anthropology* 29: 85-121.
Dwyer, Claire. 1999. Veiled Meanings: Young British Muslim Women and the Negotiation of Differences. *Gender, Place and Culture* 6 (1): 5-26.
La Ferla, Ruth. 2007. We, Myself and I. *The New York Times*, April 5. http://www.nytimes.com

Mani, Bakirathi. 2003. Undressing the Diaspora. In *South Asian Women in the Diaspora*, ed. by Nirmal Puwar and Parvati Raghuram, 117-135. Oxford and New York: Berg.

Modood, Tariq. 1992. British Asian Muslims and the Rushdie Affair. In *'Race', Culture and Difference*, ed. by James Donald and Ali Rattansi, 260-277. London: Sage Publications.

—. 2001. British Asian Identities: Something Old, Something Borrowed, Something New. In *British Cultural Studies: Geography, Nationality and Identity*, ed. by David Morley and Kevin Robins, 67-78. Oxford: Oxford University Press.

Peach, Ceri. 2005. Britain's Muslim Population: An Overview. In *Muslim Britain: Communities under Pressure*, edited by Tahir Abbas, 18-30. London and New York: Zed Books.

—. 2006. Demographics of BrAsian Settlement, 1951-2001. In *A Postcolonial People: South Asians in Britain*, ed. by N. Ali, V. S. Kalra and S. Sayyid, 168-181. London: Hurst & Company.

Phillips, Deborah, Cathy Davis and Peter Ratcliffe. 2007. British Asian Narratives of Urban Space. *Transactions of the Institute of British Geographers* 32 (2): 217-234.

Robinson, David. 2005. The Search for Community Cohesion: Key Themes and Dominant Concepts of the Public Policy Agenda. *Urban Studies* 42 (8): 1411-1427.

Roy, Amit. 2005. British Asian Muslims in Identity Crisis, post 9/11. *Telegraph [Calcutta]*, January 13,
http://www.euro-islam.info/spip/article.php3?id_article=516.

Sardar, Ziauddin. 2008. *Balti Britain: A Journey through the British Asian Experience*. London: Granta.

Tarlo, Emma. 1996. *Clothing Matters: Dress and Identity in India*. Chicago: The Uiversity of Chicago Press.

Yasmin the movie: Synopsis.
http://www.yasminthemovie.co.uk/synopsis.php

CHAPTER FORTY-THREE

IN LONDON'S "DESILAND":
HOUNSLOW AS A CONTESTED SPACE
IN GAUTAM MALKANI'S *LONDONSTANI*

ANNA TOMCZAK

The word "desi" comes from "Hinglish", a variety of English spoken by South Asians, which is a blend of English, Hindi, Punjabi and Urdu. "Desi" means indigenous, authentically South Asian. Baljinder K. Mahal, the author of the book *The Queen's Hinglish: How to Speak Pukka*, states that although Hinglish used to be treated as "the lingo of the uneducated masses, [it] is now trendy" (in Gentleman 2007). Much of Gautam Malkani's novel *Londonstani* is written in Hinglish with "desi" functioning as a proud term of self-identification used by British Indian teenage residents of Hounslow, a borough of West London. Hounslow is their territory, which they treat as home and an area to be controlled, thus manifesting the type of behaviour defined in anthropology as "territoriality". The term, first used by Edward T. Hall in *The Hidden Dimension* (1966), is defined as "staking claim to a territory (…) [and the] use of space to communicate ownership/occupancy" (http://en. wikipedia.org); or: "the desire to establish and guard personal space" and a "factor in creating spatial zones" (*Dictionary of Media Studies* 2006, 235). Sociologists also refer to it as "a social system through which control is claimed by one group over a defined geographical area [which is] defended against others" (Kintrea at al. 2008). In Malkani's book, Hounslow becomes Desiland, inhabited, possessed and fought over by a few "crews", or groups of teenagers from middle-class Indian families who may think of themselves as gangsters, but who are in reality Mummy's boys.

Londonstani (2006), the debut novel by a young *Financial Times* journalist of British Indian background, arose from sociological interest and scientific investigation. As the author discloses in interviews and in the autobiographical comments provided on his website, while studying at

Cambridge and examining the subject matter of his dissertation on the "Brit-Asian rudeboy scene and the rejection of our parents' efforts to integrate with mainstream Britain" (http://www.gautammalkani.com), he happened to "over-research" the topic and collected the massive data which could not possibly be used in his diploma work. The huge literary potential of the ample material accumulated in the form of interviews and tapes found reflection in the novel, which started as non-fiction, eventually to take the shape of the first person narrated account of the desi life.

Born in 1976, with a degree in Social and Political Sciences from Christ's College (Cambridge), Malkani describes the novel in the following words:

> Basically the book tells the story of a bunch of 19-year-old middle-class mummy's boys trying to be men—which they do by asserting their cut-and-paste ethnic identities; by blending their machismo with consumerism; by trying to talk and act as if their affluent corner of a London suburb is some kind of gritty ghetto; (…) by trying to block out their intelligence; and by grating against typically overbearing mothers who would rather their sons remain boys. (http://www. gautammalkani.com)

The title *Londonstani* may suggest a debate about radical Muslims in the UK. It was not the author's intention to make a link with Islamic fundamentalism. The title is celebratory, extolling London's multiculturalism. Malkani confirms:

> 'Londonstani' is a self-referential term that basically mean[s] I'm proud to be a Londoner because it's a place where I can be both British and Asian (…). It's like desi slang for the word 'Londoner', it means the same thing (except that 'Londoner' sound[s] Victorian and cockney, whereas 'Londonstani' sound[s] much more relevant in the late 20th Century) (http://www.gautammalkani.com).

The novel's main concern is gender, with a strong emphasis on teenage visions of masculinity. However, the characters' "affluent corner of a London suburb", viewed as "some kind of gritty ghetto", becomes more than a setting. Hounslow, with its recognizable locations of underground stations, bus routes, streets, shops, schools and parks functions as a territory to be controlled and a mark of identity. For Jas, Hardjit, Amit and Ravi, the four principal characters, it is their Desiland, which they claim as their rightful possession, their spatial zone. Thus the novel can be read as an exemplification of territorial behaviour in an urban setting, in this case—young British Asians' territoriality.

The use of the word "desi" is a matter of identity as well as being an act of defiance, an attempt at rejecting various labels invented by white Britons to refer to immigrant communities. The narrator explains:

> People're always tryin to stick a label on our scene. That's the problem with havin a fuckin scene. First we was rudeboys, then we be Indian niggas, then rajamuffins, then raggastanis, Britasians, fuckin Indobrits. These days we try an use our own word for homeboy an so we just call ourselves desis but I still remember when we were happy with the word rudeboy. (Malkani 2007, 5)

Historically, rude boys (with alternative ways of spelling as one or two words) were a subculture of Jamaican origin which flourished in the 1960s and was transported to England via West Indian immigration (Hebdige 1998, 145). Its attraction stems less from the association with the marginalized and delinquent than from the glamorized image of archetypal rebels, street-wise youths with their flashy urban style. Original rude boys, self-assured, and full of bravado, were always eager to "test their strength against the law" (Hebdige 2002, 145), hence the narrator's appropriation of the term.

The phrase "Hounslow rudeboy circuit" (Malkani 2007, 104) used a number of times in the novel, suggests awareness of the area boundaries and limitation. The rudeboy circuit becomes a no-go zone for the enemies: "goras" (white people, non-desis); "coconuts" (people who are brown on the outside and white inside, i.e. Asians who have adopted the English ways and speak with "poncey Amgrez accent" (Malkani 2007, 21); as well as "ponces and lesbians". If they enter the turf, they receive a "healin"— which means severe beating. Hardjit's crew manifests equal contempt for "rednecks" who use the word Paki and coconuts, whom they easily identify by their accent, music and sartorial choices as well as cars. Jas comments on a man in a silver Peugeot 305 which stops at the red traffic light:

> You could tell from his long hair, grungy clothes, the poncey novel a newspaper on his dashboard an Coldplay album playin in his car that he was a muthafuckin coconut. So white he was inside his brown skin, he probably talked like those gorafied desis who read the news on TV (Malkani 2007, 21).

Luckily, as the narrator boasts, recently the streets of their circuit have been effectively cleaned of any coconuts or "Paki-bashing skinheads". Such awareness of clearly marked boundaries implies recognition and acceptance of the foreign land, controlled by rival groups. Southall (a district in the neighbouring borough of Ealing) is understood to be a Sikh domain and Slough as belonging to Muslims. Command and authority are wielded within the strictly designated limits thus simultaneously becoming a double-edged sword of empowerment and liminal constraint.

The Desiland of Hounslow, the territory inhabited by wealthy Asian families of different religious denominations (Hindu, Sikh, Muslim) is divided between several "crews" who engage in various forms of petty crime, one such crew being a four-person "gang" with its self-appointed ring-leader Harjit (or Hardjit—to use the preferred version of the name). Their area of responsibility is reprogramming stolen mobile phones. Hardjit is a Sikh, but, to quote Jas: "one a them Sardarjis who don't even wear a turban" (Malkani 2007, 9). With his black Dolce and Gabbana vest, a five-ounce white gold chain, a Tag Heuer watch, Nike Air Force One trainers, and a collection of Hugo Boss aftershaves, Hardjit sends an unmistakable message of conspicuous consumption. The Khanda tattooed on his right bicep, the name "Desi" sewn onto the back of his bomber jacket, a Karha (steel bracelet) round his wrist and at least one orange item of clothing worn all the time tell the word he is a Sikh. Hardjit the leader enjoys body-building and fighting and will never miss an occasion to present his martial arts in action.

The fight for supremacy presented in the book reflects an inter-Asian conflict, not rivalry between white Londoners and ethnic minorities. Unlike in the past, when this part of London witnessed some of the most savage anti-Indian racist attacks initiated and perpetrated by the National Front activists, street violence does not concern clashes between white and non-white Britons. Jas explains the situation towards the end of chapter one:

> You hardly ever saw a brown-on-white beatin these days (...). It was when all those beatins stopped that Hardjit started hooking up with the Sikh boys who ran Southall whenever they took on the Muslim boys who ran Slough. Hounslow's more a mix of Sikhs, Muslims an Hindus, you see, so the brown-on-browns tended to be one-on-ones stead a thirty desis fightin side by side. (Malkani 2007, 12)

The young narrator still remembers the events of the previous decade when the local gangs waged serious turf wars. He recalls the time when

> all the Muslim kids acted as if they were members of the Wild Apaches or the Chalvey Boys a Slough an all the Sikh kids acted as if they were members a Shere Punjab, which, depending on who you talk to, means

either 'Tigers a the Punjab' or 'Lions a the Punjab'. You could tell that the feds understood more than our parents cos every time the Sikh from Southall stormed Slough, you'd get like a hundred cops in Southall Broadway waitin for the Muslim revenge attacks. They even sent some a those Sardarji cops with turban helmets. The Jedi Knights a the Met. The feds had got some kind a Asian gang taskforce, I think. (Malkani 2007, 84)

The above reference concerns the events of 1997, when an eighty-people-strong gang calling itself "Shere-e-Punjab" came from Birmingham to fight at Slough with the Muslim "Chalvey Boyz". Some homes and cars were attacked but, to quote from a Sikh website, "A large-scale police presence prevented any deaths and more than ninety of the culprits were arrested" (http://www.sikhsangat.com). This was nothing unusual, as in the past several British cities witnessed ethnic conflict and struggle. Sociologists emphasize that street rioting, unrest and disturbances, or clashes with the police, although triggered by varied factors, reflect "in some measure an attempt by members of local communities to assert a degree of control over the urban space they occup[y]" (Mason 2000, 90) and may constitute crowd-unifying factors resting on "area-based notions of group solidarity" (Gilroy 1998, 243).

Today's fights in Hounslow resemble duels rather than street brawls. One such confrontation is presented in chapter ten. It is a one-on-one fight between Hardjit and Tariq (a Muslim boy of the same age) which takes place on the disused BMX track on the corner of Hounslow High Street and Montague Road, right outside the Holy Trinity Church, very close to Hounslow police station, with the onlookers gathering in various places nearby. The BMX track and the car parks behind High Street are a customary location for organized fights. Unfortunately the police have learned about the place so the antagonists run the risk of being interrupted. Hounslow rude boys bemoan the situation realising that a better place could not be found as they

> Couldn't go south cos that was Richmond. Too swanky, too poncey. To the east was Brentford, but that was going the way a Richmond now. To the north it belonged to the Southall desis an all the land to the west had anti-terrorist police cos a Heathrow airport. (Malkani 2007, 112)

Once again, consciousness of the area boundaries entails respectful acknowledgement of ownership limits.

Officially, the reason for the fight is "teach[ing] Tariq a lesson or two for going out with a Sikh girl an then tryin to convert her to Islam" (Malkani 2007, 80). However, as Jas admits, 'Sikh bredren're always accusing Muslim guys a tryin to convert their Sikh sisters" (Malkani 2007, 80). It is clear that the fight is meant to be a show of power and an opportunity to assert supremacy. If there are no reasons, then a reason will be created. Hardjit (as the strongest boy of the neighbourhood) customarily "settles the beef" for both Hindu and Sikh boys; and the rivals are always Muslims. There can be no mistake about ethnic and religious loyalties. For the occasion Hardjit sports an orange bandanna and a Karha, which must be covered with the sweatband not to be used as a weapon. Tariq is dressed in a shirt with the green and yellow colours of the Pakistan cricket team.

The fight is a spectacle. The Sikh-Muslim confrontation may seem (on the surface) an example of an old rivalry between members of different religious denominations; in fact it is an occasion for body display and a manifestation of sheer physical strength. Hardjit may claim the fight is "for God" (Malkani 2007, 84), but every single detail of the scenario is played for effect, starting with a calculated moment of making an appearance, down to a careful selection of individual items of his attire: "Hardjit'd just wanted to make sure his entrance to the fight was as dramatic as possible [...]. Today he'd even kept his muscles under wrap in a baggy, long-sleeve Adidas tracksuit top" (Malkani 2007, 85). His body was to be revealed at an appropriate moment, like "a new Audi concept car waitin to be unveiled at the Geneva motor show" (Malkani 2007, 85).

> He'd chosen the Adidas tracksuit top carefully this morning, standin in front a his full-length mirror an comparing it to his Nike tracksuit top (which didn't show his shoulders enough), his tight leather jacket (which showed his pecs too much), a Ted Baker top (which showed too much bicep) an his Schott bomber jacket (which didn't show anything). None o them went well with the orange bandanna he'd tied round his head. (Malkani 2007, 86)

The combat is a show, with all the necessary paraphernalia borrowed straight from a Hollywood movie including the moment of making an entrance, to the last element of body language. The narrator's description abounds in obvious references to standard film clichés assuring the reader of the make-believe world: The men "appearing over the horizon" (Malkani 2007, 99) move with a "tough-guy penguin walk" leaving behind "foiled feds an fifty burnin baddies". In a moment "their long hair [will start] blowing in the helicopter wind" (Malkani 2007, 99). They may want to make impression of being "tough guys" but the comparison to penguins undercuts the seriousness of the scene. The choice of metaphors and similes turns the drama into a comedy. The fighters are "gangsta penguins

[…] or maybe just penguins who really need a piss" (Malkani 2007, 99);
the narrator sweats "like an oily samosa" (Malkani 2007, 100); the
spectators have overdosed their aftershave (Malkani 2007, 106), and the
leading-role actor Tariq cannot make it on time because he needs to go to a
supermarket with his mum to help her with the shopping.

It is a very different scene from the battles of the past. The jocular,
self-deprecating tone of the narration adds to the overall impression of
child's play rather than any dangerous confrontation. The multi-ethnic
crowd of about thirty youngsters consisting of blacks, Chinese, Muslims
and Sikhs will savour the performance "like cricket fans who don't care
whether India or Pakistan wins […] as long as they see some good batting
skills" (Malkani 2007, 101). The police arrive and the fight is interrupted
after a few exchanges of punches. No one suffers any serious damage.
There are no blazing sirens or armed officers. Instead two policemen
politely hold the door open for the naughty boys to be taken home. The
show is over.

Undoubtedly, the novel's rendering of the issue of street gang violence
and teenage rebellion sparkles with humour and irony. However, amidst
the heroes striking poses and their cheap effects the reader may detect
demeanour so characteristic of urban youth culture—with its peer
pressure, celebration of fashion and consumerism, fascination with image,
constant invocations of cinema memories as well as various aspects of
territoriality.

In October 2008 the Joseph Rowntree Foundation published on its
website a study entitled "Young people and territoriality in British cities"
(www.jrt.org.uk). Compiled by a team of scholars from the Department of
Urban Studies of the University of Glasgow, the report presents
manifestations of territorial behaviour among young Britons aged thirteen
to mid-twenties in six selected areas. Although the findings concern the
disadvantaged locations exclusively, many of the observations together
with the concluding comments apply to the situation depicted by Malkani
in his novel. Staking a claim to a territory, its demarcation and defence are
closely linked to ideas of self-identity. A sense of ownership of the defined
zone is accompanied by a desire to protect it. Identification with a
particular area and defending its space leads to gaining respect from peers
and becomes a source of friendship and group solidarity. Territorial
behaviour often forms part and parcel of everyday activities, sometimes
leading to social exclusion and criminality.

Today's Hounslow is a prosperous area, ethnically and religiously
diverse. Out of its 220,000 inhabitants the Indian resident population

amounts to 39.000 (18, 3 %) (http://www.london.gov.uk/). The narrator presents this diversity in chapter two.

> Some houses had got Om symbols stuck on the wooden front doors behind glass porches, some a them had Khanda (...) an others had the Muslim crescent moon. All a them had satellite TV dishes next to the main bedroom window, stuck up there like framed dentists' diploma certificates. If there weren't no symbol on the front door, you could still tell if it was a desi house if there was more than one satellite dish. One for Zee TV an one for Star Plus, probly. You could tell if someone was home cos the daal an subjhi smell would mix in with the airport traffic on the Great West Road. (Malkani 2007, 17-18)

The novel's Desiland differs considerably from other areas of London with substantial non-white communities, the "twilight zones" (Mason 2000, 80) of poor housing and relatively high unemployment. Whereas the East End street gangs clearly exemplify the link between economic deprivation and limited aspirations of the young gang members, Hounslow offers an alternative story. Being an outer borough of London, largely a well-to-do residential area, it can be treated as manifestation of Asian success, seen in the high rates of home ownership and luxury lifestyle. *Londonstani*'s protagonists' parents live in spacious houses, drive the latest models of expensive vehicles with personalized number plates, pay for their children's private tuition and give them cars and Swarovski jewellery as birthday presents.

Malkani's narrative deals with a close relationship between space and a construction of collective identity. It challenges the assumption concerning the link between urban territoriality and social/economic deprivation. Young British Indians from Hounslow do not come from pathological or deviant families, neither do they suffer from lack of parental interest or educational opportunities. Their use of space communicates ownership, a sense of ethnic bonding and a search for cultural identity. The connection between proxemic manifestations and crime arises from teenage notions of machismo as well as the limited view of success, success reduced to conspicuous consumption. Malkani's characters are products of contemporary popular culture; in their designer clothes and their parents' cars they draw inspiration from advertising and film and treat Bollywood stars and media celebrities as role models. Faithful devotees of "Bling-Bling Economics" (Malkani 2007, 172) and immediate gratification, ardent admirers of luxury brands and ready cash, they subscribe to a "subculture that worships affluence" (Malkani 2007, 171) and assert their right to control the territory through spectacle and image.

The critical response to the novel, ranging from enthusiastic praise to abusive condemnation, proves topicality of the subject matter and British sensitivity towards the presentation of "ethnic minorities". The author of the present article agrees with Anna-Marie Dover, who in a review published in *The International Writers Magazine* states that Malkani's presentation of the teenage world is "both amusing and absorbing and offers us a revealing window into a new, suburban British Asian culture" (Dover, http://www.hackwriters.com/Londonstani.htm). The suburban Desiland of Hounslow owes as much to the infantile world of Disneyland as to teenage fascination with Hollywood gangster movies while the need to create neighbourhood-bound collective identity might be interpreted as "the search for secure moorings in a shifting world" (Harvey 2002, 302).

References

Dictionary of Media Studies. 2006. London: A&C Black.

Dover, Anna-Marie. Review of *Londonstani*. In *International Writers Magazine*, http://www.hackwriters.com/Londonstani.htm, (accesssed 5 Dec, 2008).

Gentleman, Amelia. 2007. 'The Queen's Hinglish' Gains in India. In *New York Times*, 21 Nov, http://www.nytimes.com, (accessed 6 June 2009).

Gilroy, Paul. 1998. *There Ain't No Black in the Union Jack*. London: Routledge.

Harvey, David. 2002. *The Condition of Postmodernity*. Oxford and Malden: Blackwell.

Hebdige, Dick. 1998. *Subculture: The Meaning of Style*. London and New York: Routledge.

—. 2002. Reggae, Rastas and Rudies. In *Resistance through Rituals. Youth Subcultures in Post-war Britain*, ed. by Stuart Hall and Tony Jefferson, 135-155. London and New York: Routledge.

Kintrea, Keith et al. 2008. Young People and Territoriality in British Cities, www.jrf.org.uk, (accessed 15 Dec, 2008).

Malkani, Gautam. 2007. *Londonstani*. London: Harper Perennial.

Mason, David. 2000. *Race and Ethnicity in Modern Britain*. Second edition. Oxford: Oxford University Press.

http://www.gautammalkani.com.

http://en.wikipedia.org.

http://www.london.gov.uk/gla/publications/factsandfigures.

http://www.sikhsangat.com.

CONTRIBUTORS

Anthony David Barker is an Associate Professor and has taught film, drama, literature and European studies at Aveiro University in Portugal, where he was elected Head of Department 1988-92. As a teacher, he runs course in film studies, contemporary drama and research methodologies, for both humanities and for business students (he directs the Languages and Business Relations programme at the University of Aveiro). A former Treasurer and President of the Portuguese Association of Anglo-American Studies, his interests include history of cinema, film narrative and genre and British and American drama. He has published recently on David Lynch, Roman Polanski, Clint Eastwood, the Japanese POW camp movie, David Mamet and Alan Ayckbourn. He has additionally edited the following collections of essays, *Europe: Fact and Fiction* (2001), *The Power and Persistence of Stereotyping (2003), Television, Aesthetics and Reality* (CSP, 2006), *Giving and Taking Offence* (2008) and *Success and Failure* (2009). The various forms of adaptation for film and television are also issues on which he has researched—for example, the adaptation history of Thackeray's *Vanity Fair* for theatre, film and television is shortly to be published. He is currently writing an article on anarchic comedy on film and his long-term projects include a book on the relationship between cinema and television since 1950 and doing further work on British television comedy series, having already published on xenophobia in situation comedy, "mockumentary" comedy and the work of Sasha Baron Cohen.

Marek Błaszak (dr hab.) is Assistant Professor at the Institute of English Philology, University of Opole. He has published a book on Ann Radcliffe's Gothic romances (1991) and a monograph entitled *Sailors, Ships and the Sea in the Novels of Captain Frederick Marryat* (2006). His articles deal with various aspects of literary output of—among other writers—Daniel Defoe, Jane Austen, Thomas Love Peacock, D. H. Lawrence, Philip Roth, and Michael Cunningham.

Emilia Borowska is a doctoral candidate at John Paul II Catholic University of Lublin, working on her dissertation concerning feminine and masculine projections of cartography, violence and becoming in postmodern American literature. Her scholarly interests include renderings of chaos in modern physics, post-structuralist philosophy and the visual arts.

Barbara Braid is an academic teacher of British and American Literature at the University of Szczecin. She graduated from John Paul II Catholic University of Lublin in 2002. She is now working on a PhD dissertation concerning representation of femininity in Neo-Victorian novels.

Marcin Cieniuch is a PhD student at Adam Mickiewicz University in Poznań. He took his first degree writing a thesis on magic realism in Salman Rushdie's novels but his further research interests have shifted towards 20th century Irish literature, poetry and prose. This was reflected in his Master's thesis which traced modernist and postmodernist tendencies comparing the work of Banville and McCabe, Heaney and Muldoon. He has also written on Longley, and as an offshoot of his interests, on Byatt's *Possession*. The general bent of his research concerns the situation of artists in culturally, ideologically and politically oppressive environment. Currently he is working on a thesis whose aim is to investigate the use of classical Greek and Roman themes in Irish poetry from post Revival period to the work of contemporary poets from both Northern Ireland and the Republic of Ireland.

Grzegorz Czemiel is working on his PhD about Ciaran Carson at the University of Warsaw. His main areas of interest, apart from Northern Irish contemporary poetry, are modern literary theory, psychoanalysis, translation studies and philosophy. He has participated in public literary discussions, translation projects and literature seminars in Poland and the UK. He has written a number of papers on poetry by Ciaran Carson, Paul Muldoon, Paula Meehan and others, as well as on translation issues. His translation achievements cover essays concerning literary theory and philosophy, as well as poems and short stories. He works actively as a professional translator, lectures at the Warsaw School of Social Sciences and Humanities and is a DJ. Grzegorz Czemiel is also laureate of the Mazowieckie Voyvodeship Stipend for Doctoral Students.

Ilona Dobosiewicz is Professor of English at the University of Opole. She is a graduate of the University of Wrocław and Illinois State University, the author of *Female Relationships in Jane Austen's Novels* (1997), *Ambivalent Feminism: Marriage and Women's Social Roles in George Eliot's Works* (2003), the co-editor of *Crossing the Borders: English Studies at the Turn of the Century* (1998), and the co-editor of the series *Readings in English and American Literature and Culture* published by the University of Opole Press. She specializes in Victorian literature.

Fernando Galván is Professor of English Literature at the University of Alcalá (Spain), and President of ESSE (European Society for the Study of English). His research interests cover a wide range of topics: from medieval and Renaissance English literature to modern and contemporary fiction in English, as well as literary theory. He has edited and translated into Spanish numerous English classics such as Sidney, Milton, Defoe, Richardson, Fielding, Wordsworth, Dickens, Wilde, Joyce, Conrad, Orwell, and Graham Greene. He has also published extensively on contemporary authors from Britain and other parts of the world (Lessing, Golding, Fowles, McEwan, Michèle Roberts, Bruce Chatwin, Rushdie, Caryl Phillips, Amit Chaudhuri, Coetzee, Cormac McCarthy). He is now working in a research project on metaphors of the postcolonial diaspora in Britain.

Radek Glabazna is currently teaching at the Department of English of the Silesian University in Opava. He graduated from this university in 2004, having completed a degree in English and Czech. He spent the next few years in Great Britain, where he completed a Master's degree in 2009 in Literature, Culture and Modernity at the University of Southampton. Most of his academic interests were formed during his sojourn at the University of Southampton. They include the relationship between modernity and postmodernity, the role of ideology in the act of interpretation, and mainly, the production of subjectivity in the contemporary British-Asian fiction. His M.A. dissertation was dedicated to subversive strategies of self-fashioning in the novels by Hanif Kureishi and Hari Kunzru. Currently he is working on his PhD at the Palacký University in Olomouc. His research focuses on the performative character of subjectivity in the contemporary British-Indian (or Pakistani) fiction, with the utmost attention paid to writers like Salman Rushdie, Amitav Ghosh or Rana Dasgupta. His interest in the literary production and cultural formations of minorities is also reflected in his article 'On stereotyped representations of Eastern

Europe in British media', which was published in the volume *Rethinking Representation* at the University of Southampton in 2008.

Magdalena Grabias-Żurek graduated from the Institute of English of Maria Curie-Sklodowska University in Lublin. She completed the course of Literary Translations at Jagiellonian University in Krakow. She is employed at the Foreign Languages Department at Maria Curie-Sklodowska University. Currently she is preparing her PhD thesis on the subject of American cinema of 1930s and 1940s. Her special interests concern the areas of cultural studies with a focus on the issues of American and European cinematic art, and poetry translation. In 2008 she was chosen by the acclaimed British rock band Caamora to translate the poem of a Polish lyricist into English. The translation appeared worldwide in the booklet being a part of the band's *Journey's End* album. In 2009 her review of the book concerning the films of Andrzej Wajda was published in a quarterly on literature and art, Akcent.

Agnieszka Kaczmarek graduated from University of Opole with a Bachelor's degree presenting a diploma paper "Evasion of Communication as Reflected in the Literary Techniques in *The Room* and *The Birthday Party* by Harold Pinter" in 2000. Two years later, she defended her MA thesis entitled "Encounters with Death in Ernest Hemingway's Selected Novels and Short Stories". In 2006, she started working in the Institute of Neophilology, in State Higher Vocational School in Nysa teaching mainly American Literature and Literary Translation. Since then, with the support of dr hab. Jacek Gutorow, she has been concentrated on a research project applying the philosophy of Max Scheler, Martin Heidegger, and Emmanuel Lévinas to William Faulkner's writing.

Katarzyna Karwowska is a PhD candidate at the Institute of English Studies, Wrocław University. She received her Master's degree in 2006 after submitting the M.A. thesis entitled "Pastoral Conventions in Selected Novels by J.M. Coetzee." Currently, under the supervision of Prof. Ewa Kębłowska-Ławniczak, she is working on her doctoral thesis and teaches undergraduate courses, including the introduction to literary studies. Her scholarly interests comprise postcolonial studies (with an emphasis on South African literature), transnational cultural studies—human geography, cultural geography, various spatially oriented theories—and environmental criticism. Her current research is on the strategies of the construction of textual spaces and places in the prose fiction by J. M. Coetzee. Maintaining the broad postcolonial and cultural perspective, she investigates the consequences of the intertextual dialogue the discussed texts enter into with particular genres and conventions and adopts the mechanisms of figurative language to the analysis of spatial representations. Her recent publication is "'Local Solution': The Pastoral Motif of Retreat and Return in J. M. Coetzee's *Life and Times of Michael K.* and *Disgrace*" (*PASE Papers 2008*, Vol. 2: Studies in culture and literature. Ed. Anna Cichoń, Ewa Kębłowska-Ławniczak. Atut, Wrocław 2009).

Ewa Kębłowska-Ławniczak is Professor of English Literature at the University of Wrocław (Poland) and Head of the English Literature and Comparative Studies Section. She has published in the fields of the Renaissance, including *Shakespeare and the Controversy over Baroque,* and contemporary drama, including *The Visual Seen and Unseen: Insights into Tom Stoppard's Art.* She has edited two collections of essays in the series of *PASE Papers in Literature and Culture;* the second (with Anna Cichoń) was published in 2009. Her recent publications on contemporary British dramatists concern the dilemmas of space and place, spatial strategies, mapping, nomadism, migration and urban setting.

Anna Kędra-Kardela, PhD, is Senior Lecturer at the Maria Curie-Skłodowska University, Lublin, Poland. Her major areas of interest include narratology, English and Anglo-Irish literature, particularly the Anglo-Irish short story, and Gothic fiction. She is an author of The Ascent of the Soul. A Study in Henry Vaughan's Silex Scintillans (Lublin: UMCS, 1992).

Aleksandra Kędzierska, President of the Polish Association for the Study of English, is Associate Professor of English Literature at the Maria Curie-Sklodowska University in Lublin (Poland). Her main field of research is British poetry of the 19th and 20th centuries, especially the works of Gerard Manley Hopkins and of the poets of the Great War. It is on these topics that she wrote many articles and published her most important books: *On the Wings of Faith: A Study of the Man-God Relationship in the Poetry of Gerard Manley* (2001) and *Isaac Rosenberg and Wilfred Owen: A Study in the Poetry of World War I* (1995). Apart from committed poetry she also explores other areas of interests such as for instance Anglo-Irish drama, Anglo-Irish poetry, children's literature, fallenness in Victorian literature, works of Oscar Wilde, literature and the Bible and modern British fiction (Pat Barker, Martin Amis, John Fowles, George Orwell, Aldous Huxley). Yet another direction of her studies is translation and in that capacity she was

Director of Multilingual Translation Workshop in Monasterevin 2008. She is Consultant of the Gerard Manley Hopkins Society and its Awardee of the O'Connor Literary Award for Scholarship and, last but not least, Member of the International Association of University Professors of English.

Agnieszka Kliś, MA, graduated from the University of Silesia in 2007 (work title: The Vampire and Society: Unattainable Freedom in Anne Rice's *The Vampire Lestat* and *The Queen of the Damned*). She is a Ph.D. student and a graduate teaching assistant in the Department of Literary and Cultural Theory, Institute of English Cultures and Literatures, University of Silesia. Her Ph.D. dissertation, on which she is working at the moment, concentrates on the field of gothic fiction, and focuses on the discourse of the other/monster. Her research interests include: contemporary British and American literature, literary theory, gothic fiction (especially the issue of transgression in gothic fiction, the liminal characters and their status, self-representation of the liminal characters via artistic/literary creation) and vampire fiction (the twentieth- and the twenty-first-century literary and cinema representations of the vampire), psychoanalysis (the works of Sigmund Freud) contemporary pop culture and theories of consumerism, postmodernism, the works of Michel Foucault (especially the concept of the repressive hypothesis) and Jean Baudrillard (especially the concept of simulacrum).

Joanna Kokot is Professor of English literature at Warmia and Mazury University in Olsztyn. Her field of research comprises English literature at the turn of the 19th century, especially the so called popular literature. Some of her publications concern the literary output of J.R.R. Tolkien, including translations of a few scholarly works devoted to this writer. Important publications include *Tekst w tekscie* (Text within text, 1992), *Gry z czytelnikiem w nowelistyce Rudyarda Kiplinga* (Plays with the reader in Rudyard Kipling's short stories, 1993), *Kronikarz z Baker Street. Strategie narracyjne w utworach Conan Doyle'a o Sherlocku Holmesie* (The Baker Street chronicler. Narrative strategies in the Sherlock Holmes tales by Arthur Conan Doyle, 1999), *"This Rough Magic". Studies in Popular Literature* (2004). Currently working on the turn-of-the-19th-century horror fiction (Bram Stoker, Arthur Machen, Algernon Blackwood, M.R. James and others).

Magda Konopka is a PhD candidate at the Institute of English Studies, Warsaw Institute. She received her MA degree in 2006 from the same faculty. Her MA thesis was devoted to tracing the connection between popular music and national identity in the United Kingdom in the 1960s. She is also a graduate of the Institute of Ethnology and Cultural Anthropology, Warsaw University. Both her MA thesis and her current research focus on the ethnographic study of the Notting Hill Carnival in London. Additionally, she is a recent graduate of University College London, where she pursued Master's course in Cultural Heritage Studies. Her academic interests include Afro-Caribbean identity in the multicultural context of contemporary Britain, carnivalisation of popular culture, preservation and display of intangible cultural heritage, popular music studies and museology.

Barbara Kowalik is Professor of British Literature at the Institute of English Studies, University of Warsaw, Poland. Her research includes medieval literature, women's writing, intersections of literature and theology, Polish-American writers, and literary theory. She is the author of *From Circle to Tangle: Space in the Poems of the "Pearl" Manuscript, A Woman's Pastoral: Dialogue with Literary Tradition in Barbara Pym's Fiction*, and *Artistry and Christianity in "Pearl"*. Her papers and reviews have been published in *REAL, Pamiętnik Literacki, Kwartalnik Neofilologiczny, Zagadnienia Rodzajów Literackich, Essays in Poetics, Akcent, Studia Anglica Posnaniensia, Medieval English Mirror, Anglica, Acta Philologica*, and *The New Review*. She was visiting professor at the Department of Polish Literature, University of Minnesota, Minneapolis, and at the Department of Polish Literature, University of Wisconsin in Milwaukee. She is a Member of *ESSE* (the European Society for the Study of English) and *IAUPE* (the International Association of University Professors of English).

Irena Księżopolska is finishing a PhD dissertation entitled "The Web of Sense: Patterns of Involution in Selected Fictions of Virginia Woolf and Vladimir Nabokov" at the Institute of English Studies, University of Warsaw. She has published articles in *Virginia Woolf Bulletin, Virginia Woolf Miscellany* and *Anglica*. Her academic interests include: modernism/ postmodernism, detective fiction, Silver Age Russian poetry, history of the Russian emigration between the wars.

Bożena Kucała, PhD, teaches nineteenth-century and contemporary English literature at the English Department of the Jagiellonian University in Kraków. Her doctoral thesis analysed the concept of history and its representations in selected twentieth-century English fiction. Her academic interests include nineteenth- and twentieth-century fiction, history and the novel, intertextuality. She has published articles (in English and Polish) on contemporary novelists, especially Graham Swift, A. S. Byatt, Peter Ackroyd and J. M. Coetzee as well as translated academic essays into Polish. She has also prepared a revised and updated edition of Bronisława Bałutowa's book *Powieść angielska XX wieku* [The English Twentieth-Century Novel] and is currently working on her own book on intertextuality in neo-Victorian fiction.

Barbara Leftih defended her PhD thesis entitled "Mapping 'the Culture of the Gaze' in American culture and literature of the late nineteenth and early twentieth centuries" in October 2009. The thesis was written under the supervision of Prof. Tadeusz Rachwał and concerned the oppositional responses to the turn-of-the-century culture of the gaze as presented in American literature and culture at the turn of the twentieth century. This analysis was influenced by a wide corpus of work on whiteness, ways of seeing and observing racial, ethnic or cultural "others", power relations between the observer and the observed, and relations between racial and ethnic groups in American society at the turn of the twentieth century. Her most recent publication is *Reforming Wasted Lives* in *Rubbish, waste and litter. Culture and its Refus(e)als* published by Wydawnictwo SWPS Academica in 2008. Her academic interests center on American literature of the late nineteenth and early twentieth centuries, especially Native American, African American and Jewish American literature of the era. Moreover, she is interested in the turn-of-the-century social reform movements and social writings of female social reformers, such as Jane Addams or Lillian Wald.

Tadeusz Lewandowski teaches at Opole University in Poland. His academic interests include gender studies, and the left-wing mass culture critique that circulated in mid-twentieth-century America.

Paweł Marcinkiewicz teaches at Opole University and other educational institutions. In 2004, he received a PhD at the Silesian University in Katowice. The field of his study was American poetry and architecture. His dissertation, *The Rhetoric of the City: Robinson Jeffers and A.R. Ammons*, has been published by Peter Lang in 2009. He is also a poet, a translator, a lexicographer and a literary critic. His recent volume of poetry, *Days*, was published in 2009. His honors and awards include The Polish Cultural Foundation Award (1997) and The Czesław Miłosz Award, a personal poetry award of the Nobel Prize winner (2000).

Maciej Masłowski received his MA from the Wrocław Institute of English Studies in 2008, having submitted a thesis entitled "'Strangeness that is almost holy': Conspiracy and the pursuit of transcendence in the selected novels of Don DeLillo." Currently, he is working on his doctoral dissertation concerning visuality and incarnation in Don DeLillo's fiction. His academic interests include connections between literature and philosophy and the problems of visual representation in contemporary American literature. He is a member of Polish Association for American Studies.

Jarosław Mihułka is a PhD student at the Institute of English Philology, University of Opole. His MA in American Literature (defended in 2005 at the University of Opole and written under the supervision of Prof. Andrzej Ciuk) entitled "Death as an omnipresent phenomenon in Edgar Allan Poe's life and his output" showed his interest in combining literature and philosophy. Now he is completing his doctoral thesis (under the supervision of Prof. Ryszard Wolny) on the eighteenth-century English graveyard poetry. His interests are mainly English pre-Romantic poetry, the concept of death in philosophy (particularly Friedrich Nietzsche and Martin Heidegger) and American romantic literature. He published his articles "Nietzschean Will to Power in Edgar Allan Poe's "Ligeia" in *Crosscurrents: Culture, Literature and Language* (R. Wolny, ed. Kielce: Wszechnica Swiętokrzyska Press, 2008. pp. 65-73) and "Śmierć w osiemnastowiecznej poezji angielskiej wobec śmierci w wirtualnym świecie XXI wieku—zmiana percepcji? [Death in the Eighteenth-Century English Poetry versus Virtual Death of the 21st century—the Change of Perception?]" in *Idea przemiany w kulturze, literaturze, języku i edukacji* (P. Fast, M. Duś, eds. Częstochowa: High School of Linguistics Press. 2008. pp. 157-70). He is a PASE member (since 2007). He works at Wszechnica Świętokrzyska in Kielce where he teaches History of American Literature, Introduction to Literary Studies and Practical English.

Małgorzata Milczarek did her PhD at Adam Mickiewicz University in Poznań, Poland. Her dissertation discusses New Woman fiction as the transition from the Victorian to the Modernist modes of narration in the novels by George Gissing, Ella Hepworth Dixon, Mona Caird, Olive Schreiner, Sarah Grand and Netta Syrett. She is currently researching New Woman, Modernist and Edwardian literature, narrative techniques and tensions between realism and narrative experiments in particular. She is also interested in the relationship between literature and music, especially in New Woman and modernist fiction

Ewa Młynarczyk is a PhD student at the Institute of English Studies of the University of Warsaw. After defending her MA thesis "The Arthurian Legend from the Victorian Perspective in Tennyson's *Idylls of the King*", in which she explored the Victorian aspects of the medieval theme as presented by the Poet Laureate, she continues her studies in the field of the 19th century literature. Her main interests include modern theories concerning the interpretation of myths as well as the transformations of mythological motifs in the Post-Romantic and Victorian British poetry. She works as a teacher of English as a foreign language at the University of Warsaw.

Joanna Mstowska graduated from Nicolaus Copernicus University in Toruń in 2008. In 2009 she started doctoral studies in British and American sea fiction. Her academic interests include sea novels of F. Marryat, J. F. Cooper and Joseph Conrad. Her MA thesis was devoted to the topos of *theatrum mundi* in the selected works of Joseph Conrad and her article concerning postcolonial aspects of Conrad's fiction has recently been published. Apart from English, she also studies Italian and is particularly interested in comparative studies of contemporary American and Italian literature. She is currently preparing an article on the image of America in the selected novels of Cesare Pavese and Andrea De Carlo.

Stankomir Nicieja, PhD, is a lecturer at the Department of Culture, School of English and American Studies, University of Opole. In 2005, he successfully defended his PhD dissertation entitled, *In the Shadow of the Iron Lady: Thatcherism as a Cultural Phenomenon and Its Representation in the Contemporary British Novel*. His academic interests include contemporary British fiction, representation of politics and nationality in literature, utopia and utopianism as well as cultural relations between China and the West.

Katarzyna Ojrzyńska is a doctoral student at the University of Lodz at the Department of Studies in Drama and pre-1800 English Literature where she teaches modern British drama and British culture. Pursuing her doctoral degree, she is now working on a dissertation on the motif of dance in the works of contemporary Irish playwrights. Her academic interests focus on modern British drama and particularly on the use of human body by the modern Irish dramatists. She has published several articles on Brian Friel and Samuel Beckett (including The Journey through the Dying World of Boghill in Samuel Beckett's Radio Play, *All That Fall*, In *Images of the City*, ed. Magdalena Cieślak and Agnieszka Rasmus. 284-293. Newcastle: Cambridge Scholars Publishing, 2009).

Maciej Piątek graduated from the Institute of English Philology at the Jagiellonian University. He wrote his MA thesis on the subject of translating Shakespeare's *Richard II* into Polish with special attention paid to the dimension of theatrical potential. He is currently studying for his doctorate dissertation devoted to the figure of the holy fool in Shakespeare's tragedies. He is particularly interested in the theatre (theoretically and practically), postmodern literature (especially Samuel Beckett and Vladimir Nabokov) and philosophy (Derrida, Foucault, Cioran, Barthes and Bataille), as well as Buddhism, Russian history and culture, negative theology and music. He has published a number of literary and philosophical essays on www.niedoczytania.pl, a paper on Milton, Shakespeare and Sidney (delivered during the first Translation Workshops organized at the Institute of English Philology, Jagiellonian University, in 2006) and a book review in *Przekładaniec*, a journal devoted to translation. He studied philosophy for three years at the Jagiellonian University and spent three months at the University of Essex as a Socrates/Erasmus student. He has been working as a translator for the past five years and translated two books for the Jagiellonian University Publishing House (on the development of Byzantine theology and on the history of the Spanish Inquisition).

Liliana Sikorska is Professor of English and head of the Department of English Literature and Literary Linguistics and acting head of the American Literature Department at the School of English, Adam Mickiewicz University, Poznań, Poland. She is the author of *An Outline History of English Literature* (1996, 2d edition 2002, third edition under the title *A Short History of English Literature*, 2007), *In a Manner of Morall Playe. Social Ideologies in Medieval Morality Plays and Interludes (1350-1517)* as well as numerous articles on medieval English Literature, primarily on drama and medieval mystical culture. Her other research interests include: medievalism, Irish literature, contemporary literature in English and literary linguistics. She has edited a number of books, including: *Aspects of Suffering. Classical Themes in the literature in English* (2004), *Ironies of Art/Tragedies of Life. Essays on Irish Literature* (2005), *A Universe of (Hi)stories. Essays on J.M. Coetzee* (2006) and *Medievalisms. The Poetics of Literary Re-Reading* (2008). She is the editor of two scholarly journals: *Medieval English Mirror* and *Studies in Literature in English*. She was a visiting scholar at the University of Florida (Gainesville), University of California at Los Angeles, Brown University (Providence), and the American University (Washington, DC). She has been invited as a guest lecturer to Germany, Sweden, Norway, Ukraine, Korea, Japan and the USA. She is a member of Medieval Academy of America, International Associations of University Professors and Agder Academy (South Norwegian Academy of Sciences and Humanities.

Tadeusz Sławek is a poet, translator, essayist, scholar and university teacher. He graduated from Jagellonian University, Kraków, first majoring in Polish (1969) and then in English (1971). Since 1971 he has been employed at Slaski University in Katowice, initially as a teacher of English. He obtained his Ph.D. in literary studies in 1978, and after winning Fulbright Scholarship he went to San Diego University for the academic year 1979-1980. He was a *visiting professor* at East Anglia University (Norwich) in 1984, got his D.Litt. in literary studies in 1986 from AMU Poznan and returned to San Diego with lectures for 1989-1990. In the 1990s he was *a visiting professor* at the universities of Naples and Padua. He was elected Rector of Slaski University and stayed in office between 1996-2002. Presently he is head of the Comparative Literature Department at Slaski University. He specializes in the history of English and American literature as well as in literary studies. He translated into Polish the works of Wendell Berry, William Blake, Allen Ginsberg, Seamus Heaney, Robinson Jeffers, Thomas Merton, Jerome Rothenberg. He also rendered the lyrics of John Lennon, Jim Morrison and Pete Sinfield. He collaborates with many Polish papers and magazines as a columnist. He is author, among others, of: *Grand Circus Hotel, The Dark Glory: Robinson Jeffers and His Philosophy of Earth, The Outlined Shadow: Phenomenology, Grammartology, Blake, Piec esejow o goscinnosci (Five Essays on Hospitality).*

Piotr Spyra is a doctoral student at the University of Lodz, Poland, where he teaches English poetry and drama. He is interested in Middle English literature, poetry in particular, literary theory and semiotics. His other interests include 19th century poetry, philosophy and early modern science. Having published a number of articles on the poetry of Alfred Tennyson, the subject of his MA thesis, he is presently working on a dissertation devoted to the four poems found in the anonymous MS Cotton Nero A.x., attributed to the so-called *Pearl-Poet*. He is the founder and acting supervisor of the Geoffrey Chaucer Student Society, an academic society aimed at promoting Middle English literature among students of English literature in Poland.

Anna Suwalska-Kołecka is Senior Lecturer at Higher Vocational State School in Płock. She graduated from the Institute of English at Gdańsk University, where she completed her PhD on the function of time and space in the plays of Tom Stoppard. She has research interests in modern British drama and literary theory, especially in the structure and presentation of time and space. Her publications in the field of modern drama include: "Tom Stoppard's *After Magritte*—The World of Uncertainty" *Acta Neophilologica* vol. III (2001). 289-299; "History in Tom Stoppard's *Arcadia.*" *Conventions and Texts.* Ed. A. Zgorzelski. Gdańsk: Wydawnictwo Uniwersytetu Gdańskiego, 2003. 88-112; "The dream-warp of the ultimate room—the problem of time in *The Invention of Love* by Tom Stoppard." *Beyond Philology. An International Journal of Linguistics, Literary Studies and English Language Teaching.* 3 (2003). 133-146; "A Knot too Tight to Undo—the Shape of Time and Space Continuum in *The Real Inspector Hound* by Tom Stoppard." *Texts of Literature. Texts of Culture.* Eds. L. Gruszewska Blaim, A. Blaim. Lublin: Wydawnictwo Uniwersytetu Marii Curie-Skłodowskiej, 2005. 61-77; "The Closed Structure of Space in Tom Stoppard's *Arcadia.*" *Studies in English Drama and Poetry.* vol. 1 Ed. J. Kazik. Łódź: Wydawnictwo Uniwersytetu Łódzkiego, 2007. 243-251; "Dots, Bricks and Beetles"—The City Rendered in Sounds: A Study of Tom Stoppard's *Albert's Bridge.*" In *Images of the City.* Eds. A. Rasmus, M. Cieślak. Newcastle: Cambridge Scholars Publishing, 2009. 294-301.

Hanna Szewczyk, MA, is a lecturer and research assistant at Maria Curie-Skłodowska University, Lublin, Poland. Her publications include: "Pout or charisma? The representations of actors and actresses in popular British film magazines." In *The Media and International Communication*, eds. B. Lewandowska-Tomaszczyk, T. Płudowski and D. Valencia Tanno, 83-93.

Frankfurt am Main: Peter Lang, 2007, „Przekładając nieprzekładalne: Lennon wg Stillera." In *Współczesna literatura brytyjska w Polsce*, ed. T. Dobrogoszcz, 65-74. Łódź: Wydawnictwo Uniwersytetu Łódzkiego, 2008; "Shabina Begum and the hijab controversy in the British press: A discursive construction of female empowerment/disempowerment." In *Literature and/in Culture*, eds. S. Wącior and G. Maziarczyk, 189-198. Lublin: Tow. Naukowe KUL, 2008. Her current research concerns various aspects of multiculturalism in post-imperial Britain, especially British Asian identities and their representation/construction in the media, literature and film, as well as the reception of Poles and Poland in the UK prior to and following Poland's accession to the EU. Her two current projects are a doctoral thesis focusing on the interplay between dress and identity in British Asian fiction and, together with prof. Irmina Wawrzyczek and dr Zbigniew Mazur, a project concerning the representation of Poles and Poland in the British press 2003-2006, funded by a ministerial grant.

Edyta Świerczyńska is a doctoral student at the University of Warsaw where she also lectures. Her research is devoted to the life and works of Charles Dickens, particularly the poetics of space as presented in his novels. Her main areas of interest include modern literary theory, Victorian art, psychoanalysis and philosophy. She has participated in a number of literature seminars concerning literature and culture of the Victorian epoch, presenting her papers on space symbolism in the works of Charles Dickens. She has recently been elected a Member of the Supervisory Committee included in the PASE Board of Management. Her publications include: "The Motif of Pilgrimage in *The Pickwick Papers* by Charles Dickens" (2007); "Earthly City or the City of God? Visions of London in *Great Expactations* by Charles Dickens" (2008); "Distorting Mirror-Charles Dickens's depiction of London and Paris in *A Tale of Two Cities*" (2009).

Anna Maria Tomczak teaches Cultural Studies at the University of Bialystok (Poland). Her research interests include literary anthropolgy, national and cultural identity in the context of post-colonial studies and inter-cultural communication. Recently published articles: "Why did they want to kill my friend? Hanif Kureishi on Muslim fundamentalism" in Wącior and Maziarczyk (eds.) *Literature and/in Culture*, Towarzystwo Naukowe KUL, Lublin 2008; "Arrested in Imagination and Actuality: Eva Hoffman's Visit to Tykocin in the New Eastern Europe" in Kalaga, Kubisz and Mydla (eds) *Repetition and Recycling in Literary and Cultural*

Dialogues, Wydawnictwo Wyższej Szkoły Lingwistycznej, Częstochowa 2008; "England and Bangladesh in Monica Ali's *Brick Lane*" in Cichoń and Kębłowska-Ławniczak (eds) *PASE Papers 2008. vol. 2 Studies in Culture and Literature*, Oficyna Wydawnicza ATUT, Wrocław 2009; "Englishness in Hanif Kureishi's *The Buddha of Suburbia*" in Reviron-Piegay (ed.) *Englishness Revisited*, Cambridge Scholars Publishing, Newcastle 2009.

Jadwiga Uchman graduated from the Institute of English Studies, University of Łódź in 1973, having presented an MA Thesis on Harold Pinter's "comedies of menace." Since that time she has been working in the same Institute, the field of her specialization being modern British drama. In 1982 she got her PhD, the subject of her thesis being the structural and thematic function of time in the poetic dramas of T. S. Eliot and Samuel Beckett. A part of her doctoral dissertation was published in1987 under the title *The Problem of Time in the Plays of Samuel Beckett.* In 1998 she published another book—*Reality, Illusion, Theatricality: A Study of Tom Stoppard,* after which she became a professor. Now she is the head of Department of Studies of Drama and Pre-18th Century British Literature.

Katarzyna Winiarska is a graduate of Institute of Philosophy, University of Warsaw (2006, *Mimesis and Mirror Metaphors in Modern French Philosophy*) and Institute of English Studies, University of Warsaw (2008, *Paradoxes of Hopkins's Aesthetics. Study in the selected works of G.M. Hopkins*). She is currently working on her PhD project concerning ocularcentric metaphors in the religious poetry from the late Victorian to the early Modern period, in which she tries to combine her philosophical and literary interests. In 2005 she was awarded a Socrates Erasmus Scholarship at Antwerp University, Belgium. Her main areas of interest are British literature of 19th and 20th century, religious poetry of 17th, 19th and 20th century, in particular works of Gerard Manley Hopkins, Catholic literary revival, religious movements in England, philosophy of representation and European art of 17th, 19th and 20th century. She works as a teacher of English at the University of Warsaw.

Ryszard W. Wolny is Professor of Literature and Culture at University of Opole. He has published over sixty scholarly articles and books on various aspects of British, American and Australian literature, which include *The Ruinous Anatomy: The Philosophy of Death in John Donne and the Earlier Seventeenth-Century English Poetry and Prose* (Perth, 1999) and *A Cry over the Abyss: The Discourse of Power in the Poetry of Robert*

Browning and Algernon Charles Swinburne (Opole, 2004). He has edited or co-edited five other books and is currently working on a monograph entitled *Patrick White: Australia's Poet of Mythical Landscapes of the Soul.*

Dagmara Zając works at the Jagiellonian University, Kraków, Poland. Her research interests focus on Gothicism as an aesthetic which transplants itself across forms and genres. She believes that a modern approach to Gothic calls for an interdisciplinary perspective, from narrative to dramatic and poetic modes, as well as from textual to visual and aural media. She is preparing her PhD dissertation on the development of narrative strategies and devices in American Gothic fiction and film. In 2009, she presented papers at international conferences: the *18th Conference of the Polish Association for the Study of English* in Opole, the *19th Conference on British and American Studies,* organized by the West University of Timisoara, Romania, the *3rd Global Conference on Fear, Horror and Terror: At the Interface* at Mansfield College, Oxford and the *3rd International Conference on "Perception(s)"* organized by the Institut Supérieur des Sciences Humaines de Tunis, Tunisia.

EDITORS

Andrzej Ciuk is Professor *Extraordinarius* and Head of the Institute of English, Opole University, Poland, since 1993. He graduated in 1974 from Adam Mickiewicz University, Poznań (M.A. in English literature, dissertation: *The Reflection of Attitudes to Courtly Love in Shakespeare's LLL, AYLI and T&C*) and received his Ph.D. in 1984 from Łódź University and D.Litt. in English literature in 1994 from Adam Mickiewicz University. He specializes in English literature, cultural studies, and most recently in Australian studies. He is the author of three books: *Mastering English through Educational Problem* (with Stanisław Jędrzejowski), 1979; *King Arthur and the Knights of the Round Table in Victorian Poetry*, 1989; and *Georgian Poetry: A Reconsideration*, 1992. The first book is a handbook for students of pedagogy who get familiar with the history of education (from Ancient times till present) and perfect their command of English up to the advanced level on the basis of the texts and exercises attached. The second book is an endeavour at disclosing the reasons of popularity of the Arthurian legends among the Victorian poets such as Alfred Tennyson, Matthew Arnold, William Morris and A. C. Swinburne. The third book is a close study of the transition period in the history of English poetry, ca. 1890-1920, with particular emphasis on 'Georgian Revolt'—the activity of a group of poets who contributed to Edward Marsh'e *Georgian Poetry*. Andrzej Ciuk also published articles on other English 19th and 20th century poets, was editor of the university periodical *Filologia Angielska* (1995-2003), and supervisor in 5 doctorates.

Katarzyna Molek-Kozakowska is Assistant Professor at the Institute of English, Opole University, Poland. She specializes in pragma-linguistics, critical discourse analysis and cultural/media studies. In her 2006 PhD dissertation, *Discursive exponents of the ideology of counterculture in Allen Ginsberg's poems*, she researched stylistic devices used for expressing ideological resistance in literary texts. She has published twenty studies of mass-mediated political discourse, focusing on strategies of valuing, persuasion, polarization and legitimization in various samples of contemporary political texts. She has presented papers on such issues as linguistic construction of national identity, rhetorical exclusion of immigrants and metaphor and personalization in political discourse. She has recently been interested in the methodology of qualitative/critical research, particularly in developing tools for stereotype research and in promoting critical media literacy.